PORTFOLIO MANAGEMENT IN PRACTICE

Volume 2

CFA Institute is the premier association for investment professionals around the world, with over 170,000 members more than 160 countries. Since 1963 the organization has developed and administered the renowned Chartered Financial Analyst Program. With a rich history of leading the investment profession, CFA Institute has set the highest standards in ethics, education, and professional excellence within the global investment community, and is the foremost authority on investment profession conduct and practice.

Each book in the CFA Institute Investment Series is geared toward industry practitioners along with graduate-level finance students and covers the most important topics in the industry. The authors of these cutting-edge books are themselves industry professionals and academics and bring their wealth of knowledge and expertise to this series.

PORTFOLIO MANAGEMENT IN PRACTICE

Volume 2

Asset Allocation

WILEY

ISBN 978-1-119-78796-9 (Hardcover)
ISBN 978-1-119-78798-3 (ePDF)
ISBN 978-1-119-78797-6 (ePub)

Printed in the United States of America.
SKY10022159_110220

PREFACE

We are pleased to bring you Asset Allocation, Volume 2 of Portfolio Management in Practice. This series of three volumes serves as a particularly important resource for investment professionals who recognize that portfolio management is an integrated set of activities. The topic coverage in the three volumes is organized according to a well-articulated portfolio management decision-making process. This organizing principle— in addition to the breadth of coverage, the currency and quality of content, and its meticulous pedagogy—distinguishes the three volumes in Portfolio Management in Practice from other investment texts that deal with portfolio management.

The content was developed in partnership by a team of distinguished academics and practitioners, chosen for their acknowledged expertise in the field, and guided by CFA Institute. It is written specifically with the investment practitioner in mind and is replete with examples and practice problems that reinforce the learning outcomes and demonstrate real-world applicability.

The CFA Program curriculum, from which the content of this book was drawn, is subjected to a rigorous review process to assure that it is:

- faithful to the findings of our ongoing industry practice analysis
- Valuable to members, employers, and investors
- Globally relevant
- Generalist (as opposed to specialist) in nature
- replete with sufficient examples and practice opportunities
- Pedagogically sound

The accompanying workbook is a useful reference that provides Learning Outcome Statements, which describe exactly what readers will learn and be able to demonstrate after mastering the accompanying material. additionally, the workbook has summary overviews and practice problems for each chapter.

We hope you will find this and other books in the CFA Institute Investment Series helpful in your efforts to grow your investment knowledge, whether you are a relatively new entrant or an experienced veteran striving to keep up to date in the ever-changing market environment. CFA Institute, as a long-term committed participant in the investment profession and a not- for-profit global membership association, is pleased to provide you with this opportunity.

CONTENTS

CHAPTER 9

Exchange-Traded Funds: Mechanics and Applications   497

ACKNOWLEDGMENTS

Special thanks to all the reviewers, advisors, and question writers who helped to ensure high practical relevance, technical correctness, and understandability of the material presented here.

We would like to thank the many others who played a role in the conception and production of this book: the Curriculum and Learning Experience team at CFA Institute with special thanks to the curriculum directors, past and present, who worked with the authors and reviewers to produce the chapters in this book, the Practice Analysis team at CFA Institute, and the Publishing and Technology team for bringing this book to production.

ABOUT THE CFA INSTITUTE INVESTMENT SERIES

CFA Institute is pleased to provide the CFA Institute Investment Series, which covers major areas in the field of investments. We provide this best-in-class series for the same reason we have been chartering investment professionals for more than 45 years: to lead the investment profession globally by setting the highest standards of ethics, education, and professional excellence.

The books in the CFA Institute Investment Series contain practical, globally relevant material. They are intended both for those contemplating entry into the extremely competitive field of investment management as well as for those seeking a means of keeping their knowledge fresh and up to date. This series was designed to be user friendly and highly relevant.

We hope you find this series helpful in your efforts to grow your investment knowledge, whether you are a relatively new entrant or an experienced veteran ethically bound to keep up to date in the ever-changing market environment. As a long-term, committed participant in the investment profession and a not-for-profit global membership association, CFA Institute is pleased to provide you with this opportunity.

THE TEXTS

Corporate Finance: A Practical Approach is a solid foundation for those looking to achieve lasting business growth. In today's competitive business environment, companies must find innovative ways to enable rapid and sustainable growth. This text equips readers with the foundational knowledge and tools for making smart business decisions and formulating strategies to maximize company value. It covers everything from managing relationships between stakeholders to evaluating merger and acquisition bids, as well as the companies behind them. Through extensive use of real-world examples, readers will gain critical perspective into interpreting corporate financial data, evaluating projects, and allocating funds in ways that increase corporate value. Readers will gain insights into the tools and strategies used in modern corporate financial management.

Equity Asset Valuation is a particularly cogent and important resource for anyone involved in estimating the value of securities and understanding security pricing. A well-informed professional knows that the common forms of equity valuation—dividend discount modeling, free cash flow modeling, price/earnings modeling, and residual income modeling—can all be reconciled with one another under certain assumptions. With a deep understanding of the underlying assumptions, the professional investor can better understand what other investors assume when calculating their valuation estimates. This text has a global orientation, including emerging markets.

Fixed Income Analysis has been at the forefront of new concepts in recent years, and this particular text offers some of the most recent material for the seasoned professional who is not a fixed-income specialist. The application of option and derivative technology to the once staid province of fixed income has helped contribute to an explosion of thought in this area. Professionals have been challenged to stay up to speed with credit derivatives, swaptions, collateralized mortgage securities, mortgage-backed securities, and other vehicles, and this explosion of products has strained the world's financial markets and tested central banks to provide sufficient oversight. Armed with a thorough grasp of the new exposures, the professional investor is much better able to anticipate and understand the challenges our central bankers and markets face.

International Financial Statement Analysis is designed to address the ever-increasing need for investment professionals and students to think about financial statement analysis from a global perspective. The text is a practically oriented introduction to financial statement analysis that is distinguished by its combination of a true international orientation, a structured presentation style, and abundant illustrations and tools covering concepts as they are introduced in the text. The authors cover this discipline comprehensively and with an eye to ensuring the reader's success at all levels in the complex world of financial statement analysis.

Investments: Principles of Portfolio and Equity Analysis provides an accessible yet rigorous introduction to portfolio and equity analysis. Portfolio planning and portfolio management are presented within a context of up-to-date, global coverage of security markets, trading, and market-related concepts and products. The essentials of equity analysis and valuation are explained in detail and profusely illustrated. The book includes coverage of practitioner-important but often neglected topics, such as industry analysis. Throughout, the focus is on the practical application of key concepts with examples drawn from both emerging and developed markets. Each chapter affords the reader many opportunities to self-check his or her understanding of topics.

All books in the CFA Institute Investment Series are available through all major booksellers. And, all titles are available on the Wiley Custom Select platform at http://customselect.wiley.com/ where individual chapters for all the books may be mixed and matched to create custom textbooks for the classroom.

CHAPTER 1

BASICS OF PORTFOLIO PLANNING AND CONSTRUCTION

Alistair Byrne, PhD, CFA
Frank E. Smudde, MSc, CFA

LEARNING OUTCOMES

The candidate should be able to:

- describe the reasons for a written investment policy statement (IPS);
- describe the major components of an IPS;
- describe risk and return objectives and how they may be developed for a client;
- distinguish between the willingness and the ability (capacity) to take risk in analyzing an investor's financial risk tolerance;
- describe the investment constraints of liquidity, time horizon, tax concerns, legal and regulatory factors, and unique circumstances and their implications for the choice of portfolio assets;
- explain the specification of asset classes in relation to asset allocation;
- describe the principles of portfolio construction and the role of asset allocation in relation to the IPS;
- describe how environmental, social, and governance (ESG) considerations may be integrated into portfolio planning and construction.

1. INTRODUCTION

To build a suitable portfolio for a client, investment advisers should first seek to understand the client's investment goals, resources, circumstances, and constraints. Investors can be

Portfolio Management, Second Edition, by Alistair Byrne, PhD, CFA, and Frank E. Smudde, MSc, CFA.

categorized into broad groups based on shared characteristics with respect to these factors (e.g., various types of individual investors and institutional investors). Even investors within a given type, however, will invariably have a number of distinctive requirements. In this chapter, we consider in detail the planning for investment success based on an individualized understanding of the client.

This chapter is organized as follows: Section 2 discusses the investment policy statement, a written document that captures the client's investment objectives and the constraints. Section 3 discusses the portfolio construction process, including the first step of specifying a strategic asset allocation for the client. Section 4 concludes and summarizes the chapter.

2. PORTFOLIO PLANNING

Portfolio planning can be defined as a program developed in advance of constructing a portfolio that is expected to define the client's investment objectives. The written document governing this process is the investment policy statement (IPS). The IPS is sometimes complemented by a document outlining policy on **sustainable investing**—distinguishing between companies (or sectors) that either can or cannot efficiently manage their financial, environmental, and human capital resources to generate attractive long-term profitability.[1] Policies on sustainable investing may also be integrated within the IPS itself. In the remainder of this chapter, the integration of sustainable investing within the IPS will be our working assumption.

2.1. The Investment Policy Statement

The IPS is the starting point of the portfolio management process. Without a full understanding of the client's situation and requirements, it is unlikely that successful results will be achieved. "Success" can be defined as a client achieving his or her important investment goals using means that he or she is comfortable with (in terms of risks taken and other concerns). The IPS essentially communicates a plan for achieving investment success.

The IPS is typically developed following a fact-finding discussion with the client. This fact-finding discussion can include the use of a questionnaire designed to articulate the client's risk tolerance as well as specific circumstances. In the case of institutional clients, the fact finding may involve asset–liability management studies, identification of liquidity needs, and a wide range of tax and legal considerations.

The IPS can take a variety of forms.[2] A typical format will include the client's investment objectives and the constraints that apply to the client's portfolio.

The client's objectives are specified in terms of risk tolerance and return requirements. These must be consistent with each other: a client is unlikely to be able to find a portfolio

---

[1]In practice, the term "sustainable investing" is sometimes synonymous with "responsible investing" or "socially responsible investing."

[2]In this chapter, an IPS is assumed to be a document governing investment management activities covering all or most of the financial wealth of a client. In many practical contexts, investment professionals work with investment mandates that only cover parts of a client's wealth or financial risk. Governance documents such as "Limited Partnership Agreements" and "Investment Management Agreements" will govern such mandates. Their contents are to a large degree comparable to the contents of the IPS as described in this chapter.

that offers a relatively high expected return without taking on a relatively high level of expected risk. As part of their financial planning, clients may specify specific spending goals, each of which could have different risk tolerance and return objectives.

The constraints section covers factors that need to be taken into account when constructing a portfolio for the client that meets the objectives. The typical categories are liquidity requirements, time horizon, regulatory requirements, tax status, and unique needs. The constraints may be internal (i.e., set by the client), or external (i.e., set by law or regulation). These are discussed in detail below.

Having a well-constructed IPS for all clients should be standard procedure for an investment manager. The investment manager should build the portfolio with reference to the IPS and be able to refer to it to assess the suitability of a particular investment for the client. In some cases, the need for the IPS goes beyond simply being a matter of standard procedure. In some countries, the IPS (or an equivalent document) is a legal or regulatory requirement. For example, UK pension schemes must have a statement of investment principles under the Pensions Act 1995 (Section 35), and this statement is in essence an IPS. The UK Financial Services Authority also has requirements for investment firms to "know their customers." The European Union's Markets in Financial Instruments Directive ("MiFID") requires firms to assign clients to categories, such as eligible counterparties, institutional clients, and retail clients.

In the case of an institution, such as a pension plan or university endowment, the IPS may set out the governance arrangements that apply to the investment funds. For example, this information could cover the investment committee's approach to appointing and reviewing investment managers for the portfolio, and the discretion that those managers have.

The IPS should be reviewed on a regular basis to ensure that it remains consistent with the client's circumstances and requirements. For example, the UK Pensions Regulator suggests that a pension scheme's statements of investment principles—a form of IPS—should be reviewed at least every three years. The IPS should also be reviewed if the manager becomes aware of a material change in the client's circumstances, or on the initiative of the client when his or her objectives, time horizon, or liquidity needs change.

2.2. Major Components of an IPS

There is no single standard format for an IPS. Many IPS and investment governance documents with a similar purpose (as noted previously), however, include the following sections:

- *Introduction*. This section describes the client.
- *Statement of Purpose*. This section states the purpose of the IPS.
- *Statement of Duties and Responsibilities*. This section details the duties and responsibilities of the client, the custodian of the client's assets, and the investment managers.
- *Procedures*. This section explains the steps to take to keep the IPS current and the procedures to follow to respond to various contingencies.
- *Investment Objectives*. This section explains the client's objectives in investing.
- *Investment Constraints*. This section presents the factors that constrain the client in seeking to achieve the investment objectives.

- *Investment Guidelines*. This section provides information about how policy should be executed (e.g., on the permissible use of leverage and derivatives) and on specific types of assets excluded from investment, if any.
- *Evaluation and Review*. This section provides guidance on obtaining feedback on investment results.
- *Appendices*: (A) Strategic Asset Allocation (B) Rebalancing Policy. Many investors specify a strategic asset allocation (SAA), also known as the policy portfolio, which is the baseline allocation of portfolio assets to asset classes in view of the investor's investment objectives and the investor's policy with respect to rebalancing asset class weights. This SAA may include a statement of policy concerning hedging risks such as currency risk and interest rate risk.

The sections that are most closely linked to the client's distinctive needs, and probably the most important from a planning perspective, are those dealing with investment objectives and constraints. An IPS focusing on these two elements has been called an IPS in an "objectives and constraints" format.

In the following sections, we discuss the investment objectives and constraints format of an IPS beginning with risk and return objectives. The process of developing the IPS is the basic mechanism for evaluating and trying to improve an investor's overall expected return–risk stance. In a portfolio context, return objectives and expectations must be tailored to be consistent with risk objectives. The risk and return objectives must also be consistent with the constraints that apply to the portfolio. In recent years, a large proportion of investors explicitly included non-financial considerations when formulating their investment policies. This is often referred to as sustainable investing (which we discussed earlier, as well as related terms) whereby environmental, social, and governance (ESG) considerations are reflected. Sustainable investing both recognizes that ESG considerations may eventually affect the financial risk-return profile of the portfolio and expresses societal convictions of the investor. In a survey by CFA Institute,[3] 73% of respondents indicated they take ESG factors in consideration in their investment decisions on behalf of their clients. In this chapter, we discuss sustainable investing aspects of investment policy, where relevant.

2.2.1. Risk Objectives

When constructing a portfolio for a client, it is important to ensure that the risk of the portfolio is suitable for the client. The IPS should state clearly the risk tolerance of the client. Risk objectives are specifications for portfolio risk that reflect the risk tolerance of the client. Quantitative risk objectives can be absolute or relative or a combination of the two.

Examples of an absolute risk objective would be a desire not to suffer any loss of capital or not to lose more than a given percent of capital in any 12-month period. Note that these objectives are not related to investment market performance, good or bad, and are absolute in the sense of being self-standing. The fulfillment of such objectives could be achieved by not taking any risk; for example, by investing in an insured bank certificate of deposit at a creditworthy bank. If investments in risky assets are undertaken, however, such statements would need to be restated as a probability statement to be operational (i.e., practically useful). For example, the desire not to lose more than 4 percent of capital in any 12-month period

---

[3]*Environmental, Societal, and Governance Issues in Investing: A Guide for Investment Professionals*, CFA Institute, 2015

might be restated as an objective that with 95 percent probability the portfolio not lose more than 4 percent in any 12-month period. Measures of absolute risk include the variance or standard deviation of returns and value at risk.[4]

Some clients may choose to express relative risk objectives, which relate risk relative to one or more benchmarks perceived to represent appropriate risk standards. For example, investments in large-cap UK equities could be benchmarked to an equity market index, such as the FTSE 100 Index. The S&P 500 Index could be used as a benchmark for large-cap US equities, or for investments with cash-like characteristics, the benchmark could be an interest rate such as Libor or a Treasury bill rate. For risk relative to a benchmark, the measure could be tracking risk, or tracking error.[5] In practice, such risk objectives are used in situations where the total wealth management activities on behalf of a client are divided into partial mandates.

For institutional clients, the benchmark may be linked to some form of liability the institution has. For example, a pension plan must meet the pension payments as they come due and the risk objective will be to minimize the probability that it will fail to do so. A related return objective might be to outperform the discount rate used in finding the present value of liabilities over a multi-year time horizon.

When a policy portfolio (that is, a specified set of long-term asset class weightings and hedge ratios) is used, the risk objective may be expressed as a desire for the portfolio return to be within a band of plus or minus X percent of the benchmark return calculated by assigning an index or benchmark to represent each asset class present in the policy portfolio. Again, this objective has to be interpreted as a statement of probability; for example, a 95 percent probability that the portfolio return will be within X percent of the benchmark return over a stated time period. Example 1 reviews this material.

EXAMPLE 1   Types of Risk Objectives

A Japanese institutional investor has a portfolio valued at ¥10 billion. The investor expresses his first risk objective as a desire not to lose more than ¥1 billion in the coming 12-month period. The investor specifies a second risk objective of achieving returns within 4 percent of the return to the TOPIX stock market index, which is the investor's benchmark. Based on this information, address the following:

1. A. Characterize the first risk objective as absolute or relative.
    B. Give an example of how the risk objective could be restated in a practical manner.

2. A. Characterize the second risk objective as absolute or relative.
    B. Identify a measure for quantifying the risk objective.

---

[4]**Value at risk** is a money measure of the minimum value of losses expected during a specified time period at a given level of probability.
[5]**Tracking risk** (sometimes called **tracking error**) is the standard deviation of the differences between a portfolio's returns and its benchmark's returns.

Solutions:

1. A. This is an absolute risk objective.
   B. This risk objective could be restated in a practical manner by specifying that the 12-month 95 percent value at risk of the portfolio must not be more than ¥1 billion.

2. A. This is a relative risk objective.
   B. This risk objective could be quantified using the tracking risk as a measure. For example, assuming returns follow a normal distribution, an expected tracking risk of 2 percent would imply a return within 4 percent of the index return approximately 95 percent of the time. Remember that tracking risk is stated as a one standard deviation measure.

A client's overall risk tolerance is a function of the client's ability to bear (accept) risk and his or her "risk attitude," which might be considered as the client's willingness to take risk. For ease of expression, from this point on we will refer to ability to bear risk and willingness to take risk as the two components of risk tolerance. Above average ability to bear risk and above average willingness to take risk imply above average risk tolerance. Below average ability to bear risk and below average willingness to take risk imply below average risk tolerance. These interactions are shown in Exhibit 1.

EXHIBIT 1.   Risk Tolerance

	Ability to Bear Risk	
Willingness to Take Risk	**Below Average**	**Above Average**
Below Average	Below-average risk tolerance	Resolution needed
Above Average	Resolution needed	Above-average risk tolerance

The *ability* to bear risk is measured mainly in terms of objective factors, such as time horizon, expected income, and the level of wealth relative to liabilities. For example, an investor with a 20-year time horizon can be considered to have a greater ability to bear risk, other things being equal, than an investor with a 2-year horizon. This difference is because over 20 years there is more scope for losses to be recovered or other adjustments to circumstances to be made than there is over two years.

Similarly, an investor whose assets are comfortably in excess of their liabilities has more ability to bear risk than an investor whose wealth and expected future expenditure are more closely balanced. For example, a wealthy individual who can sustain a comfortable lifestyle after a very substantial investment loss has a relatively high ability to bear risk. A pension plan that has a large surplus of assets over liabilities has a relatively high ability to bear risk.

The *willingness* to take risk, or risk attitude, is a more subjective factor based on the client's psychology and perhaps also his or her current circumstances. Although the list of factors that are related to an individual's risk attitude remains open to debate, it is believed that some psychological factors, such as personality type, self-esteem, and inclination to independent thinking, are correlated with risk attitude. Some individuals are comfortable taking financial and investment risk, whereas others find it distressing. Although there is no single agreed-upon method for measuring risk tolerance, a willingness to take risk may be gauged by discussing risk with the client or by asking the client to complete a psychometric questionnaire. For example, financial planning academic John Grable and collaborators have developed 13-item and 5-item risk attitude questionnaires that have undergone some level of technical validation. The five-item questionnaire is shown in Exhibit 2.

EXHIBIT 2.   A Five-Item Risk Assessment Instrument

1. Investing is too difficult to understand.
    a. Strongly agree
    b. Tend to agree
    c. Tend to disagree
    d. Strongly disagree

2. I am more comfortable putting my money in a bank account than in the stock market.
    a. Strongly agree
    b. Tend to agree
    c. Tend to disagree
    d. Strongly disagree

3. When I think of the word "risk" the term "loss" comes to mind immediately.
    a. Strongly agree
    b. Tend to agree
    c. Tend to disagree
    d. Strongly disagree

4. Making money in stocks and bonds is based on luck.
    a. Strongly agree
    b. Tend to agree
    c. Tend to disagree
    d. Strongly disagree

5. In terms of investing, safety is more important than returns.
    a. Strongly agree
    b. Tend to agree
    c. Tend to disagree
    d. Strongly disagree

Source: Grable and Joo (2004).

The responses, a), b), c), and d), are coded 1, 2, 3, and 4, respectively, and summed. The lowest score is 5 and the highest score is 20, with higher scores indicating greater risk tolerance. For two random samples drawn from the faculty and staff of large US universities ($n = 406$), the mean score was 12.86 with a standard deviation of 3.01 and a median (i.e., most frequently observed) score of 13.

Note that a question, such as the first one in Exhibit 2, indicates that risk attitude may be associated with non-psychological factors (such as level of financial knowledge and understanding and decision-making style) as well as psychological factors.

The adviser needs to examine whether a client's ability to accept risk is consistent with the client's willingness to take risk. For example, a wealthy investor with a 20-year time horizon, who is thus able to take risk, may also be comfortable taking risk; in this case the factors are consistent. If the wealthy investor has a low willingness to take risk, there would be a conflict.

In the institutional context, there could also be conflict between ability and willingness to take risk. In addition, different stakeholders within the institution may take different views. For example, the trustees of a well-funded pension plan may desire a low-risk approach to safeguard the funding of the scheme and beneficiaries of the scheme may take a similar view. The sponsor, however, may wish a higher-risk/higher-return approach in an attempt to reduce future funding costs. When a trustee bears a fiduciary responsibility to pension beneficiaries and the interests of the pension sponsor and the pension beneficiaries conflict, the trustee should act in the best interests of the beneficiaries.

When ability to take risk and willingness to take risk are consistent, the investment adviser's task is the simplest. When ability to take risk is below average and willingness to take risk is above average, the investor's risk tolerance should be assessed as below average overall. When ability to take risk is above average but willingness is below average, the portfolio manager or adviser may seek to counsel the client and explain the conflict and its implications. For example, the adviser could outline the reasons why the client is considered to have a high ability to take risk and explain the likely consequences, in terms of reduced expected return, of not taking risk. The investment adviser, however, should not aim to change a client's willingness to take risk that is not a result of a miscalculation or misperception. Modification of elements of personality is not within the purview of the investment adviser's role. The prudent approach is to reach a conclusion about risk tolerance consistent with the lower of the two factors (ability and willingness) and to document the decisions made.

Example 2 is the first of a set that follows the analysis of an investment client through the preparation of the major elements of an IPS.

EXAMPLE 2   The Case of Henri Gascon: Risk Tolerance

Henri Gascon is an energy trader who works for a major French oil company based in Paris. He is 30 years old and married with one son, aged 5. Gascon has decided that it is time to review his financial situation and consults a financial adviser. The financial adviser notes the following aspects of Gascon's situation:

- Gascon's annual salary of €250,000 is more than sufficient to cover the family's outgoings.
- Gascon owns his apartment outright and has €1,000,000 of savings.
- Gascon perceives that his job is reasonably secure.
- Gascon has a good knowledge of financial matters and is confident that equity markets will deliver positive returns over the longer term.

- In the risk tolerance questionnaire, Gascon strongly disagrees with the statements that "making money in stocks and bonds is based on luck" and that "in terms of investing, safety is more important than returns."
- Gascon expects that most of his savings will be used to fund his retirement, which he hopes to start at age 50.

Based only on the information given, which of the following statements is *most* accurate?

A. Gascon has a low ability to take risk, but a high willingness to take risk.
B. Gascon has a high ability to take risk, but a low willingness to take risk.
C. Gascon has a high ability to take risk, and a high willingness to take risk.

Solution: C is correct. Gascon has a high income relative to outgoings, a high level of assets, a secure job, and a time horizon of 20 years. This information suggests a high *ability* to take risk. At the same time, Gascon is knowledgeable and confident about financial markets and responds to the questionnaire with answers that suggest risk tolerance. This result suggests he also has a high *willingness* to take risk.

EXAMPLE 3   The Case of Jacques Gascon: Risk Tolerance

Henri Gascon is so pleased with the services provided by the financial adviser, that he suggests to his brother Jacques that he should also consult the adviser. Jacques thinks it is a good idea. Jacques is a self-employed computer consultant also based in Paris. He is 40 years old and divorced with four children, aged between 12 and 16. The financial adviser notes the following aspects of Jacques' situation:

- Jacques' consultancy earnings average €40,000 per annum, but are quite volatile.
- Jacques is required to pay €10,000 per year to his ex-wife and children.
- Jacques has a mortgage on his apartment of €100,000 and €10,000 of savings.
- Jacques has a good knowledge of financial matters and expects that equity markets will deliver very high returns over the longer term.
- In the risk tolerance questionnaire, Jacques strongly disagrees with the statements "I am more comfortable putting my money in a bank account than in the stock market" and "When I think of the word "risk" the term "loss" comes to mind immediately."
- Jacques expects that most of his savings will be required to support his children at university.

Based on the above information, which statement is correct?

A. Jacques has a low ability to take risk, but a high willingness to take risk.
B. Jacques has a high ability to take risk, but a low willingness to take risk.
C. Jacques has a high ability to take risk, and a high willingness to take risk.

Solution: A is correct. Jacques does not have a particularly high income, his income is unstable, and he has reasonably high outgoings for his mortgage and maintenance payments. His investment time horizon is approximately two to six years given the ages of his children and his desire to support them at university. This finely balanced financial situation and short time horizon suggests a low ability to take risk. In contrast, his expectations for financial market returns and risk tolerance questionnaire answers suggest a high willingness to take risk. The financial adviser may wish to explain to Jacques how finely balanced his financial situation is and suggest that, despite his desire to take more risk, a relatively cautious portfolio might be the most appropriate approach to take.

2.2.2. Return Objectives

A client's return objectives can be stated in a number of ways. Similar to risk objectives, return objectives may be stated on an absolute or a relative basis.

As an example of an absolute objective, the client may want to achieve a particular percentage rate of return, for example, X percent. This could be a nominal rate of return or be expressed in real (inflation-adjusted) terms.

Alternatively, the return objective can be stated on a relative basis, for example, relative to a benchmark return. The benchmark could be an equity market index, such as the S&P 500 or the FTSE 100, or a cash rate of interest such as Libor. A relative return objective might be stated as, for example, a desire to outperform the benchmark index by one percentage point per year.

Some institutions also set their return objective relative to a peer group or universe of managers; for example, an endowment aiming for a return that is in the top 50 percent of returns of similar institutions, or a private equity mandate aiming for returns in the top quartile among the private equity universe. This objective can be problematic when limited information is known about the investment strategies or the returns calculation methodology being used by peers, and we must bear in mind the impossibility of *all* institutions being "above average." Furthermore, a good benchmark should be investable—that is, able to be replicated by the investor—and a peer benchmark typically does not meet that criterion.

In each case, the return requirement can be stated before or after fees. Care should be taken that the fee basis used is clear and understood by both the manager and client. The return can also be stated on either a pre- or post-tax basis when the investor is required to pay tax. For a taxable investor, the baseline is to state and analyze returns on an after-tax basis.

The return objective could be a required return—that is, the amount the investor needs to earn to meet a particular future goal—such as a certain level of retirement income.

The manager or adviser must ensure that the return objective is realistic. Care should be taken that client and manager are in agreement on whether the return objective is nominal (which is more convenient for measurement purposes) or real (i.e., inflation-adjusted, which usually relates better to the objective). It must be consistent with the client's risk objective (high expected returns are unlikely to be possible without high levels of risk) and also with the current economic and market environment. For example, 15 percent nominal returns might be possible when inflation is 10 percent, but will be unlikely when inflation is 3 percent.

When a client has unrealistic return expectations, the manager or adviser will need to counsel them about what is achievable in the current market environment and within the client's tolerance for risk.

EXAMPLE 4   The Case of Henri Gascon: Return Objectives

Having assessed his risk tolerance, Henri Gascon now begins to discuss his retirement income needs with the financial adviser. He wishes to retire at age 50, which is 20 years from now. His salary meets current and expected future expenditure requirements, but he does not expect to be able to make any additional pension contributions to his fund. Gascon sets aside €100,000 of his savings as an emergency fund to be held in cash. The remaining €900,000 is invested for his retirement.

Gascon estimates that a before-tax amount of €2,000,000 in today's money will be sufficient to fund his retirement income needs. The financial adviser expects inflation to average 2 percent per year over the next 20 years. Pension fund contributions and pension fund returns in France are exempt from tax, but pension fund distributions are taxable upon retirement.

1. Which of the following is closest to the amount of money Gascon will have to accumulate in nominal terms by his retirement date to meet his retirement income objective (i.e., expressed in money of the day in 20 years)?
   A. €900,000
   B. €2,000,000
   C. €3,000,000

2. Which of the following is closest to the annual rate of return that Gascon must earn on his pension portfolio to meet his retirement income objective?
   A. 2.0%
   B. 6.2%
   C. 8.1%

Solution to 1. C is correct. At 2 percent annual inflation, €2,000,000 in today's money equates to €2,971,895 in 20 years measured in money of the day [2m × $(1 + 2\%)^{20}$].

Solution to 2. B is correct. €900,000 growing at 6.2 percent per year for 20 years will accumulate to €2,997,318, which is just above the required amount. (The solution of 6.2 percent comes from €2,997,318/€900,000 = $(1 + X)^{20}$, where X is the required rate of return.)

In the following sections, we analyze five major types of constraints on portfolio selection: liquidity, time horizon, tax concerns, legal and regulatory factors, and unique circumstances.

2.2.3. Liquidity Requirements

The IPS should state what the likely requirements are to withdraw funds from the portfolio. Examples for an individual investor would be outlays for covering health care payments or tuition fees. For institutions, it could be spending rules and requirements for endowment funds, the existence of claims coming due in the case of property and casualty insurance, or benefit payments for pension funds and life insurance companies.

When the client does have such a requirement, the manager should allocate part of the portfolio to cover the liability. This part of the portfolio will be invested in assets that are liquid—that is, easily converted to cash—and have low risk when the liquidity need is actually present (e.g., a bond maturing at the time when private education expenses will be incurred), so that their value is known with reasonable certainty. For example, the asset allocation in the insurance portfolios of US insurer Progressive Corporation (see Exhibit 3) shows a large allocation to fixed-income investments (called "Fixed maturities" by the company), some of which are either highly liquid or have a short maturity. These investments enable the company, in the case of automobile insurance, to pay claims for which the timing is unpredictable.

EXHIBIT 3.   Asset Allocation of Progressive Corporation

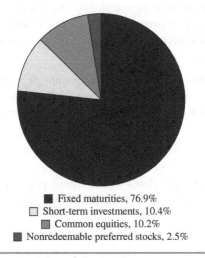

Fixed maturities, 76.9%
Short-term investments, 10.4%
Common equities, 10.2%
Nonredeemable preferred stocks, 2.5%

Source: Progressive Corporation, 2018 Second Quarter Report.

2.2.4. Time Horizon

The IPS should state the time horizon over which the investor is investing. It may be the period over which the portfolio is accumulating before any assets need to be withdrawn; it could also be the period until the client's circumstances are likely to change. For example, a 55-year-old pension plan investor hoping to retire at age 65 has a ten-year horizon. The portfolio may not be liquidated at age 65, but its structure may need to change, for example, as the investor begins to draw an income from the fund.

The time horizon of the investor will affect the nature of investments used in the portfolio. Illiquid or risky investments may be unsuitable for an investor with a short time horizon because the investor may not have enough time to recover from investment losses, for example. Such investments, however, may be suitable for an investor with a longer horizon, especially if the risky investments are expected to have higher returns.

EXAMPLE 5   Investment Time Horizon

1. Frank Johnson is investing for retirement and has a 20-year horizon. He has an average risk tolerance. Which investment is likely to be the *least* suitable for a major allocation in Johnson's portfolio?
   A. Listed equities
   B. Private equity
   C. US Treasury bills

2. Al Smith has to pay a large tax bill in six months and wants to invest the money in the meantime. Which investment is likely to be the *least* suitable for a major allocation in Smith's portfolio?
   A. Listed equities
   B. Private equity
   C. US Treasury bills

Solution to 1: C is correct. With a 20-year horizon and average risk tolerance, Johnson can accept the additional risk of listed equities and private equity compared with US Treasury bills.

Solution to 2: B is correct. Private equity is risky, has no public market, and is the least liquid among the assets mentioned.

2.2.5. Tax Concerns

Tax status varies among investors. Some investors will be subject to taxation on investment returns and some will not. For example, in many countries returns to pension funds are exempt from tax. Some investors will face a different tax rate on income (dividends and interest payments) than they do on capital gains (associated with increases in asset prices). Typically, when there is a differential, income is taxed more highly than gains. Gains may be subject to a lower rate of tax or part or all of the gain may be exempt from taxation. Furthermore, income may be taxed as it is earned, whereas gains may be taxed when they are realized. Hence, in such cases there is a time value of money benefit in the deferment of taxation of gains relative to income.

In many cases, the portfolio should reflect the tax status of the client. For example, a taxable investor may wish to hold a portfolio that emphasizes capital gains and receives little income. A taxable investor based in the United States is also likely to consider including U.S. municipal bonds ("munis") in his or her portfolio because interest income from munis, unlike from treasuries and corporate bonds, is exempt from taxes. A tax-exempt investor, such as a pension fund, will be relatively indifferent to the form of returns.

2.2.6. Legal and Regulatory Factors

The IPS should state any legal and regulatory restrictions that constrain how the portfolio is invested.

In some countries, such institutional investors as pension funds are subject to restrictions on the composition of the portfolio. For example, there may be a limit on the proportion of equities or other risky assets in the portfolio, or on the proportion of the portfolio that may be invested overseas. The United States has no limits on pension fund asset allocation but some countries do, examples of which are shown in Exhibit 4. Pension funds also often face restrictions on the percentage of assets that can be invested in securities issued by the plan sponsor, so-called **self-investment limits**.

EXHIBIT 4.   Examples of Pension Fund Investment Restrictions

Country	Listed Equity	Real Estate	Government Bonds	Corporate Bonds	Foreign Currency Exposure
Switzerland	50%	30%	100%	100%	Unhedged 30%
Japan	100%	Not permitted	100%	100%	No limits
South Africa	75%	25%	100%	75%	25%

Source: OECD Survey of Investment Regulation of Pension Funds, July 2018.

When an individual has access to material nonpublic information about a particular security, this situation may also form a constraint. For example, the directors of a public company may need to refrain from trading the company's stock at certain points of the year before financial results are published. The IPS should note this constraint so that the portfolio manager does not inadvertently trade the stock on the client's behalf.

2.2.7. Unique Circumstances

This section of the IPS should cover any other aspect of the client's circumstances, including beliefs and values, that is likely to have a material impact on the composition of the portfolio. A client may have considerations derived from his or her religion or ethical values that could constrain investment choices. For instance, an investor seeking compliance with Shari'a (the Islamic law) will avoid investing in businesses and financial instruments inconsistent with Shari'a, such as casinos and bonds, because Shari'a prohibits gambling and lending money on interest. Similarly, an investor may wish to avoid investments that he or she believes are inconsistent with their faith. Charitable and pension fund investors may have constituencies that want to express their values in an investment portfolio.

Whether rooted in religious beliefs or not, a client may have personal objections to certain products (e.g., weapons, tobacco, gambling) or practices (e.g., environmental impact of business activities, human impact of government policies, labor standards), which could lead to the exclusion of certain companies, countries, or types of securities (e.g., interest-bearing debt) from the investable universe as well as the client's benchmark. Such considerations are often referred to as ESG (environmental, social, governance), and investing in accordance with such considerations is referred to as SRI (socially responsible investing).

There are several implementation approaches in which ESG considerations can be expressed in an investment portfolio. The oldest form is **negative screening** (or **exclusionary screening**), which refers to the practice of excluding certain sectors or excluding companies that deviate from accepted standards or norms. Exclusion based on *values*, such as exclusion of gambling, alcohol, and tobacco-related companies, relate to an investor's moral or ethical beliefs in a company's or sector's business. Exclusion based on standards and norms refers to business practices that an investor does not want to be associated with from either a reputational or financial risk point of view. These practices may include harmful production processes, corruption, and land ownership issues.

Another common approach is **best-in-class**, whereby investors seek to identify companies within an industry that rank (or score) most favorably based on ESG considerations. Under this approach, investor portfolios would include only securities of those companies that exceed a certain threshold when evaluating ESG considerations. **Shareholder engagement** (sometimes call *active ownership*) is the practice of entering into a dialogue with companies (including with respect to ESG issues). Note that this is a different approach than best-in-class selection, where securities companies that do not meet investor standards are excluded. Generally speaking, the IPS should contain guidelines on shareholder voting behavior.

While exclusionary screening and best-in-class eliminate investment options, **thematic investing** and **impact investing** focus on investment in objectives, themes, and trends that relate positively to ESG issues. An example of a thematic investment (i.e., related to a business theme or societal trend) that considers ESG would be investments in alternative energy providers. In impact investing, an investment is selected primarily on its expected social or environmental benefits with measurable investment returns.

The final ESG implementation approach, **ESG integration**, refers to the integration of qualitative and quantitative ESG factors into traditional security and industry analysis. The focus of ESG integration is to identify risks and opportunities arising from ESG factors and to determine whether a company is properly managing its ESG resources in accordance with a sustainable business model. Examples of ESG integration may include potential earnings per share dilution due to a company's overly generous options program for key executives; a company's poor environmental safety or labor standards potentially resulting in a large future liability that affects the company's profitability and financial condition; or a company's technology leadership position in a certain production process technology may give a company a competitive advantage once new regulations come into place.

These ESG implementation approaches may impact a portfolio manager's investment universe and, in some cases, the manner in which investment management firms operate. The growth of ESG investing has resulted in the development of new investment management services, such as data providers specializing in quantitative and qualitative data on sustainability and governance aspects of businesses. Data quality, however, needs to be judged carefully in each case: disclosure standards differ across jurisdictions; data services companies may have limited coverage of a relevant investment universe; and data item definitions may differ. Nevertheless, the availability of such data makes it possible to estimate certain ESG considerations (e.g., the CO_2 footprint of an investment portfolio) and implement these considerations as a constraint in the portfolio construction process.

EXAMPLE 6   Ethical Preferences

The F&C Responsible UK Equity Growth Fund is designed for investors who wish to have ethical and environmental principles applied to the selection of their investments. The fund's managers apply both positive (characteristics to be emphasized in the portfolio) and negative (characteristics to be avoided in the portfolio) screening criteria:

Positive criteria

- Supplies the basic necessities of life (e.g., healthy food, housing, clothing, water, energy, communication, health care, public transport, safety, personal finance, education)
- Offers product choices for ethical and sustainable lifestyles (e.g. fair trade, organic)
- Improves quality of life through the responsible use of new technologies
- Shows good environmental management
- Actively addresses climate change (e.g., renewable energy, energy efficiency)
- Promotes and protects human rights
- Supports good employment practices
- Provides a positive impact on local communities
- Maintains good relations with customers and suppliers
- Applies effective anti-corruption controls
- Uses transparent communication

Negative criteria

- Tobacco production
- Alcohol production
- Gambling
- Violent material
- Manufacture and sale of weapons
- Unnecessary exploitation of animals
- Nuclear power generation
- Poor environmental practices
- Human rights abuses
- Poor relations with employees, customers or suppliers

[Excerpted from F&C documents; www.fandc.com/new/Advisor/Default.aspx? ID=79620.]

When the portfolio represents only part of the client's total wealth, there may be aspects or portions of wealth not under the control of the manager that have implications for the portfolio. For example, an employee of a public company whose labor income and retirement income provision are reliant on that company and who may have substantial investment exposure to the company through employee share options and stock holdings, may decide that their portfolio should not invest additional amounts in that stock. An entrepreneur may be reluctant to see his or her portfolio invested in the shares of competing businesses or in any business that has risk exposures aligned with his or her entrepreneurial venture.

A client's income may rely on a particular industry or asset class. Appropriate diversification requires that industry or asset class to be de-emphasized in the client's investments. For example, a stockbroker should consider having a relatively low weighting in equities, as his skills and thus income-generating ability are worth less when equities do not perform well. Employees should similarly be wary of having concentrated share positions in the equity of the company they work for. If the employer encounters difficulties, not only may the employee lose his or her job, but their investment portfolio could also suffer a significant loss of value.

2.3. Gathering Client Information

As noted above, it is important for portfolio managers and investment advisers to know their clients. For example, in the EU, MiFID II requires financial intermediaries to undertake substantial fact finding. This is required not only in the case of full service wealth management or in the context of an IPS, but also in "lighter" forms of financial intermediation, such as advisory relationships (in which clients make investment decisions after consultation with their investment adviser or broker) or execution-only relationships (in which the client makes his investment decisions independently).

An exercise in fact finding about the customer should take place at the beginning of the client relationship. This will involve gathering information about the client's circumstances as well as discussing the client's objectives and requirements.

Important data to gather from a client should cover family and employment situation as well as financial information. If the client is an individual, it may also be necessary to know about the situation and requirements of the client's spouse or other family members. The health of the client and his or her dependents is also relevant information. In an institutional relationship, it will be important to know about key stakeholders in the organization and what their perspective and requirements are. Information gathering may be done in an informal way or may involve structured interviews or questionnaires or analysis of data. Many advisers will capture data electronically and use special systems that record data and produce customized reports.

Good record keeping is very important, and may be crucial in a case in which any aspect of the client relationship comes into dispute at a later stage.

EXAMPLE 7 Henri Gascon: Description of Constraints

Henri Gascon continues to discuss his investment requirements with the financial adviser. The financial adviser begins to draft the constraints section of the IPS.

Gascon expects that he will continue to work for the oil company and that his relatively high income will continue for the foreseeable future. Gascon and his wife do not plan to have any additional children, but expect that their son will go to a university at age 18. They expect that their son's education costs can be met out of their salary income.

Gascon's emergency reserve of €100,000 is considered to be sufficient as a reserve for unforeseen expenditures and emergencies. His retirement savings of €900,000 has been contributed to his defined-contribution pension plan account to fund his retirement. Under French regulation, pension fund contributions are paid from gross income (i.e., income prior to deduction of tax) and pension fund returns are exempt from tax, but pension payments from a fund to retirees are taxed as income to the retiree.

With respect to Gascon's retirement savings portfolio, refer back to Example 2 as needed and address the following:

1. As concerns liquidity,
   A. a maximum of 50 percent of the portfolio should be invested in liquid assets.
   B. the portfolio should be invested entirely in liquid assets because of high spending needs.
   C. the portfolio has no need for liquidity because there are no short-term spending requirements.

2. The investment time horizon is closest to
   A. 5 years.
   B. 20 years.
   C. 40 years.

3. As concerns taxation, the portfolio
   A. should emphasize capital gains because income is taxable.
   B. should emphasize income because capital gains are taxable.
   C. is tax exempt and thus indifferent between income and capital gains.

4. The principle legal and regulatory factors applying to the portfolio are
   A. US Securities laws.
   B. European banking laws.
   C. French pension fund regulations.

5. As concerns unique needs, the portfolio should
   A. have a high weighting in oil and other commodity stocks.
   B. be invested only in responsible and sustainable investments.
   C. not have significant exposure to oil and other commodity stocks.

Solution to 1. C is correct. The assets are for retirement use, which is 20 years away. Any short-term spending needs will be met from other assets or income.

Solution to 2. B is correct. The relevant time horizon is to the retirement date, which is 20 years away. The assets may not be liquidated at that point, but a restructuring of the portfolio is to be expected as Gascon starts to draw an income from it.

Solution to 3. C is correct. Because no tax is paid in the pension fund, it does not matter whether returns come in the form of income or capital gains.

Solution to 4. C is correct. The management of the portfolio will have to comply with any rules relating the French pension funds.

Solution to 5. C is correct. Gascon's human capital (i.e., future labor income) is affected by the prospects of the oil industry. If his portfolio has significant exposure to oil stocks, he would be increasing a risk exposure he already has.

Example 8, the final one based on Henri Gascon, shows how the information obtained from the fact-finding exercises might be incorporated into the objectives and constraints section of an IPS.

EXAMPLE 8   Henri Gascon: Outline of an IPS

Following is a simplified excerpt from the IPS the adviser prepares for Henri Gascon, covering objectives and constraints.

Risk Objectives:
- The portfolio may take on relatively high amounts of risk in seeking to meet the return requirements. With a 20-year time horizon and significant assets and income,

the client has an above average ability to take risk. The client is a knowledgeable investor, with an above average willingness to take risk. Hence, the client's risk tolerance is above average, explaining the above portfolio risk objective.
- The portfolio should be well diversified with respect to asset classes and concentration of positions within an asset class. Although the client has above average risk tolerance, his investment assets should be diversified to control the risk of catastrophic loss.

Return Objectives:
- The portfolio's long-term return requirement is 6.2 percent per year, in nominal terms and net of fees, to meet the client's retirement income goal.

Constraints:
- *Liquidity*: The portfolio consists of pension fund assets and there is no need for liquidity in the short to medium term.
- *Time Horizon*: The portfolio will be invested with a 20-year time horizon. The client intends to retire in 20 years, at which time an income will be drawn from the portfolio.
- *Tax Status*: Under French law, contributions to the fund are made gross of tax and returns in the fund are tax-free. Hence, the client is indifferent between income and capital gains in the fund.
- *Legal and Regulatory Factors*: The management of the portfolio must comply with French pension fund regulations.
- *Unique Needs*: The client is an executive in the oil industry. The portfolio should strive to minimize additional exposures to oil and related stocks.

3. PORTFOLIO CONSTRUCTION

Once the IPS has been compiled, the investment manager can construct a suitable portfolio. Strategic asset allocation is a traditional focus of the first steps in portfolio construction. The strategic asset allocation is stated in terms of percent allocations to asset classes. An **asset class** is a category of assets that have similar characteristics, attributes, and risk/return relationships. The **strategic asset allocation** (SAA) is the set of exposures to IPS-permissible asset classes that is expected to achieve the client's long-term objectives given the client's risk profile and investment constraints. An SAA could include a policy of hedging portfolio risks not explicitly covered by asset class weights. The obvious examples are hedge ratios for foreign currency exposure, or the management of interest rate risk resulting from asset-liability mismatch, and the hedging of inflation risk. So-called "overlay" portfolios of derivatives are often used for this purpose.

The focus on the SAA is the result of a number of important investment principles. One principle is that a portfolio's systematic risk accounts for most of its change in value over the long term. **Systematic risk** is risk related to the economic system (e.g., risk related to business cycle) that cannot be eliminated by holding a diversified portfolio. This risk is different from **nonsystematic risk**, which is the unique risks of particular assets, which may be avoided by holding other assets with offsetting risks. A second principle is that the returns to groups of similar assets (e.g., long-term debt claims) predictably reflect exposures to certain sets of systematic factors (e.g., for the debt claims, unexpected changes in the interest rate). Thus, the SAA is a means of providing the investor with exposure to the systematic risks of asset classes in proportions that meet the risk and return objectives.

The process of formulating a strategic asset allocation is based on the IPS, already discussed, and capital market expectations, introduced in Section 3.1. How to make the strategic asset allocation operational with a rebalancing policy and a translation into actual investment portfolios will be described in Section 3.3. Section 3.4 lists some alternatives to the approach chosen and describes some portfolio construction techniques.

3.1. Capital Market Expectations

Capital market expectations are the investor's expectations concerning the risk and return prospects of asset classes, however broadly or narrowly the investor defines those asset classes. When associated with the client's investment objectives, the result is the strategic asset allocation that is expected to allow the client to achieve his or her investment objectives (at least under normal capital market conditions).

Traditionally, capital market expectations are quantified in terms of asset class expected returns, standard deviation of returns, and correlations among pairs of asset classes. Formally, the expected return of an asset class consists of the risk-free rate and one or more risk premium(s) associated with the asset class. Expected returns are in practice developed in a variety of ways, including the use of historical estimates, economic analysis, and various kinds of valuation models. Standard deviations and correlation estimates are frequently based on historical data and risk models.

3.2. The Strategic Asset Allocation

Traditionally, investors have distinguished cash, equities, bonds (government and corporate), and real estate as the major asset classes. In recent years, this list has been expanded with private equity, hedge funds, high yield and emerging market bonds, and commodities. In addition, such assets as art and intellectual property rights may be considered asset classes for those investors prepared to take a more innovative approach and to accept some illiquidity. Combining such new asset classes as well as hedge funds and private equity under the header "alternative investments" has become accepted practice.

As the strategic asset allocation is built up by asset classes, the decision about how to define those asset classes is an important one. Defining the asset classes also determines the extent to which the investor controls the risk and return characteristics of the eventual investment portfolio. For example, separating bonds into government bonds and corporate bonds, and then further separating corporate bonds into investment grade and non-investment grade (high yield) and government bonds into domestic and foreign government bonds, creates four bond categories for which risk–return expectations can be expressed and correlations with other asset classes (and, in an asset–liability management context, with the liabilities) can be estimated. An investment manager who wants to explicitly consider the risk–return characteristics of those bond categories in the strategic asset allocation may choose to treat them as distinct asset classes. Similarly, in equities some investors distinguish between emerging market and developed market equities, between domestic and international equities, or between large-cap and small-cap equities. In some regulatory environments for institutional investors, asset-class definitions are mandatory, thereby forcing investment managers to articulate risk–return expectations (and apply risk management) on the asset classes specified. Conversely, a broader categorization of asset classes leaves the allocation between different categories of bonds and equities, for example, to managers responsible for these asset classes.

When defining asset classes, a number of criteria apply. Intuitively, an asset class should contain relatively homogeneous assets while providing diversification relative to other asset classes. In statistical terms, risk and return expectations should be similar, and paired correlations of assets should be relatively high within an asset class but should be lower versus assets in other asset classes. Also, the asset classes, while being mutually exclusive, should add up to a sufficient approximation of the relevant investable universe. Applying these criteria ensures that the strategic asset allocation process has considered all available investment alternatives.

EXAMPLE 9   Specifying Asset Classes

The strategic asset allocations of many institutional investors make a distinction between domestic equities and international equities, or between developed market equities and emerging market equities. Often, equities are separated into different market capitalization brackets, resulting, for example, in an asset class such as domestic small-cap equity.

The correlation matrix in Exhibit 5 shows the paired correlations of monthly returns between different equity asset classes and other asset classes. Specifically, these correlations are measured over the period from December 2000 through August 2018. In addition, the exhibit shows the annualized volatility of monthly returns.

EXHIBIT 5.   Asset Class Correlation Matrix

Correlations	US Equities	Emerging Markets Equities	European Equities	Japanese Equities	US Small-Cap Equities	Commodities	European Gov't. Bonds	US Treasuries	US Credits	US High-Yield Credit
US Equities	1.00	0.78	0.88	0.59	0.89	0.32	0.08	−0.37	0.19	0.66
Emerging Markets Equities	0.78	1.00	0.84	0.64	0.75	0.46	0.21	−0.24	0.34	0.70
European Equities	0.88	0.84	1.00	0.64	0.79	0.43	0.16	−0.28	0.29	0.68
Japanese Equities	0.59	0.64	0.64	1.00	0.57	0.32	0.24	−0.18	0.29	0.52
US Small-Cap Equities	0.89	0.75	0.79	0.57	1.00	0.32	0.09	−0.36	0.19	0.69
Commodities	0.32	0.46	0.43	0.32	0.32	1.00	0.13	−0.18	0.12	0.36
European Gov't. Bonds	0.08	0.21	0.16	0.24	0.09	0.13	1.00	0.45	0.60	0.30
US Treasuries	−0.37	−0.24	−0.28	−0.18	−0.36	−0.18	0.45	1.00	0.58	−0.19
US Credits	0.19	0.34	0.29	0.29	0.19	0.12	0.60	0.58	1.00	0.54
US High-Yield Credit	0.66	0.70	0.68	0.52	0.69	0.36	0.30	−0.19	0.54	1.00
Volatility	14.3%	21.6%	18.4%	15.6%	18.4%	22.3%	4.9%	4.4%	5.5%	9.3%

Correlations and volatilities have been calculated using monthly returns from December 2000 through August 2018, unhedged, in USD.
Sources: MSCI Bloomberg, S&P.

Based only on the information given, address the following:

1. Contrast the correlations between equity asset classes with the correlations between equity asset classes and US Treasuries.
2. The monthly returns of which equity asset class differ the most from US equities?

Solution to 1: The matrix reveals very strong correlation between the equity asset classes. For example, the correlation between European equities and US equities is 0.88. The correlation of equities with bonds, however, is much lower. For example, US equities, emerging markets equities, European equities, and Japanese equities all have negative correlation with US government bonds (−0.37, −0.24 and −0.28, and −0.18, respectively). It is worth noting, however, that correlations can vary through time and the values shown may be specific to the sample period used.

Solution to 2: Among equity asset classes as listed in the table, the correlation between US and Japanese equities is the lowest, at 0.59. By contrast, correlations between US equities and emerging markets, European and US small cap equities are 0.78 or higher.

Using correlation as a metric, Example 9 tends to indicate that only emerging markets were well differentiated from European equities. So, why do investors still often subdivide equities? Apart from any regulatory reasons, one explanation might be that this decomposition into smaller asset classes corresponds to the way the asset allocation is structured in portfolios. Many investment managers have expertise exclusively in specific areas of the market, such as emerging market equities, US small-cap equity, or international investment-grade credit. Bringing the asset class definitions of the asset allocation in line with investment products actually available in the market may simplify matters from an organizational perspective.

The risk–return profile of the strategic asset allocation depends on the expected returns and risks of the individual asset classes, as well as the correlation between those asset classes. In general, adding assets classes with low correlation improves the risk–return trade-off (more return for similar risk). Typically, the strategic asset allocation for risk-averse investors will have a large weight in government bonds and cash, whereas those with more willingness and ability to take risk will have more of their assets in risky asset classes, such as equities and many types of alternative investments.

It is customary to represent asset classes using benchmarks and universes calculated by providers such as FTSE, MSCI, or Bloomberg. An exclusionary screening or a best-in-class policy (discussed previously) limits the number of securities to choose from, potentially impacting the risk and expected return estimates for these asset classes. Some examples of exclusions may be controversial weaponry or tobacco companies, or investments in certain countries. When such exclusions apply, risk and return estimates based on non-traditional ("off-the-shelf") asset class benchmarks may not be applicable. Separate benchmark indices reflecting the exclusions may be available from the providers to mitigate this issue.

ABP is the pension fund for the Dutch government sector employees. The fund offers teachers, police officers, the military, and other civil servants a defined benefit pension plan, aiming for a pension of 70% of the average career real income for employees. As of the first quarter of 2018, ABP had €405 billion under management. The strategic asset allocation[6] as of this period is shown in Exhibit 6.

EXHIBIT 6   Strategic Asset Allocation for ABP

Real assets	
Equities, developed countries	27%
Equities, emerging markets	9%
Real estate	10%
Private Equity	5%
Hedge Funds	4%
Commodities	5%
Infrastructure	3%
Total real assets	***63%***
Fixed-income securities	
Government bonds	13%
Corporate bonds	13%
Inflation-linked bonds	8%
Emerging market bonds	3%
Total fixed-income securities	***37%***
Total	100%

Source: ABP Quarterly Report Q1 2018.

A strategic asset allocation results from combining the constraints and objectives articulated in the IPS and long-term capital market expectations regarding the asset classes. The strategic asset allocation or policy portfolio will subsequently be implemented into real portfolios. Exhibit 7 illustrates conceptually how investment objectives and constraints and long-term capital market expectations combine into a policy portfolio.

EXHIBIT 7.   Strategic Asset Allocation Process

---

[6]ABP defines an asset class category called "real assets," which contains asset classes (not fixed-income securities) that are expected to perform well in times of inflation, but considered a major risk. The use of the term "real assets" differs from the use elsewhere in the CFA curriculum.

In some frameworks used in practice, the asset allocation is an integral part of the investment policy statement. This presentation, however, keeps the asset allocation separate from the investment policy statement because clients' investment objectives and constraints qualitatively differ in nature from capital market expectations, thus requiring different types of analysis, different sources of information, and different review cycles.

The combination of investment objectives/constraints and capital market expectations theoretically occurs using optimization techniques. In this section we apply mean–variance optimization to an sample set of investment objectives and constraints, using an investment universe with associated market expectations. We assume that investors choosing from a range of asset allocations with similar returns would prefer those with lower risk. Choosing from allocations with similar levels of risk, investors would prefer those with the highest return. Formally, investors' risk and return objectives can be described as a utility function, in which utility increases with higher expected returns and lower risk. This assumption could yield an expected utility equation such as that shown in Equation 1.[7]

$$U_p = E(R_p) - \lambda \sigma_p^2 \tag{1}$$

where

$$U_p = \text{the investor's expected utility from the portfolio}$$
$$E(R_p) = \text{the expected return of the portfolio}$$
$$\sigma_p = \text{the standard deviation of returns of the portfolio}$$
$$\lambda = \text{a measure of the investor's risk aversion}$$

This utility function expresses a positive relationship between utility and expected portfolio return (i.e., higher expected return increases utility, all else equal) and a negative relationship between utility and volatility of portfolio return as measured by the variance of portfolio returns. The stronger the negative relationship, the greater the investor's risk aversion. The portfolio is understood to represent a particular asset allocation. The asset allocation providing the highest expected utility is the one that is optimal for the investor given his or her risk aversion.

For different values of U_p, a line can be plotted that links those combinations of risk and expected return that produces that level of utility: an indifference curve. An investor would attain equal utility from all risk/return combinations on that curve.

Capital market expectations, specified in asset classes' expected returns, standard deviations of return, and correlations, translate into an efficient frontier of portfolios. A multi-asset class portfolio's expected return is given by

$$E(R_p) = \sum_{i=1}^{n} w_i E(R_i) \tag{2}$$

where w_i equals the weight of asset class i in the portfolio, and its risk is given by

$$\sigma_p = \sqrt{\sum_{i=1}^{n} \sum_{j=1}^{n} w_{p,i} w_{p,j} \text{Cov}(R_i, R_j)} \tag{3}$$

---

[7]Sharpe, Chen, Pinto, and McLeavey (2007).

The covariance between the returns on asset classes i and j is given by the product of the correlation between the two asset classes and their standard deviations of return:

$$\text{Cov}(R_i, R_j) = \rho_{i,j}\sigma_i\sigma_j \tag{4}$$

where

$\text{Cov}(R_i, R_j)$ = the covariance between the return of asset classes i and j

$\rho_{i,j}$ = the correlation between the returns of asset classes i and j

The resulting portfolios can be represented as a scatter of dots in a chart depicting their risk and expected return. As a portfolio's risk is a positive function of the risk of its assets and the correlations among them, a portfolio consisting of lowly correlated risky assets has lower risk than one with similarly risky assets with high correlation. It is therefore possible to construct different portfolios with equal expected returns but with different levels of risk. The line that connects those portfolios with the minimal risk for each level of expected return (above that of the **minimum-variance portfolio**—the portfolio with the minimum variance for each given level of expected return) is the efficient frontier. Clearly, the efficient frontier will move "upward" as more lowly correlated assets with sufficient expected return are added to the mix because it lowers the risk in the portfolios for equal expected returns. Similarly, when return expectations increase for asset classes while volatility and correlation assumptions remain unchanged, the efficient frontier will move upward because each portfolio is able to generate higher returns for the same level of risk.

Both the efficient frontier and a range of indifference curves can be plotted in the risk–return space. In Exhibit 8, the dark curves that are concave from below represent efficient frontiers associated with different assumed expected returns. The lighter colored curves are indifference curves. The point where the efficient frontier intersects with the indifference curve with the highest utility attainable (i.e., the point of tangency) represents the optimal asset allocation for the client/investor. In Exhibit 8, efficient frontier 1 has a point of tangency with indifference curve 1. Higher levels of utility, such as those associated with indifference curve 0, can apparently not be reached with the assets underlying the efficient frontier. It is clear that when capital market expectations change, this change moves the efficient frontier away from its original location. In the chart, this movement is illustrated by efficient frontier 2, which incorporates different capital market expectations. This new efficient frontier has a point of tangency with indifference curve 2, which is associated with a lower level of expected utility. Because the point of tangency represents the strategic asset allocation, it implies the asset allocation should be adjusted. Similarly, should investment objectives or constraints change, the indifference curves will change their shape and location. This change will again move the point of tangency, and hence change the asset allocation.

EXHIBIT 8.   Strategic Asset Allocation Efficient Frontier

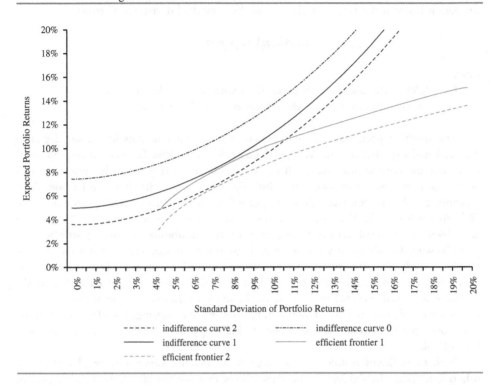

This framework describes how investor objectives and capital market expectations should theoretically be reconciled. It will, however, not be the exact procedure that in practice will be followed. First, an IPS does not necessarily translate the client's investment objectives and constraint into a utility function. Rather, an IPS gives threshold levels for risk and expected return, combined with a number of additional constraints that cannot be captured in this model. Second, the model illustrated is a single-period model, whereas in practice, the constraints from the IPS will make it more appropriate to use multi-period models. Multi-period problems can be more effectively addressed using simulation.

EXAMPLE 10   Approaching an SAA for a Private Investor

Rainer Gottschalk recently sold his local home construction company in the south of Germany to a large homebuilder with a nationwide reach. Upon selling his company, he accepted a job as regional manager for that nationwide homebuilder. He is now considering his and his family's financial future. He looks forward to his new job, where he likes his new role, and which provides him with income to fulfill his family's short-term and medium-term liquidity needs. He feels strongly that he should not invest the proceeds of the sale of his company in real estate because his income already depends on the state of the real estate market. Also, reflecting family values, he feels strongly his savings should not support the tobacco industry. He therefore wants his equity allocation to exclude any stocks of tobacco product manufacturers or retailers. He consults a financial adviser from his bank about how to invest his money to retire in good wealth in 20 years.

The IPS they develop suggests a return objective of 5 percent, with a standard deviation of 10 percent. The bank's asset management division provides Gottschalk and his adviser with the following data (Exhibit 9, Panel 1) on market expectations. The advisor estimates that excluding the tobacco industry from the investment universe affects expected equity returns of European equities by –0.2% and annual standard deviation by +0.1%. The impact on emerging market equities, and on the correlation structure, was considered negligible. Gottschalk accepts the results of these calculations as shown in Exhibit 9, Panel 2.

EXHIBIT 9.   Risk, Return, and Correlation Estimates

			Correlation Matrix		
	Expected Return	Standard Deviation	European Equities	Emerging Mkt Equities	European Govt Bonds
Panel 1					
European equities	6.0%	15.0%	1.00	0.78	–0.08
Emerging market equities	8.0%	20.1%	0.78	1.00	–0.07
European government bonds	2.0%	7.8%	–0.08	–0.07	1.00
Panel 2					
European equities	5.8%	15.1%	1.00	0.78	–0.08
Emerging market equities	8.0%	20.1%	0.78	1.00	–0.07
European government bonds	2.00%	7.8%	–0.08	–0.07	1.00

Standard deviation and correlation calculated over the period March 1999–August 2018. All data in unhedged euros.
Sources: MSCI, Bloomberg

To illustrate the possibilities, the adviser presents Gottschalk with the following plot (Exhibit 10), in which the points forming the shaded curve outline the risk–return characteristics of the portfolios that can be constructed out of the three asset classes. An imaginary line linking the points with the lowest standard deviation for each attainable level of return would be the efficient frontier. The two straight lines show the risk and return objectives. Gottschalk should aim for portfolios that offer an expected return of at least 6 percent (the straight horizontal line or above) and a standard deviation of return of 12 percent or lower (the straight vertical line to the left).

EXHIBIT 10.   Efficient Frontier

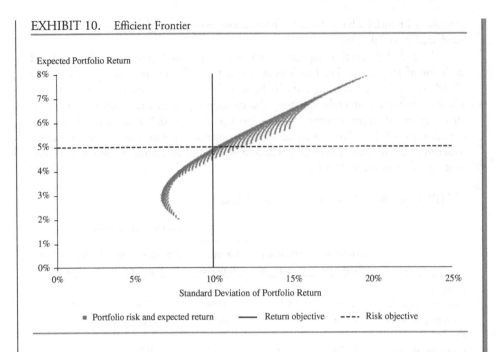

Expected Portfolio Return

Standard Deviation of Portfolio Return

■ Portfolio risk and expected return   ——— Return objective   - - - - Risk objective

Exhibit 10 shows that no portfolio satisfies the two objectives (return of 5% and standard deviation of 10%) exactly, as the highest expected return that can be attained at a maximum volatility of 10% is 4.9%. This difference, Gottschalk and the advisor agree, is acceptable. The portfolio that would correspond with this expected return consists of 16 percent European stocks, 38 percent emerging market equities, and 46 percent government bonds.

3.3. Steps Toward an Actual Portfolio

The strategic asset allocation in itself does not yet represent an actual investment portfolio. It is the first step in implementing an investment strategy. For quantitatively oriented portfolio managers, the next step is often risk budgeting.

As used in this chapter, **risk budgeting** is the process of deciding on the amount of risk to assume in a portfolio (the overall risk budget), and subdividing that risk over the sources of investment return (e.g., strategic asset allocation, tactical asset allocation, and security selection). Because the decision about the total amount of risk to be taken is made in constructing the IPS, at this stage we are concerned about the subdivision of that risk.

Apart from the exposures to systematic risk factors specified in the strategic asset allocation, the returns of an investment strategy depend on two other sources: tactical asset allocation and security selection. **Tactical asset allocation** is the decision to deliberately deviate from the policy exposures to systematic risk factors (i.e., the policy weights of asset classes) with the intent to add value based on forecasts of the near-term returns of those asset classes. For instance, an investor may decide to temporarily invest more of the portfolio in equities than the SAA prescribes if the investor anticipates that equities will deliver a higher return over the short term than other asset classes. **Security selection** is an attempt to generate higher returns than the asset class benchmark by selecting securities with a higher expected return. For example, an investment manager may decide to add more IBM stock in his portfolio than the weight in his equity benchmark if he expects this stock to do better than the benchmark. To fund this purchase, he may sell another stock expected to do worse than either the benchmark or IBM. Obviously, deciding to deviate from policy weights or to select securities aiming to beat the benchmark creates additional uncertainty about returns. This risk is over and above the risk inherent in the policy portfolio. Hence, an investment policy should set risk limits and desired payoffs for each of these three activities.

Risk budgeting implies that the portfolio manager has to choose, for every asset class, whether to deploy security selection as a return generator. This choice is generally referred to as the choice between active or passive management. Contrary to strategic asset allocation, where exposures to sources of systematic risk are selected and sized, security selection is not rewarded with a long-run payoff to risk. Security selection is a zero-sum game: All investors in an asset class are competing with each to identify a typically limited number of assets that are misvalued. In total, the gross returns of all market participants average out to the market return (the reward for taking systematic risk). This implies that the average active investor will match the market return, and that one investor's gain versus the market return is the other investor's loss versus the market return. However, because active managers tend to trade more and have to pay people (including themselves) to generate investment ideas or information leading to such ideas, the average active manager will underperform the market, net of costs. This does not imply, however, that there are no skillful investment managers who, with some consistency, beat their benchmarks. Neither does it imply that all passive managers will be able to match the benchmark. The higher the turnover of an index, the more trading costs a passive manager will incur, making the task of matching the return of an index more difficult.

The likelihood of adding a significant amount of value from security selection depends on the skills of the manager and the informational efficiency of the market for the asset class his skill relates to. The more efficient an asset class or a subset of that asset class (such as a regional stock, bond, or real estate market or a size category within the stock market), the more skillful an asset manager has to be to add value. Broadly speaking, an efficient market is a market in which prices, on average, very quickly reflect newly available information. That requires a sizeable participation of investors trading risk against expected return, acting on rational expectations, using the same or similar pricing models, and having equal opportunities to access relevant information. Clearly, the market for US large-capitalization equities would be quite efficient. By contrast, some regional bond and equity markets do not have the technical and regulatory systems for information dissemination that are sufficient to serve all investors on a timely basis. Skilled managers should be able to exploit the resulting inefficiencies.

Sometimes the choice between active and passive management is actually made implicitly when the asset class is included in the asset allocation. The markets for some assets—such as those for non-listed real estate and infrastructure assets—are so illiquid that it is very difficult to buy a diversified exposure. As a result, participating in that market is not possible without engaging in security selection.

As the portfolio is constructed and its value changes with the returns of the asset classes and securities in which it is invested, the weights of the asset classes will gradually deviate from the policy weights in the strategic asset allocation. This process is referred to as drift.

Periodically, or when a certain threshold deviation from the policy weight (the bandwidth) has been breached, the portfolio should be rebalanced back to the policy weights. The set of rules that guide the process of restoring the portfolio's original exposures to systematic risk factors is known as the **rebalancing policy**. Even absent a formal risk budget, formulating a rebalancing policy is an important element of risk management, as the following example illustrates.

EXAMPLE 11   Strategic and Tactical Asset Allocation for a European Charity

A European charity has an asset allocation at the beginning of the year consisting of the asset classes and weights shown in Exhibit 11.

EXHIBIT 11.   Asset Allocation of a European Charity (beginning of year)

Asset Class	Policy Weight	Corridor (+/–)	Upper Limit	Lower Limit
European equities	30.0%	2.0%	32.0%	28.0%
International equities	15.0%	2.0%	17.0%	13.0%
European government bonds	20.0%	2.0%	22.0%	18.0%
Corporate bonds	20.0%	2.0%	22.0%	18.0%
Cash and money market instruments	15.0%	2.0%	17.0%	13.0%
Total	100.0%			

As Exhibit 11 reveals, the charity has a policy that the asset class weights cannot deviate from the policy weights by more than 2 percent (the corridor). The resulting upper and lower limits for the asset class weights are shown in the rightmost columns of the table. There are two reasons for asset class actual weights to deviate from policy weights: by deliberate choice (tactical asset allocation or market timing) and as a result of divergence of the returns of the different asset classes (drift). In this example, the asset class weights start the year exactly in line with policy weights.

After half a year, the investment portfolio is as shown in Exhibit 12.

EXHIBIT 12.   Asset Allocation for a European Charity (6 months later)

Asset Class	Policy Weight	Corridor (+/–)	Upper Limit	Lower Limit	Period Return	Ending Weight
European equities	30.0%	2.0%	32.0%	28.0%	15.0%	32.4%
International equities	15.0%	2.0%	17.0%	13.0%	10.0%	15.5%
European government bonds	20.0%	2.0%	22.0%	18.0%	0.5%	18.9%
Corporate bonds	20.0%	2.0%	22.0%	18.0%	1.5%	19.1%
Cash and money market instruments	15.0%	2.0%	17.0%	13.0%	1.0%	14.2%
Total	100.0%				6.6%	100.0%

1. Discuss the returns of the portfolio and comment on the main asset weight changes.

Solution to 1: The investment portfolio generated a return calculated on beginning (policy) weights of 6.55 percent or 6.6 percent (= 0.30 × 15% + 0.15 × 10% + 0.20 × 0.5% + 0.20 × 1.5% + 0.15 × 1.0%), mainly driven by a strong equity market. Bond returns were more subdued, leading to considerable drift in asset class weights. In particular, the European equity weight breached the upper limit of its allowed actual weight.

The investment committee decides against reducing European equities back to policy weight and adding to the fixed-income and cash investments toward policy weights. Although this rebalancing would be prudent, the committee decides to engage in tactical asset allocation based on the view that this market will continue to be strong over the course of the year. It decides to just bring European equities back to within its bandwidth (a 32 percent portfolio weight) and add the proceeds to cash. Exhibit 13 shows the outcome after another half year.

EXHIBIT 13.   Asset Allocation for a European Charity (an additional 6 months later)

Asset Class	Policy Weight	Starting Weight	Corridor (+/−)	Upper Limit	Lower Limit	Period Return	Ending Weight
European equities	30.0%	32.0%	2.0%	32.0%	28.0%	−9.0%	29.7%
International equities	15.0%	15.5%	2.0%	17.0%	13.0%	−6.0%	14.9%
European government bonds	20.0%	18.9%	2.0%	22.0%	18.0%	4.0%	20.0%
Corporate bonds	20.0%	19.1%	2.0%	22.0%	18.0%	4.0%	20.2%
Cash and money market instruments	15.0%	14.6%	2.0%	17.0%	13.0%	2.0%	15.2%
Total	100.0%					−2.0%	100.0%

The prior decision not to rebalance to policy weights did not have a positive result. Contrary to the expectations of the investment committee, both European and international equities performed poorly while bonds recovered. The return of the portfolio was −2.0 percent.

2. How much of this return can be attributed to tactical asset allocation?

Solution to 2: Because tactical asset allocation is the deliberate decision to deviate from policy weights, the return contribution from tactical asset allocation is equal to the difference between the actual return, and the return that would have been made if the asset class weights were equal to the policy weights. Exhibit 14 shows the difference to be −0.30 percent.

EXHIBIT 14.   Returns to Tactical Asset Allocation

Asset Class	Policy Weight I	Starting Weight II	Weights Difference III (= II − I)	Period Return IV	TAA Contribution V (= III × IV)
European equities	30.0%	32.0%	2.0%	−9.0%	−0.18%
International equities	15.0%	15.5%	0.5%	−6.0%	−0.03%
European government bonds	20.0%	18.9%	−1.1%	4.0%	−0.05%
Corporate bonds	20.0%	19.1%	−0.9%	4.0%	−0.04%
Cash and money market instruments	15.0%	14.6%	−0.4%	2.0%	−0.01%
Total	100.0%			−2.0%	−0.30%

The process of executing an investment strategy continues with selecting the appropriate manager(s) for each asset class and allocating funds to them. The investment portfolio management process is then well into the execution stage.

The investment managers' performance will be monitored, as well as the results of the tactical and strategic asset allocation. When asset class weights move outside their corridors, money is transferred from the asset classes that have become too large compared with the SAA to those that fall short. Managers as well as the strategic asset allocation will be reviewed on the basis of the outcome of the monitoring process. In addition, capital market expectations may change, as may the circumstances and objectives of the client. These changes could result in an adjustment of the strategic asset allocation.

3.4. ESG Considerations in Portfolio Planning and Construction

The implementation of a policy on sustainable investing affects both strategic asset allocation and implementation of the portfolio construction process. The ESG implementation approaches described previously require a set of instructions for investment managers with regards to the selection of securities, the exercise of shareholder rights, and the selection of investment strategies. Typical examples of ESG issues that help formulate a sustainable investing policy are shown in Exhibit 15.

EXHIBIT 15.   Examples of ESG Issues

Environmental Issues	Social Issues	Governance Issues
• Climate change and carbon emissions • Air and water pollution • Biodiversity • Deforestation • Energy efficiency • Waste management • Water scarcity	• Customer satisfaction • Data protection and privacy • Gender and diversity • Employee engagement • Community relations • Human rights • Labor standards	• Board composition • Audit committee structure • Bribery and corruption • Executive compensation • Lobbying • Political contributions • Whistleblower schemes

The list of ESG issues in Exhibit 15 is not exhaustive. Structured, numeric data can be processed for most of these issues (e.g., executive salaries and bonuses, carbon footprint, employee turnover, and employee absenteeism). However, such data is often not required to be disclosed by companies. Many organizations and regulatory bodies have derived frameworks setting out standards on a number of these issues—examples include the Principles of Responsible Investment, the UN Global Compact, and the OECD Guidelines for Multinational Enterprises. Such standards help form the basis of SRI policies for asset owners. In turn, asset owners may exclude or engage with companies in accordance with these issues, or demand that their selected investment managers consider these issues in their investment process.

We previously discussed that the limitation in the investment universe using either exclusionary screening or best-in-class policies affects the expected returns and risk. When selecting or instructing active or passive managers, these managers will clearly want to see their performance measured against a benchmark that reflects the limited universe. There are benchmarks and investment vehicles (both active and passive) available, particularly in equities, that reflect many commonly excluded companies or sectors. For best-in-class inclusion policy, there is no established set of broadly agreed rules; thus asset management products associated with such a policy are customized.

Shareholder engagement requires good cooperation between investor (client) and investment manager. Engagement efforts are time-consuming and the interest in such efforts is often that of clients, rather than that of the investment managers. Clients and investment managers have to be clear with each other about the exercise of voting rights, filing shareholder proposals or entering into conversations with company management. It may be that the engagement and voting is delegated by the client to the investment manager and implemented according to the manager's stewardship policy. Alternatively, the client may instruct some proxy agent to vote on its behalf and according to its own stewardship policies.

Selecting thematic investments, particularly in liquid asset classes, requires finding specialist managers who can identify the right opportunities and manage thematic investment portfolios. In particular, an allocation to thematic investments will bias the total asset class portfolio toward a particular theme, so it is important for the investment manager to demonstrate the impact of the thematic investment on the total risk-return profile of the portfolio. Impact investing specifically selects investment opportunities based on their potential to positively affect ESG issues.

The effort and costs associated with limiting the investment universe as part of sustainable investing suggests a negative impact on investment returns. Sustainable investing proponents argue, however, that potential improvements in governance and the avoidance of risks by companies that screen favorably improve returns. Significant empirical research has been conducted on the performance of ESG factors in equities, including the return differences of ESG equity portfolios relative to mainstream equity portfolios. Academic research remains mixed on the impact of ESG factors on portfolio returns.

3.5. Alternative Portfolio Organizing Principles

The portfolio planning and construction framework presented so far relies on a somewhat rigid process. Nonetheless, there are two newer, less structured developments that deserve specific mention.

The first development is the growth in the offering of exchange-traded funds, or ETFs, in combination with algorithm-based financial advice (or robo-advice). ETFs are funds that track the performance of an asset class index or sub-index, are easily tradeable, and relatively cheap compared to actively managed funds or managed accounts. The broad array of ETF offerings, covering the main equity and fixed-income indices as well as commodities, enable retail investors to obtain fast, inexpensive, and liquid exposure to asset classes. Robo-advice has further reduced the costs for retail investors to create a well-diversified portfolio.

The second development relates to criticism of asset class return forecasts over relevant time horizons, and the perceived instability of asset class correlations and volatilities. Some market participants argue that poor investment portfolio results reflect the sensitivity of modern portfolio theory-based portfolio construction methodologies to small errors in return forecasts or estimated correlations. In response, practitioners developed an investment approach where asset classes were weighted according to risk contribution. This approach is known as *risk parity investing*. Proponents of risk parity investing argue that traditionally constructed portfolios have considerable risk from equities. That is, the typically high (60% or more) weight of equities in institutional portfolios understates the risk impact: equities tend to be much more volatile than fixed income. Opponents of risk parity argue that following the global financial crisis of 2007–2009, favorable results of risk parity portfolios were caused by the long period of decline in interest rates that benefited bond market performance.

4. CONCLUSION AND SUMMARY

In this chapter, we have discussed construction of a client's investment policy statement, including discussion of risk and return objectives and the various constraints that will apply to the portfolio. We have also discussed the portfolio construction process, with emphasis on the strategic asset allocation decisions that must be made.

- The IPS is the starting point of the portfolio management process. Without a full understanding of the client's situation and requirements, it is unlikely that successful results will be achieved.
- The IPS can take a variety of forms. A typical format will include the client's investment objectives and also list the constraints that apply to the client's portfolio.
- The client's objectives are specified in terms of risk tolerance and return requirements.
- The constraints section covers factors that need to be considered when constructing a portfolio for the client that meets the objectives. The typical constraint categories are liquidity requirements, time horizon, regulatory requirements, tax status, and unique needs.
- Clients may have personal objections to certain products or practices, which could lead to the exclusion of certain companies, countries, or types of securities from the investable universe as well as the client's benchmark. Such considerations are often referred to as ESG (environmental, social, governance).
- ESG considerations can be integrated into an investment policy by exclusionary screening, best-in-class selection, active ownership, thematic and impact investing, and ESG integration in security analysis.
- Risk objectives are specifications for portfolio risk that reflect the risk tolerance of the client. Quantitative risk objectives can be absolute or relative or a combination of the two.

- The client's overall risk tolerance is a function of the client's ability to accept risk and their "risk attitude," which can be considered the client's willingness to take risk.
- The client's return objectives can be stated on an absolute or a relative basis. As an example of an absolute objective, the client may want to achieve a particular percentage rate of return. Alternatively, the return objective can be stated on a relative basis, for example, relative to a benchmark return.
- The liquidity section of the IPS should state what the client's requirements are to draw cash from the portfolio.
- The time horizon section of the IPS should state the time horizon over which the investor is investing. This horizon may be the period during which the portfolio is accumulating before any assets need to be withdrawn.
- Tax status varies among investors and a client's tax status should be stated in the IPS.
- The IPS should state any legal or regulatory restrictions that constrain the investment of the portfolio.
- The unique circumstances section of the IPS should cover any other aspect of a client's circumstances that is likely to have a material impact on the composition of the portfolio. Certain ESG implementation approaches, such as negative (exclusionary) screening, best-in-class, thematic investing, impact investing, and ESG integration may be discussed in this section.
- Asset classes are the building blocks of an asset allocation. An asset class is a category of assets that have similar characteristics, attributes, and risk/return relationships. Traditionally, investors have distinguished cash, equities, bonds, and real estate as the major asset classes.
- A strategic asset allocation results from combining the constraints and objectives articulated in the IPS and capital market expectations regarding the asset classes.
- As time goes on, a client's asset allocation will drift from the target allocation, and the amount of allowable drift as well as a rebalancing policy should be formalized.
- In addition to taking systematic risk, an investment committee may choose to take tactical asset allocation risk or security selection risk. The amount of return attributable to these decisions can be measured.
- ESG considerations may be integrated into the portfolio planning and construction process. Such considerations can be difficult given that ESG data is often not required to be disclosed by companies. ESG implementation approaches require a set of instructions for investment managers with regards to the selection of securities, the exercise of shareholder rights, and the selection of investment strategies.

REFERENCES

Grable, John E., and Soo-Hyun Joo. 2004. "Environmental and Biopsychosocial Factors Associated with Financial Risk Tolerance." *Financial Counseling and Planning* 15 (1): 73–82.

Sharpe, William F., Peng Chen, Jerald E. Pinto, and Dennis W. McLeavey. 2007. "Asset Allocation." In *Managing Investment Portfolios: A Dynamic Process*. 3rd ed. New York: Wiley.

Waring, M. Barton, and Laurence B. Siegel. 2003. "The Dimensions of Active Management." *Journal of Portfolio Management* 29 (3): 35–51.

Waring, M. Barton, Duane Whitney, John Pirone, and Charles Castille. 2000. "Optimizing Manager Structure and Budgeting Manager Risk." *Journal of Portfolio Management* 26 (3): 90–104.

PRACTICE PROBLEMS

1. Which of the following is *least important* as a reason for a written investment policy statement (IPS)?
   A. The IPS may be required by regulation.
   B. Having a written IPS is part of best practice for a portfolio manager.
   C. Having a written IPS ensures the client's risk and return objectives can be achieved.

2. Which of the following *best* describes the underlying rationale for a written investment policy statement (IPS)?
   A. A written IPS communicates a plan for trying to achieve investment success.
   B. A written IPS provides investment managers with a ready defense against client lawsuits.
   C. A written IPS allows investment managers to instruct clients about the proper use and purpose of investments.

3. A written investment policy statement (IPS) is *most likely* to succeed if:
   A. it is created by a software program to assure consistent quality.
   B. it is a collaborative effort of the client and the portfolio manager.
   C. it reflects the investment philosophy of the portfolio manager.

4. The section of the investment policy statement (IPS) that provides information about how policy may be executed, including restrictions and exclusions, is *best* described as the:
   A. *Investment Objectives.*
   B. *Investment Guidelines.*
   C. *Statement of Duties and Responsibilities.*

5. Which of the following is *least likely* to be placed in the appendices to an investment policy statement (IPS)?
   A. *Rebalancing Policy*
   B. *Strategic Asset Allocation*
   C. *Statement of Duties and Responsibilities*

6. Which of the following typical topics in an investment policy statement (IPS) is *most closely* linked to the client's "distinctive needs"?
   A. *Procedures*
   B. *Investment Guidelines*
   C. *Statement of Duties and Responsibilities*

7. An investment policy statement that includes a return objective of outperforming the FTSE 100 by 120 basis points is *best* characterized as having a(n):
   A. relative return objective.
   B. absolute return objective.
   C. arbitrage-based return objective.

8. Risk assessment questionnaires for investment management clients are *most* useful in measuring:
   A. value at risk.
   B. ability to take risk.
   C. willingness to take risk.

9. Which of the following is *best* characterized as a relative risk objective?
   A. Value at risk for the fund will not exceed US$3 million.
   B. The fund will not underperform the DAX by more than 250 basis points.
   C. The fund will not lose more than €2.5 million in the coming 12-month period.

10. In preparing an investment policy statement, which of the following is *most difficult* to quantify?
    A. Time horizon
    B. Ability to accept risk
    C. Willingness to accept risk

11. After interviewing a client in order to prepare a written investment policy statement (IPS), you have established the following:
    • The client has earnings that vary dramatically between £30,000 and £70,000 (pre-tax) depending on weather patterns in Britain.
    • In three of the previous five years, the after-tax income of the client has been less than £20,000.
    • The client's mother is dependent on her son (the client) for approximately £9,000 per year support.
    • The client's own subsistence needs are approximately £12,000 per year.
    • The client has more than 10 years' experience trading investments including commodity futures, stock options, and selling stock short.
    • The client's responses to a standard risk assessment questionnaire suggest he has above average risk tolerance.

    The client is *best* described as having a:
    A. low ability to take risk, but a high willingness to take risk.
    B. high ability to take risk, but a low willingness to take risk.
    C. high ability to take risk and a high willingness to take risk.

12. After interviewing a client in order to prepare a written investment policy statement (IPS), you have established the following:
    • The client has earnings that have exceeded €120,000 (pre-tax) each year for the past five years.
    • She has no dependents.
    • The client's subsistence needs are approximately €45,000 per year.
    • The client states that she feels uncomfortable with her lack of understanding of securities markets.
    • All of the client's current savings are invested in short-term securities guaranteed by an agency of her national government.
    • The client's responses to a standard risk assessment questionnaire suggest she has low risk tolerance.

    The client is *best* described as having a:
    A. low ability to take risk, but a high willingness to take risk.
    B. high ability to take risk, but a low willingness to take risk.
    C. high ability to take risk and a high willingness to take risk.

13. A client who is a 34-year-old widow with two healthy young children (aged 5 and 7) has asked you to help her form an investment policy statement. She has been employed as an administrative assistant in a bureau of her national government for the previous 12 years. She has two primary financial goals—her retirement and providing for the college education of her children. This client's time horizon is *best* described as being:
     A. long term.
     B. short term.
     C. medium term.

14. The timing of payouts for property and casualty insurers is unpredictable ("lumpy") in comparison with the timing of payouts for life insurance companies. Therefore, in general, property and casualty insurers have:
     A. lower liquidity needs than life insurance companies.
     B. greater liquidity needs than life insurance companies.
     C. a higher return objective than life insurance companies.

15. A client who is a director of a publicly listed corporation is required by law to refrain from trading that company's stock at certain points of the year when disclosure of financial results are pending. In preparing a written investment policy statement (IPS) for this client, this restriction on trading:
     A. is irrelevant to the IPS.
     B. should be included in the IPS.
     C. makes it illegal for the portfolio manager to work with this client.

16. Consider the pairwise correlations of monthly returns of the following asset classes:

	Brazilian Equities	East Asian Equities	European Equities	US Equities
Brazilian equities	1.00	0.70	0.85	0.76
East Asian equities	0.70	1.00	0.91	0.88
European equities	0.85	0.91	1.00	0.90
US equities	0.76	0.88	0.90	1.00

     Based solely on the information in the above table, which equity asset class is *most sharply* distinguished from US equities?
     A. Brazilian equities.
     B. European equities.
     C. East Asian equities.

17. Returns on asset classes are *best* described as being a function of:
     A. the failure of arbitrage.
     B. exposure to the idiosyncratic risks of those asset classes.
     C. exposure to sets of systematic factors relevant to those asset classes.

18. In defining asset classes as part of the strategic asset allocation decision, pairwise correlations within asset classes should generally be:
    A. equal to correlations among asset classes.
    B. lower than correlations among asset classes.
    C. higher than correlations among asset classes.

19. Tactical asset allocation is *best* described as:
    A. attempts to exploit arbitrage possibilities among asset classes.
    B. the decision to deliberately deviate from the policy portfolio.
    C. selecting asset classes with the desired exposures to sources of systematic risk in an investment portfolio.

CHAPTER 2

SECURITY MARKET INDEXES

Paul D. Kaplan, PhD, CFA
Dorothy C. Kelly, CFA

LEARNING OUTCOMES

The candidate should be able to:

- describe a security market index;
- calculate and interpret the value, price return, and total return of an index;
- describe the choices and issues in index construction and management;
- compare the different weighting methods used in index construction;
- calculate and analyze the value and return of an index given its weighting method;
- describe rebalancing and reconstitution of an index;
- describe uses of security market indexes;
- describe types of equity indexes;
- describe types of fixed-income indexes;
- describe indexes representing alternative investments;
- compare types of security market indexes.

1. INTRODUCTION

Investors gather and analyze vast amounts of information about security markets on a continual basis. Because this work can be both time consuming and data intensive, investors often use a single measure that consolidates this information and reflects the performance of an entire security market.

Security market indexes were first introduced as a simple measure to reflect the performance of the US stock market. Since then, security market indexes have evolved into important multi-purpose tools that help investors track the performance of various security markets, estimate risk, and evaluate the performance of investment managers. They also form the basis for new investment products.

Portfolio Management, Second Edition, by Paul D. Kaplan, PhD, CFA, and Dorothy C. Kelly, CFA. Copyright © 2019 by CFA Institute.

in·dex, *noun* (*pl.*in·dex·es *or* in·di·ces) Latin *indic-, index,* from *indicare* to indicate: an indicator, sign, or measure of something.

Origin of Market Indexes

Investors had access to regularly published data on individual security prices in London as early as 1698, but nearly 200 years passed before they had access to a simple indicator to reflect security market information. To give readers a sense of how the US stock market in general performed on a given day, publishers Charles H. Dow and Edward D. Jones introduced the Dow Jones Average, the world's first security market index, in 1884. The index, which appeared in *The Customers' Afternoon Letter,* consisted of the stocks of nine railroads and two industrial companies. It eventually became the Dow Jones Transportation Average. Convinced that industrial companies, rather than railroads, would be "the great speculative market" of the future, Dow and Jones introduced a second index in May 1896—the Dow Jones Industrial Average (DJIA). It had an initial value of 40.94 and consisted of 12 stocks from major US industries. Today, investors can choose from among thousands of indexes to measure and monitor different security markets and asset classes.

This chapter is organized as follows. Section 2 defines a security market index and explains how to calculate the price return and total return of an index for a single period and over multiple periods. Section 3 describes how indexes are constructed and managed. Section 4 discusses the use of market indexes. Sections 5, 6, and 7 discuss various types of indexes, and the final section summarizes the chapter. Practice problems follow the conclusions and summary.

2. INDEX DEFINITION AND CALCULATIONS OF VALUE AND RETURNS

A **security market index** represents a given security market, market segment, or asset class. Most indexes are constructed as portfolios of marketable securities.

The value of an index is calculated on a regular basis using either the actual or estimated market prices of the individual securities, known as **constituent securities**, within the index. For each security market index, investors may encounter two versions of the same index (i.e., an index with identical constituent securities and weights): one version based on price return and one version based on total return. As the name suggests, a **price return index**, also known as a **price index**, reflects *only* the prices of the constituent securities within the index. A **total return index**, in contrast, reflects not only the prices of the constituent securities but also the reinvestment of all income received since inception.

At inception, the values of the price and total return versions of an index are equal. As time passes, however, the value of the total return index, which includes the reinvestment of all dividends and/or interest received, will exceed the value of the price return index by an increasing amount. A look at how the values of each version are calculated over multiple periods illustrates why.

The value of a price return index is calculated as:

$$V_{PRI} = \frac{\sum_{i=1}^{N} n_i P_i}{D} \tag{1}$$

where

V_{PRI} = the value of the price return index

n_i = the number of units of constituent security i held in the index portfolio

N = the number of constituent securities in the index

P_i = the unit price of constituent security i

D = the value of the divisor

The **divisor** is a number initially chosen at inception. It is frequently chosen so that the price index has a convenient initial value, such as 1,000. The index provider then adjusts the value of the divisor as necessary to avoid changes in the index value that are unrelated to changes in the prices of its constituent securities. For example, when changing index constituents, the index provider may adjust the divisor so that the value of the index with the new constituents equals the value of the index prior to the changes.

Index return calculations, like calculations of investment portfolio returns, may measure price return or total return. **Price return** measures only price appreciation or percentage change in price. **Total return** measures price appreciation plus interest, dividends, and other distributions.

2.1. Calculation of Single-Period Returns

For a security market index, price return can be calculated in two ways: either the percentage change in value of the price return index, or the weighted average of price returns of the constituent securities. The price return of an index can be expressed as:

$$PR_I = \frac{V_{PRI1} - V_{PRI0}}{V_{PRI0}} \tag{2}$$

where

PR_I = the price return of the index portfolio (as a decimal number, i.e., 12 percent is 0.12)

V_{PRI1} = the value of the price return index at the end of the period

V_{PRI0} = the value of the price return index at the beginning of the period

Similarly, the price return of each constituent security can be expressed as:

$$PR_i = \frac{P_{i1} - P_{i0}}{P_{i0}} \tag{3}$$

where
PR_i = the price return of constituent security i (as a decimal number)
P_{i1} = the price of constituent security i at the end of the period
P_{i0} = the price of constituent security i at the beginning of the period

Because the price return of the index equals the weighted average of price returns of the individual securities, we can write:

$$PR_I = \sum_{i=1}^{N} w_i PR_i = \sum_{i=1}^{N} w_i \left(\frac{P_{i1} - P_{i0}}{P_{i0}} \right) \tag{4}$$

where:
PR_I = the price return of index portfolio (as a decimal number)
PR_i = the price return of constituent security i (as a decimal number)
N = the number of individual securities in the index
w_i = the weight of security i (the fraction of the index portfolio allocated to security i)
P_{i1} = the price of constituent security i at the end of the period
P_{i0} = the price of constituent security i at the beginning of the period

Equation 4 can be rewritten simply as:

$$PR_I = w_1 PR_1 + w_2 PR_2 + \ldots + w_N PR_N \tag{5}$$

where
PR_I = the price return of index portfolio (as a decimal number)
PR_i = the price return of constituent security i (as a decimal number)
w_i = the weight of security i (the fraction of the index portfolio allocated to security i)
N = the number of securities in the index

Total return measures price appreciation plus interest, dividends, and other distributions. Thus, the **total return** of an index is the price appreciation, or change in the value of the price return index, plus income (dividends and/or interest) over the period, expressed as a percentage of the beginning value of the price return index. The total return of an index can be expressed as:

$$TR_I = \frac{V_{PRI1} - V_{PRI0} + Inc_I}{V_{PRI0}} \tag{6}$$

where
TR_I = the total return of the index portfolio (as a decimal number)
V_{PRI1} = the value of the price return index at the end of the period
V_{PRI0} = the value of the price return index at the beginning of the period
Inc_I = the total income (dividends and/or interest) from all securities in the index held over the period

The total return of an index can also be calculated as the weighted average of total returns of the constituent securities. The total return of each constituent security in the index is calculated as:

$$TR_i = \frac{P_{1i} - P_{0i} + Inc_i}{P_{0i}} \tag{7}$$

where

$\quad TR_i$ = the total return of constituent security i (as a decimal number)
$\quad P_{1i}$ = the price of constituent security i at the end of the period
$\quad P_{0i}$ = the price of constituent security i at the beginning of the period
$\quad Inc_i$ = the total income (dividends and/or interest) from security i over the period

Because the total return of an index can be calculated as the weighted average of total returns of the constituent securities, we can express total return as:

$$TR_I = \sum_{i=1}^{N} w_i TR_i = \sum_{i=1}^{N} w_i \left(\frac{P_{1i} - P_{0i} + Inc_i}{P_{0i}} \right) \tag{8}$$

Equation 8 can be rewritten simply as

$$TR_I = w_1 TR_1 + w_2 TR_2 + \ldots + w_N TR_N \tag{9}$$

where

$\quad TR_I$ = the total return of the index portfolio (as a decimal number)
$\quad TR_i$ = the total return of constituent security i (as a decimal number)
$\quad w_i$ = the weight of security i (the fraction of the index portfolio allocated to security i)
$\quad N$ = the number of securities in the index

2.2. Calculation of Index Values over Multiple Time Periods

The calculation of index values over multiple time periods requires geometrically linking the series of index returns. With a series of price returns for an index, we can calculate the value of the price return index with the following equation:

$$V_{PRIT} = V_{PRI0}(1 + PR_{I1})(1 + PR_{I2})\ldots(1 + PR_{IT}) \tag{10}$$

where

$\quad V_{PRI0}$ = the value of the price return index at inception
$\quad V_{PRIT}$ = the value of the price return index at time t
$\quad PR_{IT}$ = the price return (as a decimal number) on the index over period t, $t = 1, 2, \ldots, T$

For an index with an inception value set to 1,000 and price returns of 5 percent and 3 percent for Periods 1 and 2 respectively, the values of the price return index would be calculated as follows:

Period	Return (%)	Calculation	Ending Value
0		1,000(1.00)	1,000.00
1	5.00	1,000(1.05)	1,050.00
2	3.00	1,000(1.05)(1.03)	1,081.50

Similarly, the series of total returns for an index is used to calculate the value of the total return index with the following equation:

$$V_{TRIT} = V_{TRI0}(1 + TR_{I1})(1 + TR_{I2})...(1 + TR_{IT}) \qquad (11)$$

where
V_{TRI0} = the value of the index at inception
V_{TRIT} = the value of the total return index at time t
TR_{IT} = the total return (as a decimal number) on the index over period t, $t = 1, 2, ..., T$

Suppose that the same index yields an additional 1.5 percent return from income in Period 1 and an additional 2.0 percent return from income in Period 2, bringing the total returns for Periods 1 and 2, respectively, to 6.5 percent and 5 percent. The values of the total return index would be calculated as follows:

Period	Return (%)	Calculation	Ending Value
0		1,000(1.00)	1,000.00
1	6.50	1,000(1.065)	1,065.00
2	5.00	1,000(1.065)(1.05)	1,118.25

As illustrated above, as time passes, the value of the total return index, which includes the reinvestment of all dividends and/or interest received, exceeds the value of the price return index by an increasing amount.

3. INDEX CONSTRUCTION AND MANAGEMENT

Constructing and managing a security market index is similar to constructing and managing a portfolio of securities. Index providers must decide the following:

1. Which target market should the index represent?
2. Which securities should be selected from that target market?
3. How much weight should be allocated to each security in the index?
4. When should the index be rebalanced?
5. When should the security selection and weighting decision be re-examined?

3.1. Target Market and Security Selection

The first decision in index construction is identifying the target market, market segment, or asset class that the index is intended to represent. The target market may be defined very broadly or narrowly. It may be based on asset class (e.g., equities, fixed income, real estate, commodities, hedge funds); geographic region (e.g., Japan, South Africa, Latin America, Europe); the exchange on which the securities are traded (e.g., Shanghai, Toronto, Tokyo), and/or other characteristics (e.g., economic sector, company size, investment style, duration, or credit quality).

The target market determines the investment universe and the securities available for inclusion in the index. Once the investment universe is identified, the number of securities and the specific securities to include in the index must be determined. The constituent securities could be nearly all those in the target market or a representative sample of the target market. Some equity indexes, such as the S&P 500 Index and the FTSE 100, fix the number of securities included in the index and indicate this number in the name of the index. Other indexes allow the number of securities to vary to reflect changes in the target market or to maintain a certain percentage of the target market. For example, the Tokyo Stock Price Index (TOPIX) represents and includes all of the largest stocks, known as the First Section, listed on the Tokyo Stock Exchange. To be included in the First Section—and thus the TOPIX—stocks must meet certain criteria, such as the number of shares outstanding, the number of shareholders, and market capitalization. Stocks that no longer meet the criteria are removed from the First Section and also the TOPIX. Objective or mechanical rules determine the constituent securities of most, but not all, indexes. The S&P Bombay Stock Exchange Sensitive Index, also called the S&P BSE SENSEX and the S&P 500, for example, use a selection committee and more subjective decision-making rules to determine constituent securities.

3.2. Index Weighting

The weighting decision determines how much of each security to include in the index and has a substantial impact on an index's value. Index providers use a number of methods to weight the constituent securities in an index. Indexes can be price weighted, equal weighted, market-capitalization weighted, or fundamentally weighted. Each weighting method has its advantages and disadvantages.

3.2.1. Price Weighting
The simplest method to weight an index and the one used by Charles Dow to construct the Dow Jones Industrial Average is **price weighting**. In price weighting, the weight on each constituent security is determined by dividing its price by the sum of all the prices of the constituent securities. The weight is calculated using the following formula:

$$w_i^P = \frac{P_i}{\sum_{i=1}^{N} P_i} \tag{12}$$

Exhibit 1 illustrates the values, weights, and single-period returns following inception of a price-weighted equity index with five constituent securities. The value of the price-weighted index is determined by dividing the sum of the security values (101.50) by the divisor, which is typically set at inception to equal the initial number of securities in the index. Thus, in our example, the divisor is 5 and the initial value of the index is calculated as $101.50 \div 5 = 20.30$.

EXHIBIT 1   Example of a Price-Weighted Equity Index

Security	Shares in Index	BOP Price	Value (Shares × BOP Price)	BOP Weight (%)	EOP Price	Dividends Per Share	Value (Shares × EOP Price)	Total Dividends	Price Return (%)	Total Return (%)	BOP Weight × Price Return (%)	BOP Weight × Total Return (%)	EOP Weight (%)
A	1	50.00	50.00	49.26	55.00	0.75	55.00	0.75	10.00	11.50	4.93	5.66	52.38
B	1	25.00	25.00	24.63	22.00	0.10	22.00	0.10	−12.00	−11.60	−2.96	−2.86	20.95
C	1	12.50	12.50	12.32	8.00	0.00	8.00	0.00	−36.00	−36.00	−4.43	−4.43	7.62
D	1	10.00	10.00	9.85	14.00	0.05	14.00	0.05	40.00	40.50	3.94	3.99	13.33
E	1	4.00	4.00	3.94	6.00	0.00	6.00	0.00	50.00	50.00	1.97	1.97	5.72
Total			**101.50**	**100.00**			**105.00**	**0.90**	**3.45**	**4.33**	**3.45**	**4.33**	**100.00**
Index Value			20.30				21.00	0.18	3.45	4.33			

Divisor = 5

BOP = Beginning of period

EOP = End of period

Type of Index	BOP Value	Return (%)	EOP Value
Price Return	20.30	3.45	21.00
Total Return	20.30	4.33	21.18

As illustrated in this exhibit, Security A, which has the highest price, also has the highest weighting and thus will have the greatest impact on the return of the index. Note how both the price return and the total return of the index are calculated on the basis of the corresponding returns on the constituent securities.

A property unique to price-weighted indexes is that a stock split on one constituent security changes the weights on all the securities in the index.[1] To prevent the stock split and the resulting new weights from changing the value of the index, the index provider must adjust the value of the divisor as illustrated in Exhibit 2. Given a 2-for-1 split in Security A, the divisor is adjusted by dividing the sum of the constituent prices *after* the split (77.50) by the value of the index *before* the split (21.00). This adjustment results in changing the divisor from 5 to 3.69 so that the index value is maintained at 21.00.

The primary advantage of price weighting is its simplicity. The main disadvantage of price weighting is that it results in arbitrary weights for each security. In particular, a stock split in any one security causes arbitrary changes in the weights of all the constituents' securities.

EXHIBIT 2   Impact of 2-for-1 Split in Security A

Security	Price before Split	Weight before Split (%)	Price after Split	Weight after Split (%)
A	55.00	52.38	27.50	35.48
B	22.00	20.95	22.00	28.39
C	8.00	7.62	8.00	10.32
D	14.00	13.33	14.00	18.07
E	6.00	5.72	6.00	7.74
Total	105.00	100.00	77.50	100.00
Divisor	5.00		3.69	
Index Value	21.00		21.00	

3.2.2. Equal Weighting

Another simple index weighting method is **equal weighting**. This method assigns an equal weight to each constituent security at inception. The weights are calculated as:

$$w_i^E = \frac{1}{N} \tag{13}$$

where

w_i = fraction of the portfolio that is allocated to security i or weight of security i

N = number of securities in the index

To construct an equal-weighted index from the five securities in Exhibit 1, the index provider allocates one-fifth (20 percent) of the value of the index (at the beginning of the period) to each security. Dividing the value allocated to each security by each security's individual share price determines the number of shares of each security to include in the index. Unlike a price-weighted index, where the weights are arbitrarily determined by the market prices, the weights in an equal-weighted index are arbitrarily assigned by the index provider.

Exhibit 3 illustrates the values, weights, and single-period returns following inception of an equal-weighted index with the same constituent securities as those in Exhibit 1. This example assumes a beginning index portfolio value of 10,000 (i.e., an investment of 2,000 in each security). To set the initial value of the index to 1,000, the divisor is set to 10 (10,000 ÷ 10 = 1,000).

---

[1]A stock split is an increase in the number of shares outstanding and a proportionate decrease in the price per share such that the total market value of equity, as well as investors' proportionate ownership in the company, does not change.

EXHIBIT 3   Example of an Equal-Weighted Equity Index

Security	Shares in Index	BOP Price	Value (Shares × BOP Price)	Weight (%)	EOP Price	Dividends Per Share	Total Dividends	Value (Shares × EOP Price)	Price Return (%)	Total Return (%)	Weight × Price Return (%)	Weight × Total Return (%)	EOP Weight (%)
A	40	50.00	2,000	20.00	55.00	0.75	30	2,200	10.00	11.50	2.00	2.30	19.93
B	80	25.00	2,000	20.00	22.00	0.10	8	1,760	−12.00	−11.60	−2.40	−2.32	15.94
C	160	12.50	2,000	20.00	8.00	0.00	0	1,280	−36.00	−36.00	−7.20	−7.20	11.60
D	200	10.00	2,000	20.00	14.00	0.05	10	2,800	40.00	40.50	8.00	8.10	25.36
E	500	4.00	2,000	20.00	6.00	0.00	0	3,000	50.00	50.00	10.00	10.00	27.17
Total			10,000	100.00			48	11,040	10.40	10.88	10.40	10.88	100.00
Index Value			1,000				4.80	1,104	10.40	10.88			

Divisor = 10

BOP = Beginning of period
EOP = End of period

Type of Index	BOP Value	Return (%)	EOP Value
Price Return	1,000.00	10.40	1,104.00
Total Return	1,000.00	10.88	1,108.80

Exhibits 1 and 3 demonstrate how different weighting methods result in different returns. The 10.4 percent price return of the equal-weighted index shown in Exhibit 3 differs significantly from the 3.45 percent price return of the price-weighted index in Exhibit 1.

Like price weighting, the primary advantage of equal weighting is its simplicity. Equal weighting, however, has a number of disadvantages. First, securities that constitute the largest fraction of the target market value are underrepresented, and securities that constitute a small fraction of the target market value are overrepresented. Second, after the index is constructed and the prices of constituent securities change, the index is no longer equally weighted. Therefore, maintaining equal weights requires frequent adjustments (rebalancing) to the index.

3.2.3. Market-Capitalization Weighting

In **market-capitalization weighting**, or value weighting, the weight on each constituent security is determined by dividing its market capitalization by the total market capitalization (the sum of the market capitalization) of all the securities in the index. Market capitalization or value is calculated by multiplying the number of shares outstanding by the market price per share.

The market-capitalization weight of security i is:

$$w_i^M = \frac{Q_i P_i}{\sum_{j=1}^{N} Q_j P_j} \tag{14}$$

where

w_i = fraction of the portfolio that is allocated to security i or weight of security i
Q_i = number of shares outstanding of security i
P_i = share price of security i
N = number of securities in the index

Exhibit 4 illustrates the values, weights, and single-period returns following inception of a market-capitalization-weighted index for the same five-security market. Security A, with 3,000 shares outstanding and a price of 50 per share, has a market capitalization of 150,000 or 26.29 percent (150,000/570,500) of the entire index portfolio. The resulting index weights in the exhibit reflect the relative value of each security as measured by its market capitalization.

EXHIBIT 4   Example of a Market-Capitalization-Weighted Equity Index

Stock	Shares Out-standing	BOP Price	BOP Market Cap	BOP Weight (%)	EOP Price	Dividends Per Share	EOP Market Cap	Total Dividends	Price Return (%)	Total Return (%)	BOP Weight × Price Return (%)	BOP Weight × Total Return (%)	EOP Weight (%)
A	3,000	50.00	150,000	26.29	55.00	0.75	165,000	2,250	10.00	11.50	2.63	3.02	28.50
B	10,000	25.00	250,000	43.82	22.00	0.10	220,000	1,000	−12.00	−11.60	−5.26	−5.08	38.00
C	5,000	12.50	62,500	10.96	8.00	0.00	40,000	0	−36.00	−36.00	−3.95	−3.95	6.91
D	8,000	10.00	80,000	14.02	14.00	0.05	112,000	400	40.00	40.50	5.61	5.68	19.34
E	7,000	4.00	28,000	4.91	6.00	0.00	42,000	0	50.00	50.00	2.46	2.46	7.25
Total			**570,500**	**100.00**			**579,000**	**3,650**	**1.49**	**2.13**	**1.49**	**2.13**	**100.00**
Index Value			**1,000**				**1,014.90**	**6.40**					

Divisor = 570.50

BOP = Beginning of period

EOP = End of period

Type of Index	BOP Value	Return (%)	EOP Value
Price Return	1,000.00	1.49	1,014.90
Total Return	1,000.00	2.13	1,021.30

As shown in Exhibits 1, 3, and 4, the weighting method affects the index's returns. The price and total returns of the market-capitalization index in Exhibit 4 (1.49 percent and 2.13 percent, respectively) differ significantly from those of the price-weighted (3.45 percent and 4.33 percent, respectively) and equal-weighted (10.40 percent and 10.88 percent respectively) indexes. To understand the source and magnitude of the difference, compare the weights and returns of each security under each of the weighting methods. The weight of Security A, for example, ranges from 49.26 percent in the price-weighted index to 20 percent in the equal-weighted index. With a price return of 10 percent, Security A contributes 4.93 percent to the price return of the price-weighted index, 2.00 percent to the price return of the equal-weighted index, and 2.63 percent to the price return of the market-capitalization-weighted index. With a total return of 11.50 percent, Security A contributes 5.66 percent to the total return of the price-weighted index, 2.30 percent to the total return of the equal-weighted index, and 3.02 percent to the total return of the market-capitalization-weighted index.

3.2.3.1. Float-Adjusted Market-Capitalization Weighting

In **float-adjusted market-capitalization weighting**, the weight on each constituent security is determined by adjusting its market capitalization for its **market float**. Typically, market float is the number of shares of the constituent security that are available to the investing public. For companies that are closely held, only a portion of the shares outstanding are available to the investing public (the rest are held by a small group of controlling investors). In addition to excluding shares held by controlling shareholders, most float-adjusted market-capitalization-weighted indexes also exclude shares held by other corporations and governments. Some providers of indexes that are designed to represent the investment opportunities of global investors further reduce the number of shares included in the index by excluding shares that are not available to foreigner investors. The index providers may refer to these indexes as "free-float-adjusted market-capitalization-weighted indexes."

Float-adjusted market-capitalization-weighted indexes reflect the shares available for public trading by multiplying the market price per share by the number of shares available to the investing public (i.e., the float-adjusted market capitalization) rather than the total number of shares outstanding (total market capitalization). Currently, most market-capitalization-weighted indexes are float adjusted. Therefore, unless otherwise indicated, for the remainder of this chapter, "market-capitalization" weighting refers to float-adjusted market-capitalization weighting.

The float-adjusted market-capitalization weight of security i is calculated as:

$$w_i^M = \frac{f_i Q_i P_i}{\sum_{j=1}^{N} f_j Q_j P_j} \tag{15}$$

where

f_i = fraction of shares outstanding in the market float

w_i = fraction of the portfolio that is allocated to security i or weight of security i

Q_i = number of shares outstanding of security i

P_i = share price of security i

N = number of securities in the index

Exhibit 5 illustrates the values, weights, and single-period returns following inception of a float-adjusted market-capitalization-weighted equity index using the same five securities as before. The low percentage of shares of Security D in the market float compared with the number of shares outstanding indicates that the security is closely held.

EXHIBIT 5　Example of Float-Adjusted Marker-Capitalization-Weighted Equity Index

Stock	Shares Out-standing	% Shares in Market Float	Shares in Index	BOP Price	BOP Float-Adjusted Market Cap	BOP Weight (%)	EOP Price	Dividends Per Share	Ending Float-Adjusted Market Cap	Total Dividends	Price Return (%)	Total Return (%)	BOP Weight × Price Return (%)	BOP Weight × Total Return (%)	EOP Weight (%)
A	3,000	100	3,000	50.00	150,000	35.40	55.00	0.75	165,000	2,250	10.00	11.50	3.54	4.07	39.61
B	10,000	70	7,000	25.00	175,000	41.31	22.00	0.10	154,000	700	−12.00	−11.60	−4.96	−4.79	36.97
C	5,000	90	4,500	12.50	56,250	13.28	8.00	0.00	36,000	0	−36.00	−36.00	−4.78	−4.78	8.64
D	8,000	25	2,000	10.00	20,000	4.72	14.00	0.05	28,000	100	40.00	40.50	1.89	1.91	6.72
E	7,000	80	5,600	4.00	22,400	5.29	6.00	0.00	33,600	0	50.00	50.00	2.65	2.65	8.06
Total					**423,650**	**100.00**			**416,600**	**3,050**	**−1.66**	**−0.94**			**100.00**
Index Value					**1,000**				**983.36**	**7.20**					

Divisor = 423.65

BOP = Beginning of period

EOP = End of period

Type of Index	Initial Value	Return (%)	Ending Value
Price Return	1,000.00	−1.66	983.36
Total Return	1,000.00	−0.94	990.56

The primary advantage of market-capitalization weighting (including float adjusted) is that constituent securities are held in proportion to their value in the target market. The primary disadvantage is that constituent securities whose prices have risen the most (or fallen the most) have a greater (or lower) weight in the index (i.e., as a security's price rises relative to other securities in the index, its weight increases; and as its price decreases in value relative to other securities in the index, its weight decreases). This weighting method leads to overweighting stocks that have risen in price (and may be overvalued) and underweighting stocks that have declined in price (and may be undervalued). The effect of this weighting method is similar to a momentum investment strategy in that over time, the securities that have risen in price the most will have the largest weights in the index.

3.2.4. Fundamental Weighting

Fundamental weighting attempts to address the disadvantages of market-capitalization weighting by using measures of a company's size that are independent of its security price to determine the weight on each constituent security. These measures include book value, cash flow, revenues, earnings, dividends, and number of employees.

Some fundamental indexes use a single measure, such as total dividends, to weight the constituent securities, whereas others combine the weights from several measures to form a composite value that is used for weighting.

Letting F_i denote a given fundamental size measure of company i, the fundamental weight on security i is:

$$w_i^F = \frac{F_i}{\sum_{j=1}^{N} F_j} \tag{16}$$

Relative to a market-capitalization-weighted index, a fundamental index with weights based on such an item as earnings will result in greater weights on constituent securities with earnings yields (earnings divided by price) that are higher than the earnings yield of the overall market-weighted portfolio. Similarly, stocks with earnings yields less than the yield on the overall market-weighted portfolio will have lower weights. For example, suppose there are two stocks in an index. Stock A has a market capitalization of €200 million, Stock B has a market capitalization of €800 million, and their aggregate market capitalization is €1 billion (€1,000 million). Both companies have earnings of €20 million and aggregate earnings of €40 million. Thus, Stock A has an earnings yield of 10 percent (20/200) and Stock B has an earnings yield of 2.5 percent (20/800). The earnings weight of Stock A is 50 percent (20/40), which is higher than its market-capitalization weight of 20 percent (200/1,000). The earnings weight of Stock B is 50 percent (20/40), which is less than its market-capitalization weight of 80 percent (800/1,000). Relative to the market-cap-weighted index, the earnings-weighted index over-weights the high-yield Stock A and under-weights the low-yield Stock B.

The most important property of fundamental weighting is that it leads to indexes that have a "value" tilt. That is, a fundamentally weighted index has ratios of book value, earnings, dividends, etc. to market value that are higher than its market-capitalization-weighted counterpart. Also, in contrast to the momentum "effect" of market-capitalization-weighted indexes, fundamentally weighted indexes generally will have a contrarian "effect" in that the portfolio weights will shift away from securities that have increased in relative value and toward securities that have fallen in relative value whenever the portfolio is rebalanced.

3.3. Index Management: Rebalancing and Reconstitution

So far, we have discussed index construction. Index management entails the two remaining questions:

- When should the index be rebalanced?
- When should the security selection and weighting decisions be re-examined?

3.3.1. Rebalancing

Rebalancing refers to adjusting the weights of the constituent securities in the index. To maintain the weight of each security consistent with the index's weighting method, the index provider rebalances the index by adjusting the weights of the constituent securities on a regularly scheduled basis (rebalancing dates)—usually quarterly. Rebalancing is necessary because the weights of the constituent securities change as their market prices change. Note, for example, that the weights of the securities in the equal-weighted index (Exhibit 3) at the end of the period are no longer equal (i.e., 20 percent):

Security A	19.93%
Security B	15.94
Security C	11.60
Security D	25.36
Security E	27.17

In rebalancing the index, the weights of Securities D and E (which had the highest returns) would be decreased and the weights of Securities A, B, and C (which had the lowest returns) would be increased. Thus, rebalancing creates turnover within an index.

Price-weighted indexes are not rebalanced because the weight of each constituent security is determined by its price. For market-capitalization-weighted indexes, rebalancing is less of a concern because the indexes largely rebalance themselves. In our market-capitalization index, for example, the weight of Security C automatically declined from 10.96 percent to 6.91 percent, reflecting the 36 percent decline in its market price. Market-capitalization weights are only adjusted to reflect mergers, acquisitions, liquidations, and other corporate actions between rebalancing dates.

3.3.2. Reconstitution

Reconstitution is the process of changing the constituent securities in an index. It is similar to a portfolio manager deciding to change the securities in his or her portfolio. Reconstitution is part of the rebalancing cycle. The reconstitution date is the date on which index providers review the constituent securities, re-apply the initial criteria for inclusion in the index, and select which securities to retain, remove, or add. Constituent securities that no longer meet the criteria are replaced with securities that do meet the criteria. Once the revised list of constituent securities is determined, the weighting method is re-applied. Indexes are reconstituted to reflect changes in the target market (bankruptcies, de-listings, mergers, acquisitions, etc.) and/or to reflect the judgment of the selection committee.

Reconstitution creates turnover in a number of different ways, particularly for market-capitalization-weighted indexes. When one security is removed and another is added, the index provider has to change the weights of the other securities in order to maintain the market-capitalization weighting of the index.

The frequency of reconstitution is a major issue for widely used indexes and their constituent securities. The Russell 2000 Index, for example, reconstitutes annually. It is used as a benchmark by numerous investment funds, and each year, prior to the index's reconstitution, the managers of these funds buy stocks they think will be added to the index—driving those stocks' prices up—and sell stocks they think will be deleted from the index—driving those stocks' prices down. Exhibit 6 illustrates a historical example of the potential impact of these decisions. Beginning in late April 2009, some managers began acquiring and bidding up the price of Uranium Energy Corporation (UEC) because they believed that it would be included in the reconstituted Russell 2000 Index. On 12 June, Russell listed UEC as a preliminary addition to the Russell 2000 Index and the Russell 3000 Index.[2] By that time, the stock value had increased by more than 300 percent. Investors continued to bid up the stock price in the weeks following the announcement, and the stock closed on the reconstitution date of 30 June at USD2.90, up nearly 400 percent for the quarter.

EXHIBIT 6   Three-Month Performance of Uranium Energy Corporation and NASDAQ April through June 2009

Sources: Yahoo! Finance and Capital IQ.

---

[2]According to the press release, final membership in the index would be published after market close on Friday, 26 June.

4. USES OF MARKET INDEXES

Indexes were initially created to give a sense of how a particular security market performed on a given day. With the development of modern financial theory, their uses in investment management have expanded significantly. Some of the major uses of indexes include:

- gauges of market sentiment;
- proxies for measuring and modeling returns, systematic risk, and risk-adjusted performance;
- proxies for asset classes in asset allocation models;
- benchmarks for actively managed portfolios; and
- model portfolios for such investment products as index funds and exchange-traded funds (ETFs).

Investors using security market indexes must be familiar with how various indexes are constructed in order to select the index or indexes most appropriate for their needs.

4.1. Gauges of Market Sentiment

The original purpose of stock market indexes was to provide a gauge of investor confidence or market sentiment. As indicators of the collective opinion of market participants, indexes reflect investor attitudes and behavior. The Dow Jones Industrial Average has a long history, is frequently quoted in the media, and remains a popular gauge of market sentiment. It may not accurately reflect the overall attitude of investors or the "market," however, because the index consists of only 30 of the thousands of US stocks traded each day.

4.2. Proxies for Measuring and Modeling Returns, Systematic Risk, and Risk-Adjusted Performance

The capital asset pricing model (CAPM) defines beta as the systematic risk of a security with respect to the entire market. The market portfolio in the CAPM consists of all risky securities. To represent the performance of the market portfolio, investors use a broad index. For example, the Tokyo Price Index (TOPIX) and the S&P 500 often serve as proxies for the market portfolio in Japan and the United States, respectively, and are used for measuring and modeling systematic risk and market returns.

Security market indexes also serve as market proxies when measuring risk-adjusted performance. The beta of an actively managed portfolio allows investors to form a passive alternative with the same level of systematic risk. For example, if the beta of an actively managed portfolio of global stocks is 0.95 with respect to the MSCI World Index, investors can create a passive portfolio with the same systematic risk by investing 95 percent of their portfolio in an MSCI World Index fund and holding the remaining 5 percent in cash. Alpha, the difference between the return of the actively managed portfolio and the return of the passive portfolio, is a measure of risk-adjusted return or investment performance. Alpha can be the result of manager skill (or lack thereof), transaction costs, and fees.

4.3. Proxies for Asset Classes in Asset Allocation Models

Because indexes exhibit the risk and return profiles of select groups of securities, they play a critical role as proxies for asset classes in asset allocation models. They provide the historical data used to model the risks and returns of different asset classes.

4.4. Benchmarks for Actively Managed Portfolios

Investors often use indexes as benchmarks to evaluate the performance of active portfolio managers. The index selected as the benchmark should reflect the investment strategy used by the manager. For example, an active manager investing in global small-capitalization stocks should be evaluated using a benchmark index, such as the FTSE Global Small Cap Index, which includes approximately 4,400 liquid small-capitalization stocks across 47 countries as of August 2018.

The choice of an index to use as a benchmark is important because an inappropriate index could lead to incorrect conclusions regarding an active manager's investment performance. Suppose that the small-cap manager underperformed the small-cap index but outperformed a broad equity market index. If investors use the broad market index as a benchmark, they might conclude that the small-cap manager is earning his or her fees and should be retained or given additional assets to invest. Using the small-cap index as a benchmark might lead to a very different conclusion.

4.5. Model Portfolios for Investment Products

Indexes also serve as the basis for the development of new investment products. Using indexes as benchmarks for actively managed portfolios has led some investors to conclude that they should invest in the benchmarks instead. Based on the CAPM's conclusion that investors should hold the market portfolio, broad market index funds have been developed to function as proxies for the market portfolio.

Investment management firms initially developed and managed index portfolios for institutional investors. Eventually, mutual fund companies introduced index funds for individual investors. Subsequently, investment management firms introduced exchange-traded funds, which are managed the same way as index mutual funds but trade like stocks.

The first ETFs were based on existing indexes. As the popularity of ETFs increased, index providers created new indexes for the specific purpose of forming ETFs, leading to the creation of numerous narrowly defined indexes with corresponding ETFs. The VanEck Vectors Vietnam ETF, for example, allows investors to invest in the equity market of Vietnam.

The choice of indexes to meet the needs of investors is extensive. Index providers are constantly looking for opportunities to develop indexes to meet the needs of investors.

5. EQUITY INDEXES

A wide variety of equity indexes exist, including broad market, multi-market, sector, and style indexes.

5.1. Broad Market Indexes

A broad equity market index, as its name suggests, represents an entire given equity market and typically includes securities representing more than 90 percent of the selected market. For example, the Shanghai Stock Exchange Composite Index (SSE) is a market-capitalization-weighted index of all shares that trade on the Shanghai Stock Exchange. In the United States, the Wilshire 5000 Total Market Index is a market-capitalization-weighted index that includes all US equities with readily available prices and is designed to represent the entire US equity market.[3] The Russell 3000, consisting of the largest 3,000 stocks by market capitalization, represents approximately 98 percent of the US equity market.

5.2. Multi-Market Indexes

Multi-market indexes usually comprise indexes from different countries and regions and are designed to represent multiple security markets. Multi-market indexes may represent multiple national markets, geographic regions, economic development groups, and, in some cases, the entire world. World indexes are of importance to investors who take a global approach to equity investing without any particular bias toward a particular country or region. A number of index providers publish families of multi-market equity indexes.

MSCI offers a number of multi-market indexes. As shown in Exhibit 7, MSCI classifies countries and regions along two dimensions: level of economic development and geographic region. Developmental groups, which MSCI refers to as market classifications, include developed markets, emerging markets, and frontier markets. The geographic regions are largely divided by longitudinal lines of the globe: the Americas, Europe with Africa, and Asia with the Pacific. MSCI provides country- and region-specific indexes for each of the developed and emerging markets within its multi-market indexes. MSCI periodically reviews the classifications of markets in its indexes for movement from frontier markets to emerging markets and from emerging markets to developed markets and reconstitutes the indexes accordingly.

EXHIBIT 7   MSCI Global Investable Market Indexes (as of October 2018)

Developed Markets

Americas	Europe and Middle East	Pacific
Canada, United States	Austria, Belgium, Denmark, Finland, France, Germany, Ireland, Israel, Italy, Netherlands, Norway, Portugal, Spain, Sweden, Switzerland, United Kingdom	Australia, Hong Kong SAR, Japan, New Zealand, Singapore

Emerging Markets

Americas	Europe, Middle East, Africa	Asia
Brazil, Chile, Colombia, Mexico, Peru	Czech Republic, Egypt, Greece, Hungary, Poland, Qatar, Russia, South Africa, Turkey, United Arab Emirates	Chinese mainland, India, Indonesia, South Korea, Malaysia, Pakistan, Philippines, Taiwan region, Thailand

---

[3]Despite its name, the Wilshire 5000 has no constraint on the number of securities that can be included. It included approximately 5,000 securities at inception.

Frontier Markets

Americas	Europe & CIS	Africa	Middle East	Asia
Argentina	Croatia, Estonia, Lithuania, Kazakhstan, Romania, Serbia, Slovenia	Kenya, Mauritius, Morocco, Nigeria, Tunisia, WAEMU[1]	Bahrain, Jordan, Kuwait, Lebanon, Oman	Bangladesh, Sri Lanka, Vietnam

MSCI Standalone Market Indexes[2]

Europe, Middle East, and Africa	Americas	Europe and CIS	Africa	Middle East
Saudi Arabia	Jamaica, Panama,[3] Trinidad & Tobago	Bosnia Herzegovina, Bulgaria, Ukraine	Botswana, Ghana, Zimbabwe	Palestine

[1] The West African Economic and Monetary Union (WAEMU) consists of the following countries: Benin, Burkina Faso, Ivory Coast, Guinea-Bissau, Mali, Niger, Senegal, and Togo. Currently the MSCI WAEMU Indexes include securities classified in Senegal, Ivory Coast, and Burkina Faso.

[2] The MSCI Standalone Market Indexes are not included in the MSCI Emerging Markets Index or MSCI Frontier Markets Index. However, these indexes use either the Emerging Markets or the Frontier Markets methodological criteria concerning size and liquidity.

[3] MSCI Panama Index has been launched as a Standalone Market Index.

Source: Adapted from MSCI (https://www.msci.com/en/market-cap-weighted-indexes), October 2018.

5.2.1. Fundamental Weighting in Multi-Market Indexes

Some index providers weight the securities within each country/region by market capitalization and then weight each country/region in the overall index in proportion to its relative GDP, effectively creating fundamental weighting in multi-market indexes. GDP-weighted indexes were some of the first fundamentally weighted indexes created. Introduced in 1987 by MSCI to address the 60 percent weight of Japanese equities in the market-capitalization-weighted MSCI EAFE Index at the time, GDP-weighted indexes reduced the allocation to Japanese equities by half.[4]

5.3. Sector Indexes

Sector indexes represent and track different economic sectors—such as consumer goods, energy, finance, health care, and technology—on either a national, regional, or global basis. Because different sectors of the economy behave differently over the course of the business cycle, some investors may seek to overweight or underweight their exposure to particular sectors.

Sector indexes are organized as families; each index within the family represents an economic sector. Typically, the aggregation of a sector index family is equivalent to a broad market index. Economic sector classification can be applied on a global, regional, or country-specific basis, but no universally agreed upon sector classification method exists.

---

[4]Steven A. Schoenfeld, *Active Index Investing* (Hoboken, NJ: John Wiley & Sons, 2004):220.

Sector indexes play an important role in performance analysis because they provide a means to determine whether a portfolio manager is more successful at stock selection or sector allocation. Sector indexes also serve as model portfolios for sector-specific ETFs and other investment products.

5.4. Style Indexes

Style indexes represent groups of securities classified according to market capitalization, value, growth, or a combination of these characteristics. They are intended to reflect the investing styles of certain investors, such as the growth investor, value investor, and small-cap investor.

5.4.1. Market Capitalization

Market-capitalization indexes represent securities categorized according to the major capitalization categories: large cap, midcap, and small cap. With no universal definition of these categories, the indexes differ on the distinctions between large cap and midcap and between midcap and small cap, as well as the minimum market-capitalization size required to be included in a small-cap index. Classification into categories can be based on absolute market capitalization (e.g., below €100 million) or relative market capitalization (e.g., the smallest 2,500 stocks).

5.4.2. Value/Growth Classification

Some indexes represent categories of stocks based on their classifications as either value or growth stocks. Different index providers use different factors and valuation ratios (low price-to-book ratios, low price-to-earnings ratios, high dividend yields, etc.) to distinguish between value and growth equities.

5.4.3. Market Capitalization and Value/Growth Classification

Combining the three market-capitalization groups with value and growth classifications results in six basic style index categories:

- Large-Cap Value
- Mid-Cap Value
- Small-Cap Value

- Large-Cap Growth
- Mid-Cap Growth
- Small-Cap Growth

Because indexes use different size and valuation classifications, the constituents of indexes designed to represent a given style, such as small-cap value, may differ—sometimes substantially.

Because valuation ratios and market capitalizations change over time, stocks frequently migrate from one style index category to another on reconstitution dates. As a result, style indexes generally have much higher turnover than do broad market indexes.

6. FIXED-INCOME INDEXES

A wide variety of fixed-income indexes exists, but the nature of the fixed-income markets and fixed-income securities leads to some very important challenges to fixed-income index construction and replication. These challenges are the number of securities in the fixed-income universe, the availability of pricing data, and the liquidity of the securities.

6.1. Construction

The fixed-income universe includes securities issued by governments, government agencies, and corporations. Each of these entities may issue a variety of fixed-income securities with different characteristics. As a result, the number of fixed-income securities is many times larger than the number of equity securities. To represent a specific fixed-income market or segment, indexes may include thousands of different securities. Over time, these fixed-income securities mature, and issuers offer new securities to meet their financing needs, leading to turnover in fixed-income indexes.

Another challenge in index construction is that fixed-income markets are predominantly dealer markets. This means that firms (dealers) are assigned to specific securities and are responsible for creating liquid markets for those securities by purchasing and selling them from their inventory. In addition, many securities do not trade frequently and, as a result, are relatively illiquid. As a result, index providers must contact dealers to obtain current prices on constituent securities to update the index or they must estimate the prices of constituent securities using the prices of traded fixed-income securities with similar characteristics.

These challenges can result in indexes with dissimilar numbers of bonds representing the same markets. The large number of fixed-income securities—combined with the lack of liquidity of some securities—has made it more costly and difficult, compared with equity indexes, for investors to replicate fixed-income indexes and duplicate their performance.

6.2. Types of Fixed-Income Indexes

The wide variety of fixed-income securities, ranging from zero-coupon bonds to bonds with embedded options (i.e., callable or putable bonds), results in a number of different types of fixed-income indexes. Similar to equities, fixed-income securities can be categorized according to the issuer's economic sector, the issuer's geographic region, or the economic development of the issuer's geographic region. Fixed-income securities can also be classified along the following dimensions:

- type of issuer (government, government agency, corporation);
- type of financing (general obligation, collateralized);
- currency of payments;
- maturity;
- credit quality (investment grade, high yield, credit agency ratings); and
- absence or presence of inflation protection.

Fixed-income indexes are based on these various dimensions and can be categorized as follows:

- aggregate or broad market indexes;
- market sector indexes;
- style indexes;
- economic sector indexes; and
- specialized indexes such as high-yield, inflation-linked, and emerging market indexes.

The first fixed-income index created, the Bloomberg Barclays US Aggregate Bond Index (formerly the Barclays Capital Aggregate Bond Index), is an example of a single-country aggregate index. Designed to represent the broad market of US fixed-income securities, it comprises approximately 8,000 securities, including US Treasury, government-related, corporate, mortgage-backed, asset-backed, and commercial mortgage-backed securities.

Aggregate indexes can be subdivided by market sector (government, government agency, collateralized, corporate); style (maturity, credit quality); economic sector, or some other characteristic to create more narrowly defined indexes. A common distinction reflected in indexes is between investment grade (e.g., those with a Standard & Poor's credit rating of BBB– or better) and high-yield securities. Investment-grade indexes are typically further subdivided by maturity (i.e., short, intermediate, or long) and by credit rating (e.g., AAA, BBB, etc.).[5] The wide variety of fixed-income indexes reflects the partitioning of fixed-income securities on the basis of a variety of dimensions.

Exhibit 8 illustrates how the major types of fixed-income indexes can be organized on the basis of various dimensions.

EXHIBIT 8   Dimensions of Fixed-Income Indexes

Market	Global			
	Regional			
	Country or currency zone			
Type	Corporate	Collateralized *Securitized* *Mortgage-backed*	Government agency	Government
Maturity	For example, 1–3, 3–5, 5–7, 7–10, 10+ years; short-term, medium-term, or long-term			
Credit quality	For example, AAA, AA, A, BBB, etc.; Aaa, Aa, A, Baa, etc.; investment grade, high yield			

All aggregate indexes include a variety of market sectors and credit ratings. The breakdown of the Bloomberg Barclays Global Aggregate Bond Index by market sectors and by credit rating is shown in Exhibit 9 and Exhibit 10, respectively.

---

[5]Credit ratings are discussed in depth in the Level I CFA Program chapter "Fundamentals of Credit Analysis."

EXHIBIT 9   Market Sector Breakdown of the Bloomberg Barclays Global Aggregate Bond Index

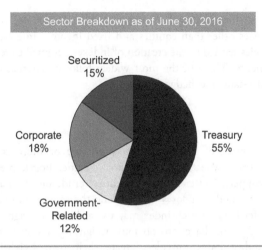

EXHIBIT 10   Credit Breakdown of the Bloomberg Barclays Global Aggregate Bond Index

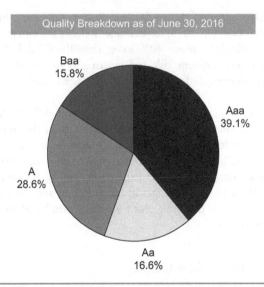

7. INDEXES FOR ALTERNATIVE INVESTMENTS

Many investors seek to lower the risk or enhance the performance of their portfolios by investing in assets classes other than equities and fixed income. Interest in alternative assets and investment strategies has led to the creation of indexes designed to represent broad classes of alternative investments. Three of the most widely followed alternative investment classes are commodities, real estate, and hedge funds.

7.1. Commodity Indexes

Commodity indexes consist of futures contracts on one or more commodities, such as agricultural products (rice, wheat, sugar), livestock (cattle, hogs), precious and common metals (gold, silver, copper), and energy commodities (crude oil, natural gas).

Although some commodity indexes may include the same commodities, the returns of these indexes may differ because each index may use a different weighting method. Because commodity indexes do not have an obvious weighting mechanism, such as market capitalization, commodity index providers create their own weighting methods. Some indexes, such as the Thomson Reuters/Core Commodity CRB Index (TR/CC CRB Index), formerly known as the Commodity Research Bureau (CRB) Index, contain a fixed number of commodities that are weighted equally. The S&P GSCI uses a combination of liquidity measures and world production values in its weighting scheme and allocates more weight to commodities that have risen in price. Other indexes have fixed weights that are determined by a committee.

The different weighting methods can also lead to large differences in exposure to specific commodities. The S&P GSCI in 2018, for example, weights the energy-sector approximately 50% higher and the agriculture sector 40% lower than the CRB Index. These differences result in indexes with very different risk and return profiles. Unlike commodity indexes, broad equity and fixed-income indexes that target the same markets share similar risk and return profiles.

The performance of commodity indexes can also be quite different from their underlying commodities because the indexes consist of futures contracts on the commodities rather than the actual commodities. Index returns are affected by factors other than changes in the prices of the underlying commodities because futures contracts must be continually "rolled over" (i.e., replacing a contract nearing expiration with a new contract). Commodity index returns reflect the risk-free interest rate, the changes in future prices, and the roll yield. Therefore, a commodity index return can be quite different from the return based on changes in the prices of the underlying commodities.

7.2. Real Estate Investment Trust Indexes

Real estate indexes represent not only the market for real estate securities but also the market for real estate—a highly illiquid market and asset class with infrequent transactions and pricing information. Real estate indexes can be categorized as appraisal indexes, repeat sales indexes, and real estate investment trust (REIT) indexes.

REIT indexes consist of shares of publicly traded REITs. REITS are public or private corporations organized specifically to invest in real estate, either through ownership of properties or investment in mortgages. Shares of public REITs are traded on the world's various stock exchanges and are a popular choice for investing in commercial real estate properties. Because REIT indexes are based on publicly traded REITs with continuous market pricing, the value of REIT indexes is calculated continuously.

The FTSE EPRA/NAREIT global family of REIT indexes shown in Exhibit 11 seeks to represent trends in real estate stocks worldwide and includes representation from the European Public Real Estate Association (EPRA) and the National Association of Real Estate Investment Trusts (NAREIT).

EXHIBIT 11   The FTSE EPRA/NAREIT Global REIT Index Family

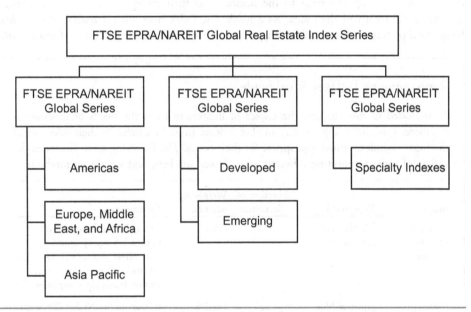

Source: FTSE International ("FTSE EPRA/NAREIT Global & Global Ex US Indices" Factsheet 2009). "FTSE®" is a trademark of the London Stock Exchange Plc, "NAREIT®" is a trademark of the National Association of Real Estate Investment Trusts ("NAREIT"), and "EPRA®" is a trademark of the European Public Real Estate Association ("EPRA") and all are used by FTSE International Limited ("FTSE") under license.

7.3. Hedge Fund Indexes

Hedge fund indexes reflect the returns on hedge funds. **Hedge funds** are private investment vehicles that typically use leverage and long and short investment strategies.

A number of research organizations maintain databases of hedge fund returns and summarize these returns into indexes. These database indexes are designed to represent the performance of the hedge funds on a very broad global level (hedge funds in general) or the strategy level. Most of these indexes are equal weighted and represent the performance of the hedge funds within a particular database.

Most research organizations rely on the voluntary cooperation of hedge funds to compile performance data. As unregulated entities, however, hedge funds are not required to report their performance to any party other than their investors. Therefore, each hedge fund decides to which database(s) it will report its performance. As a result, rather than index providers determining the constituents, the constituents determine the index.

Frequently, a hedge fund reports its performance to only one database. The result is little overlap of funds covered by the different indexes. With little overlap between their constituents, different global hedge fund indexes may reflect very different performance for the hedge fund industry over the same period of time.

Another consequence of the voluntary performance reporting is the potential for survivorship bias and, therefore, inaccurate performance representation. This means that hedge funds with poor performance may be less likely to report their performance to the database or may stop reporting to the database, so their returns may be excluded when measuring the return of the index. As a result, the index may not accurately reflect actual hedge fund performance so much as the performance of hedge funds that are performing well.

Representative Indexes Worldwide

As indicated in this chapter, the choice of indexes to meet the needs of investors is extensive. Investors using security market indexes must be careful in their selection of the index or indexes most appropriate for their needs. The following table illustrates the variety of indexes reflecting different asset classes, markets, and weighting methods.

Index	Representing	Number of Securities	Weighting Method	Comments
Dow Jones Industrial Average	US blue chip companies	30	Price	The oldest and most widely known US equity index. *Wall Street Journal* editors choose 30 stocks from among large, mature blue-chip companies.
Nikkei Stock Average	Japanese blue chip companies	225	Modified price	Known as the Nikkei 225 and originally formulated by Dow Jones & Company. Because of extreme variation in price levels of component securities, some high-priced shares are weighted as a fraction of share price.
TOPIX	All companies listed on the Tokyo Stock Exchange First Section	Varies	Float-adjusted market cap	Represents about 93 percent of the market value of all Japanese equities. Contains a large number of very small, illiquid stocks, making exact replication difficult.
MSCI All Country World Index	Stocks of 23 developed and 24 emerging markets	Varies	Free-float-adjusted market cap	Composed of companies representative of the market structure of developed and emerging market countries in the Americas, Europe/Middle East, and Asia/Pacific regions. Price return and total return versions available in both USD and local currencies.

Index	Representing	Number of Securities	Weighting Method	Comments
S&P Developed Ex-US BMI Energy Sector Index	Energy sector of developed global markets outside the United States	Varies	Float-adjusted market cap	Serves as a model portfolio for the SPDR® S&P Energy Sector Exchange-Traded Fund (ETF).
Bloomberg Barclays Global Aggregate Bond Index	Investment-grade bonds in the North American, European, and Asian markets	Varies	Market cap	Formerly known as Lehman Brothers Global Aggregate Bond Index.
Markit iBoxx Euro High-Yield Bond Indexes	Sub-investment-grade euro-denominated corporate bonds	Varies	Market cap and variations	Rebalanced monthly. Represents tradable part of market. Price and total return versions available with such analytical values as yield, duration, modified duration, and convexity. Provides platform for research and structured products.
FTSE EPRA/ NAREIT Global Real Estate Index	Real estate securities in the North American, European, and Asian markets	Varies	Float-adjusted market cap	The stocks of REITs that constitute the index trade on public stock exchanges and may be constituents of equity market indexes.
HFRX Global Hedge Fund Index	Overall composition of the HFR database	Varies	Asset weighted	Comprises all eligible hedge fund strategies. Examples include convertible arbitrage, distressed securities, market neutral, event driven, macro, and relative value arbitrage. Constituent strategies are asset weighted on the basis of asset distribution within the hedge fund industry.
HFRX Equal Weighted Strategies EUR Index	Overall composition of the HFR database	Varies	Equal weighted	Denominated in euros and is constructed from the same strategies as the HFRX Global Hedge Fund Index.
Morningstar Style Indexes	US stocks classified by market cap and value/ growth orientation	Varies	Float-adjusted market cap	The nine indexes defined by combinations of market cap (large, mid, and small) and value/ growth orientation (value, core, growth) have mutually exclusive constituents and are exhaustive with respect to the Morningstar US Market Index. Each is a model portfolio for one of the iShares Morningstar ETFs.

SUMMARY

This chapter explains and illustrates the construction, management, and uses of security market indexes. It also discusses various types of indexes. Security market indexes are invaluable tools for investors, who can select from among thousands of indexes representing a variety of security markets, market segments, and asset classes. These indexes range from those representing the global market for major asset classes to those representing alternative investments in specific geographic markets. To benefit from the use of security market indexes, investors must understand their construction and determine whether the selected index is appropriate for their purposes. Frequently, an index that is well suited for one purpose may not be well suited for other purposes. Users of indexes must be familiar with how various indexes are constructed in order to select the index or indexes most appropriate for their needs.

Among the key points made in this chapter are the following:

- Security market indexes are intended to measure the values of different target markets (security markets, market segments, or asset classes).
- The constituent securities selected for inclusion in the security market index are intended to represent the target market.
- A price return index reflects only the prices of the constituent securities.
- A total return index reflects not only the prices of the constituent securities but also the reinvestment of all income received since the inception of the index.
- Methods used to weight the constituents of an index range from the very simple, such as price and equal weightings, to the more complex, such as market-capitalization and fundamental weightings.
- Choices in index construction—in particular, the choice of weighting method—affect index valuation and returns.
- Index management includes 1) periodic rebalancing to ensure that the index maintains appropriate weightings and 2) reconstitution to ensure the index represents the desired target market.
- Rebalancing and reconstitution create turnover in an index. Reconstitution can dramatically affect prices of current and prospective constituents.
- Indexes serve a variety of purposes. They gauge market sentiment and serve as benchmarks for actively managed portfolios. They act as proxies for measuring systematic risk and risk-adjusted performance. They also serve as proxies for asset classes in asset allocation models and as model portfolios for investment products.
- Investors can choose from security market indexes representing various asset classes, including equity, fixed-income, commodity, real estate, and hedge fund indexes.
- Within most asset classes, index providers offer a wide variety of indexes, ranging from broad market indexes to highly specialized indexes based on the issuer's geographic region, economic development group, or economic sector or other factors.
- Proper use of security market indexes depends on understanding their construction and management.

PRACTICE PROBLEMS

1. A security market index represents the:
   A. risk of a security market.
   B. security market as a whole.
   C. security market, market segment, or asset class.

2. Security market indexes are:
   A. constructed and managed like a portfolio of securities.
   B. simple interchangeable tools for measuring the returns of different asset classes.
   C. valued on a regular basis using the actual market prices of the constituent securities.

3. When creating a security market index, an index provider must first determine the:
   A. target market.
   B. appropriate weighting method.
   C. number of constituent securities.

4. One month after inception, the price return version and total return version of a single index (consisting of identical securities and weights) will be equal if:
   A. market prices have not changed.
   B. capital gains are offset by capital losses.
   C. the securities do not pay dividends or interest.

5. The values of a price return index and a total return index consisting of identical equal-weighted dividend-paying equities will be equal:
   A. only at inception.
   B. at inception and on rebalancing dates.
   C. at inception and on reconstitution dates.

6. An analyst gathers the following information for an equal-weighted index comprised of assets Able, Baker, and Charlie:

Security	Beginning of Period Price (€)	End of Period Price (€)	Total Dividends (€)
Able	10.00	12.00	0.75
Baker	20.00	19.00	1.00
Charlie	30.00	30.00	2.00

The price return of the index is:
   A. 1.7%.
   B. 5.0%.
   C. 11.4%.

7. An analyst gathers the following information for an equal-weighted index comprised of assets Able, Baker, and Charlie:

Security	Beginning of Period Price (€)	End of Period Price (€)	Total Dividends (€)
Able	10.00	12.00	0.75
Baker	20.00	19.00	1.00
Charlie	30.00	30.00	2.00

The total return of the index is:
A. 5.0%.
B. 7.9%.
C. 11.4%.

8. An analyst gathers the following information for a price-weighted index comprised of securities ABC, DEF, and GHI:

Security	Beginning of Period Price (£)	End of Period Price (£)	Total Dividends (£)
ABC	25.00	27.00	1.00
DEF	35.00	25.00	1.50
GHI	15.00	16.00	1.00

The price return of the index is:
A. −4.6%.
B. −9.3%.
C. −13.9%.

9. An analyst gathers the following information for a market-capitalization-weighted index comprised of securities MNO, QRS, and XYZ:

Security	Beginning of Period Price (¥)	End of Period Price (¥)	Dividends per Share (¥)	Shares Outstanding
MNO	2,500	2,700	100	5,000
QRS	3,500	2,500	150	7,500
XYZ	1,500	1,600	100	10,000

The price return of the index is:
A. −9.33%.
B. −10.23%.
C. −13.90%.

10. An analyst gathers the following information for a market-capitalization-weighted index comprised of securities MNO, QRS, and XYZ:

Security	Beginning of Period Price (¥)	End of Period Price (¥)	Dividends Per Share (¥)	Shares Outstanding
MNO	2,500	2,700	100	5,000
QRS	3,500	2,500	150	7,500
XYZ	1,500	1,600	100	10,000

The total return of the index is:
A. 1.04%.
B. −5.35%.
C. −10.23%.

11. When creating a security market index, the target market:
A. determines the investment universe.
B. is usually a broadly defined asset class.
C. determines the number of securities to be included in the index.

12. An analyst gathers the following data for a price-weighted index:

Security	Beginning of Period		End of Period	
	Price (€)	Shares Outstanding	Price (€)	Shares Outstanding
A	20.00	300	22.00	300
B	50.00	300	48.00	300
C	26.00	2,000	30.00	2,000

The price return of the index over the period is:
A. 4.2%.
B. 7.1%.
C. 21.4%.

13. An analyst gathers the following data for a value-weighted index:

Security	Beginning of Period		End of Period	
	Price (£)	Shares Outstanding	Price (£)	Shares Outstanding
A	20.00	300	22.00	300
B	50.00	300	48.00	300
C	26.00	2,000	30.00	2,000

The return on the value-weighted index over the period is:
A. 7.1%.
B. 11.0%.
C. 21.4%.

14. An analyst gathers the following data for an equally-weighted index:

	Beginning of Period		End of Period	
Security	Price (¥)	Shares Outstanding	Price (¥)	Shares Outstanding
A	20.00	300	22.00	300
B	50.00	300	48.00	300
C	26.00	2,000	30.00	2,000

The return on the index over the period is:
A. 4.2%.
B. 6.8%.
C. 7.1%.

15. Which of the following index weighting methods requires an adjustment to the divisor after a stock split?
A. Price weighting
B. Fundamental weighting
C. Market-capitalization weighting

16. If the price return of an equal-weighted index exceeds that of a market-capitalization-weighted index comprised of the same securities, the *most likely* explanation is:
A. stock splits.
B. dividend distributions.
C. outperformance of small-market-capitalization stocks.

17. A float-adjusted market-capitalization-weighted index weights each of its constituent securities by its price and:
A. its trading volume.
B. the number of its shares outstanding.
C. the number of its shares available to the investing public.

18. Which of the following index weighting methods is *most likely* subject to a value tilt?
A. Equal weighting
B. Fundamental weighting
C. Market-capitalization weighting

19. Rebalancing an index is the process of periodically adjusting the constituent:
A. securities' weights to optimize investment performance.
B. securities to maintain consistency with the target market.
C. securities' weights to maintain consistency with the index's weighting method.

20. Which of the following index weighting methods requires the *most frequent* rebalancing?
A. Price weighting
B. Equal weighting
C. Market-capitalization weighting

21. Reconstitution of a security market index reduces:
    A. portfolio turnover.
    B. the need for rebalancing.
    C. the likelihood that the index includes securities that are not representative of the target market.

22. Security market indexes are used as:
    A. measures of investment returns.
    B. proxies to measure unsystematic risk.
    C. proxies for specific asset classes in asset allocation models.

23. Uses of market indexes do not include serving as a:
    A. measure of systemic risk.
    B. basis for new investment products.
    C. benchmark for evaluating portfolio performance.

24. Which of the following statements regarding sector indexes is *most accurate*? Sector indexes:
    A. track different economic sectors and cannot be aggregated to represent the equivalent of a broad market index.
    B. provide a means to determine whether an active investment manager is more successful at stock selection or sector allocation.
    C. apply a universally agreed upon sector classification system to identify the constituent securities of specific economic sectors, such as consumer goods, energy, finance, health care.

25. Which of the following is an example of a style index? An index based on:
    A. geography.
    B. economic sector.
    C. market capitalization.

26. Which of the following statements regarding fixed-income indexes is *most accurate*?
    A. Liquidity issues make it difficult for investors to easily replicate fixed-income indexes.
    B. Rebalancing and reconstitution are the only sources of turnover in fixed-income indexes.
    C. Fixed-income indexes representing the same target market hold similar numbers of bonds.

27. An aggregate fixed-income index:
    A. comprises corporate and asset-backed securities.
    B. represents the market of government-issued securities.
    C. can be subdivided by market or economic sector to create more narrowly defined indexes.

28. Fixed-income indexes are *least likely* constructed on the basis of:
    A. maturity.
    B. type of issuer.
    C. coupon frequency.

29. Commodity index values are based on:
    A. futures contract prices.
    B. the market price of the specific commodity.
    C. the average market price of a basket of similar commodities.

30. Which of the following statements is *most accurate*?
    A. Commodity indexes all share similar weighting methods.
    B. Commodity indexes containing the same underlying commodities offer similar returns.
    C. The performance of commodity indexes can be quite different from that of the underlying commodities.

31. Which of the following is *not* a real estate index category?
    A. Appraisal index
    B. Initial sales index
    C. Repeat sales index

32. A unique feature of hedge fund indexes is that they:
    A. are frequently equal weighted.
    B. are determined by the constituents of the index.
    C. reflect the value of private rather than public investments.

33. The returns of hedge fund indexes are *most likely*:
    A. biased upward.
    B. biased downward.
    C. similar across different index providers.

34. In comparison to equity indexes, the constituent securities of fixed-income indexes are:
    A. more liquid.
    B. easier to price.
    C. drawn from a larger investment universe.

CHAPTER 3

CAPITAL MARKET EXPECTATIONS, PART 1: FRAMEWORK AND MACRO CONSIDERATIONS

Christopher D. Piros, PhD, CFA

Parts of this chapter have been adapted from a former Capital Market Expectations chapter authored by John P. Calverley, Alan M. Meder, CPA, CFA, Brian D. Singer, CFA, and Renato Staub, PhD.

LEARNING OUTCOMES

The candidate should be able to:

- discuss the role of, and a framework for, capital market expectations in the portfolio management process;
- discuss challenges in developing capital market forecasts;
- explain how exogenous shocks may affect economic growth trends;
- discuss the application of economic growth trend analysis to the formulation of capital market expectations;
- compare major approaches to economic forecasting;
- discuss how business cycles affect short- and long-term expectations;
- explain the relationship of inflation to the business cycle and the implications of inflation for cash, bonds, equity, and real estate returns;
- discuss the effects of monetary and fiscal policy on business cycles;
- interpret the shape of the yield curve as an economic predictor and discuss the relationship between the yield curve and fiscal and monetary policy;
- identify and interpret macroeconomic, interest rate, and exchange rate linkages between economies.

1. INTRODUCTION

A noted investment authority has written that the "fundamental law of investing is the uncertainty of the future."[1] Investors have no choice but to forecast elements of the future because nearly all investment decisions look toward it. Specifically, investment decisions incorporate the decision maker's expectations concerning factors and events believed to affect investment values. The decision maker integrates these views into expectations about the risk and return prospects of individual assets and groups of assets.

This chapter's focus is **capital market expectations** (CME): expectations concerning the risk and return prospects of asset classes, however broadly or narrowly the investor defines those asset classes. Capital market expectations are an essential input to formulating a strategic asset allocation. For example, if an investor's investment policy statement specifies and defines eight permissible asset classes, the investor will need to have formulated long-term expectations concerning each of those asset classes. The investor may also act on short-term expectations. Insights into capital markets gleaned during CME setting should also help in formulating the expectations concerning individual assets that are needed in security selection and valuation.

This is the first of two chapters on capital market expectations. A central theme of both chapters is that a disciplined approach to setting expectations will be rewarded. With that in mind, Section 2 of this chapter presents a general framework for developing capital market expectations and alerts the reader to the range of problems and pitfalls that await investors and analysts in this arena. Section 3 focuses on the use of macroeconomic analysis in setting expectations. The second of the two CME chapters builds on this foundation to address setting expectations for specific asset classes: equities, fixed income, real estate, and currencies. Various analytical tools are reviewed as needed throughout both chapters.

2. FRAMEWORK AND CHALLENGES

In this section, we provide a guide to collecting, organizing, combining, and interpreting investment information. After outlining the process, we turn to a discussion of typical problems and challenges to formulating the most informed judgments possible.

Before laying out the framework, we must be clear about what it needs to accomplish. The ultimate objective is to develop a set of projections with which to make informed investment decisions, specifically asset allocation decisions. As obvious as this goal may seem, it has important implications.

Asset allocation is the primary determinant of long-run portfolio performance.[2] The projections underlying these decisions are among the most important determinants of whether investors achieve their long-term goals. It thus follows that it is vital to get the long-run *level* of returns (approximately) right. Until the late 1990s, it was standard practice for institutional investors to extrapolate historical return data into forecasts. At the height of the technology bubble,[3] this practice led many to project double-digit portfolio returns into the indefinite future. Such inflated projections allowed institutions to underfund their obligations

---

[1]Peter L. Bernstein in the foreword to Rapaport and Mauboussin (2001), p. xiii.
[2]See Brinson, Hood, and Beebower (1986) and Ibbotson and Kaplan (2000).
[3]Explosive growth of the internet in the late 1990s was accompanied by soaring valuations for virtually any internet-related investment. The NASDAQ composite index, which was very heavily weighted in technology stocks, nearly quintupled from 1997 to early 2000, then gave up all of those gains by mid-2002. A variety of names have been given to this episode including the tech or technology bubble.

and/or set unrealistic goals, many of which have had to be scaled back. Since that time, most institutions have adopted explicitly forward-looking methods of the type(s) discussed in our two CME chapters, and return projections have declined sharply. Indeed, as of the beginning of 2018, consensus rate of return projections seemed to imply that US private foundations, which must distribute at least 5% of assets annually, could struggle to prudently generate long-run returns sufficient to cover their required distributions, their expenses, and inflation. To reiterate, projecting a realistic overall level of returns has to be a top priority.

As appealing as it is to think we could project asset returns with precision, that idea is unrealistic. Even the most sophisticated methods are likely to be subject to frustratingly large forecast errors over relevant horizons. We should, of course, seek to limit our forecast errors. We should not, however, put undue emphasis on the precision of projections for individual asset classes. Far more important objectives are to ensure internal consistency across asset classes (**cross-sectional consistency**) and over various time horizons (**intertemporal consistency**). This emphasis stems once again from the primary use of the projections—asset allocation decisions. Inconsistency across asset classes is likely to result in portfolios with poor risk–return characteristics over any horizon, whereas intertemporal inconsistency is likely to distort the connection between portfolio decisions and investment horizon.

Our discussion adopts the perspective of an analyst or team responsible for developing projections to be used by the firm's investment professionals in advising and/or managing portfolios for its clients. As the setting of explicit capital market expectations has become both more common and more sophisticated, many asset managers have adopted this centralized approach, enabling them to leverage the requisite expertise and deliver more consistent advice to all their clients.

2.1. A Framework for Developing Capital Market Expectations

The following is a framework for a disciplined approach to setting CME.

1. *Specify the set of expectations needed, including the time horizon(s) to which they apply.* This step requires the analyst to formulate an explicit list of the asset classes and investment horizon(s) for which projections are needed.
2. *Research the historical record.* Most forecasts have some connection to the past. For many markets, the historical record contains useful information on the asset's investment characteristics, suggesting at least some possible ranges for future results. Beyond the raw historical facts, the analyst should seek to identify and understand the factors that affect asset class returns.
3. *Specify the method(s) and/or model(s) to be used and their information requirements.* The analyst or team responsible for developing CME should be explicit about the method(s) and/or model(s) that will be used and should be able to justify the selection.
4. *Determine the best sources for information needs.* The analyst or team must identify those sources that provide the most accurate and timely information tailored to their needs.
5. *Interpret the current investment environment using the selected data and methods, applying experience and judgment.* Care should be taken to apply a common set of assumptions, compatible methodologies, and consistent judgments in order to ensure mutually consistent projections across asset classes and over time horizons.
6. *Provide the set of expectations needed, documenting conclusions.* The projections should be accompanied by the reasoning and assumptions behind them.

7. *Monitor actual outcomes and compare them with expectations, providing feedback to improve the expectations-setting process.* The most effective practice is likely to synchronize this step with the expectations-setting process, monitoring and reviewing outcomes on the same cycle as the projections are updated, although several cycles may be required to validate conclusions.

The first step in the CME framework requires the analyst to define the universe of asset classes for which she will develop expectations. The universe should include all of the asset classes that will typically be accorded a distinct allocation in client portfolios. To put it another way, the universe needs to reflect the key dimensions of decision-making in the firm's investment process. On the other hand, the universe should be as small as possible because even pared down to minimum needs, the expectations-setting process can be quite challenging.

Steps 2 and 3 in the process involve understanding the historical performance of the asset classes and researching their return drivers. The information that needs to be collected mirrors considerations that defined the universe of assets in step 1. The more granular the classification of assets, the more granular the breakdown of information will need to be to support the investment process. Except in the simplest of cases, the analyst will need to slice the data in multiple dimensions. Among these are the following:

- Geography: global, regional, domestic versus non-domestic, economic blocs (e.g., the European Union), individual countries;
- Major asset classes: equity, fixed income, real assets;
- Sub-asset classes:
  - Equities: styles, sizes, sectors, industries;
  - Fixed income: maturities, credit quality, securitization, fixed versus floating, nominal or inflation-protected;
  - Real assets: real estate, commodities, timber.

How each analyst approaches this task depends on the hierarchy of decisions in their investment process. One firm may prioritize segmenting the global equity market by Global Industry Classification Standard (GIC) sector, with geographic distinctions accorded secondary consideration, while another firm prioritizes decisions with respect to geography considering sector breakdowns as secondary.[4]

In Step 3, the analyst needs to be sensitive to the fact that both the effectiveness of forecasting approaches and relationships among variables are related to the investor's time horizon. As an example, a discounted cash flow approach to setting equity market expectations is usually considered to be most appropriate to long-range forecasting. If forecasts are also to be made for shorter, finite horizons, intertemporal consistency dictates that the method used for those projections must be calibrated so that its projections converge to the long-range forecast as the horizon extends.

Executing the fourth step—determining the best information sources—requires researching the quality of alternative data sources and striving to fully understand the data. Using flawed or misunderstood data is a recipe for faulty analysis. Furthermore, analysts should be alert to new, superior data sources. Large, commercially available databases and reputable financial publications are likely the best avenue for obtaining widely disseminated information covering the broad spectrum of asset classes and geographies. Trade publications, academic

---

[4]There is extensive literature on the relative importance of country versus industry factors in global equity markets. Marcelo, Quiros, and Martins (2013) summarized the evidence as "vast and contradictory."

studies, government and central bank reports, corporate filings, and broker/dealer and third-party research often provide more specialized information. Appropriate data frequencies must be selected. Daily series are of more use for setting shorter-term expectations. Monthly, quarterly, or annual data series are useful for setting longer-term CME.

The first four steps lay the foundation for the heart of the process: the fifth and sixth steps. Monitoring and interpreting the economic and market environment and assessing the implications for relevant investments are activities the analyst should be doing every day. In essence, step five could be labeled "implement your investment/research process" and step six could be labeled "at designated times, synthesize, document, and defend your views." Perhaps what most distinguishes these steps from the day-to-day investment process is that the analyst must make simultaneous projections for all asset classes and all designated, concrete horizons.

Finally, in step 7 we use experience to improve the expectations-setting process. We measure our previously formed expectations against actual results to assess the level of accuracy the process is delivering. Generally, good forecasts are:

- unbiased, objective, and well researched;
- efficient, in the sense of minimizing the size of forecast errors; and
- internally consistent, both cross-sectionally and intertemporally.

Although it is important to monitor outcomes for ways in which our forecasting process can be improved, our ability to assess the accuracy of our forecasts may be severely limited. A standard rule of thumb in statistics is that we need at least 30 observations to meaningfully test a hypothesis. Quantitative evaluation of forecast errors in real time may be of limited value in refining a process that is already reasonably well constructed (i.e., not subject to obvious gross errors). Hence, the most valuable part of the feedback loop will often be qualitative and judgmental.

EXAMPLE 1   Capital Market Expectations Setting: Information Requirements

Consider two investment strategists charged with developing capital market expectations for their firms, John Pearson and Michael Wu. Pearson works for a bank trust department that runs US balanced separately managed accounts (SMAs) for high-net-worth individuals. These accounts' mandates restrict investments to US equities, US investment-grade fixed-income instruments, and prime US money market instruments. The investment objective is long-term capital growth and income. In contrast, Wu works for a large Hong Kong SAR–based, internationally focused asset manager that uses the following types of assets within its investment process:

Equities	Fixed Income	Alternative Investments
Asian equities	Eurozone sovereign	Eastern European
Eurozone	US government	venture capital
US large-cap		New Zealand timber
US small-cap		US commercial real
Canadian large-cap		estate

Wu's firm runs SMAs with generally long-term time horizons and global tactical asset allocation (GTAA) programs. Compare and contrast the information and knowledge requirements of Pearson and Wu.

Guideline answer:
Pearson's in-depth information requirements relate to US equity and fixed-income markets. By contrast, Wu's information requirements relate not only to US and non-US equity and fixed-income markets but also to three alternative investment types with non-public markets, located on three different continents. Wu has a more urgent need to be current on political, social, economic, and trading-oriented operational details worldwide than Pearson. Given their respective investment time horizons, Pearson's focus is on the long term whereas Wu needs to focus not only on the long term but also on near-term disequilibria among markets (for GTAA decisions). One challenge that Pearson has in US fixed-income markets that Wu does not face is the need to cover corporate and municipal as well as government debt securities. Nevertheless, Wu's overall information and knowledge requirements are clearly more demanding than Pearson's.

2.2. Challenges in Forecasting

A range of problems can frustrate analysts' expectations-setting efforts. Expectations reflecting faulty analysis or assumptions may cause a portfolio manager to construct a portfolio that is inappropriate for the client. At the least, the portfolio manager may incur the costs of changing portfolio composition without any offsetting benefits. The following sections provide guidance on points that warrant special caution. The discussion focuses on problems in the use of data and on analyst mistakes and biases.

2.2.1. Limitations of Economic Data

The analyst needs to understand the definition, construction, timeliness, and accuracy of any data used, including any biases. The time lag with which economic data are collected, processed, and disseminated can impede their use because data that are not timely may be of little value in assessing current conditions. Some economic data may be reported with a lag as short as one week, whereas other important data may be reported with a lag of more than a quarter. The International Monetary Fund sometimes reports data for developing economies with a lag of two years or more. Older data increase the uncertainty concerning the current state of the economy with respect to that variable.

Furthermore, one or more official revisions to initial data values are common. Sometimes these revisions are substantial, which may give rise to significantly different inferences. Often only the most recent data point is revised. Other series are subject to periodic "benchmark revisions" that simultaneously revise all or a portion of the historical data series. In either case—routine updating of the most recent release or benchmark revision—the analyst must be aware that using revised data as if it were known at the time to which it applies often suggests strong historical relationships that are unreliable for forecasting.

Definitions and calculation methods change too. For example, the US Bureau of Labor Statistics (BLS) made significant changes to the Consumer Price Index for All Urban Consumers (CPI-U) in 1983 (treatment of owner-occupied housing) and again in 1991 (regression-based product quality adjustments). Analysts should also be aware that suppliers of economic and financial indexes periodically **re-base** these indexes, meaning that the specific period used as the base of the index is changed. Analysts should take care to avoid inadvertently mixing data relating to different base periods.

2.2.2. Data Measurement Errors and Biases

Analysts need to be aware of possible biases and/or errors in data series, including the following:

- **Transcription errors**. These are errors in gathering and recording data.
- **Survivorship bias**. This bias arises when a data series reflects only entities that survived to the end of the period. Without correction, statistics from such data can be misleading. Data on alternative assets such as hedge funds are notorious for survivorship bias.
- **Appraisal (smoothed) data**. For certain assets without liquid public markets, notably but not only real estate, appraisal data are used in lieu of transaction data. Appraised values tend to be less volatile than market-determined values. As a result, measured volatilities are biased downward and correlations with other assets tend to be understated.

2.2.3. The Limitations of Historical Estimates

Although history is often a helpful guide, the past should not be extrapolated uncritically. There are two primary issues with respect to using historical data. First, the data may not be representative of the future period for which an analyst needs to forecast. Second, even if the data are representative of the future, statistics calculated from that data may be poor estimates of the desired metrics. Both of these issues can be addressed to some extent by imposing structure (that is, a model) on how data is presumed to have been generated in the past and how it is expected to be generated in the future.

Changes in technological, political, legal, and regulatory environments; disruptions such as wars and other calamities; and changes in policy stances can all alter risk–return relationships. Such shifts are known as changes in **regime** (the governing set of relationships) and give rise to the statistical problem of **nonstationarity** (meaning, informally, that different parts of a data series reflect different underlying statistical properties). Statistical tools are available to help identify and model such changes or turning points.

A practical approach for an analyst to decide whether to use the whole of a long data series or only part of it involves answering two questions.

1. Is there any reason to believe that the entirety of the sample period is no longer relevant? In other words, has there been a fundamental regime change (such as political, economic, market, or asset class structure) during the sample period?
2. Do the data support the hypothesis that such a change has occurred?

If the answer to both questions is yes, the analyst should use only that part of the time series that appears relevant to the present. Alternatively, he may apply statistical techniques that account for regime changes in the past data as well as the possibility of subsequent regime changes. Exhibit 1 illustrates examples of changes in regime.

EXHIBIT 1   Regimes and the Relevance of Historical Bond Returns

In the 1970s, oil price shocks combined with accommodative monetary policy by the US Federal Reserve fueled sharply rising inflation. In 1980, the Fed abruptly shifted to an aggressively tight stance. After the initial shock of sharply higher interest rates, US bond yields trended downward for roughly 35 years as the Fed kept downward pressure on inflation. Throughout the 1980s and 1990s, the Fed eased monetary policy in the aftermath of the technology bubble. Then, switching to an extraordinarily expansionary policy in the midst of the 2008–2009 global financial crisis, the Fed reduced its policy rate to 0% in December 2008. Subsequently, it aggressively bought Treasury bonds and mortgage-backed securities. The Fed finally raised its policy rate target in December 2015. In October 2017, it stopped rolling over maturing bonds, allowing its balance sheet to shrink, albeit very slowly. It can be argued that bond returns from the 1970s through 2015 reflect at least three distinct regimes: the inflationary 1970s with accommodative Fed policy, the 1980–2008 period of disinflationary policy and secularly falling yields, and the unprecedented 2009–2015 period of zero interest rates and explosive liquidity provision. As of mid-2018, nominal interest rates were still negative in some developed markets, and major central banks including the Fed were aiming to "normalize" policy over the next few years. There is ample reason to believe that future bond returns will reflect a regime like none before.

In general, the analyst should use the longest data history for which there is reasonable assurance of stationarity. This guideline follows from the fact that sample statistics from a longer history are more precise than those with fewer observations. Although it is tempting to assume that using higher-frequency data (e.g., monthly rather than annual observations) will also provide more-precise estimates, this assumption is not necessarily true. Although higher-frequency data improve the precision of sample variances, covariances, and correlations, they do *not* improve the precision of the sample mean.

When many variables are considered, a large number of observations may be a statistical necessity. For example, to calculate a sample covariance matrix, the number of observations must exceed the number of variables (assets). Otherwise, some asset combinations (i.e., portfolios) will spuriously appear to have zero volatility. This problem arises frequently in investment analysis, and a remedy is available. Covariance matrices are routinely estimated even for huge numbers of assets by assuming that returns are driven by a smaller set of common factors plus uncorrelated asset-specific components.

As the frequency of observations increases, the likelihood increases that data may be asynchronous (i.e., not simultaneous or concurrent in time) across variables. This means that data points for different variables may not reflect exactly the same period even though they are labeled as if they do. For example, daily data from different countries are typically asynchronous because of time zone differences. Asynchronicity can be a significant problem for daily, and perhaps even weekly data, because it distorts measured correlations and induces lead–lag relationships that might not exist if the data were measured synchronously. Lower-frequency data (e.g., monthly or quarterly) are less susceptible to asynchrony, although it can still arise. For example, two series that are released and labeled as monthly could reflect data collected at different times of the month.

As a final note on historical data, some care should be taken with respect to whether data are normally distributed. Historical asset returns, in particular, routinely exhibit skewness and "fat tails," which cause them to fail formal tests of normality. The cost in terms of analytical complexity of accounting for non-normality, however, can be quite high. As a practical matter, the added complexity is often not worth the cost.[5]

2.2.4. *Ex Post* Risk Can Be a Biased Measure of *Ex Ante Risk*

In interpreting historical prices and returns over a given sample period, the analyst needs to evaluate whether asset prices reflected the possibility of a very negative event that did not materialize during the period. This phenomenon is often referred to as the "peso problem." Looking backward, we are likely to underestimate *ex ante* risk and overestimate *ex ante* anticipated returns. The key point is that high *ex post* returns that reflect fears of adverse events that did not materialize provide a poor estimate of *ex ante* expected returns.

The 1970s Peso Devaluation

In the mid-1970s, the Mexican peso was pegged to the US dollar, but peso-denominated interest rates were persistently well above corresponding dollar rates because investors feared the Mexican government would devalue the peso. In 1976, the peso was indeed devalued by nearly 50%, but data from before that event would suggest that holding the peso was a high expected return, low risk strategy.

The opposite situation is also a problem, especially for risk measures that consider only the subset of worst-case outcomes (e.g., value at risk, or VaR). If our data series includes even one observation of a rare event, we may substantially overstate the likelihood of such events happening in the future. Within a finite sample, the observed frequency of this bad outcome will far exceed its true probability. As a simple example, there were 21 trading days in July 2018. On 26 July, the price of Facebook stock closed down 19%. Based on this sample, the (interpolated) daily 5% VaR on Facebook stock is 17.3%. That is, an investor in Facebook shares would expect to lose at least 17.3% once every 20 days.

2.2.5. Biases in Analysts' Methods

Analysts naturally search for relationships that will help in developing better capital market expectations. Among the preventable biases that the analyst may introduce are the following:

- **Data-mining bias** arises from repeatedly searching a dataset until a statistically significant pattern emerges. It is almost inevitable that some relationship will appear. Such patterns cannot be expected to have predictive value. Lack of an explicit economic rationale for a variable's usefulness is a warning sign of a data-mining problem: no story, no future.[6] Of course, the analyst must be wary of inventing the story after discovering the relationship and bear in mind that correlation does not imply causation.

---

[5]See Chapter 5 of Stewart, Piros, and Heisler (forthcoming 2019) for discussion of the effect of alternative probability distributions on asset allocation decisions.
[6]See McQueen and Thorley (1999).

- **Time-period bias** relates to results that are period specific. Research findings often turn out to be sensitive to the selection of specific starting and/or ending dates.

Small Cap Outperformance and Time-Period Bias

Evidence suggesting that small-cap stocks outperform large-cap stocks over time (the so-called small firm effect) is very sensitive to the choice of sample period. From 1926 through 1974, US small-cap stocks outperformed large caps by 0.43% per year, but if we skip the Great Depression and start in 1932, the differential becomes 3.49% per year. Similarly, small caps outperformed by 3.46% per year from 1975 through 2016 but by only 0.09% per year from 1984 through 2016. In the nine years from 1975 through 1983, small caps outperformed by 16.85% per year![7]

How might analysts avoid using an irrelevant variable in a forecasting model? The analyst should scrutinize the variable selection process for data-mining bias and be able to provide an economic rationale for the variable's usefulness in a forecasting model. A further practical check is to examine the forecasting relationship out of sample (i.e., on data that was not used to estimate the relationship).

2.2.6. The Failure to Account for Conditioning Information

The discussion of regimes introduced the notion that assets' risk and return characteristics vary with the economic and market environment. That fact explains why economic analysis is important in expectation setting. The analyst should not ignore relevant information or analysis in formulating expectations. Unconditional forecasts, which dilute this information by averaging over environments, can lead to misperception of prospective risk and return. Exhibit 2 illustrates how an analyst may use conditioning information.

EXHIBIT 2   Incorporating Conditioning Information

Noah Sota uses the CAPM to set capital market expectations. He estimates that one asset class has a beta of 0.8 in economic expansions and 1.2 in recessions. The expected return on the market is 12% in an expansion and 4% in a recession. The risk-free rate is assumed to be constant at 2%. Expansion and recession are equally likely. Sota aims to calculate the unconditional expected return for the asset class.

The conditional expected returns on the asset are 10% = 2% + 0.8 × (12% − 2%) in an expansion and 4.4% = 2% + 1.2 × (4% − 2%) in a recession. Weighting by the probabilities of expansion and recession, the unconditional expected return is 7.2% = [(0.5 × 10%) + (0.5 × 4.4%)].

---

[7]Source: Ibbotson Associates database (Morningstar). Returns calculated by the author.

EXAMPLE 2   Ignoring Conditioning Information

Following on from the scenario in Exhibit 2, one of Noah Sota's colleagues suggests an alternative approach to calculate the unconditional expected return for the asset class. His method is to calculate the unconditional beta to be used in the CAPM formula, $1.0 = (0.5 \times 0.8) + (0.5 \times 1.2)$. He then works out the unconditional expected return on the market portfolio, $8\% = (0.5 \times 12\%) + (0.5 \times 4\%)$. Finally, using the unconditional beta and the unconditional market return, he calculates the unconditional expected return on the asset class as $8.0\% = 2.0\% + 1.0 \times (8\% - 2\%)$.

Explain why the alternative approach is right or wrong.

Guideline answer:
The approach suggested by Sota's colleague is wrong. It ignores the fact that the market excess return and the asset's beta vary with the business cycle. The expected return of 8% calculated this way would overestimate the (unconditional) expected return on this asset class. Such a return forecast would ignore the fact that the beta differs for expansion (0.8) and recession (1.2).

2.2.7. Misinterpretation of Correlations

When a variable A is found to be significantly correlated with another variable B, there are at least four possible explanations: (1) A predicts B, (2) B predicts A, (3) a third variable C predicts both A and B, or (4) the relationship is spurious. The observed correlation alone does not allow us to distinguish among these situations. Consequently, correlation relationships should not be used in a predictive model without investigating the underlying linkages.

Although apparently significant correlations can be spurious, it is also true that lack of a strong correlation can be misleading. A negligible measured correlation may reflect a strong but *nonlinear* relationship. Analysts should explore this possibility if they have a solid reason for believing a relationship exists.

2.2.8. Psychological Biases

The behavioral finance literature documents a long and growing list of psychological biases that can affect investment decisions. Only a few of the more prominent ones that could undermine the analyst's ability to make accurate and unbiased forecasts are outlined here. Furthermore, note that the literature contains various names and definitions of behavioral biases, which are not necessarily mutually exclusive.

- **Anchoring bias** is the tendency to give disproportionate weight to the first information received or first number envisioned, which is then adjusted. Such adjustment is often insufficient, and approximations are consequently biased. Analysts can try to avoid anchoring bias by consciously attempting to avoid premature conclusions.
- **Status quo bias** reflects the tendency for forecasts to perpetuate recent observations—that is, to avoid making changes and preserve the status quo, and/or to accept a default option. This bias may reflect greater pain from errors of commission (making a change) than from

errors of omission (doing nothing). Status quo bias can be mitigated by disciplined effort to avoid "anchoring" on the status quo.

- **Confirmation bias** is the tendency to seek and overweight evidence or information that confirms one's existing or preferred beliefs and to discount evidence that contradicts those beliefs. This bias can be mitigated by examining all evidence with equal rigor and/or debating with a knowledgeable person capable of arguing against one's own views.
- **Overconfidence bias** is unwarranted confidence in one's own intuitive reasoning, judgment, knowledge, and/or ability. This bias may lead an analyst to overestimate the accuracy of her forecasts and/or fail to consider a sufficiently broad range of possible outcomes or scenarios. Analysts may not only fail to fully account for uncertainty about which they are aware (sometimes described as "known unknowns") but they also are very likely to ignore the possibility of uncertainties about which they are not even aware (sometimes described as "unknown unknowns").
- **Prudence bias** reflects the tendency to temper forecasts so that they do not appear extreme or the tendency to be overly cautious in forecasting. In decision-making contexts, one may be too cautious when making decisions that could damage one's career or reputation. This bias can be mitigated by conscious effort to identify plausible scenarios that would give rise to more extreme outcomes and to give greater weight to such scenarios in the forecast.
- **Availability bias** is the tendency to be overly influenced by events that have left a strong impression and/or for which it is easy to recall an example. Recent events may likewise be overemphasized. The effect of this bias can be mitigated by attempting to base conclusions on objective evidence and analytical procedures.

EXAMPLE 3   Biases in Forecasting and Decision-Making

Cynthia Casey is a London-based investment adviser with a clientele of ultra-high-net-worth individuals in the UK, the US, and the EU. Within the equity portion of her portfolios, she rarely deviates significantly from the country weightings of the MSCI World Index, even though more often than not she tilts the allocation in the right direction. Hence, she can claim a good tactical track record despite having added little value in terms of return through tactical allocation. Because most investors have an implicit "home bias," her European clients tend to view their portfolios as significantly overweight the US (nearly 50% of the World index) and are happy because the US market outperformed the MSCI World ex-US Index by about 4% per year over the 10 years ending September 2018. Conversely, her US clients are unhappy because Casey persistently projected US outperformance but maintained what they instinctively perceive as a significant underweight in the United States. Citing year-to-date performance as of 28 September 2018—US up 9%, World ex-US down 1%, with 10 of 15 European markets down in local currencies—Casey's US clients are pressuring her to aggressively increase allocations to US equities. Although experience has taught her to be wary of chasing a strong market, Casey vividly remembers losing clients in the late 1990s because she doubted that the explosive rally in technology stocks would be sustained. With that in mind, she has looked for and found a rationale for a bullish view on US stocks—very robust year-to-date earnings growth.

What psychological biases are Casey and her clients exhibiting?

Guideline answer:
Casey's clients are implicitly anchoring their expectations on the performance of their respective domestic markets. In pressing Casey to increase the allocation to US stocks based on recent outperformance, her US clients are clearly projecting continuation of the trend, a status quo bias. Casey herself is exhibiting several biases. Prudence bias is apparent in the fact that she has a good record of projecting the correct direction of relative performance among markets but has not translated that into reallocations large enough to add meaningful value. We cannot assess whether that bias affects the magnitude of her forecasts, the extent to which she responds to the opportunities, or both. Losing clients when she doubted the sustainability of the late 1990s technology rally made a very strong impression on Casey, so much so that she has apparently convinced herself to look for a reason to believe the recent relative performance trends will persist. This is indicative of availability bias. Searching for evidence to support a favored view (continued strength of the US market) is a clear sign of confirmation bias, whereas finding support for that view in the recent strength of earnings growth reflects status quo bias.

2.2.9. Model Uncertainty

The analyst usually encounters at least three kinds of uncertainty in conducting an analysis. **Model uncertainty** pertains to whether a selected model is structurally and/or conceptually correct. **Parameter uncertainty** arises because a quantitative model's parameters are invariably estimated with error. **Input uncertainty** concerns whether the inputs are correct. Any or all of these may give rise to erroneous forecasts and/or cause the unwary analyst to overestimate the accuracy and reliability of his forecasts.

The effects of parameter uncertainty can be mitigated through due attention to estimation errors. Input uncertainty arises primarily from the need to proxy for an unobservable variable such as "the market portfolio" in the CAPM. Whether or not this is a serious issue depends on the context. It is a problem if the analyst wants to test the validity of the underlying theory or identify "anomalies" relative to the model. It is less of an issue if the analyst is merely focused on useful empirical relationships rather than proof of concept/theory. Model uncertainty is potentially the most serious issue because the wrong model may lead an analyst to fundamentally flawed conclusions.

Our discussion of the limitations of historical data touched on a model that led many investors far astray in the late 1990s. Up to that point, the implicit model used by many, if not most, institutional investors for setting long-term equity expectations was, "The *ex ante* expected return is, was, and always will be a constant number μ, and the best estimate of that number is the mean over the longest sample available." As the market soared in the late 1990s, the historical estimate of μ rose steadily, leading investors to shift more heavily into equities, which fueled further price appreciation and more reallocation toward equities, and so on, until the technology bubble burst. Ironically, belief in the sanctity of historical estimates coincided with the diametrically opposed notion that the "new economy" made historical economic and market relationships obsolete. There seemed to be no limits to growth or to valuations, at least in some segments of the market. But, of course, there were. This description of the technology bubble illustrates the breakdown of a particular forecasting model. It is not a literal description of anyone's thought process. For various reasons, however—competitive pressures, status quo/availability/prudence biases—many investors acted *as if* they were following the model.

Another flawed model unraveled during the global financial crisis of 2007–2009. One component of that model was the notion that housing price declines are geographically isolated events: There was no risk of a nationwide housing slump. A second component involved "originate to sell" loan pipelines: businesses that made loans with the intention of immediately selling them to investors and therefore had very little incentive to vet loan quality. A third component was the notion that the macro risk of an ever-growing supply of increasingly poor-quality mortgages could be diversified away by progressive layers of securitization. End investors were implicitly sold the notion that the securities were low risk because numerous computer simulations showed that the "micro" risk of individual loans was well diversified. The macro risk of a housing crisis, however, was not reflected in prices and yields—until, of course, the model proved to be flawed. The scenario highlighted here provides another illustration of a particular model breaking down. In this case, it was a flawed model of risk and diversification, and its breakdown was one of many aspects of the financial crisis.

3. ECONOMIC AND MARKET ANALYSIS

The previous section outlined various pitfalls in forecasting. Each of these is important. Yet they pale in comparison to a fundamental mistake: losing sight of the fact that investment outcomes are inherently linked to the economy. The technology bubble and the global financial crisis offer two extreme illustrations of the consequences of falling into this trap. Less dramatic, but still consequential, instances of this mistake regularly contribute to the differential investment performance that separates "winners" and "losers." The remainder of this chapter is dedicated to effective incorporation of economic and market analysis into capital market expectations.

3.1. The Role of Economic Analysis

History has shown that there is a direct yet variable relationship among actual realized asset returns, expectations for future asset returns, and economic activity. Analysts need to be familiar with the historical relationships that empirical research has uncovered concerning the direction, strength, and lead–lag relationships between economic variables and capital market returns.

The analyst who understands which economic variables may be most relevant to the current economic environment has a competitive advantage, as does the analyst who can discern or forecast changes in acceleration and deceleration of a trend.

Economic output has both cyclical and trend growth components. Trend growth is of obvious relevance for setting long-term return expectations for asset classes such as equities. Cyclical variation affects variables such as corporate profits and interest rates, which are directly related to asset class returns and risk. In the following sections, we address trend growth, business cycles, the role of monetary and fiscal policies, and international interactions.

3.2. Analysis of Economic Growth

The economic growth trend is the long-term average growth path of GDP around which the economy experiences semi-regular business cycles. The analyst needs to understand and analyze both the trend and the cycles. Though each could exist without the other, they are related.

It might seem that trends are inherently easier to forecast than cycles. After all, trends are about long-term averages, whereas cycles are about shorter-term movements and turning points. The assumption that trends are easier to forecast would be true if trend growth rates were constant. But trend growth rates do change, which is what makes forecasting them relevant for investment analysis. Some changes are fairly easy to forecast because they are driven by slowly evolving and easily observable factors such as demographics. Trend changes that arise from significant "exogenous shocks" to underlying economic and/or market relationships are not only impossible to foresee but also difficult to identify, assess, and quantify until the change is well-established and retrospectively revealed in the data. Virtually by definition, the effect of truly exogenous shocks on the level and/or growth rate of the economy will not have been built into asset prices in advance—although the risk of such events will likely have been reflected in prices to some degree.

3.2.1. Exogenous Shocks to Growth

Shocks arise from various sources. Some are purely domestic. Others are transmitted from other parts of the globe. Some are negative for potential growth, while others enhance it. Significant shocks typically arise from the following:

- **Policy changes.** Elements of pro-growth government policies include sound fiscal policy, minimal intrusion on the private sector, encouraging competition within the private sector, support for infrastructure and human capital development, and sound tax policies. Any significant, unexpected change in these policies that is likely to persist will change the expected trend rate of growth. The overhaul of US business taxes at the end of 2017, although not entirely unexpected, was intended to be a pro-growth change in policy. On the other hand, standard economic arguments indicate that erecting trade barriers will diminish trend growth.
- **New products and technologies.** Creation and assimilation of new products, markets, and technologies enhances potential growth. Consider the printing press, steam engine, telegraph and telephone, railroad, automobile, airplane, transistor, random-access memory (RAM), integrated circuits, internet, wireless communication (radio, TV, smartphone), rockets, and satellites, to name just a few.
- **Geopolitics.** Geopolitical conflict has the potential to reduce growth by diverting resources to less economically productive uses (e.g., accumulating and maintaining weapons, discouraging beneficial trade). The fall of the Berlin wall, which triggered German reunification and a "peace dividend" for governments as they cut defense spending, was a growth-enhancing geopolitical shock. Interestingly, geopolitical tensions (e.g., the space race) can also spur innovation that results in growth-enhancing technologies.
- **Natural disasters.** Natural disasters destroy productive capacity. In the short run, a disaster is likely to reduce growth, but it may actually enhance long-run growth if old capacity is replaced with more efficient facilities.
- **Natural resources/critical inputs.** Discovery of new natural resources or of new ways to recover them (e.g., fracking) can be expected to enhance potential growth, directly via

production of those resources and indirectly by reducing the cost of production for other products. Conversely, sustained reduction in the supply of important resources diminishes growth (e.g., the OPEC oil shock in 1973).

- **Financial crises.** The financial system allows the economy to channel resources to their most efficient use. Financial crises arise when market participants lose confidence in others' ability (or willingness) to meet their obligations and cease to provide funding—first to specific counterparties and then more broadly as potential losses cascade through the system. As discussed in Exhibit 3, a financial crisis may affect both the level of output and the trend growth rate.

EXHIBIT 3   Trend Growth after a Financial Crisis

An extensive study of growth and debt dynamics in the wake of the 2007–2009 global financial crisis identified three types of crises:

- Type 1: A persistent (permanent, one-time) decline in the level of output, but the subsequent trend rate of growth is unchanged.
- Type 2: No persistent decline in the level of output, but the subsequent trend rate of growth is reduced.
- Type 3: Both a persistent decline in the level of output and a reduction in the subsequent trend rate of growth.

The Eurozone experienced a sharp, apparently permanent drop in output after the global financial crisis, and subsequent growth was markedly lower than before the crisis, suggesting a Type 3 crisis.

The Eurozone's stagnant growth may be traced to structural problems in conjunction with policy missteps. Structural issues included rigid labor markets, a relatively rapid aging of the population, legal and regulatory barriers, cultural differences among countries, use of a common currency in dissimilar economies, and lack of a unified fiscal policy. In terms of policy response, the European Central Bank was slow to cut rates, was slow to expand its balance sheet, and failed to sustain that expansion. Insolvent banks were allowed to remain operational, thwarting deleveraging of the financial system. In part as the result of a lack of fiscal integration that would have facilitated cross-country transfers, several countries were forced to adopt drastic budget cuts that magnified the impact on their particular economies, the differential impact across countries, and the consequences of structural impediments.

Note: See Luigi Buttiglione, Philip R. Lane, Lucrezia Reichlin, and Vincent Reinhart, "Deleveraging? What Deleveraging?," September 2014, International Center for Monetary and Banking Studies.

It should be clear that any of the shocks listed would likely constitute a "regime change" as discussed earlier.

EXAMPLE 4   Impact of Exogenous Shocks on Trend Growth

Philippe Leblanc, an analyst focusing on economic forecasting, recently read about a discovery by scientists at a major university that may allow the efficiency of solar panels to double every two to three years, a result similar to Moore's Law with respect to computer chips. In further reading, he found new research at Tsinghua University that may rapidly increase the distance over which electricity can be transmitted.

What implications should Leblanc draw with regard to growth trends if either, or both, of these developments come to fruition? What government policy changes might offset the impact?

Guideline answer:

Either of these developments would be expected to increase trend growth. They would be especially powerful together. Rapid increases in solar panel efficiency would drive down the cost of energy over time, especially in areas with long days and intense sunlight. The closer to the equator, the larger the potential effect. The developments would also make it increasingly possible to bring large-scale power production to remote areas, thereby expanding the range and scale of economically viable businesses in those areas. Extending the range of electrical transmission would allow moving lower-cost energy (regardless of how it is generated) to where it is most efficiently used. A variety of government actions could undermine the pro-growth nature of these developments; for example, tariffs on solar panels, restrictions on electrical transmission lines, subsidies to support less efficient energy sources, failure to protect intellectual property rights, or prohibition on transfer of technology.

3.2.2. Application of Growth Analysis to Capital Market Expectations

The expected trend rate of economic growth is a key consideration in a variety of contexts. First, it is an important input to discounted cash flow models of expected return. The trend growth rate imposes discipline on forecasts of fundamental metrics such as earnings because these must be kept consistent with aggregate long-run growth at the trend rate. Second, a country with a higher trend rate of growth may offer equity investors a particularly good return if that growth has not already been priced into the market. Third, a higher trend rate of growth in the economy allows actual growth to be faster before accelerating inflation becomes a significant concern. This fact is especially important in projecting the likely path of monetary policy and bond yields. Fourth, theory implies, and empirical evidence confirms, that the average level of real government bond yields is linked to the trend growth rate. Faster trend growth implies higher average real yields.

Most countries have had periods of faster and slower trend growth during their development. Emerging countries often experience rapid growth as they catch up with the leading industrial countries, but the more developed they become, the more likely it is that their growth will slow.

3.2.2.1. A Decomposition of GDP Growth and Its Use in Forecasting

The simplest way to analyze an economy's aggregate trend growth is to split it into the following components:

- growth from labor inputs, consisting of
  - growth in potential labor force size and
  - growth in actual labor force participation, plus

- growth from labor productivity, consisting of
  - growth from increasing capital inputs and
  - growth in total factor productivity.

Labor input encompasses both the number of workers and the average number of hours they work. Growth in the potential labor force size is driven by demographics such as the population's age distribution, net migration, and workplace norms such as the length of the work week. All of these factors tend to change slowly, making growth in the potential labor force relatively predictable. Trends in net migration and workplace norms, however, may change abruptly in response to sudden structural changes, such as changes in government policies.

Labor force participation primarily reflects labor versus leisure decisions by workers. All else the same, we should expect labor force participation to decline (or at least grow more slowly) as a country becomes more affluent. On the other hand, rising real wages tend to attract workers back into the labor force. Social norms and government policies also play a large role.

Growth in labor productivity comes from investment in additional capital per worker ("capital deepening") and from increases in **total factor productivity** (TFP), which is often taken to be synonymous with technological improvement.[8] Government policy (e.g., regulations) can also influence TFP. In historical analyses, TFP is often measured as a "residual"—that is, output growth that is not accounted for by the other factors.

The trend rate of growth in mature, developed markets is generally fairly stable. As a result, extrapolating past trends in the components outlined in the foregoing can be expected to provide a reasonable initial estimate of the future growth trend. This forecast should then be adjusted to reflect observable information indicating how future patterns are likely to differ from past patterns. This same approach can be applied to less developed markets. It must be recognized, however, that these economies are likely to be undergoing rapid structural changes that may require the analyst to make more significant adjustments relative to past trends.

3.2.2.2. Anchoring Asset Returns to Trend Growth

Both theory and empirical evidence indicate that the average level of real (nominal) default-free bond yields is linked to the trend rate of real (nominal) growth.[9] To put it another way, bond yields will be pulled toward this level over time. Thus, the trend rate of growth provides an important anchor for estimating bond returns over horizons long enough for this reversion

---

[8]Total factor productivity captures a variety of effects, such as the impact of adding not just *more* physical capital (i.e., "capital deepening") but *better* capital, as well as the impact of increasingly skilled labor (i.e., increases in "human capital"). Earlier chapters provide a more granular breakdown of the drivers/ components of growth.

[9]With regard to nominal yields and growth, it is assumed that inflation is sufficiently well behaved.

to prevail over cyclical and short-term forces. Intertemporal consistency demands that this anchor be factored into forecasts even for shorter horizons.

The trend growth rate also provides an anchor for long-run equity appreciation.[10] We can express the aggregate market value of equity, V^e, as the product of three factors: the level of nominal GDP, the share of profits in the economy, S^k (earnings/GDP), and the P/E ratio (*PE*).

$$V_t^e = GDP_t \times S_t^k \times PE_t$$

It is clear that over long periods, capital's share of income cannot continually increase or decrease. The same is true for the P/E multiple applied to earnings. As a result, in the long run, the growth rate of the total value of equity in an economy is linked to the growth rate of GDP. Over finite horizons, the way in which the share of capital and the P/E multiple are expected to change will also affect the forecast of the total value of equity, as well as its corresponding growth rate over that period.

This argument applies to the capital appreciation component of equity returns. It does not supply a way to estimate the other component: the dividend yield. An estimate for the dividend yield (annual dividends/market value) can be obtained by noting that the dividend yield equals the dividend payout ratio (dividends/profit) divided by the profit multiple (market value/profit). The analyst may set any two of these three ratios and infer the third.

EXAMPLE 5   Long-Run Equity Returns and Economic Growth

In January 2000, Alena Bjornsdottir, CFA, was updating her firm's projections for US equity returns. The firm had always used the historical average return with little adjustment. Bjornsdottir was aware that historical averages are subject to large sampling errors and was especially concerned about this fact because of the sequence of very high returns in the late 1990s. She decided to examine whether US equity returns since World War II had been consistent with economic growth. For the period 1946–1999, the continuously compounded (i.e., logarithmic) return was 12.18% per annum, which reflected the following components:

Real GDP Growth	Inflation	EPS/GDP (Chg)	P/E (Chg)	Dividend Yield
3.14%	4.12%	0.00%	0.95%	3.97%

Questions:
1. What conclusion was Bjornsdottir likely have drawn from this analysis?
2. If she believed that in the long run that the US labor input would grow by 0.9% per annum and labor productivity by 1.5%, that inflation would be 2.1%, that the dividend yield would be 2.25%, and that there would be no further growth in P/E, what is likely to have been her baseline projection for continuously compounded long-term US equity returns?
3. In light of her analysis, how might she have adjusted her baseline projection?

---

[10]See Stewart, Piros, and Heisler (forthcoming 2019) for more thorough development of these arguments.

Guideline answers:

1. Bjornsdottir is likely have concluded that the post-war stock return exceeded what would have been consistent with growth of the economy. In particular, the rising P/E added 0.95% of "extra" return per year for 54 years, adding 51.3% ($= 54 \times 0.95\%$) to the cumulative, continuously compounded return and leaving the market 67% ($\exp[51.3\%] = 1.67$) above "fair value."

2. Her baseline projection is likely to have been $6.75\% = 0.9\% + 1.5\% + 2.1\% + 2.25\%$.

3. She is likely to have adjusted her projection downward to some degree to reflect the likelihood that the effect of the P/E would decline toward zero over time. Assuming, for example, that this would occur over 30 years would imply reducing the baseline projection by $1.71\% = (51.3\%/30)$ per year.

Note: The P/E impact was actually eliminated by the end of 2005. Had Bjornsdottir anticipated such a rapid correction, she would have needed to reduce her projection by $10.26\% = 51.3\%/5$ per year to $-3.51\% = 6.75\% - 10.26\%$.

Studies have shown that countries with higher economic growth rates do not reliably generate higher equity market returns.[11] A partial explanation is likely to be that the higher growth rate was already reflected in market prices. The sources of growth may be a second factor. Stock market returns ultimately reflect the rate of return on invested capital. If the capital stock is growing rapidly, the rate of return on invested capital may be driven down. Both of these explanations are consistent with the arguments outlined earlier. High growth need not translate one-for-one into higher return unless it can be expected to continue forever. Declining return on investment essentially means that either GDP growth slows or profits decline as a share of GDP, or both. And, of course, valuation multiples do matter.

3.3. Approaches to Economic Forecasting

Whereas the trend growth rate is a long-term average and reflects only the supply side of the economy, most macroeconomic forecasting focuses on short- to intermediate-term fluctuations around the trend—that is, the business cycle. These fluctuations are usually ascribed primarily to shifts in aggregate demand, although shifts in the short-term aggregate supply curve also play a role.

Before discussing the business cycle, we outline the main approaches available for tracking and projecting these movements. There are at least three distinct approaches:

- Econometric models: the most formal and mathematical.
- Indicators: variables that lead, lag, or coincide with turns in the economy.
- Checklists: subjective integration of the answers to relevant questions.

These approaches are not mutually exclusive. Indeed, thorough analysis is likely to incorporate elements of all three.

---

[11]Joachim Klement, "What's Growth Got to Do With It? Equity Returns and Economic Growth," *Journal of Investing* (Summer 2015) is one such study covering 44 countries.

3.3.1. Econometric Modeling

Econometrics is the application of statistical methods to model relationships among economic variables. **Structural models** specify functional relationships among variables based on economic theory. The functional form and parameters of these models are derived from the underlying theory. **Reduced-form models** have a looser connection to theory. As the name suggests, some such models are simply more-compact representations of underlying structural models. At the other end of the spectrum are models that are essentially data driven, with only a heuristic rationale for selection of variables and/or functional forms.

Econometric models vary from small models with a handful of equations to large, complex models with hundreds of equations. They are all used in essentially the same way, however. The estimated system of equations is used to forecast the future values of economic variables, with the forecaster supplying values for the exogenous variables. For example, such a model may require the forecaster to enter exchange rates, interest rates, commodity prices, and/or policy variables. The model then uses the estimated past relationships to forecast the future. It is important to consider that the forecaster's future values for the exogenous variables are themselves subject to estimation error. This fact will increase the variability of potential forecast errors of the endogenous variables beyond what results from errors in the estimated parameter values. The analyst should examine a realistic range of values for the exogenous variables to assess the forecast's sensitivity to these inputs.

Econometric models are widely regarded as very useful for simulating the effects of changes in key variables. The great merit of the econometric approach is that it constrains the forecaster to a certain degree of consistency and also challenges the modeler to reassess prior views based on what the model concludes. It does have important limitations, however. Econometric models require the user to find adequate measures for the real-world activities and relationships to be modeled. These measures may be unavailable. Variables may also be measured with error. Relationships among the variables may change over time because of changes in economic structure and/or because the model may have been based on faulty assumptions as to how the world works. As a result, the econometric model may be mis-specified. In practice, therefore, skillful econometric modelers monitor the model's recent forecasts for signs of systematic errors. Persistent forecast errors should ideally lead to a complete overhaul of the model. In practice, however, a more pragmatic approach is often adopted: Past forecast errors are incorporated into the model as an additional explanatory variable.

3.3.2. Economic Indicators

Economic indicators are economic statistics published by official agencies and/or private organizations. These indicators contain information on an economy's recent past activity or its current or future position in the business cycle. Lagging economic indicators and coincident indicators reflect recent past and current economic activity, respectively. A **leading economic indicator** (LEI) moves ahead of the business cycle by a fairly consistent time interval. Most analysts focus primarily on leading indicators because they purport to provide information about upcoming changes in economic activity, inflation, interest rates, and security prices.

Leading indicator–based analysis is the simplest forecasting approach to use because it requires following only a limited number of statistics. It also has the advantage of not requiring the analyst to make assumptions about the path of exogenous variables. Analysts use both individual LEIs and composite LEIs, reflecting a collection of economic data releases combined to give an overall reading. The OECD composite LEI for each country or region is based on five to nine variables such as share prices, manufacturing metrics, inflation, interest rates, and monetary data that exhibit cyclical fluctuations similar to GDP, with peaks and troughs occurring six to nine months earlier with reasonable consistency. Individual LEIs can also be combined into a so-called **diffusion index**, which measures how many indicators are pointing up and how many down. For example, if 7 out of 10 are pointing upward, then the odds are that the economy is accelerating.

One of the drawbacks of the (composite) leading indicator methodology is that the entire history may be revised each month. As a result, the most recently published historical indicator series will almost certainly appear to have fit past business cycles (i.e., GDP) better than it actually did in real time. This distortion is known as "look ahead" bias. Correspondingly, the LEI may be less reliable in predicting the current/next cycle than history suggests.

Business cycle indicators have been published for decades. A new methodology for tracking the business cycle, known generically as "nowcasting," emerged in the United States in the wake of the global financial crisis. The best-known of these forecasts, the Federal Reserve Bank of Atlanta's "GDPNow," was first published on 1 May 2014 for the second quarter of that year. The objective is to forecast GDP for the current quarter (which will not be released until after quarter-end) based on data as it is released throughout the quarter. To do this, the Atlanta Fed attempts to use the same methodology and data as will be used by the Bureau of Economic Analysis (BEA) to estimate GDP, replacing data that has not yet been released with forecasts based on the data already observed. As the quarter progresses, more of the actual data will have been observed, and GDPNow should, at least on average, converge to what will be released by the BEA.

BEA releases of estimates

The BEA releases a sequence of three GDP estimates for each quarter. The first, labeled the "advance" estimate, is released four weeks after the end of the quarter and tends to have the greatest market impact. The "preliminary" estimate is released a month later, and the "final" estimate comes at the end of the following quarter. The Atlanta Fed's GDPNow is actually a forecast of the BEA's advance estimate, not of the final GDP release.

It remains to be seen how useful nowcasting will be for investment analysts. It has a couple of clear advantages: It is updated in real time, and it is focused directly on a variable of primary interest (GDP and its components). Nowcasting is not designed to be predictive of anything beyond the end of the current quarter, however. In addition, it tends to be very volatile until a significant portion of the data for the quarter has been observed, at which point it may have lost some of its usefulness as a guide for investment decisions.

3.3.3. Checklist Approach

Formally or informally, many forecasters consider a whole range of economic data to assess the economy's future position. Checklist assessments are straightforward but time-consuming because they require continually monitoring the widest possible range of data. The data may then be extrapolated into forecasts via objective statistical methods, such as time-series analysis, or via more subjective or judgmental means. An analyst may then assess whether the measures are in an equilibrium state or nearer to an extreme reading.

The subjectivity of the checklist approach is perhaps its main weakness. The checklist's strength is its flexibility. It allows the forecaster to quickly take into account changes in economic structure by changing the variables or the weights assigned to variables within the analysis.

3.3.4. Economic Forecasting Approaches: Summary of Strengths and Weaknesses

Exhibit 4 summarizes the advantages and disadvantages of forecasting using econometric models, leading indicators, and checklists.

EXHIBIT 4   Economic Forecasting Approaches: Strengths and Weaknesses

Strengths	Weaknesses
Econometric Models Approach	
• Models can be quite robust, with many factors included to approximate reality.	• Complex and time-consuming to formulate.
• New data may be collected and consistently used within models to quickly generate output.	• Data inputs not easy to forecast.
• Delivers quantitative estimates of impact of changes in exogenous variables.	• Relationships not static. Model may be mis-specified.
• Imposes discipline/consistency on analysis.	• May give false sense of precision.
	• Rarely forecasts turning points well.
Leading Indicator–Based Approach	
• Usually intuitive and simple in construction.	• History subject to frequent revision.
• Focuses primarily on identifying turning points.	• "Current" data not reliable as input for historical analysis.
• May be available from third parties. Easy to track.	• Overfitted in-sample. Likely overstates forecast accuracy.
	• Can provide false signals.
	• May provide little more than binary (no/yes) directional guidance.
Checklist Approach	
• Limited complexity.	• Subjective. Arbitrary. Judgmental.
• Flexible.	• Time-consuming.
• Structural changes easily incorporated.	• Manual process limits depth of analysis. No clear mechanism for combining disparate information.
• Items easily added/dropped.	
• Can draw on any information, from any source, as desired.	• Imposes no consistency of analysis across items or at different points in time. May allow use of biased and/or inconsistent views, theories, assumptions.
• Breadth: Can include virtually any topics, perspectives, theories, and assumptions.	

EXAMPLE 6   Approaches to Forecasting

Sara Izek and Adam Berke are members of the asset allocation committee at Cycle Point Advisors, which emphasizes the business cycle within its tactical asset allocation process. Berke has developed a time series model of the business cycle that uses a published LEI series as a key input. He presents forecasts based on the model at each asset allocation meeting. Izek is eclectic in her approach, preferring to sample research from a wide variety of sources each month and then focus on whatever perspectives and results seem most interesting. She usually brings a stack of charts she has copied to the asset allocation meeting.

Questions:
1. Which of the main forecasting approaches (or combination of approaches) best describe(s) each analyst's own practice?
2. What strength(s) are likely to have appealed to each analyst?
3. What weaknesses might each analyst be overlooking?

Guideline answers:
1. Berke uses the econometric modeling approach in conjunction with the LEI approach. Izek's practice is essentially a checklist approach.
2. Berke is probably attracted to the quantitative output provided by a model, the consistency and discipline it imposes on the process, and the ability to generate explicit forecasts. He may have included the LEI in the model because it is designed to capture cyclical turning points or simply because doing so improves the model's statistical fit of the model.
   Izek is probably drawn to the flexibility of the checklist approach with respect to what is included/excluded and how to evaluate the information.
3. Berke may be overlooking potential mis-specification of his model, which is apt to make his forecasts systematically inaccurate (i.e., biased). He may also be failing to recognize the likely magnitude of the forecast errors that will be present even if the model is unbiased (i.e., overestimating the precision of the forecasts). By using the historical LEI series as an input to the model, he may be incorporating look-ahead bias into the model.
   Izek is likely overlooking the subjective, judgmental, and idiosyncratic nature of her approach. Her practice of basing her "checklist" on what seems most interesting in other analysts' current research makes her process especially vulnerable to inconsistency and cognitive biases.

3.4. Business Cycle Analysis

The trend rate of economic growth provides a vital anchor for setting very long-run investment expectations, which in turn provide a starting point for developing projections over short- to intermediate-term horizons. Virtually by definition, deviations from trend wash out in the long run, making information about the current economic and market environment of limited value over very long horizons. Over short to intermediate horizons, however, such information can be very important. From a macroeconomic perspective, the most useful such information typically pertains to fluctuations associated with the **business cycle**.

It is useful to think of fluctuations in economic activity as a superposition of many cycles varying in frequency from very short (days) to very long (decades), each with stochastic amplitude. The business cycle is not a specific, well-defined cycle. It is the result of many intermediate frequency cycles that jointly generate most of the variation in aggregate economic activity (i.e., GDP) around the trend. This fact explains why historical business cycles have varied in both duration and intensity—each was a different realization of a range of underlying stochastic cycles. It also helps to explain why it is difficult to project turning points in real time.

Business cycle peaks and troughs

The best-known record of business cycle peaks and troughs is published for the United States by the National Bureau of Economic research (NBER). According to NBER, the United States has experienced 66 complete business cycles since 1854, averaging 56 months from peak to peak. The longest cycle was 128 months, the shortest only 17 months. Fifty percent of the cycles lasted between 38 and 69 months. On average, the cycle's contraction phase (peak to trough) lasted 17 months, whereas the expansion phase (trough to peak) lasted 39 months.

At a fundamental level, the business cycle arises in response to the interaction of uncertainty, expectational errors, and rigidities that prevent instantaneous adjustment to unexpected events. It reflects decisions that

a. are made based on imperfect information and/or analysis with the expectation of future benefits,
b. require significant current resources and/or time to implement, and
c. are difficult and/or costly to reverse.

Such decisions are, broadly defined, investment decisions. Much of the uncertainty that sustains the cycle is endogenous to the system. Competitors, suppliers, employers, creditors, customers, and policymakers do not behave as expected. Prices and quantities adjust more or less than expected. Other sources of uncertainty are more exogenous. Technological breakthroughs threaten to disrupt whole industries and/or create new ones. Fracking, gene sequencing, e-commerce, "big data," digital advertising, cybersecurity, 3-D printing, the internet of things, and driverless cars are among those now playing out. Weather patterns affect agriculture, construction, and transportation. Natural disasters devastate local economies. Political and geopolitical shifts favor some entities and disadvantage others. And, of course, shocks in one part of the global economy are often transmitted to other parts of the world through trade relations, financial markets, and the prices of goods and services.

Numerous variables can be used to monitor the business cycle. Among them are GDP growth, industrial production (IP), employment/unemployment, purchasing managers indexes, orders for durable goods, the output gap (the difference between GDP estimated as if the economy were on its trend growth path and the actual value of GDP), and the leading indicator indexes discussed earlier.

3.4.1. Phases of the Business Cycle

There are various ways to delineate phases of the business cycle. The most obvious is to divide it into two primary segments (the expansion and the contraction) with two key turning points at which growth changes sign (the peak and the trough). These two periods are fairly easy to identify, at least in retrospect. Subdividing the cycle more finely is more ambiguous, even in retrospect, because it requires identifying more nuanced changes such as acceleration or deceleration of growth without a change in direction. Nonetheless, it is useful to divide the cycle into several phases distinguished through both economic and financial market characteristics. For the purpose of setting expectations for capital markets, we use five phases of the business cycle here: initial recovery, early expansion, late expansion, slowdown, and contraction. The first four occur within the overall expansion.

1. **Initial recovery.** This period is usually a short phase of a few months beginning at the trough of the cycle in which the economy picks up, business confidence rises, stimulative policies are still in place, the output gap is large, and inflation is typically decelerating. Recovery is often supported by an upturn in spending on housing and consumer durables.
   Capital market effects: Short-term rates and government bond yields are low. Bond yields may continue to decline in anticipation of further disinflation but are likely to be bottoming. Stock markets may rise briskly as fears of a longer recession (or even a depression) dissipate. Cyclical assets—and riskier assets, such as small stocks, higher-yield corporate bonds, and emerging market equities and bonds—attract investors and typically perform well.

2. **Early expansion.** The economy is gaining some momentum, unemployment starts to fall but the output gap remains negative, consumers borrow and spend, and businesses step up production and investment. Profits typically rise rapidly. Demand for housing and consumer durables is strong.
   Capital market effects: Short rates are moving up as the central bank starts to withdraw stimulus put in place during the recession. Longer-maturity bond yields are likely to be stable or rising slightly. The yield curve is flattening. Stocks trend upward.

3. **Late expansion.** The output gap has closed, and the economy is increasingly in danger of overheating. A boom mentality prevails. Unemployment is low, profits are strong, both wages and inflation are rising, and capacity pressures boost investment spending. Debt coverage ratios may deteriorate as balance sheets expand and interest rates rise. The central bank may aim for a "soft landing" while fiscal balances improve.
   Capital market effects: Interest rates are typically rising as monetary policy becomes restrictive. Bond yields are usually rising, more slowly than short rates, so the yield curve continues to flatten. Private sector borrowing puts pressure on credit markets. Stock markets often rise but may be volatile as nervous investors endeavor to detect signs of looming deceleration. Cyclical assets may underperform while inflation hedges such as commodities outperform.

4. **Slowdown.** The economy is slowing and approaching the eventual peak, usually in response to rising interest rates, fewer viable investment projects, and accumulated debt. It is especially vulnerable to a shock at this juncture. Business confidence wavers. Inflation often continues to rise as firms raise prices in an attempt to stay ahead of rising costs imposed by other firms doing the same.

   Capital market effects: Short-term interest rates are high, perhaps still rising, but likely to peak. Government bond yields top out at the first clear sign of a slowing economy and may then decline sharply. The yield curve may invert, especially if the central bank continues to exert upward pressure on short rates. Credit spreads, especially for weaker credits generally widen. The stock market may fall, with interest-sensitive stocks such as utilities and "quality" stocks with stable earnings performing best.

5. **Contraction.** Recessions typically last 12 to 18 months. Investment spending, broadly defined, typically leads the contraction. Firms cut production sharply. Once the recession is confirmed, the central bank eases monetary policy. Profits drop sharply. Tightening credit magnifies downward pressure on the economy. Recessions are often punctuated by major bankruptcies, incidents of uncovered fraud, exposure of aggressive accounting practices, or a financial crisis. Unemployment can rise quickly, impairing household financial positions.

   Capital market effects: Short-term interest rates drop during this phase, as do bond yields. The yield curve steepens substantially. The stock market declines in the earlier stages of the contraction but usually starts to rise in the later stages, well before the recovery emerges. Credit spreads typically widen and remain elevated until signs of a trough emerge and it becomes apparent that firms will be able to roll over near-term debt maturities.

3.4.2. Market Expectations and the Business Cycle

This description of a typical business cycle may suggest that forming capital market expectations for short and intermediate horizons should be relatively straightforward. If an investor can identify the current phase of the cycle and correctly predict when the next phase will begin, is it not easy to make money? Unfortunately, it is not that simple.

First, the phases of the business cycle vary in length and amplitude. Recessions can be steep, and downturns (such as in the 1930s and in 2007–2009) can be frightening. On the other hand, recessions also can be short lived, with only a small decline in output and only a modest rise in unemployment. Sometimes, the weakest phase of the cycle does not even involve a recession but merely a period of slower economic growth or a "growth recession." Similarly, expansions vary in length and intensity.

Second, it is not always easy to distinguish between cyclical forces and secular forces acting on the economy and the markets. The prolonged recovery following the 2007–2009 global financial crisis is a prime example. Interest rates and inflation went far lower and remained extraordinarily low far longer than virtually anyone would have predicted based on a purely cyclical view.

Third, although the connection between the real economy and capital market returns is strong, it is subject to substantial uncertainty. Capital market prices reflect a composite of investors' expectations and attitudes toward risk with respect to all future horizons. How, when, and by how much the markets respond to the business cycle are as uncertain as the cycle itself—perhaps more so.

What does all of this variation and uncertainty imply for setting capital market projections? First, as with virtually any investment information, business cycle analysis generates a noisy signal with respect to prospective opportunities. Second, the signal is likely to be most reliable (a higher "signal-to-noise" ratio), and hence most valuable, over horizons within the range of likely expansion and contraction phases—perhaps one to three years. Returns over substantially shorter horizons are likely to be driven primarily by market reactions to more transitory developments, undermining the cycle's predictive value. On the other hand, as the forecast horizon extends beyond this range, it becomes increasingly likely that one or more turning points will occur within the horizon, implying returns that increasingly reflect averaging over the cycle.

EXAMPLE 7   Cycles, Horizons, and Expectations

Lee Kim uses a statistical model that divides the business cycle into two "regimes": expansion and contraction. The expected (continuously compounded) return on equities is +2% per month during expansions and −2% per month during contractions. Consistent with NBER's historical record (see earlier sidebar), the probabilities of transitioning between regimes imply that expansions last 39 months on average, whereas contractions average 20 months. Correspondingly, over the long run, the economy expands roughly two-thirds of the time and contracts one-third of the time. Hence, the long-term expected equity return is 0.67% = [(2% × 2/3) + (−2% × 1/3)] per month, or 8% per year. Kim's model indicates that the economy recently transitioned into contraction. For the upcoming asset allocation committee meeting, he will prepare equity return forecasts for horizons of 3 months, 1 year, 5 years, and 10 years.

Explain how you would expect the choice of time horizon to affect Kim's projections.

Guideline answer:

The longer the horizon, the more likely that one or more transitions will occur between contraction and expansion; more generally, the more likely it is that the horizon spans more than one business cycle phase or even more than one full cycle. As a result, the longer the horizon, the more Kim's forecast should reflect averaging over periods of expansion and contraction and the closer it will be to the "information-less" average of 8% per year.

Over the next three months, it is highly likely that the economy will remain in contraction, so Kim's forecast for that period should be very close to −2% per month [cumulatively −6%]. Because contractions last 20 months on average in the model, Kim's forecast for a one-year horizon should reflect only a modestly higher probability of having transitioned to expansion at some point within the period. So, his forecast might be −18% (an average of −1.5% per month) instead of −24% (−2% per month). Over a five-year horizon, it is very likely that the economy will have spent time in both contraction and expansion. As a result, Kim's forecast will put significant weight on each phase. Because the economy starts in contraction (i.e., the starting point is not random), the weight on that phase will probably be somewhat higher than its long-term frequency of 1/3, say 0.40. This assumption implies a forecast of 4.8% per year [= 12 × [(0.6 × 2%) + (0.4 × −2%)]]. Over a 10-year horizon, the frequency of expansion and contraction months is likely to be very close to the 2-to-1 long-run ratio. So, Kim's forecast should be very close to 8% per year.

3.4.3. Inflation and Deflation: Trends and Relation to the Business Cycle

Until the early 20th century, the money supply was largely dictated by the supply of specie—gold and/or silver used in coins and to back bank deposits. Periods of both inflation and deflation were common. Today, currencies are backed by the credibility of governments and central banks rather than specie, and people expect the prices of goods and services to trend upward. Persistent deflation is rare. Expectation of an upward trend in prices reflects recognition of an asymmetry in a central bank's so-called "reaction function." It is generally accepted that a central bank's policy tools are more effective in slowing economic activity than in accelerating sluggish activity. Hence, central banks may tend to be more aggressive in combating downward pressure on demand than in reining in strong demand. In addition, it is widely believed that outright deflation damages the economy because it undermines:

- debt-financed investments. Servicing and repayment of nominally fixed debt becomes more onerous as nominal income flows and the nominal value of real assets both decline; and
- the power of central banks. In a deflationary environment, interest rates fall to levels close to (or even below) zero. When interest rates are already very low, the central bank has less leeway to stimulate the economy by lowering interest rates.

In contrast, moderate inflation is generally considered to impose only modest costs on the economy. Both the differential effectiveness of policy and the differential costs of inflation versus deflation suggest that central banks will, implicitly or explicitly, target positive inflation, and investors set their expectations accordingly. The result is that asset prices in general and bond yields in particular generally build in compensation for a positive average inflation rate.

Inflation is procyclical, accelerating in the later stages of the business cycle when the output gap has closed and decelerating when, during a recession or the early years afterward, there is a large output gap, which puts downward pressure on wages and prices. If the central bank's target is credible, the average rate of inflation over the cycle should be near the target.

Because the cyclical pattern of inflation is well known, inflation expectations will also be procyclical. It is important, however, to differentiate inflation expectations by horizon. Very long-term inflation expectations should be virtually unaffected by cyclical fluctuations provided investors maintain confidence in the central bank's target. Short horizon expectations will tend to have about the same amplitude as actual inflation. Inflation, and therefore inflation expectations, over intermediate horizons will be a blend of the different phases of the current and subsequent cycles. Hence, the amplitude of expectations will decline with horizon—again, provided investors do not lose confidence in the central bank's target.

The pattern just described implies a "horizon structure" of inflation expectations that is countercyclical—upward sloping at the trough of the business cycle and inverted at the peak. Because inflation expectations are an important component of bond yields, this countercyclical pattern is one of the reasons that the yield curve's slope is countercyclical.[12]

---

[12] As will be discussed later, compensation for taking duration risk (the "term premium") is procyclical. As a result, an inverted "horizon structure" of expected inflation does not necessarily imply an inverted yield curve.

To assess the effect of inflation on asset classes, we must consider both the cash flows and the discount rates. We consider "cash," nominal bonds, stocks, and real estate.

- *Cash:* In this context, cash is taken to mean short-term interest-bearing instruments, not currency or zero-interest deposits. As long as short-term interest rates adjust with expected inflation, cash is essentially a zero-duration, inflation-protected asset that earns a floating real rate. Inflation above or below expectation contributes to temporary fluctuations in the realized real return. Because central banks aim to stabilize actual and expected inflation, they tend to make the real rate on cash procyclical around a long-term level consistent with their target inflation rate. Hence, cash is relatively attractive (unattractive) in a rising (declining) rate environment. Deflation may make cash particularly attractive if a zero-lower-bound is binding on the nominal interest rate. Otherwise deflation is simply a component of the required short-term real rate.
- *Bonds:* Because the cash flows are fixed in nominal terms, the effect of inflation is transmitted solely through the discount rates (i.e., the yield curve). Rising (falling) inflation induces capital losses (gains) as the expected inflation component of yields rises (falls). If inflation remains within the expected cyclical range, shorter-term yields rise/fall more than longer yields but have less price impact as a result of shorter duration. If, however, inflation moves out of the expected range, longer-term yields may rise/fall more sharply as investors reassess the likelihood of a change in the long-run average level of inflation. Persistent deflation benefits the highest-quality bonds because it increases the purchasing power of the cash flows, but it is likely to impair the creditworthiness of lower-quality debt.
- *Stocks:* As long as inflation stays within the expected cyclical range, there should be little effect on stocks because both expected future cash flows (earnings and dividends) and associated discount rates rise/fall in line with the horizon structure of inflation expectations. Signs that inflation is moving out of the expected range, however, indicate a potential threat. Unexpectedly high and/or rapidly rising inflation could mean that the central bank needs to act to slow the economy, whereas very low and/or falling inflation (possibly deflation) threatens a recession and a decline in asset prices. Within the stock market, higher inflation benefits firms that are able to pass along rising costs, whereas deflation is especially detrimental for asset-intensive, commodity-producing, and/or highly leveraged firms.
- *Real estate:* Short- to intermediate-term nominal cash flows are generally dictated by existing leases, with the speed of adjustment depending on the type of real estate asset held. As long as inflation remains within the expected range, renewal of leases will likely generate rental income rising with expected inflation, accompanied by stable asset values. Higher-than-expected inflation is likely to coincide with high demand for real estate, expectations that rental income will rise even faster than general inflation, and rising property values. The impact may be quite idiosyncratic, however, depending on the length of leases, the existing supply of similar properties, and the likelihood of new supply hitting the market when leases come up for renewal. On the other hand, unexpectedly low inflation (or deflation) will put downward pressure on expected rental income and property values, especially for less-than-prime properties, which may have to cut rents sharply to avoid rising vacancies.

EXAMPLE 8   Inflation

Kesia Jabari believes the quantitative easing undertaken by major central banks in the wake of the global financial crisis is finally about to induce a surge in inflation. She believes that without extraordinary policy actions from the central banks, the inflation rate will ultimately rise to the upper end of central banks' tolerance ranges at the peak of the current business cycle.

Assuming Jabari is correct, discuss the likely implications for floating-rate instruments ("cash"), bonds, stocks, and real estate if:

a. the market shares Jabari's view, or
b. once inflation begins to rise, the market doubts that the central banks will be able to contain it.

Guideline answer:

a. If the market agrees with Jabari, then the relationship of inflation and the asset classes to the business cycle should be fairly normal. Short-term rates and bond yields will rise with inflation expectations. The yield curve should flatten because long-term inflation expectations should remain well anchored. Floating-rate instruments (cash) will be relatively attractive, and intermediate maturities ("the belly of the curve") will be the most vulnerable. In general, the rise in inflation should not have much independent impact on stocks or real estate because both cash flows and discount rates will be expected to rise. Firms with pricing power and real estate with relatively short lease-renewal cycles are set to perform best.

b. If the market doubts that central banks can contain inflation within previously perceived tolerances, then long-run inflation expectations will rise and the yield curve may steepen rather than flatten, at least initially. Floating-rate instruments will still be relatively attractive, but now it is the longest maturities that will be the most vulnerable. Stocks are likely to suffer because the market expects central banks to be aggressive in fighting inflation. Real estate with long-term leases and little long-term, fixed-rate debt will suffer. Real estate with substantial long-term, fixed-rate debt should do relatively well, especially high-quality properties with little new supply nearby, which are likely to avoid significant vacancies even in a recession.

In the interest of completeness, we should note a caveat before leaving the topic of inflation. The preceding discussion implicitly assumes that the short-run aggregate supply curve is upward sloping and that the business cycle is primarily driven by fluctuations in aggregate demand. Together, these assumptions imply that inflation is pro-cyclical. Although globalization may have reduced the sensitivity of domestic prices to domestic output, it seems unlikely that domestic output/growth no longer matters. Thus, the aggregate supply curve may be *flatter* but is unlikely to be *flat*. With regard to what drives the cycle, if aggregate supply shocks predominate, then inflation will tend to be *counter*cyclical, reflecting alternating periods of "stagflation" and disinflationary boom. The 1970s oil crisis is a prime example. This pattern is more likely to be the exception rather than the rule, however.

3.5. Analysis of Monetary and Fiscal Policy

Actual and anticipated actions by monetary and fiscal authorities affect the decisions and actions of all other participants in the economy and the markets. As a result, it is somewhat difficult to isolate their role(s) from our broader discussion. Indeed, the foregoing sections have made numerous references to these policies. Nonetheless it is worthwhile to focus directly on these policies from the perspective of setting capital market expectations.

Monetary policy is often used as a mechanism for intervention in the business cycle. Indeed, this use is inherent in the mandates of most central banks to maintain price stability and/or growth consistent with the economy's potential. Each central bank interprets its mandate somewhat differently, sets its own operational objectives and guidelines, and selects its own mix of the tools (e.g., policy rates and liquidity provision) at its disposal. The common theme is that central banks virtually always aim to moderate the cyclical behavior of growth and inflation, in both directions. Thus, monetary policy aims to be countercyclical. The impact of monetary policy, however, is famously subject to "long and variable lags," as well as substantial uncertainty. As a result, a central bank's ability to fine-tune the economy is limited, and there is always risk that policy measures will exacerbate rather than moderate the business cycle. This risk is greatest at the top of the cycle, when the central bank may overestimate the economy's momentum and/or underestimate the effects of restrictive policies. In such situations, monetary policy may trigger a contraction that it cannot immediately counteract. In contrast, expansionary monetary policy rarely, if ever, suffices to turn a contraction into a strong recovery. This asymmetry is captured in a classic analogy: Expansionary policy is like "pushing" on a string, whereas restrictive policy is like "pulling" on a string.

Fiscal policy (government spending and taxation) can also be used to counteract cyclical fluctuations in the economy. Aside from extreme situations, however—such as the Great Depression of the 1930s and recovery from the 2007–2009 global financial crisis—fiscal policy typically addresses objectives other than regulating short-term growth, for at least two main reasons. First, in all but the most authoritarian regimes, the fiscal decision-making process is too lengthy to make timely adjustments to aggregate spending and taxation aimed at short-term objectives. Second, frequent changes of a meaningful magnitude would be disruptive to the ongoing process of providing and funding government services.

Notwithstanding these considerations, fiscal policy often does play a role in mitigating cyclical fluctuations. Progressive tax regimes imply that the effective tax rate on the private sector is pro-cyclical—rising as the economy expands and falling as the economy contracts. Similarly, means-based transfer payments vary inversely with the economy, helping to mitigate fluctuations in disposable income for the most vulnerable households. The effect of these so-called automatic stabilizers should not be overlooked in setting expectations for the economy and the markets.

From the perspective of an investment analyst focused on establishing expectations for broad asset classes, having a handle on monetary policy is mission-critical with respect to cyclical patterns. Under normal conditions, fiscal adjustments are important but likely to be secondary considerations. The reverse is likely with respect to assessing the long run. Of course, if a major change in fiscal stance is contemplated or has been implemented, the impact warrants significant attention with respect to all horizons. The major overhaul of the US tax code at the end of 2017 is a good example of these points. It almost certainly provided a short-term stimulus, especially with respect to capital expenditures. But it was not a short-term policy adjustment. It was the most significant change to the tax code in decades, a major structural change that may affect the path of both the economy and the markets for many years.

3.5.1. Monetary Policy

Central banks can, and do, carry out their mandates somewhat differently. In general, they seek to mitigate extremes in inflation and/or growth via countercyclical policy measures. As a generic illustration of how this might work, we briefly review the **Taylor rule**. In the current context, it can be viewed as a tool for assessing a central bank's stance and a guide to predicting how that stance is likely to evolve.

In essence, the Taylor rule links a central bank's target short-term nominal interest rate to the expected growth rate of the economy and inflation, relative to trend growth and the central bank's inflation target.

$$i^* = r_{neutral} + \pi_e + 0.5(\widehat{Y}_e - \widehat{Y}_{trend}) + 0.5(\pi_e - \pi_{target})$$

Where

i^* = target nominal policy rate

$r_{neutral}$ = real policy rate that would be targeted if growth is expected to be at trend and inflation on target

π_e, π_{target} = respectively, the expected and target inflation rates

$\widehat{Y}_e, \widehat{Y}_{trend}$ = respectively, the expected and trend real GDP growth rates

The rule can be re-expressed in terms of the real, inflation-adjusted target rate by moving the expected inflation rate to the left-hand side of the equation.

$$i^* - \pi_e = r_{neutral} + 0.5(\widehat{Y}_e - \widehat{Y}_{trend}) + 0.5(\pi_e - \pi_{target})$$

From this rearrangement, we see that the real, inflation-adjusted policy rate deviates from neutral by one-half the amount by which growth and inflation deviate from their respective targets. As an example, suppose the neutral real policy rate is 2.25%, the target inflation rate is 2%, and trend growth is estimated to be 2.5%. If growth is expected to be 3.5% and inflation is expected to be 3%, the Taylor rule would call for a 6.25% nominal policy rate:

$$2.25\% + 3\% + 0.5\ (3.5\% - 2.5\%) + 0.5\ (3.0\% - 2.0\%) = 6.25\%$$

With expected inflation at 3%, this calculation corresponds to a 3.25% real policy rate.

Even if a central bank were to set its policy rate according to the Taylor rule, there could still be substantial judgment left in the process. None of the inputs to the rule are objectively observable. To make the rule operational, policymakers and their staffs have to specify how the requisite expectations will be generated, and by whom. Whose estimate of trend growth is to be used? What is the appropriate neutral real policy rate? Over what horizon(s) do the expectations apply? Models could be developed to answer all these questions, but there would be judgments to be made in doing so. The upshot for the investment analyst is that monetary policy cannot be reduced to a simple equation. The Taylor rule, or some customized variant, provides a good framework for analyzing the thrust and likely evolution of monetary policy, but the analyst must pay careful attention to situational signals from the central bank. This is why, for example, the investment community literally scrutinizes every word in the Federal

Reserve's post-meeting statements and speeches by officials, looking for any hint of a change in the Fed's own interpretation of the environment.

EXAMPLE 9   Policies and the Business Cycle

Albert Grant, CFA, is an institutional portfolio strategist at Camford Advisors. After a period of trend growth, inflation at the central bank's target, and neutral monetary policy, the economy has been hit by a substantial deflationary shock.

Questions:
1. How are monetary and fiscal policies likely to respond to the shock?

Camford's economics department estimates that growth is now 1% below trend and inflation is 2% below the central bank's target. Camford's chief investment officer (CIO) has asked Grant to put together a projection of the likely path of policy rates for the next five years.

2. If Grant believes the central bank will respond in accordance with the Taylor rule, what other information will he need in order to project the path of policy rates?
3. What pattern should Grant expect for growth, inflation, and market interest rates if the central bank does *not* respond to the shock?
4. Assuming the central bank does respond and that its reaction function is well approximated by the Taylor rule, how will this alter Grant's expectations regarding the paths of growth, inflation, and short-term rates over the next five years?

Guideline answers:
1. A countercyclical response can be expected from both monetary and fiscal policy. Assuming the central bank uses a policy rate target as its primary tool, it will cut that rate. On the fiscal side, there may be no explicit expansionary policy action (tax cut or spending increase), but automatic stabilizers built into tax and transfer programs can be expected to cushion the shock's impact on private sector disposable incomes.
2. Grant will need to know what values the central bank uses for the neutral real rate, trend growth rate, and inflation target. He will also need to know how the central bank forms its expectations of growth and inflation. Finally, he will need to know how growth and inflation are likely to evolve, including how they will be affected by the path of policy rates.
3. The deflationary shock is very likely to induce a contractionary phase of the business cycle, putting additional downward pressure on growth and inflation. Short-term market interest rates will be dragged downward by weak demand and inflation. Risky asset prices are likely to fall sharply. A deep and/or protracted recession may be required before conditions conducive to recovery are in place. Grant should therefore expect a deep "U-shaped" path for growth, inflation, and short-term rates.

4. If the central bank responds as expected, it will push short-term rates down farther and faster than they would otherwise fall in an effort to mitigate the downward momentum of growth and inflation. If the central bank correctly calibrates its policy, growth and inflation should decline less, bottom out sooner, and recover more quickly toward trend growth and the target inflation level, respectively, than in the absence of a policy response. Whereas the central bank is virtually certain to drive short rates down farther and faster, it may be inclined to let the market dictate the pace at which rates eventually rise. That is, it may simply "accommodate" the need for higher rates rather than risk unduly restraining the recovery once it is established.

3.5.2. What Happens When Interest Rates Are Zero or Negative?

Prior to the 2007–2009 global financial crisis, it was generally accepted that central banks could not successfully implement negative interest rate policies. Belief in a "zero lower bound" on policy rates assumed that individuals would choose to hold currency (coins and notes) if faced with earning a negative interest rate on short-term instruments, including deposits. The move toward holding currency would drain deposits and reserves from the banking system, causing bank balance sheets to shrink. The resulting credit contraction would put upward pressure on interest rates, thwarting the central bank's attempt to maintain negative rates. The contraction of credit would likely also put additional downward pressure on economic growth, thereby reinforcing the need for stimulative policies.

This line of reasoning raised questions about the effectiveness of traditional monetary policy when the economy is so weak that economic growth fails to respond to (nominal) interest rates approaching zero. Following the global financial crisis, central banks faced with this situation pursued less conventional measures.

One important measure was quantitative easing (QE), in which central banks committed to large-scale, ongoing purchases of high-quality domestic fixed-income securities. These purchases were funded by creating an equally large quantity of bank reserves in the form of central bank deposits. As a result of QE, central bank balance sheets and bank reserves grew significantly and sovereign bond yields fell. QE was pursued by (among others) the US Federal Reserve, the European Central Bank, the Bank of Japan, and the Bank of England.

Conventional reasoning suggests that QE should have resulted in the desired growth in nominal spending. In theory, banks could use the increased reserves to extend loans, and low interest rates would stimulate businesses and households to borrow. The borrowing was expected to fund capital expenditure by businesses as well as current consumption and purchases of durables (e.g., houses and cars) by households, thereby stimulating the economy. With interest rates low, investors were expected to bid up the prices of stocks and real estate. Although asset prices did increase and businesses that could issue bonds borrowed heavily, proceeds were more often used to fund dividends and stock buybacks rather than capital expenditures. At the same time, household spending ability was significantly curtailed by the legacy of the global financial crisis.

Whether or not QE was effective remains subject to debate. To achieve desired levels of economic growth, central banks tried the previously unthinkable: targeting negative interest rates. The central banks of Denmark, Sweden, Japan, Switzerland, and the euro area were among those that adopted negative policy rates. Contrary to the notion of a "zero lower bound," negative policy rates proved to be sustainable.

The move into currency did not occur as expected because the scale and speed of transactions inherent in modern economies cannot be supported using physical cash as the primary method of exchange.[13] Trillions of dollars change hands daily to facilitate trade in goods, services, and financial instruments, and these transactions cannot be accomplished using physical cash. Bank deposits and bank reserves held at the central bank, rather than as vault cash, have an implicit yield or convenience value that cash does not. As long as this value exceeds the explicit cost of holding those deposits—in the form of a negative interest rate—there is no incentive to convert deposits into cash. In such circumstances, negative policy rates may be achievable and sustainable.

In theory, using negative nominal rates to stimulate an economy should work similarly to using low but still positive rates. Businesses and consumers are encouraged to hold fewer deposits for transaction purposes; investors are encouraged to seek higher expected returns on other assets; consumers are encouraged to save less and/or borrow more against future income; businesses are encouraged to invest in profitable projects; and banks are encouraged to use their reserves in support of larger loan books. All of this is expected to stimulate economic growth.

For consumers, investors, businesses, and banks to behave as described, however, each must believe they will be adequately rewarded for taking the inherent risks. In a negative interest rate environment, these entities are likely to have greater levels of uncertainty as to whether they will be adequately compensated for risks taken, and therefore they may not act as desired by monetary policy makers. As a result, the effectiveness of expansionary monetary policy is more tenuous at low and negative interest rate levels than at higher interest rate levels.

3.5.3. Implications of Negative Interest Rates for Capital Market Expectations

Long-run capital market expectations typically take the level of the "risk-free rate" as a baseline to which various risk premiums are added to arrive at long-run expected returns for risky assets such as long-term bonds and equities. The implicit assumption is that the risk-free rate is at its long-term equilibrium level. When short-term rates are negative, the long-run equilibrium short-term rate can be used as the baseline rate in these models instead of the observed negative rate. This rate can be estimated using the neutral policy rate ($r_{neutral}$) in the Taylor rule (or more generally in the central bank's presumed reaction function), adjusted for a modest spread between policy rates and default-free rates available to investors.

In forming capital market expectations for shorter time horizons, analysts and investors must consider the expected path of interest rates. Paths should be considered that, on average, converge to the long-run equilibrium rate estimate. With negative policy rates in place, this approach means a negative starting point. In theory, many possible scenarios, each appropriately weighted by its likelihood, should be considered. In practice, it may suffice to consider only a few scenarios. Because shorter horizons provide less opportunity for the

---

[13]It should also be noted that banks were reluctant to directly impose negative rates on their retail and commercial deposit customers. In general, rates on these accounts remained non-negative. Thus, the aggregate incentive to move into cash was mitigated somewhat. Various fees (e.g., for overdraft protection) and conditions imposed on the accounts (e.g., compensating balance requirements), however, may still have resulted in a net cost for deposit customers.

impact of events to average out, the shorter the forecast horizon, the more important it is to consider deviations from the most likely path.

Negative policy rates are expected to produce asset class returns similar to those occurring in the contraction and early recovery phrases of a "more normal" business/policy cycle. Although such historical periods may provide a reasonable starting point in formulating appropriate scenarios, it is important to note that negative rate periods may indicate severe distress in the economy and thus involve greater uncertainty regarding the timing and strength of recovery.

Key considerations when forming capital market expectations in a negative interest rate environment include the following:

- Historical data are less likely to be reliable.
  - Useful data may exist on only a few historical business cycles, which may not include instances of negative rates. In addition, fundamental structural/institutional changes in markets and the economy may have occurred since this data was generated.
  - Quantitative models, especially statistical models, tend to break down in situations that differ from those on which they were estimated/calibrated.
  - Forecasting must account for differences between the current environment and historical averages. Historical averages, which average out differences across phases of the cycle, will be even less reliable than usual.

- The effects of other monetary policy measures occurring simultaneously (e.g., quantitative easing) may distort market relationships such as the shape of the yield curve or the performance of specific sectors.

Incorporating uncertain dynamics, including negative interest rates, into capital market expectations over finite horizons is much more difficult than projecting long-term average levels. The challenge arises from the fact that asset prices depend not only on investor expectations regarding longer term "equilibrium" levels but also on the path taken to get there.

3.5.4. The Monetary and Fiscal Policy Mix

Fiscal policy is inherently political. Central banks ultimately derive their powers from governments, but most strive to be, or at least appear to be, independent of the political process in order to maintain credibility. As a result, to the extent that monetary and fiscal policy are coordinated, it is usually the case that the central bank takes the expected fiscal stance as given in formulating its own policy and disdains guidance from politicians regarding its policy.

The mix of monetary and fiscal policies has its most apparent impact on the level of interest rates and the shape of the yield curve. We first consider the effect of persistently loose or tight policies on the average level of rates. All else the same, loose fiscal policies (large deficits) increase the level of *real* interest rates because the domestic private sector must be induced to save more/investing less and/or additional capital must be attracted from abroad. Conversely, tight fiscal policies reduce real rates. Persistently loose monetary policy generally results in higher actual and expected inflation. Attempts by the central bank to hold down nominal rates will prove self-defeating, ultimately resulting in higher rather than lower nominal interest rates.[14] Conversely, persistently tight monetary policy ultimately reduces

---

[14]This was one of the crucial insights presented in Friedman (1968).

actual and expected inflation resulting in lower, rather than higher, nominal rates. Exhibit 5 summarizes the impact of persistent policy mixes on the level of real and nominal rates. In each case, the impact on real rates and on expected inflation is clear. Two cases involve a mix of loose and tight policy. In these cases, the combined impact could be higher or lower nominal rates. Nominal rates are labeled as "mid" level for these cases.

EXHIBIT 5   Effect of Persistent Policy Mix on the Average Level of Rates

		Fiscal Policy	
		Loose	**Tight**
Monetary Policy	**Loose**	High Real Rates	Low Real Rates
		+	+
		High Expected Inflation	High Expected Inflation
		=	=
		High Nominal Rates	Mid Nominal Rates
	Tight	High Real Rates	Low Real Rates
		+	+
		Low Expected Inflation	Low Expected Inflation
		=	=
		Mid Nominal Rates	Low Nominal Rates

The second impact of policy is on the slope of the yield curve. The slope of the term structure of (default-free) interest rates depends primarily on (1) the expected future path of short-term rates and (2) a risk premium required to compensate for the greater price volatility inherent in longer-maturity bonds. The maturity premium explains why the term structure is normally upward sloping. Changes in the curve's slope—flattening and steepening—are primarily driven by the evolution of short rate expectations, which are mainly driven by the business cycle and policies. This dynamic was described in an earlier discussion on business cycles. Exhibit 6 summarizes the main points regarding the evolution of rates, policy, and the yield curve.

EXHIBIT 6   Rates, Policy, and the Yield Curve over the Business Cycle

Cycle Phase	Monetary Policy & Automatic Stabilizers	Money Market Rates	Bond Yields and the Yield Curve
Initial Recovery	Stimulative stance. Transitioning to tightening mode.	Low/bottoming. Increases expected over progressively shorter horizons.	Long rates bottoming. Shortest yields begin to rise first. Curve is steep.
Early expansion	Withdrawing stimulus	Moving up. Pace may be expected to accelerate.	Yields rising. Possibly stable at longest maturities. Front section of yield curve steepening, back half likely flattening.
Late expansion	Becoming restrictive	Above average and rising. Expectations tempered by eventual peak/decline.	Rising. Pace slows. Curve flattening from longest maturities inward.

Cycle Phase	Monetary Policy & Automatic Stabilizers	Money Market Rates	Bond Yields and the Yield Curve
Slowdown	Tight. Tax revenues may surge as accumulated capital gains are realized.	Approaching/reaching peak.	Peak. May then decline sharply. Curve flat to inverted.
Contraction	Progressively more stimulative. Aiming to counteract downward momentum.	Declining.	Declining. Curve steepening. Likely steepest on cusp of Initial Recovery phase.

There is a third factor related to monetary and fiscal policy that may, or may not, be significant with respect to the shape of the yield curve and the effectiveness of policy: the relative supply of (government) bonds at various maturities. Does it matter what maturities the government issues in order to fund deficits? Does it matter what maturities the central bank chooses to buy/sell in its open market operations or its quantitative easing? There is no clear answer. The issue became important, however, in the wake of the global financial crisis for at least two reasons.

First, although it is now apparent that there is no clear lower bound on nominal interest rates, the effectiveness of conventional interest rate policies at very low rate levels remains in question. In particular, the central bank's ability to influence long-term rates may be even more tenuous than usual. Second, governments have run, and continue to run, large deficits while quantitative easing by major central banks has caused them to accumulate massive holdings of government debt (and other securities), which they may ultimately need or want to sell. If relative supply of debt along the yield curve really matters, then how governments fund their deficits in the future and how the central banks manage the maturity of their holdings could have significant implications for the yield curve and the broader financial markets.

It is difficult to draw firm conclusions with respect to maturity management. The existing evidence in conjunction with broader observation of markets, however, suggests the following: Sufficiently large purchases/sales at different maturities are likely to have a meaningful effect on the curve while they are occurring, but the effect is unlikely to be sustained for long once the buy/sell operation ends. To put it another way, a sufficiently large *flow* of supply may have a noticeable impact on relative yields, but discrete changes in the quantity of each maturity outstanding are much less likely to have a lasting impact. Government bonds are very liquid, and investors can and do move up and down the yield curve to exploit even very small yield differentials. Having said that, an important caveat pertaining to very long maturities is appropriate. Pension funds and other entities with very long-dated liabilities need correspondingly very long-maturity assets. Severely limiting the available supply of those assets would undoubtedly drive down their yield. Low yields at the very long end of the UK yield curve have been attributed to this effect at various times.

As a final comment on the interaction of monetary and fiscal policy, we acknowledge the potential for politicization of the central bank. If the level of government debt is high relative to the economy (GDP), and especially if it is also rising because of large fiscal deficits, there is a risk that the central bank may be coerced into inflating away the real value of the debt with very accommodative monetary policy. The risk that this dynamic *may* subsequently occur is almost certain to steepen the yield curve. If it *does* occur, such an event is likely to lead to an inflationary spiral, as higher inflation leads to higher nominal rates, which lead to faster accumulation of debt, which call forth even more accommodative monetary policy, and so on.

3.5.5. The Shape of the Yield Curve and the Business Cycle

The shape of the yield curve is frequently cited as a predictor of economic growth and as an indicator of where the economy is in the business cycle. Both casual observation and formal econometric analysis support its usefulness (an extensive bibliography is available at www.newyorkfed.org). The underlying rationale was summarized earlier in Exhibit 6. In simplest terms, the curve tends to be steep at the bottom of the cycle, flatten during the expansion until it is very flat or even inverted at the peak, and re-steepen during the subsequent contraction. Because expectations with respect to the path of short-term rates are the primary determinant of the curve's shape, the shape of the curve contains information about how market participants perceive the state and likely evolution of the economy as well as the impact they expect policymakers to have on that path. Thus, the empirical link between the shape of the yield curve and subsequent growth passes the test set out earlier for a good model—there is a solid rationale for believing it should be predictive. One must, of course, be aware that very few macroeconomic variables are truly exogenous and very few endogenous variables are completely unaffected by the past. "A" (shape of the yield curve) may predict "B" (growth next period), but it may also be the case that "B" predicts "A" in the period after that. The point is that the analyst should be aware of the fact that both the shape of the yield curve and economic growth (i.e., the business cycle) are endogenous within the economy. This is not to suggest throwing out a useful relationship but merely a reminder to interpret results with care.

EXAMPLE 10   The Business Cycle and the Yield Curve

Camford's quantitative analysis team helped Albert Grant incorporate the central bank's reaction function into a reduced-form model of growth and inflation. With this model, he will be able to project the path of short-term rates in the wake of the deflationary shock described in Example 9. Camford's CIO has now asked him to extend the analysis to project the path of bond yields as well.

Questions:
1. What will Grant need in order to project the path of bond yields?
2. Even before he can undertake the formal analysis, a large client asks Grant to explain the likely implications for the yield curve. What can he say?

Guideline answers:
1. Grant will need a model linking bond yields to the policy rate. In essence, he needs a model of the yield curve.
2. Following the deflationary shock, the economy is very likely to enter into the contraction phase of the business cycle. The central bank will be cutting the policy rate, perhaps sharply. Long-term yields could drop even faster initially as the market anticipates that policy, but then the curve will steepen as the central bank

> cuts rates because long-maturity yields will incorporate the expectation of short-term rates rising again once the economy gains sufficient traction. The curve will likely reach its steepest point near the trough of the policy cycle and then gradually flatten as the economy gains strength and the central bank begins to tighten policy.

3.6. International Interactions

In general, the dependence of any particular country on international interactions is a function of its relative size and its degree of specialization. Large countries with diverse economies, such as the so-called G–7 (the United States, United Kingdom, Germany, France, Italy, Japan, and Canada), tend to be less influenced by developments elsewhere than smaller economies, such as Chile, whose output depends significantly on a few commodities like copper. Nonetheless, increasing globalization of trade, capital flows, and direct investment in recent decades has increased the importance of international interactions for nearly all countries.

3.6.1. Macroeconomic Linkages

Macroeconomic linkages between countries are expressed through their respective current and capital accounts. The current account reflects net exports of goods and services, net investment income flows, and unilateral transfers. The capital account, which for the purposes of this discussion also includes what is known as the financial account, reflects net investment flows for Foreign Direct Investment (FDI)—purchase and sale of productive assets across borders—and Portfolio Investment (PI) flows involving transactions in financial assets. By construction, if a country has a surplus on current account, it must have a matching deficit on capital account, or vice versa. Anything that affects one account must induce an equal and opposite change in the other account.

A nation's current and capital accounts are linked to the broader economy by the fact that net exports, virtually always the most significant component of the current account, contributes directly to aggregate demand for the nation's output. National income accounting also implies the following important relationship among net exports $(X - M)$, saving (S), investment (I), and the government surplus $(T - G)$:

$$(X - M) = (S - I) + (T - G)$$

Net exports always equal net private saving (the excess of domestic private saving over investment spending) plus the government surplus. Anything that changes net exports must also change net private saving, the government surplus, or both. Conversely, changes in either of these will be transmitted to the rest of the world through the current account. Of course, because the current account and capital accounts are mirror images, we can reverse all the signs in the foregoing equation and make corresponding statements about the capital account. A surplus on capital account is how a nation funds an excess of investment and government spending over domestic saving plus taxes.

There are four primary mechanisms by which the current and capital accounts are kept in balance: changes in income (GDP), relative prices, interest rates and asset prices, and exchange rates. Strictly speaking, all of these tools can play a role in both the real economy (the current account and FDI) and the financial markets, and they are determined simultaneously. However, markets do not all move at the same pace. In particular, investment markets adjust much more quickly than the real economy. In the short run, interest rates, exchange rates, and financial asset prices must adjust to keep the capital account in balance with the more slowly evolving current account. Meanwhile, the current account, in conjunction with real output and the relative prices of goods and services, tends to reflect secular trends and the pace of the business cycle.

EXAMPLE 11   International Macroeconomic Linkages

A large, diversified economy recently instituted a substantial tax cut, primarily aimed at reducing business taxes. Some provisions of the new law were designed to stem the tide of domestic firms moving production facilities abroad and encourage an increase in corporate investment in the domestic economy. There was no reduction in government spending. Prior to the tax cut, the country had both a current account deficit and a government deficit.

Questions:
1. What impact is this tax cut likely to have on
    a. the country's current account balance?
    b. the country's capital account balance?
    c. growth in other countries?
    d. the current and capital accounts of other countries?

2. What adjustments is the tax cut likely to induce in the financial markets?

Guideline answers:
1. a. The deficit on current account will almost certainly increase. The government deficit will increase which, all else the same, will result in a one-for-one increase in the current account deficit. If the tax cut works as intended, domestic investment will increase, reducing net private saving and further increasing the current account deficit. Private saving will increase as a result of rising income (GDP), which will diminish the impact on the current account somewhat. Unless saving increases by the full amount of the tax cut plus the increase in investment spending, however, the net effect will be an increase in the current account deficit. In principle, this increase could be thwarted by movements in the financial markets that make it impossible to fund it, but this is unlikely.
    b. Because the current account deficit will increase, the country's capital account surplus must increase by the same amount. In effect, the tax cut will be funded primarily by borrowing from abroad and/or selling assets to non-domestic investors. Part of the adjustment is likely to come from a reduction in FDI by domestic firms (i.e., purchases of productive assets abroad) provided the new tax provisions work as intended.

    c. Growth in other countries is likely to increase as the tax cut stimulates demand for their exports and that increase in turn generates additional demand within their domestic economies.

    d. In the aggregate, other countries must already be running current account surpluses and capital account deficits matching the balances of the country that has cut taxes. Their aggregate current account surplus and capital account deficit will increase by the same amount as the increase in current account deficit and capital account surplus of the tax-cutting country.

2. The country must attract additional capital flows from abroad. This endeavor is likely to be facilitated, at least in part, by the expectation of rising after-tax profits resulting from the business taxes. Equity values should therefore rise. The adjustment may also require interest rates and bond yields to rise relative to the rest of the world. The impact on the exchange rate is less clear. Because the current account and the capital account represent exactly offsetting flows, there is no *a priori* change in demand for the currency. The net impact will be determined by what investors *expect* to happen. (See the following section for a discussion of exchange rate linkages.)

3.6.2. Interest Rate/Exchange Rate Linkages

One of the linkages of greatest concern to investors involves interest rates and exchange rates. The two are inextricably linked. This fact is perhaps most evident in the proposition that a country cannot simultaneously

- allow unrestricted capital flows;
- maintain a fixed exchange rate; and
- pursue an independent monetary policy.

    The essence of this proposition is that if the central bank attempts to push interest rates down (up), capital will flow out (in), putting downward (upward) pressure on the exchange rate, forcing the bank to buy (sell) its own currency, and thereby reversing the expansionary (contractionary) policy. Carrying this argument to its logical conclusion suggests that, with perfect capital mobility and a fixed exchange rate, "the" interest rate must be the same in countries whose currencies are pegged to each other.

    Can we extend this proposition to encompass the whole (default-free) yield curve? Yes, but in doing so, we have to be somewhat more precise. Under what conditions would two markets share a yield curve? First, there must be unrestricted capital mobility between the markets ensuring that risk-adjusted expected returns will be equalized. The second condition is more difficult: The exchange rate between the currencies must be credibly fixed *forever*.[15] That is, investors must believe there is no risk that the currencies will exchange at a different rate in the future. Otherwise, yield differentials will emerge, giving rise to differential risk and return expectations in the two markets and allowing each market to trade on its own fundamentals. Thus, it is the lack of credibly fixed exchange rates that allows (default-free) yield curves, and hence bond returns, to be less than perfectly correlated across markets.

---

[15]These conditions are necessary and sufficient for permanent convergence. See Chapter 10 of Stewart, Piros, and Heisler (forthcoming 2019) for a full exposition.

If a currency is linked to another without full credibility, then bond yields in the weaker currency are nearly always higher. This has been true even in the eurozone where, technically, separate currencies no longer exist—Greece, Italy, and Spain have always traded at meaningful, but varying, spreads over Germany and France. As long as there is no imminent risk of a devaluation, spreads at the very shortest maturities should be comparatively narrow. As demonstrated by the Greek exit ("Grexit") crisis, however, the situation changes sharply when the market perceives an imminent threat of devaluation (or a withdrawal from the common currency). Spreads then widen throughout the curve, but especially at the shortest maturities, and the curve will almost certainly invert. Why? Because in the event of a devaluation, yields in the devaluing currency will decline sharply (as the currency-risk premium collapses), generating much larger capital gains on longer-term bonds and thereby mitigating more of the currency loss.

When the exchange rate is allowed to float, the link between interest rates and exchange rates is primarily expectational. To equalize risk-adjusted expected returns across markets, interest rates must generally be higher (lower) in a currency that is expected to depreciate (appreciate). Ironically, this dynamic can lead to seemingly perverse situations in which the exchange rate "overshoots" in one direction to generate the expectation of movement in the opposite direction. The expectational linkage among exchange rates, interest rates, and asset prices is covered in detail at a later stage.

Capital mobility alone is clearly insufficient to eliminate differences in *nominal* interest rates and bond yields across countries. To a greater or lesser extent, each market responds to its own fundamentals, including policies. But what about *real* yields? We need to look at this question from two perspectives: the financial markets and the real economy.

An investor cares about the real return that she expects to earn *in her own currency*. In terms of a non-domestic asset, what matters is the *nominal* return and the change in the exchange rate. Even if non-domestic interest rates remain unchanged, the real return earned by the investor will not equal the non-domestic real interest rate unless purchasing power parity (PPP) holds over the investor's horizon. The empirical evidence overwhelmingly indicates that PPP does not hold over relevant investment horizons. Hence, we cannot rely on the simplistic notion that real interest rate differentials represent exploitable opportunities and should be eliminated by portfolio investment flows.

The preceding point is somewhat subtle and should not be construed to mean that real interest rate differentials are irrelevant for cross-market investment decisions. On the contrary, they can, but do not always, point to the likelihood of favorable *nominal* yield and exchange rate movements. The investor needs to assess non-domestic real rates from that perspective.

Ultimately, real interest rates must be consistent with the real saving and investment decisions that drive economic growth and the productivity of capital. As discussed earlier, saving and investment decisions are linked across countries through their current accounts. "Excess" saving in one country funds "excess" investment in another. In essence, there is a global market in which capital flows to where it is expected to be most productive. Although real rates around the world need not be equal, they are linked through the requirement that global savings must always equal global investment. Hence, they will tend to move together. As an example, the widespread low level of real interest rates that persisted in the aftermath of the global financial crisis was widely attributed to a very high level of global saving—primarily in Asia—and an unusually low level of capital investment in many developed markets, notably the United States.

4. SUMMARY

This is the first of two chapters on how investment professionals should address the setting of capital market expectations. The chapter began with a general framework for developing capital market expectations followed by a review of various challenges and pitfalls that analysts may encounter in the forecasting process. The remainder of the chapter focused on the use of macroeconomic analysis in setting expectations. The following are the main points covered in the chapter:

- Capital market expectations are essential inputs for strategic as well as tactical asset allocation.
- The ultimate objective is a set of projections with which to make informed investment decisions, specifically asset allocation decisions.
- Undue emphasis should not be placed on the accuracy of projections for individual asset classes. Internal consistency across asset classes (cross-sectional consistency) and over various time horizons (intertemporal consistency) are far more important objectives.
- The process of capital market expectations setting involves the following steps:
  1. Specify the set of expectations that are needed, including the time horizon(s) to which they apply.
  2. Research the historical record.
  3. Specify the method(s) and/or model(s) that will be used and their information requirements.
  4. Determine the best sources for information needs.
  5. Interpret the current investment environment using the selected data and methods, applying experience and judgment.
  6. Provide the set of expectations and document the conclusions.
  7. Monitor outcomes, compare to forecasts, and provide feedback.

- Among the challenges in setting capital market expectations are:
  - *limitations of economic data* including lack of timeliness as well as changing definitions and calculations;
  - *data measurement errors and biases* including transcription errors, survivorship bias, and appraisal (smoothed) data;
  - *limitations of historical estimates* including lack of precision, nonstationarity, asynchronous observations, and distributional considerations such as fat tails and skewness;
  - ex post *risk as a biased risk measure* such as when historical returns reflect expectations of a low-probability catastrophe that did not occur or capture a low-probability event that did happen to occur;
  - *bias in methods* including data-mining and time-period biases;
  - *failure to account for conditioning information*;
  - *misinterpretation of correlations*;
  - *psychological biases* including anchoring, status quo, confirmation, overconfidence, prudence, and availability biases.
  - *model uncertainty*.

- Losing sight of the connection between investment outcomes and the economy is a fundamental, and potentially costly, mistake in setting capital market expectations.

- Some growth trend changes are driven by slowly evolving and easily observable factors that are easy to forecast. Trend changes arising from exogenous shocks are impossible to forecast and difficult to identify, assess, and quantify until the change is well established.
- Among the most important sources of shocks are policy changes, new products and technologies, geopolitics, natural disasters, natural resources/critical inputs, and financial crises.
- An economy's aggregate trend growth rate reflects growth in labor inputs and growth in labor productivity. Extrapolating past trends in these components can provide a reasonable initial estimate of the future growth trend, which can be adjusted based on observable information. Less developed economies may require more significant adjustments because they are likely to be undergoing more rapid structural changes.
- The average level of real (nominal) default-free bond yields is linked to the trend rate of real (nominal) growth. The trend rate of growth provides an important anchor for estimating bond returns over horizons long enough for this reversion to prevail over cyclical and short-term forces.
- The trend growth rate provides an anchor for long-run equity appreciation. In the very long run, the aggregate value of equity must grow at a rate very close to the rate of GDP growth.
- There are three main approaches to economic forecasting:
  - *Econometric models*: structural and reduced-form statistical models of key variables generate quantitative estimates, impose discipline on forecasts, may be robust enough to approximate reality, and can readily forecast the impact of exogenous variables or shocks. However, they tend to be complex, time-consuming to formulate, and potentially mis-specified, and they rarely forecast turning points well.
  - *Indicators*: variables that lead, lag, or coincide with turns in the economy. This approach is the simplest, requiring only a limited number of published statistics. It can generate false signals, however, and is vulnerable to revisions that may overfit past data at the expense of the reliability of out-of-sample forecasts.
  - *Checklist(s)*: subjective integration of information deemed relevant by the analyst. This approach is the most flexible but also the most subjective. It readily adapts to a changing environment, but ongoing collection and assessment of information make it time-consuming and also limit the depth and consistency of the analysis.
- The business cycle is the result of many intermediate frequency cycles that jointly generate most of the variation in aggregate economic activity. This explains why historical business cycles have varied in both duration and intensity and why it is difficult to project turning points in real time.
- The business cycle reflects decisions that (a) are made based on imperfect information and/or analysis with the expectation of future benefits, (b) require significant current resources and/or time to implement, and (c) are difficult and/or costly to reverse. Such decisions are, broadly defined, investment decisions.
- A typical business cycle has a number of phases. We split the cycle into five phases with the following capital market implications:
  - **Initial Recovery.** Short-term interest rates and bond yields are low. Bond yields are likely to bottom. Stock markets may rise strongly. Cyclical/riskier assets such as small stocks, high-yield bonds, and emerging market securities perform well.
  - **Early Expansion.** Short rates are moving up. Longer-maturity bond yields are stable or rising slightly. Stocks are trending up.

- **Late Expansion.** Interest rates rise, and the yield curve flattens. Stock markets often rise but may be volatile. Cyclical assets may underperform while inflation hedges outperform.
- **Slowdown.** Short-term interest rates are at or nearing a peak. Government bond yields peak and may then decline sharply. The yield curve may invert. Credit spreads widen, especially for weaker credits. Stocks may fall. Interest-sensitive stocks and "quality" stocks with stable earnings perform best.
- **Contraction.** Interest rates and bond yields drop. The yield curve steepens. The stock market drops initially but usually starts to rise well before the recovery emerges. Credit spreads widen and remain elevated until clear signs of a cycle trough emerge.

- At least three factors complicate translation of business cycle information into capital market expectations and profitable investment decisions. First, the phases of the cycle vary in length and amplitude. Second, it is not always easy to distinguish between cyclical forces and secular forces acting on the economy and the markets. Third, how, when, and by how much the markets respond to the business cycle is as uncertain as the cycle itself—perhaps more so.
- Business cycle information is likely to be most reliable/valuable in setting capital market expectations over horizons within the range of likely expansion and contraction phases. Transitory developments cloud shorter-term forecasts, whereas significantly longer horizons likely cover portions of multiple cycle phases. Information about the current cyclical state of the economy has no predictive value over very long horizons.
- Monetary policy is often used as a mechanism for intervention in the business cycle. This mechanism is inherent in the mandates of most central banks to maintain price stability and/or growth consistent with potential.
- Monetary policy aims to be countercyclical, but the ability to fine-tune the economy is limited and policy measures may exacerbate rather than moderate the business cycle. This risk is greatest at the top of the cycle when the central bank may overestimate the economy's momentum and/or underestimate the potency of restrictive policies.
- Fiscal policy—government spending and taxation—can be used to counteract cyclical fluctuations in the economy. Aside from extreme situations, however, fiscal policy typically addresses objectives other than regulating short-term growth. So-called automatic stabilizers do play an important role in mitigating cyclical fluctuations.
- The Taylor rule is a useful tool for assessing a central bank's stance and for predicting how that stance is likely to evolve.
- The expectation that central banks could not implement negative policy rates proved to be unfounded in the aftermath of the 2007–2009 global financial crisis. Because major central banks combined negative policy rates with other extraordinary measures (notably quantitative easing), however, the effectiveness of the negative rate policy is unclear. The effectiveness of quantitative easing is also unclear.
- Negative interest rates, and the environment that gives rise to them, make the task of setting capital market expectations even more complex. Among the issues that arise are the following:
  - It is difficult to justify negative rates as a "risk-free rate" to which risk premiums can be added to establish long-term "equilibrium" asset class returns.
  - Historical data and quantitative models are even less likely to be reliable.
  - Market relationships (e.g., the yield curve) are likely to be distorted by other concurrent policy measures.

- The mix of monetary and fiscal policies has its most apparent effect on the average level of interest rates and inflation. Persistently loose (tight) fiscal policy increases (reduces) the average level of real interest rates. Persistently loose (tight) monetary policy increases (reduces) the average levels of actual and expected inflation. The impact on nominal rates is ambiguous if one policy is persistently tight and the other persistently loose.
- Changes in the slope of the yield curve are driven primarily by the evolution of short rate expectations, which are driven mainly by the business cycle and policies. The slope of the curve may also be affected by debt management.
- The slope of the yield curve is useful as a predictor of economic growth and as an indicator of where the economy is in the business cycle.
- Macroeconomic linkages between countries are expressed through their respective current and capital accounts.
- There are four primary mechanisms by which the current and capital accounts are kept in balance: changes in income (GDP), relative prices, interest rates and asset prices, and exchange rates.
- In the short run, interest rates, exchange rates, and financial asset prices must adjust to keep the capital account in balance with the more slowly evolving current account. The current account, in conjunction with real output and the relative prices of goods and services, tends to reflect secular trends and the pace of the business cycle.
- Interest rates and currency exchange rates are inextricably linked. This relationship is evident in the fact that a country cannot simultaneously allow unfettered capital flows, maintain a fixed exchange rate, and pursue an independent monetary policy.
- Two countries will share a default-free yield curve if (and only if) there is perfect capital mobility and the exchange rate is credibility fixed *forever*. It is the lack of credibly fixed exchange rates that allows (default-free) yield curves, and hence bond returns, to be less than perfectly correlated across markets.
- With floating exchange rates, the link between interest rates and exchange rates is primarily expectational. To equalize risk-adjusted expected returns across markets, interest rates must be higher (lower) in a currency that is expected to depreciate (appreciate). This dynamic can lead to the exchange rate "overshooting" in one direction to generate the expectation of movement in the opposite direction.
- An investor cares about the real return that he or she expects to earn *in his or her own currency*. In terms of a foreign asset, what matters is the *nominal* return and the change in the exchange rate.
- Although real interest rates around the world need not be equal, they are linked through the requirement that global savings must always equal global investment. Hence, they will tend to move together.

REFERENCES

Brinson, Gary, Randolph Hood, and Gilbert Beebower. 1986. "Determinants of Portfolio Performance." *Financial Analysts Journal* 42 (4): 39–44.

Buttiglione, Luigi, Philip R. Lane, Lucrezia Reichlin, and Vincent Reinhart. 2014. *Deleveraging? What Deleveraging?* International Center for Monetary and Banking Studies.

Friedman, Milton. 1968. "The Role of Monetary Policy." *American Economic Review* 58 (1): 1–17.

Ibbotson, Roger, and Paul Kaplan. 2000. "Does Asset Allocation Policy Explain 40, 90, or 100 Percent of Performance?" *Financial Analysts Journal* 56 (1): 26–33.

Klement, Joachim. 2015. "What's Growth Got to Do With It? Equity Returns and Economic Growth." *Journal of Investing* 24 (2): 74–78.

Marcelo, Jose Luis Miralles, Luis Miralles Quiros Jose, and Jose Luis Martins. 2013. "The Role of Country and Industry Factors During Volatile Times." *Journal of International Financial Markets, Institutions and Money* 26: 273–90.

McQueen, Grant, and Steven Thorley. 1999. "Mining Fools Gold." *Financial Analysts Journal* 55 (2): 61–72.

Rapaport, Alfred, and Michael Mauboussin. 2001. *Expectations Investing: Reading Stock Prices for Better Returns*. Boston: Harvard Business School Press.

Stewart, Scott D., Christopher D. Piros, and Jeffrey C Heisler. 2019. Forthcoming. *Portfolio Management: Theory and Practice*. Hoboken, NJ: John Wiley & Sons.

PRACTICE PROBLEMS

The following information relates to Questions 1–8

Neshie Wakuluk is an investment strategist who develops capital market expectations for an investment firm that invests across asset classes and global markets. Wakuluk started her career when the global markets were experiencing significant volatility and poor returns; as a result, she is now careful to base her conclusions on objective evidence and analytical procedures to mitigate any potential biases.

Wakuluk's approach to economic forecasting utilizes a structural model in conjunction with a diffusion index to determine the current phase of a country's business cycle. This approach has produced successful predictions in the past, thus Wakuluk has high confidence in the predictions. Wakuluk also determines whether any adjustments need to be made to her initial estimates of the respective aggregate economic growth trends based on historical rates of growth for Countries X and Y (both developed markets) and Country Z (a developing market). Exhibit 1 summarizes Wakuluk's predictions:

EXHIBIT 1   Prediction for Current Phase of the Business Cycle

Country X	Country Y	Country Z
Initial Recovery	Contraction	Late Upswing

Wakuluk assumes short-term interest rates adjust with expected inflation and are procyclical. Wakuluk reviews the historical short-term interest rate trends for each country, which further confirms her predictions shown in Exhibit 1.

Wakuluk decides to focus on Country Y to determine the path of nominal interest rates, the potential economic response of Country Y's economy to this path, and the timing for when Country Y's economy may move into the next business cycle. Wakuluk makes the following observations:

Observation 1:   Monetary policy has been persistently loose for Country Y, while fiscal policies have been persistently tight.

Observation 2:   Country Y is expected to significantly increase transfer payments and introduce a more progressive tax regime.

Observation 3:   The current yield curve for Country Y suggests that the business cycle is in the slowdown phase, with bond yields starting to reflect contractionary conditions.

1. Wakuluk *most likely* seeks to mitigate which of the following biases in developing capital market forecasts?
   A. Availability
   B. Time period
   C. Survivorship

2. Wakuluk's approach to economic forecasting:
   A. is flexible and limited in complexity.
   B. can give a false sense of precision and provide false signals.
   C. imposes no consistency of analysis across items or at different points in time.

3. Wakuluk is *most likely* to make significant adjustments to her estimate of the future growth trend for which of the following countries?
   A. Country Y only
   B. Country Z only
   C. Countries Y and Z

4. Based on Exhibit 1 and Wakuluk's assumptions about short-term rates and expected inflation, short-term rates in Country X are *most likely* to be:
   A. low and bottoming.
   B. approaching a peak.
   C. above average and rising.

5. Based on Exhibit 1, what capital market effect is Country Z *most likely* to experience in the short-term?
   A. Cyclical assets attract investors.
   B. Monetary policy becomes restrictive.
   C. The yield curve steepens substantially.

6. Based on Observation 1, fiscal and monetary policies in Country Y will *most likely* lead to:
   A. low nominal rates.
   B. high nominal rates.
   C. either high or low nominal rates.

7. Based on Observation 2, what impact will the policy changes have on the trend rate of growth for Country Y?
   A. Negative
   B. Neutral
   C. Positive

8. Based on Observation 3, Wakuluk *most likely* expects Country Y's yield curve in the near term to:
   A. invert.
   B. flatten.
   C. steepen.

The following information relates to Questions 9–10

Jennifer Wuyan is an investment strategist responsible for developing long-term capital market expectations for an investment firm that invests in domestic equities. She presents a report to the firm's investment committee describing the statistical model used to formulate capital market expectations, which is based on a dividend discount method. In the report, she notes that in developing the model, she researched the historical data seeking to identify the relevant variables and determined the best source of data for the model. She also notes her interpretation of the current economic and market environment.

9. **Explain** what additional step(s) Wuyan should have taken in the process of setting capital market expectations.

Wuyan reports that after repeatedly searching the most recent 10 years of data, she eventually identified variables that had a statistically significant relationship with equity returns. Wuyan used these variables to forecast equity returns. She documented, in a separate section of the report, a high correlation between nominal GDP and equity returns. Based on this noted high correlation, Wuyan concludes that nominal GDP predicts equity returns. Based on her statistical results, Wuyan expects equities to underperform over the next 12 months and recommends that the firm underweight equities.

Commenting on the report, John Tommanson, an investment adviser for the firm, suggests extending the starting point of the historical data back another 20 years to obtain more robust statistical results. Doing so would enable the analysis to include different economic and central bank policy environments. Tommanson is reluctant to underweight equities for his clients, citing the strong performance of equities over the last quarter, and believes the most recent quarterly data should be weighted more heavily in setting capital market expectations.

10. **Discuss** how *each* of the following forecasting challenges evident in Wuyan's report and in Tommanson's comments affects the setting of capital market expectations:
    i.   Status quo bias
    ii. Data-mining bias
    iii. Risk of regime change
    iv. Misinterpretation of correlation

Discuss how *each* of the following forecasting challenges evident in Wuyan's report and in Tommanson's comments affects the setting of capital market expectations:

Status quo bias

Data-mining bias

Risk of regime change

Misinterpretation of correlation

The following information relates to Questions 11–13

Jan Cambo is chief market strategist at a US asset management firm. While preparing a report for the upcoming investment committee meeting, Cambo updates her long-term forecast for US equity returns. As an input into her forecasting model, she uses the following long-term annualized forecasts from the firm's chief economist:

- Labor input will grow 0.5%.
- Labor productivity will grow 1.3%.
- Inflation will be 2.2%.
- Dividend yield will be 2.8%.

Based on these forecasts, Cambo predicts a long-term 9.0% annual equity return in the US market. Her forecast assumes no change in the share of profits in the economy, and she expects some contribution to equity returns from a change in the price-to-earnings ratio (P/E).

11. **Calculate** the implied contribution to Cambo's US equity return forecast from the expected change in the P/E.

At the investment committee meeting, the firm's chief economist predicts that the economy will enter the late expansion phase of the business cycle in the next 12 months.

12. **Discuss**, based on the chief economist's prediction, the implications for the following:
    i. Bond yields
    ii. Equity returns
    iii. Short-term interest rates

Discuss, based on the chief economist's prediction, the implications for the following:

Bond yields
Equity returns
Short-term interest rates

Cambo compares her business cycle forecasting approach to the approach used by the chief economist. Cambo bases her equity market forecast on a time-series model using a composite index of leading indicators as the key input, whereas the chief economist uses a detailed econometric model to generate his economic forecasts.

13. **Discuss** strengths and weaknesses of the economic forecasting approaches used by Cambo and the chief economist.

Discuss strengths and weaknesses of the economic forecasting approaches used by Cambo and the chief economist.

	Cambo's Forecasting Approach	Chief Economist's Forecasting Approach
Strengths		
Weaknesses		

The following information relates to Questions 14–16

Robert Hadpret is the chief economist at Agree Partners, an asset management firm located in the developed country of Eastland. He has prepared an economic report on Eastland for the firm's asset allocation committee. Hadpret notes that the composite index of leading economic indicators has declined for three consecutive months and that the yield curve has inverted. Private sector borrowing is also projected to decline. Based on these recent events, Hadpret predicts an economic contraction and forecasts lower inflation and possibly deflation over the next 12 months.

Helen Smitherman, a portfolio manager at Agree, considers Hadpret's economic forecast when determining the tactical allocation for the firm's Balanced Fund (the fund). Smitherman notes that the fund has considerable exposure to real estate, shares of asset-intensive and commodity-producing firms, and high-quality debt. The fund's cash holdings are at cyclical lows.

14. **Discuss** the implications of Hadpret's inflation forecast on the expected returns of the fund's holdings of:
    i.   cash.
    ii. bonds.
    iii. equities.
    iv. real estate.

Discuss the implications of Hadpret's inflation forecast on the expected returns of the fund's holdings of:

Cash
Bonds
Equities
Real Estate

In response to the projected cyclical decline in the Eastland economy and in private sector borrowing over the next year, Hadpret expects a change in the monetary and fiscal policy mix. He forecasts that the Eastland central bank will ease monetary policy. On the fiscal side, Hadpret expects the Eastland government to enact a substantial tax cut. As a result, Hadpret forecasts large government deficits that will be financed by the issuance of long-term government securities.

15. **Discuss** the relationship between the shape of the yield curve and the monetary and fiscal policy mix projected by Hadpret.

Currently, Eastland's currency is fixed relative to the currency of the country of Northland, and Eastland maintains policies that allow unrestricted capital flows. Hadpret examines the relationship between interest rates and exchange rates. He considers three possible scenarios for the Eastland economy:

Scenario 1: Shift in policy restricting capital flows
Scenario 2: Shift in policy allowing the currency to float
Scenario 3: Shift in investor belief toward a lack of full credibility that the exchange rate will be fixed forever

16. **Discuss** how interest rate and exchange rate linkages between Eastland and Northland might change under *each* scenario.
    Note: Consider *each* scenario independently.

Discuss how interest rate and exchange rate linkages between Eastland and Northland might change under *each* scenario. (Note: Consider *each* scenario independently.)

Scenario 1
Scenario 2
Scenario 3

CHAPTER 4

CAPITAL MARKET EXPECTATIONS, PART 2: FORECASTING ASSET CLASS RETURNS

Christopher D. Piros, PhD, CFA

Parts of this chapter have been adapted from a former Capital Market Expectations chapter authored by John P. Calverley, Alan M. Meder, CPA, CFA, Brian D. Singer, CFA, and Renato Staub, PhD.

LEARNING OUTCOMES

The candidate should be able to:

- discuss approaches to setting expectations for fixed-income returns;
- discuss risks faced by investors in emerging market fixed-income securities and the country risk analysis techniques used to evaluate emerging market economies;
- discuss approaches to setting expectations for equity investment market returns;
- discuss risks faced by investors in emerging market equity securities;
- explain how economic and competitive factors can affect expectations for real estate investment markets and sector returns;
- discuss major approaches to forecasting exchange rates;
- discuss methods of forecasting volatility;
- recommend and justify changes in the component weights of a global investment portfolio based on trends and expected changes in macroeconomic factors.

1. INTRODUCTION

This is the second of two chapters focusing on capital market expectations. A central theme of both chapters is that a disciplined approach to setting expectations will be rewarded. After outlining a framework for developing expectations and reviewing potential pitfalls, the first chapter focused on the use of macroeconomic analysis in setting expectations. This chapter builds on that foundation and examines setting expectations for specific asset classes—fixed income, equities, real estate, and currencies. Estimation of variance–covariance matrices is covered as well.

The chapter begins with an overview of the techniques frequently used to develop capital market expectations. The discussion of specific asset classes begins with fixed income in Section 3, followed by equities, real estate, and currencies in Sections 4–6. Estimation of variance–covariance structures is addressed in Section 7. Section 8 illustrates the use of macroeconomic analysis to develop and justify adjustments to a global portfolio.

2. OVERVIEW OF TOOLS AND APPROACHES

This section provides a brief overview of the main concepts, approaches, and tools used in professional forecasting of capital market returns. Whereas subsequent sections focus on specific asset classes, the emphasis here is on the commonality of techniques.

2.1. The Nature of the Problem

Few investment practitioners are likely to question the notion that investment opportunities change in systematic, but imperfectly predictable, ways over time. Yet the ramifications of that fact are often not explicitly recognized. Forecasting returns is not simply a matter of estimating constant, but unknown, parameters—for example, expected returns, variances, and correlations. Time horizons matter. The previous chapter highlighted two aspects of this issue: the need to ensure intertemporal consistency and the relative usefulness of specific information (e.g., the business cycle) over short, intermediate, and long horizons. The choice among forecasting techniques is effectively a choice of the information on which forecasts will be based (in statistical terms, the information on which the forecast is "conditioned") and how that information will be incorporated into the forecasts. The fact that opportunities change over time should, at least in principle, affect strategic investment decisions and how positions respond to changing forecasts.[1]

Although investment opportunities are not constant, virtually all forecasting techniques rely on notions of central tendency, toward which opportunities tend to revert over time. This fact means that although asset prices, risk premiums, volatilities, valuation ratios, and other metrics may exhibit momentum, persistence, and clustering in the short run, over sufficiently long horizons, they tend to converge to levels consistent with economic and financial fundamentals.

---

[1]For example, in general, it is not optimal to choose a portfolio on the mean–variance-efficient frontier based on forecasts for the coming period. In addition, the distinction between "strategic" and "tactical" asset allocation is less clear cut since, in general, the optimal allocation evolves with the investor's remaining investment horizon. See Piros (2015) for a non-technical exposition of these issues.

What are we trying to forecast? In principle, we are interested in the whole probability distribution of future returns. In practice, however, forecasting expected return is by far the most important consideration, both because it is the dominant driver of most investment decisions and because it is generally more difficult to forecast within practical tolerances than such risk metrics as volatility. Hence, the primary focus here is on expected return. In terms of risk metrics, we limit our attention to variances and covariances.

2.2. Approaches to Forecasting

At a very high level, there are essentially three approaches to forecasting: (1) formal tools, (2) surveys, and (3) judgment. Formal tools are established research methods amenable to precise definition and independent replication of results. Surveys involve asking a group of experts for their opinions. Judgment can be described as a qualitative synthesis of information derived from various sources and filtered through the lens of experience.

Surveys are probably most useful as a way to gauge consensus views, which can serve as inputs into formal tools and the analyst's own judgment. Judgment is always important. There is ample scope for applying judgment—in particular, economic and psychological insight—to improve forecasts and numbers, including those produced by elaborate quantitative models. In using survey results and applying their own judgment, analysts must be wary of the psychological traps discussed in the Capital Market Expectations Part 1 chapter. Beyond these brief observations, however, there is not much new to be said about surveys and judgment.

The formal forecasting tools most commonly used in forecasting capital market returns fall into three broad categories: statistical methods, discounted cash flow models, and risk premium models. The distinctions among these methods will become clear as they are discussed and applied throughout the chapter.

2.2.1. Statistical Methods

All the formal tools involve data and statistical analysis to some degree. Methods that are primarily, if not exclusively, statistical impose relatively little structure on the data. As a result, the forecasts inherit the statistical properties of the data with limited, if any, regard for economic or financial reasoning. Three types of statistical methods will be covered in this chapter. The first approach is to use well-known sample statistics, such as sample means, variances, and correlations, to describe the distribution of future returns. This is undoubtedly the clearest example of simply taking the data at face value. Unfortunately, sampling error makes some of these statistics—in particular, the sample mean—very imprecise. The second approach, **shrinkage estimation**, involves taking a weighted average of two estimates of the same parameter—one based on historical sample data and the other based on some other source or information, such as the analyst's "prior" knowledge. This "two-estimates-are-better-than-one" approach has the desirable property of reducing forecast errors relative to simple sample statistics. The third method, **time-series estimation**, involves forecasting a variable on the basis of lagged values of the variable being forecast and often lagged values of other selected variables. These models have the benefit of explicitly incorporating dynamics into the forecasting process. However, since they are reduced-form models, they may summarize the historical data well without providing much insight into the underlying drivers of the forecasts.

2.2.2. Discounted Cash Flow

Discounted cash flow (DCF) models express the idea that an asset's value is the present value of its expected cash flows. They are a basic method for establishing the intrinsic value of an asset on the basis of fundamentals and its fair required rate of return. Conversely, they are used to estimate the required rate of return implied by the asset's current price.

2.2.3. Risk Premium Models

The risk premium approach expresses the expected return on a risky asset as the sum of the risk-free rate of interest and one or more risk premiums that compensate investors for the asset's exposure to sources of *priced risk* (risk for which investors demand compensation). There are three main methods for modeling risk premiums: (1) an equilibrium model, such as the CAPM, (2) a factor model, and (3) building blocks. Each of these methods was discussed in earlier chapters. Equilibrium models and factor models both impose a structure on how returns are assumed to be generated. Hence, they can be used to generate estimates of (1) expected returns and (2) variances and covariances.

3. FORECASTING FIXED-INCOME RETURNS

There are three main ways to approach forecasting fixed-income returns. The first is discounted cash flow. This method is really the only one that is precise enough to use in support of trades involving individual fixed-income securities. This type of "micro" analysis will not be discussed in detail here since it is covered extensively elsewhere in CFA Program curriculum chapters that focus on fixed income. DCF concepts are also useful in forecasting the more aggregated performance needed to support asset allocation decisions. The second approach is the risk premium approach, which is often applied to fixed income, in part because fixed-income premiums are among the building blocks used to estimate expected returns on riskier asset classes, such as equities. The third approach is to include fixed-income asset classes in an equilibrium model. Doing so has the advantage of imposing consistency across asset classes and is especially useful as a first step in applying the Black–Litterman framework, which will be discussed in a later chapter.

3.1. Applying DCF to Fixed Income

Fixed income is really all about discounted cash flow. This stems from the facts that almost all fixed-income securities have finite maturities and that the (promised) cash flows are known, governed by explicit rules, or can be modeled with a reasonably high degree of accuracy (e.g., mortgage-backed security prepayments). Using modern arbitrage-free models, we can value virtually any fixed-income instrument. The most straightforward and, undoubtedly, most precise way to forecast fixed-income returns is to explicitly value the securities on the basis of the assumed evolution of the critical inputs to the valuation model—for example, the spot yield curve, the term structure of volatilities, and prepayment speeds. A whole distribution of returns can be generated by doing this for a variety of scenarios. As noted previously, this is essentially the only option if we need the "micro" precision of accounting for rolling down the yield curve, changes in the shape of the yield curve, changes in rate volatilities, or changes in the sensitivity of contingent cash flows. But for many purposes—for example, asset allocation—we usually do not need such granularity.

Yield to maturity (YTM)—the single discount rate that equates the present value of a bond's cash flows to its market price—is by far the most commonly quoted metric of valuation and, implicitly, of expected return for bonds. For bond portfolios, the YTM is usually calculated as if it were simply an average of the individual bonds' YTM, which is not exactly accurate but is a reasonable approximation.[2] Forecasting bond returns would be very easy if we could simply equate yield to maturity with expected return. It is not that simple, but YTM does provide a reasonable and readily available first approximation.

Assuming cash flows are received in full and on time, there are two main reasons why realized return may not equal the initial yield to maturity. First, if the investment horizon is shorter than the amount of time until the bond's maturity, any change in interest rate (i.e., the bond's YTM) will generate a capital gain or loss at the horizon. Second, the cash flows may be reinvested at rates above or below the initial YTM. The longer the horizon, the more sensitive the realized return will be to reinvestment rates. These two issues work in opposite directions: Rising (falling) rates induce capital losses (gains) but increase (decrease) reinvestment income. If the investment horizon equals the (Macaulay) duration of the bond or portfolio, the capital gain/loss and reinvestment effects will roughly offset, leaving the realized return close to the original YTM. This relationship is exact if (a) the yield curve is flat and (b) the change in rates occurs immediately in a single step. In practice, the relationship is only an approximation. Nonetheless, it provides an important insight: *Over horizons shorter than the duration, the capital gain/loss impact will tend to dominate such that rising (declining) rates imply lower (higher) return, whereas over horizons longer than the duration, the reinvestment impact will tend to dominate such that rising (declining) rates imply higher (lower) return.*

Note that the timing of rate changes matters. It will not have much effect, if any, on the capital gain/loss component because that ultimately depends on the beginning and ending values of the bond or portfolio. But it does affect the reinvestment return. The longer the horizon, the more it matters. Hence, for long-term forecasts, we should break the forecast horizon into subperiods corresponding to when we expect the largest rate changes to occur.

EXAMPLE 1   Forecasting Return Based on Yield to Maturity

Jesper Bloch works for Discrete Asset Management (DAM) in Zurich. Many of the firm's more risk-averse clients invest in a currency-hedged global government bond strategy that uses cash flows to purchase new issues and seasoned bonds all along the yield curve to maintain a roughly constant maturity and duration profile. The yield to maturity of the portfolio is 3.25% (compounded annually), and the modified duration is 4.84. DAM's chief investment officer believes global government yields are likely to rise by 200 bps over the next two years as central banks remove extraordinarily accommodative policies and inflation surges. Bloch has been asked to project approximate returns for this strategy over horizons of two, five, and seven years. What conclusions is Bloch likely to draw?

---

[2]Bear in mind that yield to maturity does not account for optionality. However, various yield measures derived from option-adjusted valuation can be viewed as conveying similar information. To keep the present discussion as simple as possible, we ignore the distinction here. If optionality is critical to the forecast, it may be necessary to apply the more granular DCF framework discussed previously.

Solution: If yields were not expected to change, the return would be very close to the yield to maturity (3.25%) over each horizon. The Macaulay duration is 5.0 (= 4.84 × 1.0325), so if the yield change occurred immediately, the capital gain/loss and reinvestment impacts on return would roughly balance over five years. Ignoring convexity (which is not given), the capital loss at the end of two years will be approximately 9.68% (= 4.84 × 2%). Assuming yields rise linearly over the initial two-year period, the higher reinvestment rates will boost the cumulative return by approximately 1.0% over two years, so the annual return over two years will be approximately −1.09% [= 3.25 + (−9.68 + 1.0)/2]. Reinvesting for three more years at the 2.0% higher rate adds another 6.0% to the cumulative return, so the five-year annual return would be approximately 2.71% [= 3.25 + (−9.68 + 1.0 + 6.0)/5]. With an additional two years of reinvestment income, the seven-year annual return would be about 3.44% [= 3.25 + (−9.68 + 1.0 + 6.0 + 4.0)/7]. As expected, the capital loss dominated the return over two years, and higher reinvestment rates dominated over seven years. The gradual nature of the yield increase extended the horizon over which the capital gain/loss and reinvestment effects would balance beyond the initial five-year Macaulay duration.

We have extended the DCF approach beyond simply finding the discount rates implied by current market prices (e.g., YTMs), which might be considered the "pure" DCF approach. For other asset classes (e.g., equities), the connection between discount rates and valuations/ returns is vague because there is so much uncertainty with respect to the cash flows. For these asset classes, discounted cash flow is essentially a conceptual framework rather than a precise valuation model. In contrast, in fixed income there is a tight connection between discount rates, valuations, and returns. We are, therefore, able to refine the "pure" DCF forecast by incorporating projections of how rates will evolve over the investment horizon. Doing so is particularly useful in formulating short-term forecasts.

3.2. The Building Block Approach to Fixed-Income Returns

The building block approach forms an estimate of expected return in terms of required compensation for specific types of risk. The required return for fixed-income asset classes has four components: the one-period default-free rate, the term premium, the credit premium, and the liquidity premium. As the names indicate, the premiums reflect compensation for interest rate risk, duration risk, credit risk, and illiquidity, respectively. Only one of the four components—the short-term default-free rate—is (potentially) observable. For example, the term premium and the credit premium are implicitly embedded in yield spreads, but they are not *equal* to observed yield spreads. Next, we will consider each of these components and summarize applicable empirical regularities.

3.2.1. The Short-term Default-free Rate
In principle, the short-term default-free rate is the rate on the highest-quality, most liquid instrument with a maturity that matches the forecast horizon. In practice, it is usually taken to be a government zero-coupon bill at a maturity that is issued frequently—say, every three months. This rate is virtually always tied closely to the central bank's policy rate and,

therefore, mirrors the cyclical dynamics of monetary policy. Secular movements are closely tied to expected inflation levels.

Under normal circumstances, the observed rate is a reasonable base on which to build expected returns for risky assets. In extreme circumstances, however, it may be necessary to adopt a normalized rate. For example, when policy rates or short-term government rates are negative, using the observed rate without adjustment may unduly reduce the required/ expected return estimate for risky instruments. An alternative to normalizing the short rate in this circumstance would be to raise the estimate of one or more of the risk premiums on the basis of the notion that the observed negative short rate reflects an elevated willingness to pay for safety or, conversely, elevated required compensation for risk.

Forecast horizons substantially longer than the maturity of the standard short-term instrument call for a different type of adjustment. There are essentially two approaches. The first is to use the yield on a longer zero-coupon bond with a maturity that matches the horizon. In theory, that is the right thing to do. It does, however, call into question the role of the term premium since the longer-term rate will already incorporate the term premium. The second approach is to replace today's observed short-term rate with an estimate of the return that would be generated by rolling the short-term instrument over the forecast horizon; that is, take account of the likely path of short-term rates. This approach does not change the interpretation of the term premium. In addition to helping establish the baseline return to which risk premiums will be added, explicitly projecting the path of short-term rates may help in estimating the term premium.

In many markets, there are futures contracts for short-term instruments. The rates implied by these contracts are frequently interpreted as the market's expected path of short-term rates. As such, they provide an excellent starting point for analysts in formulating their own projections. Some central banks—for example, the US Federal Reserve Board—publish projections of future policy rates that can also serve as a guide for analysts. Quantitative models, such as the Taylor rule, provide another tool.[3]

3.2.2. The Term Premium

The default-free spot rate curve reflects the expected path of short-term rates and the required term premiums for each maturity. It is tempting to think that given a projected path of short-term rates, we can easily deduce the term premiums from the spot curve. We can, of course, derive a set of forward rates in the usual way and subtract the projected short-term rate for each future period. Doing so would give an implied sequence of period-by-period premiums. This may be a useful exercise, but it will not give us what we really want—the expected returns for bonds of different maturities over our forecast horizon. The implication is that although the yield curve contains the information we want and may be useful in forecasting returns, we cannot derive the term premium directly from the curve itself.

A vast amount of academic research has been devoted over many decades to addressing three fundamental questions: Do term premiums exist? If so, are they constant? And if they exist, how are they related to maturity? The evidence indicates that term premiums are positive and increase with maturity, are roughly proportional to duration, and vary over time. The first of these properties implies that term premiums are important. The second allows the analyst to be pragmatic, focusing on a single term premium, which is then scaled by duration. The third property implies that basing estimates on current information is essential.

---

[3]See the Capital Market Expectations Part 1 chapter for discussion of the Taylor rule.

Ilmanen (2012) argued that there are four main drivers of the term premium for nominal bonds.

- *Level-dependent inflation uncertainty:* Inflation is arguably the main driver of long-run variation in both nominal yields and the term premium. Higher (lower) levels of inflation tend to coincide with greater (less) inflation uncertainty. Hence, nominal yields rise (fall) with inflation because of changes in both expected inflation and the inflation risk component of the term premium.
- *Ability to hedge recession risk:* In theory, assets earn a low (or negative) risk premium if they tend to perform well when the economy is weak. When growth and inflation are primarily driven by aggregate demand, nominal bond returns tend to be negatively correlated with growth and a relatively low term premium is warranted. Conversely, when growth and inflation are primarily driven by aggregate supply, nominal bond returns tend to be positively correlated with growth, necessitating a higher term premium.
- *Supply and demand:* The relative outstanding supply of short-maturity and long-maturity default-free bonds influences the slope of the yield curve.[4] This phenomenon is largely attributable to the term premium since the maturity structure of outstanding debt should have little impact on the expected future path of short-term rates.[5]
- *Cyclical effects:* The slope of the yield curve varies substantially over the business cycle: It is steep around the trough of the cycle and flat or even inverted around the peak. Much of this movement reflects changes in the expected path of short-term rates. However, it also reflects countercyclical changes in the term premium.

Although the slope of the yield curve is useful information on which to base forecasts of the term premium, other indicators work as well or better. Exhibit 1 shows correlations with subsequent excess bond returns (7- to 10-year Treasury bond return minus 3-month Treasury bill return) over 1-quarter, 1-year, and 5-year horizons for eight indicators. The indicators are listed in descending order of the (absolute value of the) correlation with one-year returns. The first four are derived from the bond market. The *ex ante* real yield has the strongest relationship over each horizon. Next on the list are the two most complex indicators. The Cochrane and Piazzesi curve factor is a composite measure capturing both the slope and the curvature of the yield curve.[6] The Kim and Wright premium is derived from a three-factor term structure model.[7] The slope of the yield curve is next on the list. Note that it has the weakest relationship over the five-year horizon. The supply indicator—the share of debt with maturity greater than 10 years—has a particularly strong relationship over the longest horizon. Since this variable tends to change gradually over time, it is not surprising that it is more closely related to long-run average returns than it is to shorter-term returns. The three

---

[4]As discussed in the Capital Market Expectations Part 1 chapter, temporary changes in the relative *flow* of bonds to the market may not have a lasting impact on the curve unless they result in a significant, permanent change in the amounts outstanding.

[5]Supply/demand effects will be more pronounced if there are reasons for certain investors to prefer or require bonds of specific maturities. This is most likely to occur at the very long end of the curve because the supply of very long-term bonds is typically limited and some institutions must fund very long-term liabilities. As an example, the long end of the UK curve was severely squeezed in the 1990s.

[6]See Cochrane and Piazzesi (2005).

[7]See Kim and Wright (2005). The three factors in the theoretical model do not correspond directly with observable variables but may be thought of as proxies for the level, slope, and curvature of the term structure.

cyclical proxies—the corporate profit-to-GDP ratio, business confidence, and the unemployment rate—are at the bottom of the list since they had the weakest correlation with return over the next year.

EXHIBIT 1   Correlations with Future Excess Bond Returns, 1962–2009

	Return Horizon		
Current Indicator	**1 Quarter**	**1 Year**	**5 Years**
Ex ante real yield	0.28	0.48	0.69
Cochrane and Piazzesi curve factor	0.24	0.44	0.32
Kim and Wright model premium*	0.25	0.43	0.34
Yield curve slope (10 year − 3 month)	0.21	0.34	0.06
Share of debt > 10 years	0.13	0.28	0.66
Corporate profit/GDP	−0.13	−0.25	−0.52
ISM business confidence	−0.10	−0.20	−0.30
Unemployment rate	0.11	0.18	0.24

*Kim and Wright model results are for 1990–2009.
Source: Ilmanen (2012, Exhibit 3.14).

3.2.3. The Credit Premium

The credit premium is the additional expected return demanded for bearing the risk of default losses—importantly, in addition to compensation for the *expected* level of losses. Both expected default losses and the credit premium are embedded in credit spreads. They cannot be recovered from those spreads unless we impose some structure (i.e., a model) on default-free rates, default probabilities, and recovery rates. The two main types of models—structural credit models and reduced-form credit models—are described in detail in other chapters.[8] In the following discussion, we will focus on the empirical behavior of the credit premium.

An analysis of 150 years of defaults among US non-financial corporate bonds showed that the severity of default losses accounted for only about half of the 1.53% average yield spread.[9] Hence, holders of corporate bonds did, on average, earn a credit premium to bear the risk of default. However, the pattern of actual defaults suggests the premium was earned very unevenly over time. In particular, high and low default rates tended to persist, causing clusters of high and low annual default rates and resultant losses. The study found that the previous year's default rate, stock market return, stock market volatility, and GDP growth rate were predictive of the subsequent year's default rate. However, the aggregate credit spread was not predictive of subsequent defaults. Contemporaneous financial market variables—stock returns, stock volatility, and the riskless rate—were significant in explaining the credit spread, but neither GDP growth nor changes in the default rate helped explain the credit spread.

---

[8] See the CFA Program curriculum chapter "Credit Analysis Models." More in-depth coverage can be found in Jarrow and van Deventer (2015).
[9] See Giesecke, Longstaff, Schaefer, and Strebulaev (2011). Default rates were measured as a fraction of the par value of outstanding bonds. The authors did not document actual recovery rates, instead assuming 50% recovery. Hence, the true level of losses could have been somewhat higher or lower.

This finding suggests that credit spreads were driven primarily by the credit risk premium and financial market conditions and only secondarily by fundamental changes in the expected level of default losses. Thus, credit spreads do contain information relevant to predicting the credit premium.

Ilmanen (2012) hypothesized that credit spreads and the credit premiums embedded in them are driven by different factors, depending on credit quality. Default rates on top-quality (AAA and AA) bonds are extremely low, so very little of the spread/premium is due to the likelihood of actual default in the absence of a change in credit quality. Instead, the main driver is "downgrade bias"—the fact that a deterioration in credit quality (resulting in a rating downgrade) is much more likely than an improvement in credit quality (leading to an upgrade) and that downgrades induce larger spread changes than upgrades do.[10] Bonds rated A and BBB have moderate default rates. They still do not have a high likelihood of actual default losses, but their prospects are more sensitive to cyclical forces and their spreads/ premiums vary more (countercyclically) over the cycle. Default losses are of utmost concern for below-investment-grade bonds. Defaults tend to cluster in times when the economy is in recession. In addition, the default rate and the severity of losses in default tend to rise and fall together. These characteristics imply big losses at the worst times, necessitating substantial compensation for this risk. Not too surprisingly, high-yield spreads/premiums tend to rise ahead of realized default rates.

Exhibit 2 shows three variables that have tended to predict excess returns (over T-bills) for an index of US investment-grade corporate bonds over the next quarter and the next year. Not surprisingly, a high corporate option-adjusted spread is bullish for corporate bond performance because it indicates a large cushion against credit losses—that is, a higher credit premium. A steep Treasury curve is also bullish because, as mentioned earlier, it tends to correspond to the trough of the business cycle when default rates begin to decline. Combining these insights with those from Exhibit 1, the implication is that a steep yield curve predicts both a high term premium and a high credit premium. Higher implied volatility in the equity market was also bullish for corporates, most likely reflecting risk-averse pricing—that is, high risk premiums—across all markets.

EXHIBIT 2   Correlations with US Investment-Grade Corporate Excess Returns, 1990–2009

Current Indicator	Return Horizon	
	1 Quarter	1 Year
Corporate option-adjusted spread	0.25	0.46
VIX implied equity volatility	0.28	0.39
Yield curve slope (10 year − 2 year)	0.20	0.27

Source: Ilmanen (2012, Exhibit 4.15).

How are credit premiums related to maturity? Aside from situations of imminent default, there is greater risk of default losses the longer one must wait for payment. We might, therefore, expect that longer-maturity corporate bonds would offer higher credit risk

---

[10]Liquidity relative to government bonds is also an important contributor to yield spreads on very high-quality private sector bonds. By definition, of course, this is really the liquidity premium, rather than part of the credit premium.

premiums. The historical evidence suggests that this has not been the case. Credit premiums tend to be especially generous at the short end of the curve. This may be due to "event risk," in the sense that a default, no matter how unlikely, could still cause a huge proportional loss but there is no way that the bond will pay more than the issuer promised. It may also be due, in part, to illiquidity since many short-maturity bonds are old issues that rarely trade as they gradually approach maturity. As a result, many portfolio managers use a strategy known as a "credit barbell" in which they concentrate credit exposure at short maturities and take interest rate/duration risk via long-maturity government bonds.

3.2.4. The Liquidity Premium

Relatively few bond issues trade actively for more than a few weeks after issuance. Secondary market trading occurs primarily in the most recently issued sovereign bonds, current coupon mortgage-backed securities, and a few of the largest high-quality corporate bonds. The liquidity of other bonds largely depends on the willingness of dealers to hold them in inventory long enough to find a buyer. In general, liquidity tends to be better for bonds that are (a) priced near par/reflective of current market levels, (b) relatively new, (c) from a relatively large issue, (d) from a well-known/frequent issuer, (e) standard/simple in structure, and (f) high quality. These factors tend to reduce the dealer's risk in holding the bond and increase the likelihood of finding a buyer quickly.

As a baseline estimate of the "pure" liquidity premium in a particular market, the analyst can look to the yield spread between fixed-rate, option-free bonds from the highest-quality issuer (virtually always the sovereign) and the next highest-quality large issuer of similar bonds (often a government agency or quasi-agency). Adjustments should then be made for the factors listed previously. In general, the impact of each factor is likely to increase disproportionately as one moves away from baseline attributes. For example, each step lower in credit quality is likely to have a bigger impact on liquidity than that of the preceding step.

EXAMPLE 2   Fixed-Income Building Blocks

Salimah Rahman works for SMECo, a Middle Eastern sovereign wealth fund. Each year, the fund's staff updates its projected returns for the following year on the basis of developments in the preceding year. The fund uses the building block approach in making its fixed-income projections. Rahman has been assigned the task of revising the key building block components for a major European bond market. The following table shows last year's values:

	Description	Value
Risk-free rate	3-month government bill	3.50%
Term premium	5-year duration	0.50%
Credit premium	Baa/BBB corporate	0.90%
Liquidity premium	Government-guaranteed agency	0.15%

Although inflation rose modestly, the central bank cut its policy rate by 50 bps in response to weakening growth. Aggregate corporate profits have remained solid, and after a modest correction, the stock market finished higher for the year. However, defaults on leveraged loans were unexpectedly high this year, and confidence surveys weakened again recently. Equity option volatility spiked mid-year but ended the year somewhat lower. The interest rate futures curve has flattened but remains upward sloping. The 10-year government yield declined only a few basis points, while the yield on comparable government agency bonds remained unchanged and corporate spreads—both nominal and option adjusted—widened.

Indicate the developments that are likely to cause Rahman to increase/decrease each of the key building blocks relative to last year.

Guideline answer:

Based on the reduction in policy rates and the flattening of the interest rate futures curve, Rahman is virtually certain to reduce the short-term rate component. Steepening of the yield curve (10-year yield barely responded to the 50 bp rate cut) indicates an increase in both the term premium and the credit premium. Declining confidence also suggests a higher term premium. Widening of credit spreads is also indicative of a higher credit premium. However, the increase in loan defaults suggests that credit losses are likely to be higher next year as well, since defaults tend to cluster. All else the same, this reduces the expected return on corporate bonds/loans. Hence, the credit premium should increase less than would otherwise be implied by the steeper yield curve and wider credit spreads. Modest widening of the government agency spread indicates an increase in the liquidity premium. The resilience of the equity market and the decline in equity option volatility suggest that investors are not demanding a general increase in risk premiums.

3.3. Risks in Emerging Market Bonds

Emerging market debt was once nearly synonymous with crisis. The Latin American debt crisis of the 1980s involved bank loans but essentially triggered development of a market for emerging market bonds. In the early 1990s, the Mexican crisis occurred. In the late 1990s, there was the Asian crisis, followed by the Russian crisis, which contributed to the turmoil that sank the giant hedge fund Long-Term Capital Management. There have been other, more isolated, events, such as Argentina's forced restructuring of its debt, but the emerging market bond market has grown, deepened, and matured. What started with only a few government issuers borrowing in hard currencies (from their perspective foreign, but widely used, currencies) has grown into a market in which corporations as well as governments issue in their local currencies and in hard currencies. The discussion here applies not just to emerging markets but also to what are known as "frontier" markets (when they are treated separately or as a subset of emerging markets).

Investing in emerging market debt involves all the same risks as investing in developed country debt, such as interest rate movements, currency movements, and potential defaults. In addition, it poses risks that are, although not entirely absent, less significant in developed markets. These risks fall roughly into two categories: (1) economic and (2) political and legal. A slightly different breakdown would be "ability to pay" and "willingness to pay."

Before discussing these country risks, note that some countries that are labeled as emerging markets may in fact be healthy, prosperous economies with strong fundamentals. Likewise, the political and legal issues discussed in this section may or may not apply to any particular country. Furthermore, these risks will, in general, apply in varying degrees across countries. Emerging markets are widely recognized as a very heterogeneous group. It is up to the analyst to assess which considerations are relevant to a particular investment decision.

3.3.1. Economic Risks/Ability to Pay

Emerging market economies as a whole have characteristics that make them potentially more vulnerable to distress and hence less likely to be able to pay their debts on time or in full, such as the following:

- Greater concentration of wealth and income; less diverse tax base
- Greater dependence on specific industries, especially cyclical industries, such as commodities and agriculture; low potential for pricing power in world markets
- Restrictions on trade, capital flows, and currency conversion
- Poor fiscal controls and monetary discipline
- Less educated and less skilled work force; poor or limited physical infrastructure; lower level of industrialization and technological sophistication
- Reliance on foreign borrowing, often in hard currencies not their own
- Small/less sophisticated financial markets and institutions
- Susceptibility to capital flight; perceived vulnerability contributing to actual vulnerability

Although history is at best an imperfect guide to the future, the analyst should examine a country's track record on critical issues. Have there been crises in the past? If so, how were they handled/resolved? Has the sovereign defaulted? Is there restructured debt? How have authorities responded to fiscal challenges? Is there inflation or currency instability?

The analyst should, of course, examine the health of the macroeconomy in some detail. A few indicative guidelines can be helpful. If there is one ratio that is most closely watched, it is the ratio of the fiscal deficit to GDP. Most emerging countries have deficits and perpetually struggle to reduce them. A persistent ratio above 4% is likely a cause for concern. A debt-to-GDP ratio exceeding 70%–80%, perhaps only mild concern for a developed market, is a sign of vulnerability for an emerging market. A persistent annual real growth rate less than 4% suggests that an emerging market is catching up with more advanced economies only slowly, if at all, and per capita income might even be falling—a potential source of political stress. Persistent current account deficits greater than 4% of GDP probably indicate lack of competitiveness. Foreign debt greater than 50% of GDP or greater than 200% of current account receipts is also a sign of danger. Finally, foreign exchange reserves less than 100% of short-term debt is risky, whereas a ratio greater than 200% is ample. It must be emphasized that the numbers given here are merely suggestive of levels that may indicate a need for further scrutiny.

When all else fails, a country may need to call on external support mechanisms. Hence, the analyst should consider whether the country has access to support from the International Monetary Fund (IMF), the World Bank, or other international agencies.

3.3.2. Political and Legal Risks/Willingness to Pay

Investors in emerging market debt may be unable to enforce their claims or recover their investments. Weak property rights laws and weak enforcement of contract laws are clearly of concern in this regard. Inability to enforce seniority structures within private sector claims is one important example. The principle of sovereign immunity makes it very difficult to force a sovereign borrower to pay its debts. Confiscation of property, nationalization of companies, and corruption are also relevant hazards. Coalition governments may also pose political instability problems. Meanwhile, the imposition of capital controls or restrictions on currency conversion may make it difficult, or even impossible, to repatriate capital.

As with economic risks, history may provide some guidance with respect to the severity of political and legal risks. The following are some pertinent questions: Is there a history of nationalization, expropriation, or other violations of property rights? How have international disputes been resolved and under which legal jurisdiction? Has the integrity of the judicial system and process been questioned? Are political institutions stable? Are they recognized as legitimate and subject to reasonable checks and balances? Has the transfer of power been peaceful, orderly, and lawful? Does the political process give rise to fragile coalitions that collapse whenever events strain the initial compromises with respect to policy?

EXAMPLE 3   Emerging Market Bonds

Belvia has big aspirations. Although still a poor country, it has been growing rapidly, averaging 6% real and 10% nominal growth for the last five years. At the beginning of this period of growth, a centrist coalition gained a narrow majority over the authoritarian, fiscally irresponsible, anti-investor, anti-business party that had been in power for decades. The government has removed the old barriers to trade, including the signing of a regional free-trade agreement, and removed capital controls. Much of its growth has been fueled by investment in its dominant industry—natural resources—financed by debt and foreign direct investment flows. These policies have been popular with the business community, as has the relaxation of regulations affecting key constituencies. Meanwhile, to ensure that prosperity flows rapidly to the people, the government has allowed redistributive social payments to grow even faster than GDP, resulting in a large and rising fiscal deficit (5% of GDP this year, projected to be 7% in two years). The current account deficit is 8% of GDP. Despite the large current account deficit, the local currency has appreciated significantly since it was allowed to float two years ago. The government has just announced that it will issue a large 10-year local currency bond under Belvian law—the first issue of its kind in many years.

Despite a very strong relationship with the bank marketing the bond, Peter Valt has decided not to invest in it. When pressed for his reasoning, what risks is he likely to identify?

Solution: There are several significant risks and warning signs. Coalition governments are often unstable, and the most likely alternative would appear to be a return to the previously dominant party that lacks fiscal discipline. That regime is likely to undo the recent pro-growth policies and might even disavow the debt, including this new bond. The bond will be governed by Belvian law, which, combined with the principle of sovereign immunity, will make it very difficult for foreigners to enforce their claims. In addition, the relaxation of regulations affecting key constituencies hints strongly at corruption and possibly at payoffs within the current regime. With respect to the economy, fiscal discipline remains poor, there is heavy reliance on a single industry, and the current account deficit is almost certainly unsustainable (e.g., over the 10-year life of this bond). In addition, the currency is very likely to be overvalued, which will both make it very difficult to broaden global competitiveness beyond natural resources and increase the investor's risk of substantial currency losses.

4. FORECASTING EQUITY RETURNS

The task of forecasting equity market returns is often the central focus of setting capital market expectations. In this section, we discuss applying each of the major methodologies to equities.

4.1. Historical Statistics Approach to Equity Returns

The *Credit Suisse Global Investment Returns Yearbook 2018*[11] updated the seminal work of Dimson, Marsh, and Staunton (2002) to include asset returns in 21 countries for the 118-year period of 1900–2017. Exhibit 3 shows the mean real return for each market portfolio centered within a 95% confidence interval. Results are also shown for a world portfolio, a world ex-US portfolio, and Europe. The portfolios are ordered from left to right on the basis of the mean return.

    The means range from a low of 5.0% for Austria to a high of 9.4% in South Africa. Note that both of these values lie within the confidence interval for every country. From a statistical perspective, there is really no difference among these markets in terms of mean real return. This illustrates the fact that sample averages, even derived from seemingly long histories, are very imprecise estimates unless the volatility of the data is small relative to the mean. Clearly that is not the case for equity returns. Nonetheless, sample means are frequently cited without regard to the quality of information they convey.

EXHIBIT 3   Historical Mean Returns with Confidence Intervals by Country, 1900–2017

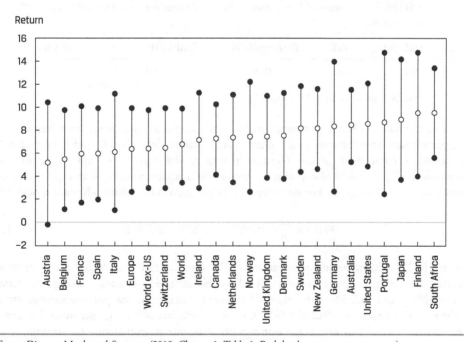

Source: Dimson, Marsh, and Staunton (2018, Chapter 1, Table 1. Real, local currency percent returns).

---

[11]Dimson, Marsh, and Staunton (2018).

As indicated in Section 2, shrinkage estimators can often provide more reliable estimates by combining the sample mean with a second estimate of the mean return. However, the application of a common shrinkage estimator confirms that there is no basis for believing that the true expected returns for the countries in Exhibit 3 are different.

4.2. DCF Approach to Equity Returns

Analysts have frequently used the Gordon (constant) growth model form of the dividend discount model, solved for the required rate of return, to formulate the long-term expected return of equity markets. Although this model is quite simple, it has a big advantage over using historical stock returns to project future returns. The vast majority of the "noise" in historical stock returns comes from fluctuations in the price-to-earnings ratio (P/E) and the ratio of earnings to GDP. Since the amount of earnings appears in the numerator of one ratio and the denominator of the other, the impact of these ratios tends to cancel out over time, leaving the relationship between equity market appreciation and GDP growth much more stable. And GDP growth itself, especially the real growth component, is much less volatile and hence relatively predictable.[12] As an illustration, Exhibit 4 shows historical volatilities (defined as the standard deviation of percentage changes) for the S&P 500 Index return, P/E, the earnings-to-GDP ratio, real US GDP growth, and inflation for 1946–2016. The Gordon growth model allows us to take advantage of this relative stability by linking long-term equity appreciation to a more stable foundation—economic growth.

EXHIBIT 4   Historical Comparison of Standard Deviations in the United States, 1946–2016

S&P 500	P/E	Earnings/GDP	Real GDP Growth	Inflation
16.1	28.5	28.9	3.0	3.2

Note: Standard deviation of % changes

In the United States and other major markets, share repurchases have become an important way for companies to distribute cash to shareholders. Grinold and Kroner (2002) provided a restatement of the Gordon growth model that takes explicit account of repurchases. Their model also provides a means for analysts to incorporate expectations of valuation levels through the familiar price-to-earnings ratio. The **Grinold–Kroner model**[13] is

$$E(R_e) \approx \frac{D}{P} + (\%\Delta E - \%\Delta S) + \%\Delta\mathrm{P/E} \tag{1}$$

where $E(R_e)$ is the expected equity return, D/P is the dividend yield, $\%\Delta E$ is the expected percentage change in total earnings, $\%\Delta S$ is the expected percentage change in shares outstanding, and $\%\Delta\mathrm{P/E}$ is the expected percentage change in the price-to-earnings ratio. The term in parentheses, $(\%\Delta E - \%\Delta S)$, is the growth rate of earnings per share. Net share repurchases ($\%\Delta S < 0$) imply that earnings per share grows faster than total earnings.

---

[12]See the previous chapter for a discussion of projecting trend growth.
[13]See Grinold and Kroner (2002) for a derivation. The model is shown here in a slightly modified form.

With a minor rearrangement of the equation, the expected return can be divided into three components:

- Expected cash flow ("income") return: $D/P - \%\Delta S$
- Expected nominal earnings growth return: $\%\Delta E$
- Expected repricing return: $\%\Delta P/E$

The expected nominal earnings growth return and the expected repricing return constitute the expected capital gains.

In principle, the Grinold–Kroner model assumes an infinite horizon. In practice, the analyst typically needs to make projections for finite horizons, perhaps several horizons. In applying the model, the analyst needs to be aware of the implications of constant growth rate assumptions over different horizons. Failure to tailor growth rates to the horizon can easily lead to implausible results. As an example, suppose the P/E is currently 16.0 and the analyst believes that it will revert to a level of 20 and be stable thereafter. The P/E growth rates for various horizons that are consistent with this view are 4.56% for 5 years, 2.26% for 10 years, 0.75% for 30 years, and an arbitrarily small positive number for a truly long-term horizon. Treating, say, the 2.26% 10-year number as if it is appropriate for the "long run" would imply an ever-rising P/E rather than convergence to a plausible long-run valuation. The only very long-run assumptions that are consistent with economically plausible relationships are $\%\Delta E$ = Nominal GDP growth, $\%\Delta S = 0$, and $\%\Delta P/E = 0$. The longer the (finite) horizon, the less the analyst's projection should deviate from these values.

EXAMPLE 4   Forecasting the Equity Return Using the Grinold–Kroner Model

Cynthia Casey uses the Grinold–Kroner model in forecasting developed market equity returns. Casey makes the following forecasts:

- a 2.25% dividend yield on Canadian equities, based on the S&P/TSE Composite Index;
- a 1% rate of net share repurchases for Canadian equities;
- a long-term corporate earnings growth rate of 6% per year, based on a 1 percentage point (pp) premium for corporate earnings growth over her expected Canadian (nominal) GDP growth rate of 5%; and
- an expansion rate for P/E multiples of 0.25% per year.

1. Based on the information given, what expected rate of return on Canadian equities is implied by Casey's assumptions?
2. Are Casey's assumptions plausible for the long run and for a 10-year horizon?

Solution to 1: The expected rate of return on Canadian equities based on Casey's assumptions would be 9.5%, calculated as

$$E(R_e) \approx 2.25\% + [6.0\% - (-1.0\%)] + 0.25\% = 9.5\%.$$

Solution to 2: Casey's assumptions are not plausible for the very long run. The assumption that earnings will grow 1% faster than GDP implies one of two things:

either an ever-rising ratio of economy-wide earnings to GDP or the earnings accruing to businesses not included in the index (e.g., private firms) continually shrinking relative to GDP. Neither is likely to persist indefinitely. Similarly, perpetual share repurchases would eventually eliminate all shares, whereas a perpetually rising P/E would lead to an arbitrarily high price per Canadian dollar of earnings per share. Based on Casey's economic growth forecast, a more reasonable long-run expected return would be 7.25% = 2.25% + 5.0%.

Casey's assumptions are plausible for a 10-year horizon. Over 10 years, the ratio of earnings to GDP would rise by roughly $10.5\% = (1.01)^{10} - 1$, shares outstanding would shrink by roughly $9.6\% = 1 - (0.99)^{10}$, and the P/E would rise by about $2.5\% = (1.0025)^{10} - 1$.

Most of the inputs to the Grinold–Kroner model are fairly readily available. Economic growth forecasts can easily be found in investment research publications, reports from such agencies as the IMF, the World Bank, and the OECD, and likely from the analyst firm's own economists. Data on the rate of share repurchases are less straightforward but are likely to be tracked by sell-side firms and occasionally mentioned in research publications. The big question is how to gauge valuation of the market in order to project changes in the P/E.

The fundamental valuation metrics used in practice typically take the form of a ratio of price to some fundamental flow variable—such as earnings, cash flow, or sales—with seemingly endless variations in how the measures are defined and calculated. Whatever the metric, the implicit assumption is that it has a well-defined long-run mean value to which it will revert. In statistical terms, it is a stationary random variable. Extensive empirical evidence indicates that these valuation measures are poor predictors of short-term performance. Over multi-year horizons, however, there is a reasonably strong tendency for extreme values to be corrected. Thus, these metrics do provide guidance for projecting intermediate-term movements in valuation.

Gauging what is or is not an extreme value is complicated by the fact that all the fundamental flow variables as well as stock prices are heavily influenced by the business cycle. One method of dealing with this issue is to "cyclically adjust" the valuation measure. The most widely known metric is the cyclically adjusted P/E (CAPE). For this measure, the current price level is divided by the average level of earnings for the last 10 years (adjusted for inflation), rather than by the most current earnings. The idea is to average away cyclical variation in earnings and provide a more reliable base against which to assess the current market price.

4.3. Risk Premium Approaches to Equity Returns

The Grinold–Kroner model and similar models are sometimes said to reflect the "supply" of equity returns since they outline the sources of return. In contrast, risk premiums reflect "demand" for returns.

4.3.1. Defining and Forecasting the Equity Premium

The term "equity premium" is most frequently used to describe the amount by which the expected return on equities exceeds the riskless rate ("equity versus bills"). However, the same term is sometimes used to refer to the amount by which the expected return on equities exceeds the expected return on default-free bonds ("equity versus bonds"). From the discussion of fixed-income building blocks in Section 3, we know that the difference between these two definitions is the term premium built into the expected return on default-free bonds. The equity-versus-bonds premium reflects an incremental/building block approach to developing expected equity returns, whereas the equity-versus-bills premium reflects a single composite premium for the risk of equity investment.

Exhibit 5 shows historical averages for both of these equity premium concepts by country for the period 1900–2017.[14] For each country, the bottom portion of the column is the realized term premium (i.e., bonds minus bills) and the top segment is the realized equity-versus-bonds premium. The whole column represents the equity-versus-bills premium. The equity-versus-bills premiums range from 3.0% to 6.3%, the equity-versus-bonds premiums range from 1.8% to 5.2%, and the term premiums range from −0.6% to 2.9%.

EXHIBIT 5   Historical Equity Premiums by Country, 1900–2017

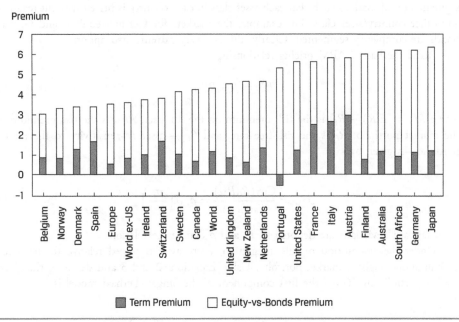

Notes: Germany excludes 1922–1923. Austria excludes 1921–1922. Returns are shown in percentages.
Source: Dimson et al. (2018, Chapter 2, Tables 8 and 9).

As with the mean equity returns in Exhibit 3, these historical premiums are subject to substantial estimation error. Statistically, there is no meaningful difference among them. Thus, the long-run cross section of returns/premiums provides virtually no reliable information with which to differentiate among countries.

---

[14]These premiums reflect geometric returns. Therefore, the equity-vs-bills premium is the sum of the term premium and the equity-vs-bonds premium. Premiums using arithmetic returns are systematically higher and are not additive.

Since equity returns are much more volatile than returns on either bills or bonds, forecasting either definition of the equity premium is just as difficult as projecting the absolute level of equity returns. That is, simply shifting to focus on risk premiums provides little, if any, specific insight with which to improve forecasts. The analyst must, therefore, use the other modes of analysis discussed here to forecast equity returns/premiums.

4.3.2. An Equilibrium Approach

There are various global/international extensions of the familiar capital asset pricing model (CAPM). We will discuss a version proposed by Singer and Terhaar (1997) that is intended to capture the impact of incomplete integration of global markets.

The Singer–Terhaar model is actually a combination of two underlying CAPM models. The first assumes that all global markets and asset classes are fully integrated. The full integration assumption allows the use of a single global market portfolio to determine equity-versus-bills risk premiums for all assets. The second underlying CAPM assumes complete segmentation of markets such that each asset class in each country is priced without regard to any other country/asset class. For example, the markets for German equities and German bonds are completely segmented. Clearly, this is a very extreme assumption.

Recall the basic CAPM pricing relationship:

$$RP_i = \beta_{i,M}RP_M \tag{2}$$

where $RP_i = [E(R_i) - R_F]$ is the risk premium on the ith asset, RP_M is the risk premium on the market portfolio, R_F is the risk-free rate, and $\beta_{i,M}$—asset i's sensitivity to the market portfolio—is given by

$$\beta_{i,M} = \frac{\text{Cov}(R_i,R_M)}{\text{Var}(R_M)} = \rho_{i,M}\left(\frac{\sigma_i}{\sigma_M}\right) \tag{3}$$

Standard deviations are denoted by σ, and ρ denotes correlation.

Under the assumption of full integration, every asset is priced relative to the global capitalization-weighted market portfolio. Using Equations 2 and 3 and denoting the global market portfolio by "GM," the first component of the Singer–Terhaar model is

$$RP_i^G = \beta_{i,GM}RP_{GM} = \rho_{i,GM}\sigma_i\left(\frac{RP_{GM}}{\sigma_{GM}}\right) \tag{4}$$

A superscript "G" has been added on the asset's risk premium to indicate that it reflects the global equilibrium. The term in parentheses on the far right is the Sharpe ratio for the global market portfolio, the risk premium per unit of global market risk.

Now consider the case of completely segmented markets. In this case, the risk premium for each asset will be determined in isolation without regard to other markets or opportunities for diversification. The risk premium will be whatever is required to induce investors with access to that market/asset to hold the existing supply. In terms of the CAPM framework, this implies treating each asset as its own "market portfolio." Formally, we can simply set β equal to 1 and ρ equal to 1 in the previous equations since each asset is perfectly correlated with itself. Using a superscript "S" to denote the segmented market equilibrium and replacing the global market portfolio with asset i itself in Equation 4, the segmented market equilibrium risk premium for asset i is

$$RP_i^S = 1 \times RP_i^S = 1 \times \sigma_i \left(\frac{RP_i^S}{\sigma_i} \right) \tag{5}$$

This is the second component of the Singer–Terhaar model. Note that the first equality in Equation 5 is an identity; it conveys no information. It reflects the fact that in a completely segmented market, the required risk premium could take any value. The second equality is more useful because it breaks the risk premium into two parts: the risk of the asset (σ_i) and the Sharpe ratio (i.e., compensation per unit of risk) in the segmented market.[15]

The final Singer–Terhaar risk premium estimate for asset i is a weighted average of the two component estimates

$$RP_i = \varphi RP_i^G + (1 - \varphi)RP_i^S \tag{6}$$

To implement the model, the analyst must supply values for the Sharpe ratios in the globally integrated market and the asset's segmented market; the degree to which the asset is globally integrated, denoted by φ; the asset's volatility; and the asset's β with respect to the global market portfolio. A pragmatic approach to specifying the Sharpe ratios for each asset under complete segmentation is to assume that compensation for non-diversifiable risk (i.e., "market risk") is the same in every market. That is, assume all the Sharpe ratios equal the global Sharpe ratio.

In practice, the analyst must make a judgment about the degree of integration/ segmentation—that is, the value of φ in the Singer–Terhaar model. With that in mind, some representative values that can serve as starting points for refinement can be helpful. Developed market equities and bonds are highly integrated, so a range of 0.75–0.90 would be reasonable for φ. Emerging markets are noticeably less integrated, especially during stressful periods, and there are likely to be greater differences among these markets, so a range of 0.50–0.75 would be reasonable for emerging market equities and bonds. Real estate market integration is increasing but remains far behind developed market financial assets, perhaps on par with emerging market stocks and bonds overall. In general, relative real estate market integration is likely to reflect the relative integration of the associated financial markets. Commodities for which there are actively traded, high-volume futures contracts should be on the higher end of the integration scale.

To illustrate the Singer–Terhaar model, suppose that an investor has developed the following projections for German shares and bonds.

	German Shares	German Bonds
Volatility (σ_i)	17.0%	7.0%
Correlation with global market ($\rho_{i,M}$)	0.70	0.50
Degree of integration (φ)	0.85	0.85
Segmented market Sharpe ratio (RP_i^S / σ_i)	0.35	0.25

---

[15] A somewhat more complex model would allow for integration of asset classes within each country. Doing so would entail incorporating local market portfolios and allowing assets to be less than perfectly correlated with those portfolios. Equation (5) would then look exactly like equation (4) with the local segmented market portfolio replacing the global market portfolio ("GM").

The risk-free rate is 3.0%, and the investor's estimate of the global Sharpe ratio is 0.30. Note that the investor expects compensation for undiversifiable risk to be higher in the German stock market and lower in the German bond market under full segmentation. The following are the fully integrated risk premiums for each of the assets (from Equation 4):

Equities: $0.70 \times 17.0\% \times 0.30 = 3.57\%$

Bonds: $0.50 \times 7.0\% \times 0.30 = 1.05\%$

The following are the fully segmented risk premiums (from Equation 5):

Equities: $17.0\% \times 0.35 = 5.95\%$

Bonds: $7.0\% \times 0.25 = 1.75\%$

Based on 85% integration ($\varphi = 0.85$), the final risk estimates (from Equation 6) would be as follows:

Equities: $(0.85 \times 3.57\%) + (1 - 0.85) \times 5.95\% = 3.93\%$

Bonds: $(0.85 \times 1.05\%) + (1 - 0.85) \times 1.75\% = 1.16\%$

Adding in the risk-free rate, the expected returns for German shares and bonds would be 6.93% and 4.16%, respectively.

Virtually all equilibrium models implicitly assume perfectly liquid markets. Thus, the analyst should assess the actual liquidity of each asset class and add appropriate liquidity premiums. Although market segmentation and market liquidity are conceptually distinct, in practice they are likely to be related. Highly integrated markets are likely to be relatively liquid, and illiquidity is one reason that a market may remain segmented.

EXAMPLE 5   Using the Singer–Terhaar Model

Stacy Adkins believes the equity market in one of the emerging markets that she models has become more fully integrated with the global market. As a result, she expects it to be more highly correlated with the global market. However, she thinks its overall volatility will decline. Her old and new estimates are as follows:

	Previous Data	New Data
Volatility (σ_i)	22.0%	18.0%
Correlation with global market ($\rho_{i,M}$)	0.50	0.70
Degree of integration (φ)	0.55	0.75
Sharpe ratio (global and segmented markets)	0.30	0.30

If she uses the Singer–Terhaar model, what will the net impact of these changes be on her risk premium estimate for this market?

> *Solution:* The segmented market risk premium will decline from 6.6% (calculated as
> 22.0% × 0.30 = 6.6%) to 5.4% (= 18% × 0.30). The fully integrated risk premium
> will increase from 3.30% (= 0.50 × 22.0% × 0.30) to 3.78% (= 0.70 × 18.0% ×
> 0.30). The weighted average premium will decline from 4.79% [= (0.55 × 3.30%) +
> (0.45 × 6.60%)] to 4.19% [= (0.75 × 3.78%) + (0.25 × 5.40%)], so the net effect is
> a decline of 60 bps.

4.4. Risks in Emerging Market Equities

Most of the issues underlying the risks of emerging market (and "frontier market" if they are classified as such) bonds also present risks for emerging market equities: more fragile economies, less stable political and policy frameworks, and weaker legal protections. However, the risks take somewhat different forms because of the different nature of equity and debt claims. Again, note that emerging markets are a very heterogeneous group. The political, legal, and economic issues that are often associated with emerging markets may not, in fact, apply to a particular market or country being analyzed.

There has been a debate about the relative importance of "country" versus "industry" risk factors in global equity markets for over 40 years. The empirical evidence has been summarized quite accurately as "vast and contradictory."[16] Both matter, but on the whole, country effects still tend to be more important than (global) industry effects. This is particularly true for emerging markets. Emerging markets are generally less fully integrated into the global economy and the global markets. Hence, local economic and market factors exert greater influence on risk and return in these markets than in developed markets.

Political, legal, and regulatory weaknesses—in the form of weak standards and/or weak enforcement—affect emerging market equity investors in various ways. The standards of corporate governance may allow interested parties to manipulate the capital structure of companies and to misuse business assets. Accounting standards may allow management and other insiders to hide or misstate important information. Weak disclosure rules may also impede transparency and favor insiders. Inadequate property rights laws, lack of enforcement, and weak checks and balances on governmental actions may permit seizure of property, nationalization of companies, and prejudicial and unpredictable regulatory actions.

Whereas the emerging market debt investor needs to focus on ability and willingness to pay specific obligations, emerging market equity investors need to focus on the many ways that the value of their ownership claims might be expropriated by the government, corporate insiders, or dominant shareholders.

EXAMPLE 6   Emerging Market Equity Risks

Bill Dwight has been discussing investment opportunities in Belvia with his colleague, Peter Valt (see Example 3). He is aware that Valt declined to buy the recently issued government bond, but he believes the country's equities may be attractive. He notes the rapid growth, substantial investment spending, free trade agreement, deregulation, and strong capital inflows as factors favoring a strong equity market. In addition, solid

---

[16]Marcelo, Quirós, and Martins (2013).

global growth has been boosting demand for Belvia's natural resources. Roughly half of the public equity market is represented by companies in the natural resources sector. The other half is a reasonably diversified mix of other industries. Many of these firms remain closely held, having floated a minority stake on the local exchange in the last few years. Listed firms are required to have published two years of financial statements conforming to standards set by the Belvia Public Accounting Board, which is made up of the heads of the three largest domestic accounting firms. With the help of a local broker, Dwight has identified a diversified basket of stocks that he intends to buy.

Discuss the risks Dwight might be overlooking.

Guideline answer:

Dwight might be overlooking several risks. He is almost certainly underestimating the vulnerability of the local economy and the vulnerability of the equity market to local developments. The economy's rapid growth is being driven by a large and growing fiscal deficit, in particular, rapidly rising redistributive social payments, and investment spending financed by foreign capital. Appreciation of the currency has made industries other than natural resources less competitive, so the free trade agreement provides little support for the economy. When the government is forced to tighten fiscal policy or capital flows shrink, the domestic economy is likely to be hit hard. Political risk is also a concern. A return to the prior regime is likely to result in a less pro-growth, less business-friendly environment, which would most likely result in attempts by foreign investors to repatriate their capital. Dwight should also have serious concerns about corporate governance, given that most listed companies are closely held, with dominant shareholders posing expropriation risk. He should also be concerned about transparency (e.g., limited history available) and accounting standards (local standards set by the auditing firms themselves).

5. FORECASTING REAL ESTATE RETURNS

Real estate is inherently quite different from equities, bonds, and cash. It is a physical asset rather than a financial asset. It is heterogeneous, indivisible, and immobile. It is a factor of production, like capital equipment and labor, and as such, it directly produces a return in the form of services. Its services can be sold but can be used/consumed only in one location. Owning and operating real estate involves operating and maintenance costs. All these factors contribute to making real estate illiquid and costly to transfer. The characteristics just described apply to direct investment in real estate (raw land, which does not produce income, is an exception). We will address the investment characteristics of equity REITs versus direct real estate, but unless otherwise stated, the focus is on directly held, unlevered, income-producing real estate.

5.1. Historical Real Estate Returns

The heterogeneity, indivisibility, immobility, and illiquidity of real estate pose a severe problem for historical analysis. Properties trade infrequently, so there is virtually no chance of getting a sequence of simultaneous, periodic (say, quarterly) transaction prices for a cross section of properties. Real estate owners/investors must rely heavily on appraisals, rather than transactions, in valuing properties. Owing to infrequent transactions and the heterogeneity of properties, these appraisals tend to reflect slowly moving averages of past market conditions. As a result, returns calculated from appraisals represent weighted averages of (unobservable) "true" returns—returns that would have been observed if there had been transaction prices— in previous periods. This averaging does not, in general, bias the mean return. It does, however, significantly distort estimates of volatility and correlations. The published return series is too smooth; that is, the usual sample volatility substantially understates the true volatility of returns. Meanwhile, by disguising the timing of response to market information, the smoothing tends to understate the strength of contemporaneous correlation with other market variables and spuriously induce a lead/lag structure of correlations.

In order to undertake any meaningful analysis of real estate as an asset class, the analyst must first deal with this data issue. It has become standard to "unsmooth" appraisal-based returns using a time-series model. Such techniques, which also apply to private equity funds, private debt funds, and hedge funds, are briefly described in a later section.

5.2. Real Estate Cycles

Real estate is subject to cycles that both drive and are driven by the business cycle. Real estate is a major factor of production in the economy. Virtually every business requires it. Every household consumes "housing services." Demand for the services provided by real estate rises and falls with the pace of economic activity. The supply of real estate is vast but essentially fixed at any point in time.[17] As a result, there is a strong cyclical pattern to property values, rents, and occupancy rates. The extent to which this pattern is observable depends on the type of real estate. As emphasized previously, changes in property values are obscured by the appraisal process, although indications can be gleaned from transactions as they occur. The extent to which actual rents and occupancy rates fully reflect the balance of supply and demand depends primarily on the type of property and the quality of the property. High-quality properties with long leases will tend to have little turnover, so fluctuations in actual rents and occupancy rates are likely to be relatively small. In contrast, demand for low-quality properties is likely to be more sensitive to the economy, leading to more substantial swings in occupancy and possibly rents as well. Properties with short leases will see rents adjust more completely to current supply/demand imbalances. Room rates and occupancy at low-quality hotels will tend to be the most volatile.

Fluctuations in the balance of supply and demand set up a classic boom–bust cycle in real estate. First, the boom: Perceptions of rising demand, property values, lease rates, and occupancy induce development of new properties. This investment spending helps drive and/or sustain economic activity, which, in turn, reinforces the perceived profitability of building new capacity. Then, the bust: Inevitably, optimistic projections lead to overbuilding and declining property values, lease rates, and occupancy. Since property has a very long life and is immobile, leases are typically for multiple years and staggered across tenants. In addition, since moving is costly for tenants, it may take many months or years for the excess supply to be absorbed.

A study by Clayton, Fabozzi, Gilberto, Gordon, Hudson-Wilson, Hughes, Liang, MacKinnon, and Mansour (2011) suggested that the US commercial real estate crash

---

[17]Yau, Schneeweis, Szado, Robinson, and Weiss (2018) found that real estate represents from one-third to as much as two-thirds of global wealth.

following the global financial crisis was the first to have been driven by the capital markets rather than by a boom–bust cycle in real estate fundamentals.[18] The catalyst was not overbuilding, Clayton et al. argued, but rather excess leverage and investment in more speculative types of properties. Consistent with that hypothesis, both the collapse in property prices and the subsequent recovery were unusually rapid. The authors attributed the accelerated response to underlying conditions to appraisers responding more vigorously to signals from the REIT and commercial mortgage-backed security markets. It remains to be seen whether this phenomenon will persist in less extreme circumstances.

5.3. Capitalization Rates

The capitalization (cap) rate, defined as net operating income (NOI) in the current period divided by the property value, is the standard valuation metric for commercial real estate. It is analogous to the earnings yield (E/P) for equities. It is not, strictly speaking, a cash flow yield because a portion of operating income may be reinvested in the property.[19] As with equities, an estimate of the long-run expected/required rate of return can be derived from this ratio by assuming a constant growth rate for NOI—that is, by applying the Gordon growth model.

$$E(R_{re}) = \text{Cap rate} + \text{NOI growth rate} \tag{7}$$

The long-run, steady-state NOI growth rate for commercial real estate as a whole should be reasonably close to the growth rate of GDP. The observation that over a 30-year period UK nominal rental income grew about 6.5% per annum, roughly 2.5% in real terms,[20] is consistent with this relationship.

Over finite horizons, it is appropriate to adjust this equation to reflect the anticipated rate of change in the cap rate.

$$E(R_{re}) = \text{Cap rate} + \text{NOI growth rate} - \%\Delta\text{Cap rate} \tag{8}$$

This equation is analogous to the Grinold–Kroner model for equities, except there is no term for share buybacks. The growth rate of NOI could, of course, be split into a real component and inflation.

Exhibit 6 shows private market cap rates as of March 2018 for US commercial properties differentiated by type, location, and quality. The rates range from 4.7% for offices in gateway cities, such as New York City, to 9.5% for skilled nursing (i.e., 24-hour old-age care) properties. There is a clear pattern of high cap rates for riskier property types (hotels versus apartments, skilled nursing facilities versus medical offices), lower-quality properties (low-productivity versus high-productivity malls), and less attractive locations (offices in secondary versus gateway cities).

---

[18]Data from the Investment Property Databank indicate that commercial property values dropped by 21.8% globally and US property values decreased by 33.2% in 2008–2009. Other countries suffered steep losses as well, notably Ireland (55.5%) and Spain (20.1%).

[19]Ilmanen (2012) indicated that the difference between cap rates and cash flow yields may be on the order of 3 percentage points. Although significant reinvestment of NOI reduces the cash flow yield, it should increase the growth rate of NOI if the investment is productive.

[20]Based on data from Investment Property Databank Limited.

EXHIBIT 6   Cap Rates (%) as of March 2018

Property Type	Average	Higher Risk	Lower Risk
Hotels	7.2	Limited Service 7.7	Full Service 7.1
Health Care	6.6	Skilled Nursing 9.5	Medical Office 5.7
Retail Malls	5.6	Low Productivity 8.8	High Productivity 5.0
Industrial	5.4		
Office	5.2	Secondary Cities 6.6	Gateway Cities 4.7
Apartments	4.8		

Source: CenterSquare Investment Management (2018). Gateway cities include Boston, Chicago, Los Angeles, New York City, San Francisco, and Washington, DC.

Retail properties provide a good example of the impact of competition on real estate. Brick-and-mortar stores have been under increasing competitive pressure from online retailers, such as Amazon. The pressure is especially intense for lower-productivity (less profitable) locations. As a result, cap rates for high- and low-productivity malls began to diverge even before the global financial crisis. In 2006, the difference in cap rates was 1.2 percentage points; by 2018, it was 3.2 percentage points.[21]

Cap rates reflect long-term discount rates. As such, we should expect them to rise and fall with the general level of long-term interest rates, which tends to make them pro-cyclical. However, they are also sensitive to credit spreads and the availability of credit. Peyton (2009) found that the spread between cap rates and the 10-year Treasury yield is positively related to the option-adjusted spread on three- to five-year B-rated corporate bonds and negatively related to ratios of household and non-financial-sector debt to GDP. The countercyclical nature of credit spreads mitigates the cyclicality of cap rates. The debt ratios are effectively proxies for the availability of debt financing for leveraged investment in real estate. Since real estate transactions typically involve substantial leverage, greater availability of debt financing is likely to translate into a lower required liquidity premium component of expected real estate returns. Not surprisingly, higher vacancy rates induce higher cap rates.

5.4. The Risk Premium Perspective on Real Estate Expected Return

As a very long-lived asset, real estate is quite sensitive to the level of long-term rates; that is, it has a high effective duration. Indeed, this is often the one and only characteristic mentioned in broad assessments of the likely performance of real estate as an asset class. Hence, real estate must earn a significant term premium. Income-earning properties are exposed to the credit risk of the tenants. In essence, a fixed-term lease with a stable stream of payments is like a corporate bond issued by the tenant secured with physical assets. The landlord must, therefore, demand a credit premium commensurate with what his or her average tenant would have to pay to issue such debt. Real estate must also earn a significant equity risk premium (relative to corporate debt) since the owner bears the full brunt of fluctuations in property values as well as uncertainty with respect to rent growth, lease rollover/termination,

---

[21]CenterSquare Investment Management (2018). These are cap rates implied by REIT pricing, which is why the 2018 differential does not exactly match the private market figures given in Exhibit 6.

and vacancies. The most volatile component of return arises, of course, from changes in property values. As noted previously, these values are strongly pro-cyclical, which implies the need for a significant equity risk premium. Combining the bond-like components (term premium plus credit premium) with a stock-like component implies a risk premium somewhere between those of corporate bonds and equities.

Liquidity is an especially important risk for direct real estate ownership. There are two main ways to view illiquidity. For publicly traded equities and bonds, the question is not whether one can sell the security quickly but, rather, at what price. For real estate, however, it may be better to think of illiquidity as a total inability to sell the asset except at randomly spaced points in time. From this perspective, the degree of liquidity depends on the average frequency of these trading opportunities. By adopting this perspective, one can ask how large the liquidity premium must be to induce investors to hold an asset with a given level of liquidity. Ang, Papanikolaou, and Westerfield (2014) analyzed this question. Their results suggest liquidity premiums on the order of 0.60% for quarterly average liquidity, 0.90% for annual liquidity, and 2%, 4%, and 6% for liquidity on average every 2, 5, and 10 years, respectively.[22] All things considered, a liquidity premium of 2%–4% would seem reasonable for commercial real estate.

5.5. Real Estate in Equilibrium

Real estate can be incorporated into an equilibrium framework (such as the Singer–Terhaar model). Indeed, doing so might be deemed a necessity given the importance of real estate in global wealth. There are, however, a few important considerations. First, the impact of smoothing must have been removed from the risk/return data and metrics used for real estate. Otherwise, inclusion of real estate will distort the results for all asset classes. Second, it is important to recognize the implicit assumption of fully liquid assets in equilibrium models. Adjusting the equilibrium for illiquidity—that is, adding a liquidity premium—is especially important for real estate and other private assets. Third, although real estate investors increasingly venture outside their home markets, real estate is still location specific and may, therefore, be more closely related to local, as opposed to global, economic/market factors than are financial claims.

5.6. Public vs. Private Real Estate

Many institutional investors and some ultra-wealthy individuals are able to assemble diversified portfolios of direct real estate holdings. Investors with smaller portfolios must typically choose between limited, undiversified direct real estate holdings or obtaining real estate exposure through financial instruments, such as REIT shares. Assessing whether these alternatives—direct real estate and REITs—have similar investment characteristics is difficult because of return smoothing, heterogeneity of properties, and variations in leverage.

A careful analysis of this issue requires (1) transaction-based returns for unlevered direct real estate holdings, (2) firm-by-firm deleveraging of REIT returns based on their individual balance sheets over time, and (3) carefully constructing direct real estate and REIT portfolios with matching property characteristics. Exhibit 7 shows the results of such an analysis.

---

[22]See Table 3 in Ang et al. (2014). The numbers cited here reflect an assumption of zero correlation between the investor's liquid and illiquid assets.

EXHIBIT 7   Direct Real Estate vs. REITs: Four Property Types, 1994–2012

	Mean Return (%)			Standard Deviation (%)		
	Direct Real Estate	REITs		Direct Real Estate	REITs	
		Unlevered	Levered		Unlevered	Levered
Aggregate	8.80	9.29		11.09	9.71	
Apartment	9.49	9.08	11.77	11.42	9.50	20.69
Office	8.43	9.37	10.49	10.97	10.58	23.78
Industrial	9.00	9.02	9.57	11.14	11.65	23.46
Retail	8.96	9.90	12.04	11.54	10.03	23.73

Source: Ling and Naranjo (2015, Table 1).

Deleveraging the REITs substantially reduces both their mean returns and their volatilities. The volatilities are roughly cut in half. Clearly, the deleveraged REIT returns are much more similar to the direct real estate returns than are the levered REIT returns. In the aggregate, REITs outperformed direct real estate by 49 bps per year with lower volatility. Looking at specific property types, REITs had higher returns and lower volatility in two categories—office and retail. Industrial REITs had essentially the same return as directly owned industrial properties but with higher volatility. Apartment REITs lagged the direct market but with significantly lower volatility.

Exhibit 7 certainly shows some interesting differences. The pattern of unlevered REIT returns by property type is not the same as for direct real estate. Retail REITs had the highest return, and industrial REITs had the lowest. Among directly owned properties, apartments had the highest return and offices the lowest. A similar mismatch appears with respect to volatilities.

Overall, this study tends to support the general conclusion reached by most comparisons: Public and private commercial real estate are different. The extent of the difference is less clear. It does appear that once we account for differences in leverage, REIT investors are not sacrificing performance to obtain the liquidity afforded by publicly traded shares. Perhaps REIT investors are able to capture a significant portion of the liquidity risk premium garnered by direct investors (because the REIT is a direct investor) as well as benefit from professional management.

What about the diversification benefits of real estate as an asset class? REITs are traded securities, and that fact shows up in their much higher short-term correlation with equities. In contrast, direct real estate is often touted as a good diversifier based on the notion that it is not very highly correlated with equities. As noted previously, the smoothed nature of most published real estate returns is a major contributor to the appearance of low correlation with financial assets, including with REITs. Once that is corrected, however, the correlation is higher, even over reasonably short horizons, such as a quarter or a year. Importantly, REITs are more highly correlated with direct real estate and less highly correlated with equities over multi-year horizons.[23] Thus, although REITs tend to act like "stocks" in the short run, they act like "real estate" in the longer run. From a strategic asset allocation perspective, REITs and direct real estate are more comparable than conventional metrics suggest.

---

[23]Stefek and Suryanarayanan (2012).

5.7. Long-Term Housing Returns

Savills World Research (2016) estimated that residential real estate accounts for 75% of the total value of developed properties globally. Most individuals' homes are their primary, perhaps only, real estate investment. A relatively new database provides a global perspective on the long-term performance of residential real estate (housing), equities, and bonds.[24] The database covers 145 years (1870–2015) and 16 countries.

Jordà, Knoll, Kuvshinov, Schularick, and Taylor (2017) found that residential real estate was the best performing asset class over the entire sample period, with a higher real return and much lower volatility than equities. However, performance characteristics differed before and after World War II:

• Residential real estate had a higher (lower) real return than equities before (after) World War II.
• Residential real estate had a higher real return than equities in every country except Switzerland, the United Kingdom, and the United States over 1950–1980 but a lower return than equities in every country for 1980–2015.
• Residential real estate and equities had similar patterns—that is, a strong correlation—prior to the war but a low correlation after the war.
• Equity returns became increasingly correlated across countries after the war, but residential real estate returns are essentially uncorrelated across countries.

Exhibit 8 shows the real returns for equities and residential real estate in each country since 1950.

EXHIBIT 8   Real Equity and Housing Returns by Country, 1950–2015

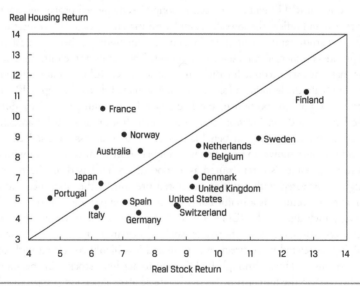

Note: Annual percentage returns are shown.
Source: Jordà et al. (2017).

---

[24]The database was developed for and is described in Jordà, Knoll, Kuvshinov, Schularick, and Taylor (2017).

EXAMPLE 7   Assessing Real Estate Investments

Tammi Sinclair, an analyst at a large retirement fund, recently attended investor presentations by three private real estate firms looking to fund new projects. Office Growth Partners specializes in building and owning low-cost, standardized office space for firms seeking to place sales representatives in the most rapidly growing small population areas across the region. Mega-Box Properties builds and owns large, custom-designed distribution facilities for multinational makers of brand-name products. The facilities are strategically located near major global transportation hubs. Exclusive Elegance Inc. develops and then manages some of the world's most luxurious, sought-after residential buildings in prime locations. It never breaks ground on a new property until at least 85% of the units have been sold and, to date, has never failed to sell out before construction is complete.

Identify important characteristics of each business that Sinclair will need to consider in establishing a required rate of return for each potential investment.

Guideline answer:
Office Growth Partners (OGP) is likely to be a very high-risk investment. It essentially chases hot markets, it builds generic office space, and its typical tenants (opportunistic sales forces) are apt to opt out as soon as the market cools. All these aspects suggest that its business is very exposed to a boom-and-bust cycle. It is likely to end up owning properties with persistently high vacancy rates and high turnover. Hence, Sinclair will likely require a rather high expected return on an investment in OGP.

Mega-Box's business should be fairly stable. The distribution centers are strategically located and designed to meet the needs of the tenant, which suggests long-term leases and low turnover will benefit both Mega-Box and the tenant firms. The average credit quality of the tenants—multinational makers of brand-name products—is likely to be solid and disciplined by the public bond and loan markets. All things considered, Sinclair should probably require a significantly lower expected return on an investment in Mega-Box than in OGP.

Exclusive Elegance appears to be even lower risk. First, it deals only in the very highest-quality, most sought-after properties in prime locations. These should be relatively immune to cyclical fluctuations. Second, it does not retain ownership of the properties, so it does not bear the equity/ownership risks. Third, it is fairly conservative in the riskiest portion of its business—developing new properties. However, Sinclair will need to investigate its record with respect to completing development projects within budget, maintaining properties, and delivering top-quality service to residents.

6. FORECASTING EXCHANGE RATES

Forecasting exchange rates is generally acknowledged to be especially difficult—so difficult that many asset managers either passively accept the impact of currency movements on their portfolio returns or routinely hedge out the currency exposure even if doing so is costly.

To get a sense for why exchange rates are so difficult to forecast, it is useful to distinguish between "money" and the currency in which it is denominated. Like equities and bonds, money is an asset denominated in a currency. Currencies are the units of account in which the prices of everything else—goods, services, real assets, financial assets, liabilities, flows, and balances—are quoted. An exchange rate movement changes the values of everything denominated in one currency relative to everything denominated in every other currency. That is a very powerful force. It works in the other direction as well. Anything that affects quantities, prices, or values within one currency relative to those in another will exert some degree of pressure on exchange rates. Perhaps even more importantly, anything that changes *expectations* of prices, quantities, or values within any currency can change expectations about the future path of currencies, causing an immediate reaction in exchange rates as people adjust their exposures.

Of course, currencies are not abstract accounting ledgers. They are inherently tied to governments, financial systems, legal systems, and geographies. The laws, regulations, customs, and conventions within and between these systems also influence exchange rates, especially when exchange rates are used as instruments or targets of policy. The consequence of all these aspects is that there is very little firm ground on which to stand for analysts trying to forecast exchange rates. The best we can hope to do is to identify the forces that are likely to be exerting the most powerful influences and assess their relative strength. On a related note, it is not possible to identify mutually exclusive approaches to exchange rate forecasting that are each complete enough to stand alone. Hence, the perspectives discussed in this section should be viewed as complementary rather than as alternatives.

6.1. Focus on Goods and Services, Trade, and the Current Account

There are three primary ways in which trade in goods and services can influence the exchange rate. The first is directly through flows. The second is through quasi-arbitrage of prices. The third is through competitiveness and sustainability.

6.1.1. Trade Flows
Trade flows do not, in general, exert a significant impact on contemporaneous exchange rate movements, provided they can be financed. Although gross trade flows may be large, net flows (exports minus imports) are typically much smaller relative to the economy and relative to actual and potential financial flows. If trade-related flows through the foreign exchange market become large relative to financing/investment flows, it is likely that a crisis is emerging.

6.1.2. Purchasing Power Parity
Purchasing power parity (PPP) is based on the notion that the prices of goods and services should change at the same rate regardless of currency denomination.[25] Thus, *the expected percentage change in the exchange rate should be equal to the difference in expected inflation rates.*

---

[25]This version of PPP is usually referred to as "relative PPP" to distinguish it from a stricter notion called "absolute PPP." Absolute PPP is an important concept but is not useful for practical forecasting. See previous CFA Program currency chapters for a broader discussion of PPP concepts.

If we define the *real exchange rate* as the ratio of price levels converted to a common currency, then PPP says that *the expected change in the real exchange rate should be zero.*

The mechanism underlying PPP is a quasi-arbitrage. Free and competitive trade should force alignment of the prices of similar products after conversion to a common currency. This is a very powerful force. It works, but it is slow and incomplete. As a result, the evidence indicates that PPP is a poor predictor of exchange rates over short to intermediate horizons but is a better guide to currency movements over progressively longer multi-year horizons.[26]

There are numerous reasons for deviations from PPP. The starting point matters. Relative PPP implicitly assumes that prices and exchange rates are already well aligned. If not, it will take time before the PPP relationship re-emerges. Not all goods are traded, and virtually every country imposes some trade barriers. PPP completely ignores the impact of capital flows, which often exert much more acute pressure on exchange rates over significant periods of time. Finally, economic developments may necessitate changes in the country's terms of trade; that is, contrary to PPP, the real exchange rate may need to change over time.

The impact of relative purchasing power on exchange rates tends to be most evident when inflation differentials are large, persistent, and driven primarily by monetary conditions. Under these conditions, PPP may describe exchange rate movements reasonably well over all but the shortest horizons. Indeed, the well-known "monetary approach" to exchange rates essentially boils down to two assumptions: (1) PPP holds, and (2) inflation is determined by the money supply.

6.1.3. Competitiveness and Sustainability of the Current Account

It is axiomatic that in the absence of capital flows prices, quantities, and exchange rates would have to adjust so that trade is always balanced. Since the prices of goods and services, production levels, and spending decisions tend to adjust only gradually, the onus of adjustment would fall primarily on exchange rates. Allowing for capital flows mitigates this pressure on exchange rates. The fact remains, however, that imposition of restrictions on capital flows will increase the sensitivity of exchange rates to the trade balance or, more generally, the current account balance.[27] This is not usually a major consideration for large, developed economies with sophisticated financial markets but can be important in small or developing economies.

Aside from the issue of restrictions on capital mobility, the extent to which the current account balance influences the exchange rate depends primarily on whether it is likely to be persistent and, if so, whether it can be sustained. These issues, in turn, depend mainly on the size of the imbalance and its source. Small current account balances—say, less than 2% of GDP—are likely to be sustainable for many years and hence would exert little influence on exchange rates. Similarly, larger imbalances that are expected to be transitory may not generate a significant, lasting impact on currencies.

The current account balance equals the difference between national saving and investment.[28] A current account surplus indicates that household saving plus business profits and the government surplus/deficit exceeds domestic investment spending. A current account

---

[26]See, for example, Abuaf and Jorion (1990); Exhibit 2 in "Currency Exchange Rates: Understanding Equilibrium Value" provides a useful visual illustration of PPP over different horizons.

[27]The Mundell–Fleming model of monetary and fiscal policy effects on the exchange rate with high/low capital mobility provides an important illustration of this point. See the CFA Program chapter "Currency Exchange Rates: Understanding Equilibrium Value."

[28]See Chapter 4 of Piros and Pinto (2013) for discussion of balance of payments accounting.

deficit reflects the opposite. A current account deficit that reflects strong, profitable investment spending is more likely to be sustainable than a deficit reflecting high household spending (low saving), low business profits, or substantial government deficits because it is likely to attract the required capital inflow for as long as attractive investment opportunities persist. A large current account surplus may not be very sustainable either because it poses a sustainability problem for deficit countries or because the surplus country becomes unwilling to maintain such a high level of aggregate saving.

Whether an imbalance is likely to persist in the absence of terms-of-trade adjustments largely depends on whether the imbalance is structural. Structural imbalances arise from (1) persistent fiscal imbalances; (2) preferences, demographics, and institutional characteristics affecting saving decisions; (3) abundance or lack of important resources; (4) availability/ absence of profitable investment opportunities associated with growth, capital deepening, and innovation; and, of course, (5) the prevailing terms of trade. Temporary imbalances mainly arise from business cycles (at home and abroad) and associated policy actions.

If a change in the (nominal) exchange rate is to bring about a necessary change in the current account balance, it will have to induce changes in spending patterns, consumption/ saving decisions, and production/investment decisions. These adjustments typically occur slowly and are often resisted by decision makers who hope they can be avoided. Rapid adjustment of the exchange rate may also be resisted because people only gradually adjust their expectations of its ultimate level. Hence, both the exchange rate and current account adjustments are likely to be gradual.

6.2. Focus on Capital Flows

Since the current account and the capital account must always balance and the drivers of the current account tend to adjust only gradually, virtually all of the short-term adjustment and much of the intermediate-term adjustment must occur in the capital account. Asset prices, interest rates, and exchange rates are all part of the equilibrating mechanism. Since a change in the exchange rate simultaneously affects the relative values of all assets denominated in different currencies, we should expect significant pressure to be exerted on the exchange rate whenever an adjustment of capital flows is required.

6.2.1. Implications of Capital Mobility

Capital seeks the highest risk-adjusted expected return. The investments available in each currency can be viewed as a portfolio. Designating one as domestic (d) and one as foreign (f), in a world of perfect capital mobility the exchange rate (expressed as domestic currency per foreign currency unit) will be driven to the point at which the expected percentage change in the exchange rate equals the "excess" risk-adjusted expected return on the domestic portfolio over the foreign portfolio. This idea can be expressed concretely using a building block approach to expected returns.

$$E(\%\Delta S_{d/f}) = (r^d - r^f) + (\text{Term}^d - \text{Term}^f) + (\text{Credit}^d - \text{Credit}^f) \\ + (\text{Equity}^d - \text{Equity}^f) + (\text{Liquid}^d - \text{Liquid}^f) \qquad (9)$$

The expected change in the exchange rate ($\%\Delta S_{d/f}$) will reflect the differences in the nominal short-term interest rates (r), term premiums (Term), credit premiums (Credit), equity premiums (Equity), and liquidity premiums (Liquid) in the two markets.

The components of this equation can be associated with the expected return on various segments of the portfolio: the money market (first term), government bonds (first and second), corporate bonds (first–third), publicly traded equities (first–fourth), and private assets (all terms), including direct investment in plant and equipment.

As an example, suppose the domestic market has a 1% higher short-term rate, a 0.25% lower term premium, a 0.50% higher credit premium, and the same equity and liquidity premiums as the foreign market. Equation 9 implies that the domestic currency must be expected to depreciate by 1.25% (= 1% − 0.25% + 0.5%)—that is, $E(\%\Delta S_{d/f}) = 1.25\%$—to equalize risk-adjusted expected returns.

It may seem counterintuitive that the domestic currency should be expected to depreciate if its portfolio offers a higher risk-adjusted expected return. The puzzle is resolved by the key phrase "driven to the point . . . " in this subsection's opening paragraph. In theory, the exchange rate will instantly move ("jump") to a level where the currency with higher (lower) risk-adjusted expected return will be so strong (weak) that it will be expected to depreciate (appreciate) going forward. This is known as the *overshooting* mechanism, introduced by Dornbusch (1976). In reality, the move will not be instantaneous, but it may occur very quickly if there is a consensus about the relative attractiveness of assets denominated in each currency. Of course, asset prices will also be adjusting.

The overshooting mechanism suggests that there are likely to be three phases in response to relative improvement in investment opportunities. First, the exchange rate will appreciate ($S_{d/f}$ will decline) as capital flows toward the more attractive market. The more vigorous the flow, the faster and greater the appreciation of the domestic currency and the more the flow will also drive up asset prices in that market. Second, in the intermediate term, there will be a period of consolidation as investors begin to question the extended level of the exchange rate and to form expectations of a reversal. Third, in the longer run, there will be a retracement of some or all of the exchange rate move depending on the extent to which underlying opportunities have been equalized by asset price adjustments. This is the phase that is reflected in Equation 9.

Importantly, these three phases imply that the relationship between currency appreciation/depreciation and apparent investment incentives will not always be in the same direction. This fact is especially important with respect to interest rate differentials since they are directly observable. At some times, higher interest rate currencies appreciate; at other times, they depreciate.

6.2.2. Uncovered Interest Rate Parity and Hot Money Flows

Uncovered interest rate parity (UIP) asserts that the expected percentage change in the exchange rate should be equal to the nominal interest rate differential. That is, only the first term in Equation 9 matters. The implicit assumption is that the response to short-term interest rate differentials will be so strong that it overwhelms all other considerations.

Contrary to UIP, the empirical evidence consistently shows that *carry trades*—borrowing in low-rate currencies and lending in high-rate currencies—earn meaningful profits on average. For example, Burnside, Eichenbaum, Kleshchelski, and Rebelo (2011) found that from February 1976 to July 2009, a strategy of rolling carry trades involving portfolios of high- and low-rate currencies returned 4.31% per annum after transaction costs versus the US dollar and 2.88% per annum versus the British pound.

The profitability of carry trades is usually ascribed to a risk premium, which is clearly consistent with the idea that the risk premiums in Equation 9 matter. The empirical results may also be capturing primarily the overshooting phase of the response to interest rate differentials. In any case, carry trades tend to be profitable on average, and UIP does not hold up well as a predictor of exchange rates.

Vigorous flows of capital in response to interest rate differentials are often referred to as *hot money flows*. Hot money flows are problematic for central banks. First, they limit the central bank's ability to run an effective monetary policy. This is the key message of the Mundell–Fleming model with respect to monetary policy in economies characterized by the free flow of capital. Second, a flood of readily available short-term financing may encourage firms to fund longer-term needs with short-term money, setting the stage for a crisis when the financing dries up. Third, the nearly inevitable overshooting of the exchange rate is likely to disrupt non-financial businesses. These issues are generally most acute for emerging markets since their economies and financial markets tend to be more fragile. Central banks often try to combat hot money flows by intervening in the currency market to offset the exchange rate impact of the flows. They may also attempt to *sterilize* the impact on domestic liquidity by selling government securities to limit the growth of bank reserves or maintain a target level of interest rates. If the hot money is flowing *out* rather than *in*, the central bank would do the opposite: sell foreign currency (thereby draining domestic liquidity) to limit/avoid depreciation of the domestic currency and buy government securities (thereby providing liquidity) to sterilize the impact on bank reserves and interest rates. In either case, if intervention is not effective or sufficient, capital controls may be imposed.

6.2.3. Portfolio Balance, Portfolio Composition, and Sustainability Issues

The earlier discussion on the implications of capital mobility implicitly introduced a portfolio balance perspective. Each country/currency has a unique portfolio of assets that makes up part of the global "market portfolio." Exchange rates provide an across-the-board mechanism for adjusting the relative sizes of these portfolios to match investors' desire to hold them. We will look at this from three angles: tactical allocations, strategic/secular allocations, and the implications of wealth transfer.

The relative sizes of different currency portfolios within the global market portfolio do not, in general, change significantly over short to intermediate horizons. Hence, investors do not need to be induced to make changes in their long-term allocations. However, they are likely to want to make tactical allocation changes in response to evolving opportunities— notably, those related to the relative strength of various economies and related policy measures. Overall, capital is likely to flow into the currencies of countries in the strongest phases of the business cycle. The attraction should be especially strong if the economic expansion is led by robust investment in real, productive assets (e.g., plant and equipment) since that can be expected to generate a new stream of long-run profits.

In the long run, the relative size of each currency portfolio depends primarily on relative trend growth rates and current account balances. Rapid economic growth is almost certain to be accompanied by an expanding share of the global market portfolio being denominated in the associated currency. Thus, investors will have to be induced to increase their strategic allocations to assets in that country/currency. All else the same, this would tend to weaken that currency—partially offsetting the increase in the currency's share of the global portfolio—and upward pressure on risk premiums in that market. However, there are several mitigating factors.

- *With growth comes wealth accumulation:* The share of global wealth owned by domestic investors will be rising along with the supply of assets denominated in their currency. Since investors generally exhibit a strong *home country bias* for domestic assets, domestic investors are likely to willingly absorb a large portion of the newly created assets.
- *Productivity-driven growth:* If high growth reflects strong productivity gains, both foreign and domestic investors are likely to willingly fund it with both financial flows and foreign direct investment.
- *Small initial weight in global portfolios:* Countries with exceptionally high trend growth rates are typically relatively small, have previously restricted foreign access to their local-currency financial markets, and/or have previously funded external deficits in major currencies (not their own). Almost by definition, these are emerging and frontier markets. Any of these factors would suggest greater capacity to increase the share of local-currency-denominated assets in global portfolios without undermining the currency.

Large, persistent current account deficits funded in local currency will also put downward pressure on the exchange rate over time as investors are required to shift strategic allocations toward that currency. Again, there are mitigating considerations.

- *The source of the deficit matters:* As discussed previously, current account deficits arising from strong investment spending are relatively easy to finance as long as they are expected to be sufficiently profitable. Deficits due to a low saving rate or weak fiscal discipline are much more problematic.
- *Special status of reserve currencies:* A few currencies—notably, the US dollar—have a special status because the bulk of official reserves are held in these currencies, the associated sovereign debt issuer is viewed as a safe haven, major commodities (e.g., oil) are priced in these currencies, and international trade transactions are often settled in them. A small current account deficit in a reserve-currency country is welcome because it helps provide liquidity to the global financial system. Historically, however, reserve currency status has not proven to be permanent.

Current account surpluses/deficits reflect a transfer of wealth from the deficit country to the surplus country. In an ideal world of fully integrated markets, perfect capital mobility, homogeneous expectations, and identical preferences,[29] a transfer of wealth would have virtually no impact on asset prices or exchange rates because everyone would be happy with the same portfolio composition. This is not the case in practice. To pick just one example, as long as investors have a home country bias, the transfer of wealth will increase the demand for the current-account-surplus country's assets and currency and decrease demand for those of the deficit country.

Does the composition of a particular currency's portfolio matter? A look back at Equation 9 suggests that it should matter to some degree. For the most part, however, we would expect asset price adjustments (changes in interest rates and risk premiums) to eliminate most of the pressure that might otherwise be exerted on the exchange rate. Nonetheless, some types of flows and holdings are often considered to be more or less supportive of the currency. Foreign direct investment flows are generally considered to be the most favorable because they indicate a long-term commitment and they contribute directly to the productivity/profitability of the economy. Similarly, investments in private real estate and private equity represent long-term capital committed to the market, although

---

[29]Note that these are essentially the assumptions underlying the standard CAPM.

they may or may not represent the creation of new real assets. Public equity would likely be considered the next most supportive of the currency. Although it is less permanent than private investments, it is still a residual claim on the profitability of the economy that does not have to be repaid. Debt has to be serviced and must either be repaid or refinanced, potentially triggering a crisis. Hence, a high and rising ratio of debt to GDP gives rise to *debt sustainability* concerns with respect to the economy. This issue could apply to private sector debt. But it is usually associated with fiscal deficits because the government is typically the largest single borrower; typically borrows to fund consumption and transfers, rather than productive investment; and may be borrowing in excess of what can be serviced without a significant increase in taxes. Finally, as noted previously with respect to hot money flows, large or rapid accumulation of short-term borrowing is usually viewed as a clear warning sign for the currency.

EXAMPLE 8   Currency Forecasts

After many years of running moderately high current account deficits (2%–4% of GDP) but doing little infrastructure investment, Atlandia plans to increase the yearly government deficit by 3% of GDP and maintain that level of deficit for the next 20 years, devoting the increase to infrastructure spending. The deficits will be financed with local-currency government debt. Pete Stevens, CFA, is faced with the task of assessing the impact of this announcement on the Atlandian currency. After talking with members of the economics department at his firm, he has established the following baseline assumptions:

- All else the same, current account deficits will persistently exceed 6% of GDP while the program is in place. Setting aside any lasting impact of the policy/spending, the current account deficit will then fall back to 3% of GDP provided the economy has remained competitive.
- Pressure on wages will boost inflation to 1.5% above the global inflation rate. Because of limitations on factor substitutability, costs in the traded good sector will rise disproportionately.
- Expectations of faster growth will raise the equity premium.
- The central bank will likely tighten policy—that is, raise rates.

Questions:
1. What would purchasing power parity imply about the exchange rate?
2. What are the implications for competitiveness for the currency?
3. What is the likely short-term impact of capital flows on the exchange rate?
4. What does the overshooting mechanism imply about the path of the exchange rate over time? How does this fit with the answers to Questions 1–3?
5. What does a sustainability perspective imply?

Solutions:
1. Purchasing power parity would imply that the Atlandian currency will depreciate by 1.5% per year. The exchange rate, quoted in domestic (Atlandian) units per foreign unit as in Equation 9, will rise by a factor of $1.015^{10} = 1.1605$,

corresponding to a 13.83% ($= 1 - 1/1.1605$) decline in the value of the domestic currency.[30]

2. Since costs in the traded sector will rise faster than inflation, the exchange rate would need to depreciate faster than PPP implies in order to maintain competitiveness. Thus, to remain competitive and re-establish a 3% current account deficit after 10 years, the *real* exchange rate needs to depreciate.

3. Both the increase in short-term rates and the increase in the equity premium are likely to induce strong short-term capital inflows even before the current account deficit actually increases. This should put significant pressure on the Atlandian currency to appreciate (i.e., the $S_{d/f}$ exchange rate will decline if the Atlandian currency is defined as the domestic currency). The initial impact may be offset to some extent by flows out of government bonds as investors push yields up in anticipation of increasing supply, but as bonds are repriced to offer a higher expected return (a higher term premium), it will reinforce the upward pressure on the exchange rate.

4. The overshooting mechanism would imply that the initial appreciation of the Atlandian currency discussed previously will extend to a level from which the currency is then expected to depreciate at a pace that equalizes risk-adjusted expected returns across markets and maintains equality between the current and capital accounts. The initial appreciation of the currency in this scenario is clearly inconsistent with PPP, but the subsequent longer-term depreciation phase (from a stronger level) is likely to bring the exchange rate into reasonable alignment with PPP and competitiveness considerations in the long run.

5. It is highly unlikely that a current account deficit in excess of 6% of GDP is sustainable for 10 years. It would entail an increase in net foreign liabilities equaling 60% ($= 6\% \times 10$) of GDP. Servicing that additional obligation would add, say, 2%–3% of GDP to the current account deficit forever. Adding that to the baseline projection of 3% would mean that the current account deficit would remain in the 5%–6% range even after the infrastructure spending ended, so net foreign liabilities would still be accumulating rapidly. Closing that gap will require a very large increase in net national saving: 5%–6% of annual GDP *in addition to* the 3% reduction in infrastructure spending when the program ends. Standard macroeconomic analysis implies that such an adjustment would require some combination of a very deep recession and a very large depreciation in the real value of the Atlandian currency (i.e., the real $S_{d/f}$ exchange rate must increase sharply). As soon as investors recognize this, a crisis is almost certain to occur. Bond yields would increase sharply, and equity prices and the currency will fall substantially.

---

[30]Note that a slightly different number is obtained if the 1.5% rate is applied directly to the foreign currency value of the Atlandian currency (i.e., the exchange rate expressed as foreign units per domestic unit). That calculation would give a cumulative depreciation of 14.03% ($= 1 - 0.985^{10}$). The difference arises because ($1/1.015$) is not exactly equal to 0.985.

7. FORECASTING VOLATILITY

In some applications, the analyst is concerned with forecasting the variance for only a single asset. More often, however, the analyst needs to forecast the variance–covariance matrix for several, perhaps many, assets in order to analyze the risk of portfolios. Estimating a single variance that is believed to be constant is straightforward: The familiar sample variance is unbiased and its precision can be enhanced by using higher-frequency data. The analyst's task becomes more complicated if the variance is not believed to be constant or the analyst needs to forecast a variance–covariance (VCV) matrix. These issues are addressed in this section. In addition, we elaborate on de-smoothing real estate and other returns.

7.1. Estimating a Constant VCV Matrix with Sample Statistics

The simplest and most heavily used method for estimating constant variances and covariances is to use the corresponding sample statistic—variance or covariance—computed from historical return data. These elements are then assembled into a VCV matrix. There are two main problems with this method, both related to sample size. First, given the short to intermediate sample periods typical in finance, the method cannot be used to estimate the VCV matrix for large numbers of assets. If the number of assets exceeds the number of historical observations, then some portfolios will erroneously appear to be riskless. Second, given typical sample sizes, this method is subject to substantial sampling error. A useful rule of thumb that addresses both of these issues is that the number of observations should be at least 10 times the number of assets in order for the sample VCV matrix to be deemed reliable. In addition, since each element is estimated without regard to any of the others, this method does not address the issue of imposing cross-sectional consistency.

7.2. VCV Matrices from Multi-Factor Models

Factor models have become the standard method of imposing structure on the VCV matrix of asset returns. From this perspective, their main advantage is that the number of assets can be very large relative to the number of observations. The key to making this work is that the covariances are fully determined by exposures to a small number of common factors whereas each variance includes an asset-specific component.

In a model with K common factors, the return on the ith asset is given by

$$r_i = \alpha_i + \sum_{k=1}^{K} \beta_{ik} F_k + \varepsilon_i \tag{10}$$

where α_i is a constant intercept, β_{ik} is the asset's sensitivity to the kth factor, F_k is the kth common factor return, and ε_i is a stochastic term with a mean of zero that is unique to the ith asset. In general, the factors will be correlated. Given the model, the variance of the ith asset is

$$\sigma_i^2 = \sum_{m=1}^{K} \sum_{n=1}^{K} \beta_{im} \beta_{in} \rho_{mn} + v_i^2 \tag{11}$$

where ρ_{mn} is the covariance between the *m*th and *n*th factors and v_i^2 is the variance of the unique component of the *i*th asset's return. The covariance between the *i*th and *j*th assets is

$$\sigma_{ij} = \sum_{m=1}^{K} \sum_{n=1}^{K} \beta_{im} \beta_{jn} \rho_{mn} \tag{12}$$

As long as none of the factors are redundant and none of the asset returns are completely determined by the factors (so $v_i^2 \neq 0$), there will not be any portfolios that erroneously appear to be riskless. That is, we will not encounter the first problem mentioned in Section 7.1, with respect to using sample statistics.

Imposing structure with a factor model makes the VCV matrix much simpler. With *N* assets, there are $[N(N-1)/2]$ distinct covariance elements in the VCV matrix. For example, if $N = 100$, there are 4,950 distinct covariances to be estimated. The factor model reduces this problem to estimating $[N \times K]$ factor sensitivities plus $[K(K+1)/2]$ elements of the factor VCV matrix, Ω. With $N = 100$ and $K = 5$, this would mean "only" 500 sensitivities and 15 elements of the factor VCV matrix—almost a 90% reduction in items to estimate. (Of course, we also need to estimate the asset-specific variance terms, v_i^2, in order to get the *N* variances, σ_i^2.) If the factors are chosen well, the factor-based VCV matrix will contain substantially less estimation error than the sample VCV matrix does.

A well-specified factor model can also improve cross-sectional consistency. To illustrate, suppose we somehow know that the true covariance of any asset *i* with any asset *j* is proportional to asset *i*'s covariance with any third asset, *k*, so

$$\frac{\sigma_{ij}}{\sigma_{ik}} = \text{Constant} \tag{13}$$

for any assets *i*, *j*, and *k*. We would want our estimates to come as close as possible to satisfying this relationship. Sample covariances computed from any given sample of returns will not, in general, do so. However, using Equation 12 with only one factor (i.e., $K = 1$) shows that the covariances from a single-factor model will satisfy

$$\frac{\sigma_{ij}}{\sigma_{ik}} = \frac{\beta_j}{\beta_k} \tag{14}$$

for all assets *i*, *j*, and *k*. Thus, in this simple example, a single-factor model imposes exactly the right cross-sectional structure.

The benefits obtained by imposing a factor structure—handling large numbers of assets, a reduced number of parameters to be estimated, imposition of cross-sectional structure, and a potentially substantial reduction of estimation error—come at a cost. In contrast to the simple example just discussed, in general, the factor model will almost certainly be mis-specified. The structure it imposes will not be exactly right. As a result, the factor-based VCV matrix is *biased*; that is, the expected value is not equal to the true (unobservable) VCV matrix of the returns. To put it differently, the matrix is not correct even "on average." The matrix is also *inconsistent*; that is, it does not converge to the true matrix as the sample size gets arbitrarily large. In contrast, the sample VCV matrix is unbiased and consistent. Thus, when we use a factor-based matrix instead of the sample VCV matrix, we are choosing to estimate something that is "not quite right" with relative precision rather than the "right thing" with a lot of noise. The point is that although factor models are very useful, they are not a panacea.

7.3. Shrinkage Estimation of VCV Matrices

As with shrinkage estimation in general, the idea here is to combine the information in the sample data, the sample VCV matrix, with an alternative estimate, the target VCV matrix—which reflects assumed "prior" knowledge of the structure of the true VCV matrix—and thereby mitigate the impact of estimation error on the final matrix. Each element (variance or covariance) of the final shrinkage estimate of the VCV matrix is simply a weighted average of the corresponding elements of the sample VCV matrix and the target VCV matrix. The same weights are used for all elements of the matrix. The analyst must determine how much weight to put on the target matrix (the "prior" knowledge) and how much weight to put on the sample data (the sample VCV matrix).

Aside from a technical condition that rules out the appearance of riskless portfolios, virtually any choice of target VCV matrix will increase (or at least not decrease) the efficiency of the estimates versus the sample VCV matrix. "Efficiency" in this context means a smaller mean-squared error (MSE), which is equal to an estimator's variance plus the square of its bias. Although the shrinkage estimator is biased, its MSE will in general be smaller than the MSE of the (unbiased) sample VCV matrix. The more plausible (and presumably less biased) the selected target matrix, the greater the improvement will be. A factor-model-based VCV matrix would be a reasonable candidate for the target.

EXAMPLE 9   Estimating the VCV Matrix

Isa Berkitz is an analyst at Barnsby & Culp (B&C), a recently formed multi-family office. Berkitz has been asked to propose the method for estimating the variance–covariance matrix to be used in B&C's asset allocation process for all clients. After examining the existing client portfolios and talking with the clients and portfolio managers, Berkitz concludes that in order to support B&C's strategic and tactical allocation needs, the VCV matrix will need to include 25 asset classes. For many of these classes, she will be able to obtain less than 10 years of monthly return data. Berkitz has decided to incorporate both the sample statistics and factor-model approaches using shrinkage estimation.

Explain the strengths and weaknesses of the two basic approaches and why Berkitz would choose to combine them using the shrinkage framework.

Solution: The VCV matrix based on sample statistics is correct on average (it is unbiased) and convergences to the true VCV matrix as the sample size gets arbitrarily large (it is "consistent"). The sample VCV method cannot be used if the number of assets exceeds the number of observations, which is not an issue in this case. However, it is subject to large sampling errors unless the number of observations is large relative to the number of assets. A 10-to-1 rule of thumb would suggest that Berkitz needs more than 250 observations (20+ years of monthly data) in order for the sample VCV matrix to give her reliable estimates, but she has at most 120 observations. In addition, the sample VCV matrix does not impose any cross-sectional consistency on the estimates. A factor-model-based VCV matrix can be used even if the number of assets exceeds the number of observations. It can substantially reduce the number of unique parameters to be estimated, it imposes cross-sectional structure, and it can substantially reduce estimation errors. However, unless the structure imposed by the factor model is exactly correct, the VCV matrix will not be correct on average (it will be biased). Shrinkage estimation—a weighted average of the sample VCV and factor-based VCV matrices—will increase (or at least not decrease) the efficiency of the estimates. In effect, the shrinkage estimator captures the benefits of each underlying methodology and mitigates their respective limitations.

7.4. Estimating Volatility from Smoothed Returns

The available return data for such asset classes as private real estate, private equity, and hedge funds generally reflect smoothing of unobservable underlying "true" returns. The smoothing dampens the volatility of the observed data and distorts correlations with other assets. Thus, the raw data tend to understate the risk and overstate the diversification benefits of these asset classes. Failure to adjust for the impact of smoothing will almost certainly lead to distorted portfolio analysis and hence poor asset allocation decisions.

The basic idea is that the observed returns are a weighted average of current and past true, unobservable returns. One of the simplest and most widely used models implies that the current observed return, R_t, is a weighted average of the current true return, r_t, and the previous observed return:

$$R_t = (1 - \lambda)r_t + \lambda R_{t-1} \tag{15}$$

where $0 < \lambda < 1$. From this equation, it can be shown that

$$\text{var}(r) = \left(\frac{1+\lambda}{1-\lambda}\right)\text{var}(R) > \text{var}(R) \tag{16}$$

As an example, if $\lambda = 0.8$, then the true variance, $\text{var}(r)$, of the asset is 9 times the variance of the observed data. Equivalently, the standard deviation is 3 times larger.

This model cannot be estimated directly because the true return, r_t, is not observable. To get around this problem, the analyst assumes a relationship between the unobservable return and one or more observable variables. For private real estate, a natural choice might be a REIT index, whereas for private equity, an index of similar publicly traded equities could be used.

EXAMPLE 10   Estimating Volatility from Smoothed Data

While developing the VCV matrix for B&C, Isa Berkitz noted that the volatilities for several asset classes—notably, real estate and private equity categories—calculated directly from available return data appear to be very low. The data are from reputable sources, but Berkitz is skeptical because similar publicly traded classes—for example, REITs and small-cap equities—exhibit much higher volatilities. What is the likely cause of the issue?

Guideline answer:
The very low volatilities are very likely due to smoothing within the reported private asset returns. That is, the observed data reflect a weighted average of current and past true returns. For real estate, this smoothing arises primarily because the underlying property values used to calculate "current" returns are based primarily on backward-looking appraisals rather than concurrent transactions.

7.5. Time-Varying Volatility: ARCH Models

The discussion up to this point has focused on estimating variances and covariances under the assumption that their true values do not change over time. It is well known, however, that financial asset returns tend to exhibit **volatility clustering**, evidenced by periods of high and low volatility. A class of models known collectively as autoregressive conditional heteroskedasticity (ARCH) models has been developed to address these time-varying volatilities.[31]

One of the simplest and most heavily used forms of this broad class of models specifies that the variance in period t is given by

$$\sigma_t^2 = \gamma + \alpha\sigma_{t-1}^2 + \beta\eta_t^2$$
$$= \gamma + (\alpha + \beta)\sigma_{t-1}^2 + \beta(\eta_t^2 - \sigma_{t-1}^2) \tag{17}$$

where α, β, and γ are non-negative parameters such that $(\alpha + \beta) < 1$. The term η_t is the unexpected component of return in period t; that is, it is a random variable with a mean of zero conditional on information at time $(t - 1)$. Rearranging the equation as in the second line shows that $(\eta_t^2 - \sigma_{t-1}^2)$ can be interpreted as the "shock" to the variance in period t. Thus, the variance in period t depends on the variance in period $(t - 1)$ plus a shock. The parameter β controls how much of the current "shock" feeds into the variance. In the extreme, if $\beta = 0$, then variance would be deterministic. The quantity $(\alpha + \beta)$ determines the extent to which the variance in future periods is influenced by the current level of volatility. The higher $(\alpha + \beta)$ is, the more the variance "remembers" what happened in the past and the more it "clusters" at high or low levels. The unconditional expected value of the variance is $[\gamma/(1 - \alpha - \beta)]$.

As an example, assume that $\gamma = 0.000002$, $\alpha = 0.9$, and $\beta = 0.08$ and that we are estimating daily equity volatility. Given these parameters, the unconditional expected value of the variance is 0.0001, implying that the daily standard deviation is 1% (0.01). Suppose the estimated variance at time $(t - 1)$ was 0.0004 $(= 0.02^2)$ and the return in period t was 3% above expectations $(\eta_t = 0.03)$. Then the variance in period t would be

$$\sigma_t^2 = 0.000002 + (0.9 \times 0.0004) + (0.08 \times 0.03^2) = 0.000434,$$

which is equivalent to a standard deviation of 2.0833%. Without the shock to the variance (i.e., with $\eta_t^2 = \sigma_{t-1}^2 = 0.0004$), the standard deviation would have been 1.9849%. Even without the shock, the volatility would have remained well above its long-run mean of 1.0%.

---

[31]Chapter 12 of Campbell, Lo, and MacKinlay (1997) provides an excellent, detailed explanation of these models. The present discussion draws on that book.

Including the shock, the volatility actually increased. Note that the impact on volatility would have been the same if the return had been 3% *below* expectations rather than above expectations.

The ARCH methodology can be extended to multiple assets—that is, to estimation of a VCV matrix. The most straightforward extensions tend to be limited to only a few assets since the number of parameters rises very rapidly. However, Engle (2002) developed a class of models with the potential to handle large matrices with relatively few parameters.

EXAMPLE 11   ARCH

Sam Akai has noticed that daily returns for a variety of asset classes tend to exhibit periods of high and low volatility but the volatility does seem to revert toward a fairly stable average level over time. Many market participants capture this tendency by estimating volatilities using a 60-day moving window. Akai notes that this method implicitly assumes volatility is constant within each 60-day window but somehow not constant from one day to the next. He has heard that ARCH models can explicitly incorporate time variation and capture the observed clustering pattern.

Explain the models to him.

Guideline answer:
The key idea is to model variance as a linear time-series process in which the current volatility depends on its own recent history or recent shocks. The shocks to volatility arise from unexpectedly large or small returns. In one of the simplest ARCH models, the current variance depends only on the variance in the previous period and the unexpected component of the current return (squared). Provided the coefficients are positive and not "too large," the variance will exhibit the properties Akai has observed: periods of time at high/low levels relative to a well-defined average level.

---

8. ADJUSTING A GLOBAL PORTFOLIO

The coverage of capital market expectations has provided an intensive examination of topics with which analysts need to be familiar in order to establish capital market expectations for client portfolios. This section brings some of this material together to illustrate how analysts can develop and justify recommendations for adjusting a portfolio. The discussion that follows is selective in the range of assets and scenarios it considers. It focuses on connecting expectations to the portfolio and is about "direction of change" rather than the details of specific forecasts.

8.1. Macro-Based Recommendations

Suppose we start with a fairly generic portfolio of global equities and bonds (we assume no other asset classes are included or considered) and we are asked to recommend changes based primarily on macroeconomic considerations. Further assume that the portfolio reflects a reasonable strategic allocation for our clients. Hence, we do not need to make any wholesale changes and can focus on incremental improvements based on assessment of current opportunities. To be specific, we limit our potential recommendations to the following:

- Change the overall allocations to equities and bonds.
- Reallocate equities/bonds between countries.
- Adjust the average credit quality of our bond portfolios.
- Adjust duration and positioning on the yield curves.
- Adjust our exposures to currencies.

To approach the task systematically, we begin with a checklist of questions.

1. Have there been significant changes in the drivers of trend growth, globally or in particular countries?
2. Are any of the markets becoming more/less globally integrated?
3. Where does each country stand within its business cycle? Are they synchronized?
4. Are monetary and fiscal policies consistent with long-term stability and the phases of the business cycle?
5. Are current account balances trending and sustainable?
6. Are any currencies under pressure to adjust or trending? Have capital flows driven any currencies to extended levels? Have any of the economies become uncompetitive/super-competitive because of currency movements?

There are certainly many more questions we could ask. In practice, the analyst will need to look into the details. But these questions suffice for our illustration. We will examine each in turn. It must be noted, however, that they are inherently interrelated.

8.1.1. Trend Growth

All else the same, an increase in trend growth favors equities because it implies more rapid long-run earnings growth. Faster growth due to productivity is especially beneficial. In contrast, higher trend growth generally results in somewhat higher real interest rates, a negative for currently outstanding bonds. Identifiable changes in trend growth that have not already been fully factored into asset prices are most likely to have arisen from a shock (e.g., new technology). A global change would provide a basis for adjusting the overall equity/bond allocation. Country-specific or regional changes provide a basis for reallocation within equities toward the markets experiencing enhanced growth prospects that have not already been reflected in market prices.

8.1.2. Global Integration

All else the same, the Singer–Terhaar model implies that when a market becomes more globally integrated, its required return should decline. As prices adjust to a lower required return, the market should deliver an even higher return than was previously expected or required by the market. Therefore, expected increases in integration provide a rationale for adjusting allocations toward those markets and reductions in markets that are already highly integrated. Doing so will typically entail a shift from developed markets to emerging markets.

8.1.3. Phases of the Business Cycle

The best time to buy equities is generally when the economy is approaching the trough of the business cycle. Valuation multiples and expected earnings growth rates are low and set to rise. The Grinold–Kroner model could be used to formalize a recommendation to buy equities. At this stage of the cycle, the term premium is high (the yield curve is steep) and the credit premium is high (credit spreads are wide). However, (short-term) interest rates are likely to start rising soon and the yield curve can be expected to flatten again as the economy gains strength. All else the same, the overall allocation to bonds will need to be reduced to facilitate the increased allocation to equities. Within the bond portfolio, overall duration should be reduced, positions with intermediate maturities should be reduced in favor of shorter maturities (and perhaps a small amount of longer maturities) to establish a "barbell" posture with the desired duration, and exposure to credit should be increased (a "down in quality" trade). The opposite recommendations would apply when the analyst judges that the economy is at or near the peak of the cycle.

To the extent that business cycles are synchronized across markets, this same prescription would apply to the overall portfolio. It is likely, however, that some markets will be out of phase—leading or lagging other markets—by enough to warrant reallocations between markets. In this case, the recommendation would be to reallocate equities from (to) markets nearest the peak (trough) of their respective cycles and to do the opposite within the bond portfolio with corresponding adjustments to duration, yield curve positioning, and credit exposure within each market.

8.1.4. Monetary and Fiscal Policies

Investors devote substantial energy dissecting every nuance of monetary and fiscal policy. If policymakers are doing what we would expect them to be doing at any particular stage of the business cycle—for example, moderate countercyclical actions and attending to longer-term objectives, such as controlling inflation and maintaining fiscal discipline—their activities may already be reflected in asset prices. In addition, the analyst should have factored expected policy actions into the assessment of trend growth and business cycles.

Significant opportunities to add value by reallocating the portfolio are more likely to arise from structural policy changes (e.g., a shift from interest rate targeting to money growth targeting, quantitative easing, and restructuring of the tax code) or evidence that the response to policy measures is not within the range of outcomes that policymakers would have expected (e.g., if massive quantitative easing induced little inflation response). Structural policy changes are clearly intentional and the impact on the economy and the markets is likely to be consistent with standard macroeconomic analysis, so the investment recommendations will follow from the implications for growth trends and business cycles. Almost by definition, standard modes of analysis may be ineffective if policy measures have not induced the expected responses. In this case, the analyst's challenge is to determine what, why, and how underlying linkages have changed and identify the value-added opportunities.

8.1.5. Current Account Balances

Current account balances ultimately reflect national saving and investment decisions, including the fiscal budget. Current accounts must, of course, net out across countries. In the short run, this is brought about in large measure by the fact that household saving and corporate profits (business saving) are effectively residuals whereas consumption and capital expenditures are more explicitly planned. Hence, purely cyclical fluctuations in the current account are just part of the business cycle. Longer-term trends in the current account require adjustments to induce deliberate changes in saving/investment decisions. A rising current account deficit will tend to put upward pressure on real required returns (downward pressure on asset prices) in order to induce a higher saving rate in the deficit country (to mitigate the widening deficit) and to attract the increased flow of capital from abroad required to fund the deficit. An expanding current account surplus will, in general, require the opposite in order to reduce "excess" saving. This suggests that the analyst should consider reallocation of portfolio assets from countries with secularly rising current account deficits to those with secularly rising current account surpluses (or narrowing deficits).

8.1.6. Capital Accounts and Currencies

Setting aside very high inflation situations in which purchasing power parity may be important even in the short term, currencies are primarily influenced by capital flows. When investors perceive that the portfolio of assets denominated in a particular currency offers a higher risk-adjusted expected return than is available in other currencies, the initial surge of capital tends to drive the exchange rate higher, often to a level from which it is more likely to depreciate rather than continue to appreciate. At that point, the underlying assets may remain attractive in their native currency but not in conjunction with the currency exposure. An analyst recommending reallocation of a portfolio toward assets denominated in a particular currency must, therefore, assess whether the attractiveness of the assets has already caused an "overshoot" in the currency or whether a case can be made that there is meaningful appreciation yet to come. In the former case, the analyst needs to consider whether the assets remain attractive after taking account of the cost of currency hedging.

There is one final question that needs to be addressed for all asset classes and currencies. The previous discussion alluded to it, but it is important enough to be asked directly: *What is already reflected in asset prices?* There is no avoiding the fact that valuations matter.

8.2. Quantifying the Views

Although the analyst may not be required to quantify the views underlying his or her recommendations, we can very briefly sketch a process that may be used for some of the tools discussed in earlier sections.

Step 1: Use appropriate techniques to estimate the VCV matrix for all asset classes.

Step 2: Use the Singer–Terhaar model and the estimated VCV matrix to determine equilibrium expected returns for all asset classes.

Step 3: Use the Grinold–Kroner model to estimate returns for equity markets based on assessments of economic growth, earnings growth, valuation multiples, dividends, and net share repurchases.

Step 4: Use the building block approach to estimate expected returns for bond classes based primarily on cyclical and policy considerations.

Step 5: Establish directional views on currencies relative to the portfolio's base currency based on the perceived attractiveness of assets and the likelihood of having overshot sustainable levels. Set modest rates of expected appreciation/depreciation.

Step 6: Incorporate a currency component into expected returns for equities and bonds.

Step 7: Use the Black–Litterman framework (described in a later chapter) to combine equilibrium expected returns from Step 2 with the expected returns determined in Steps 3–6.

SUMMARY

The following are the main points covered in the chapter.

- The choice among forecasting techniques is effectively a choice of the information on which forecasts will be conditioned and how that information will be incorporated into the forecasts.
- The formal forecasting tools most commonly used in forecasting capital market returns fall into three broad categories: statistical methods, discounted cash flow models, and risk premium models.
- Sample statistics, especially the sample mean, are subject to substantial estimation error.
- Shrinkage estimation combines two estimates (or sets of estimates) into a more precise estimate.
- Time-series estimators, which explicitly incorporate dynamics, may summarize historical data well without providing insight into the underlying drivers of forecasts.
- Discounted cash flow models are used to estimate the required return implied by an asset's current price.
- The risk premium approach expresses expected return as the sum of the risk-free rate of interest and one or more risk premiums.
- There are three methods for modeling risk premiums: equilibrium models, such as the CAPM; factor models; and building blocks.
- The DCF method is the only one that is precise enough to use in support of trades involving individual fixed-income securities.
- There are three main methods for developing expected returns for fixed-income asset classes: DCF, building blocks, and inclusion in an equilibrium model.
- As a forecast of bond return, YTM, the most commonly quoted metric, can be improved by incorporating the impact of yield changes on reinvestment of cash flows and valuation at the investment horizon.
- The building blocks for fixed-income expected returns are the short-term default-free rate, the term premium, the credit premium, and the liquidity premium.
- Term premiums are roughly proportional to duration, whereas credit premiums tend to be larger at the short end of the curve.
- Both term premiums and credit premiums are positively related to the slope of the yield curve.
- Credit spreads reflect both the credit premium (i.e., additional expected return) and expected losses due to default.
- A baseline estimate of the liquidity premium can be based on the yield spread between the highest-quality issuer in a market (usually the sovereign) and the next highest-quality large issuer (often a government agency).
- Emerging market debt exposes investors to heightened risk with respect to both ability to pay and willingness to pay, which can be associated with the economy and political/legal weaknesses, respectively.

- The Grinold–Kroner model decomposes the expected return on equities into three components: (1) expected cash flow return, composed of the dividend yield minus the rate of change in shares outstanding, (2) expected return due to nominal earnings growth, and (3) expected repricing return, reflecting the rate of change in the P/E.
- Forecasting the equity premium directly is just as difficult as projecting the absolute level of equity returns, so the building block approach provides little, if any, specific insight with which to improve equity return forecasts.
- The Singer–Terhaar version of the international capital asset pricing model combines a global CAPM equilibrium that assumes full market integration with expected returns for each asset class based on complete segmentation.
- Emerging market equities expose investors to the same underlying risks as emerging market debt does: more fragile economies, less stable political and policy frameworks, and weaker legal protections.
- Emerging market investors need to pay particular attention to the ways in which the value of their ownership claims might be expropriated. Among the areas of concern are standards of corporate governance, accounting and disclosure standards, property rights laws, and checks and balances on governmental actions.
- Historical return data for real estate is subject to substantial smoothing, which biases standard volatility estimates downward and distorts correlations with other asset classes. Meaningful analysis of real estate as an asset class requires explicit handling of this data issue.
- Real estate is subject to boom–bust cycles that both drive and are driven by the business cycle.
- The cap rate, defined as net operating income in the current period divided by the property value, is the standard valuation metric for commercial real estate.
- A model similar to the Grinold–Kroner model can be applied to estimate the expected return on real estate:

$$E(R_{re}) = \text{Cap rate} + \text{NOI growth rate} - \%\Delta\text{Cap rate}$$

- There is a clear pattern of higher cap rates for riskier property types, lower-quality properties, and less attractive locations.
- Real estate expected returns contain all the standard building block risk premiums:
  - Term premium: As a very long-lived asset with relatively stable cash flows, income-producing real estate has a high duration.
  - Credit premium: A fixed-term lease is like a corporate bond issued by the leaseholder and secured by the property.
  - Equity premium: Owners bear the risk of property value fluctuations, as well as risk associated with rent growth, lease renewal, and vacancies.
  - Liquidity premium: Real estate trades infrequently and is costly to transact.

- Currency exchange rates are especially difficult to forecast because they are tied to governments, financial systems, legal systems, and geographies. Forecasting exchange rates requires identification and assessment of the forces that are likely to exert the most influence.
- Provided they can be financed, trade flows do not usually exert a significant impact on exchange rates. International capital flows are typically larger and more volatile than trade-financing flows.

- PPP is a poor predictor of exchange rate movements over short to intermediate horizons but is a better guide to currency movements over progressively longer multi-year horizons.
- The extent to which the current account balance influences the exchange rate depends primarily on whether it is likely to be persistent and, if so, whether it can be sustained.
- Capital seeks the highest risk-adjusted expected return. In a world of perfect capital mobility, in the long run, the exchange rate will be driven to the point at which the expected percentage change equals the "excess" risk-adjusted expected return on the portfolio of assets denominated in the domestic currency over that of the portfolio of assets denominated in the foreign currency. However, in the short run, there can be an exchange rate overshoot in the opposite direction as hot money chases higher returns.
- Carry trades are profitable on average, which is contrary to the predictions of uncovered interest rate parity.
- Each country/currency has a unique portfolio of assets that makes up part of the global "market portfolio." Exchange rates provide an across-the-board mechanism for adjusting the relative sizes of these portfolios to match investors' desire to hold them.
- The portfolio balance perspective implies that exchange rates adjust in response to changes in the relative sizes and compositions of the aggregate portfolios denominated in each currency.
- The sample variance–covariance matrix is an unbiased estimate of the true VCV structure; that is, it will be correct on average.
- There are two main problems with using the sample VCV matrix as an estimate/forecast of the true VCV matrix: It cannot be used for large numbers of asset classes, and it is subject to substantial sampling error.
- Linear factor models impose structure on the VCV matrix that allows them to handle very large numbers of asset classes. The drawback is that the VCV matrix is biased and inconsistent unless the assumed structure is true.
- Shrinkage estimation of the VCV matrix is a weighted average of the sample VCV matrix and a target VCV matrix that reflects assumed "prior" knowledge of the true VCV structure.
- Failure to adjust for the impact of smoothing in observed return data for real estate and other private assets will almost certainly lead to distorted portfolio analysis and hence poor asset allocation decisions.
- Financial asset returns exhibit volatility clustering, evidenced by periods of high and low volatilities. ARCH models were developed to address these time-varying volatilities.
- One of the simplest and most used ARCH models represents today's variance as a linear combination of yesterday's variance and a new "shock" to volatility. With appropriate parameter values, the model exhibits the volatility clustering characteristic of financial asset returns.

REFERENCES

Abuaf, Niso, and Philippe Jorion. 1990. "Purchasing Power Parity in the Long Run." *Journal of Finance* (March): 157–74.

Ang, Andrew, Dimitris Papanikolaou, and Mark M. Westerfield. 2014. "Portfolio Choice with Illiquid Assets." *Management Science* 6 (11).

Burnside, Craig, Martin Eichenbaum, Isaac Kleshchelski, and Sergio Rebelo. 2011. "Do Peso Problems Explain the Returns to the Carry Trade?" *Review of Financial Studies* 24 (3): 853–91.

Campbell, John Y., Andrew W. Lo, and A. Craig MacKinlay. 1997. *The Econometrics of Financial Markets*. Princeton, NJ: Princeton University Press.

CenterSquare Investment Management Plc. 2018. "The REIT Cap Rate Perspective" (March). www.centersquare.com/documents/20182/32181/March+2018_CenterSquare+REIT+Cap+Rate+Perspective/0f802c79-00bd-4e18-8655-98ca90a87e63. Accessed January 2019.

Clayton, Jim, Frank J. Fabozzi, S. Michael Gilberto, Jacques N. Gordon, Susan Hudson-Wilson, William Hughes, Youguo Liang, Greg MacKinnon, and Asieh Mansour. 2011. "The Changing Face of Real Estate Investment Management." Special Real Estate Issue *Journal of Portfolio Management*: 12–23.

Cochrane, John H, and Monika Piazzesi. 2005. "Bond Risk Premia." *American Economic Review* (March): 138–60.

Dimson, Elroy, Paul Marsh, and Mike Staunton. 2002. *Triumph of the Optimists*. Princeton, NJ: Princeton University Press.

Dimson, Elroy, Paul Marsh, and Mike Staunton. 2018. *Credit Suisse Global Investment Returns Yearbook 2018*. Zurich: Credit Suisse Research Institute.

Dornbusch, R. Dec 1976. "Expectations and Exchange Rate Dynamics." *Journal of Political Economy* 84 (6): 1161–76.

Engle, Robert. 2002. "Dynamic Conditional Correlation: A Simple Class of Multivariate Generalized Autoregressive Conditional Heteroskedasticity Models." *Journal of Business & Economic Statistics* (July): 339–50.

Giesecke, Kay, Francis A. Longstaff, Stephen Schaefer, and Ilya Strebulaev. 2011. "Corporate Bond Default Risk: A 150-Year Perspective." *Journal of Financial Economics* 102 (2): 233–50.

Grinold, Richard, and Ken Kroner. 2002. "The Equity Risk Premium: Analyzing the Long-Run Prospects for the Stock Market." *InvestmentInsights* 5 (3).

Ilmanen, Antti. 2012. *Expected Returns on Major Asset Classes*. Charlottesville, VA: Research Foundation of CFA Institute.

Jarrow, Robert A., and Donald R. van Deventer. 2015. "Credit Analysis Models." In *Fixed Income Analysis*, 3rd ed. CFA Institute Investment Series/Wiley.

Jordà, Òscar, Katharina Knoll, Dmitry Kuvshinov, Moritz Schularick, and Alan M. Taylor. 2017. "The Rate of Return on Everything, 1870–2015." NBER Working Paper No. 24112 (December).

Kim, Don H., and Jonathan H. Wright. 2005. "An Arbitrage-Free Three-Factor Term Structure Model and the Recent Behavior of Long-Term Yields and Distant-Horizon Forward Rates." Federal Reserve Board Working Paper 2005-33 (August).

Ling, David C., and Andy Naranjo. 2015. "Returns and Information Transmission Dynamics in Public and Private Real Estate Markets." *Real Estate Economics* 43 (1): 163–208.

Marcelo, José Luis Miralles, Luis Miralles Quirós José, and José Luís Martins. 2013. "The Role of Country and Industry Factors during Volatile Times." *Journal of International Financial Markets, Institutions and Money* 26 (October): 273–90.

Peyton, Martha S. 2009. "Capital Markets Impact on Commercial Real Estate Cap Rates: A Practitioner's View." Special Real Estate Issue *Journal of Portfolio Management* 38–49.

Piros, Christopher D. 2015. "Strategic Asset Allocation: Plus ça change, plus c'est la meme chose." *Investments & Wealth Monitor* (March/April): 5–8.

Piros, Christopher D., and Jerald E. Pinto. 2013. *Economics for Investment Decision Makers Workbook: Micro, Macro, and International Economics*. Hoboken, NJ: John Wiley & Sons, Inc.

Savills World Research. 2016. *Around the World in Dollars and Cents*. London: Savills.

Singer, Brian D., and Kevin Terhaar. 1997. *Economic Foundations of Capital Market Returns*. Charlottesville, VA: Research Foundation of the Institute of Chartered Financial Analysts.

Stefek, Daniel, and Raghu Suryanarayanan. 2012. "Private and Public Real Estate: What Is the Link?" *Journal of Alternative Investments* (Winter): 66–75.

Yau, Jot K., Thomas Schneeweis, Edward A. Szado, Thomas R. Robinson, and Lisa R. Weiss. 2018. "Alternative Investments Portfolio Management." CFA Program Level III Curriculum Chapter 26.

PRACTICE PROBLEMS

1. An investor is considering adding three new securities to her internationally focused fixed-income portfolio. She considers the following non-callable securities:
   - 1-year government bond
   - 10-year government bond
   - 10-year BBB rated corporate bond

   She plans to invest equally in all three securities being analyzed or will invest in none of them at this time. She will only make the added investment provided that the expected spread/premium of the equally weighted investment is at least 1.5 percent (150bp) over the 1-year government bond. She has gathered the following information:

Risk-free interest rate (1-year, incorporating 2.6% inflation expectation)	3.8%
Term premium (10-year vs. 1-year government bond)	1%
10-year BBB credit premium (over 10-year government bond)	75bp
Estimated liquidity premium on 10-year corporate bonds	55bp

   Using only the information given, address the following problems using the risk premium approach:
   A. Calculate the expected return that an equal-weighted investment in the three securities could provide.
   B. Calculate the expected total risk premium of the three securities and determine the investor's probable course of action.

2. Jo Akumba's portfolio is invested in a range of developed market fixed-income securities. She asks her adviser about the possibility of diversifying her investments to include emerging and frontier markets government and corporate fixed-income securities. Her adviser makes the following comment regarding risk:

   "All emerging and frontier market fixed-income securities pose economic, political, and legal risk. Economic risks arise from the fact that emerging market countries have poor fiscal discipline, rely on foreign borrowing, have less diverse tax base, and significant dependence on specific industries. They are susceptible to capital flight. Their ability to pay is limited. In addition, weak property rights, weak enforcement of contract laws, and political instability pose hazards for emerging markets debt investors."

   Discuss the statement made.

3. An Australian investor currently holds a A$240 million equity portfolio. He is considering rebalancing the portfolio based on an assessment of the risk and return prospects facing the Australian economy. Information relating to the Australian investment markets and the economy has been collected in the following table:

10-Year Historical	Current	Capital Market Expectations
Average government bond yield: 2.8%	10-year government bond yield: 2.3%	Expected annual inflation: 2.3%
Average annual equity return: 4.6%	Year-over-year equity return: −9.4%	Expected equity market P/E: 14.0×
Average annual inflation rate: 2.3%	Year-over-year inflation rate: 2.1%	Expected annual income return: 2.4%
Equity market P/E (beginning of period): 15×	Current equity market P/E: 14.5×	Expected annual real earnings growth: 5.0%
Average annual dividend income return: 2.6%		
Average annual real earnings growth: 6.0%		

Using the information in the table, address the following problems:

A. Calculate the historical Australian equity risk premium using the "equity-vs-bonds" premium method.

B. Calculate the expected annual equity return using the Grinold–Kroner model (assume no change in the number of shares outstanding).

C. Using your answer to Part B, calculate the expected annual equity risk premium.

4. An analyst is reviewing various asset alternatives and is presented with the following information relating to the broad equity market of Switzerland and various industries within the Swiss market that are of particular investment interest.

Expected risk premium for overall global investable market (GIM) portfolio	3.5%
Expected standard deviation for the GIM portfolio	8.5%
Expected standard deviation for Swiss Health Care Industry equity investments	12.0%
Expected standard deviation for Swiss Watch Industry equity investments	6.0%
Expected standard deviation for Swiss Consumer Products Industry equity investments	7.5%

Assume that the Swiss market is perfectly integrated with the world markets.
Swiss Health Care has a correlation of 0.7 with the GIM portfolio.
Swiss Watch has a correlation of 0.8 with the GIM portfolio.
Swiss Consumer Products has a correlation of 0.8 with the GIM portfolio.

A. Basing your answers only upon the data presented in the table above and using the international capital asset pricing model—in particular, the Singer–Terhaar approach—estimate the expected risk premium for the following:
   i. Swiss Health Care Industry
   ii. Swiss Watch Industry
   iii. Swiss Consumer Products Industry

B. Judge which industry is most attractive from a valuation perspective.

5. Identify risks faced by investors in emerging market equities over and above those that are faced by fixed-income investors in such markets.
6. Describe the main issues that arise when conducting historical analysis of real estate returns.
7. An analyst at a real estate investment management firm seeks to establish expectations for rate of return for properties in the industrial sector over the next year. She has obtained the following information:

Current industrial sector capitalization rate ("cap" rate)	5.7%
Expected cap rate at the end of the period	5.5%
NOI growth rate (real)	1%
Inflation expectation	1.5%

Estimate the expected return from the industrial sector properties based on the data provided.
8. A client has asked his adviser to explain the key considerations in forecasting exchange rates. The adviser's firm uses two broad complementary approaches when setting expectations for exchange rate movements, namely, focus on trade in goods and services and, secondly, focus on capital flows. Identify the main considerations that the adviser should explain to the client under the two approaches.
9. Looking independently at each of the economic observations below, indicate the country where an analyst would expect to see a strengthening currency for each observation.

	Country X	Country Y
Expected inflation over next year	2.0%	3.0%
Short-term (1-month) government rate	Decrease	Increase
Expected (forward-looking) GDP growth over next year	2.0%	3.3%
New national laws have been passed that enable foreign direct investment in real estate/financial companies	Yes	No
Current account surplus (deficit)	8%	−1%

10. Fap is a small country whose currency is the Fip. Three years ago, the exchange rate was considered to be reflecting purchasing power parity (PPP). Since then, the country's inflation has exceeded inflation in the other countries by about 5% per annum. The Fip exchange rate, however, remained broadly unchanged.
   What would you have expected the Fip exchange rate to show if PPP prevailed?
   Are Fips over- or undervalued, according to PPP?

The following information relates to Questions 11–18

Richard Martin is chief investment officer for the Trunch Foundation (the foundation), which has a large, globally diversified investment portfolio. Martin meets with the foundation's fixed-income and real estate portfolio managers to review expected return forecasts and potential investments, as well as to consider short-term modifications to asset weights within the total fund strategic asset allocation.

Martin asks the real estate portfolio manager to discuss the performance characteristics of real estate. The real estate portfolio manager makes the following statements:

Statement 1: Adding traded REIT securities to an equity portfolio should substantially improve the portfolio's diversification over the next year.

Statement 2: Traded REIT securities are more highly correlated with direct real estate and less highly correlated with equities over multi-year horizons.

Martin looks over the long-run valuation metrics the manager is using for commercial real estate, shown in Exhibit 1.

EXHIBIT 1   Commercial Real Estate Valuation Metrics

Cap Rate	GDP Growth Rate
4.70%	4.60%

The real estate team uses an in-house model for private real estate to estimate the true volatility of returns over time. The model assumes that the current observed return equals the weighted average of the current true return and the previous observed return. Because the true return is not observable, the model assumes a relationship between true returns and observable REIT index returns; therefore, it uses REIT index returns as proxies for both the unobservable current true return and the previous observed return.

Martin asks the fixed-income portfolio manager to review the foundation's bond portfolios. The existing aggregate bond portfolio is broadly diversified in domestic and international developed markets. The first segment of the portfolio to be reviewed is the domestic sovereign portfolio. The bond manager notes that there is a market consensus that the domestic yield curve will likely experience a single 20 bp increase in the near term as a result of monetary tightening and then remain relatively flat and stable for the next three years. Martin then reviews duration and yield measures for the short-term domestic sovereign bond portfolio in Exhibit 2.

EXHIBIT 2   Short-Term Domestic Sovereign Bond Portfolio

Macaulay Duration	Modified Duration	Yield to Maturity
3.00	2.94	2.00%

The discussion turns to the international developed fixed-income market. The foundation invested in bonds issued by Country XYZ, a foreign developed country. XYZ's sovereign yield curve is currently upward sloping, and the yield spread between 2-year and 10-year XYZ bonds is 100 bps.

The fixed-income portfolio manager tells Martin that he is interested in a domestic market corporate bond issued by Zeus Manufacturing Corporation (ZMC). ZMC has just been downgraded two steps by a major credit rating agency. In addition to expected monetary actions that will raise short-term rates, the yield spread between three-year sovereign bonds and the next highest-quality government agency bond widened by 10 bps.

Although the foundation's fixed-income portfolios have focused primarily on developed markets, the portfolio manager presents data in Exhibit 3 on two emerging markets for Martin to consider. Both economies increased exports of their mineral resources over the last decade.

EXHIBIT 3   Emerging Market Data

Factor	Emerging Republic A	Emerging Republic B
Fiscal deficit/GDP	6.50%	8.20%
Debt/GDP	90.10%	104.20%
Current account deficit	5.20% of GDP	7.10% of GDP
Foreign exchange reserves	90.30% of short-term debt	70.10% of short-term debt

The fixed-income portfolio manager also presents information on a new investment opportunity in an international developed market. The team is considering the bonds of Xdelp, a large energy exploration and production company. Both the domestic and international markets are experiencing synchronized growth in GDP midway between the trough and the peak of the business cycle. The foreign country's government has displayed a disciplined approach to maintaining stable monetary and fiscal policies and has experienced a rising current account surplus and an appreciating currency. It is expected that with the improvements in free cash flow and earnings, the credit rating of the Xdelp bonds will be upgraded. Martin refers to the foundation's asset allocation policy in Exhibit 4 before making any changes to either the fixed-income or real estate portfolios.

EXHIBIT 4   Trunch Foundation Strategic Asset Allocation—Select Data

Asset Class	Minimum Weight	Maximum Weight	Actual Weight
Fixed income—Domestic	40.00%	80.00%	43.22%
Fixed income—International	5.00%	10.00%	6.17%
Fixed income—Emerging markets	0.00%	2.00%	0.00%
Alternatives—Real estate	2.00%	6.00%	3.34%

11. Which of the real estate portfolio manager's statements is correct?
    A. Only Statement 1
    B. Only Statement 2
    C. Both Statement 1 and Statement 2

12. Based only on Exhibit 1, the long-run expected return for commercial real estate:
    A. is approximately double the cap rate.
    B. incorporates a cap rate greater than the discount rate.
    C. needs to include the cap rate's anticipated rate of change.

13. Based on the private real estate model developed to estimate return volatility, the true variance is *most likely*:
    A. lower than the variance of the observed data.
    B. approximately equal to the variance of the observed data.
    C. greater than the variance of the observed data.

14. Based on Exhibit 2 and the anticipated effects of the monetary policy change, the expected annual return over a three-year investment horizon will *most likely* be:
    A. lower than 2.00%.
    B. approximately equal to 2.00%.
    C. greater than 2.00%.

15. Based on the building block approach to fixed-income returns, the dominant source of the yield spread for Country XYZ is *most likely* the:
    A. term premium.
    B. credit premium.
    C. liquidity premium.

16. Using the building block approach, the required rate of return for the ZMC bond will *most likely*:
    A. increase based on the change in the credit premium.
    B. decrease based on the change in the default-free rate.
    C. decrease based on the change in the liquidity premium.

17. Based only on Exhibit 3, the foundation would *most likely* consider buying bonds issued by:
    A. only Emerging Republic A.
    B. only Emerging Republic B.
    C. neither Emerging Republic A nor Emerging Republic B.

18. Based only on Exhibits 3 and 4 and the information provided by the portfolio managers, the action *most likely* to enhance returns is to:
    A. decrease existing investments in real estate by 2.00%.
    B. initiate a commitment to emerging market debt of 1.00%.
    C. increase the investments in international market bonds by 1.00%.

The following information relates to Questions 19–26

Judith Bader is a senior analyst for a company that specializes in managing international developed and emerging markets equities. Next week, Bader must present proposed changes to client portfolios to the Investment Committee, and she is preparing a presentation to support the views underlying her recommendations.

Bader begins by analyzing portfolio risk. She decides to forecast a variance–covariance matrix (VCV) for 20 asset classes, using 10 years of monthly returns and incorporating both the sample statistics and the factor-model methods. To mitigate the impact of estimation error, Bader is considering combining the results of the two methods in an alternative target VCV matrix, using shrinkage estimation.

Bader asks her research assistant to comment on the two approaches and the benefits of applying shrinkage estimation. The assistant makes the following statements:

Statement 1:   Shrinkage estimation of VCV matrices will decrease the efficiency of the estimates versus the sample VCV matrix.

Statement 2:   Your proposed approach for estimating the VCV matrix will not be reliable because a sample VCV matrix is biased and inconsistent.

Statement 3:   A factor-based VCV matrix approach may result in some portfolios that erroneously appear to be riskless if any asset returns can be completely determined by the common factors or some of the factors are redundant.

Bader then uses the Singer–Terhaar model and the final shrinkage-estimated VCV matrix to determine the equilibrium expected equity returns for all international asset classes by country. Three of the markets under consideration are located in Country A (developed market), Country B (emerging market), and Country C (emerging market). Bader projects that in relation to the global market, the equity market in Country A will remain highly integrated, the equity market in Country B will become more segmented, and the equity market in Country C will become more fully integrated.

Next, Bader applies the Grinold–Kroner model to estimate the expected equity returns for the various markets under consideration. For Country A, Bader assumes a very long-term corporate earnings growth rate of 4% per year (equal to the expected nominal GDP growth rate), a 2% rate of net share repurchases for Country A's equities, and an expansion rate for P/E multiples of 0.5% per year.

In reviewing Countries B and C, Bader's research assistant comments that emerging markets are especially risky owing to issues related to politics, competition, and accounting standards. As an example, Bader and her assistant discuss the risk implications of the following information related to Country B:

• Experiencing declining per capita income
• Expected to continue its persistent current account deficit below 2% of GDP
• Transitioning to International Financial Reporting Standards, with full convergence scheduled to be completed within two years

Bader shifts her focus to currency expectations relative to clients' base currency and summarizes her assumptions in Exhibit 1.

EXHIBIT 1   Baseline Assumptions for Currency Forecasts

	Country A	Country B	Country C
Historical current account	Persistent current account deficit of 5% of GDP	Persistent current account deficit of 2% of GDP	Persistent current account surplus of 2% of GDP
Expectation for secular trend in current account	Rising current account deficit	Narrowing current account deficit	Rising current account surplus
Long-term inflation expectation relative to global inflation	Expected to rise	Expected to keep pace	Expected to fall
Capital flows	Steady inflows	Hot money flowing out	Hot money flowing in

During a conversation about Exhibit 1, Bader and her research assistant discuss the composition of each country's currency portfolio and the potential for triggering a crisis.

Bader notes that some flows and holdings are more or less supportive of the currency, stating that investments in private equity make up the majority of Country A's currency portfolio, investments in public equity make up the majority of Country B's currency portfolio, and investments in public debt make up the majority of Country C's currency portfolio.

19. Which of the following statements made by Bader's research assistant is correct?
   A. Statement 1
   B. Statement 2
   C. Statement 3

20. Based on expectations for changes in integration with the global market, all else being equal, the Singer–Terhaar model implies that Bader should shift capital from Country A to:
   A. only Country B.
   B. only Country C.
   C. both Countries B and C.

21. Using the Grinold–Kroner model, which of the following assumptions for forecasting Country A's expected equity returns is plausible for the very long run?
   A. Rate of net share repurchases
   B. Corporate earnings growth rate
   C. Expansion rate for P/E multiples

22. Based only on the emerging markets discussion, developments in which of the following areas *most likely* signal increasing risk for Country B's equity market?
   A. Politics
   B. Competitiveness
   C. Accounting standards

23. Based on Bader's expectations for current account secular trends as shown in Exhibit 1, Bader should reallocate capital, all else being equal, from:
   A. Country A to Country C.
   B. Country B to Country A.
   C. Country C to Country A.

24. Based on Bader's inflation expectations as shown in Exhibit 1, purchasing power parity implies that which of the following countries' currencies should depreciate, all else being equal?
   A. Country A
   B. Country B
   C. Country C

25. Based on Exhibit 1, which country's central bank is *most likely* to buy domestic bonds near term to sterilize the impact of money flows on domestic liquidity?
   A. Country A
   B. Country B
   C. Country C

26. Based on the composition of each country's currency portfolio, which country is most vulnerable to a potential crisis?
   A. Country A
   B. Country B
   C. Country C

CHAPTER 5

OVERVIEW OF ASSET ALLOCATION

William W. Jennings, PhD, CFA
Eugene L. Podkaminer, CFA

LEARNING OUTCOMES

The candidate should be able to:

- describe elements of effective investment governance and investment governance considerations in asset allocation;
- prepare an economic balance sheet for a client and interpret its implications for asset allocation;
- compare the investment objectives of asset-only, liability-relative, and goals-based asset allocation approaches;
- contrast concepts of risk relevant to asset-only, liability-relative, and goals-based asset allocation approaches;
- explain how asset classes are used to represent exposures to systematic risk and discuss criteria for asset class specification;
- explain the use of risk factors in asset allocation and their relation to traditional asset class–based approaches;
- select and justify an asset allocation based on an investor's objectives and constraints;
- describe the use of the global market portfolio as a baseline portfolio in asset allocation;
- discuss strategic implementation choices in asset allocation, including passive/active choices and vehicles for implementing passive and active mandates;
- discuss strategic considerations in rebalancing asset allocations.

1. INTRODUCTION

Asset owners are concerned with accumulating and maintaining the wealth needed to meet their needs and aspirations. In that endeavor, investment portfolios—including individuals' portfolios and institutional funds—play important roles. Asset allocation is a strategic—and often a first or early—decision in portfolio construction. Because it holds that position, it is widely accepted as important and meriting careful attention. Among the questions addressed in this chapter are the following:

- What is a sound governance context for making asset allocation decisions?
- How broad a picture should an adviser have of an asset owner's assets and liabilities in recommending an asset allocation?
- How can an asset owner's objectives and sensitivities to risk be represented in asset allocation?
- What are the broad approaches available in developing an asset allocation recommendation, and when might one approach be more or less appropriate than another?
- What are the top-level decisions that need to be made in implementing a chosen asset allocation?
- How may asset allocations be rebalanced as asset prices change?

The strategic asset allocation decision determines return levels[1] in which allocations are invested, irrespective of the degree of active management. Because of its strategic importance, the investment committee, at the highest level of the governance hierarchy, typically retains approval of the strategic asset allocation decision. Often a proposal is developed only after a formal asset allocation study that incorporates obligations, objectives, and constraints; simulates possible investment outcomes over an agreed-on investment horizon; and evaluates the risk and return characteristics of the possible allocation strategies.

In providing an overview of asset allocation, this chapter's focus is the alignment of asset allocation with the asset owner's investment objectives, constraints, and overall financial condition. This is the first chapter in several sequences of chapters that address, respectively, asset allocation and portfolio management of equities, fixed income, and alternative investments. Asset allocation is also linked to other facets of portfolio management, including risk management and behavioral finance. As coverage of asset allocation progresses in the sequence of chapters, various connections to these topics, covered in detail in other areas of the curriculum, will be made.[2]

In the asset allocation sequence, the role of this chapter is the "big picture." It also offers definitions that will provide a coordinated treatment of many later topics in portfolio management. The second chapter provides the basic "how" of developing an asset allocation, and the third chapter explores various common, real-world complexities in developing an asset allocation.

This chapter is organized as follows: Section 2 explains the importance of asset allocation in investment management. Section 3 addresses the investment governance context in which asset allocation decisions are made. Section 4 considers asset allocation from the comprehensive perspective offered by the asset owner's economic balance sheet. Section 5 distinguishes three broad approaches to asset allocation and explains how they differ in investment objective and risk. In Section 6, these three approaches are discussed at a high level in relation to three cases. Section 7 provides a top-level orientation to how a chosen asset

---

[1]See Ibbotson and Kaplan (2000, p. 30) and Xiong, Ibbotson, and Chen (2010). The conclusion for the aggregate follows from the premise that active management is a zero-sum game overall (Sharpe 1991).
[2]Among these chapters, see Blanchett, Cordell, Finke, and Idzorek (2016) concerning human capital and longevity and other risks and Pompian (2011a and 2011b) and Pompian, McLean, and Byrne (2011) concerning behavioral finance.

allocation may be implemented, providing a set of definitions that underlie subsequent chapters. Section 8 discusses rebalancing considerations, and Section 9 provides a summary of the chapter.

2. ASSET ALLOCATION: IMPORTANCE IN INVESTMENT MANAGEMENT

Exhibit 1 places asset allocation in a stylized model of the investment management process viewed as an integrated set of activities aimed at attaining investor objectives.

EXHIBIT 1   The Portfolio Management Process

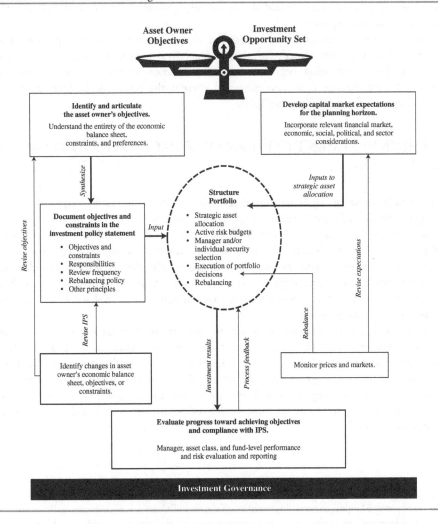

Exhibit 1 shows that an investment process that is in the asset owner's best interest rests on a foundation of good investment governance, which includes the assignment of decision-making responsibilities to qualified individuals and oversight of processes. The balance at the top of the chart suggests that the portfolio management process must reconcile (balance) investor objectives (on the left) with the possibilities offered by the investment opportunity set (on the right).

The investment process shows a sequence of activities that begins with understanding the asset owner's entire circumstance; objectives, including any constraints; and preferences. These factors, in conjunction with capital market inputs,[3] form the basis for asset allocation as a first step in portfolio construction and give a structure within which other decisions—such as the decision to invest passively or actively—take place. In the flow chart, thick lines show initial flows (or relations of logic) and thin lines show feedback flows.

Asset allocation is widely considered to be the most important decision in the investment process. The strategic asset allocation decision completely determines return levels[4] in which allocations are invested passively and also in the aggregate of all investors, irrespective of the degree of active management.

In providing an overview of asset allocation, this chapter's focus is the alignment of asset allocation with the asset owner's investment objectives, constraints, and overall financial condition. The presentation begins with an introduction to the investment governance context of asset allocation. It then moves to present the economic balance sheet as the financial context for asset allocation itself.

3. THE INVESTMENT GOVERNANCE BACKGROUND TO ASSET ALLOCATION

Investment governance represents the organization of decision-making responsibilities and oversight activities. Effective investment governance ensures that assets are invested to achieve the asset owner's investment objectives within the asset owner's risk tolerance and constraints, and in compliance with all applicable laws and regulations. In addition, effective governance ensures that decisions are made by individuals or groups with the necessary skills and capacity.

Investment performance depends on asset allocation *and* its implementation. Sound investment governance practices seek to align asset allocation and implementation to achieve the asset owner's stated goals.

Investment governance structures are relevant to both institutional and individual investors. Because such structures are often formalized and articulated in detail for defined benefit pension plans, we will build our discussion using a pension plan governance framework. Elements of pension plan governance that are not directly related to the management of plan assets—plan design, funding policy, and communications to participants—are not discussed in this chapter. Instead, we focus on those aspects of governance that directly affect the asset allocation decision.

---

[3]The set of potential inputs to portfolio construction shown in Exhibit 1 is not exhaustive. For example, for investors delegating asset management, investment managers' performance records are relevant.

[4]See Ibbotson and Kaplan (2000, p. 30) and Xiong, Ibbotson, Idzorek, and Chen (2010). The conclusion for the aggregate follows from the premise that active management is a zero-sum game overall (Sharpe 1991).

3.1. Governance Structures

Governance and management are two separate but related functions. Both are directed toward achieving the same end. But governance focuses on clarifying the mission, creating a plan, and reviewing progress toward achieving long- and short-term objectives, whereas management efforts are geared to outcomes—the execution of the plan to achieve the agreed-on goals and objectives. A common governance structure in an institutional investor context will have three levels within the governance hierarchy:

- governing investment committee
- investment staff
- third-party resources

The investment committee may be a committee of the board of directors, or the board of directors may have delegated its oversight responsibilities to an internal investment committee made up of staff. Investment staff may be large, with full in-house asset management capabilities, or small—for example, two to five investment staff responsible for overseeing external investment managers and consultants. It may even be part time—a treasurer or chief financial officer with many other, competing responsibilities. The term "third-party resources" is used to describe a range of professional resources—investment managers, investment consultants, custodians, and actuaries, for example.

Although there are many governance models in use, most effective models share six common elements. Effective governance models perform the following tasks:

1. Articulate the long- and short-term objectives of the investment program.
2. Allocate decision rights and responsibilities among the functional units in the governance hierarchy effectively, taking account of their knowledge, capacity, time, and position in the governance hierarchy.
3. Specify processes for developing and approving the investment policy statement that will govern the day-to-day operations of the investment program.
4. Specify processes for developing and approving the program's strategic asset allocation.
5. Establish a reporting framework to monitor the program's progress toward the agreed-on goals and objectives.
6. Periodically undertake a governance audit.

In the sections that follow, we will discuss selected elements from this list.

3.2. Articulating Investment Objectives

Articulating long- and short-term objectives for an investor first requires an understanding of purpose—that is, what the investor is trying to achieve. Below are examples of simple investment objective statements that can be clearly tied to purposes:

- *Defined benefit pension fund.* The investment objective of the fund is to ensure that plan assets are sufficient to meet current and future pension liabilities.
- *Endowment fund.* The investment objective of the endowment is to earn a rate of return in excess of the return required to fund, after accounting for inflation, ongoing distributions consistent with the endowment's mission.

- *Individual investor.* The investment objective is to provide for retirement at the investor's desired retirement age, family needs, and bequests, subject to stated risk tolerance and investment constraints.

A return requirement is often considered the essence of an investment objective statement, but for that portion of the objective statement to be properly understood requires additional context, including the obligations the assets are expected to fund, the nature of cash flows into and out of the fund, and the asset owner's willingness and ability to withstand interim changes in portfolio value. The ultimate goal is to find the best risk/return trade-off consistent with the asset owner's resource constraints and risk tolerance.

As an example of how the overall context can affect decision-making, the pension fund may be an active plan, with new participants added as they are hired, or it may be "frozen" (no additional benefits are being accrued by participants in the plan). The status of the plan, considered in conjunction with its funded ratio (the ratio of pension assets to pension liabilities), has a bearing on future contributions and benefit payments. The company offering the pension benefit may operate in a highly cyclical industry, where revenues ebb and flow over the course of the economic cycle. In this case, the plan sponsor may prefer a more conservative asset allocation to minimize the year-to-year fluctuations in its pension contribution.

The nature of inflows and outflows for an endowment fund can be quite different from those of a pension fund. An endowment fund may be used to support scholarships, capital improvements, or university operating expenses. The fund sponsor has some degree of control over the outflows from the fund but very little control over the timing and amounts of contributions to the fund because the contributions are typically coming from external donors.

These cash inflow and outflow characteristics must be considered when establishing the goals and objectives of the fund.

A third, inter-related aspect of defining the sponsor's goals and objectives is determining and communicating risk tolerance. There are multiple dimensions of risk to be considered: liquidity risk, volatility, risk of loss, and risk of abandoning a chosen course of action at the wrong time.

Effective investment governance requires consideration of the liquidity needs of the fund and the liquidity characteristics of the fund's investments. For example, too large an allocation to relatively illiquid assets, such as real estate or private equity, might impair the ability to make payouts in times of market stress.

A high risk/high expected return asset allocation is likely to lead to wider swings in interim valuations. Any minimum thresholds for funded status that, if breached, would trigger an adverse event, such as higher pension insurance premiums, must be considered in the asset allocation decision.

For individual investors, the risk of substantial losses may be unacceptable for a variety of financial and psychological reasons. When such losses occur after retirement, lost capital cannot be replaced with future earnings.

Asset owners have their own unique return requirements and risk sensitivities. Managing an investment program without a clear understanding of long- and short-term objectives is similar to navigating without a map: Arriving at the correct destination on time and intact is not compatible with leaving much to chance.

3.3. Allocation of Rights and Responsibilities

The rights and responsibilities necessary to execute the investment program are generally determined at the highest level of investment governance. The allocation of those rights and responsibilities among the governance units is likely to vary depending on the size of the investment program; the knowledge, skills, and abilities of the internal staff; and the amount of time staff can devote to the investment program if they have other, competing responsibilities. Above all, good governance requires that decisions be delegated to those best qualified to make an informed decision.

The resources available to an organization will affect the scope and complexity of the investment program and the allocation of rights and responsibilities. A small investment program may result in having a narrower opportunity set because of either asset size (too small to diversify across the range of asset classes and investment managers) or staffing constraints (insufficient asset size to justify a dedicated internal staff). Complex strategies may be beyond the reach of entities that have chosen not to develop investment expertise internally or whose oversight committee lacks individuals with sufficient investment understanding. Organizations willing to invest in attracting, developing, and retaining staff resources and in developing strong internal control processes, including risk management systems, are better able to adopt more complex investment programs. The largest investors, however, may find their size creates governance issues: Manager capacity constraints might lead to so many managers that it challenges the investor's oversight capacity.

Allocation of rights and responsibilities across the governance hierarchy is a key element in the success of an investment program. Effective governance requires that the individuals charged with any given decision have the required *knowledge* and expertise to thoroughly evaluate the alternative courses of action and the *capacity* to take on the ongoing responsibility of those decisions, and they must be able to execute those decisions in a timely fashion. (Individual investors engaging a private wealth manager are delegating these expertise, capacity, and execution responsibilities.)

Exhibit 2 presents a systematic way of allocating among governance units the primary duties and responsibilities of running an investment program.

EXHIBIT 2   Allocation of Rights and Responsibilities

Investment Activity	Investment Committee	Investment Staff	Third-Party Resource
Mission	Craft and approve	n/a	n/a
Investment policy statement	Approve	Draft	Consultants provide input
Asset allocation policy	Approve with input from staff and consultants	Draft with input from consultants	Consultants provide input
Investment manager and other service provider selection	Delegate to investment staff; approval authority retained for certain service providers	Research, evaluation, and selection of investment managers and service providers	Consultants provide input

Investment Activity	Investment Committee	Investment Staff	Third-Party Resource
Portfolio construction (individual asset selection)	Delegate to outside managers, or to staff if sufficient internal resources	Execution if assets are managed in-house	Execution by independent investment manager
Monitoring asset prices & portfolio rebalancing	Delegate to staff within confines of the investment policy statement	Assure that the sum of all sub-portfolios equals the desired overall portfolio positioning; approve and execute rebalancing	Consultants and custodian provide input
Risk management	Approve principles and conduct oversight	Create risk management infrastructure and design reporting	Investment manager manages portfolio within established risk guidelines; consultants may provide input and support
Investment manager monitoring	Oversight	Ongoing assessment of managers	Consultants and custodian provide input
Performance evaluation and reporting	Oversight	Evaluate manager's continued suitability for assigned role; analyze sources of portfolio return	Consultants and custodian provide input
Governance audit	Commission and assess	Responds and corrects	Investment Committee contracts with an independent third party for the audit

The available knowledge and expertise at each level of the hierarchy, the resource capacity of the decision makers, and the ability to act on a timely basis all influence the allocation of these rights and responsibilities.

3.4. Investment Policy Statement

The investment policy statement (IPS) is the foundation of an effective investment program. A well-crafted IPS can serve as a blueprint for ongoing fund management and assures stakeholders that program assets are managed with the appropriate care and diligence.

Often, the IPS itself will be a foundation document that is revised slowly over time, whereas information relating to more variable aspects of the program—the asset allocation policy and guidelines for individual investment managers—will be contained in a more easily modified appendix.

3.5. Asset Allocation and Rebalancing Policy

Because of its strategic importance, the investment committee, at the highest level of the governance hierarchy, typically retains approval of the strategic asset allocation decision. A proposal is often developed only after a formal asset allocation study that incorporates obligations, objectives, and constraints; simulates possible investment outcomes over an agreed-on investment horizon; and evaluates the risk and return characteristics of the possible allocation strategies.

Governance considerations inform not only the overall strategic asset allocation decision but also rebalancing decisions. The IPS should contain at least general orienting information relevant to rebalancing. In an institutional setting, rebalancing policy might be the responsibility of the investment committee, organizational staff, or the external consultant. Likewise, individual investors might specify that they have delegated rebalancing authority to their investment adviser. Specification of rebalancing responsibilities is good governance.

3.6. Reporting Framework

The reporting framework in a well-run investment program should be designed in a manner that enables the overseers to evaluate quickly and clearly how well the investment program is progressing toward the agreed-on goals and objectives. The reporting should be clear and concise, accurately answering the following three questions:

- Where are we now?
- Where are we relative to the goals and objectives?
- What value has been added or subtracted by management decisions?

Key elements of a reporting framework should address performance evaluation, compliance with investment guidelines, and progress toward achieving the stated goals and objectives.

- Benchmarking is necessary for performance measurement, attribution, and evaluation. Effective benchmarking allows the investment committee to evaluate staff and external managers. Two separate levels of benchmarks are appropriate: one that measures the success of the investment managers relative to the purpose for which they were hired and another to measure the gap between the policy portfolio and the portfolio as actually implemented.
- Management reporting, typically prepared by staff with input from consultants and custodians, provides responsible parties with the information necessary to understand which parts of the portfolio are performing ahead of or behind the plan and why, as well as whether assets are being managed in accordance with investment guidelines.
- Governance reporting, which addresses strengths and weaknesses in program execution, should be structured in such a way that regular committee meetings can efficiently address any concerns. Although a crisis might necessitate calling an extraordinary meeting, good governance structures minimize this need.

3.7. The Governance Audit

The purpose of the governance audit is to ensure that the established policies, procedures, and governance structures are effective. The audit should be performed by an independent third party. The governance auditor examines the fund's governing documents, assesses the capacity of the organization to execute effectively within the confines of those governing documents, and evaluates the existing portfolio for its "efficiency" given the governance constraints.

Effective investment governance ensures the durability or survivability of the investment program. An investment program must be able to survive unexpected market turmoil, and good investment governance makes certain that the consequences of such turmoil are considered before it is experienced. Good governance seeks to avoid **decision-reversal risk**— the risk of reversing a chosen course of action at exactly the wrong time, the point of maximum loss. Good investment governance also considers the effect of investment committee member and staff turnover on the durability of the investment program. Orientation sessions for new committee members and proper documentation of investment beliefs, policies, and decisions enhance the likelihood that the chosen course of action will be given sufficient time to succeed. New staff or investment committee members should be able to perceive easily the design and intent of the investment program and be able to continue to execute it. Similarly, good investment governance prevents key person risk—overreliance on any one staff member or long-term, illiquid investments dependent on a staff member.

Good governance works to assure accountability. O'Barr and Conley (1992, p. 21), who studied investment management organizations using anthropological techniques, found that blame avoidance (not accepting personal responsibility when appropriate to do so) is a common feature of institutional investors. Good governance works to prevent such behavior.

EXAMPLE 1   Investment Governance: Hypothetical Case 1

In January 2016, the Caflandia Office Workers Union Pension (COWUP) made the following announcement:

"COWUP will fully exit all hedge funds and funds of funds. Assets currently amounting to 15% of its investment program are involved. Although hedge funds are a viable strategy for some, when judged against their complexity and cost, hedge fund investment is no longer warranted for COWUP."

One week later, a financial news service reported the following:

"The COWUP decision on hedge funds was precipitated by an allegation of wrongdoing by a senior executive with hedge fund selection responsibilities in COWUP's alternative investments strategy group."

1. Considering only the first statement, state what facts would be relevant in evaluating whether the decision to exit hedge funds was consistent with effective investment governance.
2. Considering both statements, identify deficiencies in COWUP's investment governance.

Solution to 1: The knowledge, capacity, and time available within COWUP to have an effective hedge fund investment program would need to be assessed against the stated concern for complexity and cost. The investment purpose served by hedge funds in COWUP's investment program before it exited them needs to be analyzed.

Solution to 2: The second statement raises these concerns about the decision described in the first statement:

- Hiring and oversight of COWUP executives may have been inadequate.
- The initial COWUP information release was incomplete and possibly misleading. Public communications appear not to have received adequate oversight.
- Divesting hedge funds may be a reaction to the personnel issue rather than being based on investment considerations.

EXAMPLE 2   Investment Governance: Hypothetical Case 2

The imaginary country of Caflandia has a sovereign wealth fund with assets of CAF$40 billion. A governance audit includes the following:

"The professional chief investment officer (CIO) reports to a nine-member appointed investment committee board of directors headed by an executive director. Investment staff members draft asset allocation policy in conjunction with consultants and make recommendation to the investment committee; the investment committee reviews and approves policy and any changes in policy, including the strategic asset allocation. The investment committee makes manager structure, conducts manager analysis, and makes manager selection decisions. The CIO has built a staff organization, which includes heads for each major asset class. In examining decisions over the last five years, we have noted several instances in which political or non-economic considerations appear to have influenced the investment program, including the selection of local private equity investments. Generally, the board spends much of its time debating individual manager strategies for inclusion in the portfolio and in evaluating investment managers' performance with comparatively little time devoted to asset allocation or risk management."

Based on this information and that in Exhibit 2, identify sound and questionable governance practices in the management of the Caflandia sovereign wealth fund.

Solution: Sound practices: The allocation of responsibilities for asset allocation between investment staff and the investment committee is sound practice. Staff investment expertise should be reflected in the process of asset allocation policy and analysis. The investment committee assumes final responsibility for choices and decisions, which is appropriate given its position in receiving information from all parts of the organization and from all interested parties.

Questionable practices: The investment committee's level of involvement in individual manager selection and evaluation is probably too deep. Exhibit 2 indicates that these functions more effectively reside with staff. Individual manager selection is an implementation and execution decision designed to achieve strategic decisions made by the investment committee and is typically not a strategic decision itself. Manager evaluation has substantial data analysis and technical elements that can be efficiently provided by staff experts and consultants. The finding about political/non-economic influences indicates multiple problems. It confirms that the investment manager analysis and selection processes were misplaced. It also suggests that the investment committee has an inadequate set of governance principles or checks and balances as relates to the investment committee itself.

4. THE ECONOMIC BALANCE SHEET AND ASSET ALLOCATION

An accounting balance sheet reflects a point-in-time snapshot of an organization's financial condition and shows the assets, liabilities, and owners' equity recognized by accountants. An **economic balance sheet** includes conventional assets and liabilities (called "financial assets" and "financial liabilities" in this chapter) as well as additional assets and liabilities—known as

extended portfolio assets and liabilities—that are relevant in making asset allocation decisions but do not appear on conventional balance sheets.

For individual investors, extended portfolio assets include human capital (the present value of future earnings), the present value of pension income, and the present value of expected inheritances. Likewise, the present value of future consumption is an extended portfolio liability.

For an institutional investor, extended portfolio assets might include underground mineral resources or the present value of future intellectual property royalties. Extended portfolio liabilities might include the present value of prospective payouts for foundations, whereas grants payable would appear as conventional liabilities.

Theory and, increasingly, practice suggest that asset allocation should consider the full range of assets and liabilities—both the financial portfolio and extended portfolio assets and liabilities—to arrive at an appropriate asset allocation choice. For example, an asset allocation process that considers the extended balance sheet, including the sensitivity of an individual investor's earnings to equity market risk (and that of the industry in which the individual is working), may result in a more appropriate allocation to equities than one that does not.

Life-cycle balanced funds (also known as target date funds) are examples of investments that seek to coordinate asset allocation with human capital. A 2040 life-cycle balanced fund seeks to provide a retirement investment vehicle appropriate for many individuals retiring in 2040. Exhibit 3 illustrates a typical path for the composition of an individual's economic balance sheet from age 25 through age 65.

EXHIBIT 3   Human Capital (HC) and Financial Capital (FC) Relative to Total Wealth

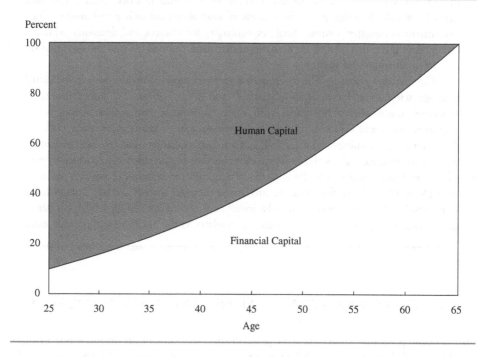

At age 25, with most of the individual's working life ahead of him, human capital dominates the economic balance sheet. As the individual progresses through life, the present

value of human capital declines as human capital is transformed into earnings. Earnings saved and invested build financial capital balances. By a retirement age of 65, the conversion of human capital to earnings and financial capital is assumed to be complete.

Life-cycle balanced funds reflect these extended portfolio assets. Research indicates that, on average, human capital is roughly 30% equity-like and 70% bond-like, with significant variation among industries.[5] Making the simplifying assumption that investors have approximately constant risk tolerance through life, their asset allocation for total overall wealth (including human capital and financial capital) should be, in theory, constant over time. In this case, the asset allocation chosen for financial capital should reflect an increasing allocation to bonds as human capital declines to age 65, holding all else constant. Exhibit 4 shows the glide path for the equity/bond allocation chosen by one US mutual fund family. The increasing allocation to bonds is consistent with the view that human capital has preponderant bond-like characteristics.

EXHIBIT 4   Glide Path of Target Date Investment Funds in One Family

Assumed Age	Equity Allocation	Bond Allocation
25	85%	15%
35	82	18
45	77	23
55	63	37
65	49	51

Note: Allocations as of 31 December 2009.
Source: Based on data in Idzorek, Stempien, and Voris (2013).

Although estimating human capital is quite complex, including human capital and other extended portfolio assets and economic liabilities in asset allocation decisions is good practice.[6]

EXAMPLE 3   The Economic Balance Sheet of Auldberg University Endowment

- *Name*: Auldberg University Endowment (AUE)
- *Narrative*: AUE was established in 1852 in Caflandia and largely serves the tiny province of Auldberg. AUE supports about one-sixth of Auldberg University's CAF $60 million operating budget; real estate income and provincial subsidies provide the

---

[5]See Blanchett and Straehl (2015) and Blanchett and Straehl (2017).

[6]Human capital is non-tradable, cannot be hedged, is subject to unspecified future taxes, and is a function of an individual's mortality. Human capital is technically defined as the net present value of an investor's future expected labor income weighted by the probability of surviving to each future age (see Ibbotson, Milevsky, Chen, and Zhu 2007). Thus, the present value of future earnings and pensions should be valued with mortality-weighted probabilities of receiving future cash flows, not the present value over life expectancy. There is meaningful extra value from the low-odds event of extreme longevity, which has an important portfolio implication in that individual investors can outlive their financial portfolios but not lifetime annuity payments.

remainder and have been relatively stable. The endowment has historically had a portfolio limited to domestic equities, bonds, and real estate holdings; that policy is under current review. Auldberg University itself (not the endowment) has a CAF$350 million investment in domestic commercial real estate assets, including office buildings and industrial parks, much of it near the campus. AUE employs a well-qualified staff with substantial diverse experience in equities, fixed income, and real estate.

- *Assets*: Endowment assets include CAF$100 million in domestic equities, CAF$60 million in domestic government debt, and CAF$40 million in Class B office real estate. The present value of expected future contributions (from real estate and provincial subsidies) is estimated to be CAF$400 million.
- *Liabilities*: These include CAF$10 million in short-term borrowings and CAF$35 million in mortgage debt related to real estate investments. Although it has no specific legal requirement, AUE has a policy to distribute to the university 5% of 36-month moving average net assets. In effect, the endowment supports $10 million of Auldberg University's annual operating budget. The present value of expected future support is CAF$450 million.

1. Prepare an economic balance sheet for AUE.
2. Describe elements in Auldberg University's investments that might affect AUE's asset allocation choices.

Solution to 1: The economic balance sheet for the endowment (given in the following table) does not include the real estate owned by Auldberg University. The economic net worth is found as a plug item $(600 - 10 - 35 - 450 = 105)$.

AUE Economic Balance Sheet (in CAF$ millions) 31 December 20x6

Assets		Liabilities and Economic Net Worth	
Financial Assets		*Financial Liabilities*	
Domestic equities	100	Short-term borrowing	10
Domestic fixed income	60	Mortgage debt	35
Class B office real estate	40		
Extended Assets		*Extended Liabilities*	
Present value of expected future contributions to AUE	400	Present value of expected future support	450
		Economic Net Worth	
		Economic net worth (Economic assets − Economic liabilities)	105
Total	600		600

Solution to 2: AUE's Class B real estate investments' value and income are likely to be stressed during the same economic circumstances as the university's own real estate investments. In such periods, the university may look to the endowment for increased operating support and AUE may not be well positioned to meet that need. Thus, the AUE's real estate investment is actually less diversifying than it may appear and the allocation to it may need to be re-examined. Similar considerations apply to AUE's holdings in equities in relation to Auldberg University's.

5. APPROACHES TO ASSET ALLOCATION

We can identify three broad approaches to asset allocation: (1) **asset-only**, (2) **liability-relative**, and (3) **goals-based**. These are decision-making frameworks that take account of or emphasize different aspects of the investment problem.

Asset-only approaches to asset allocation focus solely on the asset side of the investor's balance sheet. Liabilities are not explicitly modeled. Mean–variance optimization (MVO) is the most familiar and deeply studied asset-only approach. MVO considers only the expected returns, risks, and correlations of the asset classes in the opportunity set. In contrast, liability-relative and goals-based approaches explicitly account for the liabilities side of the economic balance sheet, dedicating assets to meet, respectively, legal liabilities and quasi-liabilities (other needs that are not strictly liabilities but are treated as such) or goals.

Liability-relative approaches to asset allocation choose an asset allocation in relation to the objective of funding liabilities. The phrase "funding of liabilities" means to provide for the money to pay liabilities when they come due. An example is surplus optimization: mean–variance optimization applied to surplus (defined as the value of the investor's assets minus the present value of the investor's liabilities). In modeling, liabilities might be represented by a short position in a bond or series of bonds matched to the present value and duration of the liabilities. Another approach involves constructing a liability-hedging portfolio focused on funding liabilities and, for any remaining balance of assets, a risky-asset portfolio (so called because it is risky or riskier in relation to liabilities—often also called a "return-seeking portfolio" because it explicitly seeks return above and beyond the liability benchmark). **Liability-driven investing** (LDI) is an investment industry term that generally encompasses asset allocation that is focused on funding an investor's liabilities. Related fixed-income techniques are covered in the fixed-income sequence under liability-based mandates.

All approaches to asset allocation can be said to address goals. In investment practice and literature, however, the term "goals based" has come to be widely associated with a particular type of approach to asset allocation and investing.

Goals-based approaches to asset allocation, as discussed here, are used primarily for individuals and families, and involve specifying asset allocations for sub-portfolios, each of which is aligned to specified goals ranging from supporting lifestyle needs to aspirational. Each goal is associated with regular, irregular, or bulleted cash flows; a distinct time horizon; and a risk tolerance level expressed as a required probability of achieving the goal.[7] For example, a middle-aged individual might specify a goal of maintaining his current lifestyle and require a high level of confidence that this goal will be attained. That same individual might express a goal of leaving a bequest to his alma mater. This would be a very long-term goal and might have a low required probability. Each goal is assigned to its own sub-portfolio, and an asset allocation strategy specific to that sub-portfolio is derived. The sum of all sub-portfolio asset allocations results in an overall strategic asset allocation for the total portfolio. **Goals-based investing** (GBI) is an investment industry term that encompasses the asset allocation focused on addressing an investor's goals.

---

[7]See Shefrin and Statman (2000) and Brunel (2015).

Institutions and Goals-Based Asset Allocation

Asset segmentation as practiced by some life insurers has some similarities to goals-based investing. Asset segmentation involves notionally or actually segmenting general account assets into sub-portfolios associated with specific lines of business or blocks of liabilities. On one hand, such an approach may be distinguished from goals-based asset allocation for individual investors in being motivated by competitive concerns (to facilitate offering competitive crediting rates on groups of contracts) rather than behavioral ones. On the other hand, Fraser and Jennings (2006) described a behaviorally motivated goals-based approach to asset allocation for foundations and endowments. Following their approach, components of an overall appropriate mean–variance optimal portfolio are allocated to time-based sub-portfolios such that uncomfortably novel or risky positions for the entity's governing body are made acceptable by being placed in longer-term sub-portfolios.

Although any asset allocation approach that considers the liabilities side of the economic balance sheet might be termed "liability relative," there are several important distinctions between liabilities for an institutional investor and goals for an individual investor. These distinctions have meaningful implications for asset allocation:[8]

- Liabilities of institutional investors are legal obligations or debts, whereas goals, such as meeting lifestyle or aspirational objectives, are not. Failing to meet them does not trigger similar consequences.
- Whereas institutional liabilities, such as life insurer obligations or pension benefit obligations, are uniform in nature (all of a single type), an individual's goals may be many and varied.
- Liabilities of institutional investors of a given type (e.g., the pension benefits owed to retirees) are often numerous and so, through averaging, may often be forecast with confidence. In contrast, individual goals are not subject to the law of large numbers and averaging. Contrast an estimate of expected death benefits payable for a group of life insurance policies against an individual's uncertainty about the resources needed in retirement: For a 65-year-old individual, the number of remaining years of life is very uncertain, but insurers can estimate the average for a group of 65-year-olds with some precision.

---

[8]See Rudd and Siegel (2013), which recognizes goals-based planning as a distinct approach. This discussion draws on Brunel (2015).

Liability-Relative and Goals-Based Approaches to Investing

Various perspectives exist concerning the relationship between liability-relative and goals-based approaches to investing. Professor Lionel Martellini summarizes one perspective in the following three statements:[9]

1. Goals-based investing is related to a new paradigm that advocates more granular and investor-centric investment solutions.
2. This new investment solutions paradigm translates into goals-based investing (GBI) approaches in individual money management, in which investors' problems can be summarized in terms of their goals, and it translates into liability-driven investing (LDI) approaches in institutional money management, where the investors' liability is treated as a proxy for their goal.
3. GBI and LDI are therefore related, but each of these approaches has its own specific characteristics. For example, GBI implies the capacity to help individual investors identify a hierarchical list of goals, with a distinction between different types of goals (affordable versus non-affordable, essential versus aspirational, etc.) for which no exact counterpart exists in institutional money management.

5.1. Relevant Objectives

All three of the asset allocation approaches listed here seek to make optimal use of the amount of risk that the asset owner is comfortable bearing to achieve stated investment objectives, although they generally define risk differently. Exhibit 5 summarizes typical objectives.

EXHIBIT 5   Asset Allocation Approaches: Investment Objective

Asset Allocation Approach	Relation to Economic Balance Sheet	Typical Objective	Typical Uses and Asset Owner Types
Asset only	Does not explicitly model liabilities or goals	Maximize Sharpe ratio for acceptable level of volatility	Liabilities or goals not defined and/or simplicity is important • Some foundations, endowments • Sovereign wealth funds • Individual investors
Liability relative	Models legal and quasi-liabilities	Fund liabilities and invest excess assets for growth	Penalty for not meeting liabilities high • Banks • Defined benefit pensions • Insurers

---

[9]Communication of 3 June 2016, used with permission.

Asset Allocation Approach	Relation to Economic Balance Sheet	Typical Objective	Typical Uses and Asset Owner Types
Goals based	Models goals	Achieve goals with specified required probabilities of success	Individual investors

In a mean–variance asset-only approach, the objective is to maximize expected portfolio return per unit of portfolio volatility over some time horizon, consistent with the investor's tolerance for risk and consistent with any constraints stated in the IPS. A portfolio's Sharpe ratio is a characteristic metric for evaluating portfolios in an asset-only mean–variance approach.

The basic objective of a liability-relative asset allocation approach is to ensure payment of liabilities when they are due.

A goals-based approach is similar to a liability-relative approach in that it also seeks to ensure that there are sufficient assets to meet the desired payouts. In goals-based approaches, however, goals are generally associated with individual sub-portfolios, and an asset allocation is designed for each sub-portfolio that reflects the time horizon and required probability of success such that the sum of the sub-portfolios addresses the totality of goals satisfactorily.

5.2. Relevant Risk Concepts

Asset-only approaches focus on asset class risk and effective combinations of asset classes. The baseline asset-only approach, mean–variance optimization, uses volatility (standard deviation) of portfolio return as a primary measure of risk, which is a function of component asset class volatilities and the correlations of asset class returns. A mean–variance asset allocation can also incorporate other risk sensitivities, including risk relative to benchmarks and downside risk. Risk relative to benchmarks is usually measured by tracking risk (tracking error). Downside risk can be represented in various ways, including semi-variance, peak-to-trough maximum drawdown, and measures that focus on the extreme (tail) segment of the downside, such as value at risk.

Mean–variance results, although often the starting point for understanding portfolio risk, are regularly augmented by Monte Carlo simulation. By providing information about how an asset allocation performs when one or more variables are changed—for example, to values representing conditions of financial market stress—simulation helps complete the picture of risk, including downside and tail risk. Insights from simulation can then be incorporated as refinements to the asset allocation.

Liability-relative approaches focus on the risk of having insufficient assets to pay obligations when due, which is a kind of shortfall risk. Other risk concerns include the volatility of contributions needed to fund liabilities. Risk in a liability-relative context is generally underpinned by the differences between asset and liability characteristics (e.g., their relative size, their interest rate sensitivity, their sensitivity to inflation).

Goals-based approaches are concerned with the risk of failing to achieve goals.[10] The risk limits can be quantified as the maximum acceptable probability of not achieving a goal.[11] The plural in "liabilities" and "goals" underscores that these risks are generally related to multiple future points in time. Overall portfolio risk is thus the weighted sum of the risks associated with each goal.

Generally, a given statistical risk measure may be relevant in any of the three approaches. For example, standard deviation can be used to assess overall portfolio volatility in asset-only

---

[10] See Das, Markowitz, Scheid, and Statman (2010), who call goals "mental accounts."
[11] See Brunel (2015).

approaches, and it may be used to measure surplus volatility (the volatility of the difference between the values of assets and liabilities) or the volatility of the funded ratio (the ratio of the values of assets and liabilities) in liability-relative asset allocation.

5.3. Modeling Asset Class Risk

Asset classes are one of the most widely used investment concepts but are often interpreted in distinct ways. Greer (1997) defines an asset class as "a set of assets that bear some fundamental economic similarities to each other, and that have characteristics that make them distinct from other assets that are not part of that class." He specifies three "super classes" of assets:

- *Capital assets*. An ongoing source of something of value (such as interest or dividends); capital assets can be valued by net present value.
- *Consumable/transformable assets*. Assets, such as commodities, that can be consumed or transformed, as part of the production process, into something else of economic value, but which do not yield an ongoing stream of value.
- *Store of value assets*. Neither income generating nor valuable as a consumable or an economic input; examples include currencies and art, whose economic value is realized through sale or exchange.

EXAMPLE 4   Asset Classes (1)

Classify the following investments based on Greer's (1997) framework, or explain how they *do not* fit in the framework:

1. Precious metals
2. Petroleum
3. Hedge funds
4. Timberland
5. Inflation-linked fixed-income securities
6. Volatility

Solutions:

1. Precious metals are a store of value asset except in certain industrial applications (e.g., palladium and platinum in the manufacture of catalytic converters).
2. Petroleum is a consumable/transformable asset; it can be consumed to generate power or provide fuel for transport.
3. Hedge funds do not fit into Greer's (1997) super class framework; a hedge fund strategy invests in underlying asset classes.
4. Timberland is a capital asset or consumable/transformable asset. It is a capital asset in the sense that timber can be harvested and replanted cyclically to generate a stream of cash flows; it is a consumable asset in that timber can be used to produce building materials/packaging or paper.
5. Inflation-linked fixed-income securities is a capital asset because cash flows can be determined based on the characteristics of the security.
6. Volatility does not fit; it is a measurable investment characteristic. Because equity volatility is the underlying for various derivative contracts and an investable risk premium may be associated with it, it is mentioned by some as an asset.

Greer (1997) approaches the classification of asset classes in an abstract or generic sense. The next question is how to specify asset classes to support the purposes of strategic asset allocation.[12] For example, if a manager lumps together very different investments, such as distressed credit and Treasury securities, into an asset class called "fixed income," asset allocation becomes less effective in diversifying and controlling risk. Furthermore, the investor needs a logical framework for distinguishing an asset class from an investment strategy. The following are five criteria that will help in effectively *specifying asset classes for the purpose of asset allocation*:[13]

1. *Assets within an asset class should be relatively homogeneous.* Assets within an asset class should have similar attributes. In the example just given, defining equities to include both real estate and common stock would result in a non-homogeneous asset class.
2. *Asset classes should be mutually exclusive.* Overlapping asset classes will reduce the effectiveness of strategic asset allocation in controlling risk and could introduce problems in developing asset class return expectations. For example, if one asset class for a US investor is domestic common equities, then world equities ex-US is more appropriate as another asset class rather than global equities, which include US equities.
3. *Asset classes should be diversifying.* For risk control purposes, an included asset class should not have extremely high expected correlations with other asset classes or with a linear combination of other asset classes. Otherwise, the included asset class will be effectively redundant in a portfolio because it will duplicate risk exposures already present. In general, a pairwise correlation above 0.95 is undesirable (given a sufficient number of observations to have confidence in the correlation estimate).
4. *The asset classes as a group should make up a preponderance of world investable wealth.* From the perspective of portfolio theory, selecting an asset allocation from a group of asset classes satisfying this criterion should tend to increase expected return for a given level of risk. Furthermore, the inclusion of more markets expands the opportunities for applying active investment strategies, assuming the decision to invest actively has been made. However, such factors as regulatory restrictions on investments and government-imposed limitations on investment by foreigners may limit the asset classes an investor can invest in.
5. *Asset classes selected for investment should have the capacity to absorb a meaningful proportion of an investor's portfolio.* Liquidity and transaction costs are both significant considerations. If liquidity and expected transaction costs for an investment of a size meaningful for an investor are unfavorable, an asset class may not be practically suitable for investment.

Note that Criteria 1 through 3 strictly focus on assets themselves, while Criterion 5, and to some extent Criterion 4, involve potential investor-specific considerations.

Asset Classes Should Be Diversifying

Pairwise asset class correlations are often useful information and are readily obtained. However, in evaluating an investment's value as a diversifier at the portfolio level, it is important to consider an asset in relation to all other assets as a group rather than in a one-by-one (pairwise) fashion. It is possible to reach limited or incorrect conclusions by solely considering pairwise correlations. To give an example, denote the returns to three assets by X, Y, and Z, respectively. Suppose that $Z = aX + bY$; a and b are constants, not both equal to

---

[12]See Kritzman (1999).

[13]As opposed to criteria for asset class definition in an absolute sense.

zero. Asset Z is an exact weighted combination of X and Y and so has no value as a diversifier added to a portfolio consisting of assets X and Y. Yet, if the correlation between X and Y is −0.5, it can be shown that Z has a correlation of just 0.5 with X as well as with Y.

Examining return series' correlations during times of financial market stress can provide practically valuable insight into potential diversification benefits beyond typical correlations that average all market conditions.

In current professional practice, the listing of asset classes often includes the following:

- *Global public equity*—composed of developed, emerging, and sometimes frontier markets and large-, mid-, and small-cap asset classes; sometimes treated as several sub-asset classes (e.g., domestic and non-domestic).
- *Global private equity*—includes venture capital, growth capital, and leveraged buyouts (investment in special situations and distressed securities often occurs within private equity structures too).
- *Global fixed income*—composed of developed and emerging market debt and further divided into sovereign, investment-grade, and high-yield sub-asset classes, and sometimes inflation-linked bonds (unless included in real assets; see the following bullet). Cash and short-duration securities can be included here.
- *Real assets*—includes assets that provide sensitivity to inflation, such as private real estate equity, private infrastructure, and commodities. Sometimes, global inflation-linked bonds are included as a real asset rather than fixed income because of their sensitivity to inflation.

Emerging Market Equities and Fixed Income

Investment practice distinguishes between developed and emerging market equities and fixed income within global equities. The distinction is based on practical differences in investment characteristics, which can be related to typical market differences including the following:

- diversification potential, which is related to the degree to which investment factors driving market returns in developed and emerging markets are not identical (a topic known as "market integration");
- perceived level of informational efficiency; and
- corporate governance, regulation, taxation, and currency convertibility.

As of mid-2016, emerging markets represent approximately 10% of world equity value based on MSCI indices.[14] In fixed income, investment opportunities have expanded as governments and corporations domiciled in emerging markets have increasingly issued debt in their own currency. Markets in local currency inflation-indexed emerging market sovereign debt have become more common.[15]

---

[14]MSCI uses three broad definitions to sort countries into developed, emerging, and frontier: 1) economic development, 2) size and liquidity requirements, and 3) market accessibility criteria (see the MSCI Market Classification Framework at www.msci.com/market-classification).

[15]For a discussion of their potential benefits, see Burger, Warnock, and Warnock (2012), Perry (2011), and Swinkels (2012). Kozhemiakin (2011) discusses how emerging market bonds can facilitate broader representation than an equity-only portfolio because some countries (e.g., Argentina) have small equity markets but larger bond markets.

"Asset classes" are, by definition, groupings of assets. Investment vehicles, such as hedge funds, that apply strategies to asset classes and/or individual investments with the objective of earning a return to investment skill or providing attractive risk characteristics may be treated as a category called "strategies" or "diversifying strategies." When that is the case, this category is assigned a percentage allocation of assets, similar to a true asset class. Economically, asset classes contrast with "strategies" by offering, in general, an inherent, non-skill-based *ex ante* expected return premium.[16]

Effective portfolio optimization and construction may be hindered by excessive asset class granularity. Consider Exhibit 6.

EXHIBIT 6   Examples of Asset Classes and Sub-Asset Classes

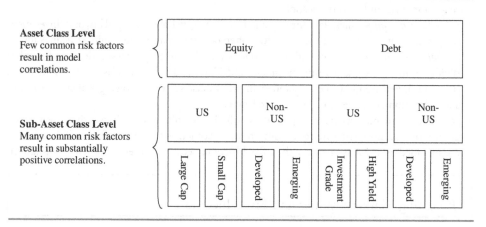

As more and more sub-asset classes are defined, they become less distinctive. In particular, the sources of risk for more broadly defined asset classes are generally better distinguished than those for narrowly defined subgroups. For example, the overlap in the sources of risk of US large-cap equity and US small-cap equity would be greater than the overlap between US and non-US equity. Using broadly defined asset classes with fewer risk source overlaps in optimization is consistent with achieving a diversified portfolio. Additionally, historical data for broadly defined asset classes may be more readily available or more reliable. The question of how much to allocate to equity versus fixed income versus other assets is far more important in strategic asset allocation than *precisely* how much to allocate to the various sub-classes of equity and fixed income. However, when the investor moves from the strategic asset allocation phase to policy implementation, sub-asset class choices become relevant.

---

[16]See Idzorek and Kowara (2013), p. 20.

EXAMPLE 5   Asset Classes (2)

Discuss a specification of asset classes that distinguishes between "domestic intermediate-duration fixed income" and "domestic long-duration fixed income." Contrast potential relevance in asset-only and liability-relative contexts.

Solution: These two groups share key risk factors, such as interest rate and credit risk. For achieving diversification in asset risk—for example, in an asset-only context—asset allocation using domestic fixed income, which includes intermediate and long duration, should be effective and simple. Subsequently, allocation within domestic fixed income could address other considerations, such as interest rate views. When investing in relation to liabilities, distinctions by duration could be of first-order importance and the specification could be relevant.

Any asset allocation, by whatever means arrived at, is expressed ultimately in terms of money allocations to assets. Traditionally—and still in common practice—asset allocation uses asset classes as the unit of analysis. Thus, mean–variance optimization based on four asset classes (e.g., global public equity, global private equity, global fixed income, and real assets) would be based on expected return, return volatility, and return correlation estimates for these asset classes. (The development of such capital market assumptions is the subject of another chapter.) Factor-based approaches, discussed in more detail later, do not use asset classes as the basis for portfolio construction. Technically, the set of achievable investment outcomes cannot be enlarged simply by developing an asset allocation by a different means (for instance, using asset classes as the unit of analysis), all else being equal, such as constraints against short selling (non-negativity constraints).[17] Put another way, adopting a factor-based asset allocation approach does not, by default, lead to superior investment outcomes.

There are allocation methods that focus on assigning investments to the investor's desired exposures to specified risk factors. These methods are premised on the observation that asset classes often exhibit some overlaps in sources of risk, as illustrated in Exhibit 7.[18]

EXHIBIT 7   Common Factor Exposures across Asset Classes

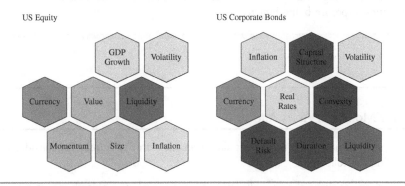

---

[17]Stated more formally and demonstrated in Idzorek and Kowara (2013).
[18]See Podkaminer (2013).

The overlaps seen in Exhibit 7 help explain the correlation of equity and credit assets. Modeling using asset classes as the unit of analysis tends to obscure the portfolio's sensitivity to overlapping risk factors, such as inflation risk in this example. As a result, controlling risk exposures may be problematic. Multifactor risk models, which have a history of use in individual asset selection, have been brought to bear on the issue of controlling systematic risk exposures in asset allocation.

In broad terms, when using factors as the units of analysis, we begin with specifying risk factors and the desired exposure to each factor. Asset classes can be described with respect to their sensitivities to each of the factors. Factors, however, are not directly investable. On that basis, asset class portfolios that isolate exposure to the risk factor are constructed; these factor portfolios involve both long and short positions. A choice of risk exposures in factor space can be mapped back to asset class space for implementation. Uses of multifactor risk models in asset allocation have been labeled "factor-based asset allocation" in contrast to "asset class-based asset allocation," which uses asset classes directly as the unit of analysis.

Factor Representation

Although risk factors can be thought of as the basic building blocks of investments, most are not directly investable. In this context, risk factors are associated with expected return premiums. Long and short positions in assets (spread positions) may be needed to isolate the respective risks and associated expected return premiums. Other risk factors may be accessed through derivatives. The following are a few examples of how risk factor exposures can be achieved.

- *Inflation.* Going long nominal Treasuries and short inflation-linked bonds isolates the inflation component.
- *Real interest rates.* Inflation-linked bonds provide a proxy for real interest rates.
- *US volatility.* VIX (Chicago Board Options Exchange Volatility Index) futures provide a proxy for implied volatility.
- *Credit spread.* Going long high-quality credit and short Treasuries/government bonds isolates credit exposure.
- *Duration.* Going long 10+ year Treasuries and short 1–3 year Treasuries isolates the duration exposure being targeted.

Factor Models in Asset Allocation

The interest in using factors for asset allocation stems from a number of considerations, including the following:

- The desire to shape the asset allocation based on goals and objectives that cannot be expressed by asset classes (such as matching liability characteristics in a liability-relative approach).

- An intense focus on portfolio risk in all of its various dimensions, helped along by availability of commercial factor-based risk measurement and management tools.
- The acknowledgment that many highly correlated so-called asset classes are better defined as parts of the same high-level asset class. For example, domestic and foreign equity may be better seen as sub-classes of global public equity.
- The realization that equity risk can be the dominant risk exposure even in a seemingly well-diversified portfolio.

6. STRATEGIC ASSET ALLOCATION

An asset allocation that arises in long-term investment planning is often called the "strategic asset allocation" or "policy portfolio": It is an asset allocation that is expected to be effective in achieving an asset owner's investment objectives, given his or her investment constraints and risk tolerance, as documented in the investment policy statement.

A theoretical underpinning for quantitative approaches to asset allocation is utility theory, which uses a utility function as a mathematical representation of preferences that incorporates the investor's risk aversion. According to utility theory, the optimal asset allocation is the one that is expected to provide the highest utility to the investor at the investor's investment time horizon. The optimization program, in broad terms, is

$$\underset{\substack{\text{Maximize} \\ \text{by choice of asset class weights}}}{\text{Maximize}}_{w_i} E[U(W_T)] = f \left(\begin{array}{c} W_0, w_i, \text{asset class return distributions,} \\ \text{degree of risk aversion} \end{array} \right)$$

$$\text{subject to} \sum_{i=1}^{n} w_i = 1 \text{ and any other constraints on } w_i$$

The first line is the objective function, and the second line consists of constraints on asset class weights; other constraints besides those on weights can also be incorporated (for example, specified levels of bond duration or portfolio yield may be targeted). With W_0 and W_T (the values of wealth today and at time horizon T, respectively) the investor's problem is to select the asset allocation that maximizes the expected utility of ending wealth, $E[U(W_T)]$, subject to the constraints that asset class weights sum to 1 and that weights observe any limits the investor places on them. Beginning wealth, asset class weights, and asset class returns imply a distribution of values for ending wealth, and the utility function assigns a value to each of them; by weighting these values by their probability of occurrence, an expected utility for the asset allocation is determined.

An expected utility framework underlies many, but not all, quantitative approaches to asset allocation. A widely used group in asset allocation consists of power utility functions,[19] which exhibit the analytically convenient characteristic that risk aversion does not depend on the level of wealth. Power utility can be approximated by mean–variance utility, which underlies mean–variance optimization.

---

[19]Power utility has the form $U = \frac{w_T^{1-\lambda}}{1-\lambda}$, where $\lambda > 0$ is the parameter of risk aversion (if $\lambda \rightarrow 0$, the investor is risk neutral).

Optimal Choice in the Simplest Case

The simplest asset allocation decision problem involves one risky asset and one risk-free asset. Let λ, μ, r_f and σ^2 represent, respectively, the investor's degree of risk aversion, the risk asset's expected return, the risk-free interest rate, and the variance of return. With mean–variance utility, the optimal allocation to the risky asset, w^*, can be shown to equal

$$w^* = \frac{1}{\lambda} \left(\frac{\mu - r_f}{\sigma^2} \right)$$

The allocation to the risky asset is inversely proportional to the investor's risk aversion and directly proportional to the risk asset's expected return per unit of risk (represented by return variance).[20]

Selection of a strategic asset allocation generally involves the following steps:[21]

1. Determine and quantify the investor's objectives. What is the pool of assets meant for (e.g., paying future benefit payments, contributing to a university's budget, securing ample assets for retirement)? What is the investor trying to achieve? What liabilities or needs or goals need to be recognized (explicitly or implicitly)? How should objectives be modeled?

2. Determine the investor's risk tolerance and how risk should be expressed and measured. What is the investor's overall tolerance for risk and specific risk sensitivities? How should these be quantified in the process of developing an appropriate asset allocation (risk measures, factor models)?

3. Determine the investment horizon(s). What are the appropriate planning horizons to use for asset allocation; that is, over what horizon(s) should the objectives and risk tolerance be evaluated?

4. Determine other constraints and the requirements they impose on asset allocation choices. What is the tax status of the investor? Should assets be managed with consideration given to ESG issues? Are there any legal and regulatory factors that need to be considered? Are any political sensitivities relevant? Are there any other constraints that the investor has imposed in the IPS and other communications?

5. Determine the approach to asset allocation that is most suitable for the investor.

6. Specify asset classes, and develop a set of capital market expectations for the specified asset classes.

7. Develop a range of potential asset allocation choices for consideration. These choices are often developed through optimization exercises. Specifics depend on the approach taken to asset allocation.

---

[20]See Ang (2014), Chapter 4, for further analysis.
[21]Arjan Berkelaar, CFA, contributed to this formulation of steps.

8. Test the robustness of the potential choices. This testing often involves conducting simulations to evaluate potential results in relation to investment objectives and risk tolerance over appropriate planning horizon(s) for the different asset allocations developed in Step 7. The sensitivity of the outcomes to changes in capital market expectations is also tested.

9. Iterate back to Step 7 until an appropriate and agreed-on asset allocation is constructed.

Subsequent chapters on asset allocation in practice will address the "how." The following sections give an indication of thematic considerations. We use investors with specific characteristics to illustrate the several approaches distinguished: sovereign wealth fund for asset-only allocation; a frozen corporate DB plan for liability-relative allocation; and an ultra-high-net-worth family for goals-based allocation. In practice, any type of investor could approach asset allocation with varying degrees of focus on modeling and integrating liabilities-side balance sheet considerations. How these cases are analyzed in this chapter should not be viewed as specifying normative limits of application for various asset allocation approaches. For example, a liability-relative perspective has wide potential relevance for institutional investors because it has the potential to incorporate all information on the economic balance sheet. Investment advisers to high-net-worth investors may choose to use any of the approaches.

6.1. Asset Only

Asset-only allocation is based on the principle of selecting portfolios that make efficient use of asset risk. The focus here is mean–variance optimization, the mainstay among such approaches. Given a set of asset classes and assumptions concerning their expected returns, volatilities, and correlations, this approach traces out an efficient frontier that consists of portfolios that are expected to offer the greatest return at each level of portfolio return volatility. The Sharpe ratio is a key descriptor of an asset allocation: If a portfolio is efficient, it has the highest Sharpe ratio among portfolios with the same volatility of return.

An example of an investor that might use an asset-only approach is the (hypothetical) Government Petroleum Fund of Caflandia (GPFC) introduced next.

Investor Case Facts: GPFC, A Sovereign Wealth Fund

- *Name*: Government Petroleum Fund of Caflandia (GPFC)
- *Narrative*: The emerging country of Caflandia has established a sovereign wealth fund to capture revenue from its abundant petroleum reserves. The government's goal in setting up the fund is to promote a fair sharing of the benefits between current and future generations (intergenerational equity) from the export of the country's petroleum resources. Caflandia's equity market represents 0.50% of global equity market capitalization. Economists estimate that distributions in the interest of intergenerational equity may need to begin in 20 years. Future distribution policy is undetermined.
- *Tax status*: Non-taxable.
- *Financial assets and financial liabilities*: Financial assets are CAF$40 billion at market value, making GPFC among the largest investors in Caflandia. GPFC has no borrowings.
- *Extended assets and liabilities*: Cash inflows from petroleum exports are assumed to grow at inflation +1% for the next 15 years and may change depending on reserves

and global commodity demand. The present value of expected future income from state-owned reserves is estimated to be CAF$60 billion. Future spending needs are positively correlated with consumer inflation and population growth. In Exhibit 8, the amount for the present value (PV) of future spending, which GPFC has not yet determined, is merely a placeholder to balance assets and liabilities; as a result, no equity is shown.

EXHIBIT 8   GPFC Economic Balance Sheet (in CAF$ billions) 31 December 20x6

Assets		Liabilities and Economic Net Worth	
Financial Assets		*Financial Liabilities*	
Investments (includes cash, equities, fixed income, and other investments)	40		
Extended Assets		*Extended Liabilities*	
PV of expected future income	60	PV of future spending	100
		Economic Net Worth	
		Economic net worth	0
Total	100		100

For GPFC, the amount and timing of funds needed for future distributions to Caflandia citizens are, as yet, unclear. GPFC can currently focus on asset risk and its efficient use to grow assets within the limits of the fund's risk tolerance. In addition to considering expected return in relation to volatility in selecting an asset allocation, GPFC might include such considerations as the following:

- diversification across global asset classes (possibly quantified as a constraint on the proportion allocated to any given asset classes);
- correlations with the petroleum sources of income to GPFC;
- the potential positive correlation of future spending with inflation and population growth in Caflandia;
- long investment horizon (as a long-term investor, GPFC may be well positioned to earn any return premium that may be associated with the relatively illiquid asset classes); and
- return outcomes in severe financial market downturns.

Suppose GPFC quantifies its risk tolerance in traditional mean–variance terms as willingness to bear portfolio volatility of up to 17% per year. This risk tolerance is partly based on GPFC's unwillingness to allow the fund to fall below 90% funded. GPFC's current strategic asset allocation, along with several alternatives that have been developed by its staff during an asset allocation review, are shown in Exhibit 9. The category "Diversifying strategies" consists of a diversified allocation to hedge funds.

EXHIBIT 9   GPFC Strategic Asset Allocation Decision[22]

| | | **Asset Allocation** | | |
| | | **Proposed** | | |
	Current	**A**	**B**	**C**
Investment				
Equities				
Domestic	50%	40%	45%	30%
Global ex-domestic		10%	20%	25%
Bonds				
Nominal	30%	30%	20%	10%
Inflation linked				10%
Real estate	20%	10%	15%	10%
Diversifying strategies		10%		15%
Portfolio statistics				
Expected arithmetic return	8.50%	8.25%	8.88%	8.20%
Volatility (standard deviation)	15.57%	14.24%	16.63%	14.06%
Sharpe ratio	0.353	0.369	0.353	0.370
One-year 5% VaR	−17.11%	−15.18%	−18.48%	−14.93%

Notes: The government bond rate is 3%. The acceptable level of volatility is ≤17% per year. The value at risk (VaR) is stated as a percent of the initial portfolio value over one year (e.g., −16% means a decline of 16%).

GPFC decides it is willing to tolerate a 5% chance of losing 22% or more of portfolio value in a given year. This risk is evaluated by examining the one-year 5% VaR of potential asset allocations.

Let us examine GPFC's decision. The current asset allocation and the alternatives developed by staff all satisfy the GPFC's tolerance for volatility and VaR limit. The staff's alternatives appear to represent incremental, rather than large-scale, changes from the current strategic asset allocation. We do not know whether capital market assumptions have changed since the current strategic asset allocation was approved.

Mix A, compared with the current asset allocation, diversifies the equity allocation to include non-domestic (global ex-domestic) equities and spreads the current allocation to real estate over real estate and diversifying strategies. Given GPFC's long investment horizon and absence of liquidity needs, an allocation to diversifying strategies at 10% should not present liquidity concerns. Because diversifying strategies are more liquid than private real estate, the

---

[22]The assumed expected returns and return volatilities are (given in that order in parentheses and expressed as decimals, rather than percentages): domestic equities (0.11, 0.25), non-domestic equities (0.09, 0.18), nominal bonds (0.05, 0.10), inflation-linked bonds (0.035, 0.06), real estate (0.075, 0.16), and diversifying strategies (0.07, 0.09). A correlation matrix with hypothetical values and a hypothetical relationship between the allocations and VaR also lies behind the exhibit. Because the purpose here is to illustrate concepts rather than mechanics, inputs are not discussed although they are very important in asset allocation.

overall liquidity profile of the fund improves. It is important to note that given the illiquid nature of real estate, it could take considerable time to reallocate from real estate to diversifying strategies. Mix A has a lower volatility (by 133 bps) than the current allocation and slightly lower tail risk (the 5% VaR for Mix A is −15%, whereas the 5% VaR for the current asset mix is −17%). Mix A's Sharpe ratio is slightly higher. On the basis of the facts given, Mix A appears to be an incremental improvement on the current asset allocation.

Compared with Mix A and the current asset allocation, Mix B increases the allocation to equities by 15 percentage points and pulls back from the allocation to bonds and, in relation to Mix A, diversifying strategies. Although Mix B has a higher expected return and its VaR is within GPFC's tolerance of 22%, Mix B's lower Sharpe ratio indicates that it makes inefficient use of its additional risk. Mix B does not appear to deserve additional consideration.

Compared with the current asset allocation and Mix A, Mix C's total allocation to equities, at 55%, is higher and the mix is more diversified considering the allocation of 25% non-domestic equities. Mix C's allocation to fixed income is 20% compared with 30% for Mix A and the current asset mix. The remaining fixed-income allocation has been diversified with an exposure to both nominal and inflation-linked bonds. The diversifying strategies allocation is funded by a combination of the reduced weights to fixed income and real estate. The following observations may be made:

- Mix C's increase in equity exposure (compared with the equity exposure of Mix A and the current mix) has merit because more equity-like choices in the asset allocation could be expected to give GPFC more exposure to such a factor as a GDP growth factor (see Exhibit 9); population growth is one driver of GDP.
- Within fixed income, Mix C's allocation to inflation-linked bonds could be expected to hedge the inflation risk inherent in future distributions.
- Mix C has the lowest volatility and the lowest VaR among the asset allocations, although the differences compared with Mix A are very small. Mix C's Sharpe ratio is comparable to (insignificantly higher than) Mix A's.

Based on the facts given, Mix A and Mix C appear to be improvements over the current mix. Mix C may have the edge over Mix A based on the discussion. As a further step in the evaluation process, GPFC may examine the robustness of the forecasted results by changing the capital market assumptions and simulating shocks to such variables as inflation. The discussion of Mix C shows that there are means for potential liability concerns (the probable sensitivity of spending to inflation and population growth) to enter decision-making even from a mean–variance optimization perspective.

EXAMPLE 6   Asset-Only Asset Allocation

1. Describe how the Sharpe ratio, considered in isolation, would rank the asset allocation in Exhibit 9.
2. State a limitation of basing a decision only on the Sharpe ratio addressed in Question 1.
3. An assertion is heard in an investment committee discussion that because the Sharpe ratio of diversifying strategies (0.55) is higher than real estate's (0.50), any

potential allocation to real estate would be better used in diversifying strategies. Describe why the argument is incomplete.

Solution to 1: The ranking by Sharpe ratios in isolation is C (3.70), A (3.69), and current and B (both 3.53). Using only the Sharpe ratio, Mix C appears superior to the other choices, but such an approach ignores several important considerations.

Solution to 2: The Sharpe ratio, while providing a means to rank choices on the basis of return per unit of volatility, does not capture other characteristics that are likely to be important to the asset owner, such as VaR and funded ratio. Furthermore, the Sharpe ratio by itself cannot confirm that the absolute level of portfolio risk is within the investor's specified range.

Solution to 3: It is true that the higher the Sharpe ratio of an investment, the greater its contribution to the Sharpe ratio of the overall portfolio, *holding all other things equal*. However, that condition is not usually true. Diversification potential in a portfolio (quantified by correlations) may differ. For example, including both diversifying strategies and real estate in an allocation may ultimately decrease portfolio-level risk through favorable correlation characteristics. Also, as in the solution to Question 2, other risk considerations besides volatility may be relevant.

Financial theory suggests that investors should consider the global market-value weighted portfolio as a baseline asset allocation. This portfolio, which sums all investable assets (global stocks, bonds, real estate, and so forth) held by investors, reflects the balancing of supply and demand across world markets. In financial theory, it is the portfolio that minimizes diversifiable risk, which in principle is uncompensated. Because of that characteristic, theory indicates that the global market portfolio should be the available portfolio that makes the most efficient use of the risk budget.[23] Other arguments for using it as a baseline include its position as a reference point for a highly diversified portfolio and the discipline it provides in relation to mitigating any investment biases, such as home-country bias (discussed below).

At a minimum, the global market portfolio serves as a starting point for discussion and ensures that the investor articulates a clear justification for moving away from global capitalization market weights. The global market portfolio is expressed in two phases. The first phase allocates assets in proportion to the global portfolio of stocks, bonds, and real assets. The second phase disaggregates each of these broad asset classes into regional, country, and security weights using capitalization weights. The second phase is typically used within a global equity portfolio where an asset owner will examine the global capitalization market weights and either accept them or alter them. Common tilts (biases) include overweighting the home-country market, value, size (small cap), and emerging markets. For many investors, allocations to foreign fixed income have been adopted more slowly than allocations to foreign equity. Most investors have at least some amount in non-home-country equity.

---

[23]According to the two-fund separation theorem, all investors optimally hold a combination of a risk-free asset and an optimal portfolio of all risky assets. This optimal portfolio is the global market value portfolio.

Home-Country Bias

A given for GPFC was that Caflandia's equity markets represent only 0.50% of the value of world equity markets. However, in all asset allocations in Exhibit 9, the share of domestic equity ranged from 50% for the current asset allocation to 30% for Mix C. The favoring of domestic over non-domestic investment relative to global market value weights is called **home-country bias** and is very common. Even relatively small economies feature pension plans, endowments, and other funds, which are disproportionately tilted toward the equity and fixed-income offerings in the domestic market. The same tendency is true for very large markets, such as the United States and the eurozone. By biasing toward the home market, asset owners may not be optimally aligning regional weights with the global market portfolio and are implicitly implementing a market view. Investment explanations for the bias, such as offsetting liabilities that are denominated in the home currency, may be relevant in some cases, however.

For reference, the MSCI All Country World Portfolio (ACWI), a proxy for the public equities portion of the global equity market portfolio, contains the following capitalization weights as of 31 December 2015:

- Developed Europe and the Middle East: 22.8%
- Developed Pacific: 11.7%
- North America: 55.9%
- Emerging markets: 9.6%

Investing in a global market portfolio faces several implementation hurdles. First, estimating the size of each asset class on a global basis is an imprecise exercise given the uneven availability of information on non-publicly traded assets. Second, the practicality of investing proportionately in residential real estate, much of which is held in individual homeowners' hands, has been questioned. Third, private commercial real estate and global private equity assets are not easily carved into pieces of a size that is accessible to most investors. Practically, proxies for the global market portfolio are often based only on traded assets, such as portfolios of exchange-traded funds (ETFs). Furthermore, some investors have implemented alternative weighting schemes, such as GDP weight or equal weight. However, it is a useful discipline to articulate a justification for any deviation from the capitalization-weighted global market portfolio.

6.2. Liability Relative

To illustrate the liability-relative approach, we take the defined benefit (DB) pension plan of (hypothetical) GPLE Corporation, with case facts given below.

A Frozen DB Plan, GPLE Corporation Pension

- *Name*: GPLE Corporation Pension
- *Narrative*: GPLE is a machine tool manufacturer with a market value of $2 billion. GPLE is the sponsor of a $1.25 billion legacy DB plan, which is now frozen (i.e., no

new plan participants and no new benefits accruing for existing plan participants). GPLE Pension has a funded ratio (the ratio of pension assets to liabilities) of 1.15. Thus, the plan is slightly overfunded. Responsibility for the plan's management rests with the firm's treasury department (which also has responsibility for GPLE Corporation treasury operations).

- *Tax status*: Non-taxable.
- *Financial assets and financial liabilities*: Assets amount to $1.25 billion at market values. Given a funded ratio of 1.15, that amount implies that liabilities are valued at about $1.087 billion. Projected distributions to pension beneficiaries have a present value of $1.087 billion at market value.

GPLE does not reflect any extended assets or liabilities; thus, economic net worth is identical to traditional accounting net worth.

EXHIBIT 10   GPLE Pension Economic Balance Sheet (in US$ billions) 31 December 20x6

Assets		Liabilities and Economic Net Worth	
Financial Assets		*Financial Liabilities*	
Pension assets	1.250	PV of pension liability	1.087
		Economic Net Worth	
		Economic net worth	0.163
Total	1.250		1.250

GPLE, the plan sponsor, receives two asset allocation recommendations. Recommendation A does not explicitly consider GPLE's pension's liabilities but is instead based on an asset-only perspective: the mean–variance efficient frontier given a set of capital market assumptions. A second recommendation, "Recommendation B," does explicitly consider liabilities, incorporating a liability-hedging portfolio based on an analysis of GPLE pension liabilities and a return-seeking portfolio.

In evaluating asset allocation choices, consider the pensioners' and the plan sponsor's interests. Pensioners want to receive the stream of promised benefits with as little risk, or chance of interruption, as possible. Risk increases as the funded ratio declines. When the funded ratio is 1.0, pension assets just cover pension liabilities with no safety buffer. When the funded ratio is less than 1.0, the plan sponsor generally needs to make up the deficit in pension assets by contributions to the plan. For example, with a 10-year investment time horizon and a choice between two asset allocations, the allocation with the lower expected present value of cumulative contributions to Year 10 would generally be preferred by the sponsor, all else being equal. In practice, all else is usually not equal. For example, the alternative with the lower *expected* present value of contributions may involve more risk to the level of contributions in adverse market conditions. For example, the 5% of *worst outcomes* for the present value of cumulative contributions may be more severe for the lower expected contribution alternative. Thus, possible asset allocations generally involve risk trade-offs.[24] Now consider the recommendations.

Recommendation A, based on asset-only analysis, involves a 65% allocation to global equities and a 35% allocation to global fixed income. Assume that this asset allocation is mean–variance efficient and has the highest Sharpe ratio among portfolios that meet the pension's assumed tolerance for asset return volatility. Capital market assumptions indicate that equities have a significantly higher expected return and volatility than fixed income.

Recommendation B, based on a liability-relative approach to asset allocation, involves an allocation of $1.125 billion to a fixed-income portfolio that is very closely matched in interest rate sensitivity to the present value of plan liabilities (and to any other liability factor risk exposures)—the liability hedging portfolio—and a $0.125 allocation to equities (the return-seeking portfolio). This is a proportional allocation of 10% to equities and 90% to fixed income. The equities allocation is believed to provide potential for increasing the size of the buffer between pension assets and liabilities with negligible risk to funded status. Recommendation B lies below the asset-only efficient frontier with a considerably lower expected return vis-à-vis Recommendation A.

What are the arguments for and against each of these recommendations? Recommendation A is expected, given capital market assumptions, to increase the size of the buffer between pension assets and liabilities. But the sponsor does not benefit from increases in the buffer if the current buffer is adequate.[25] However, with a $0.65 \times \$1.25$ billion $= \$0.8125$ allocation to equities and a current buffer of assets of $1.25 billion $- \$1.087$ billion $= \$0.163$ billion, a decline of that amount or more in equity values (a 20% decline) would put the plan into underfunded status (assuming no commensurate changes in the liability). Thus, Recommendation A creates contribution risk for the plan sponsor without a potential upside clearly benefiting either the sponsor or beneficiaries.

For Recommendation B, because the risk characteristics of the $1.125 billion fixed-income portfolio are closely matched with those of the $1.087 billion of pension liabilities with a buffer, the plan sponsor should not face any meaningful risk of needing to make further contributions to the pension. Pensioners expect the plan to be fully funded on an ongoing basis without any reliance on the sponsor's ability to make additional contributions. This is an excellent outcome for both. The pension liabilities are covered (defeased).

The example is highly stylized—the case facts were developed to make points cleanly—but does point to the potential value of managing risk in asset allocation explicitly in relation to liabilities. A typical use of fixed-income assets in liability-relative asset allocation should be noted: Liability-relative approaches to asset allocation tend to give fixed income a larger role than asset-only approaches in such cases as the one examined here because interest rates are a major financial market driver of both liability and bond values. Thus, bonds can be important in hedging liabilities, but equities can be relevant for liability hedging too. With richer case facts, as when liabilities accrue with inflation (not the case in the frozen DB example), equities may have a long-term role in matching the characteristics of liabilities. In underfunded plans, the potential upside of equities would often have greater value for the plan sponsor than in the fully funded case examined.

---

[24]Collie and Gannon (2009) explore the contribution risk trade-off considered here in more detail.

[25]Real-world complexities, such as DB plan termination to capture a positive surplus or pension risk transfer (annuitization), are beyond the scope of this chapter; generally, there are restrictions and penalties involved in such actions, and the point made here is valid.

Liability Glide Paths

If GPLE were underfunded, it might consider establishing a liability glide path. A **liability glide path** is a technique in which the plan sponsor specifies in advance the desired proportion of liability-hedging assets and return-seeking assets and the duration of the liability hedge as funded status changes and contributions are made. The technique is particularly relevant to underfunded pensions. The idea reflects the fact that the optimal asset allocation in general is sensitive to changes in the funded status of the plan. The objective is to increase the funded status by reducing surplus risk over time. Although a higher contribution rate may be necessary to align assets with liabilities, the volatility of contributions should decrease, providing more certainty for cash flow planning purposes and decreasing risk to plan participants. Eventually, GPLE would hope to achieve and maintain a sufficiently high funded ratio so that there would be minimal risk of requiring additional contributions or transferring pension risk to an annuity provider.

The importance of such characteristics as interest rate sensitivity (duration), inflation, and credit risk in constructing a liability-hedging asset portfolio suggests the relevance of risk-factor modeling in liability-relative approaches. A risk factor approach can be extended to the return-seeking portfolio in order to minimize unintentional overlap among common factors across both portfolios—for example, credit. Exploring these topics is outside the scope of the current chapter.

The next section addresses an approach to asset allocation related to liability relative in its focus on funding needs.

6.3. Goals Based

We use the hypothetical Lee family to present some thematic elements of a goals-based approach.

Investor Case Facts: The Lee Family

- *Name*: Ivy and Charles Lee
- *Narrative*: Ivy is a 54-year-old life sciences entrepreneur. Charles is 55 years old and employed as an orthopedic surgeon. They have two unmarried children aged 25 (Deborah) and 18 (David). Deborah has a daughter with physical limitations.
- *Financial assets and financial liabilities*: Portfolio of $25 million with $1 million in margin debt as well as residential real estate of $3 million with $1 million in mortgage debt.
- *Other assets and liabilities*:
  - Pre-retirement earnings are expected to total $16 million in present value terms (human capital).
  - David will soon begin studying at a four-year private university; the present value of the expected parental contribution is $250,000.

- The Lees desire to give a gift to a local art museum in five years. In present value terms, the gift is valued at $750,000.
- The Lees want to establish a trust for their granddaughter with a present value of $3 million to be funded at the death of Charles.
- The present value of future consumption expenditures is estimated at $20 million.

EXHIBIT 11   Lee Family Economic Balance Sheet (in US$ millions) 31 December 20x6

Assets		Liabilities and Economic Net Worth	
Financial Assets		*Financial Liabilities*	
Investment portfolio	25	Margin debt	1
Real estate	3	Mortgage	1
Extended Assets		*Extended Liabilities*	
Human capital	16	David's education	0.25
		Museum gift	0.75
		Special needs trust	3
		PV of future consumption	20
		Economic Net Worth	
		Economic net worth (economic assets less economic liabilities)	18
Total	**44**		**44**

The financial liabilities shown are legal liabilities. The extended liabilities include funding needs that the Lees want to meet. The balance sheet includes an estimate of the present value of future consumption, which is sometimes called the "consumption liability." The amount shown reflects expected values over their life expectancy given their ages. If they live longer, consumption needs will exceed the $20 million in the case facts and erode the $18 million in equity. If their life span is shorter, $18 million plus whatever they do not consume of the $20 million in PV of future consumption becomes part of their estate. Note that for the Lees, the value of assets exceeds the value of liabilities, resulting in a positive economic net worth (a positive difference between economic assets and economic liabilities); this is analogous to a positive owners' equity on a company's financial balance sheet.

From Exhibit 11, we can identify four goals totaling $24 million in present value terms: a lifestyle goal (assessed as a need for $20 million in present value terms), an education goal ($0.25 million), a charitable goal ($0.75 million), and the special needs trust ($3 million).

The present value of expected future earnings (human capital) at $16 million is less than the lifestyle present value of $20 million, which means that some part of the investment portfolio must fund the Lees' standard of living. It is important to note that although the Lee family has $18 million of economic net worth, most of this comes from the $16 million extended asset of human capital. Specific investment portfolio assets have not yet been dedicated to specific goals.

Goals-based asset allocation builds on several insights from behavioral finance. The approach's characteristic use of sub-portfolios is grounded in the behavioral finance insight that investors tend to ignore money's fungibility[26] and assign specific dollars to specific uses—a phenomenon known as mental accounting. Goals-based asset allocation, as described here, systemizes the fruitful use of mental accounts. This approach may help investors embrace more-optimal portfolios (as defined in an asset-only or asset–liability framework) by adding higher risk assets—that, without context, might frighten the investor—to longer-term, aspirational sub-portfolios while adopting a more conservative allocation for sub-portfolios that address lifestyle preservation.

In Exhibit 11, the Lees' lifestyle goal is split into three components: a component called "lifestyle—minimum" intended to provide protection for the Lees' lifestyle in a disaster scenario, a component called "lifestyle—baseline" to address needs outside of worst cases, and a component called "lifestyle—aspirational" that reflects a desire for a chance at a markedly higher lifestyle. These sum to the present value of future consumption shown in the preceding Exhibit 11. Exhibit 12 describes these qualitatively; a numerical characterization could be very relevant for some advisers, however. By eliciting information on the Lees' perception of the goals' importance, the investment adviser might calibrate the required probabilities of achieving the goals quantitatively. For example, the three lifestyle goals might have 99%, 90%, and 50% assigned probabilities of success, respectively.

EXHIBIT 12   Lee Family: Required Probability of Meeting Goals and Goal Time Horizons

Goal	Required Probability of Achieving	Time Horizon
Lifestyle—minimum	Extremely high	Short to distant
Lifestyle—baseline	Very high	Short to distant
Lifestyle—aspirational	Moderate	Distant
Education	Very high	Short
Trust	High	Long
Charitable	Moderate	Short

Because the Lees might delay or forego making a gift to the museum if it would affect the trust goal, the trust goal is more urgent for the Lees. Also note that although parts of the Lees' lifestyle goals run the full time horizon spectrum from short to distant, they also have significant current earnings and human capital (which transforms into earnings as time passes). This fact puts the investment portfolio's role in funding the lifestyle goal further into the future.

Goals-based approaches generally set the strategic asset allocation in a bottom-up fashion. The Lees' lifestyle goal might be addressed with three sub-portfolios, with the longest horizon sub-portfolio being less liquid and accepting more risk than the others. Although for the GPLE pension, no risk distinction was made among different parts of the pension liability vis-à-vis asset allocation, such distinctions are made in goals-based asset allocation.

---

[26]"Fungibility" is the property of an asset that a quantity of it may be replaced by another equal quantity in the satisfaction of an obligation. Thus, any 5,000 Japanese yen note can be used to pay a yen obligation of that amount, and the notes can be said to be fungible.

What about the Lees' other goals? Separate sub-portfolios could be assigned to the special needs and charitable goals with asset allocations that reflect the associated time horizons and required probabilities of not attaining these goals. A later chapter on asset allocation in practice addresses implementation processes in detail.

Types of Goals

As goals-based asset allocation has advanced, various classification systems for goals have been proposed. Two of those classification systems are as follows.

Brunel (2012):

- *Personal goals*—to meet current lifestyle requirements and unanticipated financial needs
- *Dynastic goals*—to meet descendants' needs
- *Philanthropic goals*

Chhabra (2005):

- *Personal risk bucket*—to provide protection from a dramatic decrease in lifestyle (i.e., safe-haven investments)
- *Market risk bucket*—to ensure the current lifestyle can be maintained (allocations for average risk-adjusted market returns)
- *Aspirational risk bucket*—to increase wealth substantially (greater than average risk is accepted)

EXAMPLE 7   Goals-Based Asset Allocation

The Lees are presented with the following optimized asset allocations:

Asset Allocation	Cash	Global Bonds	Global Equities	Diversifying Strategies
A	40%	50%	10%	0%
B	10%	30%	45%	15%

Assume that a portfolio of 70% global equities and 30% bonds reflects an appropriate balance of expected return and risk for the Lees with respect to a 10-year time horizon for most moderately important goals. Based on the information given:

1. What goal(s) may be addressed by Allocation A?
2. What goal(s) may be addressed by Allocation B?

Because of her industry connections in the life sciences, Ivy Lee is given the opportunity to be an early-stage venture capital investor in what she assesses is a very promising technology.

3. What insights does goals-based asset allocation offer on this opportunity?

Solution to 1: Allocation A stresses liquidity and stability. It may be appropriate to meet short-term lifestyle and education goals.

Solution to 2: Allocation B has a greater growth emphasis, although it is somewhat conservative in relation to a 70/30 equity/bond baseline. It may be appropriate for funding the trust because of the goal's long time horizon and the Lees' desire for a high probability of achieving it.

Solution to 3: Early-stage venture capital investments are both risky and illiquid; therefore, they belong in the longer-term and more risk-tolerant sub-portfolios. Ivy's decision about how much money she can commit should relate to how much excess capital remains after addressing goals that have a higher priority associated with them. Note that economic balance sheet thinking would stress that the life sciences opportunity is not particularly diversifying to her human capital.

Discount Rates and Longevity Risk

Although calculation of assets needed for sub-portfolios is outside the scope of this chapter, certain themes can be indicated. Consider a retiree with a life expectancy of 20 years. The retiree has two goals:

- To maintain his current lifestyle upon retirement. This goal has a high required probability of achievement that is evaluated at 95%.
- To gift $1 million to a university in five years. This is viewed as a "desire" rather than a "need" and has a required probability evaluated at 75%.

Suppose that the investor's adviser specifies sub-portfolios as follows:

- for the first decade of lifestyle spending, a 3% expected return;
- for the second decade of lifestyle spending, a 4.6% expected return; and
- for the planned gift to the university, a 5.4% expected return.

Based on an estimate of annual consumption needs and the amount of the gift and given expected returns for the assigned sub-portfolios, the assets to be assigned to each sub-portfolio could be calculated by discounting amounts back to the present using their expected returns. However, this approach does not reflect the asset owner's required probability of achieving a goal. The higher the probability requirement for a future cash need, the greater the amount of assets needed in relation to it. Because of the inverse relation between present value and the discount rate, to reflect a 95% required probability, for example, the discount rates could be set at a lower level so that more assets are assigned to the sub-portfolio, increasing the probability of achieving the goal to the required level of 95% level.

Another consideration in determining the amount needed for future consumption is longevity risk. Life expectancies are median (50th percentile) outcomes. The retiree may outlive his life expectancy. To address longevity risk, the calculation of the present value of liabilities might use a longer life expectancy, such as a 35-year life expectancy instead of his actuarial 20-year expectation. Another approach is to transfer the risk to an insurer by purchasing an annuity that begins in 20 years and makes payments to the retiree for as long as he lives. Longevity risk and this kind of deferred annuity (sometimes called a "longevity annuity") are discussed in another curriculum chapter on risk management.[27]

There are some drawbacks to the goals-based approach to asset allocation. One is that the sub-portfolios add complexity. Another is that goals may be ambiguous or may change over time. Goals-based approaches to asset allocation raise the question of how sub-portfolios coordinate to constitute an efficient whole. The subject will be taken up in a later chapter, but the general finding is that the amount of sub-optimality is small.[28]

7. IMPLEMENTATION CHOICES

Having established the strategic asset allocation policy, the asset owner must address additional strategic considerations before moving to implementation. One of these is the passive/active choice.

There are two dimensions of passive/active choices. One dimension relates to the management of the strategic asset allocation itself—for example, whether to deviate from it tactically or not. The second dimension relates to passive and active implementation choices in investing the allocation to a given asset class. Each of these are covered in the sections that follow.

In an advisory role, asset managers have an unequivocal responsibility to make implementation and asset selection choices that are initially, and on an ongoing basis, suitable for the client.[29]

7.1. Passive/Active Management of Asset Class Weights

Tactical asset allocation (TAA) involves deliberate short-term deviations from the strategic asset allocation. Whereas the strategic asset allocation incorporates an investor's long-term, equilibrium market expectations, tactical asset allocation involves short-term tilts away from the strategic asset mix that reflect short-term views—for example, to exploit perceived deviations from equilibrium.

Tactical asset allocation is active management at the asset class level because it involves intentional deviations from the strategic asset mix to exploit perceived opportunities in capital markets to improve the portfolio's risk–return trade-off. TAA mandates are often specified to keep deviations from the strategic asset allocation within rebalancing ranges or within risk budgets. Tactical asset allocation decisions might be responsive to price momentum, perceived asset class valuation, or the particular stage of the business cycle. A strategy incorporating deviations from the strategic asset allocation that are motivated by longer-term

---

[27]See Blanchett et al. (2016) for the management of longevity risk. Milevsky (2016) is a further reference.
[28]This is addressed technically in Das et al. (2010). See also Brunel (2015).
[29]See Standard III (C) in the Standards of Practice Handbook (CFA Institute 2014).

valuation signals or economic views is sometimes distinguished as **dynamic asset allocation** (DAA).

Tactical asset allocation may be limited to tactical changes in domestic stock–bond or stock–bond–cash allocations or may be a more comprehensive multi-asset approach, as in a global tactical asset allocation (GTAA) model. Tactical asset allocation inherently involves market timing as it involves buying and selling in anticipation of short-term changes in market direction; however, TAA usually involves smaller allocation tilts than an invested-or-not-invested market timing strategy.

Tactical asset allocation is a source of risk when calibrated against the strategic asset mix. An informed approach to tactical asset allocation recognizes the trade-off of any potential outperformance against this tracking error. Key barriers to successful tactical asset allocation are monitoring and trading costs. For some investors, higher short-term capital gains taxes will prove a significant obstacle because taxes are an additional trading cost. A program of tactical asset allocation must be evaluated through a cost–benefit lens. The relevant cost comparisons include the expected costs of simply following a rebalancing policy (without deliberate tactical deviations).

7.2. Passive/Active Management of Allocations to Asset Classes

In addition to active and passive decisions about the asset class mix, there are active and passive decisions about how to implement the individual allocations within asset classes. An allocation can be managed passively or actively or incorporate both active and passive sub-allocations. For investors who delegate asset management to external firms, these decisions would come under the heading of manager structure,[30] which includes decisions about how capital and active risk are allocated to points on the passive/active spectrum and to individual external managers selected to manage the investor's assets.[31]

With a **passive management** approach, portfolio composition does not react to changes in the investor's capital market expectations or to information on or insights into individual investments. (The word *passive* means *not reacting*.) For example, a portfolio constructed to track the returns of an index of European equities might add or drop a holding in response to a change in the index composition but not in response to changes in the manager's expectations concerning the security's investment value; the market's expectations reflected in market values and index weights are taken as is. Indexing is a common passive approach to investing. (Another example would be buying and holding a fixed portfolio of bonds to maturity.)

In contrast, a portfolio manager for an active management strategy will respond to changing capital market expectations or to investment insights resulting in changes to portfolio composition. The objective of active management is to achieve, after expenses, positive excess risk-adjusted returns relative to a passive benchmark.

The range of implementation choices can be practically viewed as falling along a passive/active spectrum because some strategies use both passive and active elements. In financial theory, the pure model of a passive approach is indexing to a broad market-cap-weighted index of risky assets—in particular, the global market portfolio. This portfolio sums all

---

[30]Manager structure is defined by the number of managers, types of managers, as well as which managers are selected.

[31]See, for example, Waring, Whitney, Pirone, and Castille (2000).

investments in index components and is macro-consistent in the sense that all investors could hold it, and it is furthermore self-rebalancing to the extent it is based on market-value-weighted indices. A buy-and-hold investment as a proxy for the global market portfolio would represent a theoretical endpoint on the passive/active spectrum. However, consider an investor who indexes an equity allocation to a broad-based value equity style index. The investment could be said to reflect an active decision in tilting an allocation toward value but be passive in implementation because it involves indexing. An even more active approach would be investing the equity allocation with managers who have a value investing approach and attempt to enhance returns through security selection. Those managers would show positive tracking risk relative to the value index in general. Unconstrained active investment would be one that is "go anywhere" or not managed with consideration of any traditional asset class benchmark (i.e., "benchmark agnostic"). The degree of active management has traditionally been quantified by tracking risk and, from a different perspective, by active share.

Indexing is generally the lowest-cost approach to investing. Indexing involves some level of transaction costs because, as securities move in and out of the index, the portfolio holdings must adjust to remain in alignment with the index. Although indexing to a market-cap-weighted index is self-rebalancing, tracking an index based on other weighting schemes requires ongoing transactions to ensure the portfolio remains in alignment with index weights. An example is tracking an equally weighted index: As changes in market prices affect the relative weights of securities in the portfolio over time, the portfolio will need to be rebalanced to restore equal weights. Portfolios tracking fixed-income indices also incur ongoing transaction costs as holdings mature, default, or are called away by their issuers.

Exhibit 13 diagrams the passive/active choice as a continuum rather than binary (0 or 1) characteristic. Tracking risk and active share are widely known quantitative measures of the degree of active management that capture different aspects of it. Each measure is shown as tending to increase from left to right on the spectrum; however, they do not increase (or decrease) in lockstep with each other, in general.

EXHIBIT 13   Passive/Active Spectrum

MOST PASSIVE (indexing to market weights)	Use of information on asset classes, investment factors, and individual investments increases is often quantified by → Increasing tracking risk relative to benchmark → → Increasing active share relative to benchmark →	MOST ACTIVE (unconstrained mandates)

Asset class allocations may be managed with different approaches on the spectrum. For example, developed market equities might be implemented purely passively, whereas emerging market bonds might be invested with an unconstrained, index-agnostic approach.

Factors that influence asset owners' decisions on where to invest on the passive/active spectrum include the following:

- *Available investments.* For example, the availability of an investable and representative index as the basis for indexing.
- *Scalability of active strategies being considered.* The prospective value added by an active strategy may begin to decline at some level of invested assets. In addition, participation in it may not be available below some asset level, a consideration for small investors.

- *The feasibility of investing passively while incorporating client-specific constraints.* For example, an investor's particular ESG investing criteria may not align with existing index products.
- *Beliefs concerning market informational efficiency.* A strong belief in market efficiency for the asset class(es) under consideration would orient the investor away from active management.
- *The trade-off of expected incremental benefits relative to incremental costs and risks of active choices.* Costs of active management include investment management costs, trading costs, and turnover-induced taxes; such costs would have to be judged relative to the lower costs of index alternatives, which vary by asset class.
- *Tax status.* Holding other variables constant, taxable investors would tend to have higher hurdles to profitable active management than tax-exempt investors.[32] For taxable investors who want to hold both passive and active investments, active investments would be held, in general, in available tax-advantaged accounts.

The curriculum chapters on equity, fixed-income, and alternative investments will explore many strategies and the nature of any active decisions involved. Investors do need to understand the nature of the active decisions involved in implementing their strategic asset allocations and their appropriateness given the factors described. Exhibit 14 shows qualitatively (rather than precisely) some choices that investors may consider for equity and fixed-income allocations. In the exhibit, non-cap-weighted indexing includes such approaches as equal weighting and quantitative rules-based indexing approaches (discussed further in the equity chapters).[33]

EXHIBIT 14   Placement on the Passive/Active Spectrum: Examples of Possible Choices

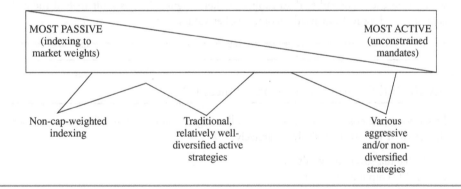

EXAMPLE 8   Implementation Choices (1)

1. Describe two kinds of passive/active choices faced by investors related to asset allocation.
2. An equity index is described as "a rules-based, transparent index designed to provide investors with an efficient way to gain exposure to large-cap and small-cap

---

[32]See Jeffrey and Arnott (1993).
[33]Podkaminer (2015) provides a survey.

stocks with low total return variability." Compared with the market-cap weighting of the parent index (with the same component securities), the weights in the low-volatility index are proportional to the inverse of return volatility, so that the highest-volatility security receives the lowest weight. Describe the active and passive aspects of a decision to invest an allocation to equities in ETFs tracking such indices.

3. Describe how investing in a GDP-weighted global bond index involves both active and passive choices.

Solution to 1: One choice relates to whether to allow active deviations from the strategic asset allocation. Tactical asset allocation and dynamic asset allocation are examples of active management of asset allocations. A second set of choices relates to where to invest allocations to asset classes along the passive/active spectrum.

Solution to 2: The active element is the decision, relative to the parent index, to overweight securities with low volatility and underweight securities with high volatility. This management of risk is distinct from reducing portfolio volatility by combining a market-cap-weighted index with a risk-free asset proxy because it implies a belief in some risk–return advantage to favoring low-volatility equities on an individual security basis. The passive element is a transparent rules-based implementation of the weighting scheme based on inverse volatilities.

Solution to 3: The passive choice is represented by the overall selection of the universe of global bonds; however, the active choice is represented by the weighting scheme, which is to use GDP rather than capital market weights. This is a tilt toward the real economy and away from fixed-income market values.

EXAMPLE 9   Implementation Choices (2)

Describe characteristic(s) of each of the following investors that are likely to influence the decision to invest passively or actively.

1. Caflandia sovereign wealth fund
2. GPLE corporate pension
3. The Lee family
4. Auldberg University Endowment

Solution:

1. For a large investor like the Caflandia sovereign wealth fund (CAF\$40 billion), the scalability of active strategies that it may wish to employ may be a consideration. If only a small percentage of portfolio assets can be invested effectively in an active strategy, for example, the potential value added for the overall portfolio may not justify the inherent costs and management time. Although the equities and fixed-income allocations could be invested using passive approaches, investments in the diversifying strategies category are commonly active.

2. The executives responsible for the GPLE corporate pension also have other, non-investment responsibilities. This is a factor favoring a more passive approach; however, choosing an outsourced chief investment officer or delegated fiduciary consultant to manage active manager selection could facilitate greater use of active investment.

3. The fact that the Lees are taxable investors is a factor generally in favor of passive management for assets not held in tax-advantaged accounts. Active management involves turnover, which gives rise to taxes.

4. According to the vignette in Example 3, the Auldberg University Endowment has substantial staff resources in equities, fixed income, and real estate. This fact suggests that passive/active decisions are relatively unconstrained by internal resources. By itself, it does not favor passive or active, but it is a factor that allows active choices to be given full consideration.

7.3. Risk Budgeting Perspectives in Asset Allocation and Implementation

Risk budgeting addresses the questions of which types of risks to take and how much of each to take. Risk budgeting provides another view of asset allocation—through a risk lens. Depending on the focus, the risk may be quantified in various ways. For example, a concern for volatility can be quantified as variance or standard deviation of returns, and a concern for tail risk can be quantified as VaR or drawdown. Risk budgets (budgets for risk taking) can be stated in absolute or in relative terms and in money or percent terms. For example, it is possible to state an overall risk budget for a portfolio in terms of volatility of returns, which would be an example of an absolute risk budget stated in percent terms (for example, 20% for portfolio return volatility). Risk budgeting is a tool that may be useful in a variety of contexts and asset allocation approaches.

Some investors may approach asset allocation with an exclusive focus on risk. A risk budgeting approach to asset allocation has been defined as an approach in which the investor specifies how risk (quantified by some measure, such as volatility) is to be distributed across assets in the portfolio, without consideration of the assets' expected returns.[34] An example is aiming for equal expected risk contributions to overall portfolio volatility from all included asset classes as an approach to diversification, which is a risk parity (or equal risk contribution) approach. A subsequent chapter in asset allocation addresses this in greater detail.

More directly related to the choice of passive/active implementation are active risk budgets and active risk budgeting. **Active risk budgeting** addresses the question of how much benchmark-relative risk an investor is willing to take in seeking to outperform a benchmark. This approach is risk budgeting stated in benchmark-relative terms. In parallel to the two dimensions of the passive/active decision outlined previously are two levels of active risk budgeting, which can be distinguished as follows:

- At the level of the overall asset allocation, active risk can be defined relative to the strategic asset allocation benchmark. This benchmark may be the strategic asset allocation weights applied to specified (often, broad-based market-cap-weighted) indices.

---

[34]See Roncalli (2013).

• At the level of individual asset classes, active risk can be defined relative to the asset class benchmark.

Active risk budgeting at the level of overall asset allocation would be relevant to tactical asset allocation. Active risk budgeting at the level of each asset class is relevant to how the allocation to those asset classes is invested. For example, it can take the form of expected-alpha versus tracking-error optimization in a manner similar to classic mean–variance optimization. If investment factor risks are the investor's focus, risk budgeting can be adapted to have a focus on allocating factor risk exposures instead. Later chapters revisit risk budgeting in investing in further detail.

8. REBALANCING: STRATEGIC CONSIDERATIONS

Rebalancing is the discipline of adjusting portfolio weights to more closely align with the strategic asset allocation. Rebalancing is a key part of the monitoring and feedback step of the portfolio construction, monitoring, and revision process. An investor's rebalancing policy is generally documented in the IPS.

Even in the absence of changing investor circumstances, a revised economic outlook, or tactical asset allocation views, normal changes in asset prices cause the portfolio asset mix to deviate from target weights. Industry practice defines "rebalancing" as portfolio adjustments triggered by such price changes. Other portfolio adjustments, even systematic ones, are not rebalancing.

Ordinary price changes cause the assets with a high forecast return to grow faster than the portfolio as a whole. Because high-return assets are typically also higher risk, in the absence of rebalancing, overall portfolio risk rises. The mix of risks within the portfolio becomes more concentrated as well. Systematic rebalancing maintains the original strategic risk exposures. The discipline of rebalancing serves to control portfolio risks that have become different from what the investor originally intended.

Consider the example from the internet bubble (1995–2001) in Exhibit 15. The example assumes a 60/40 stock/bond portfolio, in which stocks are represented by the large-cap US growth stocks that characterized the internet bubble. In Panel B, the left-hand scale and upper two lines show month-by-month total portfolio *values* with and without monthly rebalancing ("wealth rebalanced" and "wealth unrebalanced," respectively). The right-hand scale and lower two lines show month-by-month portfolio *risk* as represented by the 5th percentile drawdown (in a VaR model) with and without monthly rebalancing ("risk rebalanced" and "risk unrebalanced," respectively).

EXHIBIT 15   Rebalancing

Panel A. Asset Mix

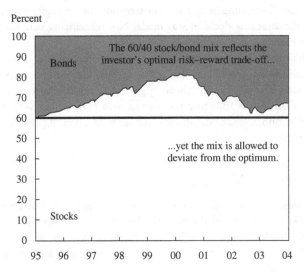

Panel B. Portfolio Value and Risk

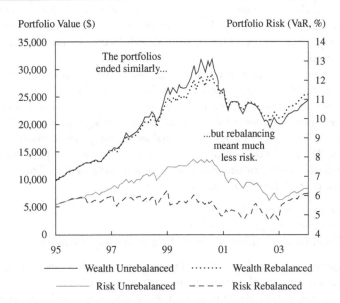

Note: The data are a 60/40 mix of the S&P 500 Growth Index and the Barclays Capital Aggregate Bond Index.

Panel A shows that, without rebalancing, the asset mix deviates dramatically from the target. Panel B shows that although the portfolios' values ended similarly (the upper two lines), disciplined rebalancing meant more-stable risks (illustrated by the lower two lines).

This risk perspective is important. Taken to the extreme, *never rebalancing* allows the high-return (and presumably higher-risk) assets to grow and dominate the portfolio. Portfolio risk rises and concentrates. Taken even further, such a philosophy of never rebalancing may suggest it would have been simpler to have invested only in the highest-expected-return asset class back when the asset mix decision was made. Not rebalancing could negate an intended level of diversification.

Because rebalancing is countercyclical, it is fundamentally a contrarian investment approach.[35] Behavioral finance tells us that such contrarianism will be uncomfortable; no one likes to sell the most recently best-performing part of the portfolio to buy the worst. Thus, rebalancing is a *discipline* of adjusting the portfolio to better align with the strategic asset allocation in both connotations of discipline—the sense of a typical practice and the sense of a strengthening regime.

8.1. A Framework for Rebalancing

The actual mechanics of rebalancing are more complex than they first appear. A number of questions arise: How often should the portfolio be rebalanced? What levels of imbalance are worth tolerating? Should the portfolio be rebalanced to the edge of the policy range or to some other point? These non-trivial questions represent the key strategic decisions in rebalancing.

The simplest approach to rebalancing is **calendar rebalancing**, which involves rebalancing a portfolio to target weights on a periodic basis—for example, monthly, quarterly, semiannually, or annually. The choice of rebalancing frequency may be linked to the schedule of portfolio reviews. Although simple, rebalancing points are arbitrary and have other disadvantages.

Percent-range rebalancing permits tighter control of the asset mix compared with calendar rebalancing. Percent-range approach involves setting rebalancing thresholds or trigger points, stated as a percentage of the portfolio's value, around target values. For example, if the target allocation to an asset class is 50% of portfolio value, **trigger points** at 45% and 55% of portfolio value define a 10 percentage point **rebalancing range** (or corridor) for the value of that asset class. The rebalancing range creates a no-trade region. The portfolio is rebalanced when an asset class's weight first passes through one of its trigger points. Focusing on percent-range rebalancing, the following questions are relevant:

- How frequently is the portfolio valued?
- What size deviation triggers rebalancing?
- Is the deviation from the target allocation fully or partially corrected?

How frequently is the portfolio valued? The percent-range discipline requires monitoring portfolio values for breaches of a trigger point at an agreed-on frequency; the more frequent the monitoring, the greater the precision in implementation. Such monitoring may be scheduled daily, weekly, monthly, quarterly, or annually. A number of considerations—

---

[35]A quantitative interpretation of rebalancing, given by Ang (2014), is that the return to rebalancing is selling out-of-the-money puts and calls.

including governance resources and asset custodian resources—can affect valuation frequency. For many investors, monthly or quarterly evaluation efficiently balances the costs and benefits of rebalancing.

What size deviation triggers rebalancing? Trigger points take into account such factors as traditional practice, transaction costs, asset class volatility, volatility of the balance of the portfolio, correlation of the asset class with the balance of the portfolio, and risk tolerance.[36]

Before the rise of modern multi-asset portfolios, the stock/bond split broadly characterized the asset allocation, and a traditional ±*x*% rebalancing band was common. These fixed ranges would apply no matter the size or volatility of the allocation target. For example, both a 40% domestic equity allocation and a 15% real asset allocation might have ±5% rebalancing ranges. Alternatively, proportional bands reflect the size of the target weight. For example, a 60% target asset class might have a ±6% band, whereas a 5% allocation would have a ±0.5% band. Proportional bands might also be set to reflect the relative volatility of the asset classes. A final approach is the use of cost–benefit analysis to set ranges.

Is the deviation from the target allocation fully or partially corrected? Once the portfolio is evaluated and an unacceptably large deviation found, the investor must determine rebalancing trade size, as well as the timeline for implementing the rebalancing. In practice, three main approaches are used: rebalance back to target weights, rebalance to range edge, or rebalance halfway between the range-edge trigger point and the target weight.

8.2. Strategic Considerations in Rebalancing

The four-part rebalancing framework just described highlights important questions to address in setting rebalancing policy. Strategic considerations generally include the following, all else being equal:

- Higher transaction costs for an asset class imply wider rebalancing ranges.
- More risk-averse investors will have tighter rebalancing ranges.
- Less correlated assets also have tighter rebalancing ranges.
- Beliefs in momentum favor wider rebalancing ranges, whereas mean reversion encourages tighter ranges.
- Illiquid investments complicate rebalancing.
- Derivatives create the possibility of synthetic rebalancing.
- Taxes, which are a cost, discourage rebalancing and encourage asymmetric and wider rebalancing ranges.

Asset class volatility is also a consideration in the size of rebalancing ranges.

A cost–benefit approach to rebalancing sets ranges, taking transaction costs, risk aversion, asset class risks, and asset class correlations into consideration. For example, an asset that is more highly correlated with the rest of the portfolio than another would merit a wider rebalancing range, all else equal, because it would be closer to being a substitute for the balance of the portfolio; thus, larger deviations would have less impact on portfolio risk.

---

[36]See Masters (2003) for details on these factors apart from traditional factors.

EXAMPLE 10   Different Rebalancing Ranges

The table shows a simple four-asset strategic mix along with rebalancing ranges created under different approaches. The width of the rebalancing range under the proportional range approach is 0.20 of the strategic target.

State a reason that could explain why the international equity range is wider than the domestic equity range using the cost–benefit approach.

Asset Class	Strategic Target	Fixed Width Ranges	Proportional Ranges (±1,000 bps)	Cost–Benefit Ranges
Domestic equity	40%	35%–45%	36%–44%	35%–45%
International equity	25%	20%–30%	22½%–27½%	19%–31%
Emerging markets	15%	10%–20%	13½%–16½%	12%–18%
Fixed income	20%	15%–25%	18%–22%	19%–21%

Solution: Higher transaction costs for international equity compared with domestic equity could explain the wider range for international equity compared with domestic equity under the cost–benefit approach. Another potential explanation relates to the possibility that international equity has a higher correlation with the balance of the portfolio (i.e., the portfolio excluding international equity) than does domestic equity (i.e., with the portfolio excluding domestic equity). If that is the case then, all else being equal, a wider band would be justified for international equity.

Investors' perspectives on capital markets can affect their approach to rebalancing. A belief in momentum and trend following, for example, encourages wider rebalancing ranges. In contrast, a belief in mean reversion encourages stricter adherence to rebalancing, including tighter ranges.

Illiquid assets complicate rebalancing. Relatively illiquid investments, such as hedge funds, private equity, or direct real estate, cannot be readily traded without substantial trading costs and/or delays. Accordingly, illiquid investments are commonly assigned wide rebalancing ranges. However, rebalancing of an illiquid asset may be affected indirectly when a highly correlated liquid asset can be traded or when exposure can be adjusted by means of positions in derivatives. For example, public equity could be reduced to offset an overweight in private equity. Rebalancing by means of highly correlated liquid assets and derivatives, however, involves some imprecision and basis risk.

This insight about liquidity is an instance where thinking ahead about rebalancing can affect the strategic asset allocation. It is one reason that allocations to illiquid assets are often smaller than if trading were possible.

Factor-based asset allocation, liability-relative investing, and goals-based investing, each a valid approach to asset allocation, can give rise to different rebalancing considerations. Factor exposures and liability hedges require monitoring (and rebalancing) the factors weights and surplus duration in addition to asset class weights. Goals-based investing in private wealth management may require both asset class rebalancing and moving funds between different goal sub-portfolios.

Tax considerations also complicate rebalancing. Rebalancing typically realizes capital gains and losses, which are taxable events in many jurisdictions. For private wealth managers, any rebalancing benefit must be compared with the tax cost. Taxes, as a cost, are much larger than other transaction costs, which often leads to wider rebalancing ranges in taxable portfolios than in tax-exempt portfolios. Because loss harvesting generates tax savings and realizing gains triggers taxes, rebalancing ranges in taxable accounts may also be asymmetric. (For example, a 25% target asset class might have an allowable range of 24%–28%, which is −1% to +3%.)

Modern cost–benefit approaches to rebalancing suggest considering derivatives as a rebalancing tool. Derivatives can often be used to rebalance synthetically at much lower transaction costs than the costs of using the underlying stocks and bonds. Using a derivatives overlay also avoids disrupting the underlying separate accounts in a multi-manager implementation of the strategic asset allocation. Tax considerations are also relevant; it may be more cost effective to reduce an exposure using a derivatives overlay than to sell the underlying asset and incur the capital gains tax liability. Lastly, trading a few derivatives may be quicker and easier than hundreds of underlying securities. Of course, using derivatives may require a higher level of risk oversight, but then risk control is the main rationale for rebalancing.

Estimates of the benefits of rebalancing vary. Many portfolios are statistically indistinguishable from each other, suggesting that much rebalancing is unnecessary. In contrast, Willenbrock (2011) demonstrates that even zero-return assets can, in theory, generate positive returns through rebalancing, which is a demonstrable (and surprising) benefit. Whatever the return estimate for the value added from rebalancing, the key takeaway is that rebalancing is chiefly about risk control, not return enhancement.

9. SUMMARY

This chapter has introduced the subject of asset allocation. Among the points made are the following:

- Effective investment governance ensures that decisions are made by individuals or groups with the necessary skills and capacity and involves articulating the long- and short-term objectives of the investment program; effectively allocating decision rights and responsibilities among the functional units in the governance hierarchy; taking account of their knowledge, capacity, time, and position on the governance hierarchy; specifying processes for developing and approving the investment policy statement, which will govern the day-to-day operation of the investment program; specifying processes for developing and approving the program's strategic asset allocation; establishing a reporting framework to monitor the program's progress toward the agreed-on goals and objectives; and periodically undertaking a governance audit.
- The economic balance sheet includes non-financial assets and liabilities that can be relevant for choosing the best asset allocation for an investor's financial portfolio.
- The investment objectives of asset-only asset allocation approaches focus on the asset side of the economic balance sheet; approaches with a liability-relative orientation focus on funding liabilities; and goals-based approaches focus on achieving financial goals.

- The risk concepts relevant to asset-only asset allocation approaches focus on asset risk; those of liability-relative asset allocation focus on risk in relation to paying liabilities; and a goals-based approach focuses on the probabilities of not achieving financial goals.
- Asset classes are the traditional units of analysis in asset allocation and reflect systematic risks with varying degrees of overlap.
- Assets within an asset class should be relatively homogeneous; asset classes should be mutually exclusive; asset classes should be diversifying; asset classes as a group should make up a preponderance of the world's investable wealth; asset classes selected for investment should have the capacity to absorb a meaningful proportion of an investor's portfolio.
- Risk factors are associated with non-diversifiable (i.e., systematic) risk and are associated with an expected return premium. The price of an asset and/or asset class may reflect more than one risk factor, and complicated spread positions may be necessary to identify and isolate particular risk factors. Their use as units of analysis in asset allocation is driven by considerations of controlling systematic risk exposures.
- The global market portfolio represents a highly diversified asset allocation that can serve as a baseline asset allocation in an asset-only approach.
- There are two dimensions of passive/active choices. One dimension relates to the management of the strategic asset allocation itself—for example, whether to deviate from it tactically or not. The second dimension relates to passive and active implementation choices in investing the allocation to a given asset class. Tactical and dynamic asset allocation relate to the first dimension; active and passive choices for implementing allocations to asset classes relate to the second dimension.
- Risk budgeting addresses the question of which types of risks to take and how much of each to take. Active risk budgeting addresses the question of how much benchmark-relative risk an investor is willing to take. At the level of the overall asset allocation, active risk can be defined relative to the strategic asset allocation benchmark. At the level of individual asset classes, active risk can be defined relative to the benchmark proxy.
- Rebalancing is the discipline of adjusting portfolio weights to more closely align with the strategic asset allocation. Rebalancing approaches include calendar-based and range-based rebalancing. Calendar-based rebalancing rebalances the portfolio to target weights on a periodic basis. Range-based rebalancing sets rebalancing thresholds or trigger points around target weights. The ranges may be fixed width, percentage based, or volatility based. Range-based rebalancing permits tighter control of the asset mix compared with calendar rebalancing.
- Strategic considerations in rebalancing include transaction costs, risk aversion, correlations among asset classes, volatility, and beliefs concerning momentum, taxation, and asset class liquidity.

REFERENCES

Ang, Andrew. 2014. *Asset Management: A Systematic Approach to Factor Investing*. New York: Oxford University Press.

Blanchett, David M., and Philip U. Straehl. 2015. "No Portfolio is an Island." *Financial Analysts Journal*, vol. 71, no. 3 (May/June): 15–33.

Blanchett, David M., and Philip U. Straehl. 2017. "Portfolio Implications of Job-Specific Human Capital Risk." *Journal of Asset Management*, vol. 18, no. 1: 1–15.

Blanchett, David M., David M. Cordell, Michael S. Finke, and Thomas Idzorek. 2016. "Risk Management for Individuals." CFA Institute.

Brunel, Jean L.P. 2012. "Goals-Based Wealth Management in Practice." *Conference Proceedings Quarterly*, vol. 29, no. 1 (March): 57–65.

Brunel, Jean L.P. 2015. *Goals-Based Wealth Management: An Integrated and Practical Approach to Changing the Structure of Wealth Advisory Practices.* Hoboken, NJ: John Wiley.

Burger, John D., Francis E. Warnock, and Veronica Cacdac Warnock. 2012. "Emerging Local Currency Bond Markets." *Financial Analysts Journal*, vol. 68, no. 4 (July/August): 73–93.

Chhabra, Ashvin. 2005. "Beyond Markowitz: A Comprehensive Wealth Allocation Framework for Individual Investors." *Journal of Wealth Management*, vol. 7, no. 4 (Spring): 8–34.

Collie, Bob, and James A. Gannon. 2009. "Liability-Responsive Asset Allocation: A Dynamic Approach to Pension Plan Management." Russell Investments Insights (April).

Das, Sanjiv, Harry Markowitz, Jonathan Scheid, and Meir Statman. 2010. "Portfolio Optimization with Mental Accounts." *Journal of Financial and Quantitative Analysis*, vol. 45, no. 2 (April): 311–334.

Fraser, Steve P., and William W. Jennings. 2006. "Behavioral Asset Allocation for Foundations and Endowments." *Journal of Wealth Management*, vol. 9, no. 3 (Winter): 38–50.

Greer, Robert J. 1997. "What is an Asset Class, Anyway?" *Journal of Portfolio Management*, vol. 23, no. 2 (Winter): 86–91.

Ibbotson, Roger G., and Paul D. Kaplan. 2000. "Does Asset Allocation Policy Explain 40, 90, or 100 Percent of Performance?" *Financial Analysts Journal*, vol. 56, no. 1 (January/February): 26–33.

Ibbotson, Roger G., Moshe A. Milevsky, Peng Chen, and Kevin X. Zhu. 2007. *Lifetime Financial Advice: Human Capital, Asset Allocation, and Insurance.* Charlottesville, VA: CFA Institute Research Foundation.

Idzorek, Thomas M., and Maciej Kowara. 2013. "Factor-Based Asset Allocation versus Asset-Class-Based Asset Allocation." *Financial Analysts Journal*, vol. 69, no. 3 (May/June): 19–29.

Idzorek, Thomas, Jeremy Stempien, and Nathan Voris. 2013. "Bait and Switch: Glide Path Instability." *Journal of Investing*, vol. 22, no. 1 (Spring): 74–82.

Jeffrey, Robert H., and Robert D. Arnott. 1993. "Is Your Alpha Big Enough to Cover Its Taxes?" *Journal of Portfolio Management*, vol. 19, no. 3 (Spring): 15–25.

Kozhemiakin, Alexander. 2011. "Emerging Markets Local Currency Debt: Capitalizing on Improved Sovereign Fundamentals." BNY Mellon Asset Management.

Kritzman, Mark. 1999. "Toward Defining an Asset Class." *Journal of Alternative Investments*, vol. 2, no. 1 (Summer): 79–82.

Masters, Seth J. 2003. "Rebalancing." *Journal of Portfolio Management*, vol. 29, no. 3 (Spring): 52–57.

Milevsky, Moshe A. 2016. "It's Time to Retire Ruin (Probabilities)." *Financial Analysts Journal*, vol. 72, no. 2 (March/April): 8–12.

Perry, William. 2011. "The Case For Emerging Market Corporates." *Journal of Indexes*, vol. 14, no. 5 (September/October): 10–17.

Podkaminer, Eugene. 2013. "Risk Factors as Building Blocks for Portfolio Diversification: The Chemistry of Asset Allocation." CFA Institute Investment Risk and Performance papers (January).

Podkaminer, Eugene. 2015. "The Education of Beta: Can Alternative Indexes Make Your Portfolio Smarter?" *Journal of Investing*, vol. 24, no. 2 (Summer): 7–34.

Pompian, Michael M. 2011a. "The Behavioral Biases of Individuals." CFA Institute.

Pompian, Michael M. 2011b. "The Behavioral Finance Perspective." CFA Institute.

Pompian, Michael, Colin McLean, and Alistair Byrne. 2011. "Behavioral Finance and Investment Processes." CFA Institute.

Roncalli, Thierry. 2013. *Introduction to Risk Parity and Budgeting.* New York: CRC Press.

Rudd, Andrew, and Laurence B. Siegel. 2013. "Using an Economic Balance Sheet for Financial Planning." *Journal of Wealth Management*, vol. 16, no. 2 (Fall): 15–23.

Sharpe, William F. 1991. "The Arithmetic of Active Management." *Financial Analysts Journal*, vol. 47, no. 1: 7–9.

Shefrin, H., and M. Statman. 2000. "Behavioral Portfolio Theory." *Journal of Financial and Quantitative Analysis*, vol. 35, no. 2 (June): 127–151.

CFA Institute. *Standards of Practice Handbook*, 11th edition. 2014. CFA Institute.

Swinkels, Laurens. 2012. "Emerging Market Inflation-Linked Bonds." *Financial Analysts Journal*, vol. 68, no. 5 (September/October): 38–56.

Waring, M. Barton, Duane Whitney, John Pirone, and Charles Castille. 2000. "Optimizing Manager Structure and Budgeting Manager Risk." *Journal of Portfolio Management*, vol. 26, no. 3 (Spring): 90–104.

Willenbrock, Scott. 2011. "Diversification Return, Portfolio Rebalancing, and the Commodity Return Puzzle." *Financial Analysts Journal*, vol. 67, no. 4 (July/August): 42–49.

Xiong, James X., Roger G. Ibbotson, Thomas M. Idzorek, and Peng Chen. 2010. "The Equal Importance of Asset Allocation and Active Management." *Financial Analysts Journal*, vol. 66, no. 2 (March/April): 22–30.

PRACTICE PROBLEMS

The following information relates to Questions 1–8

Meg and Cramer Law, a married couple aged 42 and 44, respectively, are meeting with their new investment adviser, Daniel Raye. The Laws have worked their entire careers at Whorton Solutions (WS), a multinational technology company. The Laws have two teenage children who will soon begin college.

Raye reviews the Laws' current financial position. The Laws have an investment portfolio consisting of $800,000 in equities and $450,000 in fixed-income instruments. Raye notes that 80% of the equity portfolio consists of shares of WS. The Laws also own real estate valued at $400,000, with $225,000 in mortgage debt. Raye estimates the Laws' pre-retirement earnings from WS have a total present value of $1,025,000. He estimates the Laws' future expected consumption expenditures have a total present value of $750,000.

The Laws express a very strong desire to fund their children's college education expenses, which have an estimated present value of $275,000. The Laws also plan to fund an endowment at their alma mater in 20 years, which has an estimated present value of $500,000. The Laws tell Raye they want a high probability of success funding the endowment. Raye uses this information to prepare an economic balance sheet for the Laws.

In reviewing a financial plan written by the Laws' previous adviser, Raye notices the following asset class specifications.

Equity:	US equities
Debt:	Global investment-grade corporate bonds and real estate
Derivatives:	Primarily large-capitalization foreign equities

The previous adviser's report notes the asset class returns on equity and derivatives are highly correlated. The report also notes the asset class returns on debt have a low correlation with equity and derivative returns.

Raye is concerned that the asset allocation approach followed by the Laws' previous financial adviser resulted in an overlap in risk factors among asset classes for the portfolio. Raye plans to address this by examining the portfolio's sensitivity to various risk factors, such as inflation, liquidity, and volatility, to determine the desired exposure to each factor.

Raye concludes that a portfolio of 75% global equities and 25% bonds reflects an appropriate balance of expected return and risk for the Laws with respect to a 20-year time horizon for most moderately important goals. Raye recommends the Laws follow a goals-based approach to asset allocation and offers three possible portfolios for the Laws to consider. Selected data on the three portfolios are presented in Exhibit 1.

EXHIBIT 1   Proposed Portfolio Allocations for the Law Family

	Cash	Fixed Income	Global Equities	Diversifying Strategies*
Portfolio 1	35%	55%	10%	0%
Portfolio 2	10%	15%	65%	10%
Portfolio 3	10%	30%	40%	20%

*Diversifying strategies consists of hedge funds.

Raye uses a cost–benefit approach to rebalancing and recommends that global equities have a wider rebalancing range than the other asset classes.

1. Using the economic balance sheet approach, the Laws' economic net worth is *closest* to:
   A. $925,000.
   B. $1,425,000.
   C. $1,675,000.

2. Using an economic balance sheet, which of the Laws' current financial assets is *most concerning* from an asset allocation perspective?
   A. Equities
   B. Real estate
   C. Fixed income

3. Raye believes the previous adviser's specification for debt is incorrect given that, for purposes of asset allocation, asset classes should be:
   A. diversifying.
   B. mutually exclusive.
   C. relatively homogeneous.

4. Raye believes the previous adviser's asset class specifications for equity and derivatives are inappropriate given that, for purposes of asset allocation, asset classes should be:
   A. diversifying.
   B. mutually exclusive.
   C. relatively homogeneous.

5. To address his concern regarding the previous adviser's asset allocation approach, Raye should assess the Laws' portfolio using:
   A. a homogeneous and mutually exclusive asset class–based risk analysis.
   B. a multifactor risk model to control systematic risk factors in asset allocation.
   C. an asset class–based asset allocation approach to construct a diversified portfolio.

6. Based on Exhibit 1, which portfolio *best* meets the Laws' education goal for their children?
   A. Portfolio 1

    B. Portfolio 2

    C. Portfolio 3

7. Based on Exhibit 1, which portfolio *best* meets the Laws' goal to fund an endowment for their alma mater?

    A. Portfolio 1

    B. Portfolio 2

    C. Portfolio 3

8. Raye's approach to rebalancing global equities is consistent with:

    A. the Laws' being risk averse.

    B. global equities' having higher transaction costs than other asset classes.

    C. global equities' having lower correlations with other asset classes.

CHAPTER 6

PRINCIPLES OF ASSET ALLOCATION

Jean L.P. Brunel, CFA
Thomas M. Idzorek, CFA
John M. Mulvey, PhD

LEARNING OUTCOMES

The candidate should be able to:

- describe and critique the use of mean–variance optimization in asset allocation;
- recommend and justify an asset allocation using mean–variance optimization;
- interpret and critique an asset allocation in relation to an investor's economic balance sheet;
- discuss asset class liquidity considerations in asset allocation;
- explain absolute and relative risk budgets and their use in determining and implementing an asset allocation;
- describe how client needs and preferences regarding investment risks can be incorporated into asset allocation;
- discuss the use of Monte Carlo simulation and scenario analysis to evaluate the robustness of an asset allocation;
- describe the use of investment factors in constructing and analyzing an asset allocation;
- recommend and justify an asset allocation based on the global market portfolio;
- describe and evaluate characteristics of liabilities that are relevant to asset allocation;
- discuss approaches to liability-relative asset allocation;
- recommend and justify a liability-relative asset allocation;
- recommend and justify an asset allocation using a goals-based approach;
- describe and critique heuristic and other approaches to asset allocation;
- discuss factors affecting rebalancing policy.

1. INTRODUCTION

Determining a strategic asset allocation is arguably the most important aspect of the investment process. This chapter builds on the "Introduction to Asset Allocation" chapter and focuses on several of the primary frameworks for developing an asset allocation, including asset-only mean–variance optimization, various liability-relative asset allocation techniques, and goals-based investing. Additionally, it touches on various other asset allocation techniques used by practitioners, as well as important related topics, such as rebalancing.

The process of creating a diversified, multi-asset class portfolio typically involves two separate steps. The first step is the asset allocation decision, which can refer to both the process and the result of determining long-term (strategic) exposures to the available asset classes (or risk factors) that make up the investor's opportunity set. Asset allocation is the first and primary step in translating the client's circumstances, objectives, and constraints into an appropriate portfolio (or, for some approaches, multiple portfolios) for achieving the client's goals within the client's tolerance for risk. The second step in creating a diversified, multi-asset-class portfolio involves implementation decisions that determine the specific investments (individual securities, pooled investment vehicles, and separate accounts) that will be used to implement the targeted allocations.

Although it is possible to carry out the asset allocation process and the implementation process simultaneously, in practice, these two steps are often separated for two reasons. First, the frameworks for simultaneously determining an asset allocation and its implementation are often complex. Second, in practice, many investors prefer to revisit their strategic asset allocation policy somewhat infrequently (e.g., annually or less frequently) in a dedicated asset allocation study, while most of these same investors prefer to revisit/monitor implementation vehicles (actual investments) far more frequently (e.g., monthly or quarterly).

Section 2 covers the traditional mean–variance optimization (MVO) approach to asset allocation. We apply this approach in what is referred to as an "asset-only" setting, in which the goal is to create the most efficient mixes of asset classes in the absence of any liabilities. We highlight key criticisms of mean–variance optimization and methods used to address them. This section also covers risk budgeting in relation to asset allocation, factor-based asset allocation, and asset allocation with illiquid assets. The observation that almost all portfolios exist to help pay for what can be characterized as a "liability" leads to the next subject.

Section 3 introduces liability-relative asset allocation—including a straightforward extension of mean–variance optimization known as surplus optimization. Surplus optimiza-tion is an economic balance sheet approach extended to the liability side of the balance sheet that finds the most efficient asset class mixes in the presence of liabilities. Liability-relative optimization is simultaneously concerned with the return of the assets, the change in value of the liabilities, and how assets and liabilities interact to determine the overall value or health of the total portfolio.

Section 4 covers an increasingly popular approach to asset allocation called goals-based asset allocation. Conceptually, goals-based approaches are similar to liability-relative asset allocation in viewing risk in relation to specific needs or objectives associated with different time horizons and degrees of urgency.

Section 5 introduces some informal (heuristic) ways that asset allocations have been determined and other approaches to asset allocation that emphasize specific objectives.

Section 6 addresses the factors affecting choices that are made in developing specific policies relating to rebalancing to the strategic asset allocation. Factors discussed include transaction costs, correlations, volatility, and risk aversion.[1]

Section 7 summarizes important points and concludes the chapter.

2. DEVELOPING ASSET-ONLY ASSET ALLOCATIONS

In this section, we discuss several of the primary techniques and considerations involved in developing strategic asset allocations, leaving the issue of considering the liabilities to Section 3 and the issue of tailoring the strategic asset allocation to meet specific goals to Section 4.

We start by introducing mean–variance optimization, beginning with unconstrained optimization, prior to moving on to the more common mean–variance optimization problem in which the weights, in addition to summing to 1, are constrained to be positive (no shorting allowed). We present a detailed example, along with several variations, highlighting some of the important considerations in this approach. We also identify several criticisms of mean–variance optimization and the major ways these criticisms have been addressed in practice.

2.1. Mean–Variance Optimization: Overview

Mean–variance optimization (MVO), as introduced by Markowitz (1952, 1959), is perhaps the most common approach used in practice to develop and set asset allocation policy. Widely used on its own, MVO is also often the basis for more sophisticated approaches that overcome some of the limitations or weaknesses of MVO.

Markowitz recognized that whenever the returns of two assets are not perfectly correlated, the assets can be combined to form a portfolio whose risk (as measured by standard deviation or variance) is less than the weighted-average risk of the assets themselves. An additional and equally important observation is that as one adds assets to the portfolio, one should focus not on the individual risk characteristics of the additional assets but rather on those assets' effect on the risk characteristics of the entire portfolio. Mean–variance optimization provides us with a framework for determining how much to allocate to each asset in order to maximize the *expected* return of the portfolio for an *expected* level of risk. In this sense, mean–variance optimization is a risk-budgeting tool that helps investors to spend their risk budget—the amount of risk they are willing to assume—wisely. We emphasize the word "expected" because the inputs to mean–variance optimization are necessarily forward-looking estimates, and the resulting portfolios reflect the quality of the inputs.

Mean–variance optimization requires three sets of inputs: returns, risks (standard deviations), and pair-wise correlations for the assets in the opportunity set. The objective function is often expressed as follows:

$$U_m = E(R_m) - 0.005\lambda\sigma_m^2 \tag{1}$$

where

U_m = the investor's utility for asset mix (allocation) m

---

[1]In this chapter, "volatility" is often used synonymously with "standard deviation."

R_m = the return for asset mix m

λ = the investor's risk aversion coefficient

σ_m^2 = the expected variance of return for asset mix m

The risk aversion coefficient (λ) characterizes the investor's risk–return trade-off; in this context, it is the rate at which an investor will forgo expected return for less variance. The value of 0.005 in Equation 1 is based on the assumption that $E(R_m)$ and σ_m are expressed as percentages rather than as decimals. (In using Equation 1, omit % signs.) If those quantities were expressed as decimals, the 0.005 would change to 0.5. For example, if $E(R_m) = 0.10$, $\lambda = 2$, and $\sigma = 0.20$ (variance is 0.04), then U_m is 0.06, or 6% [$= 0.10 - 0.5(2)(0.04)$]. In this case, U_m can be interpreted as a certainty-equivalent return—that is, the utility value of the risky return offered by the asset mix, stated in terms of the risk-free return that the investor would value equally. In Equation 1, 0.005 merely scales the second term appropriately.

In words, the objective function says that the value of an asset mix for an investor is equal to the expected return of the asset mix minus a penalty that is equal to one-half of the expected variance of the asset mix scaled by the investor's risk aversion coefficient. Optimization involves selecting the asset mix with the highest such value (certainty equivalent). Smaller risk aversion coefficients result in relatively small penalties for risk, leading to aggressive asset mixes. Conversely, larger risk aversion coefficients result in relatively large penalties for risk, leading to conservative asset mixes. A value of $\lambda = 0$ corresponds to a risk-neutral investor because it implies indifference to volatility. Most investors' risk aversion is consistent with λ between 1 and 10.[2] Empirically, $\lambda = 4$ can be taken to represent a moderately risk-averse investor, although the specific value is sensitive to the opportunity set in question and to market volatility.

In the absence of constraints, there is a closed-form solution that calculates, for a given set of inputs, the single set of weights (allocation) to the assets in the opportunity set that maximizes the investor's utility. Typically, this single set of weights is relatively extreme, with very large long and short positions in each asset class. Except in the special case in which the expected returns are derived using the reverse-optimization process of Sharpe (1974), the expected-utility-maximizing weights will not add up to 100%. We elaborate on reverse optimization in Section 2.4.1.

In most real-world applications, asset allocation weights must add up to 100%, reflecting a fully invested, non-leveraged portfolio. From an optimization perspective, when seeking the asset allocation weights that maximize the investor's utility, one must constrain the asset allocation weights to sum to 1 (100%). This constraint that weights sum to 100% is referred to as the "budget constraint" or "unity constraint." The inclusion of this constraint, or any other constraint, moves us from a problem that has a closed-form solution to a problem that must be solved numerically using optimization techniques.

In contrast to the single solution (single set of weights) that is often associated with unconstrained optimization (one could create an efficient frontier using unconstrained weights, but it is seldom done in practice), Markowitz's mean–variance optimization paradigm is most often identified with an efficient frontier that plots all potential efficient asset mixes subject to some common constraints. In addition to a typical budget constraint that the weights must sum to 1 (100% in percentage terms), the next most common constraint allows only positive weights or allocations (i.e., no negative or short positions).

---

[2]See Ang (2014, p. 44).

Efficient asset mixes are combinations of the assets in the opportunity set that maximize expected return per unit of expected risk or, alternatively (and equivalently), minimize expected risk for a given level of expected return. To find all possible efficient mixes that collectively form the efficient frontier, *conceptually* the optimizer iterates through all the possible values of the risk aversion coefficient (λ) and for each value finds the combination of assets that maximizes expected utility. We have used the word *conceptually* because there are different techniques for carrying out the optimization that may vary slightly from our description, even though the solution (efficient frontier and efficient mixes) is the same. The efficient mix at the far left of the frontier with the lowest risk is referred to as the global minimum variance portfolio, while the portfolio at the far right of the frontier is the maximum expected return portfolio. In the absence of constraints beyond the budget and non-negativity constraints, the maximum expected return portfolio consists of a 100% allocation to the single asset with the highest expected return (which is not necessarily the asset with the highest level of risk).

Risk Aversion

Unfortunately, it is extremely difficult to precisely estimate a given investor's risk aversion coefficient (λ). Best practices suggest that when estimating risk aversion (or, conversely, risk tolerance), one should examine both the investor's *preference* for risk (willingness to take risk) and the investor's *capacity* for taking risk. Risk preference is a subjective measure and typically focuses on how an investor feels about and potentially reacts to the ups and downs of portfolio value. The level of return an investor hopes to earn can influence the investor's willingness to take risk, but investors must be realistic when setting such objectives. Risk capacity is an objective measure of the investor's ability to tolerate portfolio losses and the potential decrease in future consumption associated with those losses.[3] The psychometric literature has developed validated questionnaires, such as that of Grable and Joo (2004), to approximately locate an investor's risk preference, although this result then needs to be blended with risk capacity to determine risk tolerance. For individuals, risk capacity is affected by factors such as net worth, income, the size of an emergency fund in relation to consumption needs, and the rate at which the individual saves out of gross income, according to the practice of financial planners noted in Grable (2008).

With this guidance in mind, we move forward with a relatively global opportunity set, in this case defined from the point of view of an investor from the United Kingdom with an approximate 10-year time horizon. The analysis is carried out in British pounds (GBP), and none of the currency exposure is hedged. Exhibit 1 identifies 12 asset classes within the universe of available investments and a set of plausible forward-looking capital market assumptions: expected returns, standard deviations, and correlations. The chapter on capital

---

[3] *Risk preference* and *risk capacity* are sometimes referred to as the willingness and the ability to take risk, respectively.

market expectations covers how such inputs may be developed.[4] In the exhibit, three significant digits at most are shown, but the subsequent analysis is based on full precision.

Time Horizon

Mean–variance optimization is a "single-period" framework in which the single period could be a week, a month, a year, or some other time period. When working in a "strategic" setting, many practitioners typically find it most intuitive to work with annual capital market assumptions, even though the investment time horizon could be considerably longer (e.g., 10 years). If the strategic asset allocation will not be re-evaluated within a long time frame, capital market assumptions should reflect the average annual distributions of returns expected over the entire investment time horizon. In most cases, investors revisit the strategic asset allocation decision more frequently, such as annually or every three years, rerunning the analysis and making adjustments to the asset allocation; thus, the annual capital market assumption often reflects the expectations associated with the evaluation horizon (e.g., one year or three years).

EXHIBIT 1   Hypothetical UK-Based Investor's Opportunity Set with Expected Returns, Standard Deviations, and Correlations

Panel A: Expected Returns and Standard Deviations

Asset Class	Expected Return (%)	Standard Deviation (%)
UK large cap	6.6	14.8
UK mid cap	6.9	16.7
UK small cap	7.1	19.6
US equities	7.8	15.7
Europe ex UK equities	8.6	19.6
Asia Pacific ex Japan equities	8.5	20.9
Japan equities	6.4	15.2
Emerging market equities	9.0	23.0
Global REITs	9.0	22.5
Global ex UK bonds	4.0	10.4
UK bonds	2.9	6.1
Cash	2.5	0.7

---

[4]The standard deviations and correlations in Exhibit 1 are based on historical numbers, while expected returns come from reverse optimization (described later).

Panel B: Correlations

	UK Large Cap	UK Mid Cap	UK Small Cap	US Equities	Europe ex UK Equities	Asia Pacific ex Japan Equities	Japan Equities	Emerging Market Equities	Global REITs	Global ex UK Bonds	UK Bonds	Cash
UK large cap	1.00	0.86	0.79	0.76	0.88	0.82	0.55	0.78	0.64	−0.12	−0.12	−0.06
UK mid cap	0.86	1.00	0.95	0.76	0.84	0.75	0.51	0.74	0.67	−0.16	−0.10	−0.17
UK small cap	0.79	0.95	1.00	0.67	0.79	0.70	0.49	0.71	0.61	−0.22	−0.15	−0.17
US equities	0.76	0.76	0.67	1.00	0.81	0.72	0.62	0.69	0.77	0.14	0.00	−0.12
Europe ex UK equities	0.88	0.84	0.79	0.81	1.00	0.82	0.60	0.80	0.72	0.04	−0.04	−0.03
Asia Pacific ex Japan equities	0.82	0.75	0.70	0.72	0.82	1.00	0.54	0.94	0.67	0.00	−0.02	0.02
Japan equities	0.55	0.51	0.49	0.62	0.60	0.54	1.00	0.56	0.52	0.18	0.07	−0.01
Emerging market equities	0.78	0.74	0.71	0.69	0.80	0.94	0.56	1.00	0.62	−0.02	−0.03	0.04
Global REITs	0.64	0.67	0.61	0.77	0.72	0.67	0.52	0.62	1.00	0.16	0.18	−0.15
Global ex UK bonds	−0.12	−0.16	−0.22	0.14	0.04	0.00	0.18	−0.02	0.16	1.00	0.62	0.24
UK bonds	−0.12	−0.10	−0.15	0.00	−0.04	−0.02	0.07	−0.03	0.18	0.62	1.00	0.07
Cash	−0.06	−0.17	−0.17	−0.12	−0.03	0.02	−0.01	0.04	−0.15	0.24	0.07	1.00

The classification of asset classes in the universe of available investments may vary according to local practices. For example, in the United States and some other larger markets, it is common to classify equities by market capitalization, whereas the practice of classifying equities by valuation ("growth" versus "value") is less common outside of the United States. Similarly, with regard to fixed income, some asset allocators may classify bonds based on various attributes—nominal versus inflation linked, corporate versus government issued, investment grade versus non-investment grade (high yield)—and/or by maturity/duration (short, intermediate, and long). By means of the non-negativity constraint and using a reverse-optimization procedure (to be explained later) based on asset class market values to generate expected return estimates, we control the typically high sensitivity of the composition of efficient portfolios to expected return estimates (discussed further in

Section 2.4). Without such precautions, we would often find that efficient portfolios are highly concentrated in a subset of the available asset classes.

Running this set of capital market assumptions through a mean–variance optimizer with the traditional non-negativity and unity constraints produces the efficient frontier depicted in Exhibit 2. We have augmented this efficient frontier with some non-traditional information that will assist with the understanding of some key concepts related to the efficient frontier. A risk-free return of 2.5% is used in calculating the reserve-optimized expected returns as well as the Sharpe ratios in Exhibit 2.

EXHIBIT 2   Efficient Frontier—Base Case

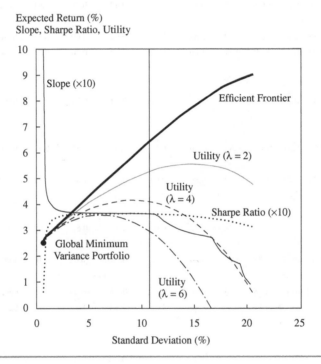

The slope of the efficient frontier is greatest at the far left of the efficient frontier, at the point representing the global minimum variance portfolio. Slope represents the rate at which expected return increases per increase in risk. As one moves to the right, in the direction of increasing risk, the slope decreases; it is lowest at the point representing the maximum return portfolio. Thus, as one moves from left to right along the efficient frontier, the investor takes on larger and larger amounts of risk for smaller and smaller increases in expected return. The "kinks" in the line representing the slope (times 10) of the efficient frontier correspond to portfolios (known as corner portfolios) in which an asset either enters or leaves the efficient mix.

For most investors, at the far left of the efficient frontier, the increases in expected return associated with small increases in expected risk represent a desirable trade-off. The risk aversion coefficient identifies the specific point on the efficient frontier at which the investor refuses to take on additional risk because he or she feels the associated increase in expected return is not high enough to compensate for the increase in risk. Of course, each investor makes this trade-off differently.

For this particular efficient frontier, the three expected utility curves plot the solution to Equation 1 for three different risk aversion coefficients: 2.0, 4.0, and 6.0, respectively.[5] For a given risk aversion coefficient, the appropriate efficient mix from the efficient frontier is simply the mix in which expected utility is highest (i.e., maximized). As illustrated in Exhibit 2, a lower risk aversion coefficient leads to a riskier (higher) point on the efficient frontier, while a higher risk aversion coefficient leads to a more conservative (lower) point on the efficient frontier.

The vertical line (at volatility of 10.88%) identifies the asset mix with the highest Sharpe ratio; it intersects the Sharpe ratio line at a value of 3.7 (an unscaled value of 0.37). This portfolio is also represented by the intersection of the slope line and the Sharpe ratio line.

Exhibit 3 is an efficient frontier asset allocation area graph. Each vertical cross section identifies the asset allocation at a point along the efficient frontier; thus, the vertical cross section at the far left, with nearly 100% cash, is the asset allocation of the minimum variance portfolio, and the vertical cross section at the far right, with 45% in emerging markets and 55% in global REITs, is the optimal asset allocation for a standard deviation of 20.5%, the highest level of portfolio volatility shown. In this example, cash is treated as a risky asset; although its return volatility is very low, because it is less than perfectly correlated with the other asset classes, mixing it with small amounts of other asset classes reduces risk further. The vertical line identifies the asset mix with the highest Sharpe ratio and corresponds to the similar line shown on the original efficient frontier graph (Exhibit 2). The asset allocation mixes are well diversified for most of the first half of the efficient frontier, and in fact, for a large portion of the efficient frontier, all 12 asset classes in our opportunity set receive a positive allocation.[6]

---

[5]Numbers have been rounded to increase readability.

[6]Studying Exhibit 3 closely, one notices distinct regime shifts where the rate at which allocations are made to asset classes changes so that a line segment with a different slope begins. These regime shifts occur at what are called *corner portfolios*. The efficient mixes between two adjacent corner portfolios are simply linear combinations of those portfolios. The efficient frontier asset allocation area graph helps to clarify this result. More formally, corner portfolios are points on the efficient frontier at which an asset class either enters or leaves the efficient mix or a constraint either becomes binding or is no longer binding.

EXHIBIT 3   Efficient Frontier Asset Allocation Area Graph—Base Case

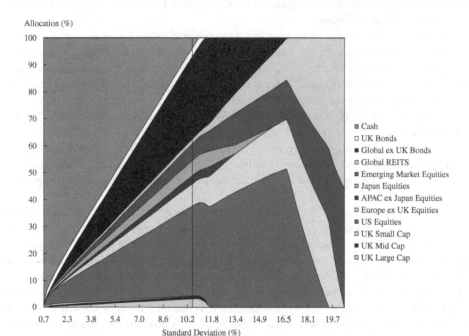

The investment characteristics of potential asset mixes based on mean–variance theory are often further investigated by means of Monte Carlo simulation, as discussed in Section 2.2. Several observations from theory and practice are relevant to narrowing the choices.

Equation 1 indicates that the basic approach to asset allocation involves estimating the investor's risk aversion parameter and then finding the efficient mix that maximizes expected utility. When the risk aversion coefficient has not been estimated, the investor may be able to identify the maximum tolerable level of portfolio return volatility. If that level is 10% per annum, for example, only the part of the efficient frontier associated with volatility less than or equal to 10% is relevant. This approach is justifiable because for a given efficient frontier, every value of the risk aversion coefficient can be associated with a value of volatility that identifies the best point on the efficient frontier for the investor; the investor may also have experience with thinking in terms of volatility. In addition, when the investor has a numerical return objective, he or she can further narrow the range of potential efficient mixes by identifying the efficient portfolios expected to meet that return objective. For example, if the return objective is 5%, one can select the asset allocation with a 5% expected return.

Example 1 illustrates the use of Equation 1 and shows the adaptability of MVO by introducing the choice problem in the context of an investor who also has a shortfall risk concern.

EXAMPLE 1   Mean–Variance-Efficient Portfolio Choice 1

An investment adviser is counseling Aimée Goddard, a client who recently inherited €1,200,000 and who has above-average risk tolerance ($\lambda = 2$). Because Goddard is young and one of her goals is to fund a comfortable retirement, she wants to earn returns that will outpace inflation in the long term. Goddard expects to liquidate €60,000 of the inherited portfolio in 12 months to fund the down payment on a house. She states that it is important for her to be able to take out the €60,000 without invading the initial capital of €1,200,000. Exhibit 4 shows three alternative strategic asset allocations.

EXHIBIT 4   Strategic Asset Allocation Choices for Goddard

Asset Allocation	Investor's Forecasts	
	Expected Return	**Standard Deviation of Return**
A	10.00%	20%
B	7.00	10
C	5.25	5

1. Based only on Goddard's risk-adjusted expected returns for the asset allocations, which asset allocation would she prefer?
2. Recommend and justify a strategic asset allocation for Goddard.

   Note: In addressing 2, calculate the minimum return, R_L, that needs to be achieved to meet the investor's objective not to invade capital, using the expression ratio $[E(R_P) - R_L]/\sigma_P$, which reflects the probability of exceeding the minimum given a normal return distribution assumption in a safety-first approach.[7]

Solution to 1: Using Equation 1,

$$
\begin{aligned}
U_m &= E(R_m) - 0.005\lambda\sigma_m^2 \\
&= E(R_m) - 0.005(2)\sigma_m^2 \\
&= E(R_m) - 0.01\sigma_m^2
\end{aligned}
$$

So Goddard's utility for Asset Allocations A, B, and C are as follows:

$$
\begin{aligned}
U_A &= E(R_A) - 0.01\sigma_A^2 \\
&= 10.0 - 0.01(20)^2 \\
&= 10.0 - 4.0 \\
&= 6.0 \text{ or } 6.0\% \\
U_B &= E(R_B) - 0.01\sigma_B^2 \\
&= 7.0 - 0.01(10)^2 \\
&= 7.0 - 1.0 \\
&= 6.0 \text{ or } 6.0\%
\end{aligned}
$$

---

[7]See the Level I CFA Program chapter "Common Probability Distributions" for coverage of Roy's safety-first criterion.

$$U_C = E(R_C) - 0.01\sigma_C^2$$
$$= 5.25 - 0.01(5)^2$$
$$= 5.25 - 0.25$$
$$= 5.0 \text{ or } 5.0\%$$

Goddard would be indifferent on their common perceived certainty-equivalent return of 6%.

Solution to 2: Because €60,000/€1,200,000 is 5.0%, for any return less than 5.0%, Goddard will need to invade principal when she liquidates €60,000. So 5% is a threshold return level.

To decide which of the three allocations is best for Goddard, we calculate the ratio $[E(R_P) - R_L]/\sigma_P$:

Allocation A: (10% − 5%)/20% = 0.25
Allocation B: (7% − 5%)/10% = 0.20
Allocation C: (5.25% − 5%)/5% = 0.05

Both Allocations A and B have the same expected utility, but Allocation A has a higher probability of meeting the threshold 5% return than Allocation B. Therefore, A would be the recommended strategic asset allocation.

There are several different approaches to determining an allocation to cash and cash equivalents, such as government bills. Exhibit 1 included cash among the assets for which we conducted an optimization to trace out an efficient frontier. The return to cash over a short time horizon is essentially certain in nominal terms. One approach to asset allocation separates out cash and cash equivalents as a (nominally) risk-free asset and calculates an efficient frontier of risky assets. Alternatively, a ray from the risk-free rate (a point on the return axis) tangent to the risky-asset efficient frontier (with cash excluded) then defines a linear efficient frontier. The efficient frontier then consists of combinations of the risk-free asset with the tangency portfolio (which has the highest Sharpe ratio among portfolios on the risky-asset efficient frontier).

A number of standard finance models (including Tobin two-fund separation) adopt this treatment of cash. According to two-fund separation, if investors can borrow or lend at the risk-free rate, they will choose the tangency portfolio for the risky-asset holdings and borrow at the risk-free rate to leverage the position in that portfolio to achieve a higher expected return, or they will split money between the tangency portfolio and the risk-free asset to reach a position with lower risk and lower expected return than that represented by the tangency portfolio. Since over horizons that are longer than the maturity of a money market instrument, the return earned would not be known, another approach that is well established in practice and reflected in Exhibit 1 is to include cash in the optimization. The amount of cash indicated by an optimization may be adjusted in light of short-term liquidity needs; for example, some financial advisers advocate that individuals hold an amount of cash equivalent to six months of expenses. All of these approaches are reasonable alternatives in practice.

Although we will treat cash as a risky asset in the following discussions, in Example 2, we stop to show the application of the alternative approach based on distinguishing a risk-free asset.

EXAMPLE 2   A Strategic Asset Allocation Based on Distinguishing a Nominal Risk-Free Asset

The Caflandia Foundation for the Fine Arts (CFFA) is a hypothetical charitable organization established to provide funding to Caflandia museums for their art acquisition programs.

CFFA's overall investment objective is to maintain its portfolio's real purchasing power after distributions. CFFA targets a 4% annual distribution of assets. CFFA has the following current specific investment policies.

Return objective
CFFA's assets shall be invested with the objective of earning an average nominal 6.5% annual return. This level reflects a spending rate of 4%, an expected inflation rate of 2%, and a 40 bp cost of earning investment returns. The calculation is $(1.04)(1.02)$ $(1.004) - 1 = 0.065$, or 6.5%.

Risk considerations
CFFA's assets shall be invested to minimize the level of standard deviation of return subject to satisfying the expected return objective.

The investment office of CFFA distinguishes a nominally risk-free asset. As of the date of the optimization, the risk-free rate is determined to be 2.2%.

Exhibit 5 gives key outputs from a mean–variance optimization in which asset class weights are constrained to be non-negative.

EXHIBIT 5   Corner Portfolios Defining the Risky-Asset Efficient Frontier

Portfolio Number	Expected Nominal Returns	Standard Deviation	Sharpe Ratio
1	9.50%	18.00%	0.406
2	8.90	15.98	0.419
3	8.61	15.20	0.422
4	7.24	11.65	0.433
5	5.61	7.89	0.432
6	5.49	7.65	0.430
7	3.61	5.39	0.262

The portfolios shown are corner portfolios (see footnote 6), which as a group define the risky-asset efficient frontier in the sense that any portfolio on the frontier is a combination of the two corner portfolios that bracket it in terms of expected return.

Based only on the facts given, determine the most appropriate strategic asset allocation for CFFA given its stated investment policies.

Solution: An 85%/15% combination of Portfolio 4 and the risk-free asset is the most appropriate asset allocation. This combination has the required 6.5% expected return with the minimum level of risk. Stated another way, this combination defines the efficient portfolio at a 6.5% level of expected return based on the linear efficient frontier created by the introduction of a risk-free asset.

Note that Portfolio 4 has the highest Sharpe ratio and is the tangency portfolio. With an expected return of 7.24%, it can be combined with the risk-free asset, with a return of 2.2%, to achieve an expected return of 6.5%:

$$6.50 = 7.24w + 2.2(1 - w)$$
$$w = 0.853$$

Placing about 85% of assets in Portfolio 4 and 15% in the risk-free asset achieves an efficient portfolio with expected return of 6.4 with a volatility of $0.853(11.65) = 9.94\%$. (The risk-free asset has no return volatility by assumption and, also by assumption, zero correlation with any risky portfolio return.) This portfolio lies on a linear efficient frontier formed by a ray from the risk-free rate to the tangency portfolio and can be shown to have the same Sharpe ratio as the tangency portfolio, 0.433. The combination of Portfolio 4 with Portfolio 5 to achieve a 6.5% expected return would have a lower Sharpe ratio and would not lie on the efficient frontier.

Asset allocation decisions have traditionally been made considering only the investor's investment portfolio (and financial liabilities) and not the total picture that includes human capital and other non-traded assets (and liabilities), which are missing in a traditional balance sheet. Taking such extended assets and liabilities into account can lead to improved asset allocation decisions, however.

Depending on the nature of an individual's career, human capital can provide relatively stable cash flows similar to bond payments. At the other extreme, the cash flows from human capital can be much more volatile and uncertain, reflecting a lumpy, commission-based pay structure or perhaps a career in a seasonal business. For many individuals working in stable job markets, the cash flows associated with their human capital are somewhat like those of an inflation-linked bond, relatively consistent and tending to increase with inflation. If human capital is a relatively large component of the individual's total economic worth, accounting for this type of hidden asset in an asset allocation setting is extremely important and would presumably increase the individual's capacity to take on risk.

Let us look at a hypothetical example. Emma Beel is a 45-year-old tenured university professor in London. Capital market assumptions are as before (see Exhibit 1). Beel has GBP 1,500,000 in liquid financial assets, largely due to a best-selling book. Her employment as a tenured university professor is viewed as very secure and produces cash flows that resemble those of a very large, inflation-adjusted, long-duration bond portfolio. The net present value of her human capital is estimated at GBP 500,000. Beel inherited her grandmother's home on the edge of the city, valued at GBP 750,000. The results of a risk tolerance questionnaire that considers both risk preference and risk capacity suggest that Beel should have an asset allocation involving moderate risk. Furthermore, given our earlier assumption that the collective market risk aversion coefficient is 4.0, we assume that the risk aversion coefficient of a moderately risk-averse investor is approximately 4.0, from a total wealth perspective.

To account for Beel's human capital and residential real estate, these two asset classes were modeled and added to the optimization. Beel's human capital of GBP 500,000 was modeled as 70% UK long-duration inflation-linked bonds, 15% UK corporate bonds, and 15% UK equities.[8] Residential real estate was modeled based on a de-smoothed residential

---

[8]These weights were used to create the return composite representing Beel's human capital that was used in the asset allocation optimization.

property index for London. (We will leave the complexities of modeling liabilities to Section 3.) Beel's assets include those shown in Exhibit 6.

EXHIBIT 6   Emma Beel's Assets

Asset	Value (GBP)	Percentage
Liquid financial assets	1,500,000	54.55
UK residential real estate	750,000	27.27
Human capital	500,000	18.18
	2,750,000	100

Beel's UK residential real estate (representing the London house) and human capital were added to the optimization opportunity set. Additionally, working under the assumption that Beel's house and human capital are non-tradable assets, the optimizer was forced to allocate 27.27% or more to UK residential real estate and 18.18% to human capital and then determined the optimal asset allocation based on a risk aversion coefficient of 4. Beel's expected utility is maximized by an efficient asset allocation with volatility of approximately 8.2%. Exhibit 7 displays the resulting asset allocation area graph.

EXHIBIT 7   Efficient Frontier Asset Allocation Area Graph—Balance Sheet Approach

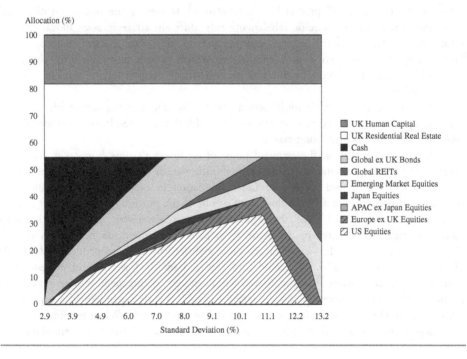

Looking past the constrained allocations to human capital and UK residential real estate, the remaining allocations associated with Beel's liquid financial assets do not include UK

equities or UK fixed income. Each of these three asset classes is relatively highly correlated with either UK residential real estate or UK human capital.[9]

2.2. Monte Carlo Simulation

Monte Carlo simulation complements MVO by addressing the limitations of MVO as a single-period framework. Additionally, in the case in which the investor's risk tolerance is either unknown or in need of further validation, Monte Carlo simulation can help paint a realistic picture of potential future outcomes, including the likelihood of meeting various goals, the distribution of the portfolio's expected value through time, and potential maximum drawdowns. Simulation also provides a tool for investigating the effects of trading/rebalancing costs and taxes and the interaction of evolving financial markets with asset allocation. It is important to note that not all Monte Carlo simulation tools are the same: They vary significantly in their ability to model non-normal multivariate returns, serial and cross-correlations, tax rates, distribution requirements, an evolving asset allocation schedule (target-date glide path), non-traditional investments (e.g., annuities), and human capital (based on age, geography, education, and/or occupation).

Using Monte Carlo simulation, an investment adviser can effectively grapple with a range of practical issues that are difficult or impossible to formulate analytically. Consider rebalancing to a strategic asset allocation for a taxable investor. We can readily calculate the impact of taxes during a single time period. Also, in a single-period setting, as assumed by MVO, rebalancing is irrelevant. In the multi-period world of most investment problems, however, the portfolio will predictably be rebalanced, triggering the realization of capital gains and losses. Given a specific rebalancing rule, different strategic asset allocations will result in different patterns of tax payments (and different transaction costs too). Formulating the multi-period problem mathematically would be a daunting challenge. We could more easily incorporate the interaction between rebalancing and taxes in a Monte Carlo simulation.

We will examine a simple multi-period problem to illustrate the use of Monte Carlo simulation, evaluating the range of outcomes for wealth that may result from a strategic asset allocation (and not incorporating taxes).

The value of wealth at the terminal point of an investor's time horizon is a possible criterion for choosing among asset allocations. Future wealth incorporates the interaction of risk and return. The need for Monte Carlo simulation in evaluating an asset allocation depends on whether there are cash flows into or out of the portfolio over time. For a given asset allocation with no cash flows, the sequence of returns is irrelevant; ending wealth will be path independent (unaffected by the sequence or path of returns through time). With cash flows, the sequence is also irrelevant if simulated returns are independent, identically distributed random variables. We could find expected terminal wealth and percentiles of terminal wealth analytically.[10] Investors save/deposit money in and spend money out of their portfolios; thus, in the more typical case, terminal wealth is path dependent (the sequence of returns matters) because of the interaction of cash flows and returns. When terminal wealth is path dependent, an analytical approach is not feasible but Monte Carlo simulation is.

---

[9]For additional information on applying a total balance sheet approach, see, for example, Blanchett and Straehl (2015) or Rudd and Siegel (2013).

[10]Making a plausible statistical assumption, such as a lognormal distribution, for ending wealth.

Example 3 applies Monte Carlo simulation to evaluate the strategic asset allocation of an investor who regularly withdraws from the portfolio.

EXAMPLE 3   Monte Carlo Simulation for a Retirement Portfolio with a Proposed Asset Allocation

---

Malala Ali, a resident of the hypothetical country of Caflandia, has sought the advice of an investment adviser concerning her retirement portfolio. At the end of 2017, she is 65 years old and holds a portfolio valued at CAF$1 million. Ali would like to withdraw CAF$40,000 a year to supplement the corporate pension she has begun to receive. Given her health and family history, Ali believes she should plan for a retirement lasting 25 years. She is also concerned about passing along a portion of her portfolio to the families of her three children; she hopes that at least the portfolio's current real value can go to them. Consulting with her adviser, Ali has expressed this desire quantitatively: She wants the median value of her bequest to her children to be no less than her portfolio's current value of CAF$1 million in real terms. The median is the 50th percentile outcome. The asset allocation of her retirement portfolio is currently 50/50 Caflandia equities/Caflandia intermediate-term government bonds. Ali and her adviser have decided on the following set of capital market expectations (Exhibit 8):

EXHIBIT 8   Caflandia Capital Market Expectations

Asset Class	Investor's Forecasts	
	Expected Return	Standard Deviation of Return
Caflandia equities	9.4%	20.4%
Caflandia bonds	5.6%	4.1%
Inflation	2.6%	

The predicted correlation between returns of Caflandia equities and Caflandia intermediate-term government bonds is 0.15.

With the current asset allocation, the expected nominal return on Ali's retirement portfolio is 7.5% with a standard deviation of 11%. Exhibit 9 gives the results of the Monte Carlo simulation.[11] In Exhibit 9, the lowest curve represents, at various ages, levels of real wealth at or below which the 10% of worst real wealth outcomes lie (i.e., the 10th percentile for real wealth); curves above that represent, respectively, 25th, 50th, 75th, and 90th percentiles for real wealth.

---

[11]Note that the *y*-axis in this exhibit is specified using a logarithmic scale. The quantity CAF$1 million is the same distance from CAF$100,000 as CAF$10 million is from CAF$1 million because CAF$1 million is 10 times CAF$100,000, just as CAF$10 million is 10 times CAF$1 million. CAF$100,000 is 10^5, and CAF $1 million is 10^6. In Exhibit 9, a distance halfway between the CAF$100,000 and CAF$1 million hatch marks is $10^{5.5}$ = CAF$316,228.

EXHIBIT 9   Monte Carlo Simulation of Ending Real Wealth with Annual Cash Outflows

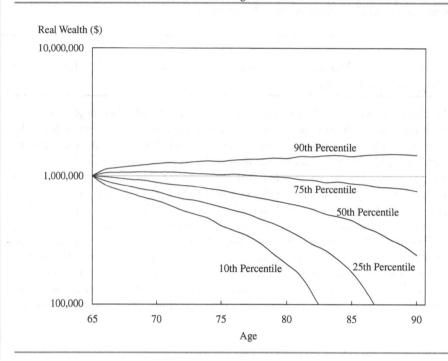

Based on the information given, address the following:

1. Justify the presentation of ending wealth in terms of real rather than nominal wealth in Exhibit 9.
2. Is the current asset allocation expected to satisfy Ali's investment objectives?

Solution to 1: Ali wants the median real value of her bequest to her children to be "no less than her portfolio's current value of CAF$1 million." We need to state future amounts in terms of today's values (i.e., in real dollars) to assess the purchasing power of those amounts relative to CAF$1 million today. Exhibit 9 thus gives the results of the Monte Carlo simulation in real dollar terms. The median real wealth at age 90 is clearly well below the target ending wealth of real CAF$1 million.

Solution to 2: From Exhibit 9, we see that the median terminal (at age 90) value of the retirement portfolio in real dollars is less than the stated bequest goal of CAF$1 million. Therefore, the most likely bequest is less than the amount Ali has said she wants. The current asset allocation is not expected to satisfy all her investment objectives. Although one potential lever would be to invest more aggressively, given Ali's age and risk tolerance, this approach seems imprudent. An adviser may need to counsel that the desired size of the bequest may be unrealistic given Ali's desired income to support her expenditures. Ali will likely need to make a relatively tough choice between her living standard (spending less) and her desire to leave a CAF$1 million bequest in real terms. A third alternative would be to delay retirement, which may or may not be feasible.

2.3. Criticisms of Mean–Variance Optimization

With this initial understanding of mean–variance optimization, we can now elaborate on some of the most common criticisms of it. The following criticisms and the ways they have been addressed motivate the balance of the coverage of MVO:

1. The outputs (asset allocations) are highly sensitive to small changes in the inputs.
2. The asset allocations tend to be highly concentrated in a subset of the available asset classes.
3. Many investors are concerned about more than the mean and variance of returns, the focus of MVO.
4. Although the asset allocations may appear diversified across assets, the sources of risk may not be diversified.
5. Most portfolios exist to pay for a liability or consumption series, and MVO allocations are not directly connected to what influences the value of the liability or the consumption series.
6. MVO is a single-period framework that does not take account of trading/rebalancing costs and taxes.

In the rest of Section 2, we look at various approaches to addressing criticisms 1 and 2, giving some attention also to criticisms 3 and 4. Sections 3 and 4 present approaches to addressing criticism 5. "Asset Allocation with Real World Constraints" addresses some aspects of criticism 6.

It is important to understand that the first criticism above is not unique to MVO. Any optimization model that uses forward-looking quantities as inputs faces similar consequences of treating input values as capable of being determined with certainty. Sensitivity to errors in inputs is a problem that cannot be fully solved because it is inherent in the structure of optimization models that use as inputs forecasts of uncertain quantities.

To illustrate the importance of the quality of inputs, the sensitivity of asset weights in efficient portfolios to small changes in inputs, and the propensity of mean–variance optimization to allocate to a relatively small subset of the available asset classes, we made changes to the expected return of two asset classes in our base-case UK-centric opportunity set in Exhibit 1. We increased the expected return of Asia Pacific ex Japan equities from 8.5% to 9.0% and decreased the expected return of Europe ex UK equities from 8.6% to 8.1% (both changes are approximately 50 bps). We left all of the other inputs unchanged and reran the optimization. The efficient frontier as depicted in mean–variance space appears virtually unchanged (not shown); however, the efficient asset mixes of this new efficient frontier are dramatically different. Exhibit 10 displays the efficient frontier asset allocation area graph based on the slightly changed capital market assumptions. Notice the dramatic difference between Exhibit 10 and Exhibit 3. The small change in return assumptions has driven UK large cap, Europe ex-UK equities, and emerging market equities out of the efficient mixes, and the efficient mixes are now highly concentrated in a smaller subset of the available asset classes. Given that the expected returns of UK large cap and emerging market equities were unchanged, their disappearance from the efficient frontier is not intuitive.

EXHIBIT 10   Efficient Frontier Asset Allocation Area Graph—Changed Expected Returns

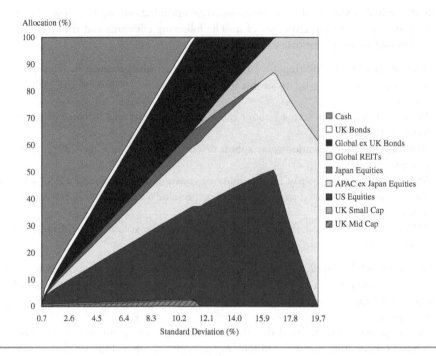

To aid with the comparison of Exhibit 10 with Exhibit 3, we identified three specific efficient asset allocation mixes and compared the version based on the ad hoc modification of expected returns to that of the base case. This comparison is shown in Exhibit 11.

EXHIBIT 11   Comparison of Select Efficient Asset Allocations—Ad Hoc Return Modification Allocations vs. Base-Case Allocations

	Modified 25/75	Base Case 25/75	Difference	Modified 50/50	Base Case 50/50	Difference	Modified 75/25	Base Case 75/25	Difference
UK large cap	0.0%	1.2%	−1.2%	0.0%	2.5%	−2.5%	0.0%	0.0%	0.0%
UK mid cap	0.8%	0.6%	0.3%	1.7%	0.8%	0.9%	0.0%	0.0%	0.0%
UK small cap	0.5%	0.5%	−0.1%	0.4%	0.4%	0.0%	0.0%	0.0%	0.0%
US equities	13.7%	13.8%	−0.1%	26.6%	26.8%	−0.2%	40.1%	40.5%	−0.4%
Europe ex UK equities	0.0%	2.7%	−2.7%	0.0%	6.5%	−6.5%	0.0%	13.2%	−13.2%

	Modified 25/75	Base Case 25/75	Difference	Modified 50/50	Base Case 50/50	Difference	Modified 75/25	Base Case 75/25	Difference
Asia Pacific ex Japan equities	7.5%	1.0%	6.5%	16.6%	2.3%	14.2%	26.8%	1.5%	25.3%
Japan equities	2.2%	2.3%	−0.1%	4.5%	4.5%	0.0%	4.4%	4.3%	0.1%
Emerging market equities	0.0%	2.0%	−2.0%	0.0%	4.9%	−4.9%	0.0%	10.0%	−10.0%
Global REITs	0.3%	0.9%	−0.6%	0.2%	1.4%	−1.3%	3.8%	5.6%	−1.8%
Global ex UK bonds	10.9%	10.6%	0.3%	24.7%	23.9%	0.7%	25.0%	25.0%	0.0%
UK bonds	2.5%	2.7%	−0.2%	2.4%	3.0%	−0.6%	0.0%	0.0%	0.0%
Cash	61.6%	61.7%	−0.1%	22.9%	23.1%	−0.1%	0.0%	0.0%	0.0%
Subtotal equities	25.0%	25.0%		50.0%	50.0%		75.0%	75.0%	
Subtotal fixed income	75.0%	75.0%		50.0%	50.0%		25.0%	25.0%	

2.4. Addressing the Criticisms of Mean–Variance Optimization

In this section, we explore several methods for overcoming some of the potential short-comings of mean–variance optimization. Techniques that address the first two criticisms mostly take three approaches: improving the quality of inputs, constraining the optimization, and treating the efficient frontier as a statistical construct. These approaches are treated in the following three subsections.

In MVO, the composition of efficient portfolios is typically more sensitive to expected return estimates than it is to estimates of volatilities and correlations. Furthermore, expected returns are generally more difficult to estimate accurately than are volatilities and correlations. Thus, in addressing the first criticism of MVO—that outputs are highly sensitive to small changes in inputs—the chapter will focus on expected return inputs. However, volatility and correlation inputs are also sources of potential error.

2.4.1. Reverse Optimization
Reverse optimization is a powerful tool that helps explain the implied returns associated with any portfolio. It can be used to estimate expected returns for use in a forward-looking optimization. MVO solves for optimal asset weights based on expected returns, covariances, and a risk aversion coefficient. Based on predetermined inputs, an optimizer solves for the

optimal asset allocation weights. As the name implies, *reverse* optimization works in the opposite direction. Reverse optimization takes as its inputs a set of asset allocation weights *that are assumed to be optimal* and, with the additional inputs of covariances and the risk aversion coefficient, solves for expected returns. These reverse-optimized returns are sometimes referred to as implied or imputed returns.

When using reverse optimization to estimate a set of expected returns for use in a forward-looking optimization, the most common set of starting weights is the observed market-capitalization value of the assets or asset classes that form the opportunity set. The market capitalization of a given asset or asset classes should reflect the collective information of market participants. In representing the world market portfolio, the use of non-overlapping asset classes representing the majority of the world's investable assets is most consistent with theory.

Some practitioners will find the link between reverse optimization and CAPM equilibrium elegant, while others will see it as a shortcoming. For those who truly object to the use of market-capitalization weights in estimating inputs, the mechanics of reverse optimization can work with any set of starting weights—such as those of an existing policy portfolio, the average asset allocation policy of a peer group, or a fundamental weighting scheme. For those with more minor objections, we will shortly introduce the Black–Litterman model, which allows the expression of alternative forecasts or views.

In order to apply reverse optimization, one must create a working version of the all-inclusive market portfolio based on the constituents of the opportunity set. The market size or capitalization for most of the traditional stock and bond asset classes can be easily inferred from the various indexes that are used as asset class proxies. Many broad market-capitalization-weighted indexes report that they comprise over 95% of the securities, by market capitalization, of the asset classes they are attempting to represent. Exhibit 12 lists approximate values and weights for the 12 asset classes in our opportunity set, uses the weights associated with the asset classes to form a working version of the global market portfolio, and then uses the beta of each asset relative to our working version of the global market portfolio to infer what expected returns would be if all assets were priced by the CAPM according to their market beta. We assume a risk-free rate of 2.5% and a global market risk premium of 4%. Note that expected returns are rounded to one decimal place from the more precise values shown later (in Exhibit 13); expected returns cannot in every case be exactly reproduced based on Exhibit 12 alone because of the approximations mentioned. Also, notice in the final row of Exhibit 12 that the weighted average return and beta of the assets are 6.5% and 1, respectively.

EXHIBIT 12   Reverse-Optimization Example (Market Capitalization in £ billions)

Asset Class	Mkt Cap	Weight	Return $E[R_i]$		Risk-Free Rate r_f		Beta $\beta_{i,mkt}$	Market Risk Premium
UK large cap	£1,354.06	3.2%	6.62%	=	2.5%	+	1.03	(4%)
UK mid cap	£369.61	0.9%	6.92%	=	2.5%	+	1.11	(4%)
UK small cap	£108.24	0.3%	7.07%	=	2.5%	+	1.14	(4%)
US equities	£14,411.66	34.4%	7.84%	=	2.5%	+	1.33	(4%)
Europe ex UK equities	£3,640.48	8.7%	8.63%	=	2.5%	+	1.53	(4%)

Asset Class	Mkt Cap	Weight	Return $E[R_i]$		Risk-Free Rate r_f		Beta $\beta_{i,mkt}$	Market Risk Premium
Asia Pacific ex Japan equities	£1,304.81	3.1%	8.51%	=	2.5%	+	1.50	(4%)
Japan equities	£2,747.63	6.6%	6.43%	=	2.5%	+	0.98	(4%)
Emerging market equities	£2,448.60	5.9%	8.94%	=	2.5%	+	1.61	(4%)
Global REITs	£732.65	1.8%	9.04%	=	2.5%	+	1.64	(4%)
Global ex UK bonds	£13,318.58	31.8%	4.05%	=	2.5%	+	0.39	(4%)
UK bonds	£1,320.71	3.2%	2.95%	=	2.5%	+	0.112	(4%)
Cash	£83.00	0.2%	2.50%	=	2.5%	+	0.00	(4%)
	£41,840.04	100.0%	6.50%				1	

Notes: For the Mkt Cap and Weight columns, the final row is the simple sum. For the Return and Beta columns, the final row is the weighted average.

Looking back at our original asset allocation area graph (Exhibit 3), the reason for the well-behaved and well-diversified asset allocation mixes is now clear. By using reverse optimization, we are consistently relating assets' expected returns to their systematic risk. If there isn't a consistent relationship between the expected return and systematic risk, the optimizer will see this inconsistency as an opportunity and seek to take advantage of the more attractive attributes. This effect was clearly visible in our second asset allocation area graph after we altered the expected returns of Asia Pacific ex Japan equities and Europe ex UK equities.

As alluded to earlier, some practitioners find that the reverse-optimization process leads to a nice starting point, but they often have alternative forecasts or views regarding the expected return of one or more of the asset classes that differ from the returns implied by reverse optimization based on market-capitalization weights. One example of having views that differ from the reverse-optimized returns has already been illustrated, when we altered the returns of Asia Pacific ex Japan equities and Europe ex UK equities by approximately 50 bps. Unfortunately, due to the sensitivity of mean–variance optimization to small changes in inputs, directly altering the expected returns caused relatively extreme and unintuitive changes in the resulting asset allocations. If one has strong views on expected returns that differ from the reverse-optimized returns, an alternative or additional approach is needed; the next section presents one alternative.

2.4.2. Black–Litterman Model

A complementary addition to reverse optimization is the Black–Litterman model, created by Fischer Black and Robert Litterman (see Black and Litterman 1990, 1991, 1992). Although the Black–Litterman model is often characterized as an asset allocation model, it is really a model for deriving a set of expected returns that can be used in an unconstrained or constrained optimization setting. The Black–Litterman model starts with excess returns (in excess of the risk-free rate) produced from reverse optimization and then provides a technique for altering reverse-optimized expected returns in such a way that they reflect an investor's own distinctive views yet still behave well in an optimizer.

The Black–Litterman model has helped make the mean–variance optimization framework more useful. It enables investors to combine their unique forecasts of expected returns with reverse-optimized returns in an elegant manner. When coupled with a mean–variance or related framework, the resulting Black–Litterman expected returns often lead to well-diversified asset allocations by improving the consistency between each asset class's expected return and its contribution to systematic risk. These asset allocations are grounded in economic reality—via the market capitalization of the assets typically used in the reverse-optimization process—but still reflect the information contained in the investor's unique forecasts (or views) of expected return.

The mathematical details of the Black–Litterman model are beyond the scope of this chapter, but many practitioners have access to asset allocation software that includes the Black–Litterman model.[12] To assist with an intuitive understanding of the model and to show the model's ability to blend new information (views) with reverse-optimized returns, we present an example based on the earlier views regarding the expected returns of Asia Pacific ex Japan equities and Europe ex UK equities. The Black–Litterman model has two methods for accepting views: one in which an absolute return forecast is associated with a given asset class and one in which the return differential of an asset (or group of assets) is expressed relative to another asset (or group of assets). Using the relative view format of the Black–Litterman model, we expressed the view that we believe Asia Pacific ex Japan equities will outperform Europe ex UK equities by 100 bps. We placed this view into the Black–Litterman model, which blends reverse-optimized returns with such views to create a new, mixed estimate.

Exhibit 13 compares the Black–Litterman model returns to the original reverse-optimized returns (as in Exhibit 12 but showing returns to the second decimal place based on calculations with full precision). The model accounts for the correlations of the assets with each other, and as one might expect, all of the returns change slightly (the change in return on cash was extremely small).

EXHIBIT 13   Comparison of Black–Litterman and Reverse-Optimized Returns

Asset Class	Reverse-Optimized Returns	Black–Litterman Returns	Difference
UK large cap	6.62%	6.60%	−0.02%
UK mid cap	6.92	6.87	−0.05
UK small cap	7.08	7.03	−0.05
US equities	7.81	7.76	−0.05
Europe ex UK equities	8.62	8.44	−0.18
Asia Pacific ex Japan equities	8.53	8.90	0.37
Japan equities	6.39	6.37	−0.02
Emerging market equities	8.96	9.30	0.33
Global REITs	9.02	9.00	−0.01
Global ex UK bonds	4.03	4.00	−0.03
UK bonds	2.94	2.95	0.01
Cash	2.50	2.50	0.00

---

[12]For those interested in the mathematical details of the Black–Litterman model, see Idzorek (2007); a prepublication version is available here: http://corporate.morningstar.com/ib/documents/Methodology Documents/IBBAssociates/BlackLitterman.pdf.

Next, we created another efficient frontier asset allocation area graph based on these new returns from the Black–Litterman model, as shown in Exhibit 14. The allocations look relatively similar to those depicted in Exhibit 3. However, if you compare the allocations to Asia Pacific ex Japan equities and Europe ex UK equities to their allocations in the original efficient frontier asset allocation graph, you will notice that allocations to Asia Pacific ex Japan equities have increased across the frontier and allocations to Europe ex UK equities have decreased across the frontier with very little impact on the other asset allocations.

EXHIBIT 14   Efficient Frontier Asset Allocation Area Graph, Black–Litterman Returns

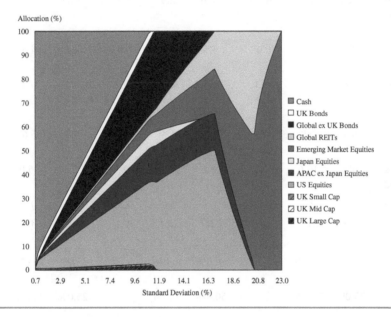

As before, to aid in the comparison of Exhibit 14 (Black–Litterman allocations) with Exhibit 3 (the base-case allocations), we identified three specific mixes in Exhibit 14 and compared those efficient asset allocation mixes based on the expected returns from the Black–Litterman model to those of the base case. The results are shown in Exhibit 15.

EXHIBIT 15   Comparison of Select Efficient Asset Allocations, Black–Litterman Allocations vs. Base-Case Allocations

	Modified 25/75	Base Case 25/75	Difference	Modified 50/50	Base Case 50/50	Difference	Modified 75/25	Base Case 75/25	Difference
UK large cap	0.4%	1.2%	−0.8%	1.4%	2.5%	−1.1%	0.0%	0.0%	0.0%
UK mid cap	0.4	0.6	−0.2	0.5	0.8	−0.3	0.0	0.0	0.0
UK small cap	0.4	0.5	−0.1	0.2	0.4	−0.2	0.0	0.0	0.0

	Modified 25/75	Base Case 25/75	Difference	Modified 50/50	Base Case 50/50	Difference	Modified 75/25	Base Case 75/25	Difference
US equities	13.8	13.8	0.0	26.8	26.8	0.0	40.0	40.5	−0.5
Europe ex UK equities	0.0	2.7	−2.7	0.0	6.5	−6.5	0.0	13.2	−13.2
Asia Pacific ex Japan equities	5.2	1.0	4.2	10.8	2.3	8.5	15.4	1.5	14.0
Japan equities	2.2	2.3	0.0	4.5	4.5	0.0	4.2	4.3	−0.1
Emerging market equities	1.8	2.0	−0.1	4.6	4.9	−0.2	9.8	10.0	−0.1
Global REITs	0.8	0.9	−0.1	1.3	1.4	−0.2	5.5	5.6	−0.1
Global ex UK bonds	10.3	10.6	−0.2	23.6	23.9	−0.3	25.0	25.0	0.0
UK bonds	3.1	2.7	0.3	3.5	3.0	0.5	0.0	0.0	0.0
Cash	61.6	61.7	−0.1	22.9	23.1	−0.1	0.0	0.0	0.0
Subtotal equities	25.0%	25.0%		50.0%	50.0%		75.0%	75.0%	
Subtotal fixed income	75.0%	75.0%		50.0%	50.0%		25.0%	25.0%	

2.4.3. Adding Constraints beyond the Budget Constraints

When running an optimization, in addition to the typical budget constraint and the non-negativity constraint, one can impose additional constraints. There are two primary reasons practitioners typically apply additional constraints: (1) to incorporate real-world constraints into the optimization problem and (2) to help overcome some of the potential shortcomings of mean–variance optimization elaborated above (input quality, input sensitivity, and highly concentrated allocations).

Most commercial optimizers accommodate a wide range of constraints. Typical constraints include the following:

1. Specify a set allocation to a specific asset—for example, 30% to real estate or 45% to human capital. This kind of constraint is typically used when one wants to include a non-tradable asset in the asset allocation decision and optimize around the non-tradable asset.

2. Specify an asset allocation range for an asset—for example, the emerging market allocation must be between 5% and 20%. This specification could be used to accommodate a constraint created by an investment policy, or it might reflect the user's desire to control the output of the optimization.
3. Specify an upper limit, due to liquidity considerations, on an alternative asset class, such as private equity or hedge funds.
4. Specify the relative allocation of two or more assets—for example, the allocation to emerging market equities must be less than the allocation to developed equities.
5. In a liability-relative (or surplus) optimization setting, one can constrain the optimizer to hold one or more assets representing the systematic characteristics of the liability short. (We elaborate on this scenario in Section 3.)

In general, good constraints are those that model the actual circumstances/context in which one is attempting to set asset allocation policy. In contrast, constraints that are simply intended to control the output of a mean–variance optimization should be used cautiously. A perceived need to add constraints to control the MVO output would suggest a need to revisit one's inputs. If a very large number of constraints are imposed, one is no longer optimizing but rather specifying an asset allocation through a series of binding constraints.

2.4.4. Resampled Mean–Variance Optimization

Another technique used by asset allocators is called resampled mean–variance optimization (or sometimes "resampling" for short).[13] Resampled mean–variance optimization combines Markowitz's mean–variance optimization framework with Monte Carlo simulation and, all else equal, leads to more-diversified asset allocations. In contrast to reverse optimization, the Black–Litterman model, and constraints, resampled mean–variance optimization is an attempt to build a better optimizer that recognizes that forward-looking inputs are inherently subject to error.

Resampling uses Monte Carlo simulation to estimate a large number of potential capital market assumptions for mean–variance optimization and, eventually, for the resampled frontier. Conceptually, resampling is a large-scale sensitivity analysis in which hundreds or perhaps thousands of variations on baseline capital market assumptions lead to an equal number of mean–variance optimization frontiers based on the Monte Carlo–generated capital market assumptions. These intermediate frontiers are referred to as simulated frontiers. The resulting asset allocations, or portfolio weights, from these simulated frontiers are saved and averaged (using a variety of methods). To draw the resampled frontier, the averaged asset allocations are coupled with the starting capital market assumptions.

To illustrate how resampling can be used with other techniques, we conducted a resampled mean–variance optimization using the Black–Litterman returns from Exhibit 10, above. Exhibit 16 provides the asset allocation area graph from this optimization. Notice that the resulting asset allocations are smoother than in any of the previous asset allocation area graphs. Additionally, relative to Exhibit 15, based on the same inputs, the smallest allocations have increased in size while the largest allocations have decreased somewhat.

---

[13]The current embodiments of resampling grew out of the work of Jobson and Korkie (1980, 1981); Jorion (1992); DiBartolomeo (1993); and Michaud (1998).

EXHIBIT 16   Efficient Frontier Asset Allocation Area Graph, Black–Litterman Returns with
Resampling

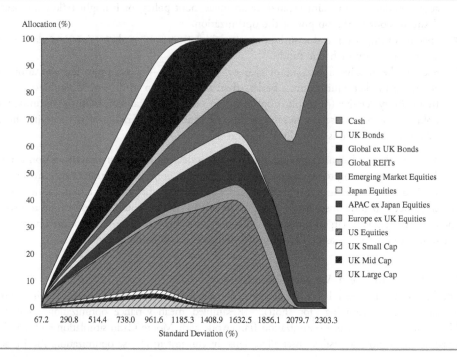

The asset allocations from resampling as depicted in Exhibit 16 are appealing. Criticisms include the following: (1) Some frontiers have concave "bumps" where expected return decreases as expected risk increases; (2) the "riskier" asset allocations are over-diversified; (3) the asset allocations inherit the estimation errors in the original inputs; and (4) the approach lacks a foundation in theory.[14]

2.4.5. Other Non-Normal Optimization Approaches

From our list of shortcomings/criticisms of mean–variance optimization, the third is that investor preferences may go beyond the first two moments (mean and variance) of a portfolio's return distribution. The third and fourth moments are, respectively, skewness and kurtosis. Skewness measures the degree to which return distributions are asymmetrical, and kurtosis measures the thickness of the distributions' tails (i.e., how frequently extreme events occur). A normal distribution is fully explained by the first two moments because the skewness and (excess) kurtosis of the normal distribution are both zero.

Returning to the discussion of Equation 1, the mean–variance optimization program involves maximizing expected utility, which is equal to expected return minus a penalty for risk, where risk is measured as variance (standard deviation). Unfortunately, variance or standard deviation is an incomplete measure of risk when returns are not normally distributed. By studying historical return distributions for the major asset classes and comparing those historical distributions to normal distributions, one will quickly see that,

---

[14]For more details, see Scherer (2002).

historically, asset class returns are not normally distributed. In fact, empirically extreme returns seem to occur approximately 10 times more often than the normal distribution would suggest. Coupling this finding with the asymmetrical risk preferences observed in investors—whereby the pain of a loss is approximately twice as significant as the joy from an equivalent gain (according to Prospect theory)—has led to more complex utility functions and optimizers that expressly account for non-normal returns and asymmetric risk preference.[15] A number of variations of these more sophisticated optimization techniques have been put forth, making them challenging to cover. In general, most of them consider the non-normal return distribution characteristics and use a more sophisticated definition of risk, such as conditional value-at-risk. We view these as important advancements in the toolkit available to practitioners.

Exhibit 17 summarizes selected extensions of quantitative asset allocation approaches outside the sphere of traditional mean–variance optimization.

EXHIBIT 17   Selected Non-Mean–Variance Developments

Key Non-Normal Frameworks	Research/Recommended Reading
Mean–semivariance optimization	Markowitz (1959)
Mean–conditional value-at-risk optimization	Goldberg, Hayes, and Mahmoud (2013)
	Rockafellar and Uryasev (2000)
	Xiong and Idzorek (2011)
Mean–variance-skewness optimization	Briec, Kerstens, and Jokung (2007)
	Harvey, Liechty, Liechty, and Müller (2010)
Mean–variance-skewness-kurtosis optimization	Athayde and Flôres (2003)
	Beardsley, Field, and Xiao (2012)

Long-Term versus Short-Term Inputs

Strategic asset allocation is often described as "long term," while tactical asset allocation involves short-term movements away from the strategic asset allocation. In this context, "long term" is often defined as 10 or perhaps 20 or more years, yet in practice, very few asset allocators revisit their strategic asset allocation this infrequently. Many asset allocators update their strategic asset allocation annually, which makes it a bit more challenging to distinguish between strategic and tactical asset allocations. This frequent revisiting of the asset allocation policy brings up important questions about the time horizon associated with the inputs. In general, long-term (10-plus-year) capital market assumptions that ignore current market conditions, such as valuation levels, the business cycle, and interest rates, are often thought of as *unconditional* inputs. Unconditional inputs focus on the average capital market assumptions over the 10-plus-year time horizon. In contrast, shorter-term capital market assumptions that

---

[15]For more on prospect theory, see Kahneman and Tversky (1979) and Tversky and Kahneman (1992).

explicitly attempt to incorporate current market conditions (i.e., that are "conditioned" on them) are conditional inputs. For example, a practitioner who believes that the market is overvalued and that as a result we are entering a period of low returns, high volatility, and high correlations might prefer to use conditional inputs that reflect these beliefs.[16]

EXAMPLE 4   Problems in Mean–Variance Optimization

In a presentation to US-based investment clients on asset allocation, the results of two asset allocation exercises are shown, as presented in Exhibit 18.

EXHIBIT 18   Asset Allocation Choices

Panel A: Area Graph 1

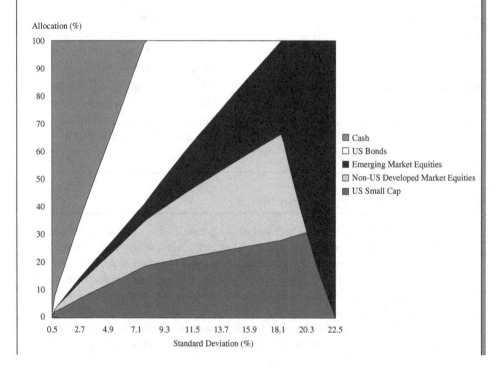

---

[16]Relatedly, Chow, Jacquier, Kritzman, and Lowry (1999) showed a procedure for blending the optimal portfolios for periods of normal and high return volatility. The approach accounts for the tendency of asset returns to be more highly correlated during times of high volatility.

Panel B: Area Graph 2

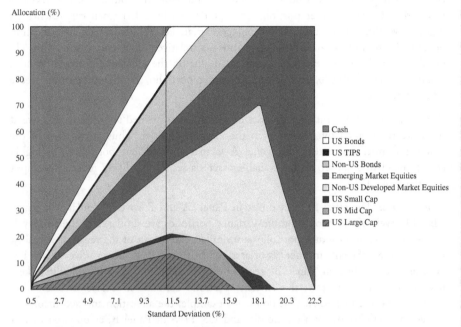

1. Based on Panel A, address the following:
   A. Based on mean–variance analysis, what is the asset allocation that would most likely be selected by a risk-neutral investor?
   B. Based only on the information that can be inferred from Panel A, discuss the investment characteristics of non-US developed market equity (NUSD) in efficient portfolios.
   C. Critique the efficient asset mixes represented in Panel A.

2. Compare the asset allocations shown in Panel A with the corresponding asset allocations shown in Panel B. (Include a comparison of the panels at the level of risk indicated by the line in Panel B.)

3.
   A. Identify three techniques that the asset allocations in Panel B might have incorporated to improve the characteristics relative to those of Panel A.
   B. Discuss how the techniques described in your answer to 3A address the high input sensitivity of MVO.

Solution to 1A: For a risk-neutral investor, the optimal asset allocation is 100% invested in emerging market equities. For a risk-neutral investor ($\lambda = 0$), expected utility is simply equal to expected return. The efficient asset allocation that maximizes expected return is the one with the highest level of volatility, as indicated on the *x*-axis. Panel A shows that that asset allocation consists entirely of emerging market equities.

Solution to 1B: The weights of NUSD as the efficient frontier moves from its minimum to its maximum risk point suggest NUSD's investment characteristics. This asset class is neither the lowest-volatility asset (which can be inferred to be cash) nor the highest-volatility asset (which is emerging market equity). At the point of the peak of NUSD, when the weight in NUSD is about to begin its decline in higher-risk efficient portfolios, US bonds drop out of the efficient frontier. Further, NUSD leaves the efficient frontier portfolio at a point at which US small cap reaches its highest weight. These observations suggest that NUSD provided diversification benefits in portfolios including US bonds—a relatively low correlation with US bonds can be inferred—that are lost at this point on the efficient frontier. Beyond a volatility level of 20.3%, representing a corner portfolio, NUSD drops out of the efficient frontier.

Solution to 1C: Of the nine asset classes in the investor's defined opportunity set, five at most are represented by portfolios on the efficient frontier. Thus, a criticism of the efficient frontier associated with Panel A is that the efficient portfolios are highly concentrated in a subset of the available asset classes, which likely reflects the input sensitivity of MVO.

Solution to 2: The efficient asset mixes in Panels A and B cover a similar risk range: The risk levels of the two minimum-variance portfolios are similar, and the risk levels of the two maximum-return portfolios are similar. Over most of the range of volatility, however, the efficient frontier associated with Panel B is better diversified. For example, at the line in Panel B, representing a moderate level of volatility likely relevant to many investors, the efficient portfolio contains nine asset classes rather than four, as in Panel A. At that point, for example, the allocation to fixed income is spread over US bonds, non-US bonds, and US TIPS in Panel B, as opposed to just US bonds in Panel A.

Solution to 3A: To achieve the better-diversified efficient frontier shown in Panel B, several methods might have been used, including reverse optimization, the Black–Litterman model, and constrained asset class weights.

Solution to 3B: Reverse optimization and the Black–Litterman model address the issue of MVO's sensitivity to small differences in expected return estimates by anchoring expected returns to those implied by the asset class weights of a proxy for the global market portfolio. The Black–Litterman framework provides a disciplined way to tilt the expected return inputs in the direction of the investor's own views. These approaches address the problem by improving the balance between risk and return that is implicit in the inputs.

A very direct approach to the problem can be taken by placing constraints on weights in the optimization to force an asset class to appear in a constrained efficient frontier within some desired range of values. For example, non-US bonds did not appear in any efficient portfolio in Panel A. The investor could specify that the weight on non-US bonds be strictly positive. Another approach would be to place a maximum on the weight in US bonds to make the optimizer spread the fixed-income allocation over other fixed-income assets besides US bonds.

2.5. Allocating to Less Liquid Asset Classes

Large institutional investors have the ability to invest in less liquid asset classes, such as direct real estate, infrastructure, and private equity. These less liquid asset classes represent unique challenges to many of the common asset allocation techniques, such as mean–variance optimization.

For traditional, highly liquid asset classes, such as publicly listed equities and bonds, almost all of the major index providers have indexes that do an outstanding job of representing the performance characteristics of the asset class (and its various sub–asset classes). For example, over any reasonably long time period, the risk and return characteristics of a given asset class are nearly identical across the major global equity indexes and the correlations between the returns of the indexes are close to 1. Additionally, in most cases, there are passive, low-cost investment vehicles that allow investors to capture the performance of the asset class with very little tracking error.

Cash, the Risk-Free Asset, and Liquidity Needs

The so called "risk-free asset" has a special and somewhat tricky spot in the world of finance. Asset allocators typically use indexes for either 30-day or 90-day government bills to represent the characteristics associated with holding cash, which they may or may not treat as the risk-free asset. The volatility associated with these total return indexes is extremely low, but it isn't zero. An alternative to using a cash index as a proxy for the risk-free asset is to use a government bond with a duration/maturity that matches the time horizon of the investor. Some asset allocators like to include cash or another asset that could be considered a risk-free asset in the optimization and to allow the optimizer to determine how to mix it with the other asset classes included in the optimization. Other asset allocators prefer to exclude the risk-free asset from the optimization and allow real-world needs, such as liquidity needs, to determine how much to allocate to cash-like assets.

Illiquid assets may offer an expected return premium as compensation for illiquidity as well as diversification benefits. Determining an appropriate allocation to these assets is associated with various challenges, however. Common illiquid asset classes cannot be readily diversified to eliminate idiosyncratic risk, so representing an overall asset class performance is problematic. Furthermore, for less liquid asset classes, such as direct real estate, infrastructure, and private equity, there are, in general, far fewer indexes that attempt to represent aggregate performance. If one were to compare the performance characteristics of multiple indexes representing one of these less liquid asset classes, there would be noticeable risk and return differences, suggesting that it is difficult to accurately measure the risk and return characteristics of these asset classes. Also, due to the illiquid nature of the constituents that make up these asset classes, it is widely believed that the indexes don't accurately reflect their true volatility. In contrast to the more traditional, highly liquid asset classes, there are no low-cost passive investment vehicles that would allow investors to closely track the aggregate performance of these less liquid asset classes.

Thus, the problem is twofold: (1) Due to the lack of accurate indexes, it is more challenging to make capital market assumptions for these less liquid asset classes, and (2) even if there were accurate indexes, there are no low-cost passive investment vehicles to track them.

Compounding the asset allocator's dilemma is the fact that the risk and return characteristics associated with actual investment vehicles, such as direct real estate funds, infrastructure funds, and private equity funds, are typically significantly different from the characteristics of the asset classes themselves. For example, the private equity "asset class" should represent the risk and return characteristics of owning all private equity, just as the MSCI All Country World Index represents the risk and return characteristics of owning all public equity. Purchasing the exchange-traded fund (ETF) that tracks the MSCI All Country World Index completely diversifies public company-specific risk. This scenario is in direct contrast to the typical private equity fund, in which the risk and return characteristics are often dominated by company-specific (idiosyncratic) risk.

In addressing asset allocation involving less liquid asset classes, practical options include the following:

1. Exclude less liquid asset classes (direct real estate, infrastructure, and private equity) from the asset allocation decision and then consider real estate funds, infrastructure funds, and private equity funds as potential implementation vehicles when fulfilling the target strategic asset allocation.
2. Include less liquid asset classes in the asset allocation decision and attempt to model the inputs to represent the *specific risk* characteristics associated with the likely *implementation vehicles*.
3. Include less liquid asset classes in the asset allocation decision and attempt to model the inputs to represent the *highly diversified* characteristics associated with the *true asset classes*.

Related to this last option, some practitioners use listed real estate indexes, listed infrastructure, and public equity indexes that are deemed to have characteristics similar to their private equity counterparts to help estimate the risk of the less liquid asset classes and their correlation with the other asset classes in the opportunity set. It should be noted that the use of listed alternative indexes often violates the recommendation that asset classes be mutually exclusive—the securities in these indexes are likely also included in indexes representing other asset classes—and thus typically results in higher correlations among different asset classes, which has the negative impact of increasing input sensitivity in most optimization settings.

For investors who do not have access to direct real estate funds, infrastructure funds, and private equity funds—for example, small investors—the most common approach is to use one of the indexes based on listed equities to represent the asset class and then to implement the target allocation with a fund that invests similarly. Thus global REITs might be used to represent (approximately) global real estate.

2.6. Risk Budgeting

[A] risk budget is simply a particular allocation of portfolio risk. An optimal risk budget is simply the allocation of risk such that the first order of conditions for portfolio optimization are satisfied. The risk budgeting process is the process of finding an optimal risk budget.

Kurt Winkelmann (2003, p. 173)

As this quote from Kurt Winkelmann suggests, there are three aspects to risk budgeting:

• The risk budget identifies the total amount of risk and allocates the risk to a portfolio's constituent parts.
• An optimal risk budget allocates risk efficiently.
• The process of finding the optimal risk budget is risk budgeting.

Although its name suggests that risk budgeting is all about risk, risk budgeting is really using risk in relation to seeking return. The goal of risk budgeting is to maximize return per unit of risk—whether overall market risk in an asset allocation setting or active risk in an asset allocation implementation setting.

The ability to determine a position's marginal contribution to portfolio risk is a powerful tool that helps one to better understand the sources of risk. The marginal contribution to a type of risk is the partial derivative of the risk in question (total risk, active risk, or residual risk) with respect to the applicable type of portfolio holding (asset allocation holdings, active holdings, or residual holdings). Knowing a position's marginal contribution to risk allows one to (1) approximate the change in portfolio risk (total risk, active risk, or residual risk) due to a change in an individual holding, (2) determine which positions are optimal, and (3) create a risk budget. *Risk-budgeting tools assist in the optimal use of risk in the pursuit of return.*

Exhibit 19 contains risk-budgeting information for the Sharpe ratio–maximizing asset allocation from our original UK example. The betas are from Exhibit 12. The marginal contribution to total risk (MCTR) identifies the rate at which risk would change with a small (or marginal) change in the current weights. For asset class i, it is calculated as $\text{MCTR}_i =$ (Beta of asset class i with respect to portfolio)(Portfolio return volatility). The absolute contribution to total risk (ACTR) for an asset class measures how much it contributes to portfolio return volatility and can be calculated as the weight of the asset class in the portfolio times its marginal contribution to total risk: $\text{ACTR}_i = (\text{Weight}_i)(\text{MCTR}_i)$. Critically, beta takes account not only of the asset's own volatility but also of the asset's correlations with other portfolio assets.

The sum of the ACTR in Exhibit 19 is approximately 10.88%, which is equal to the expected standard deviation of this asset allocation mix. Dividing each ACTR by the total risk of 10.88% gives the percentage of total risk that each position contributes. Finally, an asset allocation is optimal from a risk-budgeting perspective when the ratio of excess return (over the risk-free rate) to MCTR is the same for all assets and matches the Sharpe ratio of the tangency portfolio. So in this case, which is based on reverse-optimized returns, we have an optimal risk budget.

EXHIBIT 19   Risk-Budgeting Statistics

Asset Class	Weight	MCTR	ACTR	Percent Contribution to Total Standard Deviation	Ratio of Excess Return to MCTR
UK large cap	3.2%	11.19%	0.36%	3.33%	0.368
UK mid cap	0.9	12.02	0.11	0.98	0.368
UK small cap	0.3	12.44	0.03	0.30	0.368
US equities	34.4	14.51	5.00	45.94	0.368
Europe ex UK equities	8.7	16.68	1.45	13.34	0.368

Asset Class	Weight	MCTR	ACTR	Percent Contribution to Total Standard Deviation	Ratio of Excess Return to MCTR
Asia Pacific ex Japan equities	3.1	16.35	0.51	4.69	0.368
Japan equities	6.6	10.69	0.70	6.46	0.368
Emerging market equities	5.9	17.51	1.02	9.42	0.368
Global REITs	1.8	17.79	0.31	2.86	0.368
Global ex UK bonds	31.8	4.21	1.34	12.33	0.368
UK bonds	3.2	1.22	0.04	0.35	0.368
Cash	0.2	0.00	0.00	0.00	0.368
	100.0		10.88	100.00	

For additional clarity, the following are the specific calculations used to derive the calculated values for UK large-cap equities (where we show some quantities with an extra decimal place in order to reproduce the values shown in the exhibit):

- Marginal contribution to risk (MCTR):

$$\text{Asset beta relative to portfolio} \times \text{Portfolio standard deviation}$$

$$1.0289 \times 10.876 = 11.19\%$$

- ACTR:

$$\text{Asset weight in portfolio} \times \text{MCTR}$$

$$3.2\% \times 11.19\% = 0.36\%$$

- Ratio of excess return to MCTR:

$$(\text{Expected return} - \text{Risk-free rate})/\text{MCTR}$$

$$(6.62\% - 2.5\%)/11.19\% = 0.368$$

EXAMPLE 5   Risk Budgeting in Asset Allocation

1. Describe the objective of risk budgeting in asset allocation.
2. Consider two asset classes, A and B. Asset class A has two times the weight of B in the portfolio. Under what condition would B have a larger ACTR than A?

3.   When is an asset allocation optimal from a risk-budgeting perspective?

Solution to 1: The objective of risk budgeting in asset allocation is to use risk efficiently in the pursuit of return. A risk budget specifies the total amount of risk and how much of that risk should be budgeted for each allocation.

Solution to 2: Because $ACTR_i = (Weight_i)(Beta$ with respect to portfolio$)_i$(Portfolio return volatility), the beta of B would have to be more than twice as large as the beta of A for B to contribute more to portfolio risk than A.

Solution to 3: An asset allocation is optimal when the ratio of excess return (over the risk-free rate) to MCTR is the same for all assets.

2.7. Factor-Based Asset Allocation

Until now, we have primarily focused on the mechanics of asset allocation optimization as applied to an opportunity set consisting of traditional, non-overlapping asset classes. An alternative approach used by some practitioners is to move away from an opportunity set of *asset classes* to an opportunity set consisting of investment *factors*.

In factor-based asset allocation, the factors in question are typically similar to the fundamental (or structural) factors in widely used multi-factor investment models. Factors are typically based on observed market premiums and anomalies. In addition to the all-important market (equity) exposure, typical factors used in asset allocation include size, valuation, momentum, liquidity, duration (term), credit, and volatility. Most of these factors were identified as return drivers that help to explain returns that were not explained by the CAPM. These factors can be constructed in a number of different ways, but with the exception of the market factor, typically, the factor represents what is referred to as a zero (dollar) investment, or self-financing investment, in which the underperforming attribute is sold short to finance an offsetting long position in the better-performing attribute. For example, the size factor is the combined return from shorting large-cap stocks and going long small-cap stocks (Size factor return = Small-cap stock return − Large-cap stock return). Of course, if large-cap stocks outperform small-cap stocks, the realized size return would be negative. Constructing factors in this manner removes most market exposure from the factors (because of the short positions that offset long positions); as a result, the factors generally have low correlations with the market and with one another.

We next present an example of a factor-based asset allocation optimization. Exhibit 20 shows the list of factors, how they were specified, and their historical returns and standard deviations (in excess of the risk-free rate as proxied by the return on three-month Treasury bills). The exhibit also includes historical statistics for three-month Treasury bills.

Thus far, our optimization examples have taken place in "total return space," where the expected return of each asset has equaled the expected return of the risk-free asset plus the amount of expected return in excess of the risk-free rate. In order to stay in this familiar total return space when optimizing with risk factors, the factor return needs to include the return on the assumed collateral (in this example, cash, represented by three-month Treasury bills).

This adjustment is also needed if one plans to include both risk factors and some traditional asset classes in the same optimization, so that the inputs for the risk factors and traditional asset classes are similarly specified. Alternatively, one could move in the opposite direction, subtracting the return of the three-month Treasury bills from asset class returns and then conducting the optimization in excess-return space. One way to think about a self-financing allocation to a risk factor is that in order to invest in the risk factor, one must put up an equivalent amount of collateral that is invested in cash.

EXHIBIT 20   Factors/Asset Classes, Factor Definitions, and Historical Statistics (US data, January 1979 to March 2016)

Factor/Asset Class	Factor Definition	Compound Annual Factor Return	Standard Deviation	Total Return	Standard Deviation
Treasury bonds	Long-term Treasury bonds			7.77%	5.66%
Market	Total market return – Cash	7.49%	16.56%	12.97	17.33
Size	Small cap – Large cap	0.41	10.15	5.56	10.65
Valuation	Value – Growth	0.68	9.20	5.84	9.76
Credit	Corporate – Treasury	0.70	3.51	5.87	3.84
Duration	Long Treasury bonds – Treasury bills	4.56	11.29	9.91	11.93
Mortgage	Mortgage-backed – Treasury bonds	0.30	3.38	5.45	3.83
Large growth	—	—	—	12.64	19.27
Large value	—	—	—	13.23	16.52
Small growth	—	—	—	12.30	25.59
Small value	—	—	—	14.54	19.84
Mortgage-backed sec.	—	—	—	8.09	6.98
Corporate bonds	—	—	—	8.52	7.52
Treasury bonds	—	—	—	7.77	5.66
Cash	—	—	—	5.13	1.23

Because of space considerations, we have not included the full correlation matrix, but it is worth noting that the average pair-wise correlation of the risk factor–based opportunity set (in excess of the risk-free rate collateral return) is 0.31, whereas that of the asset class–based opportunity set is 0.57. Given the low pair-wise correlations of the risk factors, there has been some debate among practitioners around whether it is better to optimize using asset classes or risk factors. The issue was clarified by Idzorek and Kowara (2013), who demonstrated that in a proper comparison, neither approach is inherently superior. To help illustrate risk factor optimization and to demonstrate that if the two opportunity sets are constructed with access to similar exposures, neither approach has an inherent advantage, we present two side-by-side optimizations. These optimizations are based on the data given in Exhibit 20.

Exhibit 21 contains the two efficient frontiers. As should be expected, given that the opportunity sets provide access to similar exposures, the two historical efficient frontiers are very similar. This result illustrates that when the same range of potential exposures is available in two opportunity sets, the risk and return possibilities are very similar.

EXHIBIT 21   Efficient Frontiers Based on Historical Capital Market Assumptions (January 1979 to March 2016)

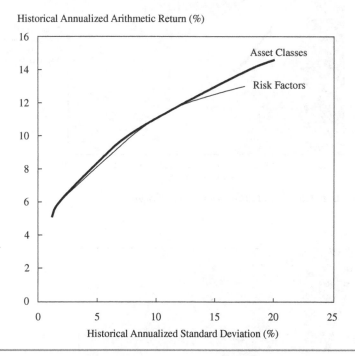

Moving to Exhibit 22, examining the two asset allocation area graphs associated with the two efficient frontiers reveals that the efficient mixes have some relatively clear similarities. For example, in Panel A (risk factors), the combined market, size, and valuation exposures mirror the pattern (allocations) in Panel B (asset classes) of combined large value and small value exposures.

EXHIBIT 22   Asset Allocation Area Graphs—Risk Factors and Asset Classes

Panel A: Risk Factor Asset Allocation Area Graph

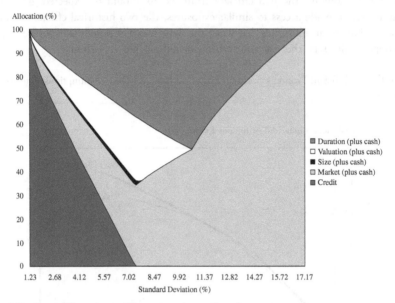

Panel B: Asset Class Asset Allocation Area Graph

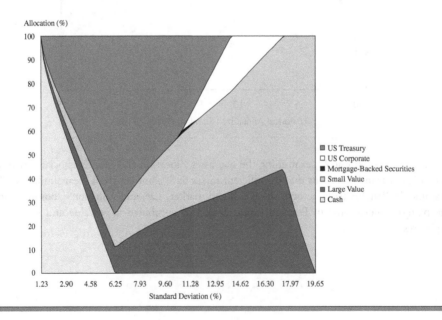

Practitioners should choose to carry out asset allocation in the particular space—risk factors or asset classes—in which they are most equipped to make capital market assumptions. Regardless of which space a practitioner prefers, expanding one's opportunity set to include new, weakly correlated risk factors or asset classes should improve the potential risk–return trade-offs.

3. DEVELOPING LIABILITY-RELATIVE ASSET ALLOCATIONS

Liability-relative asset allocation is aimed at the general issue of rendering decisions about asset allocation in conjunction with the investor's liabilities. Liability-relative investors view assets as an inventory of capital, sometimes increased by additions, which is available to achieve goals and to pay future liabilities. What is the chance that an institution's capital is sufficient to cover future cash flow liabilities? This type of question is critical for liability-relative asset allocation because many large institutional investors—for example, banks, insurance companies, and pension plans—possess legal liabilities and operate in regulated environments in which an institution's inability to meet its liabilities with current capital has serious consequences. This concern gives rise to unique risk measures, such as the probability of meeting future cash flow requirements, and the restatement of traditional risk metrics, such as volatility, in relation to liabilities.

Liability-relative methods were developed in an institutional investor context, but these ideas have also been applied to individual investors. This section will focus on institutional investors. A later section addresses a thematically similar approach with behavioral finance roots—goals-based asset allocation.

3.1. Characterizing the Liabilities

To be soundly applied, liability-relative asset allocation requires an accurate understanding of the liabilities. A liability is a promise by one party to pay a counterparty based on a prior agreement. Liabilities may be fixed or contingent. When the amounts and timing of payments are fixed in advance by the terms of a contract, the liability is said to be fixed or non-contingent. A corporate bond with a fixed coupon rate is an example.

In many cases relevant to asset allocation, payments depend upon future, uncertain events. In such cases, the liability is a contingent liability.[17] An important example involves the liabilities of a defined benefit (DB) pension plan. The plan sponsor has a legal commitment to pay the beneficiaries of the plan during their retirement years. However, the exact dates of the payments depend on the employees' retirement dates, longevity, and cash payout rules. Insurance companies' liabilities—created by the sale of insurance policies—are also contingent liabilities: The insurance company promises to pay its policyholders a specified amount contingent on the occurrence of a predefined event.

We distinguish legal liabilities from cash payments that are expected to be made in the future and are essential to the mission of an institution but are not legal liabilities. We call these quasi-liabilities. The endowment of a university can fit this category because, in many cases, the endowment contributes a major part of the university's operating budget. The endowment assures its stakeholders that it will continue to support its essential activities

---

[17]Note that the term "contingent liability" has a specific definition in accounting. We are using the term more broadly here.

through spending from the endowment capital, and failure to provide such support will often lead to changes in how the endowment is managed. Accordingly, the asset allocation decisions are made in conjunction with the university's spending rules and policies. Asset allocation is just one portion of the investment problem. Although we do not explicitly discuss them here, as suggested in Section 2, the spending needs of an individual represent another type of quasi-liability. Exhibit 23 summarizes the characteristics of liabilities that can affect asset allocation.

EXHIBIT 23   Characteristics of Liabilities That Can Affect Asset Allocation

1. Fixed versus contingent cash flows
2. Legal versus quasi-liabilities
3. Duration and convexity of liability cash flows
4. Value of liabilities as compared with the size of the sponsoring organization
5. Factors driving future liability cash flows (inflation, economic conditions, interest rates, risk premium)
6. Timing considerations, such as longevity risk
7. Regulations affecting liability cash flow calculations

The above liability characteristics are relevant to liability-relative asset allocation in various ways. For example, they affect the choice of appropriate discount rate(s) to establish the present value of the liabilities and thus the degree to which assets are adequate in relation to those liabilities. Liability characteristics determine the composition of the liability-matching portfolio and that portfolio's basis risk with respect to the liabilities. (Basis risk in this context quantifies the degree of mismatch between the hedging portfolio and the liabilities.)

We will discuss the following case study in detail. It involves a frozen pension plan for LOWTECH, a hypothetical US company. The company has decided to close its defined benefit pension plan and switch to a defined contribution plan. The DB plan has the fixed liabilities (accumulated benefit obligations) shown in Exhibit 24.

EXHIBIT 24   Projected Liability Cash Flows for Company LOWTECH (US$ billions)

		PV(Liabilities)	
Beginning of Year	Cash Outflow (Liability)	4% Discount Rate	2% Discount Rate
2015	—	$2.261	$3.039
2016	$0.100	2.352	3.10
2017	0.102	2.342	3.06
2018	0.104	2.329	3.02
2019	0.106	2.314	2.97
2020	0.108	2.297	2.92
2021	0.110	2.276	2.87
2022	0.113	2.252	2.82

		PV(Liabilities)	
Beginning of Year	**Cash Outflow (Liability)**	**4% Discount Rate**	**2% Discount Rate**
2023	0.115	2.225	2.76
2024	0.117	2.195	2.69
2025	0.120	2.161	2.63
2026	0.122	2.123	2.56
2027	0.124	2.081	2.49
2028	0.127	2.035	2.41
2029	0.129	1.984	2.33
2030	0.132	1.929	2.24
2031	0.135	1.869	2.15
2032	0.137	1.804	2.06
2033	0.140	1.733	1.96
2034	0.143	1.657	1.86
2035	0.146	1.575	1.75
2036	0.149	1.486	1.63
2037	0.152	1.391	1.52
2038	0.155	1.289	1.39
2039	0.158	1.180	1.26
2040	0.161	1.063	1.13
2041	0.164	0.938	0.98
2042	0.167	0.805	0.84
2043	0.171	0.663	0.68
2044	0.174	0.512	0.52
2045	0.178	0.352	0.36
2046	0.181	0.181	0.181

In the Cash Outflow (Liability) column, the assumption is made that payments for a given year are made at the beginning of the year (in the exhibit, outflows have a positive sign). As of the beginning of 2015, the present value of these liabilities, given a 4% discount rate for high-quality corporate bonds (required in the United States by the Pension Protection Act of 2006, which applies to private DB pension plans), is US$2.261 billion. The current market value of the assets is assumed to equal US$2.5 billion, for a surplus of US$0.239 billion. On the other hand, if the discount rate is equal to the long-term government bond rate at 2% (required before the 2006 US legislation), the surplus becomes a deficit at −$0.539 billion. In many cases, regulations set the appropriate discount rates; these rates have an impact on the determination of surplus or deficit and thus on future contribution rules.

Like other institutions with legal liabilities, the LOWTECH company must analyze its legal future cash flows under its DB pension system and evaluate them in conjunction with the current market value of its assets on an annual basis. The following steps of the valuation exercise for a DB pension plan occur on a fixed annual date:

1. Calculate the market value of assets.
2. Project liability cash flows (via actuarial principles and rules).
3. Determine an appropriate discount rate for liability cash flows.
4. Compute the present value of liabilities, the surplus value, and the funding ratio.

$$\text{Surplus} = \text{Market value (assets)} - \text{Present value (liabilities)}.$$

The surplus for the LOWTECH company is US\$2.500 billion – US\$2.261 billion = US\$0.239 billion, given the 4% discount rate assumption.

The funding ratio is another significant measure: Funding ratio = Market value (assets)/ Present value (liabilities). We say that an investor is fully funded if the investor's funding ratio equals 1 (or the surplus is 0). A state of overfunding occurs when the funding ratio is greater than 1, and a state of underfunding takes place when the funding ratio is less than 1. Based on a discount rate of 4%, the funding ratio for LOWTECH = US\$2.5 billion/US\$2.261 billion = 1.1057, so that the company is about 10.6% overfunded.

The surplus value and the funding ratio are highly dependent upon the discount rate assumption. For example, if the discount rate is equal to 2.0% (close to the 10-year US Treasury bond rate in early 2016), the surplus drops to –US\$0.539 billion and the funding ratio equals 0.8226. The company's status changes from overfunded to underfunded. The choice of discount rate is generally set by regulations and tradition. Rate assumptions are different across industries, countries, and domains. From the standpoint of economic theory, if the liability cash flows can be hedged perfectly by a set of market-priced assets, the discount rate can be determined by reference to the discount rate for the assets. For example, if the pension plan liabilities are fixed (without any uncertainty), the discount rate should be the risk-free rate with reference to the duration of the liability cash flows—for example, a five-year zero-coupon bond yield for a liability with a (modified) duration of 5. In other cases, it can be difficult to find a fully hedged portfolio because an ongoing DB pension plan's liabilities will depend upon future economic growth and inflation, which are clearly uncertain. Even a frozen pension plan can possess uncertainty due to the changing longevity of the retirees over the long-term future.

3.2. Approaches to Liability-Relative Asset Allocation

Various approaches to liability-relative asset allocation exist. These methods are influenced by tradition, regulations, and the ability of the stakeholders to understand and extend portfolio models that come from the asset-only domain.

There are several guiding principles. The first is to gain an understanding of the make-up of the investor's liabilities and especially the factors that affect the amount and timing of the cash outflows. Given this understanding, the present value of the liabilities is calculated, along with the surplus and funding ratio. These measures are used to track the results of ongoing investment and funding policies and for other tasks. Next come the decisions regarding the asset allocation taking account of the liabilities. There are a number of ways to proceed. We will discuss three major approaches:

- *Surplus optimization.* This approach involves applying mean–variance optimization (MVO) to an efficient frontier based on the volatility of the surplus ("surplus volatility," or "surplus risk") as the measure of risk. Surplus optimization is thus an extension of MVO based on asset volatility.[18] Depending on context, surplus risk may be stated in money or percentage terms ("surplus return volatility" is then another, more precise term for this measure).
- *Hedging/return-seeking portfolios approach.* This approach involves separating assets into two groups: a hedging portfolio and a return-seeking portfolio. The chapter also refers to this as the two-portfolio approach. The concept of allocating assets to two distinct portfolios can be applied for various funding ratios, but the chapter distinguishes as the basic approach the case in which there is a positive surplus available to allocate to the return-seeking portfolio.
- *Integrated asset–liability approach.* For some institutional investors, such as banks and insurance companies and long–short hedge funds, asset and liability decisions can be integrated and jointly optimized.

We cover these three approaches in turn.

3.2.1. Surplus Optimization

Surplus optimization involves adapting asset-only mean–variance optimization by substituting surplus return for asset return over any given time horizon. The quadratic optimization program involves choosing the asset allocation (mix) that maximizes expected surplus return net of a penalty for surplus return volatility at the chosen time horizon. The objective function is

$$U_m^{LR} = E(R_{s,m}) - 0.005\lambda\sigma^2(R_{s,m}) \tag{2}$$

where U_m^{LR} is the surplus objective function's expected value for a particular asset mix m; $E(R_{s,m})$ is the expected surplus return for asset mix m, with surplus return defined as (Change in asset value – Change in liability value)/(Initial asset value); and the parameter λ (lambda) indicates the investor's risk aversion. The more risk averse the investor, the greater the penalty for surplus return volatility. Note that the change in liability value (liability return) measures the time value of money for the liabilities plus any expected changes in the discount rate and future cash flows over the planning horizon.

This surplus efficient frontier approach is a straightforward extension of the asset-only portfolio model. Surplus optimization assumes that the relationship between the value of liabilities and the value of assets can be approximated through a correlation coefficient. Surplus optimization exploits natural hedges that may exist between assets and liabilities as a result of their systematic risk characteristics.

The following steps describe the surplus optimization approach:

1. Select asset categories and determine the planning horizon. One year is often chosen for the planning exercise, although funding status analysis is based on an analysis of all cash flows.

---

[18]Among the papers that discuss the surplus optimization model are Leibowitz and Henriksson (1988); Mulvey (1989, 1994); Sharpe and Tint (1990); Elton and Gruber (1992).

2. Estimate expected returns and volatilities for the asset categories and estimate liability returns (expanded matrix).
3. Determine any constraints on the investment mix.
4. Estimate the expanded correlation matrix (asset categories and liabilities) and the volatilities.[19]
5. Compute the surplus efficient frontier and compare it with the asset-only efficient frontier.
6. Select a recommended portfolio mix.

Exhibit 25 lists LOWTECH's asset categories and current allocation for a one-year planning horizon. The current allocation for other asset categories, such as cash, is zero. LOWTECH has been following an asset-only approach but has decided to adopt a liability-relative approach. The company is exploring several liability-relative approaches. With respect to surplus optimization, the trustees want to maintain surplus return volatility at a level that tightly controls the risk that the plan will become underfunded, and they would like to keep volatility of surplus below US$0.25 billion (10%).

EXHIBIT 25   Asset Categories and Current Allocation for LOWTECH

	Private Equity	Real Estate	Hedge Funds	Real Assets	US Equities	Non-US Equities (Developed Markets)	Non-US Equities (Emerging Markets)	US Corporate Bonds
Allocation	20.0%	12.0%	18.0%	7.0%	15.0%	12.0%	8.0%	8.0%

The second step is to estimate future expected asset and liability returns, the expected present value of liabilities, and the volatility of both assets and PV(liabilities). The capital market projections can be made in several ways—based on historical data, economic analysis, or expert judgment, for example. The plan sponsor and its advisers are responsible for employing one or a blend of these approaches. Exhibit 26 shows the plan sponsor's capital market assumptions over a three- to five-year horizon. Note the inclusion of the present value of liabilities in Exhibit 26.

EXHIBIT 26   LOWTECH's Capital Market Assumptions: Expected Annual Compound Returns and Volatilities

	Private Equity	Real Estate	Hedge Funds	Real Assets	US Equities	Non-US Equities (Developed Markets)	Emerging Markets	US Corporate Bonds	Cash	PV (Liabilities)
Expected returns	8.50%	7.50%	7.00%	6.00%	7.50%	7.20%	7.80%	4.90%	1.00%	4.90%
Volatilities	14.20%	9.80%	7.70%	6.10%	18.00%	19.50%	26.30%	5.60%	1.00%	5.60%

---

[19]A covariance matrix is computed by combining the correlation matrix and the volatilities.

Typically, in the third step, the investor imposes constraints on the composition of the asset mix, including policy and legal limits on the amount of capital invested in individual assets or asset categories (e.g., a constraint that an allocation to equities must not exceed 50%). In our example, we simply constrain portfolio weights to be non-negative and to sum to 1.

The fourth step is to estimate the correlation matrix and volatilities. We assume that the liabilities have the same expected returns and volatilities as US corporate bonds; thus, the expanded matrix has a column and a row for liabilities with values equal to the corporate bond values. For simplicity, the investor may employ historical performance. Exhibit 27 shows the correlation matrix of asset categories based on historical quarterly returns. Recall that we assume that liability returns (changes in liabilities) are driven by changes in the returns of US corporate bonds. An alternative approach is to deploy a set of underlying factors that drive the returns of the assets. Factors include changes in nominal and real interest rates, changes in economic activity (such as employment levels), and risk premiums. This type of factor investment model can be applied in an asset-only or a liability-relative asset allocation context.

EXHIBIT 27 Correlation Matrix of Returns

	Private Equity	Real Estate	Hedge Funds	Real Assets	US Equities	Non-US Equities (Developed Markets)	Non-US Equities (Emerging Markets)	US Corporate Bonds	Cash	PV (Liabilities)
Private equity	1	0.41	0.57	0.32	0.67	0.59	0.49	−0.27	0	−0.27
Real estate	0.41	1	0.45	0.41	0.31	0.33	0.17	−0.08	0	−0.08
Hedge funds	0.57	0.45	1	0.11	0.68	0.61	0.54	−0.23	0	−0.23
Real assets	0.32	0.41	0.11	1	0.04	0.06	−0.06	0.34	0	0.34
US equities	0.67	0.31	0.68	0.04	1	0.88	0.73	−0.38	0	−0.38
Non-US equities (developed)	0.59	0.33	0.61	0.06	0.88	1	0.81	−0.39	0	−0.39
Non-US equities (emerging)	0.49	0.17	0.54	−0.06	0.73	0.81	1	−0.44	0	−0.44
US corporate bonds	−0.27	−0.08	−0.23	0.34	−0.38	−0.39	−0.44	1	0	1
Cash	0	0	0	0	0	0	0	0	1	0
PV (liabilities)	−0.27	−0.08	−0.23	0.34	−0.38	−0.39	−0.44	1	0	1

Exhibit 28 shows a surplus efficient frontier that results from the optimization program based on the inputs from Exhibits 26 and 27. Surplus risk (i.e., volatility of surplus) in money terms (US$ billions) is on the x-axis, and expected surplus in money terms (US$ billions) is on the y-axis. By presenting the efficient frontier in money terms, we can associate the level of risk with the level of plan surplus, US$0.239 billion. Like the asset-only efficient frontier, the surplus efficient frontier has a concave shape.

EXHIBIT 28   Surplus Efficient Frontier

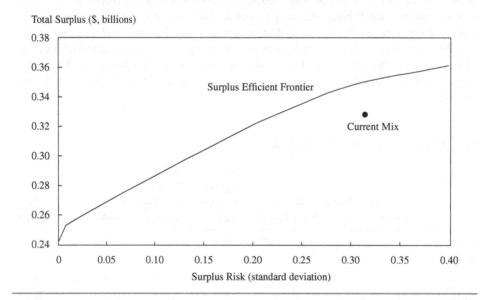

The first observation is that the current mix in Exhibit 28 lies below the surplus efficient frontier and is thus suboptimal.[20] We can attain the same expected total surplus as that of the current mix at a lower level of surplus volatility by choosing the portfolio on the efficient frontier at the current mix's level of expected total surplus. Another observation is that by uncovering the implications of asset mixes for surplus and surplus volatility, this approach allows the deliberate choice of an asset allocation in terms of the tolerable level of risk in relation to liabilities. It may be the case, for example, that neither the surplus volatility of the current mix nor that of the efficient mix with equal expected surplus is the appropriate level of surplus risk for the pension.

The surplus efficient frontier in Exhibit 28 shows efficient reward–risk combinations but does not indicate the asset class composition of the combinations. Exhibit 29 shows the asset class weights for surplus efficient portfolios.

---

[20]The current mix can also be shown to lie below the asset-only mean–variance frontier.

EXHIBIT 29   Surplus Efficient Frontier Asset Allocation Area Graph

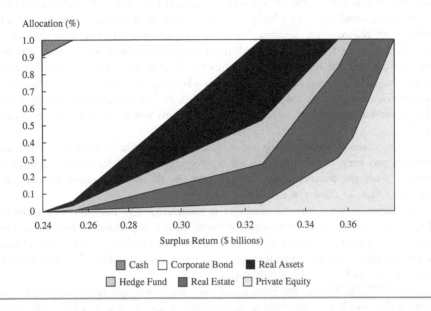

Exhibit 30, showing weights for portfolios on the usual *asset-only* efficient frontier based on the same capital market assumptions reflected in Exhibit 29, makes the point that efficient portfolios from the two perspectives are meaningfully different.[21]

EXHIBIT 30   Asset-Only Efficient Frontier Asset Allocation Area Graph

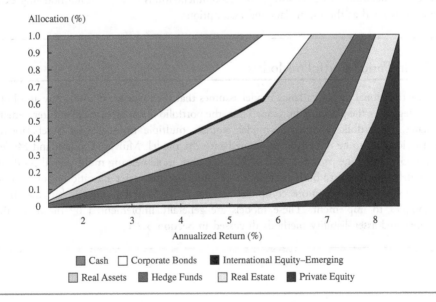

---

[21]In Exhibit 30, the annualized percentage returns can be equated to monetary surplus returns by multiplying by the asset value, US$2.5 billion.

The asset mixes are very different on the conservative side of the two frontiers. The most conservative mix for the surplus efficient frontier (in Exhibit 29) consists mostly of the US corporate bond index (the hedging asset) because it results in the lowest volatility of surplus over the one-year horizon. Bonds are positively correlated with changes in the present value of the frozen liability cash flows (because the liabilities indicate negative cash flows). In contrast, the most conservative mix for the asset-only efficient frontier (in Exhibit 30) consists chiefly of cash. As long as there is a hedging asset and adequate asset value, the investor can achieve a very low volatility of surplus, and for conservative investors, the asset value at the horizon will be uncertain but the surplus will be constant (or as constant as possible).

The two asset mixes (asset-only and surplus) become similar as the degree of risk aversion decreases, and they are identical for the most aggressive portfolio (private equity). Bonds disappear from the frontier about halfway between the most conservative and the most aggressive mixes, as shown in Exhibits 29 and 30.

To summarize, the current asset mix is moderately aggressive and below the surplus efficient frontier. Thus, a mean–variance improvement is possible: either higher expected surplus with the same surplus risk or lower surplus risk for the same expected surplus. The current portfolio is also poorly hedged with regard to surplus volatility; the hedging asset (long bonds in this case) has a low commitment.

The LOWTECH plan has been frozen, and the investment committee is interested in lowering the volatility of the surplus. Accordingly, it seems appropriate to choose an asset allocation toward the left-hand side of the surplus efficient frontier. For instance, a surplus efficient portfolio with about 60% bonds and the remainder in other assets (as can be approximately identified from Exhibit 29) will drop surplus volatility by about 50%.

In the end, the investment committee for the plan sponsor and its advisers and stakeholders are responsible for rendering the best decision, taking into account all of the above considerations. And as always, the recommendations of a portfolio-modeling exercise are only as good as the input data and assumptions.

Multi-Period Portfolio Models

The traditional mean–variance model assumes that the investor follows a buy-and-hold strategy over the planning horizon. Thus, the portfolio is not rebalanced at intermediate dates. A portfolio investment model requires multiple time periods if rebalancing decisions are to be directly incorporated into the model. Mulvey, Pauling, and Madey (2003) discuss the pros and cons of building and implementing multi-period portfolio models. Applicable to both asset-only and liability-relative asset allocation, multi-period portfolio models are more comprehensive than single-period models but are more complex to implement. These models are generally implemented by means of the integrated asset–liability methods discussed in Section 3.2.1

EXAMPLE 6 Surplus Optimization

1. Explain how surplus optimization solutions differ from mean–variance optimizations based on asset class risk alone.
2. What is a liability return?
3. Compare the composition of a surplus optimal portfolio at two points on the surplus efficient frontier. In particular, take one point at the lower left of the surplus frontier (surplus return = US$0.26 billion) and the other point higher on the surplus efficient frontier (surplus return = US$0.32 billion). Refer to Exhibit 29. Explain the observed relationship in terms of the use of corporate bonds as the hedging asset for the liabilities.

Solution to 1: The surplus optimization model considers the impact of asset decisions on the (Market value of assets − Present value of liabilities) at the planning horizon.

Solution to 2: Liability returns measure the time value of money for the liabilities plus any expected changes in the discount rate over the planning horizon.

Solution to 3: Whereas the portfolio at the US$0.26 billion surplus return point on the efficient frontier has a substantial position in corporate bonds, the efficient mix with US$0.32 billion surplus return does not include them. The observed relationship that the allocation to corporate bonds declines with increasing surplus return can be explained by the positive correlation of bond price with the present value of liabilities. The hedging asset (corporate bonds) is employed to a greater degree at the low end of the surplus efficient frontier.

3.2.2. Hedging/Return-Seeking Portfolio Approach

In this approach, the liability-relative asset allocation task is divided into two parts. We distinguish as "basic" the two-portfolio approach in the case in which there is a surplus available to allocate to a return-seeking portfolio and as "variants" the approach as applied when there is not a positive surplus. In the basic case, the first part of the asset allocation task consists of hedging the liabilities through a hedging portfolio. In the second part, the surplus (or some part of it) is allocated to a return-seeking portfolio, which can be managed independently of the hedging portfolio (for example, using mean–variance optimization or another method). An essential issue involves the composition of the hedging portfolio. In some cases, such as the LOWTECH frozen DB pension plan, the hedging portfolio is straightforward to identify. The designated cash flows can be hedged via cash flow matching, duration matching, or immunization (as explained in the fixed-income chapters). This hedge will support the future cash flows with little or no risk.

In LOWTECH's application of the basic two-portfolio approach, the small surplus causes the pension plan to invest most of its capital in the hedging portfolio. The hedging portfolio can be approximated by the long-bond indexed investment as a first cut. Thus, given a 4% discount rate, US$2.261 billion is placed in long bonds. The remaining US$0.239 billion is invested in a portfolio of higher expected return assets, such as stocks, real estate, and hedge funds. This approach guarantees that the capital is adequate to pay future liabilities, as long as the hedging portfolio does not experience defaults.

Note that if the discount rate were 2% rather than 4%, the pension plan would be underfunded even if all assets were placed in a hedging portfolio. In such a case, the pension plan sponsor would either develop a strategy to increase the funding ratio so that the liabilities would be eventually paid or apply a variant of the two-portfolio approach. An underfunded plan will require higher contributions from the sponsor than a plan that is fully funded or overfunded.

The basic two-portfolio approach is most appropriate for conservative investors, such as insurance companies, and for overfunded pension plans that wish to reduce or eliminate the risk of not being able to pay future liabilities.

Several variants of the two-portfolio approach are possible. These include a partial hedge, whereby capital allocated to the hedging portfolio is reduced in order to generate higher expected returns, and dynamic versions whereby the investor increases the allotment to the hedging portfolio as the funding ratio increases. The specification of this allotment is often referred to as the liability glide path. These variants do not hedge the liabilities to the full extent possible given the assets and thus are less conservative than the basic approach discussed above. Still, there can be benefits to a partial hedge when the sponsor is able to increase contributions if the funding ratio does not increase in the future to 1 or above.

In the following discussion, we focus on determining the hedging portfolio.

3.2.2.1. Forming the Hedging Portfolio

The hedging portfolio must include assets whose returns are driven by the same factor(s) that drive the returns of the liabilities. Otherwise, even if the assets and liabilities start with equal values, the assets and liabilities will likely become inconsistent over time. One example involves promises (cash outflows) that are dependent upon future inflation. The hedging portfolio in this situation would often include index-linked (inflation-linked) Treasury bonds, again cash matched to the liabilities or immunized to the degree possible.

If there is an active market for the hedging portfolio (securities) in question, the present value of future cash flows is equal to a market value of the assets contained in the hedging portfolio. In this case, the date of valuation for the assets must be the same as the date of valuation for the liabilities. Absent market values, some form of appraised value is used.

The task of forming the hedging portfolio is complicated by the discount rate assumption and by the need to identify assets that are driven by the same factors that affect the liabilities. For example, if the discount rate is set by reference to a marketable instrument, such as the long government bond index, but the liability cash flows are driven by a factor such as inflation, the hedging task may require the use of instruments beyond nominal bonds (perhaps multiple instruments, such as interest rate swaps, inflation-linked bonds, and real assets). And in many applications, the hedge cannot be fully accomplished due to the nature of the driving factors (e.g., if they are non-marketable factors, such as economic growth).

If the uncertainties in the cash flows are related to non-market factors, such as future salary increases, the discount rate will depend upon regulations and tradition. Clearly, high discount rates lead to high funding ratios and in most cases require lower contributions from the sponsoring organization (at least in the short run). Conversely, lower discount rates give rise to lower funding ratios and thereby higher contributions. In the former case, investors with high discount rates will need to generate higher asset returns to achieve their promises if the pension plan sponsor wishes to avoid future contributions. A more conservative route is to designate a lower discount rate, as is the case in much of Europe and Asia. In all cases, it is the regulator's responsibility to set the guidelines, rules, and penalties involved in determining contribution policy.

Several issues complicate the valuation of liability cash flows. In many situations, investors must satisfy their promises without being able to go to a market and purchase a security with positive cash flows equal in magnitude to the liability cash flows.

At times, uncertain liabilities can be made more certain through the law of large numbers. For example, life insurance companies promise to pay beneficiaries when a policyholder dies. The life insurance company can minimize the risk of unexpected losses by insuring large numbers of individuals. Then, valuation of liabilities will use present value of expected cash flows based on a low (or even zero) risk premium in the discount rate. The field of application of the law of large numbers can be limited. For example, averages do not eliminate longevity risk.

3.2.2.2. Limitations

The basic two-portfolio approach cannot be directly applied under several circumstances. First, if the funding ratio is less than 1, the investor cannot create a fully hedging portfolio unless there is a sufficiently large positive cash flow (contribution). In this case, the sponsor might increase contributions enough to generate a positive surplus. As an alternative, there are conditional strategies that might help improve the investor's funding ratio, such as the glide path rules.[22]

A second barrier occurs when a true hedging portfolio is unavailable. An example involves losses due to weather-related causes, such as hurricanes or earthquakes. In these cases, the investor might be able to partially hedge the portfolio with instruments that share some of the same risks. The investor has "basis risk" when imperfect hedges are employed. (As an aside, the investor might be able to set up a contract with someone who, for a fee, will take on the liability risk that cannot be hedged. Insurance contracts have this defining characteristic.)

EXAMPLE 7   The Hedging/Return-Seeking Portfolios Approach

1. Compare how surplus optimization and the hedging/return-seeking portfolio approach take account of liabilities.
2. How does funding status affect the use of the basic hedging/return-seeking portfolio approach?

Solution to 1: The surplus optimization approach links assets and the present value of liabilities through a correlation coefficient. The two-portfolio model does not require this input. Surplus optimization considers the asset allocation problem in one step; the hedging/return-seeking portfolio approach divides asset allocation into two steps.

Solution to 2: Implementation of the basic two-portfolio approach depends on having an overfunded plan. A variant of the two-portfolio approach might be applied, however. Surplus optimization does not require an overfunded status. Both approaches address the present value of liabilities, but in different ways.

---

[22]See Gannon and Collins (2009).

3.2.3. Integrated Asset–Liability Approach

The previous two approaches are most appropriate when asset allocation decisions are made after, and relatively independently of, decisions regarding the portfolio of liabilities. However, there are numerous applications of the liability-relative perspective in which the institution must render significant decisions regarding the composition of its liabilities *in conjunction with the asset allocation*. Banks, long–short hedge funds (for which short positions constitute liabilities), insurance companies, and re-insurance companies routinely fall into this situation. Within this category, the liability-relative approaches have several names, including asset–liability management (ALM) for banks and some other investors and dynamic financial analysis (DFA) for insurance companies. These approaches are often implemented in the context of multi-period models. Using the following two cases, we review the major issues.

Integrated Asset–Liability Approach for Property/Casualty Insurance Companies

A property/casualty insurance company must make asset investment decisions in conjunction with business decisions about the portfolio of insured properties, its liabilities. To that end, asset and liability decisions are frequently integrated in an enterprise risk management system. In fact, the liability portfolio is essential to the company's long-term viability. For example, a particular property/casualty (PC) insurance company might engage (accept) liabilities for catastrophic risks such as earthquakes and hurricanes. In this case, the liabilities depend upon rare events and thus are most difficult to hedge against. Specialized firms calculate insured losses for a chosen set of properties for property/casualty insurance companies, and these firms provide liability cash flows on a probabilistic (scenario) basis. In this way information is gathered about the probability of losses over the planning horizon and the estimated losses for each loss event. An important issue involves the amount of capital needed to support the indicated liabilities. This issue is addressed by evaluating the tail risks, such as the 1% Value-at-Risk or Conditional-Value-at-Risk amount. To reduce this risk, there are major advantages to forming a diversified global portfolio of liabilities and rendering asset allocation decisions in conjunction with the liability portfolio decisions. The hedging portfolio in this case is not well defined. Therefore, it is difficult to hedge liabilities for a book of catastrophic risk policies. Liabilities might be addressed via customized products or by purchasing re-insurance. The assets and liabilities are integrated so that the worst-case events can be analyzed with regard to both sides of the balance sheet.

Integrated Asset–Liability Approach for Banks

Large global banks are often required to analyze their ability to withstand stress scenarios, in accordance with the Basel III framework. These institutions must be able to show that their current capital is adequate to withstand losses in their business units, such as asset trading, in conjunction with increases in liabilities. The chief risk officer evaluates these scenarios by means of integrated asset–liability approaches. The asset and liability decisions are linked in an enterprise manner. Both the portfolio of assets and the portfolio of liabilities have major impacts on the organization's risk. Thus, decisions to take on new products or expand an existing product—thereby generating liabilities—must take into account the associated decisions on the asset side. The integrated asset–liability management system provides a mechanism for discovering the optimal mix of assets and liabilities (products). These applications often employ multi-period models via a set of projected scenarios.

Decisions about asset allocation will affect the amount of business available to a financial intermediary, such as a bank or insurance company. Similarly, decisions about the portfolio of liabilities and concentration risks will feed back to the asset allocation decisions. Accordingly, we can set up a linked portfolio model. In a similar fashion, the performance of the assets of an institution possessing quasi-liabilities, such as a university endowment, will affect the spending rules for the institution. We can reduce worst-case outcomes by adjusting spending during crash periods, for example. Portfolio models linked to liabilities can provide significant information, helping the institution make the best compromise decisions for both the assets and the liabilities under its control. The twin goals are to maximize the growth of surplus over time subject to constraints on worst-case and other risk measures relative to the institution's surplus.

3.2.4. Comparing the Approaches

We have introduced three approaches for addressing asset allocation decisions in the context of liability issues; Exhibit 31 summarizes their characteristics. Each of these approaches has been applied in practice. The surplus optimization approach is a straightforward extension of the traditional (asset-only) mean–variance model. Surplus optimization demonstrates the importance of the hedging asset for risk-averse investors and provides choices for investors who are less risk averse in the asset mixes located on the middle and the right-hand side of the efficient frontier. The assumptions are similar to those of the traditional Markowitz model, where the inputs are expected returns and a covariance matrix. Thus, the assets and liabilities are linked through correlation conditions. The second approach, separating assets into two buckets, has the advantage of simplicity. The basic approach is most appropriate for conservative investors, such as life insurance companies, and for overfunded/fully funded institutional investors that can fully hedge their liabilities. Another advantage of this approach is a focus on the hedging portfolio and its composition. The hedging portfolio can be constructed using a factor model and then linked to the assets via the same factors. Unfortunately, underfunded investors do not have the luxury of fully hedging their liabilities and investing the surplus in the risky portion; they must apply variants of the two-portfolio approach. The third approach, integrating the liability portfolio with the asset portfolio, is the most comprehensive of the three. It requires a formal method for selecting liabilities and for linking the asset performance with changes in the liability values. This approach can be implemented in a factor-based model, linking the assets and liabilities to the underlying driving factors. It has the potential to improve the institution's overall surplus. It does not require the linear correlation assumption and is capable of modeling transaction costs, turnover constraints, and other real-world constraints. The capital required for this approach is often determined by reference to the output of integrated asset–liability systems in banks and property/casualty insurance and re-insurance companies.

EXHIBIT 31   Characteristics of the Three Liability-Relative Asset Allocation Approaches

Surplus Optimization	Hedging/Return-Seeking Portfolios	Integrated Asset–Liability Portfolios
Simplicity	Simplicity	Increased complexity
Linear correlation	Linear or non-linear correlation	Linear or non-linear correlation
All levels of risk	Conservative level of risk	All levels of risk
Any funded ratio	Positive funded ratio for basic approach	Any funded ratio
Single period	Single period	Multiple periods

EXAMPLE 8   Liability-Relative Asset Allocation: Major Approaches

1. Discuss how the probability of not being able to pay future liabilities when they come due is or is not addressed by each of the major approaches to liability-relative asset allocation.
2. What are the advantages of the three approaches for investors who are more interested in protecting the surplus than growing their assets? Assume that the investor has a positive surplus.

Solution to 1: Such issues are best addressed by means of multi-period integrated asset–liability models. Surplus optimization and the two-portfolio approach, being single-period models, have difficulty estimating the probability of meeting future obligations.

Solution to 2: The three liability-relative approaches are appropriate for conservative investors (investors who are more interested in protecting the surplus than growing their assets). All of the three approaches force investors to understand the nature of their liabilities. This type of information can help inform the decision-making process.

3.3. Examining the Robustness of Asset Allocation Alternatives

As part of a liability-relative asset allocation study, the institutional investor can evaluate performance over selected events and "simulated" historical time periods. Each of the selected events can be interpreted as a "what if" sensitivity analysis. For example, we might wish to consider the effect of a 100 bp increase in interest rates across all maturities—that is, a parallel shift in the yield curve. This event would have a significant impact on the value of government bonds, clearly. Also, there would be a corresponding positive impact on the present discounted value of liabilities that are discounted at the government bond rate. The effect on other liability-relative asset allocation elements is less direct, and assumptions must be made. Suppose, for example, that the investor must discount at the high-quality corporate rate. In that case, we need to estimate the effect of changing government rates on corporate rates. These designated studies are part of the stress tests required by banking and other regulators.

Another type of event study is the construction of scenarios based on carefully selected historical time periods. For example, we might select late 2008 as a reference point. In such a scenario, we are interested in the changes in the economic factors and the associated changes in the values of the institution's assets and liabilities. What would be the impact on our current (or projected) portfolio—assets and PV(liabilities)—if the conditions seen in late 2008 occurred again?

A more comprehensive method for examining robustness involves setting up a multi-stage simulation analysis. Here, we use scenarios to model uncertainty and replace decisions with "rules." The process begins with a set of scenarios for the underlying driving economic factors. Each scenario designates a path for the asset returns and the liability values at each stage of the planning horizon. The result is a set of probabilistic outcomes for the institutional investor's asset portfolio and the cash flows for its liabilities. In such modeling, one must take care to be consistent between asset returns and corresponding liabilities within a scenario; for example, if interest rates are a common factor driving both asset performance and the PV (liabilities), the interest rate effects should be based on the same assumptions.

Through the scenario analysis, the probability of both good and bad outcomes can be estimated. For example, we can measure the probability that an institutional investor will make a capital contribution in the future. Exhibit 32 shows the decision structure for the simulation of an insurance company over several periods, including modeling of the company's business strategy and the required capital rules.

To evaluate robustness, we can apply the simulation system with different assumptions. For instance, if we change the expected return of US equities, what is the effect on the probability of meeting the liabilities over an extended horizon, such as 10 years? This type of sensitivity analysis is routinely done in conjunction with the modeling exercise.

EXHIBIT 32   Simulation Analysis

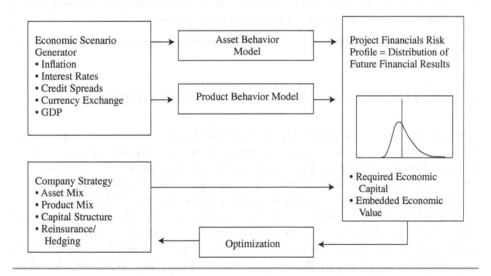

3.4. Factor Modeling in Liability-Relative Approaches

A factor-based approach for liability-relative asset allocation has gained interest and credibility for several reasons. First, in many applications, the liability cash flows are dependent on multiple uncertainties. The two primary macro factors are future economic conditions and inflation. Many pension payments to beneficiaries will be based on inflation and salary changes over the employees' work span. A fully hedged portfolio cannot be constructed when the liabilities are impacted by these uncertain factors. Recall that a hedged portfolio can be constructed for a frozen plan with fixed liabilities. For ongoing pension schemes, the best that can be done is to add asset categories to the portfolio that are positively correlated with the underlying driving risk factors, such as inflation-linked bonds. A factor-based approach can be implemented with any of the three liability-relative asset allocation methods discussed above.

EXAMPLE 9   Robustness and Risk Assessment in Liability-Relative Asset Allocation

---

What types of sensitivity analysis can be evaluated with a multi-period ALM simulation system?

Solution: To provide estimates of the probability of meeting future obligations and the distribution of outcomes, several types of sensitivity analysis are likely to be performed.

- For example, the expected returns could be increased or decreased to evaluate the impact on future contributions to the plan.
- Likewise, by analyzing historical events, the investor can estimate the size of losses during crash periods and make decisions about the best asset allocation to protect against these worst-case events. Multiple risk measures over time (temporal risk measures) can be readily included in a simulation system.

---

4. DEVELOPING GOALS-BASED ASSET ALLOCATIONS

In this section, we review the concept of goals-based asset allocation, focusing first on the rationale behind this different approach and its investment implications. We then discuss the major elements of the process, illustrating them with specific, simplified examples when necessary. We conclude with a discussion of the applicability of the approach and its major shortcomings.

A goals-based asset allocation process disaggregates the investor's portfolio into a number of sub-portfolios, each of which is designed to fund an individual goal (or "mental account") with its own time horizon and required probability of success. The literature behind the development of this approach is very rich. Initially, goals-based wealth management was specifically proposed by a small group of practitioners,[23] each of whom offered his own solution for taking into account the tendency of individuals to classify money into non-fungible mental accounts. Shefrin and Statman (2000) developed the concept of the

---

[23]See Brunel (2003, 2005); Nevins (2004); Pompian and Longo (2004); Chhabra (2005).

behavioral portfolio, which can be related to the Maslow (1943) hierarchy of needs. Das, Markowitz, Scheid, and Statman (2010, 2011) showed that traditional and behavioral finance could be viewed as equivalent if one were prepared to change the definition of risk from volatility of returns to the probability of not achieving a goal.[24] The essential point is that optimality requires both a suitably structured portfolio that can meet the given need *and* the correct capital allocation based on an appropriate discount rate, reflecting considerations of time horizon and the required probability of success.

Individuals have needs that are different from those of institutions. The most important difference is that individuals often have multiple goals, each with its own time horizon and its own "urgency," which can be expressed as a specific required probability of success. Exhibit 33 summarizes differences in institutional and individual investor definitions of goals. An individual's goals are not necessarily mutually compatible in two senses: The investor may not be able to address them all given the financial assets available, and there may be internal contradictions among the goals. An alternative process using one set of overall investment objectives—and thus effectively ignoring or "averaging" the different time horizons and required probabilities of success of individual goals—ostensibly loses the granular nature of client goals; as a result, the inherent complexities of the investment problem are less likely to be addressed fully. An approach that breaks the problem into sub-portfolios carries a higher chance of fully addressing an investor's goals, although it may require several iterations to ensure that the investor's portfolio is internally consistent and satisfactory.

EXHIBIT 33   Institutional and Individual Ways of Defining Goals

	Institutions	**Individuals**
Goals	Single	Multiple
Time horizon	Single	Multiple
Risk measure	Volatility (return or surplus)	Probability of missing goal
Return determination	Mathematical expectations[a]	Minimum expectations
Risk determination	Top-down/bottom-up	Bottom-up
Tax status	Single, often tax-exempt	Mostly taxable

[a] "Mathematical expectations" here means the weighted expected return of portfolio components.

The characteristics of individuals' goals have three major implications for an investment process that attempts to address the characteristics directly:

- The overall portfolio needs to be divided into sub-portfolios to permit each goal to be addressed individually.
- Both taxable and tax-exempt investments are important.
- Probability- and horizon-adjusted expectations (called "minimum expectations" in Exhibit 33) replace the typical use of mathematically expected average returns in determining the appropriate funding cost for the goal (or "discount rate" for future cash flows).

Compared with average return expectations—the median or average return anticipated for a combination of assets that is appropriate to address a goal—minimum expectations reflect a

---

[24]We apologize to these authors for grossly oversimplifying their work, but our aim is to make their insights more readily available without going into excruciating detail.

more complex concept. Minimum expectations are defined as the minimum return expected to be earned over the given time horizon with a given minimum required probability of success.

To illustrate, assume that a portfolio associated with a goal has an expected return of 7% with 10% expected volatility and the investor has indicated that the goal is to be met over the next five years with at least 90% confidence. Over the next five years, that portfolio is expected to produce returns of 35% with a volatility of 22.4%.[25] In short, this portfolio is expected to experience an average compound return of only 1.3% per year over five years with a probability of 90%; this result is quite a bit lower than the portfolio's average 7% expected return (see Exhibit 34). Thus, rather than discounting expected cash outflows by 7% to compute the dollar amount needed to defease the goal over that five-year horizon, one must use a considerably lower discount rate and by implication reserve a higher level of capital to meet that goal. Under moderate simplifying assumptions, that computation is valid whether or not return and volatility numbers are pretax or after-tax. Exhibit 34 shows, for the case of a normal distribution of returns, a return level that is expected to be exceeded 90% of the time (the 40% of the probability that lies between the vertical lines plus the 50% to the right of the median).

EXHIBIT 34   Probability-Weighted Return vs. Expected (= Median) Return

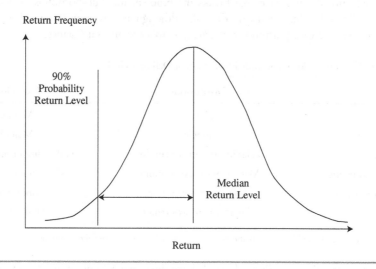

4.1. The Goals-Based Asset Allocation Process

Investment advisers taking a goals-based approach to investing client assets may implement this approach in a variety of ways. Exhibit 35 illustrates the major elements of the goals-based asset allocation process described in this chapter. Ostensibly, there are two fundamental parts to this process. The first centers on the creation of portfolio modules, while the second involves identifying client goals and matching each of these goals to the appropriate sub-portfolio of a suitable asset size.

---

[25]The return is the product of the annual return times the number of years, while the volatility is the product of the annual volatility times the square root of the number of years (under the assumption of independently and identically distributed returns).

EXHIBIT 35   A Stylized Representation of the Goals-Based Asset Allocation Process

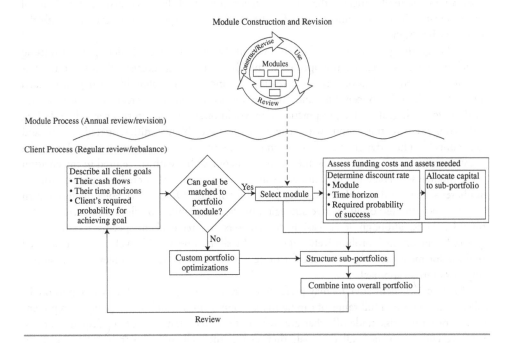

Determining the lowest-cost funding for any given goal requires the formulation of an optimized portfolio that will be used to defease that goal optimally in the sense that risks are not taken for which the investor is not fairly compensated. Note that this process is most often generic and internal to the adviser and his or her firm. The adviser will typically not create a specific sub-portfolio for each goal of each client but rather will select, from a pre-established set, one of a few modules—or model portfolios—that best meet each goal.[26] As discussed above, adjusting the expected return on that portfolio to account for the time horizon and the required probability of success allows one to formulate the relevant discount rate which, when applied to the expected cash flows, will help determine the capital required at the outset. That capital will then be invested in the optimized portfolio asset allocation, where the balance will decline until the end of the horizon, when it runs out.[27] Note that the process is somewhat iterative because individual investors may describe a certain horizon as set when in fact they view it as "the next *x* years," with the horizon rolling by one year every year.

---

[26]See the next paragraph for a discussion of when it makes sense to create specific optimal sub-portfolios.

[27]An important reason for the use of a declining-balance portfolio relates to the need for individuals and families to plan for the transfer of assets at death. In order for the income from assets to be used by an individual, these assets must be in the individual's name, or at least in a structure of which he or she is a beneficiary. Such assets would then be a part of the estate of the individual. Using a declining-balance portfolio allows the individual to receive the income—and some of the principal liquidated every year— while still ensuring that the amount of assets kept in the individual's name remains as low as appropriate given the individual's goals. An exception to this scenario would be the case of families whose income needs are so modest in relation to total assets that there is no need to provide income in planning for generational transfers or families that have such large eventual philanthropic intentions that assets kept in some beneficiaries' names are meant to be transferred to charity at death.

Note also that discounting needs based on probability- and horizon-adjusted minimum expectations naturally means that these expectations will be exceeded under "normal circumstances." Thus, it is not unusual for the funding for a goal to seem excessive with the benefit of hindsight.

Although the great majority of advisers will likely create individual client portfolios using model portfolios—precisely, pre-optimized modules—a greater degree of customization is possible. Such customization involves creating specific sub-portfolios for each goal of each client. Indeed, it is conceivable, and mathematically possible, to create an optimal sub-portfolio for each goal. In fact, in practice, one would often proceed in this way when dealing with complex situations and with clients who have highly differentiated needs and constraints.[28] The adviser may find it impossible to use pre-optimized modules if the investment constraints imposed by the client are incompatible with those used in the creation of the module set. These might include, for instance, geographical or credit emphases—or de-emphases—that conflict with the market portfolio concept. Other restrictions might concern base currency, the use of alternative strategies, or the acceptability of illiquid investments, for example. Thus, although it is feasible for advisers to create client-specific modules, this approach can become prohibitively expensive. In short, one would likely use standardized modules for most individuals, except for those whose situation is so complex as to require a fully customized approach.

Many multi-client advisers may prefer to create a set of "goal modules" whose purpose is, collectively, to cover a full range of capital market opportunities and, individually, to represent a series of return–risk trade-offs that are sufficiently differentiated to offer adequate but not excessive choices to meet all the goals they expect their clients to express. These modules should therefore collectively appear to create a form of efficient frontier, though the frontier they depict in fact does not exist because the modules may well be based on substantially different sets of optimization constraints.

The two most significant differences from one module to the next, besides the implied return–risk trade-offs, are liquidity requirements and the eligibility of certain asset classes or strategies. Additionally, while intra–asset class allocation to individual sub–asset classes or strategies may typically be guided by the market portfolio for that asset class, one can conceive of instances where the selection of a specific sub–asset class or strategy is justified, even though the asset class per se may seem inappropriate. For instance, one might agree to hold high-yield bonds in an equity-dominated portfolio because of the equity risk factor exposure inherent in lower-credit fixed income. Conversely, the fixed-income market portfolio might be limited to investment-grade bonds and possibly the base-currency-hedged variant of non-domestic investment-grade bonds. We will return to the construction of these modules in Section 4.5.

4.2. Describing Client Goals

At this point, it is important to note that individual investors do not always consider all goals as being equal and similarly well-formulated in their own minds. Thus, while certain investors will have a well-thought-out set of goals—which may at times not be simultaneously

---

[28]Note that such an approach, being more complex, is also costlier. It would therefore be more likely to be economically feasible for those advisory clients who also have the ability to pay a higher fee.

achievable given the financial assets available—others will focus only on a few "urgent" goals and keep other requirements in the background.

Thus, a first step is to distinguish between goals for which anticipated cash flows are available—whether regularly or irregularly timed across the horizon or represented by a bullet payment at some future point—and those we call "labeled goals," for which details are considerably less precise. The term "labeled" here simply means that the individual has certain "investment features" in mind—such as minimal risk, capital preservation, purchasing power preservation, and long-term growth—but has not articulated the actual need that stands behind each label. The individual may already have mentally allocated some portion of his or her assets, in currency or percentage terms, to one or several of these labels. For cash flow–based goals,[29] the time horizon over which the goal is to be met is usually not difficult to ascertain: It is either the period over which cash outflows are expected to be made or the point in time at which a bullet payment is expected. More complex, however, is the issue of the urgency of the goal and thus of the required minimum probability of success.

By working to preserve a human (as opposed to a technical) tone in the advisory conversations, the adviser can serve the client without forcing him or her to come up with a quantified probability of success. The adviser may start with the simple observation that there are two fundamental types of goals: those that one seeks to achieve and those whose consequences one seeks to avoid. Dividing the goals the investor seeks to achieve into "needs, wants, wishes, and dreams" provides the adviser with an initial sense of the urgency of each goal. A need typically must be met and so should command a 90%–99% probability of success, while at the other end of the spectrum, it is an unfortunate fact that we all live with unfulfilled dreams, whose required probabilities of success probably fall below 60%. A parallel —and analogous—structure can be created to deal with goals one seeks to avoid:[30] "nightmares, fears, worries, and concerns," with similar implications in terms of required probabilities of success. In short, while some discussion of probability level may well take place, it can be informed and guided by the use of commonly accepted everyday words that will ensure that the outcome is internally consistent. The adviser avoids the use of jargon, which many clients dislike, and yet is able to provide professional advice.[31]

The simplest way to bring this concept to life is to work with a basic case study. Imagine a family, the Smiths, with financial assets of US$25 million. (For the sake of simplicity, we are assuming that they do not pay taxes and that all assets are owned in a single structure.) The parents are in their mid-fifties, and the household spends about US $500,000 a year. They expect that inflation will average about 2% per year for the

---

[29]Note that all cash flows do not have to be negative (i.e., outflows). One can easily imagine circumstances where certain future inflows are anticipated and yet are not seen, individually, as sufficient to meet the specified goal.

[30]Although negative goals may sound surprising, they do exist and play a double role. First, when a negative goal is explicitly stated, it can be "replaced" by a specific positive goal: Avoiding the nightmare of running out of capital, for example, can be turned into the need to meet a certain expense budget. Second, negative goals serve as a useful feedback loop to check the internal consistency of the investor's goal set.

[31]Note that the adviser can also identify a series of "secondary" words to help determine whether a need, for instance, means that the required probability of success should be set at 99%, 95%, or 90%. An *indispensable* need could require a 99% probability of being met, while an *urgent* need might require only a 95% probability of success, and a *serious* need a 90% probability.

foreseeable future. They express four important goals and are concerned that they may not be able to meet all of them:

1. They *need* a 95% chance of being able to maintain their current expenditures over the next five years.
2. They *want* an 85% chance of being able to maintain their current expenditures over the ensuing 25 years, which they see as a reasonable estimate of their joint life expectancy.
3. They *need* a 90% chance of being able to transfer US$10 million to their children in 10 years.
4. They *wish* to have a 75% chance to be able to create a family foundation, which they wish to fund with US$10 million in 20 years.

EXAMPLE 10   Understanding Client Goals

1. A client describes a desire to have a reserve of €2 million for business opportunities that may develop when he retires in five years. What are the important features of this goal?
2. A 70-year-old client discusses the need to be able to maintain her lifestyle for the balance of her life and wishes to leave US$3 million to be split among her three grandchildren at her death. What are the important features of this situation?

Solution to 1: The time horizon is five years. Words such as "desire" in describing a goal, compared with expressions indicating "need," indicate that there is room for "error" in the event that capital markets are not supportive. The portfolio required to meet the goal described as a desire will likely be able to involve a riskier profile. One would want to verify this assumption by comparing the size of that goal compared with the total financial assets available to the client.

Solution to 2: The key takeaway is that although the two goals have the same time horizon, the two portfolios designed to defease them will have potentially significantly different risk profiles. The time horizon is approximately 20 years. The first goal relates to maintaining the client's lifestyle and must be defeased with an appropriately structured portfolio. The second goal, relating to the wish to leave some money to grandchildren, will allow more room for risk taking.

4.3. Constructing Sub-Portfolios

Having defined the needs of the investor in as much detail as possible, the next step in the process is to identify the amount of money that needs to be allocated to each goal and the asset allocation that will apply to that sum. For most advisers, the process will start with a set of sub-portfolio modules (such as those we briefly discussed in Section 4.1 and will study in more depth in Section 4.5). When using a set of pre-optimized modules, the adviser will then need to identify the module best suited to each of the specific goals of the client. That process is always driven by the client's time horizon and required probability of success, and it involves identifying the module that offers the highest possible return given the investor's risk tolerance as characterized by a given required probability of success over a given time horizon.

To illustrate, consider the set of six modules shown in Exhibit 36;[32] these modules result from an optimization process that will be explained later.[33] In the exhibit, the entries for minimum expected return are shown rounded to one decimal place; subsequent calculations for required capital are based on full precision.

EXHIBIT 36.   "Highest Probability- and Horizon-Adjusted Return" Sub-Portfolio Module under Different Horizon and Probability Scenarios

	A	B	C	D	E	F
Portfolio Characteristics						
Expected return	4.3%	5.5%	6.4%	7.2%	8.0%	8.7%
Expected volatility	2.7%	4.5%	6.0%	7.5%	10.0%	12.5%
Annualized Minimum Expectation Returns						
Time Horizon (years)			5			
Required Success						
99%	1.5%	0.9%	0.2%	–0.6%	–2.4%	–4.3%
95	2.3	2.2	2.0	1.7	0.7	–0.5
90	2.7	3.0	3.0	2.9	2.3	1.5
75	3.5	4.2	4.6	4.9	5.0	4.9
Time Horizon (years)			10			
Required Success						
99%	2.3%	2.2%	2.0%	1.7%	0.7%	–0.5%
90	3.2	3.7	4.0	4.1	4.0	3.6
75	3.7	4.6	5.1	5.6	5.9	6.0%
60	4.1	5.2	5.9	6.6	7.2	7.7
Time Horizon (years)			20			
Required Success						
95%	3.3%	3.9%	4.2%	4.4%	4.4%	4.1%
90	3.5	4.3	4.7	5.0	5.2	5.1
85	3.7	4.5	5.0	5.4	5.7	5.8
75	3.9	4.9	5.5	6.0	6.5	6.8

---

[32]The different ranges of required probabilities of success for various time horizons reflect the fact that the differentiation across modules can occur more or less rapidly, reflecting the different ratios of return per unit of risk.

[33]Exhibit 38 presents the details of the asset allocation of these modules and the constraints underpinning their optimization.

	A	B	C	D	E	F
Time Horizon (years)			25			
Required Success						
95%	3.4%	4.1%	4.4%	4.7%	4.7%	4.6%
90	3.6	4.4	4.9	5.2	5.5	5.5
85	3.7	4.6	5.2	5.6	6.0	6.1
75	3.9	4.9	5.6	6.2	6.7	7.0

In Exhibit 36, the top section, on portfolio characteristics, presents the expected return and expected volatility of each module. Below that are four sections, one for each of four time horizons: 5, 10, 20, and 25 years. In a given section, the entries are the returns that are expected for a given required probability of achieving success. For example, at a 10-year horizon and a 90% required probability of success, Modules A, B, C, D, E, and F are expected to return, respectively, 3.2%, 3.7%, 4.0%, 4.1%, 4.0%, and 3.6%. In this case, Module D would be selected to address a goal with this time horizon and required probability of success because its 4.1% expected return is higher than those of all the other modules. Thus, Module D offers the lowest "funding cost" for the given goal. The highest expected return translates to the lowest initially required capital when the expected cash flows associated with the goal are discounted using that expected return.

EXAMPLE 11   Selecting a Module

Address the following module selection problems using Exhibit 36:

1. A client describes a desire to have a reserve of €2 million for business opportunities that may develop when he retires in five years. Assume that the word "desire" points to a wish to which the adviser will ascribe a probability of 75%.
2. A 70-year-old client with a 20-year life expectancy discusses the need to be able to maintain her lifestyle for the balance of her life and wishes to leave US$3 million to be split among her three grandchildren at her death.

Solution to 1: The time horizon is five years. Exhibit 36 shows that Module E has the highest expected return (5.0%) over the five-year period and with the assumed 75% required probability of success.

Solution to 2: The time horizon is 20 years. The first goal is a need, while the second is a wish. We assume a required probability of success of 95% for a need and 75% for a wish. Exhibit 36 shows that Module D provides the highest horizon- and required-probability-adjusted return (4.4%) for the first goal. Module F is better suited to the second goal because, even though the second goal has the same time horizon, it involves only a 75% required probability of success; the appropriately adjusted return is 6.8%, markedly the highest, which means the initially required capital is lower.

Returning to the Smiths, let us use that same set of modules to look at their four specific goals. The results of our analysis are presented in Exhibit 37.

1. The first goal is a need, with a five-year time horizon and a 95% required probability of success. Looking at the 95% required probability line in the five-year time horizon section of Exhibit 36, we can see that the module with the highest expected return on a time horizon- and required probability-adjusted basis is Module A and that the appropriately adjusted expected return for that module is 2.3%. Discounting a US$500,000 annual cash flow, inflated by 2% a year from Year 2 onwards, required a US$2,430,000 initial investment. This amount represents 9.7% of the total financial wealth of the Smiths.

2. The second goal is a want, with a 25-year time horizon and an 85% required probability of success. The corresponding line of the table in Exhibit 36 points to Module F and a discount rate of 6.1%. Discounting their current expenses with the same assumption over the 25 years starting in Year 6 with a 6.1% rate points to an initially required capital of US$6,275,000, representing 25.1% of the Smiths' wealth.

3. The third goal is another need, with a 10-year time horizon and a 90% required probability of success. Module D is the best module, and the US$6,671,000 required capital reflects the discounting of a US$10 million payment in 10 years at the 4.1% indicated in Exhibit 36.

4. Finally, the fourth goal is a wish with a 20-year time horizon and a 75% required probability of success. Module F is again the best module, and the discounting of a US$10 million payment 20 years from now at the 6.8% expected return from Exhibit 36 points to a required capital of US$2,679,000 today.

Note that different goals may, in fact, be optimally addressed using the same module; thus, an individual module may be used more than once in the allocation of the individual's overall financial assets. Here, Goals 2 and 4 can both be met with the riskiest of the six modules, although their time horizons differ, as do the required probabilities of success, with Goal 2 being characterized as a want and Goal 4 as a wish.

EXHIBIT 37   Module Selection and Dollar Allocations (US$ thousands)

	Total Financial Assets					25,000
	Goals					**Overall Asset Allocation**
	1	**2**	**3**	**4**	**Surplus**	
Horizon (years)	5	25	10	20		
Required probability of success	95%	85%	90%	75%	$E(R_t)$	7.2%
Discount rate	2.3%	6.1%	4.1%	6.8%	$\sigma(R_t)$	8.0%
Module	**A**	**F**	**D**	**F**	**C**	
Required capital						
In currency	2,430	6,275	6,671	2,679	6,945	25,000
As a % of total	9.7%	25.1%	26.7%	10.7%	27.8%	100.0%

Note also that the Smiths' earlier worry, that they might not be able to meet all their goals, can be addressed easily. Our assumptions suggest that, in fact, they have excess capital representing 27.8% of their total financial wealth. They can either revisit their current goals and bring the timing of payments forward or raise their probability of success. The case suggests that they would rather think of additional goals but will want to give themselves some time to refine their intentions. Their adviser then suggests that a "middle of the road" module be used as a "labeled goal" for that interim period, and they call this module (Module C) "capital preservation."

4.4. The Overall Portfolio

Assuming the same six modules, with their detailed composition shown in Exhibit 38, one can then derive the overall asset allocation by aggregating the individual exposures to the various modules. In short, the overall allocation is simply the weighted average exposure to each of the asset classes or strategies within each module, with the weight being the percentage of financial assets allocated to each module. Exhibit 39 presents these computations and the overall asset allocation, which is given in bold in the right-most column. The overall portfolio's expected return and volatility are also shown. In Exhibit 38, liquidity[34] is measured as one minus the ratio of the average number of days that might be needed to liquidate a position to the number of trading days in a year. (Note that the column B values add up to 101 because of rounding.)

EXHIBIT 38   Asset Allocation of Each Module

	A	B	C	D	E	F
Portfolio Characteristics						
Expected return	4.3%	5.5%	6.4%	7.2%	8.0%	8.7%
Expected volatility	2.7%	4.5%	6.0%	7.5%	10.0%	12.5%
Expected liquidity	100.0%	96.6%	90.0%	86.1%	83.6%	80.0%
Portfolio Allocations						
Cash	80%	26%	3%	1%	1%	1%
Global investment-grade bonds	20	44	45	25	0	0
Global high-yield bonds	0	5	11	25	34	4
Lower-volatility alternatives	0	9	13	0	0	0
Global developed equities	0	9	13	19	34	64
Global emerging equities	0	2	2	3	6	11
Equity-based alternatives	0	0	0	8	0	0
Illiquid global equities	0	0	5	10	15	20
Trading strategy alternatives	0	1	3	6	7	0
Global real estate	0	5	5	3	3	0
Total	100%	100%	100%	100%	100%	100%

---

[34]Note that we need to incorporate some estimate of liquidity for all asset classes and strategies to ensure that the client's and the goals' liquidity constraints can be met.

EXHIBIT 39   Goals-Based Asset Allocation (US$ thousands)

	Total Financial Assets				25,000	
	Goals					Overall Asset Allocation
	1	2	3	4	Surplus	
Horizon	5	25	10	20		
Required success	95%	85%	90%	75%	$E(R_t)$	7.2%
Discount rate	2.3%	6.1%	4.1%	6.8%	$\sigma(R_t)$	8.0%
Module	**A**	**F**	**D**	**F**	**C**	
Required capital						
In currency	2,430	6,275	6,671	2,679	6,945	25,000
As a % of total	9.7	25.1	26.7	10.7	27.8	100.0
Cash	80%	1%	1%	1%	3%	**9%**
Global investment-grade bonds	20	0	25	0	45	**24**
Global high-yield bonds	0	4	25	4	11	**12**
Lower-volatility alternatives	0	0	0	0	13	**4**
Global developed equities	0	64	19	64	13	**28**
Global emerging equities	0	11	3	11	2	**5**
Equity-based alternatives	0	0	8	0	0	**2**
Illiquid global equities	0	20	10	20	5	**10**
Trading strategy alternatives[a]	0	0	6	0	3	**3**
Global real estate	0	0	3	0	5	**2**
Total	100	100	100	100	100	**100**

[a] "Trading strategy alternatives" refers to discretionary or systematic trading strategies such as global macro and managed futures.

4.5. Revisiting the Module Process in Detail

Having explained and illustrated the client process in Exhibit 35, we now explore how modules are developed. Creating an appropriate set of optimized modules starts with the formulation of capital market assumptions. Exhibit 40 presents a possible set of forward-looking pretax capital market expectations for expected return, volatility, and liquidity[35] in Panel A and a historical 15-year correlation matrix in Panel B.[36]

---

[35]For clients who might invest in traditional asset classes by means of vehicles such as mutual funds or ETFs, these asset classes can be treated as providing virtually instant liquidity. For clients with particularly large asset pools who might use separately managed accounts, the liquidity factor for high-yield or emerging market bonds, small-capitalization equities, and certain real assets might be adjusted downward.

[36]For illiquid equities, data availability reduces the time period to seven years. The correlation matrix is based on the 15 years ending with March 2016.

EXHIBIT 40   Example of Capital Market Expectations for a Possible
Asset Class Universe

Panel A

| | Expected | | |
	Return	Volatility	Liquidity
Cash	4.0%	3.0%	100%
Global investment-grade bonds	5.5	6.5	100
Global high-yield bonds	7.0	10.0	100
Lower-volatility alternatives	5.5	5.0	65
Global developed equities	8.0	16.0	100
Global emerging equities	9.5	22.0	100
Equity-based alternatives	6.0	8.0	65
Illiquid global equities	11.0	30.0	0
Trading strategy alternatives	6.5	10.0	80
Global real estate	7.0	15.0	100

Panel B

| | Global | | Lower-Volatility Alts | Global | | Equity-Based Alts | Trading Strategy Alts | Illiquid Equities | Global Real Estate |
	Cash	IG Bonds	HY Bonds		Developed Equities	Emerging Equities				
Cash	1.00	0.00	−0.12	0.08	−0.06	−0.04	0.02	0.04	−0.26	−0.01
Global investment-grade bonds	0.00	1.00	0.27	0.14	0.28	0.09	0.07	0.16	0.20	0.24
Global high-yield bonds	−0.12	0.27	1.00	0.46	0.70	0.17	0.31	−0.08	0.35	0.28
Lower-volatility alternatives	0.08	0.14	0.46	1.00	0.44	0.61	0.86	0.12	0.65	0.47
Global developed equities	−0.06	0.28	0.70	0.44	1.00	0.17	0.32	−0.03	0.47	0.38
Global emerging equities	−0.04	0.09	0.17	0.61	0.17	1.00	0.72	−0.03	0.67	0.49
Equity-based alternatives	0.02	0.07	0.31	0.86	0.32	0.72	1.00	0.11	0.72	0.45
Trading strategy alternatives	0.04	0.16	−0.08	0.12	−0.03	−0.03	0.11	1.00	−0.09	0.07

				Global						Global
		IG	HY	Lower-Volatility	Developed	Emerging	Equity-Based	Trading Strategy	Illiquid	Real
	Cash	Bonds	Bonds	Alts	Equities	Equities	Alts	Alts	Equities	Estate
Illiquid global equities	−0.26	0.20	0.35	0.65	0.47	0.67	0.72	−0.09	**1.00**	0.88
Global real estate	−0.01	0.24	0.28	0.47	0.38	0.49	0.45	0.07	0.88	**1.00**

Ostensibly, in the real world, the process ought to be associated with a set of after-tax expectations, which usually cannot be limited to broad asset classes or sub–asset classes. Indeed, the tax impact of management processes within individual asset classes or strategies (for instance, index replication, index replication with systematic tax-loss harvesting, broadly diversified portfolios, or concentrated portfolios) requires that each management process within each asset class or strategy be given its own expected return and volatility. We will dispense with that step here for the sake of simplicity, both in absolute terms and with respect to jurisdictional differences.

Exhibit 41 presents a possible set of such modules based on the capital market expectations from Exhibit 40. The optimization uses a mean–variance process and is subject to a variety of constraints that are meant to reflect both market portfolio considerations and reasonable asset class or strategy suitability given the goals that we expect to correspond to various points on the frontier. Note that the frontier is not "efficient" in the traditional sense of the term because the constraints applied to the portfolios differ from one to the next. Three elements within the set of constraints deserve special mention. The first is the need to be concerned with the liquidity of the various strategies: It would make little sense, even if it were appropriate based on other considerations, to include any material exposure to illiquid equities in a declining-balance portfolio expected to "mature" within 10 years, for instance. Any exposure thus selected would be bound to increase through time because portfolio liquidation focuses on more-liquid assets. The second relates to strategies whose return distributions are known not to be "normal." This point applies particularly to a number of alternative strategies that suffer from skew and kurtosis,[37] which a mean–variance optimization process does not take into account (see Section 2.4.4). Finally, the constraints contain a measure of drawdown control to alleviate the problems potentially associated with portfolios that, although apparently optimal, appear too risky in overly challenging market circumstances. Drawdown controls are an important element in that they help deal with the often-observed asymmetric tolerance of investors for volatility: upward volatility is much preferred to downward volatility.

---

[37] Kat (2003) described the challenge, and Davies, Kat, and Lu (2009) presented a solution that involves the use of mean–variance-skew-kurtosis optimization, which is typically too complex for most real-life circumstances.

EXHIBIT 41   Six Possible Sub-Portfolio Modules

	A	B	C	D	E	F
Portfolio Characteristics						
Expected return	4.3%	5.5%	6.4%	7.2%	8.0%	8.7%
Expected volatility	2.7	4.5	6.0	7.5	10.0	12.5
Expected liquidity	100.0	96.6	90.0	86.1	83.6	80.0
Portfolio Allocations						
Cash	80%	26%	3%	1%	1%	1%
Global investment-grade bonds	20	44	45	25	0	0
Global high-yield bonds	0	5	11	25	34	4
Lower-volatility alternatives	0	9	13	0	0	0
Global developed equities	0	9	13	19	34	64
Global emerging equities	0	2	2	3	6	11
Equity-based alternatives	0	0	0	8	0	0
Illiquid global equities	0	0	5	10	15	20
Trading strategy alternatives	0	1	3	6	7	0
Global real estate	0	5	5	3	3	0
Total	100%	100%	100%	100%	100%	100%
Constraints						
Maximum volatility	3.0%	4.5%	6.0%	7.5%	10.0%	12.5%
Minimum liquidity	100.0	95.0	90.0	85.0	80.0	70.0
Maximum alternatives	0.0	10.0	20.0	30.0	30.0	30.0
Minimum cash	80.0	20.0	0.3	0.5	0.7	1.0
Maximum HY as a percent of total fixed income	0.0	10.0	20.0	50.0	100.0	100.0
Maximum equity spectrum	0.0	10.0	20.0	40.0	75.0	100.0
Maximum EM as a percent of public equities	15.0	15.0	15.0	15.0	15.0	15.0
Maximum illiquid equities	0.0	0.0	5.0	10.0	15.0	20.0
Maximum trading as a percent of equity spectrum	0.0	10.0	15.0	15.0	20.0	25.0
Maximum real estate	0.0	5.0	10.0	15.0	20.0	25.0
Escrow cash as a percent of illiquid equities	5.0	5.0	5.0	5.0	5.0	5.0
Maximum probability of return < drawdown	1.0	1.5	2.0	2.0	2.5	2.5
Drawdown horizon	3	3	3	3	3	3
Drawdown amount	0.0	−5.0	−7.5	−10.0	−15.0	−20.0

The six sub-portfolios shown in Exhibit 41 satisfy two major design goals: First, they cover a wide spectrum of the investment universe, ranging from a nearly all-cash portfolio (Portfolio A) to an all-equity alternative (Portfolio F). Second, they are sufficiently differentiated to avoid creating distinctions without real differences. These portfolios are graphed in Exhibit 42.

EXHIBIT 42   Sub-Portfolio Modules Cover a Full Range

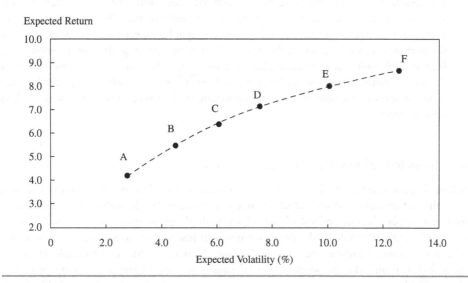

Returning to an earlier point about "labeled goals," one can easily imagine "aspirations" to describe each of these modules, ranging from "immediate- to short-term lifestyle" for Module A to "aggressive growth" for Module F. Module B might be labeled "long-term lifestyle," while C and D might represent forms of capital preservation and E a form of "balanced growth."

A final point deserves special emphasis: Modules need to be revisited on a periodic basis. While equilibrium assumptions will likely not change much from one year to the next, the need to identify one's position with respect to a "normal" market cycle can lead to modest changes in forward-looking assumptions. It would indeed be foolish to keep using long-term equilibrium assumptions when it becomes clear that one is closer to a market top than to a market bottom. The question of the suitability of revisions becomes moot when using a systematic approach such as the Black–Litterman model. One may also need to review the continued suitability of constraints, not to mention (when applicable) the fact that the make-up of the market portfolio may change in terms of geography or credit distribution.

4.6. Periodically Revisiting the Overall Asset Allocation

Once set, the goals-based allocation must be regularly reviewed. Two considerations dominate:

1. Goals with an initially fixed time horizon are not necessarily one year closer to maturity after a year. Superficially, one would expect that someone who says that his or her need is to meet lifestyle expenditures over the next five years, for instance, means exactly this. Accordingly, next year, the time horizon should shift down to four years. Yet experience suggests that certain horizons are "placeholders": One year on, the time horizon remains five years. This is particularly—and understandably—relevant when the horizon reflects the anticipated death of an individual.

2. The preference for upward rather than downward volatility, combined with perceptions that goals may have higher required probabilities of success than is truly the case, leads to portfolios that typically outperform the discount rate used to compute the required initial capital. Thus, one would expect there to be some need for portfolio rebalancing when the assets allocated to certain goals appear excessive, at least in probability- and horizon-adjusted terms. This situation gives rise to important discussions with taxable clients because any form of portfolio rebalancing is inherently more complex and costly in a taxable environment than when taxes do not come into consideration.

4.7. Issues Related to Goals-Based Asset Allocation

Although goals-based asset allocation offers an elegant and mathematically sound way to deal with the circumstances of individuals, it is not a panacea. By definition, goals-based asset allocation applies best to individuals who have multiple goals, time horizons, and urgency levels. The classic example of the professional who is just starting to save for retirement and who has no other significant goal (as in the case of Aimée Goddard in Example 1) can be easily handled with the traditional financial tools discussed in the earlier sections of this chapter.[38] However, one should always be cautious to ensure that there is no "hidden" goal that should be brought out and that the apparently "single" retirement goal is not in fact an aggregation of several elements with different levels of urgency, if not also different time horizons. Single-goal circumstances may still be helped by the goals-based asset allocation process when there are sustainability or behavioral questions. In that case, one can look at the single goal as being made up of several similar goals over successive time periods with different required probabilities of success. For instance, one might apply a higher sense of urgency— and thus require a lower risk profile—to contributions made in the first few years, on the ground that adverse market circumstances might negatively affect the willingness of the client to stay with the program. In many ways, this approach can be seen as a conceptual analog to the dollar-cost-averaging investment framework.

Goals-based asset allocation is ideally suited to situations involving multiple goals, time horizons, and urgency levels, whether the assets are large or more modest. In fact, in cases where "human capital" is considered, a multi-goal approach can help investors understand the various trade-offs they face. Ostensibly, the larger the assets, the more complex the nature of the investment problem, the more diverse the list of investment structures, and the more one should expect a client-focused approach to offer useful benefits. However, the ratio of cash outflows to assets under consideration is a more germane issue than the overall size of the asset pool.

---

[38]However, an adviser may find it appropriate to help the individual divide the funds he or she believes are needed for retirement into several categories. For instance, there may be some incompressible lifestyle expenditure that represents a minimum required spending level, but there may also be some luxury or at least compressible spending that does not have such a high level of urgency or that applies over a different time frame (say, the early or late years). Thus, one could still describe the problem as involving multiple goals, multiple time horizons, and multiple urgency levels. Then, one could compare the costs associated with the funding of these goals and have the individual weigh potential future satisfaction against the loss of current purchasing power.

Advisers using goals-based wealth management must contend with a considerably higher level of business management complexity. They will naturally expect to have a different policy for each client and potentially more than one policy per client. Thus, managing these portfolios day to day and satisfying the usual regulatory requirement that all clients be treated in an equivalent manner can appear to be a major quandary.

Typically, the solution would involve developing a systematic approach to decision-making such that it remains practical for advisers to formulate truly individual policies that reflect their investment insights. Exhibit 43 offers a graphical overview of advisers' activities, divided into those that involve "firm-wide" processes, defined as areas where no real customization is warranted, and those that must remain "client focused." The result is analogous to a customized racing bicycle, whose parts are mass produced but then combined into a truly unique bike custom-designed for the individual racer.

EXHIBIT 43   Goals-Based Wealth Management Advisory Overview

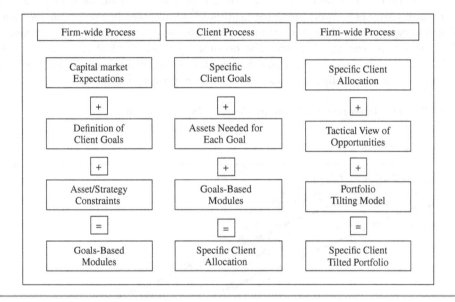

5. HEURISTICS AND OTHER APPROACHES TO ASSET ALLOCATION

In addition to the various asset allocation approaches already covered, a variety of heuristics (rules that provide a reasonable but not necessarily optimal solution) and other techniques deserve mention:

5.1. The "120 minus your age" rule

The phrase "120 minus your age" is a heuristic for inferring a hidden, age-driven risk tolerance coefficient that then leads directly to an age-based stock versus fixed income split: 120 − Age = Percentage allocated to stocks. Thus, a 25-year-old man would allocate 95% of his investment portfolio to stocks. Although we are aware of no theoretic basis for this heuristic—or its older and newer cousins, "100 minus your age" and "125 minus your age," respectively—it results in a linear decrease in equity exposure that seems to fit the general equity glide paths associated with target-date funds, including those that are based on a total balance sheet approach that includes human capital. A number of target-date funds (sometimes called life-cycle or age-based funds) and some target-date index providers report that their glide path (the age-based change in equity exposure) is based on the evolution of an individual's human capital. For example, one set of indexes[39] explicitly targets an investable proxy for the world market portfolio in which the glide path is the result of the evolving relationship of financial capital to human capital.[40]

Exhibit 44 displays the glide paths of the 60 largest target-date fund families in the United States. The retirement year (typically part of the fund's name) on the *x*-axis denotes the year in which the investor is expected to retire, which is almost always assumed to be the year the investor turns 65. Thus, as of 2016, the 2060 allocations correspond to a 21-year-old investor (79% equity, using the heuristic), whereas the 2005 allocation corresponds to a 76-year-old investor (24% equity, using the heuristic).[41] One dashed line represents the equity allocation based on the "100 minus your age" heuristic, while another dashed line represents the "120 minus your age" heuristic. The heuristic lines lack some of the nuances of the various glide path lines, but it would appear that an age-based heuristic leads to asset allocations that are broadly similar to those used by target-date funds.

EXHIBIT 44   Target-Date Funds and Age Heuristics (as of January 2016)

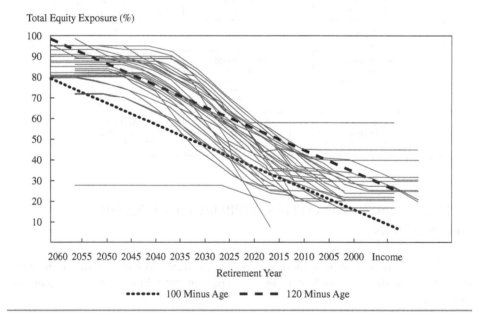

[39]Morningstar's Lifetime Allocation (target-date) indexes.
[40]See Idzorek (2008).
[41]Many target-date funds continue to offer a "2005" vintage that would have been marketed/sold to people retiring in 2005.

5.2. The 60/40 stock/bond heuristic

Some investors choose to skip the various optimization techniques and simply adopt an asset allocation consisting of 60% equities and 40% fixed income.

The equity allocation is viewed as supplying a long-term growth foundation, and the fixed-income allocation as supplying risk reduction benefits. If the stock and bond allocations are themselves diversified, an overall diversified portfolio should result.

There is some evidence that the global financial asset market portfolio is close to this prototypical 60/40 split. Exhibit 45 displays the estimated market value of eight major components of the market portfolio from 1990 to 2012. In approximately 7 of the 23 years, equities, private equity, and real estate account for slightly more than 60%, while for the rest of the time, the combined percentage is slightly less.

EXHIBIT 45   Global Market Portfolio, 1990 to 2012

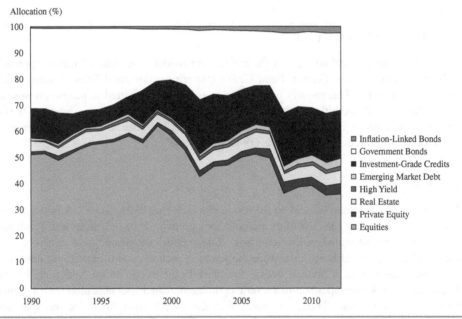

Source: Doeswijk, Lam, and Swinkels (2014).

5.3. The endowment model

An approach to asset allocation that emphasizes large allocations to non-traditional investments, including equity-oriented investments driven by investment manager skill (e.g., private equities), has come to be known as the endowment model or Yale model. The label "Yale model" reflects the fact that the Yale University Investments Office under David Swensen pioneered the approach in the 1990s; the label "endowment model" reflects the influence of this approach among US university endowments. Swensen (2009) stated that most investors should not pursue the Yale model but should instead embrace a simpler asset allocation implemented with low-cost funds. Besides high allocations to non-traditional assets and a commitment to active management, the approach characteristically seeks to earn illiquidity premiums, which endowments with long time horizons are well positioned to capture. Exhibit 46, showing the Yale endowment asset allocation, makes these points. In the exhibit, "absolute return" indicates investment in event-driven and value-driven strategies.

EXHIBIT 46　Yale University Endowment Asset Allocation as of June 2014

	Yale University	US Educational Institution Mean
Absolute return	17.4%	23.3%
Domestic equity	3.9	19.3
Fixed income	4.9	9.3
Foreign equity	11.5	22.0
Natural resources	8.2	8.5
Private equity	33.0	10.0
Real estate	17.6	4.2
Cash	3.5	3.5

Source: Yale University (2014, p. 13).

In almost diametrical contrast to the endowment model is the asset allocation approach of Norway's Government Pension Fund Global (Statens pensjonsfond Utland), often called the Norway model.[42] This model's asset allocation is highly committed to passive investment in publicly traded securities (subject to environmental, social, and governance [ESG] concerns), reflecting a belief in the market's informational efficiency. Since 2009, the asset allocation has followed an approximate 60/40 stock/bond mix.

5.4. Risk parity

A risk parity asset allocation is based on the notion that each asset (asset class or risk factor) should contribute equally to the total risk of the portfolio for a portfolio to be well diversified. Recall that in Section 2, we identified various criticisms and potential shortcomings of mean–variance optimization, one of which was that, while the resulting asset allocations may appear diversified across assets, the sources of risk may not be diversified. In the section on risk budgeting, Exhibit 19 contained a risk decomposition of a reverse-optimization-based asset allocation from a United Kingdom–based investor. There, we noted that the overall equity/fixed income split was approximately 54% equities and 46% fixed income, yet of the 10% standard deviation, approximately 74% of the risk came from equities while only 26% came from fixed income.

Risk parity is a relatively controversial approach. Although there are several variants, the most common risk parity approach has the following mathematical form:

$$w_i \times \text{Cov}(r_i, r_P) = \frac{1}{n}\sigma_P^2 \tag{3}$$

where
　w_i = the weight of asset i
　$\text{Cov}(r_i, r_P)$ = the covariance of asset i with the portfolio
　n = the number of assets
　σ_P^2 = the variance of the portfolio

[42]See Curtis (2012).

In general, there is not a closed-form solution to the problem, and it must be solved using some form of optimization (mathematical programming). Prior to Markowitz's development of mean–variance optimization, which simultaneously considered both risk and return, most asset allocation approaches focused only on return *and ignored risk* (or accounted for it in an ad hoc manner). The primary criticism of risk parity is that it makes the opposite mistake: It *ignores expected returns*. In general, most of the rules-based risk approaches—such as other forms of volatility weighting, minimum volatility, and target volatility—suffer from this shortcoming.

With risk parity, the contribution to risk is highly dependent on the formation of the opportunity set. For example, if the opportunity set consists of seven equity asset classes and three fixed-income asset classes, intuitively, 70% of risk will come from the equities and 30% of risk will come from fixed income. Conversely, if the opportunity set consists of three equity asset classes and seven fixed-income asset classes, intuitively, 70% of risk will come from fixed income and 30% of risk will come from equities. The point is that practitioners of risk parity must be very cognizant of the formation of their opportunity set.

Exhibit 47 gives a US-centric example consisting of five equity asset classes and three fixed-income asset classes. A constrained optimization routine (weights must sum to 100%) was used to determine the weight to each asset class, such that all asset classes contributed the same amount to total risk. In this case, each asset class contributed 0.8%, resulting in an asset allocation with a total standard deviation of 6.41%. In this example, 5/8 of total risk comes from equity asset classes and 3/8 comes from fixed-income asset classes. Earlier, we explained that reverse optimization can be used to infer the expected return of any set of presumed efficient weights. In Exhibit 47, based on a total market risk premium of 2.13% and a risk-free rate of 3%, we inferred the reverse-optimized total returns (final column). In this case, these seem to be relatively reasonable expected returns.

EXHIBIT 47   Risk Parity Portfolio Weights and Risk-Budgeting Statistics Based on Reverse-Optimized Returns

Asset Class	Weight	Marginal Contribution to Total Risk (MCTR)	ACTR	Percentage Contribution to Total Standard Deviation	Reverse-Optimized Total Returns
US large-cap equities	7.7%	10.43%	0.80%	12.50%	6.47%
US mid-cap equities	6.1	13.03	0.80	12.50	7.33
US small-cap equities	5.9	13.61	0.80	12.50	7.52
Non-US developed market equities	5.6	14.38	0.80	12.50	7.78
Emerging market equities	4.5	17.74	0.80	12.50	8.89
Non-US bonds	15.5	5.17	0.80	12.50	4.72
US TIPS	23.9	3.36	0.80	12.50	4.12
US bonds	30.8	2.60	0.80	12.50	3.86
Total	100.0%		6.41%	100.00%	5.13%

After deriving a risk parity–based asset allocation, the next step in the process is to borrow (use leverage) or to lend (save a portion of wealth, presumably in cash) so that the overall portfolio corresponds to the investor's risk appetite. Continuing with our example, the market risk premium is 2.13% (above the assumed risk-free rate of 3%) and the market variance is 0.41% (i.e., 6.41% squared); thus, the implied market trade-off of expected return (in excess of the risk-free rate) for risk is 2.13% divided by 0.41%, which equals approximately 5.2. Investors with a greater appetite for risk than the market as a whole would borrow money to lever up the risk parity portfolios, while investors with a lower appetite for risk would invest a portion of their wealth in cash.

Back tests of levered risk parity portfolios have produced promising results, although critics of these back tests argue that they suffer from look-back bias and are very dependent on the ability to use extremely large amounts of leverage at low borrow rates (which may not have been feasible); see, for example, Anderson, Bianchi, and Goldberg (2012). Proponents of risk parity have suggested that the idea of "leverage aversion" contributes to the success of the strategy. Black (1972) suggested that restrictions on leverage and a general aversion to leverage may cause return-seeking investors to pursue higher-returning assets, such as stocks. All else equal, this behavior would reduce the price of bonds, thus allowing the investor to buy bonds at a small discount, hold them to maturity, and realize the full value of the bond. Asness, Frazzini, and Pedersen (2012) have offered this idea as a potential explanation for why a levered (bond-centric) asset allocation might outperform an equity-centric asset allocation with equivalent or similar risk.

5.5. The 1/N rule

One of the simplest asset allocation heuristics involves equally weighting allocations to assets. DeMiguel, Garlappi, and Uppal (2009) define an approach in which $1/N$ of wealth is allocated to each of N assets available for investment at each rebalancing date. Calendar rebalancing to equal weighting at quarterly intervals is one common rebalancing discipline used. By treating all assets as indistinguishable in terms of mean returns, volatility, and correlations, in principle, $1/N$ rule portfolios should be dominated by methods that optimize asset class weights to exploit differences in investment characteristics. In empirical studies comparing approaches, however, the $1/N$ rule has been found to perform considerably better, based on Sharpe ratios and certainty equivalents, than theory might suggest. One possible explanation is that the $1/N$ rule sidesteps problems caused by optimizing when there is estimation error in inputs.

6. PORTFOLIO REBALANCING IN PRACTICE

The chapter "Introduction to Asset Allocation" provided an introduction to rebalancing, including some detailed comments on strategic considerations. This section aims to present useful additional insight and information.

Meanings of "Rebalancing"

Rebalancing has been defined as the discipline of adjusting portfolio weights to more closely align with the strategic asset allocation. In that sense, rebalancing includes policy regarding the correction of any drift away from strategic asset allocation weights resulting from market price movements and the passage of time for finite-lived assets, such as bonds. In liability-relative asset allocation, adjusting a liability-hedging portfolio to account for changes in net duration exposures from the passage of time, for example, would fall under the rubric of rebalancing.

Some use the term "rebalancing" more expansively, to include the combined effects on asset class weights not only of rebalancing in the above sense but also of active allocation activities. In that sense, rebalancing would include tactical allocations. Although rebalancing policy can be established to accommodate tactical adjustments, tactical asset allocation per se is not covered under "rebalancing" as the term is used here.

Changes in asset allocation weights in response to changes in client circumstances, goals, or other client factors are sometimes also referred to as "rebalancing" (especially if the adjustments are minor). These activities fall under the scope of client monitoring and asset allocation review, as described elsewhere in the CFA curriculum.

An appropriate rebalancing policy involves a weighing of benefits and costs. Benefits depend on the idea that if an investor's strategic asset allocation is optimal, then any divergence in the portfolio from that asset allocation represents an expected utility loss to the investor. Rebalancing benefits the investor by reducing the present value of expected losses from not tracking the optimum. In theory, the basic cost of not rebalancing is this present value of expected utility losses from straying from the optimum.[43]

Apart from the above considerations of trade-offs, disciplined rebalancing has tended to reduce risk while incrementally adding to returns. Several interpretations of this empirical finding have been offered, including the following:

- *Rebalancing earns a diversification return.* The compound growth rate of a portfolio is greater than the weighted average compound growth rates of the component portfolio holdings (given positive expected returns and positive asset weights). Given sufficiently low transaction costs, this effect leads to what has been called a *diversification return* to frequent rebalancing to a well-diversified portfolio.[44]
- *Rebalancing earns a return from being short volatility.* In the case of a portfolio consisting of a risky asset and a risk-free asset, the return to a rebalanced portfolio can be replicated by creating a buy-and-hold position in the portfolio, writing out-of-the-money puts and calls on the risky asset, and investing the premiums in risk-free bonds.[45] As the value of puts and calls is positively related to volatility, such a position is called being short volatility (or being short gamma, by reference to the option Greeks).

---

[43]See Leland (2000).

[44]See Willenbrock (2011). This phenomenon was called *rebalancing return* by Mulvey and Kim (2009). Luenberger (2013) suggests that the phenomenon could be exploited by a strategy of buying high-volatility assets and rebalancing often, a process he called *volatility pumping.*

[45]As shown in Ang (2014, pp. 135–139).

Practice appears not to have produced a consensus on the most appropriate rebalancing discipline. "Introduction to Asset Allocation" defined and discussed calendar rebalancing[46]— sometimes mentioned as common in portfolios managed for individual investors—and percent-range rebalancing. Calendar rebalancing involves lower overhead because of lower monitoring costs. Percent-range rebalancing is a more disciplined risk control policy, however, because it makes rebalancing contingent on market movements. Without weighing costs and benefits in the abstract, Exhibit 48 assumes percent-range rebalancing and summarizes the effects of each of several key factors on the corridor width of an asset class, holding all else equal, except for the factor of the asset class's own volatility.[47] For taxable investors, transactions trigger capital gains in jurisdictions that tax them; therefore, for such investors, higher tax rates on capital gains should also be associated with wider corridors.

EXHIBIT 48   Factors Affecting the Optimal Corridor Width of an Asset Class

Factor	Effect on Optimal Width of Corridor (All Else Equal)	Intuition
Factors Positively Related to Optimal Corridor Width		
Transaction costs	The higher the transaction costs, the wider the optimal corridor.	High transaction costs set a high hurdle for rebalancing benefits to overcome.
Risk tolerance	The higher the risk tolerance, the wider the optimal corridor.	Higher risk tolerance means less sensitivity to divergences from the target allocation.
Correlation with the rest of the portfolio	The higher the correlation, the wider the optimal corridor.	When asset classes move in sync, further divergence from target weights is less likely.
Factors Inversely Related to Optimal Corridor Width		
Volatility of the rest of the portfolio	The higher the volatility, the narrower the optimal corridor.	Higher volatility makes large divergences from the strategic asset allocation more likely.

Among positive factors, the cases of transaction costs and risk tolerance are obvious. Transaction costs can be reduced to the extent that portfolio cash flows can be used to rebalance. The case of correlation is less obvious. Because of correlations, the rebalancing triggers among different asset classes are linked.

Consider correlation in a two–asset class scenario. Suppose one asset class is above its target weight, so the other asset class is below its target weight. A further increase in the value of the overweight asset class implies, on average, a smaller divergence in the asset mix if the asset classes' returns are more highly positively correlated (because the denominator in computing the overweight asset class's weight is the sum of the values of the two asset classes). In a multi-asset-class scenario, all pair-wise asset class correlations would need to be considered, making the interpretation of correlations complex. To expand the application of the two-asset case's intuition, one simplification involves considering the balance of a portfolio to be a single hypothetical asset and computing an asset class's correlation with it.

---

[46]Rebalancing a portfolio to target weights on a periodic basis—for example, monthly, quarterly, semiannually, or annually.

[47]See Masters (2003).

As indicated in Exhibit 48, the higher the volatility of the rest of the portfolio, excluding the asset class being considered, the more likely a large divergence from the strategic asset allocation becomes. That consideration should point to a narrower optimal corridor, all else being equal.

In the case of an asset class's own volatility, "holding all else equal" is not practically meaningful. If rebalancing did not involve transaction costs, then higher volatility would lead to a narrower corridor, all else equal, for a risk-averse investor.[48] Higher volatility implies that if an asset class is not brought back into the optimal range after a given move away from it, the chance of an even further divergence from optimal is greater. In other words, higher volatility makes large divergence from the strategic asset allocation more likely. However, reducing a corridor's width means more frequent rebalancing and higher transaction costs. Thus, the effect of volatility on optimal corridor width involves a trade-off between controlling transaction costs and controlling risk. Conclusions also depend on the assumptions made about asset price return dynamics.

In practice, corridor width is often specified to be proportionally greater, the higher an asset class's volatility, with a focus on transaction cost control. In *volatility-based rebalancing*, corridor width is set proportionally to the asset class's own volatility. In one variation of *equal probability rebalancing* (McCalla 1997), the manager specifies a corridor for each asset class in terms of a common multiple of the standard deviation of the asset class's returns such that, under a normal probability assumption, each asset class is equally likely to trigger rebalancing.

EXAMPLE 12   Tolerance Bands for an Asset Allocation

An investment committee is reviewing the following strategic asset allocation:

Domestic equities 50% ± 5% (i.e., 45% to 55% of portfolio value)
International equities 15% ± 1.5%
Domestic bonds 35% ± 3.5%

The market for the domestic bonds is relatively illiquid. The committee views the above corridors as appropriate *if* each asset class's risk and transaction cost characteristics remain unchanged. The committee now wants to account for differences among the asset classes in setting the corridors.

Evaluate the implications of the following sets of facts for the stated tolerance bands, given an all-else-equal assumption in each case:

1. Tax rates for international equities increase by 10 percentage points.
2. Transaction costs in international equities increase by 20% relative to domestic equities, but the correlation of international equities with domestic equities and bonds declines. What is the expected effect on the tolerance band for international equities?
3. The volatility of domestic bonds increases. What is the expected effect on their tolerance band? Assume that domestic bonds are relatively illiquid.

Solution to 1: The tolerance band for international equities should increase if the entity is a taxable investor.

---

[48]As in Masters (2003).

Solution to 2: Increased transaction costs point to widening the tolerance band for international equities, but declining correlations point to narrowing it. The overall effect is indeterminate.

Solution to 3: Given that the market for domestic bonds is relatively illiquid, the increase in volatility suggests widening the rebalancing band. Containing transaction costs is more important than the expected utility losses from allowing a larger divergence from the strategic asset allocation.

One decision involved in rebalancing policy is whether to adjust asset class holdings to their target proportions, to the limits of the corridors, or to within the corridors but not to target weights. Compared with rebalancing to target weights, rebalancing to the upper or lower limit of the allowed range results in less close alignment with target proportions but lower transaction costs—an especially important consideration in the case of relatively illiquid assets. The choice among alternatives may be influenced by judgmental tactical considerations.

Because one rebalancing decision affects later rebalancing decisions, the optimal rebalancing decisions at different points in time are linked. However, optimal rebalancing in a multi-period, multi-asset case is an unsolved problem.

The analysis of Dybvig (2005) suggests that fixed transaction costs favor rebalancing to the target weights and variable transaction costs favor rebalancing to the nearest corridor border (the interior of the corridor being therefore a "no trade zone"). A number of studies have contrasted rebalancing to target weights and rebalancing to the allowed range based on particular asset classes, time periods, and measures of the benefits of rebalancing. These studies have reached a variety of conclusions, suggesting that no simple, empirically based advice can be provided.

Rebalancing in a Goals-Based Approach

The use of probability- and horizon-adjusted discount rates to size the various goal-defeasing sub-portfolios means that portfolios will usually produce returns that are higher than assumed. Thus, as time passes, the dollars allocated to the various sub-portfolios—other than labeled-goal portfolios—may be expected to exceed the actual requirements. For example, in average markets, returns should exceed the conservative requirements of a goal associated with a 90% required probability of success. Sub-portfolios with shorter time horizons for goals with high required probabilities of success will tend to contain relatively low-risk assets, whereas riskier assets may have high allocations in longer-horizon portfolios for goals with lower required probabilities of success. Thus, there is a greater chance that the exposure to lower-risk assets will creep up before one experiences the same for riskier assets. Thus, failing to rebalance the portfolio will gradually move it down the risk axis—and the defined efficient frontier—and thus lead the client to take less risk than he or she can bear.

7. CONCLUSIONS

This chapter has surveyed how appropriate asset allocations can be determined to meet the needs of a variety of investors. Among the major points made have been the following:

- The objective function of asset-only mean–variance optimization is to maximize the expected return of the asset mix minus a penalty that depends on risk aversion and the expected variance of the asset mix.
- Criticisms of MVO include the following:
  - The outputs (asset allocations) are highly sensitive to small changes in the inputs.
  - The asset allocations are highly concentrated in a subset of the available asset classes.
  - Investors are often concerned with characteristics of asset class returns such as skewness and kurtosis that are not accounted for in MVO.
  - While the asset allocations may appear diversified across assets, the sources of risk may not be diversified.
  - MVO allocations may have no direct connection to the factors affecting any liability or consumption streams.
  - MVO is a single-period framework that tends to ignore trading/rebalancing costs and taxes.
- Deriving expected returns by reverse optimization or by reverse optimization tilted toward an investor's views on asset returns (the Black–Litterman model) is one means of addressing the tendency of MVO to produce efficient portfolios that are not well diversified.
- Placing constraints on asset class weights to prevent extremely concentrated portfolios and resampling inputs are other ways of addressing the same concern.
- For some relatively illiquid asset classes, a satisfactory proxy may not be available; including such asset classes in the optimization may therefore be problematic.
- Risk budgeting is a means of making optimal use of risk in the pursuit of return. A risk budget is optimal when the ratio of excess return to marginal contribution to total risk is the same for all assets in the portfolio.
- Characteristics of liabilities that affect asset allocation in liability-relative asset allocation include the following:
  - Fixed versus contingent cash flows
  - Legal versus quasi-liabilities
  - Duration and convexity of liability cash flows
  - Value of liabilities as compared with the size of the sponsoring organization
  - Factors driving future liability cash flows (inflation, economic conditions, interest rates, risk premium)
  - Timing considerations, such as longevity risk
  - Regulations affecting liability cash flow calculations
- Approaches to liability-relative asset allocation include surplus optimization, a hedging/return-seeking portfolios approach, and an integrated asset–liability approach.
- Surplus optimization involves MVO applied to surplus returns
- A hedging/return-seeking portfolios approach assigns assets to one of two portfolios. The objective of the hedging portfolio is to hedge the investor's liability stream. Any remaining funds are invested in the return-seeking portfolio.
- An integrated asset–liability approach integrates and jointly optimizes asset and liability decisions.

- A goals-based asset allocation process combines into an overall portfolio a number of sub-portfolios, each of which is designed to fund an individual goal with its own time horizon and required probability of success.
- In the implementation, there are two fundamental parts to the asset allocation process. The first centers on the creation of portfolio modules, while the second relates to the identification of client goals and the matching of these goals to the appropriate sub-portfolios to which suitable levels of capital are allocated.
- Other approaches to asset allocation include "120 minus your age," 60/40 stocks/bonds, the endowment model, risk parity, and the $1/N$ rule.
- Disciplined rebalancing has tended to reduce risk while incrementally adding to returns. Interpretations of this empirical finding include that rebalancing earns a diversification return, that rebalancing earns a return from being short volatility, and that rebalancing earns a return to supplying liquidity to the market.
- Factors positively related to optimal corridor width include transaction costs, risk tolerance, and an asset class's correlation with the rest of the portfolio. The higher the correlation, the wider the optimal corridor, because when asset classes move in sync, further divergence from target weights is less likely.
- The volatility of the rest of the portfolio (outside of the asset class under consideration) is inversely related to optimal corridor width.
- An asset class's own volatility involves a trade-off between transaction costs and risk control. The width of the optimal tolerance band increases with transaction costs for volatility-based rebalancing.

REFERENCES

Anderson, Robert M., Stephen W. Bianchi, and Lisa R. Goldberg. 2012. "Will My Risk Parity Strategy Outperform?" *Financial Analysts Journal*, vol. 68, no. 6 (November/December): 75–93.

Ang, Andrew. 2014. *Asset Management*. New York: Oxford University Press.

Asness, Clifford S., Andrea Frazzini, and Lasse H. Pedersen. 2012. "Leverage Aversion and Risk Parity." *Financial Analysts Journal*, vol. 68, no. 1 (January/February): 47–59.

Athayde, Gustavo M. de, and Renato G. Flôres Jr. 2003. "Incorporating Skewness and Kurtosis in Portfolio Optimization: A Multideminsional Efficient Set." In *Advances in Portfolio Construction and Implementation*, edited by Stephen Satchell and Alan Scowcroft. Oxford, UK: Butterworth–Heinemann.

Beardsley, Xiaoxin W., Brian Field, and Mingqing Xiao. 2012. "Mean–Variance-Skewness-Kurtosis Portfolio Optimization with Return and Liquidity." *Communications in Mathematical Finance*, vol. 1, no. 1: 13–49.

Black, Fischer. 1972. "Capital market equilibrium with restricted borrowing." *Journal of Business*, vol. 45, no. 3: 444–455.

Black, Fischer, and Robert Litterman. 1990. "Asset Allocation: Combining Investors Views with Market Equilibrium." Fixed Income Research, Goldman, Sachs & Company, September.

Black, Fischer, and Robert Litterman. 1991. "Global Asset Allocation with Equities, Bonds, and Currencies." Fixed Income Research, Goldman, Sachs & Company, October.

Black, Fischer, and Robert Litterman. 1992. "Global Portfolio Optimization." *Financial Analysts Journal*, vol. 48, no. 5 (September/October): 28–43.

Blanchett, David M., and Philip U. Straehl. 2015. "No Portfolio is an Island." *Financial Analysts Journal*, vol. 71, no. 3 (May/June): 15–33.

Briec, W., K. Kerstens, and O. Jokung. 2007. "Mean–Variance-Skewness Portfolio Performance Gauging: A General Shortage Function and Dual Approach." *Management Science*, vol. 53, no. 1 (January): 135–149.

Brunel, Jean L.P. 2003. "Revisiting the Asset Allocation Challenge through a Behavioral Finance Lens." *Journal of Wealth Management*, vol. 6, no. 2 (Fall): 10–20.

Brunel, Jean L.P. 2005. "A Behavioral Finance Approach to Strategic Asset Allocation—A Case Study." *Journal of Investment Consulting*, vol. 7, no. 3 (Winter): 61–69.

Chhabra, Ashvin. 2005. "Beyond Markowitz: A Comprehensive Wealth Allocation Framework for Individual Investors." *Journal of Wealth Management*, vol. 7, no. 4 (Spring): 8–34.

Chow, George, Eric Jacquier, Mark Kritzman, and Kenneth Lowry. 1999. "Optimal Portfolios in Good Times and Bad." *Financial Analysts Journal*, vol. 55, no. 3 (May/June): 65–73.

Curtis, Gregory. 2012. "Yale versus Norway." White Paper 55, Greycourt (September).

Das, Sanjiv, Harry Markowitz, Jonathan Scheid, and Meir Statman. 2010. "Portfolio Optimization with Mental Accounts." *Journal of Financial and Quantitative Analysis*, vol. 45, no. 2 (April): 311–334.

Das, Sanjiv, Harry Markowitz, Jonathan Scheid, and Meir Statman. 2011. "Portfolios for Investors Who Want to Reach Their Goals While Staying on the Mean–Variance Efficient Frontier." *Journal of Wealth Management*, vol. 14, no. 2 (Fall): 25–31.

Davies, Ryan, Harry M. Kat, and Sa Lu. 2009. "Fund of Hedge Funds Portfolio Selection: A Multiple-Objective Approach." *Journal of Derivatives & Hedge Funds*, vol. 15, no. 2: 91–115.

DeMiguel, V., L. Garlappi, and R. Uppal. 2009. "Optimal versus Naive Diversification: How Inefficient Is the 1/*N* Portfolio Strategy?" *Review of Financial Studies*, vol. 22, no. 5: 1915–1953.

DiBartolomeo, Dan. 1993. "Portfolio Optimization: The Robust Solution." Prudential Securities Quantitative Conference. Available online at http://www.northinfo.com/documents/45.pdf.

Doeswijk, Ronald, Trevin Lam, and Laurens Swinkels. 2014. "The Global Multi-Asset Market Portfolio, 1959–2012." *Financial Analysts Journal*, vol. 70, no. 2 (March/April): 26–41.

Dybvig, Philip H. 2005. "Mean-variance portfolio rebalancing with transaction costs." Working paper, Washington University in Saint Louis.

Elton, Edwin J., and Martin J. Gruber. 1992. "Optimal Investment Strategies with Investor Liabilities." *Journal of Banking & Finance*, vol. 16, no. 5: 869–890.

Gannon, James A., and Bob Collins. 2009. "Liability-Responsive Asset Allocation." Russell Research Viewpoint.

Goldberg, Lisa R., Michael Y. Hayes, and Ola Mahmoud. 2013. "Minimizing Shortfall." *Quantitative Finance*, vol. 13, no. 10: 1533–1545.

Grable, John E. 2008. "RiskCAT: A Framework for Identifying Maximum Risk Thresholds in Personal Portfolios." *Journal of Financial Planning*, vol. 21, no. 10: 52–62.

Grable, John E., and Soo-Hyun Joo. 2004. "Environmental and Biopsychosocial Factors Associated with Financial Risk Tolerance." *Financial Counseling and Planning*, vol. 15, no. 1: 73–88.

Harvey, Campbell R., John C. Liechty, Merrill W. Liechty, and Peter Müller. 2010. "Portfolio Selection with Higher Moments." *Quantitative Finance*, vol. 10, no. 5 (May): 469–485.

Idzorek, Thomas. 2008. "Lifetime Asset Allocations: Methodologies for Target Maturity Funds." Ibbotson Associates Research Report.

Idzorek, Thomas M., and Maciej Kowara. 2013. "Factor-Based Asset Allocation vs. Asset-Class-Based Asset Allocation." *Financial Analysts Journal*, vol. 69, no. 3 (May/June): 19–29.

Jobson, David J., and Bob Korkie. 1980. "Estimation for Markowitz Efficient Portfolios." *Journal of the American Statistical Association*, vol. 75, no. 371 (September): 544–554.

Jobson, David J., and Bob Korkie. 1981. "Putting Markowitz Theory to Work." *Journal of Portfolio Management*, vol. 7, no. 4 (Summer): 70–74.

Jorion, Phillipe. 1992. "Portfolio Optimization in Practice." *Financial Analysts Journal*, vol. 48, no. 1 (January/February): 68–74.

Kahneman, Daniel, and Amos Tversky. 1979. "Prospect Theory: An Analysis of Decision under Risk." *Econometrica*, vol. 47, no. 2: 263–292.

Kat, Harry M. 2003. "10 Things That Investors Should Know about Hedge Funds." *Journal of Wealth Management*, vol. 5, no. 4 (Spring): 72–81.

Leibowitz, Martin L., and Roy D. Henriksson. 1988. "Portfolio Optimization Within a Surplus Framework." *Financial Analysts Journal*, vol. 44, no. 2: 43–51.

Leland, Hayne. 2000. "Optimal Portfolio Implementation with Transaction Costs and Capital Gains Taxes." Working paper, University of California, Berkeley.

Luenberger, David G. 2013. *Investment Science*, 2nd ed. New York: Oxford University Press.

Markowitz, Harry M. 1952. "Portfolio Selection." *Journal of Finance*, vol. 7, no. 1 (March): 77–91.

Markowitz, Harry M. 1959. *Portfolio Selection: Efficient Diversification of Investments*. New York: John Wiley & Sons.

Maslow, A.H. 1943. "A Theory of Human Motivation." *Psychological Review*, vol. 50, no. 4: 370–396.

Masters, Seth J. 2003. "Rebalancing." *Journal of Portfolio Management*, vol. 29, no. 3: 52–57.

McCalla, Douglas B. 1997. "Enhancing the Efficient Frontier with Portfolio Rebalancing." *Journal of Pension Plan Investing*, vol. 1, no. 4: 16–32.

Michaud, Richard O. 1998. *Efficient Asset Management*. Boston: Harvard Business School Press.

Mulvey, John M. 1989. "A Surplus Optimization Perspective." *Investment Management Review*, vol. 3: 31–39.

Mulvey, John M. 1994. "An Asset-Liability System." *Interfaces*, vol. 24, no. 3: 22–33.

Mulvey, J.M., and W. Kim. 2009. "Constantly Rebalanced Portfolio—Is Mean Reversion Necessary?" in Rama Cont, ed. *Encyclopedia of Quantitative Finance*, vol 2, Hoboken, NJ: John Wiley & Sons.

Mulvey, John M., Bill Pauling, and Ron E. Madey. 2003. "Advantages of Multi-Period Portfolio Models." *Journal of Portfolio Management*, vol. 29, no. 2 (Winter): 35–45.

Nevins, Daniel. 2004. "Goal-Based Investing: Integrating Traditional and Behavioral Finance." *Journal of Wealth Management*, vol. 6, no. 4 (Spring): 8–23.

Pompian, Michael M., and John B. Longo. 2004. "A New Paradigm for Practical Application of Behavioral Finance." *Journal of Wealth Management*, vol. 7, no. 2 (Fall): 9–15.

Rockafellar, R. Tyrrell, and Stanislav Uryasev. 2000. "Optimization of Conditional Value-at-Risk." *Journal of Risk*, vol. 2, no. 3 (Spring): 21–41.

Rudd, Andrew, and Laurence B. Siegel. 2013. "Using an Economic Balance Sheet for Financial Planning." *Journal of Wealth Management*, vol. 16, no. 2 (Fall): 15–23.

Scherer, Bernd. 2002. "Portfolio Resampling: Review and Critique." *Financial Analysts Journal*, vol. 58, no. 6 (November/December): 98–109.

Sharpe, William. 1974. "Imputing Expected Security Returns from Portfolio Composition." *Journal of Financial and Quantitative Analysis*, vol. 9, no. 3 (June): 463–472.

Sharpe, William, and Lawrence G. Tint. 1990. "Liabilities: A New Approach." *Journal of Portfolio Management*, vol. 16, no. 2: 5–10.

Shefrin, H. and M. Statman. 2000. "Behavioral Portfolio Theory." *Journal of Financial and Quantitative Analysis*, vol. 35, no. 2: 127–151.

Swensen, D. 2009. *Pioneering Portfolio Management: An Unconventional Approach to Institutional Investment*, 2nd ed. New York: Free Press.

Tversky, Amos, and Daniel Kahneman. 1992. "Advances in prospect theory: Cumulative representation of uncertainty." *Journal of Risk and Uncertainty*, vol. 5, no. 4: 297–323.

Willenbrock, Scott. 2011. "Diversification Return, Portfolio Rebalancing, and the Commodity Return Puzzle." *Financial Analysts Journal*, vol. 67, no. 4 (July/August): 42–49.

Winkelmann, Kurt. 2003. "Developing an Optimal Active Risk Budget," in *Modern Investment Management: An Equilibrium Approach* Bob Litterman, ed. New York: John Wiley & Sons.

Xiong, James X., and Thomas M. Idzorek. 2011. "The Impact of Skewness and Fat Tails on the Asset Allocation Decision." *Financial Analysts Journal*, vol. 67, no. 2 (March/April): 23–35.

Yale University. 2014. "The Yale Endowment 2014" (http://investments.yale.edu/s/Yale_Endowment_14.pdf).

PRACTICE PROBLEMS

The following information relates to questions 1–8

Megan Beade and Hanna Müller are senior analysts for a large, multi-divisional money management firm. Beade supports the institutional portfolio managers, and Müller does the same for the private wealth portfolio managers.

Beade reviews the asset allocation in Exhibit 1, derived from a mean–variance optimization (MVO) model for an institutional client, noting that details of the MVO are lacking.

EXHIBIT 1   Asset Allocation and Market Weights (in percent)

Asset Classes	Asset Allocation	Investable Global Market Weights
Cash	0	—
US bonds	30	17
US TIPS	0	3
Non-US bonds	0	22
Emerging market equity	25	5
Non-US developed equity	20	29
US small- and mid-cap equity	25	4
US large-cap equity	0	20

The firm's policy is to rebalance a portfolio when the asset class weight falls outside of a corridor around the target allocation. The width of each corridor is customized for each client and proportional to the target allocation. The width of each corridor is customized for each client and proportional to the target allocation. Beade recommends wider corridor widths for high-risk asset classes, narrower corridor widths for less liquid asset classes, and narrower corridor widths for taxable clients with high capital gains tax rates.

One client sponsors a defined benefit pension plan where the present value of the liabilities is $241 million and the market value of plan assets is $205 million. Beade expects interest rates to rise and both the present value of plan liabilities and the market value of plan assets to decrease by $25 million, changing the pension plan's funding ratio.

Beade uses a surplus optimization approach to liability-relative asset allocation based on the objective function

$$U_m^{LR} = E(R_{s,m}) - 0.005\lambda\sigma^2(R_{s,m})$$

where $E(R_{s,m})$ is the expected surplus return for portfolio m, λ is the risk aversion coefficient, and $\sigma^2(R_{s,m})$ is the variance of the surplus return. Beade establishes the expected surplus return and surplus variance for three different asset allocations, shown in Exhibit 2. Given $\lambda = 1.50$, she chooses the optimal asset mix.

EXHIBIT 2   Expected Surplus Return and Volatility for Three Portfolios

	Return	Standard Deviation
Portfolio 1	13.00%	24%
Portfolio 2	12.00%	18%
Portfolio 3	11.00%	19%

Client Haunani Kealoha has a large fixed obligation due in 10 years. Beade assesses that Kealoha has substantially more funds than are required to meet the fixed obligation. The client wants to earn a competitive risk-adjusted rate of return while maintaining a high level of certainty that there will be sufficient assets to meet the fixed obligation.

In the private wealth area, the firm has designed five sub-portfolios with differing asset allocations that are used to fund different client goals over a five-year horizon. Exhibit 3 shows the expected returns and volatilities of the sub-portfolios and the probabilities that the sub-portfolios will exceed an expected minimum return. Client Luis Rodríguez wants to satisfy two goals. Goal 1 requires a conservative portfolio providing the highest possible minimum return that will be met at least 95% of the time. Goal 2 requires a riskier portfolio that provides the highest minimum return that will be exceeded at least 85% of the time.

EXHIBIT 3   Characteristics of Sub-Portfolios

Sub-Portfolio	A	B	C	D	E
Expected return, in percent	4.60	5.80	7.00	8.20	9.40
Expected volatility, in percent	3.46	5.51	8.08	10.80	13.59
Required Success Rate	Minimum Expected Return for Success Rate				
99%	1.00	0.07	−1.40	−3.04	−4.74
95%	2.05	1.75	1.06	0.25	−0.60
90%	2.62	2.64	2.37	2.01	1.61
85%	3.00	3.25	3.26	3.19	3.10
75%	3.56	4.14	4.56	4.94	5.30

Müller uses a risk parity asset allocation approach with a client's four–asset class portfolio. The expected return of the domestic bond asset class is the lowest of the asset classes, and the returns of the domestic bond asset class have the lowest covariance with other asset class returns. Müller estimates the weight that should be placed on domestic bonds.

Müller and a client discuss other approaches to asset allocation that are not based on optimization models or goals-based models. Müller makes the following comments to the client:

Comment 1.   An advantage of the "120 minus your age" heuristic over the 60/40 stock/bond heuristic is that it incorporates an age-based stock/bond allocation.

Comment 2.   The Yale model emphasizes traditional investments and a commitment to active management.

Comment 3.   A client's asset allocation using the $1/N$ rule depends on the investment characteristics of each asset class.

1. The asset allocation in Exhibit 1 *most likely* resulted from a mean–variance optimization using:
   A. historical data.
   B. reverse optimization.
   C. Black–Litterman inputs.

2. For clients concerned about rebalancing-related transactions costs, which of Beade's suggested changes in the corridor width of the rebalancing policy is correct? The change with respect to:
   A. high-risk asset classes.
   B. less liquid asset classes.
   C. taxable clients with high capital gains tax rates.

3. Based on Beade's interest rate expectations, the pension plan's funding ratio will:
   A. decrease.
   B. remain unchanged.
   C. increase.

4. Based on Exhibit 2, which portfolio provides the greatest objective function expected value?
   A. Portfolio 1
   B. Portfolio 2
   C. Portfolio 3

5. The asset allocation approach most appropriate for client Kealoha is *best* described as:
   A. a surplus optimization approach.
   B. an integrated asset–liability approach.
   C. a hedging/return-seeking portfolios approach.

6. Based on Exhibit 3, which sub-portfolios *best* meet the two goals expressed by client Rodríguez?
   A. Sub-Portfolio A for Goal 1 and Sub-Portfolio C for Goal 2
   B. Sub-Portfolio B for Goal 1 and Sub-Portfolio C for Goal 2
   C. Sub-Portfolio E for Goal 1 and Sub-Portfolio A for Goal 2

7. In the risk parity asset allocation approach that Müller uses, the weight that Müller places on domestic bonds should be:
   A. less than 25%.
   B. equal to 25%.
   C. greater than 25%.

8. Which of Müller's comments about the other approaches to asset allocation is correct?
   A. Comment 1
   B. Comment 2
   C. Comment 3

The following information relates to questions 9–13

Investment adviser Carl Monteo determines client asset allocations using quantitative techniques such as mean–variance optimization (MVO) and risk budgets. Monteo is reviewing the allocations of three clients. Exhibit 1 shows the expected return and standard deviation of returns for three strategic asset allocations that apply to several of Monteo's clients.

EXHIBIT 1   Strategic Asset Allocation Alternatives

	Adviser's Forecasts	
Asset Allocation	Expected Return (%)	Standard Deviation of Returns (%)
A	10	12.0
B	8	8.0
C	6	2.0

Monteo interviews client Mary Perkins and develops a detailed assessment of her risk preference and capacity for risk, which is needed to apply MVO to asset allocation. Monteo estimates the risk aversion coefficient (λ) for Perkins to be 8 and uses the following utility function to determine a preferred asset allocation for Perkins:

$$U_m = E(R_m) - 0.005\lambda\sigma_m^2$$

Another client, Lars Velky, represents Velky Partners (VP), a large institutional investor with $500 million in investable assets. Velky is interested in adding less liquid asset classes, such as direct real estate, infrastructure, and private equity, to VP's portfolio. Velky and Monteo discuss the considerations involved in applying many of the common asset allocation techniques, such as MVO, to these asset classes. Before making any changes to the portfolio, Monteo asks Velky about his knowledge of risk budgeting. Velky makes the following statements:

Statement 1.   An optimum risk budget minimizes total risk.
Statement 2.   Risk budgeting decomposes total portfolio risk into its constituent parts.
Statement 3.   An asset allocation is optimal from a risk-budgeting perspective when the ratio of excess return to marginal contribution to risk is different for all assets in the portfolio.

Monteo meets with a third client, Jayanta Chaterji, an individual investor. Monteo and Chaterji discuss mean–variance optimization. Chaterji expresses concern about using the output of MVOs for two reasons:

Criticism 1: The asset allocations are highly sensitive to changes in the model inputs.
Criticism 2: The asset allocations tend to be highly dispersed across all available asset classes.

Monteo and Chaterji also discuss other approaches to asset allocation. Chaterji tells Monteo that he understands the factor-based approach to asset allocation to have two key characteristics:

Characteristic 1.   The factors commonly used in the factor-based approach generally have low correlations with the market and with each other.

Characteristic 2.   The factors commonly used in the factor-based approach are typically different from the fundamental or structural factors used in multifactor models.

Monteo concludes the meeting with Chaterji after sharing his views on the factor-based approach.

9.   Based on Exhibit 1 and the risk aversion coefficient, the preferred asset allocation for Perkins is:
   A.   Asset Allocation A.
   B.   Asset Allocation B.
   C.   Asset Allocation C.

10.   In their discussion of the asset classes that Velky is interested in adding to the VP portfolio, Monteo should tell Velky that:
   A.   these asset classes can be readily diversified to eliminate idiosyncratic risk.
   B.   indexes are available for these asset classes that do an outstanding job of representing the performance characteristics of the asset classes.
   C.   the risk and return characteristics associated with actual investment vehicles for these asset classes are typically significantly different from the characteristics of the asset classes themselves.

11.   Which of Velky's statements about risk budgeting is correct?
   A.   Statement 1
   B.   Statement 2
   C.   Statement 3

12.   Which of Chaterji's criticisms of MVO is/are valid?
   A.   Only Criticism 1
   B.   Only Criticism 2
   C.   Both Criticism 1 and Criticism 2

13.   Which of the characteristics put forth by Chaterji to describe the factor-based approach is/are correct?
   A.   Only Characteristic 1
   B.   Only Characteristic 2
   C.   Both Characteristic 1 and Characteristic 2

14.   John Tomb is an investment advisor at an asset management firm. He is developing an asset allocation for James Youngmall, a client of the firm. Tomb considers two possible allocations for Youngmall. Allocation A consists of four asset classes: cash, US bonds, US equities, and global equities. Allocation B includes these same four asset classes, as well as global bonds. Youngmall has a relatively low risk tolerance with a risk aversion coefficient (λ) of 7. Tomb runs mean–variance optimization (MVO) to maximize the following utility function to determine the preferred allocation for Youngmall:

$$U_m = E(R_m) - 0.005\lambda\sigma_m^2$$

The resulting MVO statistics for the two asset allocations are presented in Exhibit 1.

EXHIBIT 1   MVO Portfolio Statistics

	Allocation A	Allocation B
Expected return	6.7%	5.9%
Expected standard deviation	11.9%	10.7%

Determine which allocation in Exhibit 1 Tomb should recommend to Youngmall. **Justify** your response.

Determine which allocation in Exhibit 1 Tomb should recommend to Youngmall. (circle one)

Allocation A	Allocation B

Justify your response.

15. Walker Patel is a portfolio manager at an investment management firm. After successfully implementing mean–variance optimization (MVO), he wants to apply reverse optimization to his portfolio. For each asset class in the portfolio, Patel obtains market capitalization data, betas computed relative to a global market portfolio, and expected returns. This information, along with the MVO asset allocation results, are presented in Exhibit 1.

EXHIBIT 1   Asset Class Data and MVO Asset Allocation Results

Asset Class	Market Cap (trillions)	Beta	Expected Returns	MVO Asset Allocation
Cash	$4.2	0.0	2.0%	10%
US bonds	$26.8	0.5	4.5%	20%
US equities	$22.2	1.4	8.6%	35%
Global equities	$27.5	1.7	10.5%	20%
Global bonds	$27.1	0.6	4.7%	15%
Total	$107.8			

The risk-free rate is 2.0%, and the global market risk premium is 5.5%.
Contrast, using the information provided above, the results of a reverse optimization approach with that of the MVO approach for each of the following:
   i.   The asset allocation mix
   ii. The values of the expected returns for US equities and global bonds
Justify your response.

16. Viktoria Johansson is newly appointed as manager of ABC Corporation's pension fund. The current market value of the fund's assets is $10 billion, and the present value of the fund's liabilities is $8.5 billion. The fund has historically been managed using an asset-only approach, but Johansson recommends to ABC's board of directors that they adopt a liability-relative approach, specifically the hedging/return-seeking portfolios approach.

Johansson assumes that the returns of the fund's liabilities are driven by changes in the returns of index-linked government bonds. Exhibit 1 presents three potential asset allocation choices for the fund.

EXHIBIT 1   Potential Asset Allocations Choices for ABC Corp's Pension Fund

Asset Class	Allocation 1	Allocation 2	Allocation 3
Cash	15%	5%	0%
Index-linked government bonds	70%	15%	85%
Corporate bonds	0%	30%	5%
Equities	15%	50%	10%
Portfolio Statistics			
Expected return	3.4%	6.2%	3.6%
Expected standard deviation	7.0%	12.0%	8.5%

Determine which asset allocation in Exhibit 1 would be *most appropriate* for Johansson given her recommendation. **Justify** your response.

Determine which asset allocation in Exhibit 1 would be *most appropriate* for Johansson given her recommendation.
(circle one)

           Allocation 1   Allocation 2   Allocation 3

Justify your response.

The following information relates to Questions 17 and 18

Mike and Kerry Armstrong are a married couple who recently retired with total assets of $8 million. The Armstrongs meet with their financial advisor, Brent Abbott, to discuss three of their financial goals during their retirement.

Goal 1: An 85% chance of purchasing a vacation home for $5 million in five years.

Goal 2: A 99% chance of being able to maintain their current annual expenditures of $100,000 for the next 10 years, assuming annual inflation of 3% from Year 2 onward.

Goal 3: A 75% chance of being able to donate $10 million to charitable foundations in 25 years.

Abbott suggests using a goals-based approach to construct a portfolio. He develops a set of sub-portfolio modules, presented in Exhibit 1. Abbott suggests investing any excess capital in Module A.

EXHIBIT 1   "Highest Probability- and Horizon-Adjusted Return" Sub-Portfolio Modules under
Different Horizon and Probability Scenarios

Portfolio Characteristics	A	B	C	D
Expected return	6.5%	7.9%	8.5%	8.8%
Expected volatility	6.0%	7.7%	8.8%	9.7%
	Annualized Minimum Expectation Returns			
Time Horizon	5 Years			
Required Success				
99%	0.3%	−0.1%	−0.7%	−1.3%
85%	3.7%	4.3%	4.4%	4.3%
75%	4.7%	5.6%	5.8%	5.9%
Time Horizon	10 Years			
Required Success				
99%	2.1%	2.2%	2.0%	1.7%
85%	4.5%	5.4%	5.6%	5.6%
75%	5.2%	6.3%	6.6%	6.7%
Time Horizon	25 Years			
Required Success				
99%	3.7%	4.3%	4.4%	4.3%
85%	5.3%	6.3%	6.7%	6.8%
75%	5.7%	6.9%	7.3%	7.5%

17. **Select**, for each of Armstrong's three goals, which sub-portfolio module from Exhibit 1
Abbott should choose in constructing a portfolio. **Justify** each selection.

Select, for each of Armstrong's three goals, which sub-portfolio module from Exhibit 1 Abbott should
choose in constructing a portfolio.
(circle one module for each goal)

Goal 1	Goal 2	Goal 3
Module A	Module A	Module A
Module B	Module B	Module B
Module C	Module C	Module C
Module D	Module D	Module D

Justify each selection.

18. **Construct** the overall goals-based asset allocation for the Armstrongs given their three goals and Abbott's suggestion for investing any excess capital. **Show** your calculations.

Construct the overall goals-based asset allocation for the Armstrongs given their three goals and Abbott's suggestion for investing any excess capital.

(insert the percentage of the total assets to be invested in each module)

Module A	Module B	Module C	Module D

Show your calculations.

CHAPTER 7

ASSET ALLOCATION WITH REAL-WORLD CONSTRAINTS

Peter Mladina
Brian J. Murphy, CFA
Mark Ruloff, FSA, EA, CERA

LEARNING OUTCOMES

The candidate should be able to:

- discuss asset size, liquidity needs, time horizon, and regulatory or other considerations as constraints on asset allocation;
- discuss tax considerations in asset allocation and rebalancing;
- recommend and justify revisions to an asset allocation given change(s) in investment objectives and/or constraints;
- discuss the use of short-term shifts in asset allocation;
- identify behavioral biases that arise in asset allocation and recommend methods to overcome them.

1. INTRODUCTION

This chapter illustrates ways in which the asset allocation process must be adapted to accommodate specific asset owner circumstances and constraints. It addresses adaptations to the asset allocation inputs given an asset owner's asset size, liquidity, and time horizon as well as external constraints that may affect the asset allocation choice (Section 2). We also discuss the ways in which taxes influence the asset allocation process for the taxable investor (Section 3). In addition, we discuss the circumstances that should trigger a re-evaluation of the long-term strategic asset allocation (Section 4), when and how an asset owner might want to make short-term shifts in asset allocation (Section 5), and how innate investor behaviors can interfere with successful long-term planning for the investment portfolio (Section 6). Throughout the chapter, we illustrate the application of these concepts using a series of hypothetical investors.

2. CONSTRAINTS IN ASSET ALLOCATION

General asset allocation principles assume that all asset owners have equal ability to access the entirety of the investment opportunity set, and that it is merely a matter of finding that combination of asset classes that best meets the wants, needs, and obligations of the asset owner. In practice, however, it is not so simple. An asset owner must consider a number of constraints when modeling and choosing among asset allocation alternatives. Some of the most important are asset size, liquidity needs, taxes, and time horizon. Moreover, regulatory and other external considerations may influence the investment opportunity set or the optimal asset allocation decision.

2.1. Asset Size

The size of an asset owner's portfolio has implications for asset allocation. It may limit the opportunity set—the asset classes accessible to the asset owner—by virtue of the scale needed to invest successfully in certain asset classes or by the availability of investment vehicles necessary to implement the asset allocation.

Economies and diseconomies of scale are perhaps the most important factors relevant to understanding asset size as a constraint. The size of an asset owner's investment pool may be too small—or too large—to capture the returns of certain asset classes or strategies efficiently. Asset owners with larger portfolios can generally consider a broader set of asset classes and strategies. On the one hand, they are more likely to have sufficient governance capacity— sophistication and staff resources—to develop the required knowledge base for the more complex asset classes and investment vehicles. They also have sufficient size to build a diversified portfolio of investment strategies, many of which have substantial minimum investment requirements. On the other hand, some asset owners may have portfolios that are *too* large; their desired minimum investment may exhaust the capacity of active external investment managers in certain asset classes and strategies. Although "too large" and "too small" are not rigidly defined, the following example illustrates the difficulty of investing a very large portfolio. Consider an asset owner with an investment portfolio of US$25 billion who is seeking to make a 5% investment in global small-cap stocks:

- The median total market capitalization of the stocks in the S&P Global SmallCap is approximately US$555 million.
- Assume a small-cap manager operates a 50-stock portfolio and is willing to own 3% of the market cap of any one of its portfolio companies. Their average position size would be US $17 million, and an effective level of assets under management (AUM) would be on the order of US$850 million. Beyond that level, the manager may be forced to expand the portfolio beyond 50 stocks or to hold position sizes greater than 3% of a company's market cap, which could then create liquidity issues for the manager.
- Now, our US$25 billion fund is looking to allocate US$1.25 billion to small-cap stocks (US$25 billion × 5%). They want to diversify this allocation across three or four active managers—a reasonable allocation of governance resources in the context of all of the

fund's investment activities. The average allocation per manager is approximately US$300 to US$400 million, which would constitute between 35% and 50% of each manager's AUM. This exposes both the asset owner and the investment manager to an undesirable level of operational risk.

Although many large asset owners have found effective ways to implement a small-cap allocation, this example illustrates some of the issues associated with managing a large asset pool. These include such practical considerations as the number of investment managers that might need to be hired to fulfill an investment allocation and the ability of the asset owner to identify and monitor the required number of managers.

Research has shown that investment managers tend to incur certain disadvantages from increasing scale: Growth in AUM leads to larger trade sizes, incurring greater price impact; capital inflows may cause active investment managers to pursue ideas outside of their core investment theses; and organizational hierarchies may slow down decision-making and reduce incentives.[1] Asset *owners,* however, are found to have *increasing* returns to scale, as discussed below.

A study of pension plan size and performance (using data spanning 1990–2008) found that large defined benefit plans outperformed smaller ones by 45–50 basis points per year on a risk-adjusted basis.[2] The gains are derived from a combination of cost savings related to internal management, a greater ability to negotiate fees with external managers, and the ability to support larger allocations to private equity and real estate investments. As fund size increases, the "per participant" costs of a larger governance infrastructure decline and the plan sponsor can allocate resources away from such asset classes as small-cap stocks, which are sensitive to diseconomies of scale, to such other areas as private equity funds or co-investments where they are more likely to realize scale-related benefits.

Whereas owners of large asset pools may achieve these operating efficiencies, scale may also impose obstacles related to the liquidity and trading costs of the underlying asset. Above some size, it becomes difficult to deploy capital effectively in certain active investment strategies. As illustrated in Exhibit 1, owners of very large portfolios may face size constraints in allocating to active equity strategies. The studies referenced earlier noted that these asset owners frequently choose to invest passively in developed equity markets where their size inhibits alpha potential. The asset owner's finite resources can then be allocated instead toward such strategies as private equity, hedge funds, and infrastructure, where their scale and resources provide a competitive advantage.

EXHIBIT 1   Asset Size and Investor Constraints

Asset Class	Investor Constraints by Size
• Cash equivalents and money market funds • Large-cap developed market equity • Small-cap developed market equity • Emerging market equity	No size constraints. Generally accessible to large and small asset owners, although the very large asset owner may be constrained in the amount of assets allocated to certain active strategies and managers.

---

[1] See Stein (2002); Chen, Hong, Huang, and Kubik (2004); and Pollet and Wilson (2008).
[2] See Dyck and Pomorski (2011). The median plan in this study was just over US$2 billion. The 25th percentile plan was US$780 million, and the 75th percentile plan was US$6.375 billion.

Asset Class	Investor Constraints by Size
• Developed market sovereign bonds • Investment-grade bonds • Non-investment-grade bonds • Private real estate equity	Generally accessible to large and small asset owners, although to achieve prudent diversification, smaller asset owners may need to implement via a commingled vehicle.
Alternative Investments • Hedge funds • Private debt • Private equity • Infrastructure • Timberland and farmland	May be accessible to large and small asset owners, although if offered as private investment vehicles, there may be legal minimum qualifications that exclude smaller asset owners. The ability to successfully invest in these asset classes may also be limited by the asset owner's level of investment understanding/expertise. Prudent diversification may require that smaller asset owners implement via a commingled vehicle, such as a fund of funds, or an ancillary access channel, such as a liquid alternatives vehicle or an alternatives ETF. For very large funds, the allocation may be constrained by the number of funds available.

Even in these strategies, very large asset owners may be constrained by scale. In smaller or less liquid markets, can a large asset owner invest enough that the exposure contributes a material benefit to the broader portfolio? For example, a sovereign wealth fund or large public pension plan may not find enough attractive hedge fund managers to fulfill their desired allocation to hedge funds. True alpha is rare, limiting the opportunity set. Asset owners who find that they have to split their mandate into many smaller pieces may end up with an index-like portfolio but with high active management fees; one manager's active bets may cancel out those of another active manager. A manager mix with no true alpha becomes index-like because the uncompensated, idiosyncratic return variation is diversified away. A much smaller allocation may be achievable, but it may be too small to meaningfully affect the risk and return characteristics of the overall portfolio. More broadly, a very large size makes it more difficult to benefit from opportunistic investments in smaller niche markets or from skilled investment managers who have a small set of unique ideas or concentrated bets. No hard and fast rules exist to determine whether a particular asset owner is too small or too large to effectively access an asset class. Greater governance resources more commonly found among owners of larger asset pools create the capacity to pursue the more complex investment opportunities, but the asset owner may still need to find creative ways to implement the desired allocation. Each asset owner has a unique set of knowledge and constraints that will influence the opportunity set.

Smaller asset owners (typically institutions with less than US$500 million in assets, and private wealth investors with less than US$25 million in assets) also find that their opportunity set may be constrained by the size of their investment portfolio. This is primarily a function of the more limited governance infrastructure typical of smaller asset owners: They may be too small to adequately diversify across the range of asset classes and investment managers or may have staffing constraints (insufficient asset size to justify a dedicated internal staff). Complex strategies may be beyond the reach of asset owners that have chosen not to develop investment expertise internally or where the oversight committee lacks individuals with sufficient investment understanding. In some asset classes and strategies, commingled investment vehicles can be used to achieve the needed diversification, provided the governing documents do not prohibit their use.

Access to other asset classes and strategies—private equity, private real estate, hedge funds, and infrastructure—may still be constrained for smaller asset owners. The commingled vehicles through which these strategies are offered typically require high minimum investments. For successful private equity and hedge fund managers, in particular, minimum investments can be in the tens of millions of (US) dollars, even for funds of funds.

Regulatory restrictions can also impose a size constraint. In the United Kingdom, for example, an asset owner in a private investment vehicle must qualify as an elective professional client, meaning they must meet two of the following three conditions:

1. The client has carried out transactions, in significant size, on the relevant market at an average frequency of 10 per quarter over the previous four quarters.
2. The size of the client's financial instrument portfolio exceeds €500,000.
3. The client works or has worked in the financial sector for at least one year in a professional position, which requires knowledge of the transactions or services envisaged.

In the United States, investors must be either accredited or qualified purchasers to invest in many private equity and hedge fund vehicles. To be a qualified purchaser, a natural person must have at least US$5 million in investments, a company must have at least US$25 million in investable assets, and an investment manager must have at least US$25 million under management. In Hong Kong SAR, the Securities and Futures Commission requires that an investor must meet the qualifications of a "Professional Investor" to invest in certain categories of assets. A Professional Investor is generally defined as a trust with total assets of not less than HK$40 million, an individual with a portfolio not less than HK$8 million, or a corporation or partnership with a portfolio not less than HK$8 million or total assets of not less than HK$40 million. The size constraints related to these asset classes suggest that smaller asset owners have real challenges achieving an effective private equity or hedge fund allocation.

Asset size as a constraint is often a more acute issue for individual investors than institutional asset owners. Wealthy families may pool assets through such vehicles as family limited partnerships, investment companies, fund of funds, or other forms of commingled vehicles to hold their assets. These pooled vehicles can then access investment vehicles, asset classes, and strategies that individual family members may not have portfolios large enough to access on their own.

Where Asset Size Constrains Investment Opportunity

As of early 2016, the 10 largest sovereign wealth funds globally each exceed US$400 billion in assets. For a fund of this size, a 5% allocation to hedge funds (the average sovereign wealth fund allocation) would imply US$20 *billion* to be deployed. The global hedge fund industry manages approximately US$2.8 trillion in total; 73% of the funds manage less than US$100 million. The remaining 27% of the funds (roughly 3,000) manage 72% of the industry's AUM; their implied average AUM is therefore US$670 million. If we assume that the asset owner would want to be no more than 20% of a firm's AUM, we can infer that the average investment might be approximately US$130 million. With US$20 billion to deploy, the fund would need to invest with nearly 150 funds to achieve a 5% allocation to hedge funds.

Sources: Sovereign Wealth Fund Institute, BarclayHedge, Eurekahedge (2016).

EXAMPLE 1   Asset Size Constraints in Asset Allocation

1. Akkarat Aromdee is the recently retired president of Alpha Beverage, a producer and distributor of energy drinks throughout Southeast Asia. Upon retiring, the company provided a lump sum retirement payment of THB880,000,000 (equivalent to €20 million), which was rolled over to a tax-deferred individual retirement savings plan. Aside from these assets, Aromdee owns company stock worth about THB70,000,000. The stock is infrequently traded. He has consulted with an investment adviser, and they are reviewing the following asset allocation proposal:

Global equities	40%
Global high-yield bonds	15%
Domestic intermediate bonds	30%
Hedge funds	10%
Private equity	5%

Describe asset size constraints that Aromdee might encounter in implementing this asset allocation. Discuss possible means to address them.

2. The CAF$40 billion Government Petroleum Fund of Caflandia is overseen by a nine-member Investment Committee. The chief investment officer has a staff with sector heads in global equities, global bonds, real estate, hedge funds, and derivatives. The majority of assets are managed by outside investment managers. The Investment Committee, of which you are a member, approves the asset allocation policy and makes manager selection decisions. Staff has recommended an increase in the private equity allocation from its current 0% to 15%, to be implemented over the next 12 to 36 months. The head of global equities will oversee the implementation of the private equity allocation.

   Given the asset size of the fund, formulate a set of questions regarding the feasibility of this recommendation that you would like staff to address at the next Investment Committee meeting.

3. The Courneuve University Endowment has US$250 million in assets. The current allocation is 65% global large-capitalization stocks and 35% high-quality bonds, with a duration target of 5.0 years. The University has adopted a 5% spending policy. University enrollment is stable and expected to remain so. A capital spending initiative of US$100 million for new science buildings in the next three to seven years is being discussed, but it has not yet been approved. The University has no dedicated investment staff and makes limited use of external resources. Investment recommendations are formulated by the University's treasurer and approved by the Investment Committee, composed entirely of external board members.

The new president of the University has stated that he feels the current policy is overly restrictive, and he would like to see a more diversified program that takes advantage of the types of investment strategies used by large endowment programs. Choosing from among the following asset classes, propose a set of asset classes to be considered in the revised asset allocation. Justify your response.

- Cash equivalents and money market funds
- Large-cap developed market equity
- Small-cap developed market equity
- Emerging market equity
- Developed market sovereign bonds
- Investment-grade bonds

- Non-investment-grade bonds
- Private real estate equity
- Hedge funds
- Private debt
- Private equity

Solution to 1: With a THB88 million (€2 million) allocation to hedge funds and a THB44 million (€1 million) allocation to private equity funds, Aromdee may encounter restrictions on his eligibility to invest in the private investment vehicles typically used for hedge fund and private equity investment. To the extent he is eligible to invest in hedge funds and/or private equity funds, a fund-of-funds or similar commingled arrangement would be essential to achieving an appropriate level of diversification. Additionally, it is essential that he and his adviser develop the necessary level of expertise to invest in these alternative assets. To achieve a prudent level of diversification, the allocation to global high-yield bonds would most likely need to be accomplished via a commingled investment vehicle.

Solution to 2: Questions regarding the feasibility of the recommendation include the following:

- How many private equity funds do you expect to invest in to achieve the 15% allocation to private equity?
- What is the anticipated average allocation to each fund?
- Are there a sufficient number of high-quality private equity funds willing to accept an allocation of that size?
- What expertise exists at the staff or board level to conduct due diligence on private equity investment funds?
- What resources does the staff have to oversee the increased allocation to private equity?

Solution to 3: Asset size and limited governance resources are significant constraints on the investment opportunity set available to the Endowment. The asset allocation should emphasize large and liquid investments, such as cash equivalents, developed and emerging market equity, and sovereign and investment-grade bonds. Some small portion of assets, however, could be allocated to commingled investments in real estate, private equity, or hedge funds. Given the University's limited staff resources, it is necessary to ensure that the board members have the level of expertise necessary to select and monitor these more complex asset classes. The Endowment might also consider engaging an outside expert to advise on investment activities in these asset classes.

2.2. Liquidity

Two dimensions of liquidity must be considered when developing an asset-appropriate allocation solution: the liquidity needs of the asset owner and the liquidity characteristics of the asset classes in the opportunity set. Integrating the two dimensions is an essential element of successful investment planning.

The need for liquidity in an investment portfolio will vary greatly by asset owner and by the goals the assets are set aside to achieve. For example, a bank will typically have a very large portfolio supporting its day-to-day operations. That portfolio is likely to experience very high turnover and a very high need for liquidity; therefore, the investment portfolio must hold high-quality, very short-term, and highly liquid assets.

The same bank may have another designated investment pool one level removed from operating assets. Although the liquidity requirements for this portfolio may be lower, the investments most likely feature a high degree of liquidity—a substantial allocation to investment-grade bonds, perhaps with a slight extension of maturity. For its longer-term investment portfolio, the bank may choose to allocate some portion of its portfolio to less liquid investments. The opportunity set for each portfolio will be constrained by applicable banking laws and regulations.

Long-term investors, such as sovereign wealth funds and endowment funds, can generally exploit illiquidity premiums available in such asset classes as private equity, real estate, and infrastructure investments. However, pension plans may be limited in the amount of illiquidity they can absorb. For example, a frozen pension plan may anticipate the possibility of eliminating its pension obligation completely by purchasing a group annuity and relinquishing the responsibility for making pension payments to an insurance company. If there is a significant probability that the company will take this step in the near term, liquidity of plan assets will become a primary concern; and if there is a substantial allocation to illiquid assets, the plan sponsor may be unable to execute the desired annuity purchase transaction.

Liquidity needs must also consider the particular circumstances and financial strength of the asset owner and what resources they may have beyond those held in the investment portfolio. The following examples illustrate this point:

- A university must consider its prospects for future enrollments and the extent to which it relies on tuition to meet operating needs. If the university experiences a significant drop in enrollment, perhaps because of a poor economic environment, or takes on a new capital improvement project, the asset allocation policy for the endowment should reflect the increased probability of higher outflows to support university operations.
- A foundation whose mission supports medical research in a field in which a break-through appears imminent may desire a higher level of liquidity to fund critical projects than would a foundation that supports ongoing community efforts.
- An insurance company whose business is predominantly life or auto insurance, where losses are actuarially predictable, can absorb more liquidity risk than a property/casualty reinsurer whose losses are subject to unpredictable events, such as natural disasters.
- A family with several children nearing college-age will have higher liquidity needs than a couple of the same age and circumstances with no children.

When assessing the appropriateness of any given asset class for a given asset owner, it is wise to evaluate potential liquidity needs in the context of an extreme market stress event. The market losses of the 2008–2009 global financial crisis were extreme. Simultaneously, other forces exacerbated investors' distress: Many university endowments were called upon to provide an increased level of operating support; insurers dipped into reserves to offset operating losses; community foundations found their beneficiaries in even greater need of financial support; and some individual investors experienced setbacks that caused them to move, if only temporarily, from being net contributors to net spenders of financial wealth. A successful asset allocation effort will stress the proposed allocation; it will anticipate, where possible, the likely behavior of other facets of the saving/spending equation during times of stress.

It is also important to consider the intersection of asset class and investor liquidity in the context of the asset owner's governance capacity. Although the mission of the organization or trust may allow for a certain level of illiquidity, if those responsible for the oversight of the investment program do not have the mental fortitude or discipline to maintain course through the crisis, illiquid and less liquid investments are unlikely to produce the rewards typically expected of these exposures. Although rates of return may be mean-reverting, wealth is not. Losses resulting from panic selling during times of stress become permanent losses; there are fewer assets left to earn returns in a post-crash recovery.

The Case of Vanishing Liquidity

In the global financial crisis of 2008–2009, many investors learned painful truths about liquidity. When most needed—whether to rebalance or to meet spending obligations—it can evaporate. As investors liquidated their most liquid assets to meet financial obligations (or to raise cash in fear of further market declines), the remaining less liquid assets in their portfolios became an ever-larger percentage of the portfolio. Many investors were forced to sell private partnership interests on the secondary market at steeply discounted prices. Others defaulted on outstanding private fund capital commitments by refusing to honor future obligations.

Similarly, illiquidity became a substantial problem during the Asian currency crisis of 1997–1998 and again with the Russian debt default and Long-Term Capital Management (LTCM) crisis of 1998. In the following paragraphs, we describe several "liquidity crises" that are often used in stress testing asset allocation choices.

The Asian Currency Crisis of 1997

In the spring of 1997, Thailand spent billions to defend the Thai baht against speculative attacks, finally capitulating and devaluing the baht in July 1997. This triggered a series of moves throughout the region to defend currencies against speculators. Ultimately, these efforts were unsuccessful and many countries abandoned the effort and allowed their currencies to float freely. The Philippines, Indonesia, and South Korea abandoned their pegs against the US dollar. On 27 October 1997, rattled by the currency crisis, Asian and European markets declined sharply in advance of the opening of the US markets. The S&P 500 declined nearly 7%, and trading on US stock markets was suspended.

The Russian Debt/LTCM Crisis of August 1998

On 17 August 1998, the Russian government defaulted on its short-term debt. This unprecedented default of a sovereign debtor roiled the global bond markets. A global flight-to-quality ensued, which caused credit spreads to widen and liquidity to evaporate. Highly levered investors experienced significant losses. Long-Term Capital Management, with reported notional exposure of over US$125 billion (a 25-to-1 leverage ratio), exacerbated these price declines as they faced their own liquidity crisis and were forced to liquidate large relative value, distressed, convertible arbitrage, merger arbitrage, and equity positions. Ultimately, the magnitude of the liquidity squeeze for LTCM and the risk of potential disruption to global markets caused the New York branch of the Federal Reserve Bank to orchestrate a disciplined, structured bailout of the LTCM fund.

Financial markets are increasingly linked across borders and asset classes; as a result, changes in liquidity conditions in one country can directly affect liquidity conditions elsewhere. These linkages do improve access to financing and capital markets, but they also show that a liquidity problem in one part of the world can ripple across the globe—increasing volatility, creating higher execution costs for investors, and possibly leading to a reduction in credit availability and a decline in economic activity.

EXAMPLE 2   Liquidity Constraints in Asset Allocation

The Frentel Furniture Pension Fund has £200 million frozen in a defined benefit pension plan that is 85% funded. The plan has a provision that allows employees to elect a lump sum distribution of their pension benefit at retirement. The company is strong financially and is committed to fully funding the pension obligations over time. However, they also want to minimize cash contributions to the plan. Few governance resources are allocated to the pension fund, and there is no dedicated staff for pension investment activities. The current asset allocation is as shown:

Global equities	20%
Private equity	10%
Real estate	10%
Infrastructure	5%
Hedge funds	15%
Bonds	40%

The company expects to reduce their employee headcount sometime in the next three to five years, and they are tentatively planning incentives to encourage employees to retire early.

Discuss the appropriateness of the current asset allocation strategy for the pension fund, including benefits and concerns.

Solution: In addition to the size constraints a £200 million (≈US$250 million) plan faces when attempting to invest in real estate, private equity, infrastructure, and hedge funds, the likelihood of early retirement incentives and lump-sum distribution requests in the next three to five years indicates a need for increased sensitivity to liquidity concerns. Investments in private equity, infrastructure, and real estate may be unsuitable for the plan given their less liquid nature. Although hedge fund investments would likely be accessible via a commingled vehicle, the liquidity of the commingled vehicle should be evaluated to determine if it is consistent with the liquidity needs of the plan.

2.3. Time Horizon

An asset owner's time horizon is a critical constraint that must be considered in any asset allocation exercise. A liability to be paid at a given point in the future or a goal to be funded by a specified date each define the asset owner's horizon, thus becoming a basic input to the asset allocation solution. The changing composition of the asset owner's assets and liabilities must also be considered. As time progresses, the character of both *assets* (human capital) and *liabilities* changes.

Changing Human Capital

When asset allocation considers such extended portfolio assets as human capital, the optimal allocation of financial capital can change through time (Bodie, Merton, and Samuelson 1992). Assuming no change in the investor's utility function, as human capital—with its predominately bond-like risk—declines over time, the asset allocation for financial capital would reflect an increasing allocation to bonds. This is a prime example of how time horizon can influence asset allocation.

Changing Character of Liabilities

The changing character of liabilities through time will also affect the asset allocation aligned to fund those liabilities.

As an example, the term structure of liabilities changes as they approach maturity. A pension benefit program is a simple way to illustrate this point. When the employee base is young and retirements are far into the future, the liability can be hedged with long-term bonds. As the employee base ages and prospective retirements are not so far into the future, the liability is more comparable to intermediate- or even short-term bonds. When retirements are imminent, the structure of the liabilities can be characterized as cash-like, and an optimal asset allocation would also have cash-like characteristics.

Similarly, the overall profile of an individual investor's liabilities changes with the progression of time, particularly for investors with finite investment horizons. Nearer-term goals and liabilities move from partially funded to fully funded, while other, longer-term goals and liabilities move progressively closer to funding. As the relative weights of the goals to be funded shift and the time horizon associated with certain goals shortens, the aggregate asset allocation must be adapted if it is to remain aligned with the individual's goals.

Time horizon is also likely to affect the manner in which an investor prioritizes certain goals and liabilities. This will influence the desired risk profile of the assets aligned to fund them. Consider a 75-year-old retired investor with two goals:

1. Fund consumption needs through age 95
2. Fund consumption needs from age 95 through age 105

He most likely assigns a much higher priority to funding goal 1, given the lower probability that he will live beyond age 95.[3] Let's also assume that he has sufficient assets to fund goal 1 and to partially fund goal 2. The higher priority assigned to goal 1 indicates he is less willing to take risk, and this sub-portfolio will be invested more conservatively. Now consider goal 2: Given the low probability of living past 95 and the fact that he does not currently have sufficient assets to fund that goal, the sub-portfolio assigned to goal 2 is likely to have a more growth-oriented asset allocation. The priority of a given goal can change as the investor's time horizon shortens—or lengthens.

Consider the hypothetical investors Ivy and Charles Lee from the chapter "Introduction to Asset Allocation." Ivy is a 54-year-old life science entrepreneur. Charles is a 55-year-old orthopedic surgeon. They have two unmarried children aged 25 (Deborah) and 18 (David). Deborah has a daughter with physical limitations. Four goals have been identified for the Lees:

1. Lifestyle/future consumption needs
2. College education for son David, 18 years old
3. Charitable gift to a local art museum in 5 years
4. Special needs trust for their granddaughter, to be funded at the death of Charles

The lifestyle/consumption goal is split into three components: required minimum consumption requirements (a worst-case scenario of reduced lifestyle), baseline consumption needs (maintaining current standard of living), and aspirational consumption needs (an improved standard of living). At age 54, the risk preferences assigned to these goals might look something like the following:

Lifestyle Goals	Risk Preference	Asset Allocation	Sub-Portfolio as % of Total*
Required minimum	Conservative	100% bonds and cash	65%
Baseline	Moderate	60% equities/40% bonds	10%
Aspirational	Aggressive	100% equities	4%
College education	Conservative	100% bonds and cash	1%
Charitable gift (aspirational)	Aggressive	100% equities	5%
Special needs trust	Moderate	60% equities/40% bonds	15%
Aggregate portfolio		≈25% equities/75% bonds and cash	100%

* The present value of each goal as a proportion of the total portfolio.

The asset allocation for the total portfolio aggregates the asset allocations for each of the goal-aligned sub-portfolios, weighted by the present value of each goal. For the Lees, this is an overall asset allocation of about 25% equities and 75% bonds and cash. (Each goal is discounted to its present value by expected return of its respective goal-aligned sub-portfolio.)

Move forward 20 years. The Lees are now in their mid-70s, and their life expectancy is about 12 years. Their son has completed his college education and is successfully established in his own career. The charitable gift has been made. These two goals have been realized.

---

[3] A 75-year-old US American male has a life expectancy of 11.1 years, per the Social Security Administration's 2014 "Actuarial Life Tables," https://www.ssa.gov/oact/STATS/table4c6_2014.html (Accessed 22 Nov 2018).

The assets needed to fund the baseline consumption goal are significantly reduced because fewer future consumption years need to be funded. The special needs trust for their granddaughter remains a high priority. Although the Lee's risk preferences for these goals have not changed, the overall asset allocation *will* change because the total portfolio is an aggregated mix of the remaining goal-aligned sub-portfolios, weighted by their current present values:

Lifestyle Goals	Risk Preference	Asset Allocation	Sub-Portfolio as % of Total*
Required minimum	Conservative	100% bonds and cash	54%
Baseline	Moderate	60% equities/40% bonds	9%
Aspirational	Aggressive	100% equities	3%
Special needs trust	Moderate	60% equities/40% bonds	34%
Aggregate portfolio		≈30% equities/70% bonds and cash	100%

* The present value of each goal as a proportion of the total portfolio. The implied assumption is that current assets are sufficient to fund all goals, provided the Lees adopt an aggressive asset allocation strategy for the aspirational and charitable gifting goals. If the value of current assets exceeds the present value of all goals, the Lees would have greater flexibility to adopt a lower risk preference for some or all goals.

Although for ease of illustration our example assumed the Lee's risk preferences remained the same, this is not likely to be the case in the real world. Required minimum and baseline consumption goals would remain very important; there is less flexibility to withstand losses caused by either reduced earnings potential or lower likelihood of the market regaining lost ground within the shorter horizon. The aspirational lifestyle goal is likely to be a much lower priority, and it may have been eliminated altogether. The special needs trust may have a higher (or lower) priority as the needs of the granddaughter and the ability of her parents to provide for her needs after their death become more evident. The preferred asset allocation for each of these goals will shift over the course of the investor's lifetime.

As an investor's time horizon shifts, both human capital and financial market considerations, along with changes in the investor's priorities, will most likely lead to different asset allocation decisions.

EXAMPLE 3   Time Horizon Constraints in Asset Allocation

Akkarat Aromdee, the recently retired president of Alpha Beverage, is 67 years old with a remaining life expectancy of 15 years. Upon his retirement two years ago, he established a charitable foundation and funded it with THB600 million (≈US$17.3 million). The remaining financial assets, THB350 million (≈US$10 million), were transferred to a trust that will allow him to draw a lifetime income. The assets are invested 100% in fixed-income securities, consistent with Aromdee's desire for a high level of certainty in meeting his goals. He is a widower with no children. His consumption needs are estimated at THB20 million annually. Assets remaining in the trust at his death will pass to the charities named in the trust.

While vacationing in Ko Samui, Aromdee met and later married a 45-year-old woman with two teenage children. She has limited financial assets of her own.

Upon returning from his honeymoon, Aromdee meets with his investment adviser. He intends to pay the college expenses of his new stepchildren—THB2 million annually for eight years, beginning five years from now. He would also like to ensure that his portfolio can provide a modest lifetime income for his wife after his death.

Discuss how these changed circumstances are likely to influence Aromdee's asset allocation.

Solution: At the time Aromdee established the trust, the investment horizon was 15 years and his annual consumption expenditures could easily be funded from the trust. His desire to support his new family introduces two new horizons to be considered: In five years, the trust will begin making annual payments of THB2 million to fund college expenses, and the trust will continue to make distributions to his wife after his death, though at a reduced rate. When the trust needed to support only his consumption requirements, a conservative asset allocation was appropriate. However, the payment of college expenses will reduce his margin of safety and the lengthening of the investment horizon suggests that he should consider adding equity-oriented investments to the asset mix to provide for growth in assets over time.

Time Diversification of Risk

In practice, investors often align lower risk/lower return assets with short-term goals and liabilities and higher risk/higher return assets with long-term goals and liabilities. It is generally believed that longer-horizon goals can tolerate the higher volatility associated with higher risk/higher return assets as below average and above average returns even out over time. This is the notion of time diversification.

Mean–variance optimization, typically conducted using a multi-year time horizon, assumes that asset returns follow a random walk; returns in Year X are independent of returns in Year X – 1. Under this baseline assumption, there *is* no reduction in risk with longer time horizons.[4] Although the *probability* of reduced wealth or of a shortfall in funding a goal or liability (based on the mean of the distribution of possible outcomes) may be lower at longer time horizons, the dispersion of possible outcomes widens as the investment horizon expands. Thus, the *magnitude* of potential loss or shortfall can be greater.

Consider the choice of investing US$100,000 in an S&P 500 Index fund with a 10% expected return and 15% standard deviation versus a risk-free asset with a 3% annual return.[5] The table below compares the return of the risk-free asset over various time horizons, with the range of predicted returns for the S&P 500 Index fund at a 95% confidence interval. Although the *mean* return of the distribution of S&P 500 returns exceeds that of the risk-free asset in each time period (thus the notion that the volatility of higher risk, higher return assets evens out over time), the lower boundary of expected S&P 500 returns is less than the initial investment for all periods less than 10 years! The lower boundary of the S&P 500 outcomes does not exceed the ending

[4]See Samuelson (1963) and Samuelson (1969).
[5]This example is drawn from Kritzman (2015).

wealth of the risk-free investment until the investment horizon is extended to 20 years. If the confidence interval is expanded to 99%, the lower boundary of S&P 500 outcomes falls below the initial investment up until and through 20 years!

	Ending Wealth (US$)		
	S&P 500		
	95% Confidence Interval		
	Lower Boundary	**Upper Boundary**	**Risk-Free Asset**
1 year	81,980	147,596	103,000
5 years	83,456	310,792	115,927
10 years	102,367	657,196	134,392
15 years	133,776	130,4376	155,797
20 years	180,651	2,565,345	180,611

Although one-year returns are largely independent, there is some evidence that risky asset returns can display mean-reverting tendencies over intermediate to longer time horizons. An assumption of mean-reverting risky asset returns would support the conventional arguments for funding long-term goals and liabilities with higher risk/ higher return assets, and it would also support a reduction in the allocation to these riskier assets as the time horizon shortens.

2.4. Regulatory and Other External Constraints

Just as an integrated asset/liability approach to asset allocation is likely to result in a different allocation decision than what might have been selected in an asset-only context, external considerations may also influence the asset allocation decision. Local laws and regulations can have a material effect on an investor's asset allocation decisions.

Pension funds, insurance companies, sovereign wealth funds, and endowments and foundations are each subject to externally imposed constraints that are likely to tilt their asset allocation decision away from what may have been selected in a pure asset/liability context.

2.4.1. Insurance Companies

Unlike pension fund or endowment assets—which are legally distinct from the assets of the sponsoring entity—insurance companies' investment activities are an integral part of their day-to-day operations. Although skilled underwriting may be the focus of the firm as the key to profitability, investment returns are often a material contributor to profits or losses. Regulatory requirements and accounting treatment vary from country to country, but insurers are most often highly focused on matching assets to the projected, probabilistic cash flows of the risks they are underwriting. Fixed-income assets, therefore, are typically the largest component of an insurance company's asset base, and investing with skill in this asset class is a key to competitive pricing and success. In some regions, the relevant accounting treatment may be a book value approach, rendering variability in the market pricing of assets to be a secondary consideration as long as an asset does not have to have its book value written down as "other than temporarily impaired" ("OTTI"). Risk considerations for an insurance company include the need for capital to pay policyholder benefits and other factors that directly influence the company's financial strength ratings. Some of the key considerations are risk-based capital measures, yield, liquidity, the potential for forced liquidation of assets to fund negative claims development, and credit ratings.

Additionally, allocations to certain asset classes are often constrained by a regulator. For example, the maximum limit on equity exposure is often 10%, but it ranges as high as 30% in Switzerland and 50% in Mexico. Israel and Korea impose a limit of 15% on real estate investments.[6] Restrictions on non-publicly traded securities might also limit the allocation to such assets as private equity, for example, and there may also be limits on the allocation to high-yield bonds. Insurance regulators generally set a minimum capital level for each insurer based on that insurer's mix of assets, liabilities, and risk. Many countries are moving to Solvency II regulatory standards designed to harmonize risk-based capital requirements for insurance companies across countries.[7] Asset classes are often treated differently for purposes of determining whether an insurer meets risk-based capital requirements.

2.4.2. Pension Funds

Pension fund asset allocation decisions may be constrained by regulation and influenced by tax rules.[8] Some countries regulate maximum or minimum percentages in certain asset classes. For example, Japanese pension funds must hold a certain minimum percentage of assets in Japanese bonds in order to maintain their tax-exempt status. Canada allows a maximum of 10% of market value invested in any one entity or related entities; Switzerland generally limits real estate investments to 30%; Estonia allows a maximum of 75% of assets invested in public equity with no limit on foreign investments; and Brazil allows a maximum of 70% in public equity with a maximum of 10% in foreign public equity.[9] Ukraine limits bond investments to no more than 40%.

Pension funds are also subject to a wide array of funding, accounting, reporting, and tax constraints that may influence the asset allocation decision. (For example, US public pension funding and public and corporate accounting rules favor equity investments—higher equity allocations support a higher discount rate—and thus lower pension cost. Loss recognition is deferred until later through the smoothing mechanism.) The plan sponsor's appetite for risk is defined in part by these constraints, and the choice among asset allocation alternatives is often influenced by funding and financial statement considerations, such as the anticipated contributions, the volatility of anticipated contributions, or the forecasted pension expense or income under a given asset allocation scenario. The specific constraints vary by jurisdiction, and companies with plans in multiple jurisdictions must satisfy the rules and regulations of each jurisdiction while making sound financial decisions for the organization as a whole.

Exhibit 2 illustrates how funding considerations may affect the asset allocation decision. In this chart, risk is defined as the probability of contributions exceeding some threshold amount. In this case, the risk threshold is specified as the 95th percentile of the present value of contributions—that point on the distribution of possible contributions (using Monte Carlo

---

[6]https://www.oecd.org/finance/private-pensions/Regulation-of-Insurance-Company-and-Pension-Fund-Investment.pdf (September 2015)–accessed 23 November 2018.

[7]Solvency II is an EU legislative program implemented in all 28 member states, including the United Kingdom, in January 2016. It introduces a new, harmonized EU-wide insurance regulatory regime.

[8]Information in this section is based on the OECD "Annual Survey of Investment Regulation of Pension Funds" (2017).

[9]Foreign investment is restricted to MERCOSUR countries for equities (other asset classes are more flexible).

simulation) where the plan sponsor can be 95% certain that contributions will not exceed that amount.

Assume that an allocation of 70% equities/30% aggregate bonds represents the most efficient portfolio for the plan sponsor's desired level of risk in an asset optimization framework. In Exhibit 2, we can see that the 70% equity/30% aggregate bond mix (Portfolio A) is associated with a present value (PV) of expected contributions of approximately US $51 million (y-axis) and a 95% confidence level that contributions will not exceed approximately US$275 million (x-axis)—Portfolio A in Exhibit 2. If the plan sponsor were to shift to longer-duration bonds (from aggregate to long bonds) to better match the duration of liabilities—Portfolio D_1 on Exhibit 2—the PV of expected contributions declines by approximately US$5 million and the 95% confidence threshold improves to approximately US$265 million. In fact, Portfolio D_1 results in nearly the lowest PV of contributions for this plan sponsor. (Note that the vertical axis is ordered from highest contributions at the bottom and lowest contributions at the top, consistent with the notion of lower contributions as a better outcome.)

EXHIBIT 2   Efficient Frontiers Where Risk Is Defined as the Risk of Large Contributions

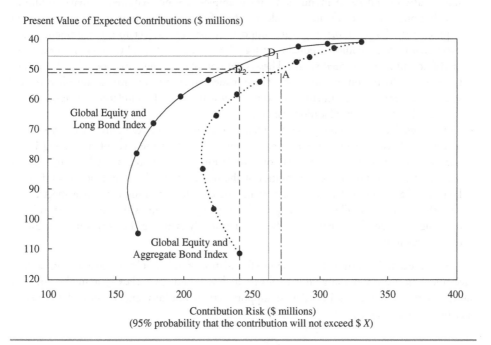

Present Value of Expected Contributions ($ millions)

Contribution Risk ($ millions)
(95% probability that the contribution will not exceed $ X)

Now consider Portfolio D_2, 60% equities/40% long bonds. Reducing the equity exposure from 70% to 60% lowers the contribution risk significantly, with only marginally higher expected PV of contributions than Portfolio A. (A lower equity allocation implies a lower expected rate of return, which increases the PV of contributions. However, the lower equity allocation also reduces the probability that less-than-expected returns will lead to unexpectedly large contributions.) The sponsor that wishes to reduce contribution risk substantially is likely to give serious consideration to moving from Portfolio A to Portfolio D_2.

By iterating through various efficient frontiers using different definitions of risk, the sponsor is able to better understand the risk and reward trade-offs of alternative asset allocation choices. The regulatory or tax constraints on minimum and maximum contributions, or on minimum required funded levels, or other values that are important to the plan sponsor, can be factored into the simulations so the sponsor can better understand how these constraints might affect the risk and reward trade-offs.

2.4.3. Endowments and Foundations

Endowments and foundations are often established with the expectation that they will exist in perpetuity and thus can invest with a long investment horizon. In addition, the sponsoring entity often has more flexibility over payments from the fund than does a pension plan sponsor or insurance company. As a result, endowments and foundations generally can adopt a higher-risk asset allocation than other institutions. However, two categories of externally imposed constraints may influence the asset allocation decisions of an endowment or foundation: tax incentives and credit-worthiness considerations.

- *Tax incentives.* Although some endowments and foundations—US public foundations and some Austrian and Asian foundations, for example—are not required to make minimum distributions, many countries provide tax benefits tied to certain minimum spending requirements. For example, a private foundation may be subject to a requirement that it make charitable expenditures equal to at least 5% of the market value of its assets each year or risk losing its tax-favored status. These spending requirements may be relaxed if certain types of socially responsible investments are made, which can, in turn, create a bias toward socially responsible investments for some endowments and foundations, irrespective of their merits in an asset allocation context.
- *Credit considerations.* Although endowments and foundations typically have a very long investment horizon, sometimes external factors may restrict the level of risk-taking in the portfolio. For example, endowment or foundation assets are often used to support the balance sheet and borrowing capabilities of the university or the foundation organization. Lenders often require that the borrower maintain certain minimum balance sheet ratios. Therefore, the asset allocation adopted by the organization will consider the risks of breaking these bond covenants or otherwise negatively affecting the borrowing capabilities of the organization.

As an example, although a hospital foundation fund would normally have a long investment horizon and the ability to invest in less liquid asset classes, it might limit the allocation to illiquid assets in order to support certain liquidity and balance sheet metrics specified by its lender(s).

2.4.4. Sovereign Wealth Funds

Although every sovereign wealth fund (SWF) is unique with respect to its mission and objectives, some broad generalizations can be made with respect to the external constraints that may affect a fund's asset allocation choices. In general, SWFs are government-owned pools of capital invested on behalf of the peoples of their states or countries, investing with a long-term orientation. They are not generally seeking to defease a set of liabilities or known obligations as is common with pension funds and, to a lesser extent, endowment funds.

The governing entities adopt regulations that constrain the opportunity set for asset allocation. For example, the Korean SWF KIC cannot invest in Korean won-denominated domestic assets;[10] and the Norwegian SWF NBIM is not permitted to invest in any alternative asset class other than real estate, which is limited to no more than 7% of assets.[11] Furthermore, as publicly owned entities, SWFs are typically subject to broad public scrutiny and tend to adopt a lower-risk asset allocation than might otherwise be considered appropriate given their long-term investment horizon in order to avoid reputation risk.

In addition to the broad constraints of asset size, liquidity, time horizon, and regulations, there may be cultural or religious factors which also constrain the asset allocation choices. Environmental, social, and governance (ESG) considerations are becoming increasingly important to institutional and individual investors alike. Sharia law, for example, prohibits investment in any business that has links to pork, alcohol, tobacco, pornography, prostitution, gambling, or weaponry, and it constrains investments in most businesses that operate on interest payments (like major Western banks and mortgage providers) and in businesses that transfer risk (such as major Western insurers).[12]

ESG goals are not typically modeled during the asset allocation decision process. Instead, these goals may be achieved through the implementation of the asset allocation, or the asset owner may choose to set aside a targeted portion of the assets for these missions. The asset allocation process would treat this "set-aside" in much the same way that a concentrated stock position might be handled: The risk, return, and correlation characteristics of this holding are specified; the "set aside" asset becomes an asset class in the investor's opportunity set; and the asset allocation constraints will designate a certain minimum investment in this asset class.

EXAMPLE 4   External Constraints and Asset Allocation

1. An insurance company has traditionally invested its pension plan using the asset allocation strategy adopted for its insurance assets: The pension assets are 95% invested in high-quality intermediate duration bonds and 5% in global equities. The duration of pension liabilities is approximately 25 years. Until now, the company has always made contributions sufficient to maintain a fully funded status. Although the company has a strong capability to fund the plan adequately and a relatively high tolerance for variability in asset returns, as part of a refinement in corporate strategy, management is now seeking to reduce long-term expected future cash contributions. Management is willing to accept more risk in the asset return, but they would like to limit contribution risk and the risk to the plan's funded status. The Investment Committee is considering three asset allocation proposals for the pension plan:

    A. Maintain the current asset allocation with the same bond portfolio duration.

    B. Increase the equity allocation and lengthen the bond portfolio duration to increase the hedge of the duration risk in the liabilities.

---

[10]https://mpra.ub.uni-muenchen.de/44028/1/MPRA_paper_44028.pdf (accessed 23 November 2018). Note: In principle, KIC must invest only in assets denominated in foreign currencies. If KIC manages KRW-denominated assets temporarily for an unavoidable reason, it must be either in the form of bank deposits or passively held public debt.

[11]https://www.nbim.no/en/investments/investment-strategy/ (accessed 23 November 2018).

[12]Islamic Investment Network (www.islamicinvestmentnetwork.com/sharialaw.php).

     C. Maintain the current asset allocation of 95% bonds and 5% global equities, but increase the duration of bond investments.

     Discuss the merits of each proposal.

2. A multinational corporation headquartered in Mexico has acquired a former competitor in the United States. It will maintain both the US pension plan with US$250 million in assets and the Mexican pension plan with MXN$18,600 million in assets (≈US$1 billion). Both plans are 95% funded and have similar liability profiles. The Mexican pension trust has an asset allocation policy of 30% equities (10% invested in the Mexican equity market and 20% in equity markets outside Mexico), 10% hedge funds, 10% private equity, and 50% bonds. The treasurer has proposed that the company adopt a consistent asset allocation policy across all of the company's pension plans worldwide.

     Critique the treasurer's proposal.

Solution to 1: Given the intermediate duration bond allocation, Proposal A fails to consider the mismatch between pension assets and liabilities and risks a reduction in the funded status and *increased* contributions if bond yields decline. (If yields decline across the curve, the shorter duration bond portfolio will fail to hedge the increase in liabilities.) To meet the objective of lower future contributions, the asset allocation must include a higher allocation to equities. Proposal B has this higher allocation, and the extension of duration in the bond portfolio in Proposal B reduces balance sheet and surplus risk relative to the pension liabilities. The net effect could be a reduction in short-term contribution risk; moreover, if the greater expected return on equities is realized, it should result in reduced contributions to the plan over the long term. Proposal C improves the hedging of the liabilities, and it may result in a modest improvement in the expected return on assets if the yield curve is upward-sloping. However, the expected return on Proposal C is likely lower than the expected return of Proposal B and is therefore unlikely to achieve the same magnitude of reduction in future cash contributions. Proposal C would be appropriate if the goal was focused on reducing surplus risk rather than reducing long-term contributions.

Solution to 2: The treasurer's proposal fails to consider the relative asset size of the two pension plans as well as the likelihood that plans in different jurisdictions may be subject to different funding, regulatory, and financial reporting requirements. The US pension plan may be unable to effectively access certain alternative asset classes, such as private equity, infrastructure, and hedge funds. Although economies of scale may be realized if management of the pension assets is consolidated under one team, the legal and regulatory differences of the markets in which they operate mean that the asset allocation policy must be customized to each plan.

3. ASSET ALLOCATION FOR THE TAXABLE INVESTOR

Portfolio theory developed in a frictionless world. But in the real world, taxes on income and capital gains can erode the returns achieved by taxable investors. The asset owner who ignores taxes during the asset allocation process is overlooking an economic variable that can materially alter the outcome. Although tax adjustments can be made after the asset allocation has been determined, this is a suboptimal approach because the pre-tax and after-tax risk and return characteristics of each asset class can be materially different.

Some assets are less tax efficient than others because of the character of their returns—the contribution of interest, dividends, and realized or unrealized capital gains to the total return. Interest income is usually taxed in the tax year it is received, and it often faces the highest tax rates. Therefore, assets that generate returns largely comprised of interest income tend to be less tax efficient in many countries.[13] Jurisdictional rules can also affect how the returns of certain assets are taxed. In the United States, for example, the interest income from state and local government bonds is generally exempt from federal income taxation. As a result, these bonds often constitute a large portion of a US high-net-worth investor's bond allocation. Preferred stocks, often used in lieu of bonds as an income-producing asset, are also eligible for more favorable tax treatment in many jurisdictions, where the income from preferred shares may be taxed at more favorable dividend tax rates.

The tax environment is complex. Different countries have different tax rules and rates, and these rules and rates can change frequently. However, looking across the major economies, there are some high-level commonalities in how investment returns are taxed. Interest income is taxed typically (but not always) at progressively higher income tax rates. Dividend income and capital gains are taxed typically (but not always) at lower tax rates than those applied to interest income and earned income (wages and salaries, for example). Capital losses can be used to offset capital gains (and sometimes income). Generally, interest income incurs the highest tax rate, with dividend income taxed at a lower rate in some countries, and long-term capital gains receive the most favorable tax treatment in many jurisdictions. Once we move beyond these general commonalities, however, the details of tax treatment among countries quickly diverge.

Entities and accounts can be subject to different tax rules. For example, retirement savings accounts may be tax deferred or tax exempt, with implications for the optimal asset allocation solution. These rules provide opportunities for strategic asset *location*—placing less tax-efficient assets in tax-advantaged accounts.

We will provide a general framework for considering taxes in asset allocation. We will not survey global tax regimes or incorporate all potential tax complexities into the asset allocation solution. When considering taxes in asset allocation, the objective is to model material investment-related taxes, thereby providing a closer approximation to economic reality than is represented when ignoring taxes altogether.

For simplicity, we will assume a basic tax regime that represents no single country but includes the key elements of investment-related taxes that are roughly representative of what a typical taxable asset owner in the major developed economies must contend with.

3.1. After-Tax Portfolio Optimization

After-tax portfolio optimization requires adjusting each asset class's expected return and risk for expected tax. The expected after-tax return is defined in Equation 1:

$$r_{at} = r_{pt}(1 - t) \qquad (1)$$

---

[13]See Deloitte's tax guides and country highlights: https://dits.deloitte.com/#TaxGuides.

where

r_{at} = the expected after-tax return

r_{pt} = the expected pre-tax (gross) return

t = the expected tax rate

This can be straightforward for bonds in cases where the expected return is driven by interest income. Take, for example, an investment-grade par bond with a 3% coupon expected to be held to maturity. If interest income is subject to a 40% expected tax rate, the bond has an expected after-tax return of 1.80% [0.03(1 − 0.40) = 0.018].

The expected return for equity typically includes both dividend income and price appreciation (capital gains). Equation 2 expands Equation 1 accordingly:

$$r_{at} = p_d r_{pt}(1 - t_d) + p_a r_{pt}(1 - t_{cg}) \tag{2}$$

where

p_d = the proportion of r_{pt} attributed to dividend income

p_a = the proportion of r_{pt} attributed to price appreciation

t_d = the dividend tax rate

t_{cg} = the capital gains tax rate

The treatment of the capital gains portion of equity returns can be more complex. Assuming no dividend income, a stock with an 8% expected pre-tax return that is subject to a 25% capital gains tax rate has an expected after-tax return of 6% [0.08(1 − 0.25) = 0.06]. This is an approximation satisfactory for modeling purposes.[14]

Taxable assets may have existing unrealized capital gains or losses (i.e., the cost basis is below or above market value), which come with embedded tax liabilities (or tax assets). Although there is not a clear consensus on how best to deal with existing unrealized capital gains (losses), many approaches adjust the asset's current market value for the value of the embedded tax liability (asset) to create an after-tax value. Reichenstein (2006) approximates the after-tax value by subtracting the value of the embedded capital gains tax from the market value, as if the asset were sold today. Horan and Al Zaman (2008) assume the asset is sold in the future and discount the tax liability to its present value using the asset's after-tax return as the discount rate. Turvey, Basu, and Verhoeven (2013) argue that the after-tax risk-free rate is the more appropriate discount rate because the embedded tax liability is analogous to an interest-free loan from the government, where the tax liability can be arbitraged away by dynamically investing in the risk-free asset. We will discuss how to incorporate after-tax values into the portfolio optimization process in Section 3.3, where we address strategies to reduce the impact of taxes.

The ultimate purpose of an asset can be a consideration when modeling tax adjustments. In the preceding material on asset allocation, we discussed goals-based investing. If the purpose of a given pool of assets is to fund consumption in 10 years, then that 10-year holding period may influence the estimated implied annual capital gains tax rate. If the purpose of the specified pool of assets is to fund a future gift of appreciated stock to a tax-exempt charity, then capital gains tax may be ignored altogether. Through this alignment of goals with assets, goals-based investing facilitates more-precise tax adjustments.

---

[14]A more precise estimation of the expected after-tax return also takes into account the effect of the holding period on the capital gains tax. For those interested in a more detailed discussion of these issues, see Mladina (2011).

Although correlation assumptions need not be adjusted when modeling asset allocation choices for the taxable asset owner (taxes are proportional to return; after-tax co-movements are the same as pre-tax co-movements), taxes do affect the standard deviation assumption for each asset class. The expected after-tax standard deviation is defined in Equation 3:

$$\sigma_{at} = \sigma_{pt}(1 - t) \tag{3}$$

where
σ_{at} = the expected after-tax standard deviation
σ_{pt} = the expected pre-tax standard deviation

Taxes alter the distribution of returns by both reducing the expected mean return and muting the dispersion of returns. Taxes truncate both the high and low ends of the distribution of returns, resulting in lower highs and higher lows. The effect of taxes is intuitive when considering a positive return, but the same economics apply to a negative return: Losses are muted by the same $(1 - t)$ tax adjustment. The investor is not taxed on losses but instead receives the economic benefit of a capital loss, whether realized or not. In many countries, a realized capital loss can offset a current or future realized capital gain. An unrealized capital loss captures the economic benefit of a cost basis that is above the current market value, making a portion of expected future appreciation tax free.

How does the optimal asset allocation along a pre-tax efficient frontier compare with the optimal asset allocation along an after-tax efficient frontier? Let's assume all investment assets are taxable and that cost bases equal current market values. Assume also that interest income is taxed at 40%, and dividend income and capital gains are taxed at 25%.

The asset classes we will consider include investment-grade (IG) bonds, high-yield (HY) bonds, and equity. Exhibit 3 shows the expected pre-tax returns and standard deviations for each asset class as well as the correlation matrix. Note that for ease of illustration, we have assumed that the IG bonds and HY bond returns are comprised of 100% interest income. In practice, some portion of the expected return would be eligible for capital gains tax treatment.

EXHIBIT 3   Expected Pre-Tax Return and Risk

	Return	Std. Dev.
IG bonds	3.0%	4.0%
HY bonds	5.0%	10.0%
Equity	8.0%	20.0%

Correlations	IG Bonds	HY Bonds	Equity
IG bonds	1.0	0.2	0.0
HY bonds	0.2	1.0	0.7
Equity	0.0	0.7	1.0

Employing mean–variance portfolio optimization with these pre-tax inputs, we obtain the optimal asset allocations in Exhibit 4, which shows the allocations for portfolios P1 (lowest risk), P25, P50 (median risk), P75, and P100 (highest risk)—each on an efficient frontier comprised of 100 portfolios.

EXHIBIT 4   Optimal Pre-Tax Asset Mixes

	$P1_{pt}$	$P25_{pt}$	$P50_{pt}$	$P75_{pt}$	$P100_{pt}$
IG bonds	93%	52%	25%	0%	0%
HY bonds	5%	18%	26%	33%	0%
Equity	2%	30%	49%	67%	100%

Using Equations 1, 2, and 3, we calculate the expected after-tax returns and standard deviations displayed in Exhibit 5. No adjustments are made to correlations.

EXHIBIT 5   Expected After-Tax Return and Risk

	Return	Std. Dev.
IG bonds	1.8%	2.4%
HY bonds	3.0%	6.0%
Equity	6.0%	15.0%

Portfolio optimization using these after-tax inputs produces the optimal asset allocations shown in Exhibit 6.

EXHIBIT 6   Optimal After-Tax Asset Mixes

	$P1_{at}$	$P25_{at}$	$P50_{at}$	$P75_{at}$	$P100_{at}$
IG bonds	92%	60%	38%	16%	0%
HY bonds	7%	7%	7%	7%	0%
Equity	1%	33%	55%	77%	100%

In Exhibit 7, we compare the pre-tax and after-tax efficient frontiers from these previous exhibits. Note that the portfolios at either extreme (P1 and P100) are essentially unchanged after taxes are factored into the assumptions. In portfolios P25, P50, and P75, however, you can see a significant reduction in the allocation to high-yield bonds. This is because of the heavier tax burden imposed on high-yield bonds. Although investment-grade bonds receive the same tax treatment, they are less risky than high-yield bonds and demonstrate a lower correlation with equity, so they continue to play the important role of portfolio risk reduction.

EXHIBIT 7   Pre-Tax and After-Tax Asset Allocation Comparisons

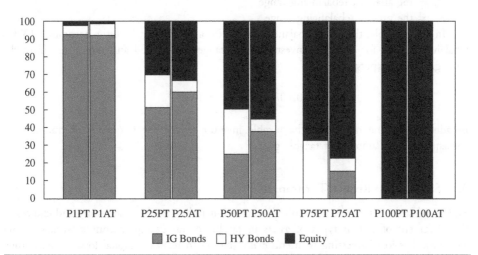

The optimal after-tax asset allocation depends on the interaction of after-tax returns, after-tax risk, and correlations. If an asset class or strategy is tax inefficient, it can still play a diversifying role in an optimal after-tax asset allocation if the asset or strategy offers sufficiently low correlations. After-tax portfolio optimization helps answer that question.

3.2. Taxes and Portfolio Rebalancing

Among tax-exempt institutional asset owners, periodic portfolio rebalancing—reallocating assets to return the portfolio to its target strategic asset allocation—is an integral part of sound portfolio management. This is no less true for taxable asset owners, but with the important distinction that more frequent rebalancing exposes the taxable asset owner to realized taxes that could have otherwise been deferred or even avoided. Whereas the tax burden incurred by liquidating assets to fund-required consumption cannot be avoided, rebalancing is discretionary; thus, the taxable asset owner should consider the trade-off between the benefits of tax minimization and the merits of maintaining the targeted asset allocation by rebalancing. The decision to rebalance and incur taxes is driven by each asset owner's unique circumstances.

Because after-tax volatility is less than pre-tax volatility (Equation 3) and asset class correlations remain the same, it takes larger asset class movements to materially alter the risk profile of the taxable portfolio. This suggests that rebalancing ranges for a taxable portfolio can be wider than those of a tax-exempt portfolio with a similar risk profile.

For example, consider a portfolio with a 50% allocation to equity, where equity returns are subject to a 25% tax rate. A tax-exempt investor may establish a target allocation to equities of 50%, with an acceptable range of 40% to 60% (50% plus or minus 10%). A taxable investor with the same target equity allocation can achieve a similar risk constraint with a range of 37% to 63% (50% plus or minus 13%). The equivalent rebalancing range for the taxable investor is derived by adjusting the permitted 10% deviation (up or down) by the tax rate, as shown in Equation 4:

$$R_{at} = R_{pt}/(1 - t) \tag{4}$$

where

    R_{at} = the after-tax rebalancing range

    R_{pt} = the pre-tax rebalancing range

In our example, the 10% rebalancing range for a tax-exempt investor becomes a 13.3% rebalancing range for a taxable investor (when ranges are viewed and monitored from the same gross return perspective):

$$0.10/(1 - 0.25) = 13.3\%$$

Broader rebalancing ranges for the taxable investor reduce the frequency of trading and, consequently, the amount of taxable gains.

3.3. Strategies to Reduce Tax Impact

Additional strategies can be used to reduce taxes, including tax-loss harvesting and choices in the placement of certain types of assets in taxable or tax-exempt accounts (strategic asset location). Tax-loss harvesting is intentionally trading to realize a capital loss, which is then used to offset a current or future realized capital gain in another part of the portfolio, thereby reducing the taxes owned by the investor. It is discussed elsewhere in the curriculum, but we address strategic asset location strategies here.

Strategic asset location refers to placing (or locating) less tax-efficient assets in accounts with more favorable tax treatment, such as retirement savings accounts.

Aggregating assets across accounts with differing tax treatment requires modifying the asset value inputs to the portfolio optimization. Assets held in tax-*exempt* accounts require no tax adjustment to their market values. Assets in tax-*deferred* accounts grow tax free but are taxed upon distribution. Because these assets cannot be distributed (and consumed) without incurring the tax, the tax burden is inseparable from the economic value of the assets. Thus, the after-tax value of assets in a tax-deferred account is defined by Equation 5:

$$v_{at} = v_{pt}(1 - t_i) \tag{5}$$

where

    v_{at} = the after-tax value of assets

    v_{pt} = the pre-tax market value of assets

    t_i = the expected income tax rate upon distribution

In our earlier example, we had three asset classes: investment-grade bonds, high-yield bonds, and equities. If we assume that each of these three asset classes can be held in either of two account types—taxable or tax-deferred—then our optimization uses six different after-tax asset classes (three asset classes times two account types). The three asset classes in taxable accounts use the after-tax return and risk inputs derived earlier. The three asset classes in tax-deferred accounts (which grow tax free) use expected pre-tax return and risk inputs. The optimization adds constraints based on the after-tax value of the assets currently available in each account type and derives the optimal after-tax asset allocation and asset location simultaneously.

As a general rule, the portion of a taxable asset owner's assets that are eligible for lower tax rates and deferred capital gains tax treatment should first be allocated to the investor's taxable accounts. For example, equities should generally be held in taxable accounts, while taxable bonds and high-turnover trading strategies should generally be located in tax-exempt and tax-deferred accounts to the extent possible.

One important exception to this general rule regarding asset location applies to assets held for near-term liquidity needs. Because tax-exempt and tax-deferred accounts may not be immediately accessible without tax penalty, a portion of the bond allocation may be held in taxable accounts if its role is to fund near-term consumption requirements.

EXAMPLE 5   Asset Allocation and the Taxable Investor

1. Sarah Moreau, 45 years old, is a mid-level manager at a consumer products company. Her investment portfolio consists entirely of tax-deferred retirement savings accounts. Through careful savings and investments, she is on track to accumulate sufficient assets to retire at age 60. Her portfolio is currently allocated as indicated below:

Investment-grade bonds	20%
High-yield bonds	20%
Common stock–dividend income strategy	30%
Common stock–total return (capital gain) strategy	30%
Total portfolio	100%

The common stock–dividend income strategy focuses on income-oriented, high-dividend-paying stocks; the common stock–total return strategy focuses on stocks that represent good, long-term opportunities but pay little to no dividend. For the purposes of this example, we will assume that the expected long-term return is equivalent between the two strategies. Moreau has a high comfort level with this portfolio and the overall level of risk it entails.

Moreau has recently inherited additional monies, doubling her investable assets. She intends to use this new, taxable portfolio to support causes important to her personally over her lifetime. There is no change in her risk tolerance. She is interviewing prospective investment managers and has asked each to recommend an asset allocation strategy for the new portfolio using the same set of asset classes. She has received the following recommendations:

	Recommendation		
	A	B	C
Investment-grade bonds	20%	40%	30%
High-yield bonds	20%	0%	0%
Common stock–dividend income strategy	30%	30%	0%
Common stock–total return (capital gain) strategy	30%	30%	70%
Total portfolio	100%	100%	100%

Which asset allocation is *most* appropriate for the new portfolio? Justify your response.

2. How should Moreau distribute these investments among her taxable and tax-exempt accounts?

3. You are a member of the Investment Committee for a multinational corporation, responsible for the supervision of two portfolios. Both portfolios were established to fund retirement benefits: One is a tax-exempt defined benefit pension fund, and the other is taxable, holding assets intended to fund non-exempt retirement benefits. The pension fund has a target allocation of 70% equities and 30% fixed income, with a +/− 5% rebalancing range. There is no formal asset allocation policy for the taxable portfolio; it has simply followed the same allocation adopted by the pension portfolio. Because of recent strong equity market returns, both portfolios are now allocated 77% to equities and 23% to bonds. Management expects that the equity markets will continue to produce strong returns in the near term. Staff has offered the following options for rebalancing the portfolios:

A. Do not rebalance.

B. Rebalance both portfolios to the 70% equity/30% fixed-income target allocation.

C. Rebalance the tax-exempt portfolio to the 70% equity/30% fixed-income target allocation, but expand the rebalancing range for the taxable portfolio.

Which recommendation is *most* appropriate? Justify your response.

Solution to 1: Recommendation C would be the most appropriate asset allocation for the new portfolio. The high-yield bond and common stock–dividend income strategies are tax disadvantaged in a taxable portfolio. (Although investment-grade bonds are also tax disadvantaged, they maintain the role of controlling portfolio risk to maintain Moreau's risk preference.) By shifting this equity-like risk to the total return common stock strategy, Moreau should achieve a greater after-tax return. Given the lower standard deviation characteristics of after-tax equity returns when held in the taxable portfolio, a higher allocation to common stocks may be justified without exceeding Moreau's desired risk level. Recommendations A and B do not consider the negative tax implications of holding the high-yield and/or common stock–dividend income strategies in a taxable portfolio. Recommendation B also fails to consider Moreau's overall risk tolerance: The volatility of the common stock–capital gain strategy is lower when held in a taxable portfolio, thus a higher allocation to this strategy can enhance returns while remaining within Moreau's overall risk tolerance.[15]

Solution to 2: If Moreau is willing to think of her investable portfolio as a single portfolio, rather than as independent "retirement" and "important causes" portfolios, she should hold the allocation to high-yield bonds and dividend-paying stocks in her tax-exempt retirement portfolio. In addition, subject to the overall volatility of the individual tax-exempt and taxable portfolios, it would be sensible to bear any increased stock risk in the taxable portfolio. A new optimization for *all* of Moreau's assets—using pre-tax and after-tax risk and return assumptions and subject to the constraint that half of the assets are held in a taxable portfolio and half are held in the tax-exempt portfolio—would more precisely allocate investments across portfolio (account) types.

---

[15]Investment-grade bonds also have lower after-tax volatility. The equivalent risk portfolios in pre-tax and after-tax environments are a function of a complex interaction of after-tax returns, standard deviations, and correlations.

Asset Location for Optimal Tax Efficiency

	Tax Advantaged Retirement Account	Taxable Account
Investment-grade bonds	X	
High-yield bonds	X	
Common stock–dividend income strategy	X	
Common stock–total return (capital gain) strategy		X

Solution to 3: Recommendation C is the most appropriate course of action. Rebalancing of the tax-exempt portfolio is unencumbered by tax considerations, and rebalancing maintains the desired level of risk. The rebalancing range for the taxable portfolio can be wider than that of the tax-exempt portfolio based on the desire to minimize avoidable taxes and the lower volatility of after-tax equity returns. Recommendation A (no rebalancing) does not address the increased level of risk in the tax-exempt portfolio that results from the increase in the stock allocation. Recommendation B would create an unnecessary tax liability for the company, given that the portfolio is still operating in a reasonable range of risk when adjusted for taxes.

Increasing Allocations to Fixed Income in Corporate Pension Plans

Increasing allocations to fixed income by defined benefit pension funds worldwide have been driven largely by a desire to better hedge plan liabilities. In some countries, accounting standards discourage de-risking. De-risking, however, is not the only argument in favor of a higher fixed-income allocation.

De-risking

There has been much discussion globally of pension plans "de-risking"—moving toward larger fixed-income allocations to better hedge liabilities, thereby reducing contribution uncertainty. Some countries' accounting rules, however—most notably those in the United States—discourage companies from moving in that direction. Under US GAAP accounting rules, for example, a higher allocation to equities allows the plan sponsor to employ a higher return assumption, thereby reducing pension cost, a non-cash expense that directly affects reported income.

For underfunded pension plans, de-risking leads to higher pension contributions. If a company has a weak core business with a higher-than-average probability of going bankrupt and makes only the minimum required contribution, it might be argued that the asset allocation decision was contrary to the interests of plan participants. If the company were to go bankrupt, the participants would get only the benefits covered by any government guaranty program. Had the company taken equity risk in the plan, there would have been a possibility of closing the funding gap, resulting in higher benefit payments.

Efficient Allocation of Risk

A higher allocation to fixed income—and a lower allocation to equity—might also be driven by corporate governance considerations. Pension investment activities are not a core competency of many companies, especially non-financial companies. Assuming that the company has a limited appetite for risk, shareholders might prefer that management allocate its risk budget to the core business of the company where they are expected to have skill, rather than to the pension fund. The rewards per unit of risk should presumably be greater in the company's core business, and the improved profitability should offset the increase in pension contributions required as a result of the lower equity allocation.

A Holistic Approach to Asset Location

Finally, some have argued that an asset allocation of 100% fixed-income securities can be justified on the premise that the company is acting as an agent for the benefit of all stakeholders, including shareholders and plan participants. This argument centers on tax-efficient asset location. A taxable investor—the shareholder and plan participant—should prefer to take his long-term equity risk in that portion of his overall portfolio where he will receive the benefit of lower capital gains rates rather than in tax-deferred accounts, the proceeds of which will be taxed at income tax rates. Consider a small business owner with US$3 million in total assets. The assets are split between a pension fund of which he is the sole participant (US$1 million) and a taxable portfolio (US$2 million). Assume that the asset allocation that represents his preferred level of risk is 67% equities and 33% fixed income. Where should this individual hold his equity exposure? As discussed, the more favorable tax treatment of equity returns argues for holding the equity exposure in his taxable account, while the investments subject to the higher tax rate should be held in the tax-deferred account—the pension plan. Theoretically, this tax efficiency argument can be extended to pension funds operated by publicly traded companies.[16]

4. REVISING THE STRATEGIC ASSET ALLOCATION

An asset owner's strategic asset allocation is not a static decision. Circumstances often arise that justify revisiting the original decision, either to confirm its appropriateness or to consider a change to the current allocation strategy. It is sound financial practice to periodically re-examine the asset allocation strategy even in the absence of one of the external factors discussed next. Many institutional asset owners typically re-visit the asset allocation policy at least once every five years through a formal asset allocation study, and all asset owners should affirm annually that the asset allocation remains appropriate given their needs and circumstances.

The circumstances that might trigger a special review of the asset allocation policy can generally be classified as relating to a change in *goals*, a change in *constraints*, or a change in *beliefs*. Among the reasons to review the strategic asset allocation are the following:

---

[16]For those interested in a more detailed discussion of this concept, see "The Case against Stock in Public Pension Funds" (Bader and Gold 2007) or the UBS Q-Series article, "Pension Fund Asset Allocation" (Cooper and Bianco 2003).

Goals

- Changes in business conditions affecting the organization supporting the fund and, therefore, expected changes in the cash flows
- A change in the investor's personal circumstances that may alter her risk appetite or risk capacity

Over an individual's lifespan, or throughout the course of an institutional fund's lifespan, it is unlikely that the investment goals and objectives will remain unchanged. An individual may get married, have children, or become disabled, for example, each of which may have implications for the asset allocation strategy.

Significant changes in the core business of an organization supporting or benefiting from the trust might prompt a re-examination of the asset allocation strategy. For example, an automobile manufacturer that has historically generated a significant portion of its revenues from its consumer finance activities may find that technology is disrupting this source of revenue as more online tools become available to car buyers. With greater uncertainty in its revenue stream, company management may move to reduce risk-taking in the pension fund in order to achieve a goal of reducing the variability in year-to-year contributions.

A university may embark on a long-term capital improvement plan that is reliant on the endowment fund for financial support. Or the university may be experiencing declining enrollments and must lean more heavily on the endowment fund to support its ongoing operational expenditures. The source of funds to a sovereign wealth fund may shrink considerably or even evaporate. When any of these, or similar, events occur or are anticipated, the existing asset allocation policy should be re-evaluated.

Constraints

A material change in any one of the constraints mentioned earlier—time horizon, liquidity needs, asset size, or regulatory or other external constraints—is also reason to re-examine the existing asset allocation policy. Some of these changes might include the following:

- Changes in the expected payments from the fund
- A significant cash inflow or unanticipated expenditure
- Changes in regulations governing donations or contributions to the fund
- Changes in time horizon resulting from the adoption of a lump sum distribution option at retirement
- Changes in asset size as a result of the merging of pension plans

Changes in the expected payments from the fund can materially affect the asset allocation strategy. For example, a university reduces its spending policy from 5% to 4% of assets annually; an individual retires early, perhaps for health reasons or an involuntary late-career layoff; or a US corporate pension sponsor reduces or freezes pension benefits because it can no longer afford increasing Pension Benefit Guaranty Corporation[17] premiums. Faced with lower payouts, the university endowment may have greater latitude to invest in less liquid segments of the market. Decisions as to how and where to invest given this greater flexibility should be made within the framework of an asset allocation study to ensure the resulting allocation achieves the optimal trade-off of risk and return.

---

[17]The Pension Benefit Guaranty Corporation insures certain US pension plan benefits.

Similarly, a significant cash inflow has the potential to materially affect the asset allocation strategy. If a university endowment fund with £500 million in assets receives a gift of £100 million, the new monies *could* be invested in parallel with the existing assets, but that fails to consider the increased earning potential of the fund and any spending requirements associated with the donation. Pausing to formally reassess the fund's goals, objectives, constraints, and opportunities through an asset allocation study allows the asset owner to consider more broadly how best to maximize this additional wealth.

A change in regulations may also give rise to a change in asset allocation policy. Examples of regulatory changes that could trigger a re-examination of the asset allocation include the following:

- Regulatory changes in the United States in 2006 mandated a change in the liability discount rate, which resulted in larger pension contributions. With higher required contributions, there was less need to reach for higher investment returns. Many US corporate pension plans began de-risking (adopting an asset allocation strategy focused on hedging the liabilities) to reduce contribution volatility.
- UK tax incentives (30% of social impact investment costs can be deducted from income tax) and relaxed regulations for institutional investors were instituted to encourage socially responsible (impact) investing.

Again, an asset allocation study to objectively evaluate the effect of these changes on the investment opportunity set can help ensure that any new investment strategies adopted are consistent with the fund's overarching goals and objectives.

Beliefs

Investment beliefs are a set of guiding principles that govern the asset owner's investment activities. Beliefs are not static, however, and changes in the economic environment and capital market expectations or a change in trustees or committee members are two factors that may lead to an altering of the principles that guide investment activities.[18]

An integral aspect of any asset allocation exercise is the forecasting of expected returns, volatilities, and correlations of the asset classes in the opportunity set. It follows, then, that a material change in the outlook for one or more of the asset classes may heavily influence the asset allocation outcome.

Consider the 2015–2016 environment relative to the environment that prevailed in 1984–2014. The 1984–2014 investing environment was characterized by declining inflation and interest rates (from the extraordinarily high levels of the 1970s and early 1980s); strong global GDP growth, aided by favorable demographics; gains in productivity; and rapid growth in China. Corporate profit growth was extremely robust, reflecting revenue growth from new markets, declining corporate taxes over the period, and improved efficiencies. Despite increased market turbulence, returns on US and Western European equities and bonds during the past 30 years were considerably higher than the long-run trend.

The environment of 2015–2016 was much less favorable for investors. The dramatic decline in inflation and interest rates ended, and labor force expansion and productivity gains stalled, with negative implications for GDP growth. The largest developed-country companies that generated much of the profits of the past 30 years were faced with competitive pressures

---

[18]For an example of an investment belief statement, see www.uss.co.uk/how-uss-invests/investment-approach/investment-beliefs-and-principles.

as emerging-market companies expanded and technology advances changed the competitive landscape. In April 2016, McKinsey Global Institute published a projection of stocks and bonds under two growth scenarios—a slow growth scenario and a moderate growth scenario (Exhibit 8). In neither instance do the expected returns of the next 30 years come close to the returns of the past 30 years.[19] Clearly, an asset allocation developed in 2010 built on return expectations based on the prior 26 years would look materially different than an asset allocation developed using more current, forward-looking return assumptions.

EXHIBIT 8   A Major Shift in Underlying Return Assumptions

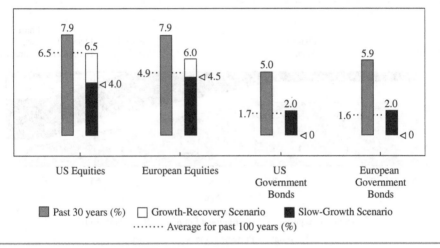

Notes:

Numbers for growth-recovery and slow-growth scenarios reflect the range between the low end of the slow-growth scenario and the high end of the growth-recovery scenario.

European equities: Weighted average real returns based on each year's Geary-Khamis purchasing power parity GDP for 14 countries in Western Europe.

US and European government bonds: Bond duration for United States is primarily 10 years; for Europe, duration varies by country but is typically 20 years.

Source: McKinsey Global Institute (www.mckinsey.com/industries/private-equity-and-principal-investors/our-insights/why-investors-may-need-to-lower-their-sights).

Finally, as new advisers or members join the Investment Committee, they bring their own beliefs and biases regarding certain investment activities. Conducting an asset allocation study to educate these new members of the oversight group and introduce them to the investment philosophy and process that has been adopted by the organization will smooth their integration into the governance system and ensure that they have a holistic view of the asset owner's goals and objectives.

In some instances, a change to an asset allocation strategy may reasonably be implemented without a formal asset allocation study. Certain milestones are reasonable points at which to implement a change in the policy, in most instances, reducing the level of risk.

---

[19]McKinsey Global Institute, "Diminishing Returns: Why Investors May Need to Lower Their Expectations" (May 2016).

(For pension funds, these "milestones" are typically related to changes in the plan's funded status.) Anticipating these milestones by putting an asset allocation policy in place that anticipates these changes allows the investor to respond more quickly to changing circumstances and in a non-reactive and objective manner. This rebalancing policy is frequently referred to as a "glide path." Target-date mutual funds common in retirement investing for individuals are one example of this approach to asset allocation. Exhibit 9 illustrates one fund company's approach to migrating the asset allocation away from equities and toward bonds as retirement approaches.

EXHIBIT 9   An Asset Allocation Glide Path

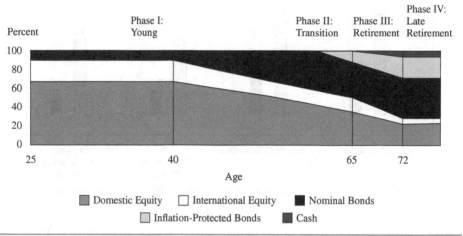

Source: Vanguard, "Target-Date Funds: A Solid Foundation for Retirement Investors" (May 2009): www.vanguard.com/jumppage/targetretirement/TRFCOMM.pdf.

In an institutional framework, the Investment Committee may specify certain funding levels it seeks to achieve. At the start of the period, an underfunded pension plan might adopt a higher equity allocation in an attempt to reduce the underfunding. If this is successful, the plan becomes better funded and there is less of a desire or need to take the higher level of equity risk. A pension fund may quickly implement "pre-programmed" asset allocation changes as the funded status of a pension plan improves. Typically, these planned reallocations are spelled out in an Investment Policy Statement.

EXAMPLE 6   Revising the Strategic Asset Allocation

1. Auldberg University Endowment Fund (AUE) has assets totaling CAF$200 million. The current asset allocation is as follows:
   - CAF$100 million in domestic equities
   - CAF$60 million in domestic government debt
   - CAF$40 million in Class B office real estate

   AUE has historically distributed to the University 5% of the 36-month moving average of net assets, contributing approximately CAF$10 million of Auldberg University's CAF$60 million annual operating budget. Real estate income (from the University's CAF$350 million direct investment in domestic commercial real estate assets, including office buildings and industrial parks, much of it near the campus) and provincial subsidies have been the main source of income to the University. Admission is free to all citizens who qualify academically.

Growth in the Caflandia economy has been fueled by low interest rates, encouraging excess real estate development. There is a strong probability that the economy will soon go into recession, negatively impacting both the property values and the income potential of the University's real estate holdings.

Gizi Horvath, a University alumnus, has recently announced an irrevocable CAF $200 million gift to AUE, to be paid in equal installments over the next five years. AUE employs a well-qualified staff with substantial diverse experience in equities, fixed income, and real estate. Staff has recommended that the gift from Ms. Horvath be invested using the same asset allocation policy that the endowment has been following successfully for the past five years. They suggest that the asset allocation policy should be revisited once the final installment has been received. Critique staff's recommendation, and identify the case facts that support your critique.

2. The Government Petroleum Fund of Caflandia (GPFC) is operating under the following asset allocation policy, which was developed with a 20-year planning horizon. Target weights and actual weights are given:

	Target Asset Allocation	Current Asset Allocation
Global equities	30%	38%
Global high-yield bonds	10%	15%
Domestic intermediate bonds	30%	25%
Hedge funds	15%	15%
Private equity	15%	7%

When this asset allocation policy was adopted 5 years ago, the petroleum revenues that support the sovereign wealth fund were projected to continue to grow for at least the next 25 years and intergenerational distributions were expected to begin in 20 years. However, since the adoption of this policy, alternate fuel sources have eroded both the price and quantity of oil exports, the economy is undergoing significant restructuring, inflows to the fund have been suspended, and distributions are expected to begin within 5 years.

What are the implications of this change in the liquidity constraints for the current asset allocation policy?

3. O-Chem Corp has a defined benefit pension plan with US$1.0 billion in assets. The plan is closed, the liabilities are frozen, and the plan is currently 65% funded. The company intends to increase cash contributions to improve the funded status of the plan and then purchase annuities to fully address all of the plan's pension obligations. As part of an asset allocation analysis conducted every five years, the company has recently decided to allocate 80% of assets to liability-matching bonds and the remaining 20% to a mix of global equities and real estate. An existing private equity portfolio is in the midst of being liquidated. This allocation reflects a desired reduction in the level of investment risk.

O-Chem has just announced an ambitious US$15 billion capital investment program to build new plants for refining and production. The CFO informed the Pension Committee that the company will be contributing to the plan only the minimum funding required by regulations for the foreseeable future. It is estimated that achieving fully funded status for the pension plan under minimum funding requirements and using the current asset allocation approach will take at least 10 years.

What are the implications of this change in funding policy for the pension plan's asset allocation strategy?

Solution to 1: The size of the anticipated contributions will double AUE's assets over the next five years, potentially increasing the opportunity set of asset classes suitable for their investment program. Given that a typical asset allocation study encompasses a long investment horizon—10 years, 20 years, or more—staff should begin to evaluate the opportunities available to them today in *anticipation* of the future cash flows. Given the material change in the economic balance sheet along with changes in the asset size, liquidity, and time horizon constraints, AUE should plan on a regular, more frequent, formal review of the asset allocation policy until the situation stabilizes. The asset allocation study should explore the feasibility of adding new asset classes as well as the ability to improve diversification within existing categories, perhaps by including non-domestic equities and bonds. Furthermore, the forecast economic environment may materially alter the outflows from the fund in support of the University's day-to-day operations. Cash flows from the University's real estate holdings are likely to decline, as are the values of those real estate assets. Given the outlook for real estate, a strong case can be made to limit or reduce the endowment's investment in real estate; moreover, consideration should be given to the effect of declining income from the current real estate investment.

Solution to 2: GPFC had adopted a long-range asset allocation policy under the expectation of continuing net cash inflows and no immediate liquidity constraints. With the change in circumstances, the need for liquidity in the fund has increased significantly. The current asset allocation policy allocates 40% of the fund's assets to less liquid asset classes—high-yield bonds, hedge funds, and private equity. Although the allocation to private equity has not been fully implemented, the fund is overweight high-yield bonds and at the target weight for hedge funds. These asset classes—or the size of the allocation to these asset classes—may no longer be appropriate for the fund given the change in circumstances.

Solution to 3: The Investment Committee should conduct a new asset allocation study to address the changes in cash flow forecasts. The lower contributions imply that the pension plan will need to rely more heavily on investment returns to reach its funding objectives. A higher allocation to return-seeking assets, such as public and private equities, is warranted. The company should suspend the current private equity liquidation plan until the new asset allocation study has been completed. A liability-matching bond portfolio is still appropriate, although less than the current 80% of assets should be allocated to this portfolio.

5. SHORT-TERM SHIFTS IN ASSET ALLOCATION

Strategic asset allocation (SAA), or policy asset allocation, represents long-term investment policy targets for asset class weights, whereas tactical asset allocation (TAA) allows short-term deviations from SAA targets.[20] TAA moves might be justified based on cyclical variations within a secular trend (e.g., stage of business or monetary cycle) or temporary price dislocations in capital markets. TAA has the objective of increasing return, or risk-adjusted return, by taking advantage of short-term economic and financial market conditions that appear more favorable to certain asset classes. In seeking to capture a short-term return opportunity, TAA decisions move the investor's risk away from the targeted risk profile. TAA is predicated on a belief that investment returns, in the short run, are predictable. (This contrasts with the random walk assumption more strongly embedded in most SAA processes.) Using either short-term views or signals, the investor actively re-weights broad asset classes, sectors, or risk factor premiums. TAA is not concerned with individual security selection. In other words, generating alpha through TAA decisions is dependent on successful market or factor timing rather than security selection. TAA is an asset-only approach. Although tactical asset allocation shifts must still conform to the risk constraints outlined in the investment policy statement, they do not expressly consider liabilities (or goals in goals-based investing).

The SAA policy portfolio is the benchmark against which TAA decisions are measured. Tactical views are developed and bets are sized relative to the asset class targets of the SAA policy portfolio. The sizes of these bets are typically subject to certain risk constraints. The most common risk constraint is a pre-established allowable range around each asset class's policy target. Other risk constraints may include either a predicted tracking error budget versus the SAA or a range of targeted risk (e.g., an allowable range of predicted volatility).

The success of TAA decisions can be evaluated in a number of ways. Three of the most common are

- a comparison of the Sharpe ratio realized under the TAA relative to the Sharpe ratio that would have been realized under the SAA;
- evaluating the information ratio or the *t*-statistic of the average excess return of the TAA portfolio relative to the SAA portfolio; and
- plotting the realized return and risk of the TAA portfolio versus the realized return and risk of portfolios along the SAA's efficient frontier. This approach is particularly useful in assessing the risk-adjusted TAA return. The TAA portfolio may have produced a higher return or a higher Sharpe ratio than the SAA portfolio, but it could be less optimal than other portfolios along the investor's efficient frontier of portfolio choices.

The composition of the portfolio's excess return over the SAA portfolio return can also be examined more closely using attribution analysis, evaluating the specific overweights and underweights that led to the performance differential.

Tactical investment decisions may incur additional costs—higher trading costs and taxes (in the case of taxable investors). Tactical investment decisions can also increase the concentration of risk relative to the policy portfolio. For example, if the tactical decision is to overweight equities, not only is the portfolio risk increased but also the diversification of risk contributions is reduced. This is particularly an issue when the SAA policy portfolio relies on

---

[20]SAA and TAA are distinct from GTAA (global tactical asset allocation), an opportunistic investment strategy that seeks to take advantage of pricing or valuation anomalies across multiple asset classes, typically equities, fixed income, and currencies.

uncorrelated asset classes. These costs should be weighed against the predictability of short-term returns.

There are two broad approaches to TAA. The first is discretionary, which relies on a qualitative interpretation of political, economic, and financial market conditions. The second is systematic, which relies on quantitative signals to capture documented return anomalies that may be inconsistent with market efficiency.

5.1. Discretionary TAA

Discretionary TAA is predicated on the existence of manager skill in predicting and timing short-term market moves away from the expected outcome for each asset class that is embedded in the SAA policy portfolio. In practice, discretionary TAA is typically used in an attempt to mitigate or hedge risk in distressed markets while enhancing return in positive return markets (i.e., an asymmetric return distribution).

Short-term forecasts consider a large number of data points that provide relevant information about current and expected political, economic, and financial market conditions that may affect short-term asset class returns. Data points might include valuations, term and credit spreads, central bank policy, GDP growth, earnings expectations, inflation expectations, and leading economic indicators. Price-to-earnings ratios, price-to-book ratios, and the dividend yield are commonly used valuation measures that can be compared to historical averages and across similar assets to inform short-to-intermediate-term tactical shifts. Term spreads provide information about the business cycle, inflation, and potential future interest rates. Credit spreads gauge default risk, borrowing conditions, and liquidity. Other data points are more directly related to current and expected GDP and earnings growth.

Short-term forecasts may also consider economic sentiment indicators. TAA often assumes a close relationship between the economy and capital market returns. Because consumer spending is a major driver of GDP in developed countries, consumer sentiment is a key consideration. Consumer confidence surveys provide insight as to the level of optimism regarding the economy and personal finances.

TAA also considers market sentiment—indicators of the optimism or pessimism of financial market participants. Data points considered in gauging market sentiment include margin borrowing, short interest, and a volatility index.

- Margin borrowing measures give an indication of the current level of bullishness, and the capacity for more or less margin borrowing has implications for future bullishness. Higher prices tend to inspire confidence and spur more buying; similarly, more buying on margin tends to spur higher prices. The aggregate level of margin can be an indicator that bullish sentiment is overdone, although the level of borrowing must be considered in the context of the rate of change in borrowing.
- Short interest measures give an indication of current bearish sentiment and also have implications for future bearishness. Although rising short interest indicates increasing negative sentiment, a high short interest ratio may be an indication of the extreme pessimism that often occurs at market lows.
- The volatility index, commonly known as the fear index, is a measure of market expectations of near-term volatility. VDAX-NEW in Germany, V2X in the United Kingdom, and VIX in the United States each measure the level of expected volatility of their respective indexes as implied by the bid/ask quotations of index options; it rises when put option buying increases and falls when call buying activity increases.

Different approaches to discretionary TAA may include different data points and relationships and also may prioritize and weight those data points differently depending on both the approach and the prevailing market environment. Despite the plethora of data inputs, the interpretation of this information is qualitative at its core.

5.2. Systematic TAA

Using signals, systematic TAA attempts to capture asset-class-level return anomalies that have been shown to have some predictability and persistence. Value and momentum, for example, are factors that have been determined to offer some level of predictability, both among securities within asset classes (for security selection) and at the asset class level (for asset class timing).

The value factor is the return of value stocks over the return of growth stocks. The momentum factor is the return of stocks with higher prior returns over the returns of stocks with lower prior returns. Value and momentum (and size) factors have been determined to have some explanatory power regarding the relative returns of equity securities within the equity asset class. Value and momentum phenomena are also present at the asset class level and can be used in making tactical asset allocation decisions across asset classes.

Valuation ratios have been shown to have some explanatory power in predicting variation in future equity returns. Predictive measures for equities include dividend yield, cash flow yield, and Shiller's earnings yield (the inverse of Shiller's P/E[21]). Sometimes these yield measures are defined as the excess of the yield over the local risk-free rate or inflation.[22]

Other asset classes have their own value signals, such as yield and carry in currencies, commodities, and/or fixed income. Carry in currencies uses short-term interest rate differentials to determine which currencies (or currency-denominated assets) to overweight (or own) and which to underweight (or sell short). Carry in commodities compares positive (backwardation) and negative (contango) roll yields to determine which commodities to own or short. And for bonds, yields-to-maturity and term premiums (yields in excess of the local risk-free rate) signal the relative attractiveness of different fixed-income markets.

Asset classes can trend positively or negatively for some time before changing course. Trend following is an investment or trading strategy based on the expectation that asset class (or asset) returns will continue in the same upward or downward trend that they have most recently exhibited.[23] A basic trend signal is the most recent 12-month return: The expectation is that the direction of the most recent 12-month returns can be expected to persist for the next 12 months. Shorter time frames and different weighting schemes can also be used. For example, another trend signal is the moving-average crossover, where the moving average price of a shorter time frame is compared with the moving average price of a longer time frame. This signals an upward (downward) trend when the moving average of the shorter time frame is above (below) the moving average of the longer time frame. Trend signals are widely used in systematic TAA. Asset classes may be ranked or categorized into positive or negative buckets based on their most recent prior 12-month performance and over- or underweighted

---

[21]A price-to-earnings ratio based on the average inflation-adjusted earnings of the previous 10 years.

[22]Return predictability for equity markets is driven by historical mean-reversion, which tends to occur over the intermediate-term. These valuation measures are often used as signals for TAA, but they can also be used to shape return expectations for SAA.

[23]Trend following is also called time-series momentum. Cross-sectional momentum describes the relative momentum returns of securities within the same asset class.

accordingly. More-complex signals for both momentum/trend signals (such as those that use different lookback periods or momentum signals correlated with earnings momentum) and value/carry are also used.

EXAMPLE 7   Short-Term Shifts in Asset Allocation

1. The investment policy for Alpha Beverage Corporation's pension fund allows staff to overweight or underweight asset classes, within pre-established bands, using a TAA model that has been approved by the Investment Committee. The asset allocation policy is reflected in Exhibit 10, and the output of the TAA model is given in Exhibit 11. Using the data presented in Exhibits 10 and 11, recommend a TAA strategy for the pension fund and justify your response.

EXHIBIT 10   Strategic Asset Allocation Policy

SAA Policy	Current Weight	Target Allocation	Upper Policy Limit	Lower Policy Limit
Investment-grade bonds	45%	40%	45%	35%
High-yield bonds	10%	10%	15%	5%
Developed markets equity	35%	40%	45%	35%
Emerging markets equity	10%	10%	15%	5%

EXHIBIT 11   Trend Signal (the positive or negative trailing 12-month excess return)

	12-Month Return	Risk-Free Return	Excess Return	Signal
Investment-grade bonds	4%	1%	3%	Long
High-yield bonds	−2%	1%	−3%	Short
Developed markets equity	5%	1%	4%	Long
Emerging markets equity	−10%	1%	−11%	Short

2. One year later, the Investment Committee for Alpha Beverage Corporation is conducting its year-end review of pension plan performance. Staff has prepared the following exhibits regarding the tactical asset allocation decisions taken during the past year. Assume that all investments are implemented using passively managed index funds. Evaluate the effectiveness of the TAA decisions.

EXHIBIT 12A

Asset Class	Asset Allocation	Calendar Year Return
Investment-grade bonds	45%	3.45%
High-yield bonds	5%	−6.07%
Developed markets equity	45%	−0.32%
Emerging markets equity	5%	−14.60%

EXHIBIT 12B

	Policy Portfolio	Realized Results
12-month return	−0.82%	0.38%
Risk-free rate	0.50%	0.50%
Standard deviation	5.80%	6.20%
Sharpe ratio	−0.23	−0.02

EXHIBIT 12C

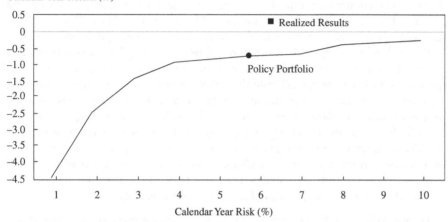

Solution to 1: The TAA decision must be taken in the context of the SAA policy constraints. Thus, although the signals for high-yield bonds and emerging market equities are negative, the minimum permissible weight in each is 5%. Similarly, although the signals for investment-grade bonds and developed markets equities are positive, the maximum permissible weight in each is 45%. Asset classes can be over- or underweighted to the full extent of the policy limits. Based on the trend signals and the policy constraints, the recommended tactical asset allocation is as follows:

- Investment-grade bonds   45% *(overweight by 5%)*
- High-yield bonds   5% *(underweight by 5%)*
- Developed markets equity   45% *(overweight by 5%)*
- Emerging markets equity   5% *(underweight by 5%)*

Solution to 2: The decision to overweight investment grade bonds and underweight emerging markets equity and high-yield bonds was a profitable one. The chosen asset allocation added approximately 120 basis points to portfolio return over the year. Although portfolio risk was elevated relative to the policy portfolio (standard deviation of 6.2% versus 5.8% for the policy portfolio), the portfolio positioning improved the fund's Sharpe ratio relative to allocations they might have selected along the efficient frontier.

A Silver Lining to the 2008–2009 Financial Crisis

Prior to 2008, corporate pension plans had begun to shift the fixed-income component of their policy portfolios from an intermediate maturity bond index to a long bond index. Despite the relatively low interest rates at the time, this move was made to better align the plans' assets with the long duration liability payment stream. The fixed-income portfolios were typically benchmarked against a long government and credit index that included both government and corporate bonds. Swaps or STRIPS* were sometimes used to extend duration.

During the financial crisis that began in 2008, these heavier and longer-duration fixed-income positions performed well relative to equities (the long government and credit index was up 8%, whereas the S&P 500 Index was down 37% in 2008), providing plan sponsors with a level of investment protection that had not been anticipated. Additionally, with its exposure to higher-returning government bonds that benefited from investors' flight to safety, this fixed-income portfolio often outperformed the liabilities. (Recall from the earlier discussion on pension regulation that pension liabilities are typically measured using corporate bond yields. Thus, liabilities rose in the face of declining corporate bond yields while the liability-hedging asset rose even further given its overall higher credit quality.) This was an unintended asset/ liability mismatch that had very positive results. Subsequent to this rally in bonds, some plan sponsors made a tactical asset allocation decision—to move out of swaps and government bonds and into physical corporate bonds (non-derivative fixed-income exposure)—locking in the gains and better hedging the liability.

* Treasury STRIPS are fixed-income securities with no interest payments that are sold at a discount to face value and mature at par. STRIPS is an acronym for Separate Trading of Registered Interest and Principal of Securities.

6. DEALING WITH BEHAVIORAL BIASES IN ASSET ALLOCATION

Although global capital markets are competitive pricing engines, human behavior can be less rational than most economic models assume. Behavioral finance—the hybrid study of financial economics and psychology—has documented a number of behavioral biases that commonly arise in investing. The CFA Program chapter "The Behavioral Biases of Individuals" discusses 16 common behavioral biases. The biases most relevant in asset allocation include loss aversion, the illusion of control, mental accounting, representativeness bias, framing, and availability bias. An effective investment program will address these decision-making risks through a formal asset allocation process with its own objective framework, governance, and controls. An important first step toward mitigating the negative effects of behavioral biases is simply acknowledging that they exist; just being aware of them can reduce their influence on decision-making. It is also possible to incorporate certain behavioral biases into the investment decision-making process to produce better outcomes. This is most commonly practiced in goals-based investing. We will discuss strategies that help deal with these common biases.

6.1. Loss Aversion

Loss-aversion bias is an emotional bias in which people tend to strongly prefer avoiding losses as opposed to achieving gains. A number of studies on loss aversion suggest that, psychologically, losses are significantly more powerful than gains. The utility derived from a gain is much lower than the utility given up with an equivalent loss. This behavior is related to the marginal utility of wealth, where each additional dollar of wealth is valued incrementally less with increasing levels of wealth.

A diversified multi-asset class portfolio is generally thought to offer an approximately symmetrical distribution of returns around a positive expected mean return. Financial market theory suggests that a rational investor would think about risk as the dispersion or uncertainty (variance) around the mean (expected) outcome. However, loss aversion suggests the investor assigns a greater weight to the negative outcomes than would be implied by the actual shape of the distribution. Looking at this another way, risk is not measured relative to the expected mean return but rather on an absolute basis, relative to a 0% return. The loss-aversion bias may interfere with an investor's ability to maintain his chosen asset allocation through periods of negative returns.

In goals-based investing, loss-aversion bias can be mitigated by framing risk in terms of shortfall probability or by funding high-priority goals with low-risk assets.

Shortfall probability is the probability that a portfolio will not achieve the return required to meet a stated goal. Where there are well-defined, discrete goals, sub-portfolios can be established for each goal and the asset allocation for that sub-portfolio would use shortfall probability as the definition of risk.

Similarly, by segregating assets into sub-portfolios aligned to goals designated by the client as high-priority and investing those assets in risk-free or low risk assets of similar duration, the adviser mitigates the loss-aversion bias associated with this particular goal—freeing up other assets to take on a more appropriate level of risk. Riskier assets can then be used to fund lower-priority and aspirational goals.

In institutional investing, loss aversion can be seen in the herding behavior among plan sponsors. Adopting an asset allocation not too different from the allocation of one's peers minimizes reputation risk.

6.2. Illusion of Control

The illusion of control is a cognitive bias—the tendency to overestimate one's ability to control events. It can be exacerbated by overconfidence, an emotional bias. If investors believe they have more or better information than what is reflected in the market, they have (excessive) confidence in their ability to generate better outcomes. They may perceive *information* in what are random price movements, which may lead to more frequent trading, greater concentration of portfolio positions, or a greater willingness to employ tactical shifts in their asset allocation. The following investor behaviors might be attributed to this illusion of control:

- Alpha-seeking behaviors, such as attempted market timing in the form of extreme tactical asset allocation shifts or all in/all out market calls—the investor who correctly anticipated a market reversal now believes he has superior insight on valuation levels.
- Alpha-seeking behaviors based on a belief of superior resources—the institutional investor who believes her internal resources give her an edge over other investors in active security selection and/or the selection of active investment managers.

- Excessive trading, use of leverage, or short selling—the long/short equity investor who moves from a normal exposure range of 65% long/20% short to 100% long/50% short.
- Reducing, eliminating, or even shorting asset classes that are a significant part of the global market portfolio based on non-consensus return and risk forecasts—the chair of a foundation's investment committee who calls for shortening the duration of the bond portfolio from six years to six months based on insights drawn from his position in the banking industry.
- Retaining a large, concentrated legacy asset that contributes diversifiable risk—the employee who fails to diversify her holding of company stock.

Hindsight bias—the tendency to perceive past investment outcomes as having been predictable—exacerbates the illusion of control.

In the asset allocation process, an investor who believes he or she has better information than others may use estimates of return and risk that produce asset allocation choices that are materially different from the market portfolio. This can result in undiversified portfolios with outsized exposures to just one or two minor asset classes, called extreme corner portfolios. Using such biased risk and return estimates results in a biased asset allocation decision—precisely what an objective asset allocation process seeks to avoid.

The illusion of control can be mitigated by using the global market portfolio as the starting point in developing the asset allocation. Building on the basic principles of CAPM, Markowitz's mean–variance theory, and efficient market theory, the global market portfolio offers a theoretically sound benchmark for asset allocation. Deviations from this baseline portfolio must be thoughtfully considered and rigorously vetted, ensuring the asset allocation process remains objective. A formal asset allocation process that employs long-term return and risk forecasts, optimization constraints anchored around asset class weights in the global market portfolio, and strict policy ranges will significantly mitigate the illusion of control bias in asset allocation.

6.3. Mental Accounting

Mental accounting is an information-processing bias in which people treat one sum of money differently from another sum based solely on the mental account the money is assigned to. Investors may separate assets or liabilities into buckets based on subjective criteria. For example, an investor may consider his retirement investment portfolio independent of the portfolio that funds his child's education, even if the combined asset allocation of the two portfolios is sub-optimal. Or an employee with significant exposure to her employer's stock through vested stock options may fail to consider this exposure alongside other assets when establishing a strategic asset allocation.

Goals-based investing incorporates mental accounting directly into the asset allocation solution. Each goal is aligned with a discrete sub-portfolio, and the investor can specify the acceptable level of risk for each goal. Provided each of the sub-portfolios lies along the same efficient frontier, the sum of the sub-portfolios will also be efficient.[24]

---

[24]This condition holds when the asset allocation process is unconstrained. With a long-only constraint, some efficiency is lost but the effect is much less significant than the loss of efficiency from inaccurately specifying risk aversion (which goals-based approaches to asset allocation attempt to mitigate). See Das, Markowitz, Scheid, and Statman (2010) and Das et al. (2011).

Concentrated stock positions also give rise to another common mental accounting issue that affects asset allocation. For example, the primary source of an entrepreneur's wealth may be a concentrated equity position in the publicly traded company he founded. The entrepreneur may prefer to retain a relatively large exposure to this one security within his broader investment portfolio despite the inherent risk. Although there may be rational reasons for this preference—including ownership control, an information advantage, and tax considerations—the desire to retain this riskier exposure is more often the result of a psychological loyalty to the asset that generated his wealth. This mental accounting bias is further reinforced by the endowment effect—the tendency to ascribe more value to an asset already owned rather than another asset one might purchase to replace it.

The concentrated stock/mental accounting bias can be accommodated in goals-based asset allocation by assigning the concentrated stock position to an aspirational goal—one that the client would *like* to achieve but to which he or she is willing to assign a lower probability of success. Whereas lifetime consumption tends to be a high-priority goal requiring a well-diversified portfolio to fund it with confidence, an aspirational goal such as a charitable gift may be an important but much less highly valued goal. It can reasonably be funded with the concentrated stock position. (This could have the additional benefit of avoiding capital gains tax altogether!)

6.4. Representativeness Bias

Representativeness, or recency, bias is the tendency to overweight the importance of the most recent observations and information relative to a longer-dated or more comprehensive set of long-term observations and information. Tactical shifts in asset allocation, those undertaken in response to recent returns or news—perhaps shifting the asset allocation toward the highest or lowest allowable ends of the policy ranges—are particularly susceptible to recency bias. Return chasing is a common manifestation of recency bias, and it results in overweighting asset classes with good recent performance.

It is believed that asset prices largely follow a random walk; past prices cannot be used to predict future returns. If this is true, then shifting the asset allocation in response to recent returns, or allowing recent returns to unduly influence the asset class assumptions used in the asset allocation process, will likely lead to sub-optimal results. *If,* however, asset class returns exhibit trending behavior, the recent past *may* contain information relevant to tactical shifts in asset allocation. And if asset class returns are mean-reverting, comparing current valuations to historical norms may signal the potential for a reversal or for above-average future returns.

Recency bias is not uniformly negative. Random walk, trending, and mean-reversion may be simultaneously relevant to the investment decision-making process, although their effect on asset prices will unfold over different time horizons. The strongest defenses against recency bias are an objective asset allocation process and a strong governance framework. It is important that the investor objectively evaluate the motivation underlying the response to recent market events. A formal asset allocation policy with pre-specified allowable ranges will constrain recency bias. A strong governance framework with the appropriate level of expertise and well-documented investment beliefs increases the likelihood that shifts in asset allocation are made objectively and in accordance with those beliefs.

6.5. Framing Bias

Framing bias is an information-processing bias in which a person may answer a question differently based solely on the way in which it is asked. One example of framing bias is common in committee-oriented decision-making processes. In instances where one individual frequently speaks first and speaks with great authority, the views of other committee members may be suppressed or biased toward this first position put on the table.

A more nuanced form of framing bias can be found in asset allocation. The investor's choice of an asset allocation may be influenced merely by the manner in which the risk-to-return trade-off is presented.

Risk can mean different things to different investors: volatility, tail risk, the permanent loss of capital, or a failure to meet financial goals. These definitions are all closely related, but the relative importance of each of these aspects can influence the investor's asset allocation choice. Further, the investor's perception of each of these risks can be influenced by the manner in which they are presented—gain and loss potential framed in money terms versus percentages, for example.

Investors are often asked to evaluate portfolio choices using expected return, with standard deviation as the sole measure of risk. Standard deviation measures the dispersion or volatility around the mean (expected) return. Other measures of risk may also be used. Value at risk (VaR) is a loss threshold: "If I choose this asset mix, I can be pretty sure that my losses will not exceed X, most of the time." More formally, VaR is the minimum loss that would be expected a certain percentage of the time over a certain period of time given the assumed market conditions. Conditional value at risk (CVaR) is the probability-weighted average of losses when the VaR threshold is breached. VaR and CVaR both measure downside or tail risk.

Exhibit 13 shows the expected return and risk for five portfolios that span an efficient frontier from P1 (lowest risk) to P100 (highest risk). A normal distribution of returns is assumed; therefore, the portfolio's VaR and CVaR are a direct function of the portfolio's expected return and standard deviation. In this case, standard deviation, VaR, and CVaR measure precisely the same risk but frame that risk differently. Standard deviation presents that risk as volatility, while VaR and CVaR present it as risk of loss. When dealing with a normal distribution, as this example presumes, the 5% VaR threshold is simply the point on the distribution 1.65 standard deviations below the expected mean return.

EXHIBIT 13   There's More Than One Way to Frame Risk

	P1	P25	P50	P75	P100
Return	3.2%	4.9%	6.0%	7.0%	8.0%
Std. Dev.	3.9%	7.8%	11.9%	15.9%	20.0%
VaR (5%)	−3.2%	−8.0%	−13.6%	−19.3%	−25.0%
CVaR (5%)	−4.8%	−11.2%	−18.5%	−25.8%	−33.2%

When viewing return and volatility alone, many investors may gravitate to P50 with its 6.0% expected return and 11.9% standard deviation. P50 represents the median risk portfolio that appeals to many investors in practice because it balances high-risk and low-risk choices with related diversification benefits. However, loss-aversion bias suggests that some investors who gravitate to the median choice might actually find the −18.5% CVaR of P50 indicative of a level of risk they find very uncomfortable. The CVaR frame intuitively communicates a different perspective of exactly the same risk that is already fully explained by standard deviation—namely, the downside or tail-risk aspects of the standard deviation and mean. With this example, you can see that how risk is framed and presented can affect the asset allocation decision.

The framing effect can be mitigated by presenting the possible asset allocation choices with multiple perspectives on the risk/reward trade-off. The most commonly used risk measure—standard deviation—can be supplemented with additional measures, such as **shortfall probability** (the probability of failing to meet a specific liability or goal)[25] and tail-risk measures (e.g., VaR and CVaR). Historical stress tests and Monte Carlo simulations can also be used to capture and communicate risk in a tangible way. These multiple perspectives of the risk and reward trade-offs among a set of asset allocation choices compel the investor to consider more carefully what outcomes are acceptable or unacceptable.

6.6. Availability Bias

Availability bias is an information-processing bias in which people take a mental shortcut when estimating the probability of an outcome based on how easily the outcome comes to mind. Easily recalled outcomes are often perceived as being more likely than those that are harder to recall or understand. For example, more recent events or events in which the investor has personally been affected are likely to be assigned a higher probability of occurring again, regardless of the objective odds of the event actually occurring.

As an example, many private equity investors experienced a liquidity squeeze during the financial crisis that began in 2008. Their equity portfolios had suffered large losses, and their private equity investments were illiquid. Worse yet, they were contractually committed to additional capital contributions to those private equity funds. At the same time, their financial obligations continued at the same or an even higher pace. Investors who personally experienced this confluence of negative events are likely to express a strong preference for liquid investments, assigning a higher probability to such an event occurring again than would an investor who had cash available to acquire the private equity interests that were sold at distressed prices.

Familiarity bias stems from availability bias: People tend to favor the familiar over the new or different because of the ease of recalling the familiar. In asset allocation, familiarity bias most commonly results in a **home bias**—a preference for securities listed on the exchanges of one's home country. However, concentrating portfolio exposure in home country securities, particularly if the home country capital markets are small, results in a less diversified, less efficient portfolio. Familiarity bias can be mitigated by using the global market portfolio as the starting point in developing the asset allocation, where deviations from this baseline portfolio must be thoughtfully considered and rigorously vetted.

Familiarity bias may also cause investors to fall into the trap of comparing their investment decisions (and performance) to others', without regard for the appropriateness of those decisions for their own specific facts and circumstances. By avoiding comparison of

---

[25]Shortfall risk and shortfall probability are often used to refer to the same concept. This author prefers shortfall probability because the measure refers to the probability of shortfall, not the magnitude of the potential shortfall. For example, you may have a low probability of shortfall but the size of the shortfall could be significant. In this case, it could be misleading to say the shortfall risk is low.

investment returns or asset allocation decisions with others, an organization is more capable of identifying the asset allocation that is best tailored to their needs.

Investment decision-making is subject to a wide range of potential behavioral biases. This is true in both private wealth *and* institutional investing. Employing a formal asset allocation process using the global market portfolio as the starting point for asset allocation modeling is a key component of ensuring the asset allocation decision is as objective as possible.

A strong governance structure, such as that discussed in the overview chapter on asset allocation, is a necessary first step to mitigating the effect that these behavioral biases may have on the long-term success of the investment program. Bringing a diverse set of views to the deliberation process brings more tools to the table to solve any problem and leads to better and more informed decision-making. A clearly stated mission—a common goal—and a commitment from committee members and other stakeholders to that mission are critically important in constraining the influence of these biases on investment decisions.

Effective Investment Governance

Six critical elements of effective investment governance are

1. clearly articulated long- and short-term investment objectives of the investment program;
2. allocation of decision rights and responsibilities among the functional units in the governance hierarchy, taking account of their knowledge, capacity, time, and position in the governance hierarchy;
3. established processes for developing and approving the investment policy statement that will govern the day-to-day operation of the investment program;
4. specified processes for developing and approving the program's strategic asset allocation;
5. a reporting framework to monitor the program's progress toward the agreed-upon goals and objectives; and
6. periodic governance audits.

EXAMPLE 8   Mitigating Behavioral Biases in Asset Allocation

Ivy Lee, the retired founder of a publicly traded company, has two primary goals for her investment assets. The first goal is to fund lifetime consumption expenditures of US$1 million per year for herself and her husband; this is a goal the Lees want to achieve with a high degree of certainty. The second goal is to provide an end-of-life gift to Auldberg University. Ivy has a diversified portfolio of stocks and bonds totaling US$5 million and a sizable position in the stock of the company she founded. The following table summarizes the facts.

Investor Profile

Annual consumption needs	US$1,000,000
Remaining years of life expectancy	40
Diversified stock holdings	US$3,000,000
Diversified bond holdings	US$2,000,000
Concentrated stock holdings	US$15,000,000
Total portfolio	US$20,000,000

Assume that a 60% equity/40% fixed-income portfolio represents the level of risk Ivy is willing to assume with respect to her consumption goal. This 60/40 portfolio offers an expected return of 6.0%. (For simplicity, this illustration ignores inflation and taxes.)

The present value of the expected consumption expenditures is US$15,949,075. This is the amount needed on hand today, which, if invested in a portfolio of 60% equities and 40% fixed income, would fully fund 40 annual cash distributions of US $1,000,000 each.[26]

The concentrated stock has a highly uncertain expected return and comes with significant idiosyncratic (stock-specific) risk. A preliminary mean–variance optimization using three "asset classes"—stocks, bonds, and the concentrated stock—results in a zero allocation to the concentrated stock position. But Ivy prefers to retain as much concentrated stock as possible because it represents her legacy and she has a strong psychological loyalty to it.

1. Describe the behavioral biases most relevant to developing an asset allocation recommendation for Ivy.
2. Recommend and justify an asset allocation for Ivy given the facts presented above.

Solution to 1: Two behavioral biases that the adviser must be aware of in developing an asset allocation recommendation for Ivy are illusion of control and mental accounting. Because Ivy was the founder of the company whose stock comprises 75% of her investment portfolio, she may believe she has more or better information about the return prospects for this portion of the portfolio. The belief that she has superior information may lead to a risk assessment that is not reflective of the true risk in the holding. Using a goals-based approach to asset allocation may help Ivy more fully understand the risks inherent in the concentrated stock position. The riskier, concentrated stock position can be assigned to a lower-priority goal, such as the gift to Auldberg University.

Solution to 2:

	Beginning Asset Allocation	**Recommended Asset Allocation**
Diversified stocks	US$3,000,000	US$9,600,000
Diversified bonds	US$2,000,000	US$6,400,000
Funding of lifestyle goal		*US$16,000,000*
Concentrated stock	US$15,000,000	US$4,000,000
Total portfolio	US$20,000,000	US$20,000,000

---

[26]Assumes cash distributions occur at the beginning of the year and the expected return is the geometric average.

It is recommended that Ivy fully fund her high-priority lifestyle consumption needs (US$15,949,075) with US$16 million in a diversified portfolio of stocks and bonds. To achieve this, US$11 million of the concentrated stock position should be sold and the proceeds added to the diversified portfolio that supports lifestyle consumption needs. The remaining US$4 million of concentrated stock can be retained to fund the aspirational goal of an end-of-life gift to Auldberg University. In this example, the adviser has employed the mental accounting bias to achieve a suitable outcome: By illustrating the dollar value needed to fund the high-priority lifetime consumption needs goal, the adviser was able to clarify for Ivy the risks in retaining the concentrated stock position. The adviser might also simulate portfolio returns and the associated probability of achieving Ivy's goals using a range of scenarios for the performance of the concentrated stock position. Framing the effect this one holding may have on the likelihood of achieving her goals may help Ivy agree to reduce the position size. Consideration of certain behavioral biases like mental accounting can improve investor outcomes when they are incorporated in an objective decision-making framework.

7. SUMMARY

- The primary constraints on an asset allocation decision are asset size, liquidity, time horizon, and other external considerations, such as taxes and regulation.
- The size of an asset owner's portfolio may limit the asset classes accessible to the asset owner. An asset owner's portfolio may be too small—or too large—to capture the returns of certain asset classes or strategies efficiently.
- Complex asset classes and investment vehicles require sufficient governance capacity.
- Large-scale asset owners may achieve operating efficiencies, but they may find it difficult to deploy capital effectively in certain active investment strategies given liquidity conditions and trading costs.
- Smaller portfolios may also be constrained by size. They may be too small to adequately diversify across the range of asset classes and investment managers, or they may have staffing constraints that prevent them from monitoring a complex investment program.
- Investors with smaller portfolios may be constrained in their ability to access private equity, private real estate, hedge funds, and infrastructure investments because of the high required minimum investments and regulatory restrictions associated with those asset classes. Wealthy families may pool assets to meet the required minimums.
- The liquidity needs of the asset owner and the liquidity characteristics of the asset classes each influence the available opportunity set.
- Liquidity needs must also take into consideration the financial strength of the investor and resources beyond those held in the investment portfolio.
- When assessing the appropriateness of any given asset class for a given investor, it is important to evaluate potential liquidity needs in the context of an extreme market stress event.

- An investor's time horizon must be considered in any asset allocation exercise. Changes in human capital and the changing character of liabilities are two important time-related constraints of asset allocation.
- External considerations—such as regulations, tax rules, funding, and financing needs—are also likely to influence the asset allocation decision.
- Taxes alter the distribution of returns by both reducing the expected mean return and muting the dispersion of returns. Asset values and asset risk and return inputs to asset allocation should be modified to reflect the tax status of the investor. Correlation assumptions do not need to be adjusted, but taxes do affect the return and the standard deviation assumptions for each asset class.
- Periodic portfolio rebalancing to return the portfolio to its target strategic asset allocation is an integral part of sound portfolio management. Taxable investors must consider the tax implications of rebalancing.
- Rebalancing thresholds may be wider for taxable portfolios because it takes larger asset class movements to materially alter the risk profile of the taxable portfolio.
- Strategic asset location is the placement of less tax-efficient assets in accounts with more-favorable tax treatment.
- An asset owner's strategic asset allocation should be re-examined periodically, even in the absence of a change in the asset owner's circumstances.
- A special review of the asset allocation policy may be triggered by a change in goals, constraints, or beliefs.
- In some situations, a change to an asset allocation strategy may be implemented without a formal asset allocation study. Anticipating key milestones that would alter the asset owner's risk appetite, and implementing pre-established changes to the asset allocation in response, is often referred to as a "glide path."
- Tactical asset allocation (TAA) allows short-term deviations from the strategic asset allocation (SAA) targets and are expected to increase risk-adjusted return. Using either short-term views or signals, the investor actively re-weights broad asset classes, sectors, or risk-factor premiums. The sizes of these deviations from the SAA are often constrained by the Investment Policy Statement.
- The success of TAA decisions is measured against the performance of the SAA policy portfolio by comparing Sharpe ratios, evaluating the information ratio or the t-statistic of the average excess return of the TAA portfolio relative to the SAA portfolio, or plotting outcomes versus the efficient frontier.
- TAA incurs trading and tax costs. Tactical trades can also increase the concentration of risk.
- Discretionary TAA relies on a qualitative interpretation of political, economic, and financial market conditions and is predicated on a belief of persistent manager skill in predicting and timing short-term market moves.
- Systematic TAA relies on quantitative signals to capture documented return anomalies that may be inconsistent with market efficiency.
- The behavioral biases most relevant in asset allocation include loss aversion, the illusion of control, mental accounting, recency bias, framing, and availability bias.
- An effective investment program will address behavioral biases through a formal asset allocation process with its own objective framework, governance, and controls.
- In goals-based investing, loss-aversion bias can be mitigated by framing risk in terms of shortfall probability or by funding high-priority goals with low-risk assets.

- The cognitive bias, illusion of control, and hindsight bias can all be mitigated by using a formal asset allocation process that uses long-term return and risk forecasts, optimization constraints anchored around asset class weights in the global market portfolio, and strict policy ranges.
- Goals-based investing incorporates the mental accounting bias directly into the asset allocation solution by aligning each goal with a discrete sub-portfolio.
- A formal asset allocation policy with pre-specified allowable ranges may constrain recency bias.
- The framing bias effect can be mitigated by presenting the possible asset allocation choices with multiple perspectives on the risk/reward trade-off.
- Familiarity bias, a form of availability bias, most commonly results in an overweight in home country securities and may also cause investors to inappropriately compare their investment decisions (and performance) to other organizations. Familiarity bias can be mitigated by using the global market portfolio as the starting point in developing the asset allocation and by carefully evaluating any potential deviations from this baseline portfolio.
- A strong governance framework with the appropriate level of expertise and well-documented investment beliefs increases the likelihood that shifts in asset allocation are made objectively and in accordance with those beliefs. This will help to mitigate the effect that behavioral biases may have on the long-term success of the investment program.

REFERENCES

Bader, Lawrence N., and Jeremy Gold. 2007. "The Case against Stock in Public Pension Funds." *Financial Analysts Journal*, vol. 63, no. 1 (January/February): 55–62.

Bodie, Zvi, Robert C. Merton, and William F. Samuelson. 1992. "Labor Supply Flexibility and Portfolio Choice in a Life Cycle Model." *Journal of Economic Dynamics & Control*, vol. 16: 427–449.

Chen, Joseph, Harrison Hong, Ming Huang, and Jeffrey Kubik. 2004. "Does Fund Size Erode Mutual Fund Performance? The Role of Liquidity and Organization." *American Economic Review*, vol. 94, no. 5: 1276–1302.

Cooper, Stephen, and David Bianco. 2003. "Q-Series™: Pension Fund Asset Allocation." UBS Investment Research (September).

Das, Sanjiv, Harry Markowitz, Jonathan Scheid, and Meir Statman. 2010. "Portfolio Optimization with Mental Accounts." *Journal of Financial and Quantitative Analysis*, vol. 45, no. 2: 311–334.

Das, Sanjiv, Harry Markowitz, Jonathan Scheid, and Meir Statman. 2011. "Portfolios for Investors Who Want to Reach Their Goals While Staying on the Mean–Variance Efficient Frontier." *Journal of Wealth Management*, vol. 14, no. 2 (Fall): 25–31.

Dyck, Alexander, and Lukasz Pomorski. 2011. "Is Bigger Better? Size and Performance in Pension Plan Management." Rotman School of Management Working Paper No. 1690724.

Horan, Stephen, and Ashraf Al Zaman. 2008. "Tax-Adjusted Portfolio Optimization and Asset Location: Extensions and Synthesis." *Journal of Wealth Management*, vol. 11, no. 3: 56–73.

Kritzman, Mark. 2015. "What Practitioners Need to Know about Time Diversification (corrected March 2015)." *Financial Analysts Journal*, vol. 71, no. 1 (January/February): 29–34.

Mladina, Peter. 2011. "Portfolio Implications of Triple Net Returns." *Journal of Wealth Management*, vol. 13, no. 4 (Spring): 51–59.

Pollet, Joshua, and Mungo Wilson. 2008. "How Does Size Affect Mutual Fund Behavior?" *Journal of Finance*, vol. 63, no. 6 (December): 2941–2969.

Reichenstein, William. 2006. "After-Tax Asset Allocation." *Financial Analysts Journal*, vol. 62, no. 4 (July/August): 14–19.

Samuelson, Paul A. 1963. "Risk and Uncertainty: A Fallacy of Large Numbers." *Scientia*, vol. 57, no. 98: 108–113.

Samuelson, Paul A. 1969. "Lifetime Portfolio Selection by Dynamic Stochastic Programming." *Review of Economics and Statistics*, vol. 51, no. 3: 239–246.

Stein, Jeremy. 2002. "Information Production and Capital Allocation: Decentralized versus Hierarchical Firms." *Journal of Finance*, vol. 57, no. 5 (October): 1891–1921.

Turvey, Philip, Anup Basu, and Peter Verhoeven. 2013. "Embedded Tax Liabilities and Portfolio Choice." *Journal of Portfolio Management*, vol. 39, no. 3: 93–101.

PRACTICE PROBLEMS

The following information relates to questions 1–6

Rebecca Mayer is an asset management consultant for institutions and high-net-worth individuals. Mayer meets with Sebastian Capara, the newly appointed Investment Committee chairman for the Kinkardeen University Endowment (KUE), a very large tax-exempt fund.

Capara and Mayer review KUE's current and strategic asset allocations, which are presented in Exhibit 1. Capara informs Mayer that over the last few years, Kinkardeen University has financed its operations primarily from tuition, with minimal need of financial support from KUE. Enrollment at the University has been rising in recent years, and the Board of Trustees expects enrollment growth to continue for the next five years. Consequently, the board expects very modest endowment support to be needed during that time. These expectations led the Investment Committee to approve a decrease in the endowment's annual spending rate starting in the next fiscal year.

EXHIBIT 1   Kinkardeen University Endowment—Strategic Asset Allocation Policy

Asset Class	Current Weight	Target Allocation	Lower Policy Limit	Upper Policy Limit
Developed markets equity	30%	30%	25%	35%
Emerging markets equity	28%	30%	25%	35%
Investment-grade bonds	15%	20%	15%	25%
Private real estate equity	15%	10%	5%	15%
Infrastructure	12%	10%	5%	15%

As an additional source of alpha, Mayer proposes tactically adjusting KUE's asset-class weights to profit from short-term return opportunities. To confirm his understanding of tactical asset allocation (TAA), Capara tells Mayer the following:

Statement 1.   The Sharpe ratio is suitable for measuring the success of TAA relative to SAA.

Statement 2.   Discretionary TAA attempts to capture asset-class-level return anomalies that have been shown to have some predictability and persistence.

Statement 3.   TAA allows a manager to deviate from the IPS asset-class upper and lower limits if the shift is expected to produce higher expected risk-adjusted returns.

Capara asks Mayer to recommend a TAA strategy based on excess return forecasts for the asset classes in KUE's portfolio, as shown in Exhibit 2.

EXHIBIT 2   Short-Term Excess Return Forecast

Asset Class	Expected Excess Return
Developed markets equity	2%
Emerging markets equity	5%
Investment-grade bonds	–3%
Private real estate equity	3%
Infrastructure	–1%

Following her consultation with Capara, Mayer meets with Roger Koval, a member of a wealthy family. Although Koval's baseline needs are secured by a family trust, Koval has a personal portfolio to fund his lifestyle goals.

In Koval's country, interest income is taxed at progressively higher income tax rates. Dividend income and long-term capital gains are taxed at lower tax rates relative to interest and earned income. In taxable accounts, realized capital losses can be used to offset current or future realized capital gains. Koval is in a high tax bracket, and his taxable account currently holds, in equal weights, high-yield bonds, investment-grade bonds, and domestic equities focused on long-term capital gains.

Koval asks Mayer about adding new asset classes to the taxable portfolio. Mayer suggests emerging markets equity given its positive short-term excess return forecast. However, Koval tells Mayer he is not interested in adding emerging markets equity to the account because he is convinced it is too risky. Koval justifies this belief by referring to significant losses the family trust suffered during the recent economic crisis.

Mayer also suggests using two mean–variance portfolio optimization scenarios for the taxable account to evaluate potential asset allocations. Mayer recommends running two optimizations: one on a pre-tax basis and another on an after-tax basis.

1. The change in the annual spending rate, in conjunction with the board's expectations regarding future enrollment and the need for endowment support, could justify that KUE's target weight for:
   A. infrastructure be increased.
   B. investment-grade bonds be increased.
   C. private real estate equity be decreased.

2. Which of Capara's statements regarding tactical asset allocation is correct?
   A. Statement 1
   B. Statement 2
   C. Statement 3

3. Based on Exhibits 1 and 2, to attempt to profit from the short-term excess return forecast, Capara should increase KUE's portfolio allocation to:
   A. developed markets equity and decrease its allocation to infrastructure.
   B. emerging markets equity and decrease its allocation to investment-grade bonds.
   C. developed markets equity and increase its allocation to private real estate equity.

4. Given Koval's current portfolio and the tax laws of the country in which he lives, Koval's portfolio would be more tax efficient if he reallocated his taxable account to hold more:
   A. high-yield bonds.
   B. investment-grade bonds.
   C. domestic equities focused on long-term capital gain opportunities.

5. Koval's attitude toward emerging markets equity reflects which of the following behavioral biases?
   A. Hindsight bias
   B. Availability bias
   C. Illusion of control

6. In both of Mayer's optimization scenarios, which of the following model inputs could be used without adjustment?
   A. Expected returns
   B. Correlation of returns
   C. Standard deviations of returns

The following information relates to questions 7–13

Elsbeth Quinn and Dean McCall are partners at Camel Asset Management (CAM). Quinn advises high-net-worth individuals, and McCall specializes in retirement plans for institutions.

Quinn meets with Neal and Karina Martin, both age 44. The Martins plan to retire at age 62. Twenty percent of the Martins' $600,000 in financial assets is held in cash and earmarked for funding their daughter Lara's university studies, which begin in one year. Lara's education and their own retirement are the Martins' highest-priority goals. Last week, the Martins learned that Lara was awarded a four-year full scholarship for university. Quinn reviews how the scholarship might affect the Martins' asset allocation strategy.

The Martins have assets in both taxable and tax-deferred accounts. For baseline retirement needs, Quinn recommends that the Martins maintain their current overall 60% equity/40% bonds (± 8% rebalancing range) strategic asset allocation. Quinn calculates that given current financial assets and expected future earnings, the Martins could reduce future retirement savings by 15% and still comfortably retire at 62. The Martins wish to allocate that 15% to a sub-portfolio with the goal of making a charitable gift to their alma mater from their estate. Although the gift is a low-priority goal, the Martins want the sub-portfolio to earn the highest return possible. Quinn promises to recommend an asset allocation strategy for the Martins' aspirational goal.

Next, Quinn discusses taxation of investments with the Martins. Their interest income is taxed at 35%, and capital gains and dividends are taxed at 20%. The Martins want to minimize taxes. Based on personal research, Neal makes the following two statements:

Statement 1.   The after-tax return volatility of assets held in taxable accounts will be less than the pre-tax return volatility.
Statement 2.   Assets that receive more favorable tax treatment should be held in tax-deferred accounts.

The equity portion of the Martins' portfolios produced an annualized return of 20% for the past three years. As a result, the Martins' equity allocation in both their taxable and tax-deferred portfolios has increased to 71%, with bonds falling to 29%. The Martins want to keep the strategic asset allocation risk levels the same in both types of retirement portfolios. Quinn discusses rebalancing; however, Neal is somewhat reluctant to take money out of stocks, expressing confidence that strong investment returns will continue.

Quinn's CAM associate, McCall, meets with Bruno Snead, the director of the Katt Company Pension Fund (KCPF). The strategic asset allocation for the fund is 65% stocks/ 35% bonds. Because of favorable returns during the past eight recession-free years, the KCPF is now overfunded. However, there are early signs of the economy weakening. Since Katt Company is in a cyclical industry, the Pension Committee is concerned about future market and economic risk and fears that the high-priority goal of maintaining a fully funded status may be adversely affected. McCall suggests to Snead that the KCPF might benefit from an updated IPS. Following a thorough review, McCall recommends a new IPS and strategic asset allocation.

The proposed IPS revisions include a plan for short-term deviations from strategic asset allocation targets. The goal is to benefit from equity market trends by automatically increasing (decreasing) the allocation to equities by 5% whenever the S&P 500 Index 50-day moving average crosses above (below) the 200-day moving average.

7. Given the change in funding of Lara's education, the Martins' strategic asset allocation would *most likely* decrease exposure to:
   A. cash.
   B. bonds.
   C. equities.

8. The *most appropriate* asset allocation for the Martins' new charitable gift sub-portfolio is:
   A. 40% equities/60% bonds.
   B. 70% equities/30% bonds.
   C. 100% equities/0% bonds.

9. Which of Neal's statements regarding the taxation of investments is correct?
   A. Statement 1 only
   B. Statement 2 only
   C. Both Statement 1 and Statement 2

10. Given the Martins' risk and tax preferences, the taxable portfolio should be rebalanced:
    A. less often than the tax-deferred portfolio.
    B. as often as the tax-deferred portfolio.
    C. more often than the tax-deferred portfolio.

11. During the rebalancing discussion, which behavioral bias does Neal exhibit?
    A. Framing bias
    B. Loss aversion
    C. Representativeness bias

12. Given McCall's IPS recommendation, the *most appropriate* new strategic asset allocation for the KCPF is:
    A. 40% stocks/60% bonds.
    B. 65% stocks/35% bonds.
    C. 75% stocks/25% bonds.

13. The proposal for short-term adjustments to the KCPF asset allocation strategy is known as:
    A. de-risking.
    B. systematic tactical asset allocation.
    C. discretionary tactical asset allocation.

The following information relates to questions 14–18

Emma Young, a 47-year-old single mother of two daughters, ages 7 and 10, recently sold a business for $5.5 million net of taxes and put the proceeds into a money market account. Her other assets include a tax-deferred retirement account worth $3.0 million, a $500,000 after-tax account designated for her daughters' education, a $400,000 after-tax account for unexpected needs, and her home, which she owns outright.

Her living expenses are fully covered by her job. Young wants to retire in 15 years and to fund her retirement from existing assets. An orphan at eight who experienced childhood financial hardships, she places a high priority on retirement security and wants to avoid losing money in any of her three accounts.

14. **Identify** the behavioral biases Young is *most likely* exhibiting.

    Justify each response.

Identify the behavioral biases Young is *most likely* exhibiting. (Circle the correct answers.)

Justify each response.

Bias	Justification
Loss Aversion	
Illusion of Control	
Mental Accounting	
Representative Bias	
Framing Bias	
Availability Bias	

A broker proposes to Young three portfolios, shown in Exhibit 1. The broker also provides Young with asset class estimated returns and portfolio standard deviations in Exhibit 2 and Exhibit 3, respectively. The broker notes that there is a $500,000 minimum investment requirement for alternative assets. Finally, because the funds in the money market account are readily investible, the broker suggests using that account only for this initial investment round.

EXHIBIT 1   Proposed Portfolios

Asset Class	Portfolio 1	Portfolio 2	Portfolio 3
Municipal Bonds	5%	35%	30%
Small-Cap Equities	50%	10%	35%
Large-Cap Equities	35%	50%	35%
Private Equity	10%	5%	0%
Total	100%	100%	100%

EXHIBIT 2   Asset Class Pre-Tax Returns

Asset Class	Pre-Tax Return
Municipal Bonds	3%
Small-Cap Equities	12%
Large-Cap Equities	10%
Private Equity	25%

EXHIBIT 3   Portfolio Standard Deviations

Proposed Portfolio	Post-Tax Standard Deviation
Portfolio 1	28.2%
Portfolio 2	16.3%
Portfolio 3	15.5%

Young wants to earn at least 6.0% after tax per year, without taking on additional incremental risk. Young's capital gains and overall tax rate is 25%.

15. **Determine** which proposed portfolio *most closely* meets Young's desired objectives. **Justify** your response.

Determine which proposed portfolio *most closely* meets Young's desired objectives. (Circle one.)

Portfolio 1	**Portfolio 2**	**Portfolio 3**

Justify your response.

The broker suggests that Young rebalance her $5.5 million money market account and the $3.0 million tax-deferred retirement account periodically in order to maintain their targeted allocations. The broker proposes the same risk profile for the equity positions with two potential target equity allocations and rebalancing ranges for the two accounts as follows:

- Alternative 1: 80% equities +/– 8.0% rebalancing range
- Alternative 2: 75% equities +/– 10.7% rebalancing range

16. **Determine** which alternative *best* fits each account. **Justify** each selection.

Determine which alternative (circle one) *best* fits each account.

Account	Alternative	Justify each selection.
$5.5 Million Account	Alternative 1	
	Alternative 2	
$3.0 Million Account	Alternative 1	
	Alternative 2	

Ten years later, Young is considering an early-retirement package offer. The package would provide continuing salary and benefits for three years. The broker recommends a special review of Young's financial plan to assess potential changes to the existing allocation strategy.

17. **Identify** the *primary* reason for the broker's reassessment of Young's circumstances. **Justify** your response.

Identify the *primary* reason for the broker's reassessment of Young's circumstances. (Circle one.)

Change in goals	Change in constraints	Change in beliefs

Justify your response.

Young decides to accept the retirement offer. Having very low liquidity needs, she wants to save part of the retirement payout for unforeseen costs that might occur more than a decade in the future. The broker's view on long-term stock market prospects is positive and recommends additional equity investment.

18. **Determine** which of Young's accounts (education, retirement, reallocated money market, or unexpected needs) is *best* suited for implementing the broker's recommendation.

Determine which of Young's accounts is *best* suited for implementing the broker's recommendation. (Circle one.)

Account	Justification
Education	
Reallocated Money Market	
Retirement	
Unexpected Needs	

The following information relates to questions 19–20

Mark DuBord, a financial adviser, works with two university foundations, the Titan State Foundation (Titan) and the Fordhart University Foundation (Fordhart). He meets with each university foundation investment committee annually to review fund objectives and constraints.

Titan's portfolio has a market value of $10 million. After his annual meeting with its investment committee, DuBord notes the following points:

- Titan must spend 3% of its beginning-of-the-year asset value annually to meet legal obligations.
- The investment committee seeks exposure to private equity investments and requests DuBord's review of the Sun-Fin Private Equity Fund as a potential new investment.
- A recent declining trend in enrollment is expected to continue. This is a concern because it has led to a loss of operating revenue from tuition.
- Regulatory sanctions and penalties are likely to result in lower donations over the next five years.

DuBord supervises two junior analysts and instructs one to formulate new allocations for Titan. This analyst proposes the allocation presented in Exhibit 1.

EXHIBIT 1 Fund Information for Titan

Fund Name	Existing Allocation	Proposed Allocation	Fund Size in Billions (AUM)	Fund Minimum Investment
Global Equity Fund	70%	70%	$25	$500,000
Investment-Grade Bond Fund	27%	17%	$50	$250,000
Sun-Fin Private Equity Fund	0%	10%	$0.40	$1,000,000
Cash Equivalent Fund	3%	3%	$50	$100,000

19. **Discuss** *two* reasons why the proposed asset allocation is inappropriate for Titan.

The Fordhart portfolio has a market value of $2 billion. After his annual meeting with its investment committee, DuBord notes the following points:

- Fordhart must spend 3% of its beginning-of-the-year asset value annually to meet legal obligations.
- The investment committee seeks exposure to private equity investments and requests that DuBord review the CFQ Private Equity Fund as a potential new investment.
- Enrollment is strong and growing, leading to increased operating revenues from tuition.
- A recent legal settlement eliminated an annual obligation of $50 million from the portfolio to support a biodigester used in the university's Center for Renewable Energy.

DuBord instructs his second junior analyst to formulate new allocations for Fordhart. This analyst proposes the allocation presented in Exhibit 2.

EXHIBIT 2 Fund Information for Fordhart

Fund Name	Existing Allocation	Proposed Allocation	Fund Size in Billions (AUM)	Fund Minimum Investment
Large-Cap Equity Fund	49%	29%	$50	$250,000
Investment-Grade Bond Fund	49%	59%	$80	$500,000
CFQ Private Equity Fund	0%	10%	$0.5	$5,000,000
Cash Equivalent Fund	2%	2%	$50	$250,000

20. **Discuss** *two* reasons why the proposed asset allocation is inappropriate for Fordhart.

CHAPTER 8

ASSET ALLOCATION TO ALTERNATIVE INVESTMENTS

Adam Kobor, PhD, CFA

Mark D. Guinney, CFA

LEARNING OUTCOMES

The candidate should be able to:

- explain the roles that alternative investments play in multi-asset portfolios;
- compare alternative investments and bonds as risk mitigators in relation to a long equity position;
- compare traditional and risk-based approaches to defining the investment opportunity set, including alternative investments;
- discuss investment considerations that are important in allocating to different types of alternative investments;
- discuss suitability considerations in allocating to alternative investments;
- discuss approaches to asset allocation to alternative investments;
- discuss the importance of liquidity planning in allocating to alternative investments;
- discuss considerations in monitoring alternative investment programs.

1. INTRODUCTION

Asset allocation is a critical decision in the investment process. The mathematical and analytical processes inherent in contemporary asset allocation techniques are complicated by the idiosyncrasies of alternative investments. Approaches to incorporating alternative assets into the strategic asset allocation have developed rapidly as allocations to assets other than

---

stocks and bonds have accelerated in the aftermath of the 2008 Global Financial Crisis. The term "alternative" understates the prominence of alternative investment allocations in many investment programs, because institutional and private clients have been increasingly turning to these investments not just to supplement traditional long-only stocks and bonds but also sometimes to replace them altogether. For example, the Yale Endowment and the Canada Pension Plan Investment Board both have close to 50% of their assets allocated to alternatives.[1] Although these two funds are admittedly outliers, between 2008 and 2017 most of the pension funds around the world substantially expanded their allocations to alternative asset classes. On average, pension funds in developed markets increased their allocation from 7.2% to 11.8% of assets under management (AUM) in 2017, a 63% increase.[2]

"Alternative" investment has no universally accepted definition. For the purposes of this chapter, alternative investments include private equity, hedge funds, real assets (including energy and commodity investments), commercial real estate, and private credit.

The chapter begins with a discussion of the role alternative assets play in a multi-asset portfolio and explores how alternatives may serve to mitigate long-only equity risk, a role traditionally held by bonds. We then consider different ways investors may define the opportunity set—through the traditional asset class lens or, more recently, using a risk- or factor-based lens. An allocation to alternatives is not for all investors, so the chapter describes issues that should be addressed when considering an allocation to alternatives. We then discuss approaches to asset allocation when incorporating alternatives in the opportunity set and the need for liquidity planning in private investment alternatives. Finally, the chapter discusses the unique monitoring requirements for an alternatives portfolio.

2. THE ROLE OF ALTERNATIVE INVESTMENTS IN A MULTI-ASSET PORTFOLIO

Allocations to alternatives are playing an increasing role in investor portfolios largely driven by the belief that these investments increase the risk-adjusted return expectations for their programs. Some allocations are driven by expectations of higher returns, while others are driven by the expected diversification (risk-reduction) benefits. In the aggregate, the portfolio's *risk-adjusted* return is expected to improve. Exhibit 1 provides a framework for how the common alternative strategies are generally perceived to affect the risk/return profile of a "typical" 60/40 portfolio of public stocks and bonds.

---

[1] Boston Consulting Group (BCG), "The Rise of Alternative Assets and Long-Term Investing" (March 2017).
[2] See Ivashina and Lerner 2018.

EXHIBIT 1   Alternative Investments in the Risk/Reward Continuum

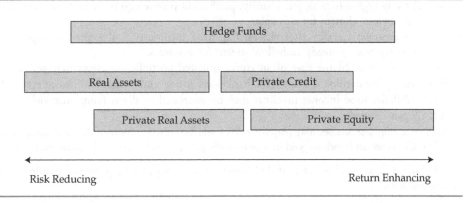

Although we present a simplified view, real assets are generally believed to mitigate the risks to the portfolio arising from unexpected inflation. At the other end of the spectrum, venture capital investments (private equity) are expected to provide a sufficient return premium over public equities to compensate for their illiquidity risk and heightened operational complexity. Hedge funds, the least homogenous of strategies, span the spectrum from "risk reducing" or diversifying (many arbitrage strategies) to "return enhancing" (e.g., an activist fund that takes significant positions in public companies with the goal of improving performance through management changes, capital allocation policies, and/or company strategy).

Risk reduction can mean different things to different investors. Institutions may choose to add non-correlated strategies to their portfolios to reduce the volatility of the overall investment program. Private clients are frequently concerned with reducing only downside volatility—the "left tail" risk associated with significant public equity market drawdowns. An insurance pool whose liabilities are sensitive to inflation might benefit from real assets that could reduce its asset–liability mismatch. Exhibit 2 provides some guidance as to how an allocator might view alternative assets vis-à-vis traditional asset classes.

EXHIBIT 2   Illustrative Capital Market Assumptions

	Traditional Assets				**Alternative Assets**					
	Public Equities	**Cash**	**Govt Bonds**	**Broad Fixed Income**	**Private Credit**	**Hedge Funds**	**Commodities**	**Public Real Estate**	**Private Real Estate**	**Private Equity**
Expected Return (Geometric Average)	6.5%	2.0%	2.3%	2.8%	6.5%	5.0%	4.5%	6.0%	5.5%	8.5%
Volatility	17.0%	1.1%	4.9%	3.4%	10.0%	8.1%	25.2%	20.4%	13.8%	15.7%
Correlation with Equities	1.00	−0.12	−0.60	−0.41	0.70	0.83	0.21	0.60	0.37	0.81
Equity Beta	1.00	−0.01	−0.17	−0.08	0.40	0.40	0.31	0.72	0.30	0.74

Source: Authors' own data.

In the context of asset allocation, investors may categorize an asset class based on the role it is expected to play in the overall portfolio. The roles and their relative importance will vary among investors, but it is common to identify the following functional roles:

- *Capital growth*: This role may be a top priority for portfolios with a long-term time horizon and relatively high-return target. Usually, public and private equity investments would be the most obvious choices for this role.
- *Income generation*: Certain asset classes, like fixed income or real estate, are capable of generating reasonably steady cash flow stream for investors.
- *Risk diversification*: In the case of an equity-oriented portfolio, investors may seek assets that diversify the dominant equity risk. Real assets and several hedge fund strategies may fit here. Similarly, fixed-income investors may be interested in diversifying pure yield curve risk via private credit.
- *Safety*: Certain asset classes may play the role of safe haven when most of the risky asset classes suffer. Government bonds or gold may potentially play such roles in a well-diversified portfolio.

Exhibit 3 illustrates how each of the alternative assets is generally perceived to fulfill these functional roles.

EXHIBIT 3   The Role of Asset Classes in a Multi-Asset Portfolio

Asset Class		Capital Growth	Income	Diversifying Public Equities	Safety
Fixed Income and Credit	Governments		M	H	H
	Inflation-Linked		M	H	H/M
	Inv.-Grade Credit		M	H	M
	High-Yield Credit		H	M	
	Private Credit		H	M	
Equities	Public Equity	H	M		
	Private Equity	H	M	M	
Real Estate	Public Real Estate	M	H	M	
	Private Real Estate	M	H	M	
Real Assets	Public Real Assets (Energy, Metal, etc.)			H	
	Private Real Assets (Timber, etc.)	H	H	H	
Hedge Funds	Absolute Return		M	H	
	Equity Long/Short			M	

Notes: H = high/strong potential to fulfill the indicated role; M = moderate potential to fulfill the indicated role.

Exhibit 4 illustrates the potential contributions the various alternative strategies might make to a portfolio dominated by equity risk. Note that the graph illustrates the *average* investment characteristics of each asset class over some extended period of time. Some assets—gold, for example—may not consistently exhibit attractive *aggregate* characteristics compared to other strategies but may serve the portfolio well during many major market shocks.

EXHIBIT 4   Diversification Potential of Various Alternative Asset Classes

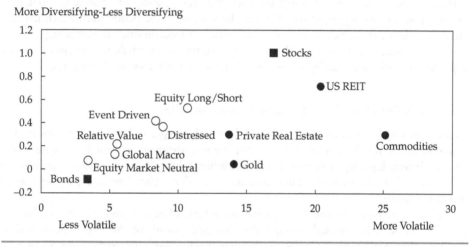

Sources: Bloomberg and authors' own data and calculations.

2.1. The Role of Private Equity in a Multi-Asset Portfolio

Private equity investments are generally viewed as a return enhancer in a portfolio of traditional assets. The expectation for a return premium over public equities stems from the illiquidity risk that comes with most forms of private equity investment. Because of the strong link between the fundamentals of private and public companies, there are limited diversification benefits when added to a portfolio that otherwise contains significant public equity exposure. Private equity volatility is not directly observable because holdings are not publicly traded. Assets tend to be valued at the lower of cost or the value at which the company raises additional capital or when ownership changes hands (e.g., through an initial public offering or a sale to a strategic buyer or to another private equity sponsor). Consequently, private equity indexes do not provide a true picture of the strategy's risk. For asset allocation exercises, volatility is often estimated using a public equity proxy with an adjustment to better represent the nature of the private equity program. For example, a proxy for early-stage venture capital might be microcap technology companies. A proxy for buyout funds might start with the volatility of a geographically relevant large-cap equity index (e.g., S&P 500, Nikkei), which is then adjusted for relative financial leverage.

2.2. The Role of Hedge Funds in a Multi-Asset Portfolio

As illustrated in Exhibit 1, hedge funds span the spectrum from being risk reducers to return enhancers. Generally speaking, long/short equity strategies are believed to deliver equity-like returns with less than full exposure to the equity premium but with an additional source of return that might come from the manager's shorting of individual stocks. Short-biased equity strategies are expected to lower a portfolio's overall equity beta while producing some measure of alpha. Arbitrage and event-driven strategies, executed properly, look to exploit small inefficiencies in the public markets while exhibiting low to no correlation with traditional asset classes. However, most hedge fund arbitrage strategies involve some degree of "short volatility" risk. Because of this "short volatility" risk, the volatility in an arbitrage strategy is non-symmetrical; the aggregate volatility may look muted if the period from which the data are drawn does not include a market stress period. "Opportunistic" strategies (e.g., global macro and managed futures), although very volatile as stand-alone strategies, provide exposures not otherwise readily accessible in traditional stock and bond strategies.

2.3. The Role of Real Assets in a Multi-Asset Portfolio

This category includes timber, commodities, farmland, energy, and infrastructure assets. The common thread for these investments is that the underlying investment is a physical asset with a relatively high degree of correlation with inflation broadly or with a sub-component of inflation, such as oil (energy funds), agricultural products (farmland), or pulp and wood products (timber).

Timber investments provide both growth and inflation-hedging properties in a multi-asset portfolio. Growth is provided through the biological growth of the tree itself as well as through the appreciation in the underlying land value. Timber's inflation-hedging characteristics are derived from the unique nature in which the value of the asset is realized: If the market for timber products is weak, the owner of the asset can leave it "on the stump" waiting for prices to rise. While waiting, the volume of the asset increases—the tree continues to grow—and there is ultimately more of the asset to sell when prices recover. At the same time, the volatility of the timber asset rises; the market for more mature timber is more volatile, and the potential loss from pests and natural disasters rises.

Commodities investments (i.e., tradable commodities) fall into the following four categories:

- Metals (gold, silver, platinum, copper)
- Energy (crude oil, natural gas, heating oil, gasoline)
- Livestock and Meat (hogs, pork bellies, live cattle)
- Agricultural (corn, soybeans, wheat, rice, cocoa, coffee, cotton, sugar)

Although it is possible to own the commodity asset directly (e.g., corn, wheat, barrel of oil), most investors will invest in commodity derivatives (i.e., futures contracts) whose price is directly related to the price of the physical commodity. Investors generally own commodities as a hedge against a core constituent of inflation measures as well as a differentiated source of alpha. Gold and other precious metals are frequently owned directly because they are thought to be a good store of value in the face of a depreciating currency. Storage and insurance costs come with owning commodities directly.

Farmland investing involves two primary approaches. The higher return/risk strategy involves owning the farmland while providing the farmer a salary for tending and selling the crops. The investor retains the commodity risk and the execution risk. This approach requires a long time horizon and has high sensitivity to natural disasters and regulatory risk, such as trade disputes. In the other main approach, the investor owns the farmland but leases the property to the farmer. The farmer retains the risk for execution and commodity prices. If an investor pursues this second strategy, farmland is more like core commercial real estate investing than a real asset (commodity) strategy.

Energy investments consist of strategies that focus on the exploration, development, transportation, and delivery of energy (primarily oil and natural gas-based energy sources but also increasingly wind, hydroelectric, and solar) as well as all the ancillary services that facilitate energy production. Investors usually do not own the land that holds the minerals. Most energy investments are executed through call-down, private equity-style funds and are usually long-dated, illiquid holdings. Energy assets are generally considered real assets because the investor owns the mineral rights to certain commodities (e.g., natural gas, oil, methane) that can be correlated with certain inflationary factors. Master limited partnerships (MLPs) are another frequently used vehicle for energy investments. MLPs generally construct and own the pipelines that carry oil or natural gas from the wellhead to the storage facility. MLPs rarely take ownership of the energy assets. The companies charge a fee based on the volume of oil/natural gas they transport. This fee is often pegged to the Producer Price Index.

Infrastructure is a strategy that typically involves the construction and maintenance of public-use projects, such as building bridges, toll roads, or airports. Because of the illiquid nature of these assets, the holding period associated with these funds can be even longer than the typical illiquid strategy, with some lasting 20 years or longer. These assets tend to generate stable or modestly growing income, and the asset itself often requires minimal upkeep or capital expenditures once built. The revenue generated by the assets tends to have high correlation with overall inflation, though it is often subject to regulatory risks because governmental agencies may be involved in price setting with certain jurisdictions and assets.

2.4. The Role of Commercial Real Estate in a Multi-Asset Portfolio

Real estate investing involves the development, acquisition, management, and disposition of commercial properties, including retail, office, industrial, housing (including apartments), and hotels. Strategies range from *core,* the ownership of fully occupied properties and collecting rents, to *opportunistic,* ground-up property development (land acquisition, construction, and sale) and/or the purchase of distressed assets with the intent to rehabilitate them.

Real estate investments are believed to provide protection against unanticipated increases in inflation. Two fundamental attributes of real estate investment contribute to this inflation protection. Well-positioned properties frequently have the ability to increase rents in response to inflationary pressures, and the value of the physical buildings may increase with inflation (properties are often valued as a function of replacement cost). In this way, real estate contributes both income and capital gain potential to a portfolio. Building a diversified private commercial real estate program can be challenging for all but the largest and most sophisticated allocators. The public real estate market is a fraction of the size of the private real estate market, but it may be easier and cheaper to build a diversified real estate investment program in some geographies (e.g., United States, Europe) via the public markets. However, private real estate can offer exposures that are difficult if not impossible to achieve through publicly-traded real estate securities. Investing directly (or in a private fund) offers customization by geography, property type, and strategy (e.g., distressed, core, development).

2.5. The Role of Private Credit in a Multi-Asset Portfolio

Private credit includes distressed investment and direct lending. Although both strategies involve the ownership of fixed-income assets, their roles in an investment program are quite different. Direct-lending assets are income-producing, and the asset owner assumes any default or recovery risks. Direct-lending assets generally behave like their public market counterparts with similar credit profiles (i.e., high-quality, direct-lending assets behave like investment-grade bonds, and low-quality, direct-lending assets behave like high-yield bonds). Distressed debt assets have a more equity-like profile. The expected return is derived from the value of a company's assets relative to its debt. Illiquidity risks are high with both strategies. Direct-lending assets have no secondary market.

Direct-lending funds provide capital to individuals and small businesses that generally cannot access more traditional lending channels. Some loans are unsecured while others might be backed by an asset, such as a house or car. Direct lending is one of the least liquid debt strategies because there is typically no secondary market for these instruments. Investors in direct-lending strategies gain access to a high-yielding but riskier segment of the debt market that is not available via the traditional public markets.

Distressed funds typically purchase the securities of an entity that is under stress and where the stress is relieved through legal restructuring or bankruptcy. The investment can take the form of debt or equity, and in many strategies, the manager often takes an active role throughout the restructuring or bankruptcy. Because many investors are precluded from owning companies or entities that are in bankruptcy or default, managers of distressed funds are often able to purchase assets (usually the debt) at a significant discount. Experience with the bankruptcy process frequently distinguishes these managers from others. Although the asset is usually a bond, distressed investments typically have low sensitivity to traditional bond risks (i.e., interest rate changes or changes in spreads) because the idiosyncratic risk of the company itself dominates all other risks.

3. DIVERSIFYING EQUITY RISK

In this section, we examine the claim that alternative assets may be better risk mitigators than government bonds. To address this question, we must agree on *which* risks alternatives are said to mitigate and on *what* time horizon is relevant. If your investment horizon is short term, volatility may be the most important risk measure. If you are a long-term investor, not achieving the long-horizon return objective may be the most relevant concern.

3.1. Volatility Reduction over the Short Time Horizon

Let's look first at the short horizon investor and consider how alternative asset classes compare to bonds as a volatility reducer in an equity-dominated portfolio. Advocates of alternative investments as risk reducers sometimes argue that alternative investments' volatilities calculated based on reported returns are significantly lower than the volatility of public equities. An immediate technical challenge is that reported returns of many alternative asset classes need an adjustment called **unsmoothing** for proper risk estimation. (Various approaches have been developed to unsmooth a return series that demonstrates serial correlation. The specifics of those approaches are beyond the scope of this chapter.) In the case of private investments, reported returns are calculated from appraisal-based valuations that may result in volatility and correlation estimates that are too low. (The underlying assumptions in most appraisal models tend to lead to gradual and incremental changes in appraised value that may not accurately capture the asset's true price realized in an actual transaction. The low volatility of the return stream may also dampen the reported correlation between the appraisal-based asset and the more volatile market-based asset.) Other factors may also contribute to underestimated risk across alternatives. For example, **survivorship bias** and **back-fill bias** (reporting returns to a database only after they are known to be good returns) in hedge fund databases can potentially lead to an understatement of downside risk. Additionally, a hedge fund "index" includes many managers whose returns exhibit low correlation; in the same way that combining stocks and bonds in a portfolio can be expected to lower overall portfolio volatility, so too does combining several hedge funds into an "index."

As an example, we build a hypothetical, equally-weighted index of long/short equity hedge funds with volatilities ranging from 6% to 11%. As shown in Exhibit 5, given the less-than-perfect correlation among the constituents of our index, the index volatility is only 4.9%:

EXHIBIT 5   Volatility Is Less Than the Sum of Its Parts

	Fund 1	Fund 2	Fund 3	Fund 4	Fund 5	Combined
Volatility	10.9%	6.5%	8.5%	9.7%	8.1%	**4.9%**
Correlation						
Fund 1		−0.02	0.14	0.00	0.15	
Fund 2			0.27	0.39	0.29	
Fund 3				0.25	−0.03	
Fund 4					0.14	

Exhibit 6 shows the correlations of fixed-income and alternative asset classes to public equities based on observed market data over 1997–2017. We also show each asset class's estimated equity beta. To estimate correlations and betas, we used unsmoothed return data for alternative asset classes. We discuss unsmoothing of returns in more detail in a later section.

EXHIBIT 6   Fixed-Income's and Alternative's Equity Beta and Correlation with Equities

Correlation

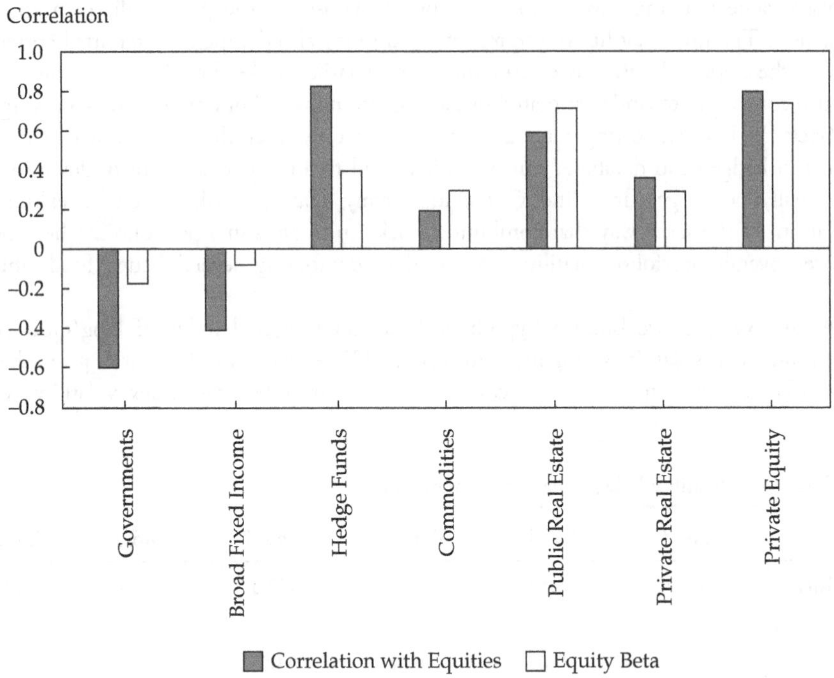

Sources: Bloomberg and authors' own data and calculations.

Most of the alternative investment categories had positive, but less than perfect, correlation with equities. Although certain alternatives (e.g., commodities, particularly gold) may rally during a public equity market downturn, other alternative investments—like hedge funds, private credit, or private equities—also experience drawdowns at the same time the equity market falls. Hedge funds and private equities have a correlation co-efficient with equities over +0.8, and this indicates a fairly strong positive relationship between public equities and these alternative investments.

Government bonds, however, have a −0.6 estimated correlation with equities, which indicates a negative relationship of moderate strength. This is consistent with the tendency for government bonds to serve as a risk haven during "risk-off" or "flight to quality" episodes.

Although correlation and beta have the same sign and are statistically interrelated, we have to remember that they quantify two different things. The correlation coefficient quantifies the strength of a linear relationship between two variables, thus playing a crucial role in portfolio diversification: The lower the correlation, the stronger the asset's diversification power. Beta, however, measures the response of an asset to a unit change in a reference index; for example, equity beta measures how various assets would respond to a 1% rise of public equities. Hedge funds' beta is estimated at around 0.4; thus, we would expect a 0.4% return (excluding manager alpha) from hedge funds if equities rose by 1%. Hedge funds' relatively low beta (0.4) and high correlation (+0.8) means that hedge funds' rise or fall is milder than those of public equities in magnitude, but this directional relationship is fairly strong in a statistical sense. Commodities also have an equity beta of similar positive magnitude (0.3), but their correlation with equities is much weaker (+0.2); so, we can expect that a much bigger portion of commodity price changes would be driven by factors unrelated to the equity markets.

In Exhibit 7, we compare the total return volatility of public equities (black bar) with volatilities of portfolios comprised of 70% equity and 30% other asset classes. Using 20 years of data, the volatility of public equities is estimated at approximately 17%. A portfolio allocated 70% to equity and 30% to cash would imply a portfolio volatility of 11.9% (70% × 17%). Portfolios of 70% equities and 30% any of the alternative asset classes also reduces portfolio volatility relative to an all-equity portfolio, but the lowest volatility of 11.1% could be achieved by combining equities with government bonds because of the negative correlation between these two asset classes.

EXHIBIT 7   Volatility of Portfolios Comprised of 70% Equities and 30% Other Asset Class

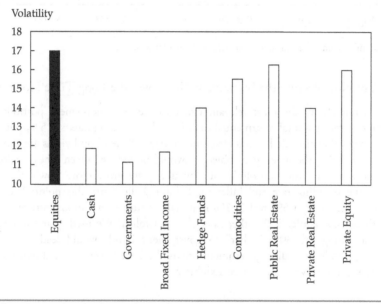

Sources: Bloomberg and authors' own data and calculations.

Bear in mind, however, that this analysis is based on 20 years of returns ending in 2017, a period that was characterized by a persistent negative equity–bond correlation. Because there was limited inflation in developed markets over this period, economic growth prospects were the dominant influence on asset prices. Positive growth surprises are good for equities (better earnings outlook) and negative for bonds (potential central bank rate increases). If inflation becomes a threat, bonds' risk mitigation power could erode. Exhibit 8 looks at the US equity–bond correlation since the 1950s. As the chart suggests, the correlation between US equities and government bonds was, in fact, positive in the 1970s through the 1990s when inflation was also more elevated.

EXHIBIT 8   Long-Term Historical Equity–Bond Correlation and Inflation

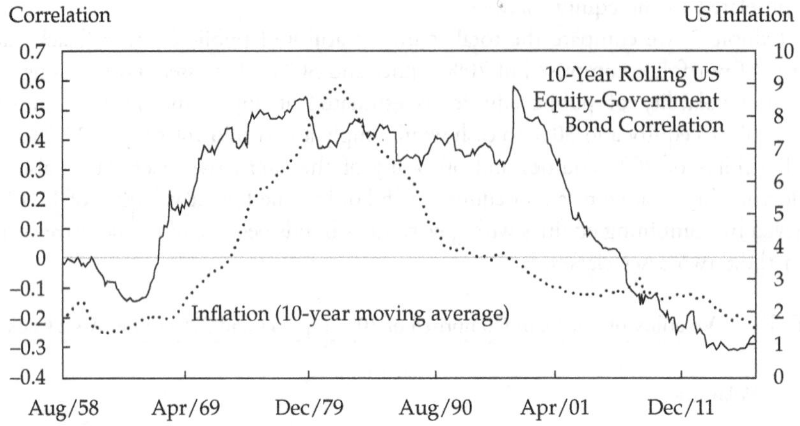

Sources: Bloomberg and the authors' own data and calculations.

3.2. Risk of Not Meeting the Investment Goals over the Long Time Horizon

Volatility is not always the most relevant risk measure. An endowment portfolio is often focused on generating a total return equal to at least the spending rate, say 5%, plus inflation to preserve real value of capital over a long time horizon. When bond yields are very low, the likelihood of meeting the investment objective would be reduced given a heavy allocation to bonds, simply because the portfolio's value would likely grow more slowly than the rate implied by the spending rate and inflation. Exhibit 9 illustrates this point: We show the probability of achieving a 5% real (7.1% nominal[3]) return over various horizons up to 10-years for three 70% equity/30% other asset class portfolios. We used quarterly rebalancing. Although allocating the 30% "other" to government bonds would lead to the greatest reduction in portfolio volatility, government bonds also have lower expected return compared to hedge funds and private equity (see Exhibit 2).

---

[3]By using the Fisher equation to combine the 5% real return and 2% inflation: $(1 + 5\%) * (1 + 2\%) - 1 = 7.1\%$.

EXHIBIT 9   The Probability of Achieving Investment Objectives over the Longer Time Horizon

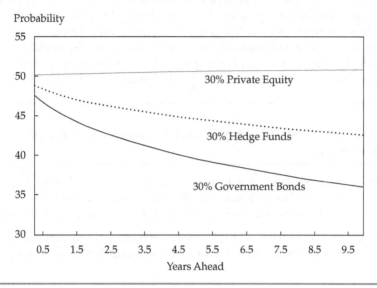

Note: Portfolios comprised of 70% equities and 30% other asset classes.
Source: Authors' calculations.

The 70% public equities/30% government bond portfolio has an expected return of 5.7%,[4] below the nominal return target of 7.1%. The 70% public equities/30% private equities portfolio has an expected geometric return of 7.2%, slightly over the return target. Both portfolios' expected returns are 50th percentile returns; there is a 50% probability that this is the return that would be realized over time. Thus, the 70% public equities/30% private equities portfolio, with a nominal expected return of 7.2%, has slightly better than a 50% probability of meeting the 7.1% nominal return target. The 70% public equities/30% government bond portfolio, with an expected return less than the nominal return target, therefore has less than a 50% probability of meeting the required return. Why does the 70% public equities/30% private equities portfolio maintain its 50%+ probability of meeting the return target over time while the probability that the 70% public equities/30% government bond portfolio meets the return target declines over time? As the time horizon lengthens, return accumulation (compounding) becomes more and more important. In a simplified way, return accumulates proportionally with time, whereas volatility scales with the square root of time. Thus, as we lengthen the time horizon, the gap between the cumulative return target and the expected return accumulation widens faster than the range of possible portfolio return outcomes. As a result, the likelihood of a low-returning portfolio catching up to the target return declines over time.

To summarize, bonds have been a more effective volatility mitigator than alternatives over shorter time horizons, but over long horizons, a heavy allocation to bonds would reduce the probability of achieving the investment goal. It is important to emphasize that volatility and the probability of achieving the target return are two very different dimensions of risk.

---

[4]Note that geometric expected return is approximated as the expected arithmetic return minus half of the investment's variance. Thus, portfolio expected geometric return is not simply the weighted average of the asset classes' expected geometric returns because portfolio variance benefits from diversification.

Volatility addresses interim fluctuations in portfolio return, whereas achieving a return target takes on increasing importance as we expand the time horizon over multiple years. Both risks are important, especially for a program that is distributing 7% of assets per year as in this example. Although the 30% allocation to private equity increases the chance of meeting the expected return, a severe and sustained short-term drawdown in the public equity markets could significantly handicap the fund's ability to achieve its long-term return objectives. This is why drawdowns (related to volatility) need to be considered and managed.

EXAMPLE 1   Mitigating Equity Risk by Allocating to Hedge Funds or Bonds

The investment committee of a major foundation is concerned about high equity valuations and would like to increase the allocation either to hedge funds or to high-grade, fixed-income assets to diversify equity risk. As the risk manager of this foundation:

1. Discuss the justifications and the limitations of using bonds to mitigate equity risk.
2. Discuss the justifications and the limitations of using hedge funds to mitigate equity risk.

Solution to 1:

- Supporting argument: Bonds have exhibited negative correlation and beta to equities in a low inflation environment, so as long as inflation stays at or below average historical levels, this negative equity–bond correlation should lead to the highest reduction in portfolio volatility.
- Limitations: The negative stock/bond correlation may be temporary, and amid high inflation the stock/bond correlation could turn positive. Furthermore, if bonds' expected return is low, a heavy allocation to bonds may reduce the probability of achieving the foundation's long-term return objectives.

Solution to 2:

- Supporting argument: With a net equity beta of around 0.3–0.4 (see Exhibit 5), hedge funds would reduce an equity-dominated portfolio's overall beta. With higher expected returns than bonds, an allocation to hedge funds would make achieving the long-term return target more feasible.
- Limitations: Although a well-constructed hedge fund portfolio may reduce portfolio volatility and beta, hedge funds are often highly actively managed, levered investment strategies, and individual hedge funds may suffer significant and permanent losses during turbulent times.

---

4. PERSPECTIVES ON THE INVESTMENT OPPORTUNITY SET

In this section, we consider how traditional approaches to asset allocation can be adapted to include alternative investments and how investors can apply risk-based approaches to incorporate alternatives in their asset allocation. This chapter extends the asset allocation framework introduced in earlier chapters on asset allocation. Although the ultimate goal of meeting the investment objectives subject to the relevant constraints remains the same, investors often face several analytical and operational challenges when introducing alternative asset classes.

4.1. Traditional Approaches to Asset Classification

When defining asset classes for the traditional approaches to asset allocation, investors may group and classify alternative assets along several dimensions. Two common approaches (in addition to the growth–income–diversification–safety roles described earlier) are with respect to the liquidity of the asset class and with respect to asset behavior under various economic conditions.

4.1.1. A Liquidity-Based Approach to Defining the Opportunity Set

Certain alternative investments, like REITs or commodity futures, are highly liquid and can be easily traded in public markets. Private investments, however, are highly illiquid and usually require long-term commitments (more than 10 years) from the investors. Of course, there are differences among various private asset classes in this respect as well: Private equity investments may require longer than a 10-year commitment, while the term of a private credit fund can be shorter, say 5 to 8 years. Although public equity and private equity may be similar asset classes from the fundamental economic point of view, they differ significantly in their liquidity characteristics.

The long investment horizon and the lack of liquidity in many of the alternative asset classes make it difficult to accurately characterize their risk characteristics for purposes of the asset allocation exercise. One approach to dealing with this issue is to make the initial asset allocation decision using only the broad, liquid asset classes in which the underlying data that drive risk, return, and correlation assumptions are robust (e.g., stocks, bonds, and real estate). A second iteration of the asset allocation exercise would break the equity/fixed-income/real estate asset allocation down further by using the asset groupings as shown in Exhibit 10, which illustrates a possible categorization of asset classes that incorporates their broad liquidity profile.

EXHIBIT 10   Major Asset Class Categories

	Equity & Equity-Like	Fixed Income & Fixed Income-Like	Real Estate
Marketable/Liquid	Public Equity Long/Short Equity Hedge Funds	Fixed Income Cash	Public Real Estate Commodities
Private/Illiquid	Private Equity	Private Credit	Private Real Estate Private Real Assets

4.1.2. An Approach Based on Expected Performance under Distinct Macroeconomic Regimes
Investors may also categorize asset classes based on how they are expected to behave under
different macroeconomic environments, and investors may assign roles to them in a broad
macroeconomic context:

- *Capital growth assets* would be expected to benefit from healthy economic growth. Public
  and private equities would belong to this category.
- *Inflation-hedging assets*—so-called "real assets" such as real estate, commodities, and natural
  resources but also inflation-linked bonds—would be expected to outperform other asset
  classes when inflation expectations rise or actual inflation exceeds expectations.
- *Deflation-hedging assets* (e.g., nominal government bonds) would be expected to outperform
  most of the other asset classes when the economy slows and inflation becomes very low or
  negative.

In Exhibit 11, we illustrate how investors may think about the expected performance of
various asset classes in a broad macroeconomic context. Each asset class is positioned along
the continuum to illustrate the macroeconomic environment in which we would expect it to
generate strong performance. Such mapping is usually based on both historical experience and
qualitative judgment. Considering fundamental economic drivers of asset classes could help
investors construct portfolios that are better diversified and more robust under various
economic conditions and scenarios.

EXHIBIT 11　Asset Classes Grouped by the Macroeconomic Environment under Which They Would
Be Expected to Generate Strong Performance

		Inflation Environment		
		Deflation	Moderate Inflation	High Inflation
Economic Environment	High Growth		Public Equity Private Equity High-Yield Bonds Private Credit	Real Estate Commodities
	Low Growth/ Recession	Government Bonds		Inflation-Linked Bonds, Gold

Source: Authors' data.

Exhibit 12 illustrates the average quarterly total return of various asset classes and
alternative strategies under stronger and weaker economic growth environments between
1997 and 2017, a period of low to moderate inflation in developed markets.

EXHIBIT 12   Historical Asset Class Performance under Stronger and Weaker Economic Growth
Periods (1997–2017)

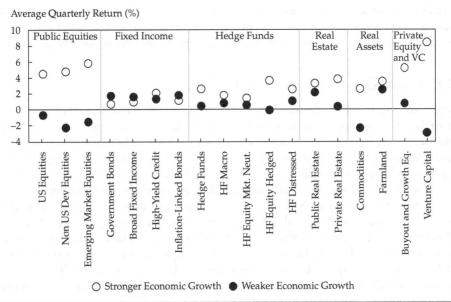

○ Stronger Economic Growth   ● Weaker Economic Growth

Notes: Strong and weak economic periods were determined using quarterly GDP data. Strong growth periods were those quarters when GDP growth exceeded the average GDP growth through the full historical sample.
Sources: The exhibit is based on the authors' calculations. Index data is based on the following. US Equities: Russell 3000; Non-US Developed Market Equities: MSCI EAFE USD Net unhedged; Emerging Market Equities: MSCI Emerging Markets Net USD unhedged; Governments: Bloomberg Barclays US Treasury Index; Broad Fixed Income: Bloomberg Barclays US Aggregate; High Yield: Bloomberg Barclays US Corporate High Yield; Inflation-Linked Bonds: Bloomberg Barclays US Government Inflation-Linked Bonds Index; Hedge Funds: HFRI; Public Real Estate: Dow Jones Equity REIT Index; Private Real Estate: NCREIF Property Index; Commodities: S&P GSCI Total Return Index; Farmland: NCREIF Farmland Index; Buyout and Growth Equities: Cambridge Associates US Private Equity Index; Venture Capital: Cambridge Associates US Venture Capital Index.

Public and private equities, hedge funds, and commodities posted strong returns amid strong economic growth conditions and weaker returns amid weaker economic conditions. Commodities exhibit a bigger disparity between returns in periods of stronger and weaker growth than does the hedge fund category.

Within fixed income, government bonds posted higher returns during periods of weaker economic growth—when investors likely reallocated from risky assets to safer assets. On the other hand, high-yield bonds (and potentially private credit, if we assume a behavior pattern similar to that of high-yield bonds) performed well during periods of stronger economic growth but posted lower returns during weaker economic periods, likely because of concerns about weakening credit quality.

Understanding how various asset classes behave under distinct macroeconomic regimes enables investors to tailor the asset allocation to align with their fundamental goals or to mitigate their fundamental risks. If the investment portfolio has a specific goal, such as hedging inflation risk, then it would be logical to build a portfolio that is dominated by asset classes that are expected to perform best amid rising inflation. Even if the portfolio's goal is to generate high return over the long run, combining "growth" asset classes with "inflation-hedging" or "deflation-hedging" asset classes could make the asset allocation more resilient to changing economic and market conditions. This approach can be extended to macroeconomic scenario analysis and stress testing when the analyst evaluates how various asset allocation options would perform under conditions of high or low economic growth and/or inflation, and it can identify which economic conditions would hurt the investment portfolio the most.

4.2. Risk-Based Approaches to Asset Classification

When we assign traditional and alternative asset classes to certain functional roles in the portfolio, or when we assess how different asset classes would perform under distinct macroeconomic regimes, we can also easily realize that many traditional and alternative asset classes share similar characteristics that can result in high correlations. We may put public equities in the same functional bucket as private equity, and we may expect elevated default rates from high-yield bonds and private credit during recessionary environments.

Exhibit 13 compares the betas of various traditional and alternative asset classes to global equities. The chart clearly shows that private equity and venture capital asset classes have global equity betas similar to public equities. On the other hand, betas of various hedge fund strategies differ significantly. Hedge fund returns, in aggregate, had a beta of 0.4. However, global macro or equity market-neutral strategies had betas as low as 0.1. The long/short "equity hedged" strategy's beta is estimated to be much higher, around 0.5, which is consistent with its long equity bias.

EXHIBIT 13   Global Equity Beta of Various Asset Classes, 1997–2017

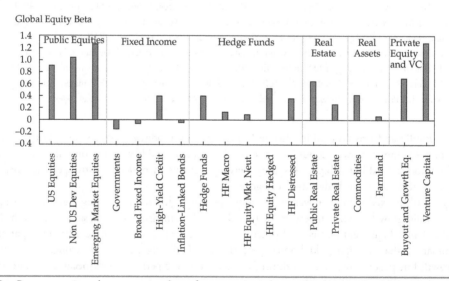

Note: Betas were estimated as a regression slope of representative index returns relative to the global equity return stream over the time period 1997–2017.

Sources: Authors' calculations; index data sources are the same as those in Exhibit 12.

Many investors have begun to view asset allocation through a risk factor lens to capture these similarities. In this section, we extend the risk factor asset allocation framework introduced in earlier chapters to alternative investments using the following risk factors:

- *Equity market return*: representative of the general direction of global equity markets, and investors may also refer to this as the best market proxy for "growth."
- *Size*: excess return of small-cap equities over large-cap equities.
- *Value*: excess return of value versus growth stocks (*negative* factor sensitivity = *growth* bias.
- *Liquidity*: the Pastor–Stambaugh liquidity factor[5]—a market-wide liquidity measure based on the excess returns of stocks with large sensitivity to changes in aggregate liquidity (less-liquid stocks) versus stocks with less sensitivity to changing liquidity (more-liquid stocks).
- *Duration*: sensitivity to 10-year government yield changes.
- *Inflation*: sensitivity to 10-year breakeven inflation changes obtained from the inflation-linked bond markets.
- *Credit spread*: sensitivity to changes in high-yield spread.
- *Currency*: sensitivity to changes in the domestic currency versus a basket of foreign currencies.

This framework can easily be extended further to other risk factors, like momentum or volatility.

Exhibit 14 illustrates risk factor sensitivities of various traditional and alternative investment strategies using a construct as discussed by Naik, Devarajan, Nowobilski, Page, and Pedersen (2016). The parameters in the table are regression coefficients based on 20 years of historical data. Quarterly index returns representing each asset class were regressed on the risk factors listed previously. Note that for conventional reasons we changed the signs of the "nominal duration" and "credit spread" sensitivities: The 4.2 duration of broad fixed income, for example, means that this asset class would experience an approximate 4.2% decline in response to a 100 bps increase in the nominal interest rates.

EXHIBIT 14   Factor Sensitivity Estimates across Various Asset Classes

Asset Classes	Equity	Size	Value	Liquidity	Nominal Duration	Inflation	Credit Spread	Currency	R-squared
US Equities	1.0								1.00
Non-US Dev Equities	0.9							0.7	0.86
Emerging Mkt Equities	1.1	0.5						0.5	0.66
Government Bonds					4.8				0.96
Broad Fixed Income					4.2		0.6		0.89
High-Yield Credit					4.1		4.2		0.95
Inflation-Linked Bonds					6.6	7.0			0.82
Hedge Funds	0.3	0.1					0.6		0.74

[5]For more details on Pastor–Stambaugh liquidity factors, see Naik et al. (2016).

Asset Classes	Equity	Size	Value	Liquidity	Nominal Duration	Inflation	Credit Spread	Currency	R-squared
HF Macro	0.2	0.2			1.9	3.1	−0.9	0.1	0.28
HF Equity Mkt. Neut.	0.1								0.14
HF Equity Hedged	0.5								0.72
HF Distressed	0.1	0.2					1.8		0.72
Commodities						18.0		0.8	0.36
Public Real Estate	0.9				4.6	0.9			0.38
Private Real Estate	0.2			0.1		2.4			0.20
Buyout & Growth Equities	0.6	0.2	−0.3	0.1					0.70
Venture Capital	0.8	0.6	−1.8	0.2					0.38

Note: Only statistically significant slopes are displayed in the exhibit. Sources are the same as those for Exhibit 12.

In a risk factor-based asset allocation framework, the factors represent the systematic risks embedded in the selected asset classes and investment strategies. The primary systematic risk factors would fully, or almost fully, explain the behavior of broad, passive traditional public asset classes. There should be a relatively larger portion of unexplained risk in the alternative asset classes. This arises from such issues as the appraisal-based valuation in real estate, the idiosyncratic risks in the portfolio companies of private equity funds, or the idiosyncratic risks in hedge funds resulting from active management. (This last one is logically intuitive if you subscribe to the belief that returns generated by hedge fund strategies should be primarily driven by *alpha* rather than systematic risk factors.)

The extension of the risk factor framework to alternative asset classes allows every asset class to be described using the same framework. Investors can therefore more clearly understand their sources of investment risk and identify the intended and unintended tilts and biases they have in the portfolio. Furthermore, a risk factor framework enables investors to more efficiently allocate capital and risk in a multi-dimensional framework (i.e., a framework that seeks to do more than simply achieve the highest return at a given level of volatility). If an investor, for example, would like to increase the portfolio's inflation risk-mitigating exposure, decomposing this specific risk factor from inflation-linked bonds, real estate, or commodity asset classes could help the investor to identify the asset classes and exposures that are most likely to facilitate that goal.

Risk factor-based approaches improve upon the traditional approaches in identifying the investment opportunity set but do have certain limitations. As mentioned earlier, a small set of systematic risk factors is insufficient to describe the historical return stream of alternative asset classes. Note that all non-zero-risk factor coefficients displayed in the table are statistically significant based on their *t*-statistics. Although our eight illustrative factors fit the total return history of traditional asset classes with *r*-squared statistics of 0.8–1.0, the *r*-squared ratios for alternative investments are lower, ranging between 0.3 and 0.7. Increasing the number of risk factors would certainly improve the goodness of fit, but too many factors could make the risk factor-based asset allocation framework difficult to handle and interpret. In addition, certain risk factor sensitivities can be quite volatile, making a "point in time" factor-based definition of an asset class a poor descriptor of the class's expected behavior. For example, the aggregate hedge fund inflation beta typically fluctuates in the range of 0.3 to 0.4, while the inflation beta of commodities fluctuates much more widely.[6]

EXAMPLE 2   Applying Risk Factors for Inflation Hedging

1. The CIO (chief investment officer) of the United Retired Workers Plan would like to reduce inflation risk in the portfolio. Based on the data displayed in Exhibit 14, which asset classes would you recommend as potential inflation-hedging tools?
2. The CIO is not only concerned about inflation but also rising interest rates. Which alternative asset classes would you recommend for consideration?

Solution to 1: Commodities and inflation-linked bonds have the highest factor sensitivity to inflation, so they are the most obvious candidates. Real estate (both public and private) also has some potential to protect against inflation. Based on the data presented, macro hedge fund strategies also exhibited a positive inflation beta, but given their active nature, further analysis may be needed before choosing them as inflation-hedging vehicles.

Solution to 2: Commodities and private real estate would be the likely asset classes to hedge against rising interest rates, given their zero-factor sensitivity to nominal duration. Some of the hedge fund strategies also show zero-factor sensitivity to duration, but the relationship may not hold true in the future given the actively managed nature of hedge funds. Although Exhibit 14 indicates equity strategies (both public and private) also show little to no sensitivity to rising interest rates (duration), bonds and equities have been more highly correlated in the past.

4.2.1. Illustration: Asset Allocation and Risk-Based Approaches

Let's look at an example of how a risk-based approach may enhance traditional asset allocation. In Exhibit 15, we show two investment portfolios, Portfolio A and Portfolio B, that have exactly the same high-level asset allocations. However, the underlying investments in the two portfolios are quite different. The fixed-income assets in Portfolio A are government bonds, while the fixed-income assets in Portfolio B are high-yield bonds. Hedge fund investments in Portfolio A are represented by very low equity beta market neutral strategies, while Portfolio B is invested in the higher beta long/short equity hedge funds. Similarly, Portfolio B's investments in real assets and private equity have higher risk than those in Portfolio A.

---

[6]For further detail on expanding asset allocation to risk allocation, we refer to Naik et al. (2016) and Cambridge Associates LLC (2013).

EXHIBIT 15   Traditional Asset Allocation and Risk Contribution Comparison

Broad Asset Classes	Asset Allocation		Underlying Investments		% Contribution to Risk	
	Portfolio A	Portfolio B	Portfolio A	Portfolio B	Portfolio A	Portfolio B
Fixed Income	20%	20%	Government Bonds	High-Yield Bonds	−6.5%	7.6%
Public Equities	20%	20%	US Equities	Non-US Developed Equities	51.4%	18.2%
Hedge Funds	20%	20%	Equity Market Neutral	Long/Short Equity	5.4%	11.1%
Real Assets	20%	20%	Inflation-linked bonds	REITs	0.7%	13.2%
Private Equity	20%	20%	Buyout	Venture Capital	48.9%	49.8%
Total	100%	100%				
				Expected Return	5.3%	8.8%
				Volatility	5.9%	16.5%
				Equity Beta	0.30	0.79

Notes: The percentage contribution to risk is a result of three components: the asset allocation to a specific asset, its volatility, and its correlation with the other assets. For fixed income, the contribution to total risk is negative in the case of Portfolio A because government bonds have negative correlations with other asset classes; however, it is positive in the case of Portfolio B because high-yield bonds have positive correlations with the other asset classes. *Source*: Authors' calculations.

As a result of these major differences between nominally similar broad asset allocations, it is not surprising that Portfolio B has higher volatility, beta, and expected return compared to Portfolio A. Let's look more closely at the risk contribution of each of the asset classes:

4.2.1.1. Portfolio A
The majority of the risk in Portfolio A comes from public and private equity. Hedge funds contribute approximately 5% to the total risk, and fixed income actually reduces risk because government bonds had negative correlations with public equities in our historical data sample.

4.2.1.2. Portfolio B
Private equity explains about half of the total portfolio risk of Portfolio B. (In this portfolio, the private equity allocation is represented by the higher risk venture capital.) Public equities, hedge funds, and real assets each contribute roughly the same to the total risk of the portfolio. This is consistent with the equity-like characteristics of the underlying assets in the portfolio. The long/short equity hedged strategy has an equity beta of around 0.5, and REITs have an equity beta of 0.9. In Portfolio B, fixed income contributes positively to total risk, consistent with high-yield bonds' positive correlation with equities over the time series.

Although the nominal asset allocations of the two portfolios are the same, the risk profile and the risk allocation among asset classes are significantly different. Let's go one step further and apply the risk factor sensitivities of Exhibit 14 to our hypothetical portfolios. Exhibit 16 shows the absolute contribution to total portfolio risk by risk factor. This approach moves beyond the borders of asset classes and aggregates the equity risk factor embedded in public equities, private equities, venture capital, and REITs into a single-factor contribution. Both portfolios are highly dominated by exposure to equity risk. Portfolio A's total risk is almost fully explained by the exposure to the equity factor, while about 70% of Portfolio B's total risk comes from the equity risk factor alone. Portfolio B also has exposure to the size and value factors, driven by the allocation to venture capital. Finally, we can also see that although Portfolio B is not directly investing in government bonds, some risk mitigation benefit still arises from the low "duration" component of high-yield bonds and REITs.

EXHIBIT 16   Absolute Contribution to Total Risk by Risk Factors

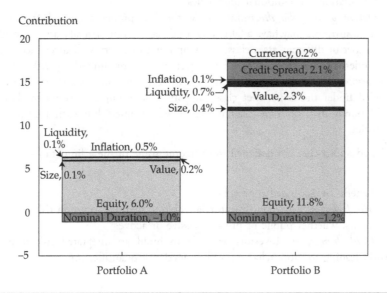

This is an extreme example (the two portfolios have vastly different expected returns), but it is useful to illustrate how factor sensitivities can be used to explore the underlying risk exposures in seemingly similar asset allocations.

4.3. Comparing Risk-Based and Traditional Approaches

Investors often employ multiple approaches in setting their asset allocation for a portfolio that includes alternative investments. When applying these various approaches, investors must consider their strengths and limitations.

4.3.1. Main Strengths of Traditional Approaches
- *Easy to communicate.* Listing the roles of various asset classes is intuitive and easy to explain to the decision makers, who often have familiarity with the traditional asset class-based approach. Scenario analyses based on historical or expected behavior of various asset classes

under different macroeconomic conditions can help to introduce quantitative aspects of the portfolio's expected performance and risk and substantiate the asset allocation proposal.

- *Relevance for liquidity management and operational considerations.* Public and private asset class mandates have vastly distinct liquidity profiles. Thus, although private and public equity would have a lot of commonality in their risk factor exposures, they would be positioned very differently from a liquidity management perspective. Similarly, investors must implement the target asset allocation by allocating to investment managers. The traditional categorization of asset classes may be necessary to identify the relevant mandates—what portion of the equity portfolio she would like to allocate to equity-oriented hedge funds rather than to long-only equity managers.

4.3.2. Main limitations of traditional approaches

- *Over-estimation of portfolio diversification.* Without a proper analytical framework for assessing risk, investors may have a false sense of diversification. An allocation spread across a large number of different asset classes may appear to be very well diversified, when, in fact, the underlying investments may be subject to the same underlying risks.
- *Obscured primary drivers of risk.* Investments with very different risk characteristics may be commingled under the same asset class category. For example, government bonds and high-yield bonds may both be classified as "fixed income," but each has distinct risk characteristics.

Risk-based approaches are designed to overcome some of these limitations.

4.3.3. Key benefits of risk-based approaches

- *Common risk factor identification.* Investors are able to identify common risk factors across all investments, whether public or private, passive or active.
- *Integrated risk framework.* Investors are able to build an integrated risk management framework, leading to more reliable portfolio-level risk quantification.

4.3.4 Key limitations of risk-based approaches

- *Sensitivity to the historical look-back period.* Empirical risk factor exposure estimations may be sensitive to the historical sample. For example, the duration of a bond portfolio or the beta of a diversified equity portfolio could be reasonably stable, but the estimated inflation sensitivity of real assets can change rapidly over time. Thus, the analyst has to be cautious when interpreting some of the risk factor sensitivities, such as the "inflation beta" of commodities.
- *Implementation hurdles.* Establishing a strategic target to different risk factors is a very important high-level decision, but converting these risk factor targets to actual investment mandates requires additional considerations, including liquidity planning, time and effort for manager selection, and rebalancing policy.

5. INVESTMENT CONSIDERATIONS RELEVANT TO THE DECISION TO INVEST IN ALTERNATIVES

In addition to the risk, return, and correlation characteristics relevant to the decision to invest in the alternative asset classes, many operational and practical complexities must be considered before finalizing a decision to invest. It is essential that the investor be fully aware of these complexities: Failure to grasp these differences between traditional and alternative investments can derail an investment program. The primary factors to consider include:

- properly defining risk characteristics;
- establishing return expectations;
- selection of the appropriate investment vehicle;
- operational liquidity issues;
- expense and fee considerations;
- tax considerations (applicable for taxable entities); and
- build vs. buy.

5.1. Risk Considerations

Mean–variance optimization (MVO), widely used in modeling asset allocation choices, cannot easily accommodate the characteristics of most alternative investments. MVO characterizes an asset's risk using standard deviation. Standard deviation is a one-dimensional view of risk and an especially poor representation of the risk characteristics of alternative investments—where assets suffer some degree of illiquidity, valuations may be subjective, and returns may be "chunky" and not normally distributed. The non-standard deviation risks are usually accommodated in an MVO framework by assigning a higher standard deviation than might be derived solely by looking at the historical returns of the asset class.

Most approaches to asset allocation assume that the portfolio's allocation to an asset class is always fully invested. Although this is not an assumption that is limited to alternatives, the problem is exaggerated with the private alternative strategies where it could take several years for capital to be invested and where capital is returned to the investor as investments are sold. Thus, it is rare that the *actual* asset allocation of a program with a significant exposure to alternatives will mirror the *modeled* asset allocation. This suggests that the investor must carefully (and continually) monitor the program's aggregate exposures to ensure that the risks are in line with the strategic asset allocation. A case in point: Some investors over-allocated to private equity, real-estate, and other call-down funds prior to 2008 in order to more quickly reach their asset allocation targets. Many of these investors then found themselves in a situation where they were receiving capital calls for these commitments during 2008 and 2009, a period where their public assets had lost considerable value and liquidity and cash were scarce. Some investors had to reduce distributions, sell illiquid investments in the secondary market at severely discounted prices, and/or walk away from their fund commitments, thereby forfeiting earlier investments.

Although every strategy (and, by extension, each individual fund) will have its own unique risk profile, we provide two examples of the complications that might be encountered when modeling an allocation to alternative investments.

5.1.1. Short-Only Strategy

A short-biased fund can provide strong diversification benefits, lowering a portfolio's aggregate exposure to the equity risk factor; however, a short-only fund has a risk profile quite unlike a long-only equity fund. Most investors understand that a long-only equity fund has theoretically infinite upside potential and a downside loss bounded by zero (assuming no leverage). A short-biased or short-only fund has the opposite distribution. A short-selling strategy is capped on its upside but has unlimited downside risk.

5.1.2. Option Payouts

Some hedge fund strategies will structure their trades as call options either by owning call options outright or by synthetically replicating a call option (e.g., convertible bond arbitrage in which the manager goes long the convertible bond, short the equity for the same underlying, and hedges the interest rate risk). If executed properly, the fund would have limited downside but unlimited upside. It is difficult, if not impossible, to accurately model such a return profile by looking simply at a fund's historical standard deviation or other risk metrics, especially if the fund's track record does not encompass a full market cycle.

5.2. Return Expectations

Given the limited return history of alternative investments (relative to stocks and bonds) and the idiosyncratic nature of alternative investment returns, no single accepted approach to developing the return expectations required in an asset allocation exercise exists. One approach that can be applied with some consistency across asset classes is a "building blocks" approach: Begin with the risk-free rate, estimate the return associated with the factor exposures relevant to the asset class (e.g., credit spreads, level and shape of the yield curve, equity, leverage, liquidity), apply an assumption for manager alpha, and deduct appropriate fees (management and incentive) and taxes. Where the portfolio already contains an allocation to alternative investments, the underlying money managers can be helpful in estimating exposures and return potential. The portfolio's current positions can be characterized by their known exposures, rather than through a generic set of exposures that may not be truly representative of the program's objectives for the asset class exposure. Say, for example, that the investor's hedge fund program deliberately excludes long/short equity hedge funds because the investor chooses to take equity risk in the long-only portion of the portfolio. The return (and risk) characteristics of this hedge fund allocation would be very different from those of a broad-based allocation to hedge funds, which typically has a significant weight to long/short equity funds.

5.3. Investment Vehicle

Most alternative investments are implemented through a private (limited) partnership that is controlled by a general partner (GP), the organization and individuals that manage the investments. The asset owner becomes a limited partner (LP) in the private partnership. The main rationale for using the limited partnership format is that it limits the investor's liability to the amount of capital that she has contributed; she is not responsible for the actions of or the debts incurred by the GP. The investor may invest directly into a manager's fund or through a fund of funds, a private partnership that invests in multiple underlying partnerships. Larger investors may also consider making co-investments alongside a manager into a portfolio company, or they may make direct private equity investments on their own.

Private limited partnerships are the dominant investment vehicle for most alternative investments in private equity, real estate, private credit, and real assets. In the United States, hedge funds will tend to employ two structures: a limited partnership (typically Delaware-based) or an offshore corporation or feeder fund (possibly based in the Cayman Islands, Bermuda, or the British Virgin Islands) that usually feeds into an underlying limited partnership (i.e., feeder fund). European hedge funds tend to register their vehicles in Ireland or Luxembourg[7] as a public limited company, a partnership limited by shares, or a special limited partnership.

There are growing opportunities to invest in alternatives using mutual funds, undertakings for collective investment in transferable securities (UCITS), and/or separately managed accounts (SMAs), although the strategies implemented through these more-liquid vehicles are unlikely to have the same risk/return profile as their less-liquid counterparts. The requirements and demands of a broader investor base have made mutual funds, UCITS, and SMAs increasingly popular. We describe the structure, benefits, and drawbacks of each of these vehicles.

5.3.1. Direct Investment in a Limited Partnership

An investor with the necessary scale and expertise can purchase limited partnership interests directly from the GP. GPs have broad discretion to select and manage the underlying investments and will typically invest a portion of their capital in the fund alongside the limited partners. Because each limited partnership follows its own distinct investment strategy, the investor must often invest in multiple partnerships to diversify idiosyncratic risk. In order to maintain the limited liability shield afforded by the limited partnership structure, the investor must not become too involved in the operation of the fund itself.

5.3.2. Funds of Funds (FOFs)

Many investors lack the necessary scale and investment/operational expertise to access, evaluate, and develop a diversified alternative investment program. An FOF pools the capital of these investors, allowing them to achieve an allocation to an asset class that would otherwise be unobtainable. An FOF manager will typically specialize in a certain alternative strategy, such as Asian private equity funds, and may invest in either many or just a handful of underlying funds. The FOF manager is responsible for sourcing, conducting due diligence on, and monitoring the underlying managers. Using an FOF simplifies the investor's accounting and reporting: Capital calls from the underlying funds are frequently consolidated into a single capital call by the FOF, and investors receive a single report consolidating the accounting and investment results of all the underlying funds. The FOF manager does charge additional fees for these services. Investors in an FOF also lose a degree of flexibility to customize their exposures.

5.3.3. SMAs/Funds of One

As large institutions and family offices increased capital allocated to the alternative investment space, many of them demanded more-favorable investment terms and conditions than those offered to smaller investors. Some alternative investment managers, interested in accessing these large pools of capital, have agreed to offer investment management services to these clients through a highly customizable SMA. SMAs have very high minimum investments and pose greater operational challenges for both the manager and the investor. In instances where an SMA is impractical, fund managers have created a "fund of one"—a limited partnership with a single

---

[7]See Eurekahedge, "2016 Key Trends in Global Hedge Funds" (August 2016).

client. These funds have many of the same benefits as an SMA but can be easier to implement. (For example, an SMA requires that the *investor* must be approved by each of the counterparties to any derivatives contracts. In a fund of one, GPs must obtain and maintain these approvals, which is something that they do in the ordinary course of running their investment businesses.)

SMAs and funds of one cannot generally avail themselves of the alignment of interests that arises from the investment of GP capital alongside that of the LPs. When other clients are invested in the GP's primary investment vehicles at the GP's standard fees and to which the GP has committed some of its own capital, there is a risk that the GP favors these other funds in allocating capital-constrained investment opportunities.

5.3.4. Mutual Funds/UCITS/Publicly Traded Funds

A number of open-ended mutual funds and UCITS seek to replicate some alternative investment strategies, particularly hedge funds. Nominally, these allow smaller investors to access asset classes that would otherwise be unavailable to them. It should be noted, however, that these vehicles often operate with regulatory restrictions that limit the fund manager's ability to implement the investment strategy offered via their primary investment vehicle. Accordingly, the investor must be cautious in considering whether the track record achieved in the manager's primary investment vehicle is representative of what might be achieved in a mutual fund, UCIT, or other publicly-traded vehicle. For example, a mutual fund that offers daily liquidity is unlikely to be a suitable investment vehicle for a distressed or activist investment fund, where the time horizon to realize investment returns may be one to two years. This "liquid-alt" space grew significantly following the Global Financial Crisis.

5.4. Liquidity

Traditional assets are generally highly liquid, and the vehicles that are typically used by investors to access the asset class (e.g., separate accounts or daily valued commingled funds, such as mutual funds and UCITS) typically do not impose additional liquidity constraints. That is not the case with many alternative assets, where both the vehicle and the underlying instruments may expose the investor to some degree of liquidity risk. We address liquidity risks at the fund and security level separately.

5.4.1. Liquidity Risks Associated with the Investment Vehicle

The most common vehicle employed by alternative asset managers is the private limited partnership previously described. (Some investors will invest via an offshore corporate structure used for certain tax and regulatory reasons. This offshore corporation is typically a "feeder" fund—a vehicle that channels investors' assets to the master limited partnership.) The private placement memorandum (PPM) details the subscription and redemption features of the partnership. Liquidity provisions differ across asset classes but are substantially similar within asset classes. Exhibit 17 details the typical liquidity considerations associated with investing in a private limited partnership. SMA liquidity provisions may be negotiated directly with the manager.

EXHIBIT 17   Typical Liquidity Provisions for Alternative Investment Vehicles

	Subscription	**Redemption**	**Lock-Up**
Hedge Funds	• Typically accept capital on a monthly or quarterly basis.	• Quarterly or annual redemptions with 30 to 90 days' notice required. • May be subject to a gate limiting the amount of fund or investor assets that can be redeemed at any one redemption date. • 10% holdback of the redemption amount pending completion of the annual audit.	• Typically one year in the US; shorter in Europe. • Redemptions prior to the lock-up period may be permitted but are subject to a penalty, typically 10%.
Private Equity, Private Credit, Real Estate, and Real Asset Funds	• Funds typically have multiple "closes." The final close for new investors is usually one year after the first close. Committed capital is called for investment in stages over a 3-year investment period.	• No redemption provisions. Fund interests may be sold on the secondary market, subject to GP approval. • Distributions paid as investments are realized over the life of the fund. Unrealized assets may be distributed in kind to the LP at fund termination.	• Typical 10-year life, with GP option to extend fund term 1 to 2 years.

5.4.1.1. Secondary Markets

Although fund terms may prevent investors from redeeming early, a small but growing secondary market for many alternative funds exists. Some brokers will match sellers and buyers of limited partnership interests, and some secondary funds' main objective is to buy limited partnership interests from the original investor. These transactions typically occur at a significant discount to the net asset value (NAV) of the fund and usually require the GP to approve the transaction.

5.4.1.2. Understanding a Drawdown Structure

Private equity/credit, private real estate, and real asset funds typically call investors' capital in stages as fund investments are identified. This investment period is specified in the PPM and typically ranges from three to five years from the initial capital call. Thus, although an investor may have committed a specified percentage of the portfolio to an asset class, the allocation may not be fully funded until some point well into the future. We will illustrate the drawdown structure for a single fund using a hypothetical commitment to a real estate fund:

The Chan Family Partnership commits €5,000,000 to Uptown Real Estate LP. The fund has a three-year investment period. When fully invested, Uptown expects to hold 12 to 15 properties. The capital call schedule for Uptown may look something like this:

- Year 1: €1,500,000 of the €5,000,000 committed is called, covering three investments
- Year 2: €2,500,000 is called, covering six investments
- Year 3: €500,000 is called, covering two investments
- Year 6: €2,000,000 is distributed by Uptown Real Estate
- More distributions in subsequent years

Expanding on this example, Exhibit 18 shows how the cash flows for our hypothetical fund might operate throughout the fund's life.

EXHIBIT 18.   Hypothetical Capital Call—Distribution Schedule

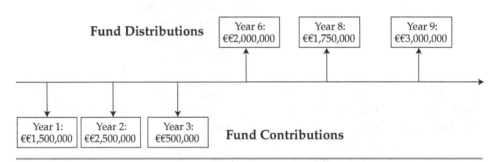

In reality, most funds will have several capital calls in a year. It is also possible that a fund may make a distribution before the final capital call occurs. Because of the highly uncertain liquidity profile of call down (or drawdown) funds (private equity/credit, real estate/real assets), it is incumbent on the investor to plan for multiple contingencies. Funds may end up calling significantly less capital than the investor assumed or may call capital at a faster pace than planned. Capital may be returned to the investor more quickly or more slowly than originally anticipated. Each of these scenarios could result in investors being under or over their target allocations. Critically, investors will want to verify that they have suitable liquidity, such that even under adverse conditions they are able to meet their capital calls. Investors who are unable to meet their capital calls may be required to forfeit their entire investment in the fund (or such other penalties as may be specified in the PPM).

The capital commitment/drawdown structure also presents potential opportunity costs for the investor. Returning to Exhibit 18, having committed €5,000,000 to Uptown Real Estate LP, the Chan Family Partnership is obligated to meet the GP's capital calls but must address the opportunity cost of having the committed capital invested in lower-returning liquid (cash) assets pending the capital call—or face the risk of having insufficient assets available to meet the capital call if the funds were invested in another asset class that has experienced a loss in the interim. Also note that only €4,500,000 of the €5,000,000 commitment was called before distributions began.

5.4.2. Liquidity Risks Associated with the Underlying Investments
The investor must be aware of any potential mismatch between the fund terms and the liquidity profile of the underlying instruments held by the fund. This is particularly important

if the investor is negotiating fund terms or if other investors have terms that may be different from his own. Because the private market funds rarely offer interim liquidity, this problem most often arises in hedge funds. We provide a few examples of the issues an investor may encounter.

5.4.2.1. Equity-Oriented Hedge Funds

The majority of assets in a typical equity-oriented hedge fund are liquid, marketable securities compatible with monthly or quarterly fund-level liquidity terms. Short positions may be notably less liquid than long positions, so funds that make greater use of short selling will have correspondingly lower overall liquidity. This should be taken into consideration when evaluating the potential for a liquidity mismatch between the fund's terms and the underlying holdings. Some otherwise liquid hedge fund strategies may own a portion of their holdings in illiquid or relatively illiquid securities. The GP may designate these securities as being held in a "side pocket." Such "side-pocketed" securities are not subject to the fund's general liquidity terms. The redeeming investor's pro rata share of the side pocket would remain in the fund and be distributed at such time as the fund manager liquidates these assets, which could take quarters or even years to accomplish. If the percentage of assets held in side pockets is large, this could render the fund's liquidity terms irrelevant. The investor must evaluate the illiquidity challenges inherent in the underlying holdings, including side pockets, in order to estimate a liquidity profile for the total portfolio.

5.4.2.2. Event-Driven Hedge Funds

Event-driven strategies, by their nature, tend to have longer investment horizons. The underlying investments in a merger arbitrage strategy, for example, are generally liquid, but the nature of the strategy is such that returns are realized in "chunks." It is in the manager's and the investor's interests to ensure that the liquidity terms provide the necessary flexibility to execute the investment thesis. A hedge fund focused on distressed investing is dealing with both the "workout" horizon (the time frame over which the negotiations between the creditors and the company are being conducted) and the lesser liquidity of the distressed assets. The fund terms for a distressed strategy are likely to be much longer than other hedge fund strategies. (In fact, many distressed funds choose to organize in a private equity fund structure.)

5.4.2.3. Relative Value Hedge Funds

Many relative value hedge funds will invest in various forms of credit, convertibles, derivatives, or equities that have limited or at least uncertain liquidity characteristics. Many funds will include provisions in the fund documents to restrict redemptions under certain scenarios so that they are not forced to sell illiquid securities at inopportune moments. Without such provisions, the fund manager may be forced to sell what securities they *can* (i.e., the more liquid holdings) rather than the securities that they *want*. This could have the unfortunate consequence of leaving remaining investors in the fund holding a sub-optimally illiquid portfolio. On the other hand, funds that deal in managed futures or similar instruments may have very flexible terms (daily or weekly liquidity, only a few days notification, etc.). This was a scenario many hedge fund managers faced during the Global Financial Crisis as investors made significant redemption requests to meet their own cash needs. The liquid funds were disproportionately affected as investors sought to raise cash wherever they could find it.

5.4.2.4. Leverage

A fund's use of leverage and its agreements with counterparties providing the leverage can also affect the alignment between fund terms and the investment strategy. If a strategy is levered, lenders have a first claim on the assets. The lenders' claims are superior to those of the LPs, and the lenders have preferential liquidity terms; most lenders can make a margin call on stocks, bonds, or derivatives positions with just two days' notice. Given that margin calls are most likely to happen when the markets (and/or the fund) are stressed, the LPs' liquidity can evaporate as the most-liquid positions in the portfolio are sold to meet margin calls. The need to de-lever and sell assets to meet margin calls will typically result in a lower return when the market eventually recovers.

5.5. Fees and Expenses

In addition to management fees of 0.5% to 2.5% of assets and incentive fees of 10% to 20% of returns, investments in alternative assets often entail higher expenses passed through to or paid directly by the investor. These fees can result in a significant variation between the gross and net of fee returns. Consider a hedge fund that was earning a 3% gross quarterly return (12.6% annualized). After deducting a 2% management and a 20% incentive fee, accrued quarterly, the net return at year-end is just 8.2%.

Fees can have a larger impact on the difference between gross and net returns for such call-down-type fund structures as private equity funds, where the management fee is charged on *committed* capital, not invested capital. If the manager is slow to deploy capital, there can be a pronounced J-curve effect (negative IRRs in the early years) that can be difficult to overcome (the adage "it takes a 100% return to recover from a 50% loss").

In addition, most alternative investment funds will pass through normal fund expenses, including legal, custodial, audit, administration, and accounting fees. For smaller funds, these additional costs can add up to another 0.5%. Larger funds can spread these same costs out over the larger asset base, and the pass-through to investors is likely to be in the range of 0.05% to 0.20% of assets. Some of these expenses have a limited life (e.g., the capitalized organizational expenses), so the impact can vary over time. Funds may also pass through to investors' costs associated with acquiring an asset, including the due diligence costs and any brokerage commissions paid. A careful evaluation of the fund's offering documents is essential to understanding the all-in cost of an investment in alternatives.

5.6. Tax Considerations

For taxable investors, the tax implications associated with many alternatives can have a significant impact on their relative attractiveness. In many instances, a tax inefficient strategy, one that generates substantial short-term gains or taxable income, can significantly erode the anticipated return benefits. This arises frequently with many hedge fund strategies, especially those funds and fund companies where tax-exempt investors dominate the client base and the fund manager may be insensitive to tax efficiency. Vehicle selection becomes an important tool to mitigate potential tax consequences. For example, certain Asia-based investors may use European or other offshore vehicles that feed into US strategies in order to mitigate US tax withholding. Conversely, some funds benefit from preferential tax treatment that might add to its relative attractiveness.

Here are a few examples of these tax considerations:

- The US tax code has provisions that favor real estate, timber, and energy investments. Timber sales, for example, are taxed at lower capital gains rates rather than as ordinary income and may benefit from a depletion deduction. Commercial and residential building assets can be depreciated according to various schedules, with the depreciation offsetting income received on those assets. Some oil and natural gas royalty owners may benefit from a depletion deduction, offsetting income generated from the sale of the oil or gas.
- Some alternative investment strategies can generate unrelated business income tax (UBIT). UBIT arises when a US tax-exempt organization engages in activities that are not related to the tax-exempt purpose of that organization. Since most tax-exempt entities seek to mitigate (if not avoid) taxes, they will want to verify whether such a fund might generate UBIT and, if so, whether the fund manager has an offshore vehicle that may shield the investor from such income.
- The taxable investor faces additional costs and operational hurdles because of the more complex tax filings. Some taxable investors must estimate their expected annual income, including income that is derived from investments. Deriving an accurate estimate can be a challenge. Unfortunately, if the misestimation is large enough it might result in tax penalties.

Tax considerations, like fees, will affect the return assumptions used in the asset allocation exercise.

5.7. Other Considerations

Although smaller investors seeking to build a diversified alternative investment program are generally constrained to use an intermediary, such as a fund of funds, large investors have the opportunity to build a program in-house and must decide whether this approach is appropriate given their governance structure. Key questions to explore in evaluating the options include the following:

- What is the likelihood that the investor can identify and gain access to the top-tier managers in the investment strategy?
  Truly differentiated strategies and top-tier managers are notoriously capacity constrained, which tends to limit the amount of assets they can reasonably manage without negatively affecting investment returns. Fund managers who recognize this problem frequently limit the number of investors that they allow into their fund and may close their doors to new clients or capital. This can make it extremely difficult for investors to find and access top-tier managers. Investors who are subject to public disclosure requirements may be rejected by a manager who believes that success is based on a proprietary informational edge that could be eroded through these required public disclosures. Many studies on alternative assets have concluded that it may not be worth the costs and resources required to be successful in this space if investors do not have access to top-tier funds.
- What is the likelihood that the investor will be accorded the access needed to conduct effective due diligence on an investment strategy?
  It is not enough to know when or if to invest with a fund manager; it is equally, if not more, important to be able to determine when to terminate the relationship. Having poor to no access to the key decision makers within the organization could make it difficult to

ascertain if the conditions have changed such that a redemption is warranted. The situation could be even worse if other clients have good (or preferential) access to the fund manager, which might result in their redeeming early, leaving other, less-informed investors subject to gates or other more-restrictive redemption terms that could be triggered.

- What skills and resources does the investor have in-house to evaluate and monitor an alternative investment program?

This question is evaluated through a consideration of the cost tradeoffs, the investment expertise of in-house staff, the desire to tailor an investment program to investor-specific wants and needs, and the degree of control.

  - Cost is typically the overriding factor in the decision to build a program in-house or buy an existing off-the-shelf product. The all-in costs of compensation, benefits, rent, technology, reporting, travel, overhead, and other miscellaneous expenses associated with managing an alternative investments program can far exceed the costs associated with running a traditional asset portfolio. However, very large organizations may be able to justify the costs of building in-house teams.
  - Investors seeking to leverage a manager's expertise through co-investments and other direct investment opportunities must build an in-house team with the expertise to evaluate specific securities and deals and must provide the infrastructure needed to support those efforts.
  - Investors who require highly customized investment programs might be poorly served by consultants or FOFs who typically gain scale and margin by providing solutions that can be broadly applied to a large number of clients. For example, an endowment that wants their alternative investment program to consider environmental, social, and governance (ESG) factors (i.e., socially responsible investing) may have a difficult time finding an investment consultant who can deliver on the client's specific ESG requirements. Or, a family office that wants to emphasize tax-efficient angel investments might need to hire in-house resources in order to find and supervise these more specialized investments.
  - Those investors who desire a high degree of control and/or influence over the implementation of the investment program are more likely to have this need met through an in-house program.

EXAMPLE 3   Considerations in Allocating to Alternative Investments

The investment committee (IC) for a small endowment has decided to invest in private equity for the first time and has agreed upon a 10% strategic target. The internal investment team comprises the CIO (chief investment officer) and two analysts. The IC asks the CIO to recommend an implementation plan at the next meeting.

1. What are the options the CIO should include in her report as it relates to vehicles, and what factors might influence the recommendation?
2. The IC provided no guidance as to expectations for when the investment program should reach its 10% target weight. What additional information should the CIO gather before presenting her plan of action?

Solution to 1: The primary considerations for the CIO include the size of the private equity allocation, the team's expertise with private equity, and the available resources.

Because this is a small endowment, it may be difficult to commit enough capital to achieve an adequate level of diversification. The size of the fund's investment team is also likely to be a concern. Unless there are financial resources to add a private equity specialist and/or employ an outside consultant, the fund-of-funds route would likely be the optimal vehicle(s) to implement a diversified private equity program.

Solution to 2: The CIO should factor in the cash flows and anticipated liquidity profile of the overall endowment in considering the speed with which they would commit to a significant PE program. If, for example, the foundation is embarking on a capital campaign and anticipated distributions are small over the next few years, then commitments may be accelerated after factoring in an appropriate vintage year diversification. (Because private investment returns are very sensitive to the fund's vintage year, it is common for investors to build up to a full allocation over a period of years, called vintage year diversification.) However, if the rest of the investment program is heavily exposed to illiquid investments (e.g., real estate, certain hedge fund strategies) and anticipated distributions to fund operating expenses are high, the CIO may want to commit at a slower pace.

EXAMPLE 4   Considerations in Allocating to Alternative Investments

A $100 million client of a family office firm has requested that all public securities investments meet certain ESG criteria. The ESG ratings will be provided by an independent third-party firm that provides a rating for most public equities and some fixed-income issuers. Moreover, the family would like to dedicate a percentage of assets to support an "environmental sustainability" impact theme.

1. Which alternative investment strategies may not be suitable for this client given the ESG requirements?
2. What additional information might the family office firm require from the client in order to meet the environmental sustainability threshold?

Solution to 1: Because the ESG criteria apply to all public securities, most hedge fund strategies would be precluded because they are typically owned in a commingled vehicle, such as a limited partnership or a mutual fund where transparency of holdings is limited and the investor has no influence over the composition of the underlying portfolio. Separate account strategies are available for certain large portfolios, but it is unlikely that a $100 million client would be eligible for a custom portfolio that would be allocating only a small asset base to any particular fund.

Solution to 2: The client and the manager would need to agree on a clear definition of environmental sustainability and the types of investments that might qualify for this theme. It is unlikely that most hedge funds, private credit, energy, or infrastructure strategies would be considered to positively impact environmental sustainability. The most likely candidates for consideration could be timber, sustainable farmland, and clean-tech funds under the venture capital category.

6. SUITABILITY CONSIDERATIONS

Alternative investments are not appropriate for all investors. We discuss briefly several *investor* characteristics that are important to a successful alternative investment program.

6.1. Investment Horizon

Investors with less than a 15-year investment horizon should generally avoid investments in private real estate, private real assets, and private equity funds. An alternative investment program in private markets may take 5 to 7 years to fully develop and another 10 to 12 years to unwind, assuming no new investments are made after the 7-year mark. Even a 10-year horizon may be too short to develop a robust private alternative investment program.

Other strategies can tolerate a shorter investment focus. Many hedge fund strategies that focus on public equities or managed futures have much shorter lock-ups (on the order of months or not at all). Some strategies can be entered and exited in shorter time frames, and the purchase or sale of limited partnership interests on the secondary market may be used to shorten the entry and exit phases of the process. However, the alternative investment program has a higher likelihood of success if the investor adopts a long-horizon approach coupled with an understanding of the underlying investment processes.

6.2. Expertise

A successful alternative investment program requires that the investor understand the risks entailed and the market environments that drive success or failure of each of the strategies. Understanding the breadth of the alternative investment opportunities and the complexity of strategies within each alternative class requires a relatively high level of investment expertise. Even if the investor is highly experienced, the risk of information asymmetry between the limited partner (LP) and the general partner (GP) is always there. A pension fund without full-time investment staff, or an individual without the resources to hire an adviser with a dedicated alternative investments team, is unlikely to have the investment expertise necessary to implement a successful alternative investment program.

Additionally, the investment philosophy of the asset owner (or its overseers) must be consistent with the principles of alternative investments. An investor whose investment philosophy is rooted in a belief that markets are fundamentally efficient may struggle to embrace an alternative investment program, where success is predicated on active management. A mismatch in philosophy could very well be a setup for failure when the alternative investments underperform traditional asset classes.

6.3. Governance

A robust investment governance framework ensures that an alternative investment program is structured to meet the needs of the investor. The following are hallmarks of a strong governance framework suitable to an alternative investment program:

- The long- and short-term objectives of the investment program are clearly articulated.
- Decision rights and responsibilities are allocated to those individuals with the knowledge, capacity, and time required to critically evaluate possible courses of action.

- A formal investment policy has been adopted to govern the day-to-day operations of the investment program.
- A reporting framework is in place to monitor the program's progress toward the agreed-on goals and objectives.

Investors without a strong governance program are less likely to develop a successful alternative investment program.

6.4. Transparency

Investors must be comfortable with less than 100% transparency into the underlying holdings of their alternative investment managers. In real estate, private equity, and real asset funds, the investor is typically buying into a "blind pool"—committing capital for investment in a portfolio of as-yet-unidentified assets. During the course of investment due diligence, the investor may have looked at the assets acquired in the manager's previous funds, but there is no assurance that the new fund will look anything like the prior funds. Hedge fund managers are generally reluctant to disclose the full portfolio to investors on an ongoing basis. Even if you were to have access to the full underlying portfolio, it is rarely apparent where the true risk exposures lie without a detailed understanding of the investment themes the manager is pursuing.

Reporting for alternative funds is often less transparent than investors are accustomed to seeing on their stock and bond portfolios. Generally, no legal requirements mandate the frequency, timing, and details of fund reporting for private investment partnerships. For many illiquid strategies (real estate/assets, private equity/credit), reporting is often received well past month- or quarter-end deadlines that investors are accustomed to with their traditional investments.

A typical hedge fund report, usually available on a quarterly basis, may detail performance, top 10 holdings, and some general commentary on the capital markets as well as some factors that influenced fund performance. The hedge fund manager may also provide a risk report that broadly outlines the major risk exposures of the fund. There is no commonality among the risk reports provided from fund to fund. This hampers an investor's efforts to develop a picture of aggregate risk exposure. Clients with separately managed accounts have access to portfolio holdings and may be able to produce their own risk reporting with a common set of risk metrics.

Private equity funds will provide more transparency into portfolio holdings, but the private equity fund report is unlikely to "slice-and-dice" the exposures by geography, sector, or industry. The investor must gather the additional information needed to develop a fuller exposure of the portfolio's risk exposures and progress toward meeting expectations. Private equity managers typically provide an abbreviated quarterly report with a more detailed annual report following the completion of the fund's annual audit.

This lack of transparency can shield questionable actions by GPs. In 2014, the US Securities and Exchange Commission found that more than 50% of private equity firms had collected or misallocated fees without proper disclosure to their clients.[8] This study and subsequent lawsuits have increased transparency within the industry, although the industry remains opaque at many levels.

Reporting for private real estate funds commonly consists of a quarterly report with details on the fund's size, progress in drawdowns, realizations to date, and valuations of

---

[8]Andrew Ceresney, "Keynote Address: Private Equity Enforcement," Securities Enforcement Forum West (12 May 2016).

unrealized investments as well as market commentary relevant to the fund's strategy. Reports typically include details on each investment such as the original acquisition cost(s), square footage, borrowing details (e.g., cost of debt, leverage ratios, and debt maturity dates), and fundamental metrics regarding the health of the properties (e.g., occupancy rates and, if appropriate, the estimated credit health of tenants). Often there is qualitative commentary on the health of the property's submarket, on anticipated next steps, and on the timing of realization(s). Reports are typically issued with a one-quarter lag to allow sufficient time to update property valuations. Annual reports, which frequently require updated third-party appraisals, may not be available until the second quarter following year end.

Investors should ensure that funds use independent administrators to calculate the fund and LPs' NAV. These administrators are also responsible for processing cash flows, including contributions, fee payments, and distributions that are consistent with the fund documents. The use of independent administrators is common practice among hedge funds. It is relatively uncommon for a fund investing in illiquid strategies (e.g., private equity/credit, real estate/ natural resources) to use an independent administrator. Funds that do not use third-party administrators have wide discretion in valuing assets. In the midst of the Great Financial Crisis, it was not uncommon for two different private equity firms with ownership interests in the same company to provide very different estimates of the company's value.

The lack of transparency common with many alternative investments can challenge risk management and performance evaluation. High-quality alternative investment managers will engage an independent and respected accounting firm to perform an annual audit of the fund; the audit report should be available to the LPs.

Regulatory requirements for mutual funds and UCITS funds require such standardized information as costs, expected risks, and performance data. Additional information may also be available on a periodic basis. Information provided to one investor should be available to all shareholders. These rules have been interpreted by some mutual fund/UCITS managers to mean that they cannot provide more-detailed, non-standardized information given the complexity of sharing it with a broad audience. This can possibly restrict the level of transparency certain shareholders can obtain for these vehicles.

EXAMPLE 5   Suitability Considerations in Allocating to Alternative Investments

The Christian family office is concerned with investor or manager fraud and so will invest only in separately managed accounts (SMAs).

1. What are the benefits and drawbacks to the use of SMAs?
2. The 75-year-old patriarch of the Christian family would like to consider a significant private equity allocation in a trust that he oversees on behalf of his youngest daughter. This would be the first alternative investment commitment made with any of the family's assets. The daughter is 40 years old. She will receive one-half of the assets outright upon his death. The remainder of the assets will be held in trust subject to the terms of the trust agreement. List some of the reasons why private equity may or may not be appropriate for this trust.

Solution to 1: Although an SMA allows for greater transparency and control of capital flows (the manager does not generally have the authority to distribute capital from the client account), it has several potential disadvantages: 1) SMAs are not available or appropriate for many alternative strategies; thus, the requirement to invest via an SMA may limit the ability to develop an optimal alternative investment program. 2) A manager cannot invest alongside the client in the client's SMA. This may reduce the alignment of interest between the manager and the client and may give rise to conflicts of interest as trades are allocated between the SMA and the manager's other funds.

Solution to 2:

- Successful private equity investment requires a long time horizon. Given the patriarch's age, it is likely that half of the trust's assets will be distributed before the private equity program has had time to mature. This may lead to an unintended doubling in the size of the private equity allocation.
- The patriarch has no experience investing in alternative assets. Unless he is willing to commit the time, money, and effort and engage an outside adviser with the relevant expertise and access to top-tier funds, the likelihood of a successful private equity investment program would be low.
- Because the beneficiary of the trust is relatively young, the time horizon of the investment likely matches the profile of the underlying investor. It may be appropriate for the trust to invest in long-dated private equity assets, provided the investment is sized appropriately and the necessary expertise has been retained.

7. ASSET ALLOCATION APPROACHES

We mentioned earlier that one approach to determining the desired allocation to the alternative asset classes is to make the initial asset allocation decision using only the broad, liquid asset classes and do a second iteration of the asset allocation exercise incorporating alternative assets. After first addressing the challenges in developing risk and return assumptions for alternative asset classes, we then discuss three primary approaches that investors use to approach this second iteration.

1. *Monte Carlo simulation.* We discuss how Monte Carlo simulation may be used to generate return scenarios that relax the assumption of normally distributed returns. We illustrate how simulation can be applied to estimate the long-term risk profile and return potential of various asset allocation alternatives, and, in particular, we evaluate whether various asset allocation alternatives would satisfy the investor's ultimate investment objectives.
2. *Optimization techniques.* Mean–variance optimization (MVO) typically over-allocates to alternative asset classes, partly because risk is underestimated because of stale or infrequent pricing and the underlying assumption that returns are normally distributed. Practitioners usually address this bias toward alternatives by establishing limits on the allocations to alternatives. Optimization methods that incorporate downside risk (mean–CVaR optimization) or take into account skew may be used to enhance the asset allocation process.
3. *Risk factor-based approaches.* Risk factor-based approaches to alternative asset allocation can be applied to develop more robust asset allocation proposals.

These analytical techniques complement each other, and investors frequently rely on all of them rather than just using one or the other. Monte Carlo simulation can provide simulated non-normal (fat-tailed) data for a mean–CVaR optimization, but simulation can also be applied to analyze the long-term behavior of various asset allocation alternatives that are the results of portfolio optimization.

7.1. Statistical Properties and Challenges of Asset Returns

Alternative investments present the modeler with a number of analytical challenges. These two are particularly relevant in the asset allocation process:

1. Appraisal-based valuations used in private alternative investments often lead to stale and/ or artificially smoothed returns. Volatility and other risk measures estimated based on these smoothed time series would potentially understate the actual, fundamental risk.
2. Although even the public asset classes can exhibit non-normal return distributions, skewness and fat tails (excess kurtosis) are more pronounced with many of the alternative investment strategies. Leverage, sensitivity to the disappearance of liquidity, and even the asymmetric nature of performance fees all contribute to additional skewness and excess kurtosis among alternative investments. This option–payoff style quality can undermine a simplistic statistical approach.

Asset allocators use various analytical approaches to mitigate the impact of these challenges.

7.1.1. Stale Pricing and Unsmoothing
Appraisal-based valuation is common in private real estate and private equity. The valuation parameter assumptions in the appraisal process change quite slowly. This has a smoothing effect on reported returns and gives the illusion that illiquid assets' performance is much less volatile than that of public marketable assets with similar fundamental characteristics. This issue also affects hedge funds in which the manager invests in illiquid or less-liquid assets whose valuations are updated infrequently or are using models with static valuation assumptions. These artificially smoothed returns can be detected by testing the return stream for serial correlation. If serial correlation is detected and found statistically significant, the analyst needs to unsmooth the returns to get a more accurate representation of the risk and return characteristics of the asset class we are modeling.

To illustrate unsmoothing, we use a simple approach described by Ang (2014). Exhibit 19 illustrates the reported quarterly return history of the Cambridge Associates Private Equity Index, as well as the unsmoothed series.[9] The annualized volatility estimated using the reported quarterly return data and scaling using the square root of time convention is 9.5%.[10] The widely accepted rule of scaling by the square root of time, however, is based on the

---

[9]We used the following formula to unsmooth the report total return time series:

$r_{t,\text{unsmoothed}} = (r_{t,\text{reported}} - s \times r_{t-1,\text{reported}})/(1-s)$, where s denotes the estimated serial correlation of the time series.

[10]To scale volatility estimates to a longer (or shorter) time horizon, the volatility can be multiplied by the square root of time. For example, if we know the quarterly volatility and want an annual volatility estimate, we would multiply the quarterly volatility estimate by the square root of 4. (This scaling convention assumes price changes are independent and returns are not serially correlated over time.)

assumption of serially uncorrelated, normally-distributed returns. In our example, the serial correlation of the quarterly reported private equity returns is 0.38, which, given the number of observations, is significant with a *t*-statistic of 4.09. Because our returns are serially correlated, we want to unsmooth the returns to get a better estimate of volatility. The volatility calculated on the unsmoothed return series is 14.0%, significantly higher than the volatility estimated from the unsmoothed data.

EXHIBIT 19   C|A Private Equity Index Quarterly Returns

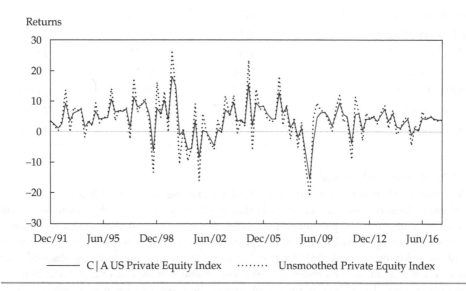

Exhibit 20 illustrates serial correlation and volatility estimates based on quarterly returns of a broad range of asset classes. Although the serial correlation of public marketable asset classes is generally low, private asset classes and some hedge fund strategies have higher serial correlations that indicate stronger smoothing effects. The higher the serial correlation in the reported return series, the larger the difference between the volatility based on the unsmoothed and reported (smoothed) return data. The impact of smoothing is the highest in the case of private investments, as suggested by the serial correlation for private real estate (0.85) and private equity (0.38). The unsmoothed volatility of private real estate is, in fact, three times the volatility that we would estimate based on the reported returns. Given the serial correlation evident in private alternative strategies, it is not surprising that the distressed hedge fund strategy exhibits higher serial correlation (0.36) than other hedge fund strategies.

EXHIBIT 20   The Effect of Serial Correlation on Volatility

Quarterly Data Dec. 1997–Sept. 2017	Serial Correlation	Volatility (reported returns)	Volatility (unsmoothed)
US Equities	0.03	17.0%	17.7%
Non-US Developed Market Equities	0.08	19.2%	20.8%
Emerging Market Equities	0.17	26.2%	30.8%
Governments	−0.01	4.9%	4.9%

Quarterly Data Dec. 1997–Sept. 2017	Serial Correlation	Volatility (reported returns)	Volatility (unsmoothed)
Broad Fixed Income	0.02	3.4%	3.5%
High-Yield Credit	0.34	10.0%	14.3%
Inflation-Linked Bonds	0.12	5.0%	5.7%
Hedge Funds—Aggregate	0.15	8.1%	9.5%
HF Macro	0.08	5.4%	5.9%
HF Equity Market Neutral	0.17	3.5%	4.1%
HF Equity Hedged	0.19	10.7%	13.1%
HF Distressed	0.36	8.9%	13.0%
Commodities	0.14	25.2%	28.8%
Public Real Estate	0.15	20.4%	24.0%
Private Real Estate	0.85	4.6%	13.8%
Private Equity	0.38	10.7%	15.7%

7.1.2. Skewness and Fat Tails

A common and convenient assumption behind asset pricing theory, as well as models applied for asset allocation and risk analytics, is that asset returns are normally distributed. Both academic researchers and practitioners are widely aware of the limitations of this assumption, but no standard quantitative method to replace this assumption of normality exists. Skewness and excess kurtosis, or so-called "fat tails," in the distributions of empirically observed asset returns may lead to underestimated downside risk measures in the case of both traditional and alternative asset classes. Non-normality of returns, however, can be more severe in private alternative asset class and certain hedge fund strategies than in most of the traditional asset classes.

In Exhibit 21, we show skewness and excess kurtosis parameters calculated based on 20 years of unsmoothed quarterly return data of various public and alternative asset classes. We also show 95% quarterly conditional value at risk (CVaR) estimates based on the assumption of normally distributed asset returns, as well as based on the observed (actual) distributions. Positive skewness indicates smaller downside risk potential, while negative skewness indicates greater downside risk potential. Excess kurtosis (i.e., a kurtosis parameter exceeding 3) similarly points toward greater downside risk than would be apparent from the numbers calculated using the assumption of normally-distributed returns. The observed (actual) CVaR estimates typically exceed the normal distribution-based CVaR figures when kurtosis is high and skewness is negative. Equity market-neutral hedge funds and private real estate have the biggest *relative* differences between the 95% normal distribution CVaR and the observed CVaR (columns C and D divided by column C). Both of these strategies have negative skewness and fairly high excess kurtosis. It's interesting to note that distressed hedge funds similarly have high kurtosis and negative skewness, but the difference in tail risk measures becomes mainly visible at the 99% confidence level, where the extreme but infrequent losses may occur.

EXHIBIT 21   Normal Distribution Assumption and Observed Downside Risk Measures

Unsmoothed Quarterly Data Dec. 1997–Sept. 2017	(A) Skewness	(B) Excess Kurtosis	(C) 95% CVaR (Normal Distribution)	(D) 95% CVaR (Observed)	(E) 99% CVaR (Normal Distribution)	(F) 99% CVaR (Observed)
US Equities	−0.51	0.43	−15.3%	−17.7%	−20.3%	−23.9%
Non-US Dev Equities	−0.19	0.29	−18.9%	−19.8%	−24.8%	−20.7%
Emerging Mkt Equities	−0.23	−0.03	−28.2%	−25.4%	−37.0%	−27.7%
Governments	0.59	0.39	−3.5%	−3.2%	−4.9%	−4.0%
Broad Fixed Income	−0.05	−0.41	−2.1%	−2.4%	−3.1%	−3.1%
High-Yield Credit	0.18	6.14	−7.9%	−9.8%	−10.8%	−19.7%
Inflation-Linked Bonds	−0.32	1.08	−4.2%	−4.2%	−5.8%	−8.1%
Hedge Funds	−0.17	1.69	−7.6%	−8.6%	−10.3%	−9.7%
HF Macro	0.36	0.85	−4.3%	−4.1%	−6.0%	−5.1%
HF Equity Market Neutral	−1.17	3.55	−2.9%	−3.9%	−4.1%	−5.4%
HF Equity Hedged	0.08	2.24	−10.8%	−10.6%	−14.5%	−12.7%
HF Distressed	−1.25	3.52	−10.8%	−11.1%	−14.5%	−16.9%
Commodities	−0.71	1.62	−28.4%	−30.6%	−36.6%	−50.6%
Public Real Estate	−0.88	4.60	−20.9%	−24.5%	−27.7%	−40.2%
Private Real Estate	−2.80	9.62	−11.3%	−15.4%	−15.3%	−27.9%
Private Equity	−0.46	2.05	−12.2%	−15.7%	−16.7%	−22.6%

Source: Authors' calculations.

To further illustrate the impact of non-normality on the downside risk, in Exhibit 22 we compare the ratio of observed to normal CVaR measures with the skewness and excess kurtosis. Although the skewness or excess kurtosis alone doesn't fully explain the relative difference between observed and normal 95% CVaR (positive skewness may compensate high excess kurtosis or vice versa), we can see the evidence that higher kurtosis or more negative skewness usually increases the likely severity of any tail risk.

EXHIBIT 22   The Impact of Skewness and Kurtosis on Tail Risk

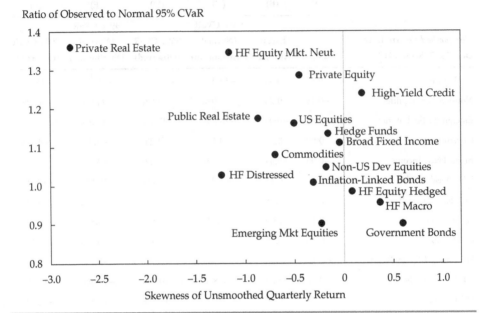

Ratio of Observed to Normal 95% CVaR

Source: Authors' calculations.

Analysts can choose to incorporate non-normality into their analyses in a few different ways. The most obvious and straightforward choice is to use empirically observed asset returns instead of working with the normal distribution. Still, in private investments where we typically have only quarterly return data, the analyses may be subject to serious limitations. Even with 20 years of quarterly return data, we have only 80 data points (and the industry has changed significantly over this time, further straining the validity of the data).

With sufficient data, analysts and researchers can capture the effects of fat tails by using advanced mathematical or statistical models:

- Time-varying volatility models (e.g., stochastic volatility), which assume that volatility is not constant over time but changes dynamically, can be used.
- Regime-switching models capture return, volatility, and correlation characteristics in different market environments (bull/bear or low volatility and moderate correlation vs. high volatility and elevated correlation). The combination of two or more normal distributions with different average returns, volatilities, and correlations could capture skewed and fat-tailed distributions.
- Extreme value theory and other fat-tailed distributions can be used when the analyst wants to focus on the behavior in the tails.

Although no single and uniformly accepted approach exists to address all of these quantitative challenges to the asset allocation exercise, a sound asset allocation process will do the following:

1. Adjust the observed asset class return data by unsmoothing the return series if the autocorrelation is significant.

2. Determine whether it is reasonable to accept an assumption of normal return distributions, in which case mean–variance optimization is appropriate to use.

3. Allow you to choose an optimization approach that takes the tail risk into account if the time series exhibits fat tails and skewness and if the potential downside risk would exceed the levels that would be observed with a normal distribution.

7.2. Monte Carlo Simulation

Monte Carlo simulation can be a very useful tool in asset allocation to alternative investments. In this section, we discuss two applications of this modeling approach. First, we discuss how we can simulate risk factor or asset return scenarios that exhibit the skewness and kurtosis commonly seen in alternative investments. Second, we illustrate simulation-based risk and return analytics over a long time horizon in a broad asset allocation context.

At a very high level, we can summarize the model construction process in the following steps:

1. Identify those variables that we would like to randomly generate in our simulation. These variables may be asset class total returns directly, or risk factors, depending on the model.
2. Establish the quantitative framework to generate realistic random scenarios for the selected asset class returns or risk factors. Here, the analyst faces several choices, including the following:
   a. What kind of time-series model are we using? Will it be a random walk? Or will it incorporate serial correlations and mean-reversion-like characteristics?
   b. What kind of distribution should we assume for the shocks or innovations to the variables? Is normal distribution reasonable? Or, will we use some fat-tailed distribution model instead?
   c. Are volatilities and correlations stable over time? Or, do they vary across time?
3. If using a risk factor approach, convert the risk factors to asset or asset class returns using a factor-based model. In this chapter, all our illustrations are based on linear factor models, but certain asset types with optionality need more-sophisticated models to incorporate convexity characteristics as well.
4. Further translate realistic asset class return scenarios into meaningful indicators. We can simultaneously model, for example, the investment portfolio and the liability of a pension fund, enabling us to assess how the funding ratio is expected to evolve over time. Or, in the case of an endowment fund, we can assess whether certain asset allocation choices would improve the probability of meeting the spending rate target while preserving the purchasing power of the asset base.

7.2.1. Simulating Skewed and Fat-Tailed Financial Variables

A fairly intuitive way of incorporating non-normal returns into the analysis is to assume that there are two (or more) possible states of the world. Individually, each state can be described by using a normal distribution (*conditional normality*), but the combination of these two distributions will not be normally distributed.[11] Next, we show a fairly simplified application

---

[11] The estimation process of such models is beyond the scope of this chapter. Readers interested in additional details are referred to Hamilton (1989) and Kim and Nelson (1999).

for the public equities and government bonds. Note that the same approach can be applied to more asset classes as well, or it can be applied to risk factor changes rather than asset class returns.

For this illustration, we assume that the capital markets can be described by two distinct regimes—a "quiet period" (Regime 1) and a high-volatility state (Regime 2). Exhibit 23 shows the quarterly return history of the US equities and government bonds as well as the model's more volatile regimes (the gray-shaded periods). It is easy to see that the Global Financial Crisis—and such earlier crisis periods as the 1997 Asian currency contagion, the 1998 Russian ruble crisis and LTCM meltdown, and the 2002 tech bubble burst—all belong to the high-volatility regimes. The mean return and volatility statistics for the full period as well as each of the two regimes can be found in Exhibit 24. Equities outperformed government bonds over the full observation period, and it's interesting to see how dynamics changed between the quiet to the volatile periods. In the quiet period (Regime 1), equities outperformed bonds by around 4.6% quarterly, whereas in the volatile period (Regime 2), government bonds outperformed equities by more than 5%. The total return volatilities also jumped dramatically when the market switched from quiet to volatile periods. In addition, the correlation between equities and bonds was near zero during the quiet period but turned significantly negative (about −0.6) during the volatile period. Finally, we estimate that the low-volatility Regime 1 prevailed 62% of the time and the high-volatility Regime 2 prevailed 38% of the time.

EXHIBIT 23   US Equities and Government Bonds Return History and Identification of High-Volatility Regimes

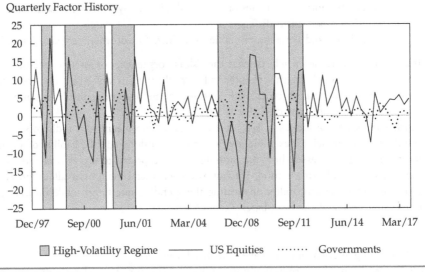

Source: Authors' calculations.

EXHIBIT 24   Return Statistics (1997–2017)

	Equities	Government Bonds
Quarterly Average Return	2.1%	1.2%
Quarterly Return Volatility	8.5%	4.5%
Skewness	−0.5	0.6
Kurtosis	0.4	0.4
Average Return in Regime 1	5.1%	0.5%
Average Return in Regime 2	−3.1%	2.4%
Volatility in Regime 1	5.5%	1.9%
Volatility in Regime 2	13.7%	3.8%
Correlation in Regime 1	0.0	
Correlation in Regime 2	−0.6	

If we want to capture only skewness and fat tails in a simulation framework, we just need the normal distribution parameters of the distinct regimes and the overall state probabilities of either Regime 1 or Regime 2. Then, the analyst would generate normally distributed random scenarios based on the different means and covariances estimated under the two (or more) regimes with the appropriate frequency of the estimated probability of being the quiet or hectic regimes. This mixture of high- and low-volatility normal distributions would lead to an altogether skewed and fat-tailed distribution of asset class return or risk factor changes. In practice, some may build a more dynamic, multi-step simulation model for a longer time horizon, in which case it's also important to estimate the probability of switching from one regime to another.

Exhibit 25 shows histograms of equity returns, overlaid with the fitted normal distribution and the combined distributions from our regime-switching model. As the chart illustrates, the combination of two normal distributions improves the distribution fit and introduces some degree of skewness and fat-tail characteristics.

EXHIBIT 25   Normal and Fat-Tailed Distribution Fit for US Equity Quarterly Returns

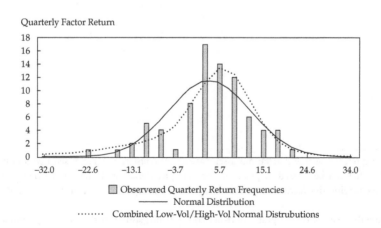

Several variations of regime-switching models are available. We have used a very basic set-up to illustrate the additional richness a regime-switching model can bring to the analysis. We could also apply a similar approach if we were to build asset classes using risk factors. We could overlay the non-normal distributions of the risk factors on the relevant asset class returns.[12]

7.2.2. Simulation for Long-Term Horizon Risk Assessment

We will now work through a practical application of Monte Carlo simulation in the context of asset allocation over a long time horizon. We simulate asset class returns in quarterly steps over a 10-year time horizon.[13] Such models exhibit some degree of mean-reversion and also capture dynamic interactions across risk factors or asset classes over multiple time periods.

The volatilities, correlations, and other parameters of the time series model are estimated based on the past 20 years of unsmoothed asset class return data. The expected returns for the selected asset classes (shown in Exhibit 26), however, are not based on historical average returns but are illustrative, forward-looking estimates. Note that these return expectations mostly assume passive investments in the specific asset class and don't include the possible value-added from (or lost through) active management. Hedge funds are the exception, of course, because by definition hedge funds are actively managed investment strategies rather than a true stand-alone asset class. The expected returns are also generally assumed to be net of fees to make them comparable across asset classes.

Asset class-level expected returns are critically important to an asset allocation exercise. Return expectations should be reflective of the current market conditions—including valuations, levels of interest rates, and spreads. Setting return expectations requires a combination of objective facts (e.g., the current yield and spread levels) and judgment (how risk factors and valuation ratios might change from the current levels over the relevant time horizon).

---

[12]In this chapter, we assume that various asset classes have constant risk factor sensitivities over time, an assumption that can be relaxed in practice. For example, Berkelaar, Kobor, and Kouwenberg (2009) present time-varying risk factors for various hedge fund strategies in a similar Monte Carlo simulation framework.

[13]To ensure that we not only capture short-horizon risks but also properly assess long-term asset return behavior characteristics, we capture the linear interdependencies among multiple time series by working with a vector-autoregressive model.

EXHIBIT 26   Asset Class Expected Returns

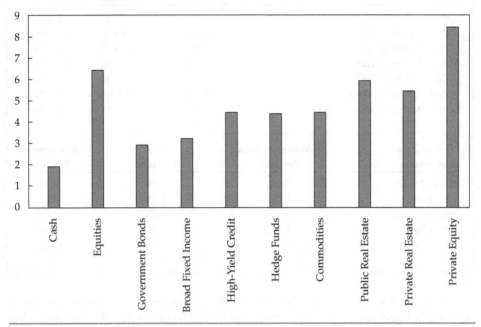

Source: Authors' data.

In this example, we compare three possible portfolios:

- A portfolio 100% invested in government bonds
- A portfolio allocated 50% to global public equities and 50% to broad fixed income
- A diversified "endowment portfolio" allocated 40% to global public equities, 15% to fixed income, 20% to broad hedge funds, 15% to private equity, 5% to private real estate, and 5% to commodities

Exhibit 27 shows the risk and return statistics for the three portfolios. VaR and CVaR downside risk measures focus over the shorter, quarterly, and 1-year time horizons. The worst drawdown and the cumulative annualized total return ranges are expressed over a 10-year time horizon.

EXHIBIT 27   Portfolio Risk and Return Estimates

	Government Bond Portfolio	50/50 Portfolio	Endowment Portfolio
Expected Geometric Return over 10 Years	2.3%	5.6%	7.0%
Annual Total Return Volatility	4.2%	6.6%	11.2%
95% VaR over Q/Q (quarter over quarter)	−3.1%	−2.9%	−4.6%
95% VaR over 1 Year	−5.2%	−4.2%	−9.1%

	Government Bond Portfolio	50/50 Portfolio	Endowment Portfolio
95% CVaR over Q/Q	−4.0%	−3.9%	−6.4%
95% CVaR over 1 Year	−6.9%	−6.6%	−13.1%
99% VaR over Q/Q	−4.5%	−4.6%	−7.5%
99% VaR over 1 Year	−7.9%	−8.1%	−15.6%
99% CVaR over Q/Q	−5.2%	−5.5%	−8.7%
99% CVaR over 1 Year	−9.2%	−10.3%	−18.7%
Worst Drawdown over 10 Years	−19.8%	−22.5%	−36.9%

10-Year Return Distribution	Government Bond Portfolio	50/50 Portfolio	Endowment Portfolio
5% Low	0.0%	2.3%	1.9%
25% Low	1.2%	4.2%	4.8%
50% (Median)	2.3%	5.6%	7.0%
75% High	3.1%	7.0%	9.1%
95% High	4.5%	9.0%	12.2%

From Exhibit 27, we see that the multi-asset endowment portfolio generates a significantly higher return than the portfolio exclusively invested in government bonds, albeit at much higher downside risk as measured by VaR, CVaR, or worst drawdown. This table alone, however, is insufficient to determine which investment alternative a particular investor should choose.

Consider the case of a university endowment fund. Let's assume that the investment objective is to support a 5% annual spending rate as well as to preserve the purchasing power of the asset base over the 10-year time horizon. We use the same simulation engine to generate the analytics of Exhibit 28. Here, we plot the expected cumulative total return within a +/− 1 standard deviation range together with the cumulative spending rate, as well as the spending rate augmented with inflation on a cumulative basis. The latter two variables represent the investment target, so we can meaningfully interpret the return potential of the two investment choices in the context of the investment objective. The 50% equities/ 50% government bond portfolio initially appeared to be a lower risk alternative in Exhibit 27, but Exhibit 28 shows that this choice is more likely to fall short of the return target, given that its median return of 5.6% is less than the nominal return target of approximately 7% (the 5% spending rate plus 2% inflation). At the same time, the endowment portfolio's 7% median return indicates that it would have a better chance of meeting the investment objective.

EXHIBIT 28   Cumulative Total Return Cones Simulated over a 10-Year Horizon

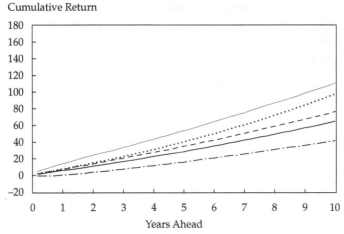

A. 50/50 Portfolio

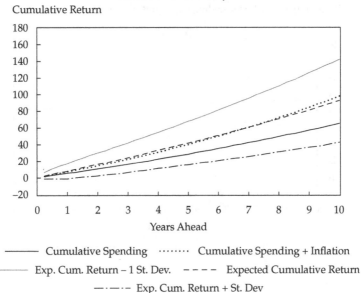

B. Endowment Portfolio

——— Cumulative Spending   ········ Cumulative Spending + Inflation

——— Exp. Cum. Return – 1 St. Dev.   – – – – Expected Cumulative Return

—·—·– Exp. Cum. Return + St. Dev

Exhibit 29 shows the probability of meeting the spending rate as well as the spending rate plus inflation at any point in time over the investment horizon. If risk is defined as the probability of falling short of meeting the return target (rather than the asset-only perspective of risk, volatility), the otherwise lower-risk 50% equities and 50% government bond portfolio becomes the higher risk alternative.

EXHIBIT 29   Estimated Probability of Achieving the Investment Goal

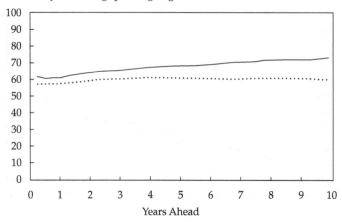

A.

Probability of meeting spending target

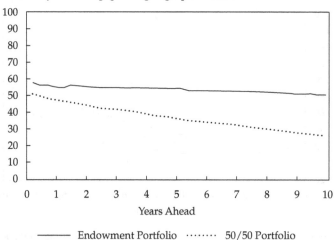

B.

Probability of meeting spending target plus inflation

——— Endowment Portfolio   ········ 50/50 Portfolio

7.3. Portfolio Optimization

Portfolio optimization for asset allocation has been covered in great detail in earlier chapters. Here we focus on some special considerations for optimization in the context of alternative investments.

7.3.1. Mean–Variance Optimization without and with Constraints

We mentioned earlier that mean–variance optimization would likely over-allocate to alternative, mainly illiquid, asset classes given their higher expected returns and potentially underestimated risk. Some investors impose minimum and maximum constraints on various asset classes to compensate for this bias. Let's consider the ramifications of this approach.

Here, the input data for our optimization are comprised of the asset class expected returns depicted in Exhibit 26, while the covariance matrix is based on the unsmoothed asset class return history over the past 20 years. Exhibit 30 shows the optimized portfolio allocations generated by the mean–variance optimization without and with constraints. Each column in these bar charts represents an optimized portfolio allocation subject to a return target. The exhibit progresses from low-return targets on the left to high-return targets on the right. In total, we show 20 possible portfolio allocations first without and then with constraints.

By reviewing Panel B of Exhibit 30, we can see that the unconstrained portfolio allocations are dominated by cash and fixed income at the lower end of the risk spectrum, and private equity becomes the dominant asset class for higher risk portfolios. Optimization is quite sensitive to the input parameters: It's quite common to see allocations concentrated in a small number of asset classes. Thus, investors shouldn't take the unconstrained output as the "best" allocation. Small changes in the input variables could lead to large changes in the asset allocations.

Because investors would potentially reject the raw, concentrated output of unconstrained mean–variance optimization, we also ran a constrained optimization where we capped private equity and hedge fund allocations at 30% each, private real estate at 15%, and major public asset classes at 50% each. The resulting constrained allocations, shown in the Panel A of Exhibit 30, are less concentrated and appear to be more diversified.

Exhibit 31 depicts the mean–variance efficient frontiers corresponding to the optimized portfolio allocations of Exhibit 30. Note that both frontiers contain 20 dots, each representing an optimized portfolio. The numbers under each bar in Exhibit 30 identify the allocation associated with each of the dots on the efficient frontiers in Exhibit 31 (e.g., the allocation associated with portfolio 20 on the efficient frontier in Exhibit 31 is the one shown at the rightmost edge of Exhibit 30).

EXHIBIT 30   Unconstrained and Constrained Asset Allocations

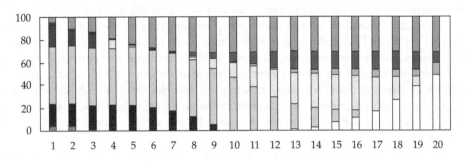

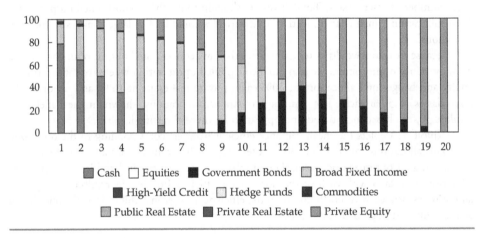

Note that the constrained efficient frontier runs below its unconstrained peer (Exhibit 31). This is not unexpected, as we artificially prohibited the optimization from selecting the most efficient allocation it could get based on the available quantitative data.

EXHIBIT 31   Unconstrained and Constrained Mean–Variance Efficient Frontiers

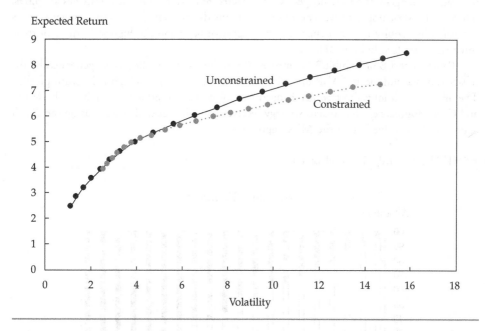

In practice, many investors are aware of the limits of the mean–variance framework—the possible underestimation of the true fundamental risks based on the reported returns of private investments—and they may also have in mind other constraints, such as capping illiquidity. Thus, introducing maximum and minimum constraints for certain asset classes may be a reasonable, although exogenous, adjustment to the quantitative optimization. However, not even constrained optimized allocations should be accepted without further scrutiny. In fact, similar volatility and expected return profiles can be achieved with a wide variety of asset allocations. So, although optimized portfolios may serve as analytical guidance, it's important to validate whether a change to an asset allocation policy results in a significant return increment and/or volatility reduction.

7.3.2. Mean–CVaR Optimization

Portfolio optimization can also improve the asset allocation decision through a risk management lens. An investor who is particularly concerned with the downside risk of a proposed asset allocation may choose to minimize the portfolio's CVaR rather than its volatility relative to a return target.[14] If the portfolio contains asset classes and investment strategies with negative skewness and long tails, the CVaR lens could materially alter the asset allocation decision. Minimizing CVaR subject to an expected return target is quantitatively much more complex than portfolio variance minimization: It requires a large number of historical or simulated return scenarios to properly incorporate potential tail risk into the optimization.[15]

---

[14]Because we are optimizing allocation to asset classes, the CVaR tail risk measure quantifies *systematic* asset class level risks. Individual asset managers or securities may impose additional idiosyncratic risk when the asset allocation is implemented in practice.

[15]Technical details are provided by Rockafellar and Uryasev (2000).

Our first illustration is applied to three hedge fund strategies: macro, equity market neutral, and long/short equity hedged. Our expected returns for the three strategies are 3.6%, 3.6%, and 6.0%, respectively. The observed return distribution for macro strategy is fairly normal, while equity market neutral exhibits negative skew and the highest kurtosis of these three strategies (see Exhibit 21).

Panels A and B of Exhibit 32 compare 20 possible portfolio allocations generated by the mean–variance and mean–CVaR optimizations, varying from low to high risk/return profiles. The allocation to long/short equity hedged (the black bar) is similar under both the MVO and CVaR approaches. The macro strategy receives a much higher allocation using the CVaR approach than it does using the MVO approach.

EXHIBIT 32   Hedge Fund Allocations

A. Mean–Variance

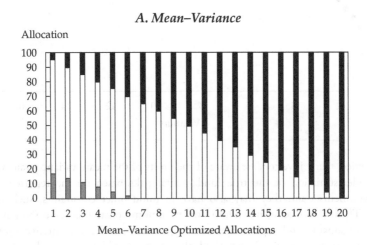

Mean–Variance Optimized Allocations

B. Mean–CVaR

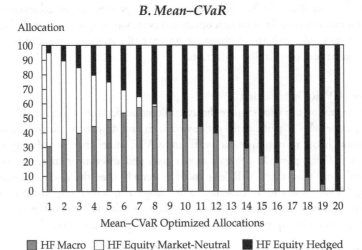

Mean–CVaR Optimized Allocations

■ HF Macro   □ HF Equity Market-Neutral   ■ HF Equity Hedged

Exhibit 33 compares portfolio #12 from the mean–variance efficient frontier to portfolio #12 from the mean–CVaR efficient frontier. Both portfolios allocated 60% to the long/short equity strategy. Under the CVaR-optimization approach, the remaining 40% of the portfolio is invested in global macro. Under the MVO approach, the remaining 40% of the portfolio is invested in equity market-neutral.

Let's compare the portfolio volatilities and downside risk measures. The mean–CVaR portfolio has higher volatility (7.8% vs 7.3%) but lower tail risk (−6.8% vs −7.7%). Exhibit 33 also shows a third portfolio, which evenly *splits* the 40% not allocated to equity-hedged between global macro and equity market neutral. The volatility of this portfolio lies between the two optimal portfolios. Although nominally more diversified than either of the #12 portfolios from the optimization, its CVaR is worse than that of the mean–CVaR optimized portfolio (but still better than that of the MVO portfolio). An investor may have qualitative considerations that warrant including this more-diversified portfolio among the options to be evaluated.

EXHIBIT 33   Mean–Variance and Mean–CVaR Efficient Hedge Fund Allocations

| | Asset Allocation | | | Portfolio Characteristics | | | |
	Macro	Equity Market Neutral	Long/Short Equity	Expected Return	Volatility	95% VaR	95% CVaR
Mean–Variance Optimal	0.0%	40.0%	60.0%	5.0%	7.3%	−3.7%	−7.7%
Mean–CVaR Optimal	40.0%	0.0%	60.0%	5.0%	7.8%	−4.1%	−6.8%
Combination	20.0%	20.0%	60.0%	5.0%	7.5%	−3.7%	−7.3%

Exhibit 34 compares the optimal allocations of a broad asset class portfolio through the mean–variance and mean–CVaR lenses. In this example, the optimal allocations were selected subject to a 6.8% expected return target. Both approaches allocated a significant portion of the portfolio to private equity and hedge funds (30% each). A notable difference, however, is in the allocation to public and private real estate. Where the MVO approach allocated 22% to the combined real estate categories, the CVaR approach allocated nothing at all to either real estate category. We can identify the reason for this by referring back to Exhibit 21: The public and private real estate categories are characterized by 99% CVaRs of −40.2% and −27.9%, respectively.

EXHIBIT 34 Mean–Variance and Mean–CVaR Efficient Multi-Asset Portfolios

| | Asset Allocation | | | | | | Portfolio Characteristics | | |
	Equities	Govt Bonds	Hedge Funds	Public Real Estate	Private Real Estate	Private Equity	Expected Return	Volatility	99% CVaR
Mean–Variance	18%	0%	30%	7%	15%	30%	6.8%	11.5%	−20.7%
Mean–CVaR	34%	6%	30%	0%	0%	30%	6.8%	12.1%	−15.6%

EXAMPLE 6   Asset Allocation Recommendation

The CIO (chief investment officer) of the International University Endowment Fund (the Fund) is preparing for the upcoming investment committee (IC) meeting. The Fund's annual asset allocation review is on the agenda, and the CIO plans to propose a new strategic asset allocation for the Fund. Subject to prudent risk-taking, the recommended asset allocation should offer

- the highest expected return and
- the highest probability of achieving the long-term 5% real return target.

The inflation assumption is 2%.

In addition, the risk in the Fund is one factor that is considered when lenders assign a risk rating to the university. The university's primary lender has proposed a loan covenant that would trigger a re-evaluation of the university's creditworthiness if the Fund incurs a loss greater than 20% over any 1-year period.

The investment staff produced the following tables to help the CIO prepare for the meeting.

| | Asset Allocation | | | | | | |
Alternative	Cash	Public Equity	Govt	Credit	Hedge Fund	Real Estate	Private Equity
A	5.0%	60.0%	30.0%	5.0%	0.0%	0.0%	0.0%
B	4.0%	50.0%	16.0%	5.0%	10.0%	5.0%	10.0%
C	2.0%	40.0%	8.0%	5.0%	18.0%	7.0%	20.0%
D	1.0%	30.0%	5.0%	4.0%	20.0%	10.0%	30.0%
E	2.0%	40.0%	3.0%	3.0%	15.0%	7.0%	30.0%
F	2.0%	50.0%	3.0%	0.0%	10.0%	5.0%	30.0%
G	1.0%	56.0%	3.0%	0.0%	10.0%	0.0%	30.0%

							Portfolio Characteristics	
							10-Year Horizon	
Alternative	**Expected Return**	**Volatility**	**1-Year 99% VaR**	**1-Year 99% CVaR**	**5th Percentile Return**	**95th Percentile Return**	**Probability of Meeting 5% Real Return**	**Probability of Purchasing Power Impairment**
A	6.0%	9.0%	−12.4%	−15.0%	1.6%	10.5%	37.0%	7.1%
B	6.7%	10.3%	−14.6%	−17.3%	2.0%	11.4%	46.1%	4.3%
C	7.1%	11.1%	−15.8%	−18.8%	2.2%	12.2%	52.1%	3.2%
D	7.4%	11.5%	−16.3%	−19.4%	2.4%	12.6%	56.1%	2.5%
E	7.7%	12.3%	−17.4%	−20.6%	2.4%	13.2%	58.8%	2.8%
F	7.8%	13.0%	−18.5%	−21.8%	2.2%	13.7%	60.8%	3.6%
G	7.9%	13.5%	−19.3%	−22.7%	2.1%	14.1%	61.0%	4.0%

Notes:

- 1-year horizon 99% VaR: the lowest return over any 1-year period at a 99% confidence level (i.e., only a 1% chance to experience a total return below this threshold).
- 1-year horizon 99% CVaR: the expected return if the return falls below the 99% VaR threshold.
- 5th and 95th percentile annualized returns over a 10-year time horizon: a 90% chance that the annualized 10-year total return will fall between these two figures
- probability of purchasing power impairment:[16] as defined by the IC, the probability of losing 40% of the endowment's purchasing power over 10 years after taking gifts to the endowment, spending from the endowment, and total return into account.

1. Which asset allocation is *most likely* to meet the committee's objective and constraints?

Solution to 1: Portfolio D. Portfolios E, F, and G have 1-year, 99% CVaRs, which, if realized, would trigger the loan covenant. Portfolio D has the next highest probability of meeting the 5% real return target and the lowest probability of purchasing power impairment. Portfolios A, B, and C have lower probabilities of meeting the return targets and higher probabilities of purchasing power impairment.

7.4. Risk Factor-Based Optimization

Increasingly, investors believe that viewing investment decisions through a risk factor lens (e.g., growth, inflation, credit risk) may improve the investment process. Separating fundamentally similar investments, like public and private equities, into distinct asset classes ignores the probability that both are exposed to the same risk factors. In this section, we will work through an asset allocation example using a risk factor lens.

---

[16]Similar measures of risk are proposed by Swensen (2009) in the context of endowment funds.

Let's assume that an investor starts the asset allocation exercise by first allocating the overall risk budget across the main risk factors.[17] Instead of setting expectations for distinct asset classes, she may start thinking about the return expectations and correlation of the fundamental risk factors. Exhibit 35 shows her return expectations for the risk factors described in Exhibit 14. In this illustration, the global equity risk factor (a practical proxy for macroeconomic-oriented "growth") is expected to generate the highest return. She expects the duration and value factors to generate negative returns because stronger economic growth fueled by advances in technology would lead to rising rates and better returns for growth stocks. She is concerned about rising inflation, so she has assigned a positive expected return to the inflation factor.

EXHIBIT 35   Expected Factor Returns

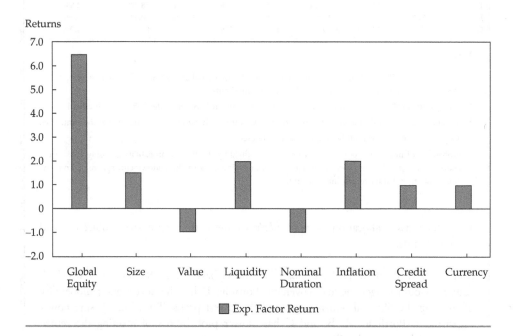

Using these returns and the historical factor volatilities and correlations, we can optimize the risk factor exposure by minimizing factor-implied risk subject to a total return target of 6.5%. The black bars in Exhibit 36 show these optimal factor exposures. Note that the target exposures of the value and nominal duration factors are positive, although the associated expected factor returns are negative. The model allocates to these factors for their diversification potential because they are negatively correlated with other risk factors. Duration and equity factors have a correlation of –0.6, whereas value and equity factors have a correlation of –0.3 based on the data used for this illustration.

We have established optimal risk factor exposures, so now we must implement this target using actual investments. Some investors may have access to only public market investments, while other investors may also have access to private illiquid investments. The gray and white

---

[17]Approaches to asset allocation and portfolio construction are expanding as the understanding of risk factors is increasing. A risk parity approach to asset allocation, for example, would allocate total risk in equal portion to the selected risk factors.

bars in Exhibit 36 illustrate the two possible implementations of the target factor exposures. Portfolio 1 assumes the investor is limited to public market investments. Portfolio 2 uses both public market investments and private, illiquid investments. The portfolio allocation details are displayed in Exhibit 37.

EXHIBIT 36   Optimal Risk Factor Allocations and Associated Asset Class Portfolios

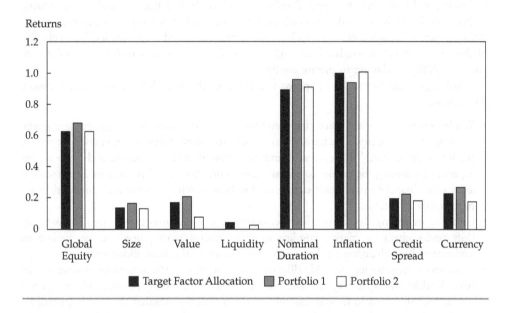

EXHIBIT 37   Asset Class Portfolios Designed Based on Optimal Risk Factor Allocations

	Portfolio 1	Portfolio 2
Domestic Equities; *Value Tilt*	21.0%	13.0%
Non-Domestic Developed Market Equities; *Value Tilt*	21.0%	13.0%
Foreign Emerging Market Equities	21.0%	12.0%
Government Bonds	0.0%	5.0%
Broad Fixed Income	10.0%	0.0%
High-Yield Credit	2.0%	3.0%
Inflation-Linked Bonds	7.0%	0.0%
Hedge Funds	15.0%	10.0%
Commodities	3.0%	4.0%
Public Real Estate	0.0%	12.0%
Private Real Estate	0.0%	13.0%
Private Equity	0.0%	15.0%
Total	**100.0%**	**100.0%**
Expected Return	6.2%	6.9%
Volatility	13.5%	13.2%

Even though they have similar factor exposures, you can see some significant differences in the asset class allocations of the two portfolios. Portfolio 1 allocates 63% to public equities, whereas Portfolio 2 allocates 35% to public equities plus 15% to private equity for its higher return potential. Portfolio 1 allocates 18% to alternatives (15% in hedge funds and 3% in commodities, two of the most liquid alternative asset classes), while Portfolio 2 has allocated 54% to alternatives (10% hedge funds, 4% commodities, 12% public real estate, 13% private real estate, and 15% private equity). Portfolio 1 achieves its inflation sensitivity by allocating to inflation-linked bonds and commodities. Portfolio 2 achieves its desired exposure to the inflation factor through a combined allocation to real estate and commodities. The volatility of the two portfolios is similar, but Portfolio 2 is able to achieve a higher expected return given its ability to allocate to private equity.

Although a risk factor-driven approach is conceptually very elegant, we must mention a few caveats:

- While generally accepted asset class definitions provide a common language among the investment community, risk factors may be defined quite differently investor-to-investor. It's important to establish a common understanding of factor definitions and factor return expectations among the parties to an asset allocation exercise. This includes an agreement as to what financial instruments can be used to best match the factor exposures if they are not directly investable.
- Correlations among risk factors, just like correlations across asset classes, may dramatically shift under changing market conditions; thus, careful testing needs to be applied to understand how changing market conditions will affect the asset allocation.
- Some factor sensitivities are stable (like the nominal interest rate sensitivity of government bonds), while others are very unstable (like the inflation sensitivity of commodities). Factor sensitivities also need to be very carefully tested to validate whether the invested portfolio would truly deliver the desired factor exposures and not deliver unintended factor returns.

EXAMPLE 7   Selecting an Asset Allocation Approach

1. You have a new client who has unexpectedly inherited a substantial sum of money. The client is in his early 30s and newly married. He has no children and no other investible assets. What asset allocation approach is most suitable for this client?

2. Your client is a tax-exempt foundation that recently received a bequest doubling its assets to €200 million. There is an outside investment adviser but no dedicated investment staff; however, the six members of the investment committee (IC) are all wealthy, sophisticated investors in their own right. The IC conducts an asset allocation study every three years and reviews the asset allocation at its annual meeting. The current asset allocation is 30% equities, 20% fixed income, 25% private equity, and 25% real estate. Three percent of assets are paid out annually in grants; this expenditure is covered by an annuity purchased some years ago. The foundation's primary investment objective is to maximize returns subject to a maximum level of volatility. A secondary consideration is the desire to avoid a permanent loss of capital. What asset allocation approach is most suitable for this client?

Solution to 1: Mean–variance optimization with Monte Carlo simulation is most appropriate for this client. He has limited investment expertise, so your first responsibility is to educate him with respect to such basic investment concepts as risk, return, and diversification. A simple MVO approach supplemented with Monte Carlo simulation to illustrate potential upside and downside of an asset allocation choice is mostly likely to serve the asset allocation and investment education needs.

Solution to 2: Given the sophistication and investment objectives of the IC members, using a mean–CVaR optimization approach is appropriate to determine the asset allocation. This client has a more sophisticated understanding of risk and will appreciate the more nuanced view of risk offered by mean–CVaR optimization. Given the portfolio's exposure to alternative investments, the asset allocation decision will be enhanced by the more detailed picture of left-tail risk offered by CVaR optimization (the risk of permanent loss) relative to mean–variance optimization. The lack of permanent staff and a once-per-year meeting schedule suggest that a risk factor-based approach may not be appropriate.

8. LIQUIDITY PLANNING

Earlier, we addressed various aspects of liquidity associated with investing in alternative asset classes. In this section, we focus on multi-year horizon liquidity planning for private investments.

When managing portfolios that contain allocations to alternative investments, managing liquidity risk takes on critical importance. We need to ensure that we have sufficient liquidity to meet interim obligations or goals, which might include:

- periodic payments to beneficiaries (e.g., a pension fund's retirement benefit payments, an endowment fund's distributions to support operating expenses, or a family office's ordinary expenses);
- portfolio rebalancing or funding new asset manager mandates; or
- fulfilling a commitment made to a private investment fund when the general partner makes the capital call.

Alternative investments pose unique liquidity challenges that must be explicitly addressed before committing to an alternative investment program. Private investments—including private equity, private real estate, private real assets, and private credit—represent the most illiquid components of an investment portfolio. Private investments usually require a long-term commitment over an 8- to 15-year time horizon. An investor contributes capital over the first few years (the investment period) and receives distributions in the later years. Combined with the call down (or drawdown) structure of a private investment fund, this creates a need to model a hypothetical path to achieving and maintaining a diversified, fully-invested allocation to private investments. Here we will explore the challenges with private investment liquidity planning with three primary considerations:

1. How to achieve and maintain the desired allocation.
2. How to handle capital calls.
3. How to plan for the unexpected.

8.1. Achieving and Maintaining the Strategic Asset Allocation

Strategic planning is required to determine the necessary annual commitments an investor should make in order to reach and maintain the long-term target asset allocation. Large private investors often use a liquidity forecasting model for their private investment programs. Here, we illustrate one such model based on work published by Takahashi and Alexander (2001). We also discuss private investment commitment pacing as an application of this model. This model is only one possible way to forecast private investment cash flows; investors may develop their own model using their own assumptions and experience.

We will illustrate this model with a hypothetical capital commitment (CC) of £100 million to a fund with a contractual term (L) of 12 years.

We begin by modeling the capital contributions (C) to the fund. Certain assumptions must be made regarding the rate of contribution (RC). We'll assume that 25% is contributed in the first year and that 50% of the remaining commitments are contributed in each of the subsequent years:

Year 1: £100 million × 25% = £25 million
Year 2: (£100 million − £25 million) × 50% = £37.5 million
Year 3: (£100 million − £25 million − £37.5 million) × 50% = £18.75 million

and so on.

The capital contribution (C) in year t can be expressed with the following formula:

$$C_t = RC_t \times (CC - PIC_t) \tag{1}$$

where PIC denotes the already paid-in capital.

Alternatively, we can express this in words:

Capital Contribution = Rate of Contribution × (Capital Commitment − Paid-in-Capital)

In practice, the investment period is often limited to a defined number of years. It's also possible that not all of the committed capital would be called.

The next step is to estimate the periodic distribution paid to investors. Distributions (D) are a function of the net asset value (NAV). From one year to the next, the NAV rises as additional capital contributions are made and as underlying investments appreciate (G). NAV declines as distributions are made (or as assets are written down).

G is equal to the expected growth rate. If the partnership investment develops as anticipated, then the fund's IRR would be equal to this rate. For our example, we set G equal to 13%.

To estimate the expected annual distribution payments, we need to make an assumption about the pattern of distributions. For example, an analyst may assume that the fund does not distribute any money in Year 1 or Year 2 but distributes 10% of the prevailing net asset value in Year 3, 20% in Year 4, 30% in Year 5, and 50% of the remaining balance in each of the remaining years. In the case of real estate funds, it is also possible that there is a pre-defined minimum annual distribution rate (called the "yield" in this context).[18] Once we have the annual rates of distribution determined, the annual amount distributed is calculated by the following formula:

$$D_t = RD_t[NAV_{t-1} \times (1 + G)] \tag{2}$$

where

$$NAV_t = [NAV_{t-1} \times (1 + G)] + C_t - D_t \tag{3}$$

Again, in words:

Distributions = Rate of Distribution at time t × [NAV × (1 + Growth Rate)], and

NAV at time 1 = prior NAV × (1 + Growth Rate) + Capital Contribution − Distributions

In Exhibit 38, we display the forecasted annual capital contributions, outstanding commitment forecast, distributions, NAV, and cumulative net cash flow for a private investment fund with a 12-year life. We assume that 25% of the committed capital is contributed in the first year and that 50% of the remaining commitments are contributed in each of the subsequent years. We set the RD_t distribution rates such that the yearly distribution rates would increase fairly gradually.[19] We assume a 13% growth rate from the investments in this fund.

---

[18]Takahashi and Alexander (2001) specify the annual rate of distribution (RD) as a function. The formula of the rate of distribution is a function of parameter called the "bow" (B). This parameter determines how early or late in the fund's life distributions would concentrate. The calculated rate of distribution is expressed by the following formula: $RD_t = (t/L)^B$. In general, if the "bow" parameter is set small, distribution rate would increase in the earlier years and investors would get their capital and gains back earlier in the fund's life. If the "bow" is set higher, the distributions would be back-loaded toward the final years and investors' capital would be invested for a longer period.

[19]We set the "bow" (B) parameter equal to 2.5.

EXHIBIT 38   Expected Annual Contribution, Outstanding Commitment, Rate of Distribution, Annual Distribution, NAV, and Net Cash Flow of a Hypothetical Private Investment Fund

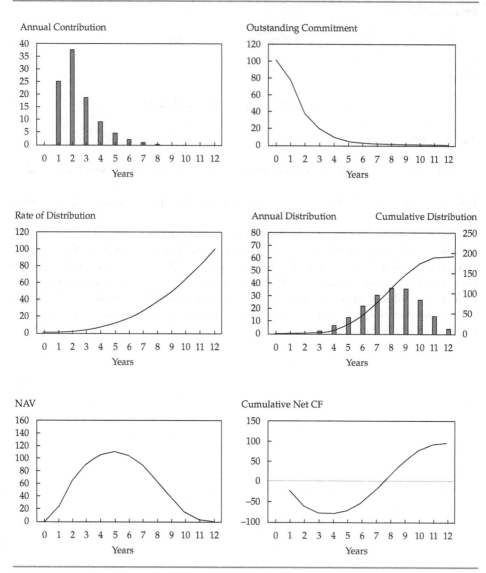

The corresponding annual RD_t rates are displayed in Exhibit 39.

EXHIBIT 39   Assumed Annual Distribution Rates (RD_t)

Year	1	2	3	4	5	6	7	8	9	10	11	12
Rate of Distribution	0%	1%	3%	6%	11%	18%	26%	36%	49%	63%	80%	100%

How does the shape of the expected rate of distribution influence NAV and the annual distribution amounts? For the sake of illustration, we can change our assumption of RD such that early year distribution rates are very low and start increasing in the second half of the fund's life.[20] The new distribution rates are shown in Exhibit 40, and Exhibit 41 shows how distributions and the NAV would react to this change.

EXHIBIT 40   Alternative Assumed Annual Distribution Rates (RD_t)

Year	1	2	3	4	5	6	7	8	9	10	11	12
Rate of Distribution	0%	0%	0%	0%	1%	3%	7%	13%	24%	40%	65%	100%

EXHIBIT 41   Rate of Distribution, Expected Annual Distribution, NAV, and Cumulative Net Cash Flow with Back-Loaded Distributions

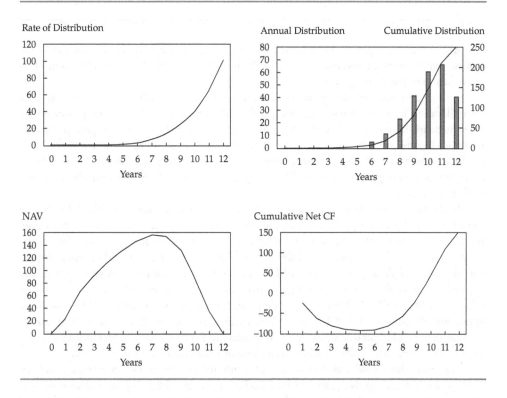

Although the annual capital contributions would not be affected, we can see that the lower distribution rate in the early years allows the NAV to grow higher. The cumulative net cash flow, however, would stay in the negative zone for a longer time.

---

[20]We set the "bow" (B) parameter equal to 5.0.

EXAMPLE 8   Liquidity Planning for Private Investments

1. The NAV of an investor's share in a private renewable energy fund was
   €30 million at the end of 2020. All capital has been called. The investor expects
   a 20% distribution to be paid at the end of 2021. The expected growth rate is
   12%. What is the expected NAV at year-end 2022?

Solution to 1: The expected NAV at year-end 2022 is €30,105,600. The expected
distribution at the end of 2021 is €6.72 million [(€30 million × 1.12) × 20%]. The
NAV at year-end 2022 is therefore [(€30 million × 1.12) × 20%] × 1.12% =
€30,105,600.

A very important practical application of such models is to help determine the size of the
annual commitment an investor needs to make in order to reach the target allocation of an
asset class over the coming years.

Let's assume that we manage an investment portfolio of £1 billion and that our strategic
asset allocation target for private equities is 20%. We currently don't have any private equity
investment in the portfolio. We also have to project the growth of the aggregate investment
portfolio, because we want to achieve the 20% allocation based on the expected *future* value
of the portfolio and of the private equity investment, not today's value. We assume an
aggregate portfolio growth rate of 6% per year, including both net contributions and
investment returns.

With these assumptions, and the private investment cash flow and NAV forecasting
model discussed previously, the investor can determine the annual commitments that would
be necessary to reach the overall target allocation. By using the same cash flow forecasting
parameters as for the analysis in Exhibit 38, we can see that a £100 million commitment
would lead the NAV to peak at around £110 million five years from now. A very rudimentary
approximation could be the following: In five years, the total portfolio size would be £1
billion × $1.06^5 \approx$ £1.338 billion; so, at that point, the total private equity NAV should be
approximately 20% × £1.338 billion = £268 million. Because we know that a £100 million
commitment would lead to an NAV of £110 million in five years, we can extrapolate to arrive
at the conclusion that a £243 million commitment today could achieve the goal.

However, this would result in a very concentrated private equity investment, with an
NAV peaking in four to five years and then declining over the following years as distributions
are made. A better practice is to spread commitments out over multiple years. A stable and
disciplined multi-year commitment schedule leads to a more stable NAV size over time. It
also achieves an important objective of diversifying exposure across vintage years. Thus, an
investor can choose to commit a target amount of around £70 million per year over a period
of four years (2017 through 2020) instead of concentrating his or her commitment in a single
year. This schedule would bring the total private equity NAV to the target 20% level over five
years. In Exhibit 42, we illustrate how the portfolio of private equity investments of different
vintage years would build up over time. We also show how the total NAV would evolve
beyond 2022 if no further capital commitment is made. As the chart suggests, the NAV
would continue to grow through 2023 but would start to decline in later years as the 2017–
2020 vintage private funds make distributions.

EXHIBIT 42   Commitment Pacing: Cumulative NAV of Private Equity Investments

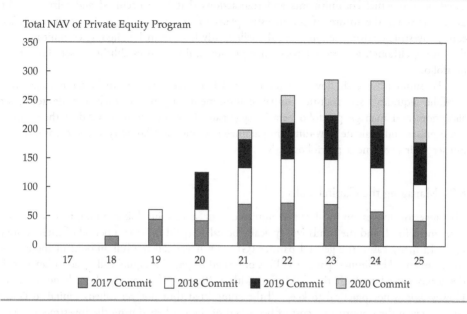

Total NAV of Private Equity Program

■ 2017 Commit   □ 2018 Commit   ■ 2019 Commit   □ 2020 Commit

In Exhibit 43, we show how private equity investments would grow as a proportion of the overall investment portfolio. As in the previous chart, we extend the forecast beyond 2022 so we can see that the proportion of private equity investments will start to decline if we don't make any further capital commitments after 2020.

EXHIBIT 43   Commitment Pacing: Private Equity NAV as % of the Total Portfolio

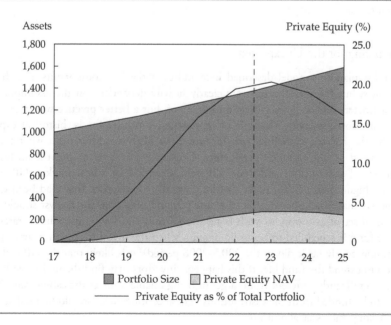

■ Portfolio Size   □ Private Equity NAV
——— Private Equity as % of Total Portfolio

The investor must review her pacing model forecast periodically, updating it as needed based on the actual commitments and transactions that have occurred and refreshing the assumptions for the future. If the investor plans to maintain a 20% allocation to private equity investments over the long run, she will clearly have to make ongoing commitments in the future, although at a slower pace once private equity is an established asset class in the portfolio.

To summarize, cash flow and pacing models enable investors to better manage their portfolio liquidity, set realistic annual commitment targets to reach the desired asset allocation, and manage portfolio beta in aggregate. Investors need to validate their model assumptions and evaluate how different parameter settings and liquidity stress scenarios could impact their investment portfolios.

8.2. Managing the Capital Calls

The investor makes an up-front commitment of a certain dollar amount to a private investment fund, and the funds will typically be called (paid in) over a period of three to four years. In many cases, the general partner (GP) will never call the full amount of the capital commitment. The limited partner (LP) is obligated to pay the capital call in accordance with the terms agreed to with the GP, often within 30 days of receiving the call notification. However, it is not practical to keep all the committed (but not yet called) capital in liquid reserves given the opportunity cost of being out of the markets during the investment phase. Investors must develop a strategy for maintaining the asset allocation while waiting for the fund to become fully invested. Capital pending investment in a private equity fund is often invested in public equities as a proxy for private equities. A similar approach may be followed in the case of other private asset classes: The investor may consider high yield as a placeholder for pending private credit investments, REITs as a placeholder for private real estate investments, and energy stocks or commodity futures as a proxy for private real asset investments.

8.3. Preparing for the Unexpected

The liquidity-planning model described here addresses the key components of cash inflows and outflows, but the model results are clearly heavily dependent on the assumptions. The model parameters can be based purely on judgment, but a better practice would be to verify estimates and forecasts with a sample of representative private funds' historical experience. Obviously, the realized cash flows in the future are likely to differ from what the model predicted based on the assumed parameters. Thus, it is advisable to run the analysis using different sets of assumptions and under different scenarios. In a bear market, GPs may call capital at a higher pace and/or make distributions at a slower pace than had been expected. This suggests that in addition to the base case scenario planning, the analyst should develop an additional set of assumptions with faster capital calls and lower distribution rates.

If the fund is scheduled to begin liquidation when the investor's public market portfolio is performing poorly (as it did in the 2007–2008 period), it is likely that the GP will exercise his option to extend the fund life. If this happens, investors may find themselves with an asset allocation significantly different from target or being unable to meet the capital calls that were intended to be funded from the distributions. These contingencies should be modeled as part of stress testing the asset allocation.

EXAMPLE 9   Private Investments, Asset Allocation, and Liquidity Planning

The Endowment Fund of the University of Guitan (the Fund) has $750 million in assets. The investment committee (IC) adopted the following strategic asset allocation four years ago. Private investments are at the lower end of the permitted range. To reach the target allocation among private investments, the investment team has made several new commitments recently, and they expect capital calls over the coming year equal to approximately about 20% of the current private asset net asset value.

	Strategic Asset Allocation Target	Permitted Range	Current Asset Allocation (%)	Current Asset Allocation ($mil)
Cash	2%	0 to 5%	3%	22.5
Public Equities (including long/short equity)	35%	30 to 40%	35%	262.5
Government Bonds	5%	4 to 10%	7%	52.5
High-Yield Credit	3%	2 to 5%	5%	37.5
Hedge Funds (excluding long/short equity)	20%	17 to 23%	23%	172.5
Private Real Estate	10%	7 to 13%	8%	60.0
Private Real Assets	5%	3 to 7%	4%	30.0
Private Equity	20%	15 to 22%	15%	112.5
Total				$750 mil
Expected Return	7.1%			
Expected Volatility	11.1%			
99% CVaR	−18.8%			
Assumed Inflation Rate	2%			

The strategic asset allocation has a 52% probability of meeting the 5% real return target (4% spend rate, 1% principal growth, and 2% inflation).

At its last meeting, the endowment committee of the board approved a temporary increase in the spending rate, raising it from 4% to 5% for the next five years to support the university's efforts to reposition itself in the face of declining enrollments. The spending rate is calculated as a percentage of the Fund's trailing 5-year average value.

The CIO (chief investment officer) has produced a capital market outlook that will guide the fund's tactical asset allocation strategy for the next several quarters. Key elements of the outlook are:

- accommodative central bank policies are ending;
- equity valuation metrics have recently set new highs;
- the economic cycle is at or near its peak (i.e., there is a meaningful probability of rising inflation and a weaker economic environment over the next several quarters); and

- returns will quite likely be lower than what has been experienced over the past five years.

She also developed the following stress scenario based on her capital market outlook:

Return Stress Scenario	
Cash	2%
Public Equities (including l/s equity)	−30%
Government Bonds	−3%
High-Yield Credit	−10%
Hedge Funds (excluding l/s equity)	−8%
Private Real Estate	0%
Private Real Assets	10%
Private Equity	−10%

1. Identify and discuss the liquidity factors that the CIO should consider as she develops her portfolio positioning strategy for the next 12 to 24 months.
2. Recommend and justify a tactical asset allocation strategy for the Fund.

Solution to 1:

- Given the market outlook, it is reasonable to assume cash flows into the fund from existing private investments will be negligible.
- The fund has next-12-month liabilities as follows:
  - Approximately $37.5 million to the university ($750 million × 5%). This is a high (conservative) estimate based on an assumption that the trailing 5-year average Fund value is less than the current $750 million.
  - Approximately $40.5 million in capital calls from private investment commitments (equally allocated across private real estate, private real assets, and private equity)

$$[(\$60m + \$30m + \$112.5m) \times 20\%]$$

  - Total liabilities next 12 months = $78 million

- Sources of immediate liquidity:
  - Cash = $22.5 million
  - Government bonds = $52.5 million
  - $75.0 million in total (less than the $78 million liability)

- Other liquidity:
  - Public equities are at the midpoint of the permitted range. The allocation could be reduced from 35% to 30% and remain within the permitted range. This would free up $37.5 million ($750 million × 5%) for reinvestment in more-defensive asset classes or to meet anticipated liquidity needs. However, if the return scenario is realized (equities down 30%), then the equity allocation will fall below the 30% minimum and additional rebalancing will be required.

- High-yield credit is at the upper end of the allowed range. The allocation could be reduced from the current 5% to 2% or 3%, freeing up an additional $15 to $22.5 million. The limited liquidity in high-yield bond markets may make this challenging.
- The hedge fund allocation is at the upper end of the allowed range. The allocation could be reduced from the current 23% to something in the range of 17% to 20% (between the lower end of the band and the target allocation). However, given the required redemption notice (generally 60 to 90 days in advance of the redemption date), if the market weakens the hedge funds might invoke any gates allowed for in their documents.
- Longer term, a temporary increase in the spending rate reduces the probability that the fund will meet its real return target. This objective would be further threatened if the inflation rate does rise as the CIO fears. The liquidity profile of the Fund's investments should prepare for the possibility that, in a bad year, they may be called upon to dip into capital to fund the spending obligation.

Solution to 2:

- The Fund should target the upper end of the ranges for cash and government bonds in light of the current high equity valuations, weakening economic outlook, and threat of rising inflation. Given rising inflation and interest rate concerns, she may also consider shortening the duration of the government bond portfolio.
- The higher cash and bond allocation will also provide the liquidity buffer needed to meet the Fund's liabilities. Additional cash might be justified to fund the known payouts.
- A high allocation to real estate could also be considered a defensive positioning, but the current 8% allocation may rise toward its 13% maximum, even without additional allocations, given the expected decline in the balance of the portfolio. In addition, tactical tilts in private asset classes are difficult to implement because it would take an extended time period to make new commitments and invest the additional capital.
- The allocations to public equities and hedge funds could be reduced to fund the increases in cash and government bonds. The following table summarizes the proposed allocation and looks at the likely end-of-year allocations if events unfold as forecast.

	Allowed Ranges			Proposed Allocation			Allocation 12 Months Forward	
	Lower Limit	Upper Limit	Current Allocation	%	$ (mil)	Expected Return Next 12 Months	%	$ (mil)
Cash	0%	5%	3%	10%	75	2%		0*
Public Equities	30%	40%	35%	30%	225	−30%	25%	157.50
Government Bonds	4%	10%	7%	10%	75	−3%	12%	72.75
High-Yield Credit	2%	5%	5%	5%	37.5	−10%	5%	33.75
Hedge Funds	17%	23%	23%	17%	127.5	−8%	19%	117.30

	Allowed Ranges			Proposed Allocation			Allocation 12 Months Forward	
	Lower Limit	Upper Limit	Current Allocation	%	$ (mil)	Expected Return Next 12 Months	%	$ (mil)
Private Real Estate	7%	13%	8%	8%	60	0%	12%	72.00
Private Real Assets	3%	7%	4%	5%	37.5	10%	8%	48.75
Private Equity	15%	22%	15%	15%	112.5	−10%	20%	123.75
Total				100%	$750.0		100%	$625.80

* Cash paid to fund liabilities ($37.5 million to the university and $40.5 million to fund private investment capital calls). Additional cash needs funded from government bond portfolio.

9. MONITORING THE INVESTMENT PROGRAM

The monitoring of an alternative investment program is time and labor intensive. Data are hard to come by and are not standardized among managers or asset classes. The analyst must spend a good amount of time gathering data and ensuring that the analysis is comparable across managers and asset classes. It is incumbent on the investor to both monitor the managers *and* the alternative investment program's progress toward the goals that were the basis for the investment in these assets.

9.1. Overall Investment Program Monitoring

When an investor makes a strategic decision to invest in alternative assets, specific goals are typically associated with the alternative investment program—return enhancement, income, risk reduction, safety, or a combination of the four. The goals may vary by asset class. A real estate program, for example, might be undertaken with the objective of replacing a portion of the fixed-income allocation—providing yield or income but also providing some measure of growth and/or inflation protection. The real estate program should be monitored relative to those goals, not simply relative to a benchmark.

We know that an alternative investment program is likely to take a number of years to reach fully-invested status. Is it reasonable to defer an assessment of the program until that point? Probably not. The investor must monitor developments in the relevant markets to ensure that the fundamental thesis underlying the decision to invest remains intact. Continuing with our real estate analogy, if real estate cap rates[21] fall to never-before-seen lows, what are the implications for the real estate's ability to continue to fulfill its intended role in the portfolio? Or if the managers hired within the real estate allocation allocate more to commercial office properties than was anticipated, what are the implications for the ability of real estate to fulfill the income-oriented goal? Only by monitoring the development of the

---

[21]The ratio of net operating income (NOI) to property asset value (the inverse of price/earnings).

portfolio(s) will the investor be able to adjust course and ensure that the allocation remains on track to achieve the goals established at the outset.

We also know that investor goals and objectives are subject to change. Perhaps a university experiences a persistent decline in enrollments and the endowment fund will be called upon to provide greater support to the university while it transitions to the new reality; what are the implications for a private equity program? Or what if the primary wage-earner in a two-parent household becomes critically ill; how might this affect the asset allocation? These types of events cannot be predicted, but it is important to continuously monitor the linkages between the asset allocation and the investor's goals, objectives, and circumstances. Particularly in the private markets—where changing course requires a long lead time and abruptly terminating an investment program can radically alter the risk and return profile of the portfolio—an early warning of an impending change can greatly improve the investor's ability to maintain the integrity of the investment program.

9.2. Performance Evaluation

Properly benchmarking an alternative investment strategy is a challenge that has important implications for judging the effectiveness of the alternative investment program. Many investors resort to custom index proxies (e.g., a static return premium over cash or equity index) or rely on peer group comparisons (e.g., Hedge Fund Research, Inc., Eurekahedge, Cambridge Private Equity Index). Both approaches have significant limitations.

Consider a private equity program benchmarked to the MSCI World Index plus 3%. This custom index may help frame the return expectation the investment committee holds with regard to its private equity assets, but it is unlikely to match the realized risk, return, and liquidity characteristics of the actual private equity program.

It is similarly challenging to develop a peer group representative of a manager's strategy given the high level of idiosyncratic risk inherent in most alternative investment funds. Existing providers follow vastly different rules in constructing these "benchmarks." They all have their own set of definitions (e.g., whether a fund is a credit fund or an event-driven fund), weighting methodology (asset weighted or equal weighted), method for dealing with potential survivorship bias, and other rules for inclusion (e.g., whether the fund is currently open or closed to new capital).

Exhibit 44 shows the returns from three different hedge fund index providers. An event-driven fund that generated a 6% return over the relevant 5-year period might look attractive if evaluated relative to the Credit Suisse index, whereas it might look subpar if evaluated relative to the Eurekahedge index. Additionally, a manager's ranking within the peer group is affected as much by what *other* managers do as by his own actions. Clearly, peer group ranking is, at best, one small part of the overall benchmarking exercise.

EXHIBIT 44   The Trouble with Peer Groups

Strategy	Provider	3-Year Annualized Return (%)	5-Year Annualized Return (%)
		ending December 31, 2017	
Equity Hedge	HFRI	5.7	6.6
	Credit Suisse	4.3	7.1
	Eurekahedge	6.5	7.8
Event-Driven	HFRI	3.8	5.9
	Credit Suisse	0.8	3.7
	Eurekahedge	6.8	7.2
Global Macro	HFRI	0.6	0.7
	Credit Suisse	2.0	2.7
	Eurekahedge	−0.1	1.2

The timing and nature of reported alternative investment returns also pose challenges to monitoring the performance of alternative investment managers. For call-down strategies such as private equity, private real estate, and real assets, tracking and calculating performance might require different systems and methodologies. Private equity, credit, and real estate returns are typically reported using internal rates of return (IRRs) rather than time-weighted returns (TWR) as is common in the liquid asset classes. IRRs are sensitive to the timing of cash flows into and out of the fund. Two managers may have similar portfolios but very different return profiles depending on their particular capital call and distribution schedule. Investors have to be wise to the ways in which a manager can bias their reported IRR. Alternative metrics, such as multiple on invested capital (MOIC) have been developed to provide an additional frame of reference. (MOIC is a private equity measure that divides the current value of the underlying companies plus any distributions received by the total invested capital.)

Pricing issues also complicate performance evaluation of most alternative strategies. Stale pricing common in many alternative strategies can distort reported returns and the associated risk metrics. Betas, correlations, Sharpe ratios, and other measures must be interpreted with a healthy degree of skepticism.

Although performance measurement has its challenges with all asset classes, relying exclusively on any single measure with alternative investments increases the likelihood of inaccurate or misleading conclusions. With respect to the more illiquid investment strategies, judgment as to whether a given fund is meeting its investment objectives should be reserved until most or even all of the investments have been monetized, and capital has been returned to the investor. If capital is returned quickly (thereby possibly producing extraordinarily high IRRs), the investor may want to put greater emphasis on the MOIC measure. Similarly, funds that return capital more slowly than expected might want to put greater weight on the IRR measure. Even a fund with both a weak MOIC and a weak IRR need the measures to be put into context. An appropriate peer group analysis can help ascertain whether the "poor" performance was common across all funds of similar vintage (perhaps suggesting a poor investment climate) or whether it was specific to that fund. Likewise, a fund that posts strong performance may simply have benefited from an ideal investment period.

Perhaps the best way to gain performance insight beyond the numbers is to develop a qualitative understanding of the underlying assets. What are the manager's expectations at the time of acquisition? How does the manager plan to add value to the investment over the holding period? What is the manager's exit strategy for the investment? The investor can monitor how the investment develops relative to the initial thesis. This type of qualitative assessment can lead to a better understanding of whether the manager did well for the right reasons, whether the manager was wrong but for the right reasons, or whether the manager was just wrong.

9.3. Monitoring the Firm and the Investment Process

In addition to monitoring the portfolio, monitoring of the investment process and the investment management firm itself are particularly important in alternative investment structures where the manager cannot be terminated easily, and the assets transferred to another manager in which the investor has more confidence. What follows is a non-exhaustive list of issues that the investor will want to monitor:

- *Key person risk*: Most alternative investment strategies depend to a large extent on the skill of a few key investment professionals. These are what are known as "key persons." Key persons are typically specified in the fund documents, with certain rights allocated to the limited partners in the event a key person leaves the firm. It is important to ensure that these investment professionals remain actively involved in the investment process. There are also other employees of the investment manager whose departure may negatively affect the operation of the business or signal an underlying problem. If, for example, the chief operating officer or chief compliance officer leaves the firm, it is important to understand why and what effect it may have on the business.
- *Alignment of interests*: Alignment of interest issues range from the complexity of the organization, structure of management fees, compensation of the investment professionals, growth in assets under management (AUM), and the amount of capital the key professionals have committed to the funds that they are managing. The investor will want to verify that the money manager's interests remain closely aligned with their own. Has the manager withdrawn a significant portion of her own capital that had been invested alongside the limited partners? If so, why? Is the manager raising a new fund? If so, what safeguards are in place to ensure that the investment professionals are not unduly distracted with fundraising, firm administration, or unfairly concentrated on managing other funds? Is the opportunity set deep enough to support the additional capital being raised? Will the funds have shared ownership interest in a given asset? If so, what conflicts of interest may arise (e.g., the manager may earn an incentive fee in one fund if the asset is sold, while it may be in the best interest of the second fund to sell the asset at a later date).
- *Style drift*: Fund documents often give managers wide latitude as to their investment options and parameters, but it is incumbent on the investor to understand where the fund manager has a competitive advantage and skill and confirm that the investments being made are consistent with the manager's edge.
- *Risk management*: The investor should understand the manager's risk management philosophy and processes and periodically confirm that the fund is abiding by them. Where a fund makes extensive use of leverage, a robust risk management framework is essential.
- *Client/asset turnover*: A critical part of the ongoing due diligence process should include a review of clients and assets. A significant gain or drop in either may be a sign of an

underlying problem. An unusual gain in assets could make it difficult for the investment professionals to invest in suitably attractive investments, potentially handicapping future performance. Conversely, significant client redemptions may force the money manager to sell attractive assets as he looks to raise cash. If this occurs during periods of market turmoil when liquidity in the market itself may be low, the manager may be forced to sell what he can rather than what he should in order to optimize performance. This could hurt the returns of non-redeeming clients and/or leave the remaining clients with illiquid holdings that might make it difficult for them to redeem in the future.

- *Client profile*: Investors will want to gauge the profile of the fund manager's other clients. Are the fund's other clients considered long-term investors, or do they have a history of redeeming at the first sign of trouble? Are they new to the alternative investment space and perhaps don't understand the nuances of the fund's strategy and risks? You may have a strong conviction in a money manager's skills, but the actions of others may affect your ability to reap the benefits of those skills. If too many of her other clients elect to redeem, the manager may invoke the gates allowed by the fund's documents or, at the extreme, liquidate the fund at what might be the worst possible moment. This was a common occurrence during 2008–2009, when investors sought to raise cash by redeeming from their more liquid fund managers. Even if a money manager weathers massive outflows, profitability and the ability to retain key talent may be at risk.

- *Service providers:* Investors will want to ensure that the fund manager has engaged independent and reputable third-party service providers, including administrators, custodians, and auditors. Although an investor may have performed extensive checks prior to investing, it is good practice to periodically verify that these relationships are intact and working well. If the service provider changes, the investor will want to understand *why*. Has the fund's AUM grown to a level that cannot be handled adequately by the current provider? Perhaps the service provider has chosen to terminate the relationship because of actions taken by the fund manager. Exploring the motivation behind a change in a service provider can uncover early warning flags deserving of further investigation.

EXAMPLE 10   Monitoring Alternative Investment Programs

1. The O'Hara family office determined that the illiquidity risk inherent in private investments is a risk that the family is ill-suited to bear. As a result, they decided several years ago to unwind their private equity program. There are still a few remaining assets in the portfolio. The CIO (chief investment officer) notices that the private equity portfolio has delivered outstanding performance lately, especially relative to other asset classes. He presents the data to his research staff and wants to revisit their decision to stop making new private equity investments. Explain why the investment results that prompted the CIO's comments should not be relied upon.

2. The ZeeZaw family office has been invested in the Warriors Fund, a relatively small distressed debt strategy, which has performed very well for a number of years. In a recent conversation with the portfolio manager, the CIO for ZeeZaw discovered that the Warriors fund will be receiving a significant investment from a large institution within the next few weeks. What are some of the risks that might

develop with the Warriors Fund as a result of this new client? What are some other issues that the CIO might want to probe with the Warriors Fund?

Solution to 1: With small, residual holdings, even a modest change in valuation can result in outsized returns; for example, a $2,000 investment that gets revalued to $3,000 would report a nominal return of 50%. The 50% return is not representative of private equity investment as a whole but is merely an artifact of the unwinding process. A more accurate picture of performance must consider the development of the fund IRR over time and consider other performance measures, such as the MOIC.

Solution to 2: The CIO should investigate whether the fund manager is able to appropriately deploy this new capital consistent with the investment process and types of investments that contributed to the Warriors Fund success. Because the fund was relatively small, a very large influx of capital might force the portfolio manager to make larger investments than is optimal or more investments than they did before. Either change without the appropriate resources could undermine future success. Finally, a large influx of cash could dilute near-term performance, especially if the funds remain undeployed for a significant period of time.

SUMMARY

- Allocations to alternatives are believed to increase a portfolio's risk-adjusted return. An investment in alternatives typically fulfills one or more of four roles in an investor's portfolio: capital growth, income generation, risk diversification, and/or safety.
- Private equity investments are generally viewed as return enhancers in a portfolio of traditional assets.
- Long/short equity strategies are generally believed to deliver equity-like returns with less than full exposure to the equity premium. Short-biased equity strategies are expected to lower a portfolio's overall equity beta while producing some measure of alpha. Arbitrage and event-driven strategies are expected to provide equity-like returns with little to no correlation with traditional asset classes.
- Real assets (e.g., commodities, farmland, timber, energy, and infrastructure assets) are generally perceived to provide a hedge against inflation.
- Timber investments provide both growth and inflation-hedging properties.
- Commodities (e.g., metals, energy, livestock, and agricultural commodities) serve as a hedge against inflation and provide a differentiated source of alpha. Certain commodity investments serve as safe havens in times of crisis.
- Farmland investing may have a commodity-like profile or a commercial real-estate-like profile.
- Energy investments are generally considered a real asset as the investor owns the mineral rights to commodities that are correlated with inflation factors.
- Infrastructure investments tend to generate stable/modestly growing income and to have high correlation with overall inflation.

- Real estate strategies range from core to opportunistic and are believed to provide protection against unanticipated increases in inflation. Core real estate strategies are more income-oriented, while opportunistic strategies rely more heavily on capital appreciation.
- Bonds have been a more effective volatility mitigator than alternatives over shorter time horizons.
- The traditional approaches to defining asset classes are easy to communicate and implement. However, they tend to over-estimate portfolio diversification and obscure primary drivers of risk.
- Typical risk factors applied to alternative investments include equity, size, value, liquidity, duration, inflation, credit spread, and currency. A benefit of the risk factor approach is that every asset class can be described using the same framework.
- Risk factor-based approaches have certain limitations. A framework with too many factors is difficult to administer and interpret, but too small a set of risk factors may not accurately describe the characteristics of alternative asset classes. Risk factor sensitivities are highly sensitive to the historical look-back period.
- Investors with less than a 15-year investment horizon should generally avoid investments in private real estate, private real asset, and private equity funds.
- Investors must consider whether they have the necessary skills, expertise, and resources to build an alternative investment program internally. Investors without a strong governance program are less likely to develop a successful alternative investment program.
- Reporting for alternative funds is often less transparent than investors are accustomed to seeing on their stock and bond portfolios. For many illiquid strategies, reporting is often received well past typical monthly or quarter-end deadlines. Full, position-level transparency is rare in many alternative strategies.
- Three primary approaches are used to determine the desired allocation to the alternative asset classes:
  - Monte Carlo simulation may be used to generate return scenarios that relax the assumption of normally distributed returns.
  - Optimization techniques, which incorporate downside risk or take into account skew, may be used to enhance the asset allocation process.
  - Risk factor-based approaches to alternative asset allocation can be applied to develop more robust asset allocation proposals.
- Two key analytical challenges in modeling allocations to alternatives include stale and/or artificially smoothed returns and return distributions that exhibit significant skewness and fat tails (or excess kurtosis).
- Artificially smoothed returns can be detected by testing the return stream for serial correlation. The analyst needs to unsmooth the returns to get a more accurate representation of the risk and return characteristics of the asset class.
- Skewness and kurtosis can be dealt with by using empirically observed asset returns because they incorporate the actual distribution. Advanced mathematical or statistical models can also be used to capture the true behavior of alternative asset classes.
- Applications of Monte Carlo simulation in allocating to alternative investments include:
  1. simulating skewed and fat-tailed financial variables by estimating the behavior of factors and/or assets in low-volatility regimes and high-volatility regimes, then generating scenarios using the different means and covariances estimated under the different regimes; and

2. simulating portfolio outcomes (+/− 1 standard deviation) to estimate the likelihood of falling short of the investment objectives.

- Unconstrained mean–variance optimization (MVO) often leads to portfolios dominated by cash and fixed income at the low-risk end of the spectrum and by private equity at the high-risk end of the spectrum. Some investors impose minimum and maximum constraints on asset classes. Slight changes in the input variables could lead to substantial changes in the asset allocations.
- Mean–CVaR optimization may be used to identify allocations that minimize downside risk rather than simply volatility.
- Investors may choose to optimize allocations to risk factors rather than asset classes. These allocations, however, must be implemented using asset classes. Portfolios with similar risk factor exposures can have vastly different asset allocations.
- Some caveats with respect to risk factor-based allocations are that investors may hold different definitions for a given risk factor, correlations among risk factors may shift under changing market conditions, and some factor sensitivities are very unstable.
- Cash flow and commitment-pacing models enable investors in private alternatives to better manage their portfolio liquidity and set realistic annual commitment targets to reach the desired asset allocation.
- An alternative investment program should be monitored relative to the goals established for the alternative investment program, not simply relative to a benchmark. The investor must monitor developments in the relevant markets to ensure that the fundamental thesis underlying the decision to invest remains intact.
- Two common benchmarking approaches to benchmarking alternative investments— custom index proxies and peer group comparisons—have significant limitations.
- IRRs are sensitive to the timing of cash flows into and out of the fund: Two managers may have similar portfolios but different return profiles depending on their capital call and distribution schedule.
- Pricing issues can distort reported returns and the associated risk metrics, such as betas, correlations, and Sharpe ratios.
- Monitoring of the firm and the investment process are particularly important in alternative investment structures where the manager cannot be terminated easily. Key elements to monitor include key person risk, alignment of interests, style drift, risk management, client/asset turnover, client profile, and service providers.

REFERENCES

Ang, A. 2011. "Illiquid Assets." *CFA Institute Conference Proceedings Quarterly* 28 (4).

Ang, A. 2014. *Asset Management: A Systematic Approach to Factor Investing.* New York: Oxford University Press.

Berkelaar, A.B., A. Kobor, and R.R.P. Kouwenberg. 2009. "Asset Allocation for Hedge Fund Strategies: How to Better Manage Tail Risk." In *The VaR Modeling Handbook: Practical Applications in Alternative Investing, Banking, Insurance, and Portfolio Management,* ed. Greg N. Gregoriou. New York: McGraw-Hill.

Cambridge Associates LLC. 2013. "From Asset Allocation to Risk Allocation – The Risk Allocation Framework."

Getmansky, M., A.W. Lo, and I. Makarov. 2004. "An Econometric Model of Serial Correlation and Illiquidity in Hedge Fund Returns." *Journal of Financial Economics* 74 (3): 529–609.

Hamilton, J.D. 1989. "A New Approach to the Economic Analysis of Nonstationary Time Series and the Business Cycle." *Econometrica* 57 (2): 357–84.

Ivashina, Victoria, and Jose Lerner. 2018. "Looking for Alternatives: Pension Investments around the World, 2008 to 2017." Federal Reserve of Boston conference paper.

Kim, C., and C.R. Nelson. 1999. *State-Space Models with Regime Switching – Classical and Gibbs-Sampling Approaches and Applications*. Cambridge, MA: MIT Press.

Liu, Y., S. Sun, R. Huang, T. Tang, and X. Wu. March 2017. "The Rise of Alternative Assets and Long-Term Investing." Boston Consulting Group.

Lo, A. 2002. "The Statistics of Sharpe Ratios." *Financial Analysts Journal* 58 (4): 36–52.

Naik, V., M. Devarajan, A. Nowobilski, S. Page, and N. Pedersen. 2016. *Factor Investing and Asset Allocation – A Business Cycle Perspective*. Charlottesville, VA: CFA Institute Research Foundation.

Rockafellar, R.T., and S. Uryasev. 2000. "Optimization of Conditional Value at Risk." *Journal of Risk* 2 (3): 21–42.

Rockafellar, R.T., and S. Uryasev. 2002. "Conditional Value at Risk for General Loss Distributions." *Journal of Banking & Finance* 26 (7): 1443–71.

Swensen, D.F. 2009. *Pioneering Portfolio Management: An Unconventional Approach to Institutional Investment*. New York: Free Press.

Takahashi, D., and S. Alexander. 2001. "Illiquid Alternative Asset Fund Modeling." Yale School of Management (January).

PRACTICE PROBLEMS

The following information relates to Questions 1–8

Kevin Kroll is the chair of the investment committee responsible for the governance of the Shire Manufacturing Corporation (SMC) defined benefit pension plan. The pension fund is currently fully funded and has followed an asset mix of 60% public equities and 40% bonds since Kroll has been chair. Kroll meets with Mary Park, an actuarial and pension consultant, to discuss issues raised at the last committee meeting.

Kroll notes that the investment committee would like to explore the benefits of adding alternative investments to the pension plan's strategic asset allocation. Kroll states:

Statement 1:   The committee would like to know which alternative asset would best mitigate the risks to the portfolio due to unexpected inflation and also have a relatively low correlation with public equities to provide diversification benefits.

The SMC pension plan has been able to fund the annual pension payments without any corporate contributions for a number of years. The committee is interested in potential changes to the asset mix that could increase the probability of achieving the long-term investment target return of 5.5% while maintaining the funded status of the plan. Park notes that fixed-income yields are expected to remain low for the foreseeable future. Kroll asks:

Statement 2:   If the public equity allocation remains at 60%, is there a single asset class that could be used for the balance of the portfolio to achieve the greatest probability of maintaining the pension funding status over a long time horizon? Under this hypothetical scenario, the balance of the portfolio can be allocated to either bonds, hedge funds, or private equities.

Park confirms with Kroll that the committee has historically used a traditional approach to define the opportunity set based on distinct macroeconomic regimes, and she proposes that a risk-based approach might be a better method. Although the traditional approach is relatively powerful for its ability to handle liquidity and manager selection issues compared to a risk-based approach, they both acknowledge that a number of limitations are associated with the existing approach.

Park presents a report (Exhibit 1) that proposes a new strategic asset allocation for the pension plan. Kroll states that one of the concerns that the investment committee will have regarding the new allocation is that the pension fund needs to be able to fund an upcoming early retirement incentive program (ERIP) that SMC will be offering to its employees within the next two years. Employees who have reached the age of 55 and whose age added to the number of years of company service sum to 75 or more can retire 10 years early and receive the defined benefit pension normally payable at age 65.

EXHIBIT 1   Proposed Asset Allocation of SMC Defined Benefit Pension Plan

Asset Class	Public Equities	Broad Fixed Income	Private Equities	Hedge Funds	Public Real Estate	Total
Target	45%	25%	10%	10%	10%	100%
Range	35%–55%	15%–35%	0%–12%	0%–12%	0%–12%	–

Kroll and Park then discuss suitability considerations related to the allocation in Exhibit 1. Kroll understands that one of the drawbacks of including the proposed alternative asset classes is that daily reporting will no longer be available. Investment reports for alternatives will likely be received after monthly or quarter-end deadlines used for the plan's traditional investments. Park emphasizes that in a typical private equity structure, the pension fund makes a commitment of capital to a blind pool as part of the private investment partnership.

In order to explain the new strategic asset allocation to the investment committee, Kroll asks Park why a risk factor-based approach should be used rather than a mean–variance-optimization technique. Park makes the following statements:

Statement 3:   Risk factor-based approaches to asset allocation produce more robust asset allocation proposals.

Statement 4:   A mean–variance optimization typically overallocates to the private alternative asset classes due to stale pricing.

Park notes that the current macroeconomic environment could lead to a bear market within a few years. Kroll asks Park to discuss the potential impact on liquidity planning associated with the actions of the fund's general partners in the forecasted environment.

Kroll concludes the meeting by reviewing the information in Exhibit 2 pertaining to three potential private equity funds analyzed by Park. Park discloses the following due diligence findings from a recent manager search: Fund A retains administrators, custodians, and auditors with impeccable reputations; Fund B has achieved its performance in a manner that appears to conflict with its reported investment philosophy; and Fund C has recently experienced the loss of three key persons.

EXHIBIT 2   Potential Private Equity Funds, Internal Rate of Return (IRR)

Private Equity Fund	Fund A	Fund B	Fund C
5-year IRR	12.9%	13.2%	13.1%

1. Based on Statement 1, Park should recommend:
   A. hedge funds.
   B. private equities.
   C. commodity futures.

2. In answering the question raised in Statement 2, Park would *most likely* recommend:
   A. bonds.
   B. hedge funds.
   C. private equities.

3. A limitation of the existing approach used by the committee to define the opportunity set is that it:
   A. is difficult to communicate.
   B. overestimates the portfolio diversification.
   C. is sensitive to the historical look-back period.

4. Based on Exhibit 1 and the proposed asset allocation, the greatest risk associated with the ERIP is:
   A. liability.
   B. leverage.
   C. liquidity.

5. The suitability concern discussed by Kroll and Park *most likely* deals with:
   A. governance.
   B. transparency.
   C. investment horizon.

6. Which of Park's statements regarding the asset allocation approaches is correct?
   A. Only Statement 3
   B. Only Statement 4
   C. Both Statement 3 and Statement 4

7. Based on the forecasted environment, liquidity planning should take into account that general partners may:
   A. call capital at a slower pace.
   B. make distributions at a faster pace.
   C. exercise an option to extend the life of the fund.

8. Based on Exhibit 2 and Park's due diligence, the pension committee should consider investing in:
   A. Fund A.
   B. Fund B.
   C. Fund C.

The following information relates to Questions 9–13

Eileen Gension is a portfolio manager for Zen-Alt Investment Consultants (Zen-Alt), which assists institutional investors with investing in alternative investments. Charles Smittand is an analyst at Zen-Alt and reports to Gension. Gension and Smittand discuss a new client, the Benziger University Endowment Fund (the fund), as well as a prospective client, the Opeptaja Pension Plan (the plan).

The fund's current portfolio is invested primarily in public equities, with the remainder invested in fixed income. The fund's investment objective is to support a 6% annual spending rate and to preserve the purchasing power of the asset base over a 10-year time horizon. The fund also wants to invest in assets that provide the highest amount of diversification against its dominant equity risk. Gension considers potential alternative investment options that would best meet the fund's diversification strategy.

In preparation for the first meeting between Zen-Alt and the fund, Gension and Smittand discuss implementing a short-biased equity strategy within the fund. Smittand makes the following three statements regarding short-biased equity strategies:

Statement 1:   Short-biased equity strategies generally provide alpha when used to diversify public equities.

Statement 2:   Short-biased equity strategies are expected to provide a higher reduction in volatility than bonds over a long time horizon.

Statement 3:   Short-biased equity strategies are expected to mitigate the risk of public equities by reducing the overall portfolio beta of the fund.

Gension directs Smittand to prepare asset allocation and portfolio characteristics data on three alternative portfolios. The fund's risk profile is one factor that potential lenders consider when assigning a risk rating to the university. A loan covenant with the university's primary lender states that a re-evaluation of the university's creditworthiness is triggered if the fund incurs a loss greater than 20% over any one-year period. Smittand states that the recommended asset allocation should achieve the following three goals, in order of priority and importance:

• Minimize the probability of triggering the primary lender's loan covenant.
• Minimize the probability of purchasing power impairment over a 10-year horizon.
• Maximize the probability of achieving a real return target of 6% over a 10-year horizon.

Smittand provides data for three alternative portfolios, which are presented in Exhibits 1 and 2.

EXHIBIT 1   Asset Allocation

Alternative Portfolio	Cash	Public Equity	Gov't.	Credit	Hedge Fund	Real Estate	Private Equity
A	4.0%	35.0%	6.0%	5.0%	20.0%	10.0%	20.0%
B	2.0%	40.0%	8.0%	3.0%	15.0%	7.0%	25.0%
C	1.0%	50.0%	3.0%	6.0%	10.0%	0.0%	30.0%

EXHIBIT 2   Portfolio Characteristics

Alternative Portfolio	1-Year 99% VaR	1-Year 99% CVaR	Probability of Meeting 6% Real Return (10-Year Horizon)	Probability of Purchasing Power Impairment (10-Year Horizon)
A	−16.3%	−19.4%	56.1%	2.5%
B	−17.4%	−20.6%	58.8%	2.8%
C	−19.3%	−22.7%	61.0%	4.0%

Notes:

- One-year horizon 99% VaR: the lowest return over any one-year period at a 99% confidence level
- One-year horizon 99% CVaR: the expected return if the return falls below the 99% VaR threshold
- Probability of purchasing power impairment: the probability of losing 40% of the fund's purchasing power over 10 years, after consideration of new gifts received by the fund, spending from the fund, and total returns

Gension next meets with the investment committee (IC) of the Opeptaja Pension Plan to discuss new opportunities in alternative investments. The plan is a $1 billion public pension fund that is required to provide detailed reports to the public and operates under specific government guidelines. The plan's IC adopted a formal investment policy that specifies an investment horizon of 20 years. The plan has a team of in-house analysts with significant experience in alternative investments.

During the meeting, the IC indicates that it is interested in investing in private real estate. Gension recommends a real estate investment managed by an experienced team with a proven track record. The investment will require multiple capital calls over the next few years. The IC proceeds to commit to the new real estate investment and seeks advice on liquidity planning related to the future capital calls.

9. Which asset class would *best* satisfy the Fund's diversification strategy?
    A. Private equity
    B. Private real estate
    C. Absolute return hedge fund

10. Which of Smittand's statements regarding short-biased equity strategies is *incorrect*?
    A. Statement 1
    B. Statement 2
    C. Statement 3

11. Based on Exhibit 2, which alternative portfolio should Gension recommend for the fund given Smittand's stated three goals?
    A. Portfolio A
    B. Portfolio B
    C. Portfolio C

12. Which of the following investor characteristics would *most likely* be a primary concern for the plan's IC with respect to investing in alternatives?
    A. Governance
    B. Transparency
    C. Investment horizon

13. With respect to liquidity planning relating to the plan's new real estate investment, Gension should recommend that the fund set aside appropriate funds and invest them in:
    A. 100% REITs.
    B. 100% cash equivalents.
    C. 80% cash equivalents and 20% REITs.

The following information relates to Questions 14–15

Ingerðria Greslö is an adviser with an investment management company and focuses on asset allocation for the company's high-net-worth investors. She prepares for a meeting with Maarten Pua, a new client who recently inherited a $10 million portfolio solely comprising public equities.

Greslö meets with Pua and proposes that she create a multi-asset portfolio by selling a portion of his equity holdings and investing the proceeds in another asset class. Greslö advises Pua that his investment objective should be to select an asset class that has a high potential to fulfill two functional roles: risk diversification and capital growth. Greslö suggests the following three asset classes:

- Public real estate
- Private real assets (timber)
- Equity long/short hedge funds

14. **Determine** which asset class is *most likely* to meet Pua's investment objective. **Justify** your response.

Determine which asset class is *most likely* to meet Pua's investment objective. (Circle one.)	**Justify** your response.
Public Real Estate	
Private Real Assets (Timber)	
Equity Long/Short Hedge Funds	

Five years after his first meeting with Pua, Greslö monitors a private real estate investment that Pua has held for one year. Until recently, the investment had been managed by a local real estate specialist who had a competitive advantage in this market; the specialist's strategy was to purchase distressed local residential housing properties, make strategic property improvements, and then sell them. Pua is one of several clients who have invested in this opportunity.

Greslö learns that the specialist recently retired and the investment is now managed by a national real estate company. The company has told investors that it now plans to invest throughout the region in both distressed housing and commercial properties. The company also lengthened the holding period for each investment property from the date of the initial capital call because of the complexity of the property renovations, and it altered the interim profit distribution targets.

15. **Discuss** the qualitative risk issues that have *most likely* materialized over the past year.

The following information relates to Questions 16–18

The Ælfheah Group is a US-based company with a relatively small pension plan. Ælfheah's investment committee (IC), whose members collectively have a relatively basic understanding of the investment process, has agreed that Ælfheah is willing to accept modest returns while the IC gains a better understanding of the process. Two key investment considerations for the IC are maintaining low overhead costs and minimizing taxes in the portfolio. Ælfheah has not been willing to incur the costs of in-house investment resources.

Qauhtèmoc Ng is the investment adviser for Ælfheah. He discusses with the IC its goal of diversifying Ælfheah's portfolio to include alternative assets. Ng suggests considering the following potential investment vehicles:

• Publicly traded US REIT
• Relative value hedge fund
• Tax-efficient angel investment

Ng explains that for the relative value hedge fund alternative, Ælfheah would be investing alongside tax-exempt investors.

16. **Determine** which of the potential investment vehicles *best* meets the investment considerations for Ælfheah. **Justify** your response. **Explain** for *each* investment not selected why the investment considerations are not met.

Determine which of the potential investment vehicles *best* meets the investment considerations for Ælfheah. (Circle one.)	Justify your response.	Explain for *each* investment not selected why the investment considerations are not met.
Publicly traded US REIT		
Relative value hedge fund		
Tax-efficient angel investment		

Ng and the IC review the optimal approach to determine the asset allocation for Ælfheah, including the traditional and risk-based approaches to defining the investment opportunity set.

17. **Determine** which approach to determine the asset allocation is *most appropriate* for Ælfheah. **Justify** your response.

Determine which approach to determine the asset allocation is *most appropriate* for Ælfheah. (Circle one.)	**Justify** your response.
Traditional	
Risk based	

The following year, Ng and the IC review the portfolio's performance. The IC has gained a better understanding of the investment process. The portfolio is meeting Ælfheah's liquidity needs, and Ng suggests that Ælfheah would benefit from diversifying into an additional alternative asset class. After discussing suitable investment vehicles for the proposed alternative asset class, Ng proposes the following three investment vehicles for further review:

- Funds of funds (FOFs)
- Separately managed accounts (SMAs)
- Undertakings for collective investment in transferable securities (UCITS)

18. **Determine** the investment vehicle that would be *most appropriate* for Ælfheah's proposed alternative asset class. **Justify** your response.

Determine the investment vehicle that would be *most appropriate* for Ælfheah's proposed alternative asset class. (Circle one.)	**Justify** your response.
FOFs	
SMAs	
UCITS	

The following information relates to Questions 19–20

Mbalenhle Calixto is a global institutional portfolio manager who prepares for an annual meeting with the investment committee (IC) of the Estevão University Endowment. The endowment has €450 million in assets, and the current asset allocation is 42% equities, 22% fixed income, 19% private equity, and 17% hedge funds.

The IC's primary investment objective is to maximize returns subject to a given level of volatility. A secondary objective is to avoid a permanent loss of capital, and the IC has indicated to Calixto its concern about left-tail risk. Calixto considers two asset allocation approaches for the endowment: mean–variance optimization (MVO) and mean–CVaR (conditional value at risk) optimization.

19. **Determine** the asset allocation approach that is *most suitable* for the Endowment. **Justify** your response.

Determine the asset allocation approach that is *most suitable* for the Endowment. (Circle one.)	**Justify** your response.
MVO	
Mean–CVaR optimization	

Calixto reviews the endowment's future liquidity requirements and analyzes one of its holdings in a private distressed debt fund. He notes the following about the fund:

- As of the most recent year end:
  - The NAV of the endowment's investment in the fund was €25,000,000.
  - All capital had been called.
- At the end of the current year, Calixto expects a distribution of 18% to be paid.
- Calixto estimates an expected growth rate of 11% for the fund.

20. **Calculate** the expected NAV of the fund at the end of the current year.

CHAPTER 9

EXCHANGE-TRADED FUNDS: MECHANICS AND APPLICATIONS

Joanne M. Hill, PhD

Dave Nadig

LEARNING OUTCOMES

The candidate should be able to:

- explain the creation/redemption process of ETFs and the function of authorized participants;
- describe how ETFs are traded in secondary markets;
- describe sources of tracking error for ETFs;
- describe factors affecting ETF bid–ask spreads;
- describe sources of ETF premiums and discounts to NAV;
- describe costs of owning an ETF;
- describe types of ETF risk;
- identify and describe portfolio uses of ETFs.

1. INTRODUCTION

Exchange-traded funds (ETFs) have grown rapidly since their invention in the early 1990s, in large part because of their low associated cost, exchange access, holdings transparency, and range of asset classes available. Growth in ETFs has also been driven by the increased use of index-based investing. ETF investors need to understand how these products work and trade and how to choose from the numerous options available. Although many ETFs are organized under the same regulation as mutual fund products, there are important differences related to trading and tax efficiency. ETFs have features that can make them more tax efficient than traditional mutual funds, and not all ETFs are organized like mutual funds. ETFs can be based on derivative strategies, use leverage and shorting, and be offered in alternate structures, such as exchange-traded notes (ETNs), which have their own unique risks.

Understanding how ETF shares are created and redeemed is key to understanding how these products can add value in a portfolio. Since so many ETFs track indexes, understanding their index tracking or tracking error is also critical. Investors should also understand how to assess an ETF's trading costs, including differences between the ETF's market price and the fair value of its portfolio holdings.

This chapter is organized as follows: Section 2 discusses ETF primary and secondary markets, including the creation/redemption process. Section 3 covers important investor considerations, such as costs and risks, when choosing an ETF. Section 4 explains how ETFs are used in strategic, tactical, and portfolio efficiency applications. Section 5 concludes and summarizes the chapter.

2. ETF MECHANICS

Exchange-traded funds function differently from mutual funds because of their structure, with the key difference in an ETF's method of share creation and redemption. Mutual fund shares must be purchased or sold at the end of the day from the fund manager (or via a broker) at the closing net asset value (NAV) of the fund's holdings, in a cash-for-shares or shares-for-cash swap. In contrast, an ETF trades intraday, or during the trading day, just like a stock. ETF shares are created or redeemed in kind, in a shares-for-shares swap.

ETFs are intrinsically linked to the creation/redemption process. Creation/redemption enables ETFs to operate at lower cost and with greater tax efficiency than mutual funds and generally keeps ETF prices in line with their NAVs. Unlike stocks, which come to market via an initial public offering of fixed size, ETFs can be created or redeemed continuously. ETF transactions take place in two interrelated markets. Understanding how this mechanism works is key to understanding both the benefits and potential risks of ETFs.

The primary market for ETF trading is that which exists on an over-the-counter basis between **authorized participants** (APs), a special group of institutional investors, and the ETF issuer, or sponsor. This process is referred to as **creation/redemption**. These primary market transactions are the only way that shares of the ETF can be created or redeemed. The "trade" in this market is in kind: A pre-specified basket of securities (which can include cash) is exchanged for a certain number of shares in the ETF.

ETF shares trade in the secondary market on exchanges. For investors, exchange trading is the only way to buy or sell ETFs. Like stocks, ETFs are bought and sold on exchanges through a brokerage account. This secondary market trading is perhaps the most novel feature of ETFs.

In-kind creation/redemption creates the unique benefits ETFs offer—as well as some of their risks. Here we explain ETFs' unique creation/redemption mechanism, the role of APs, and how the creation/redemption mechanism affects ETF design. ETF trading and settlement on primary and secondary markets is also covered.

2.1. The Creation/Redemption Process

The best way to understand the creation/redemption process is to step through the process from an investor's perspective.

Imagine you're an investor and you want to invest in an ETF. The process is simple: You place a buy order in your brokerage account the same way you would place an order to buy any publicly listed equity security, and your broker submits that order to the public market to find a willing seller: another investor or a market maker (i.e., a broker/dealer who stands ready to take the opposite side of the transaction). The order is executed, and you receive shares of the ETF in your brokerage account just as if you transacted in a stock.

At this point, the ETF manager (also referred to as the ETF issuer or sponsor) is not involved in the transaction. The ETF issuer does not know that you have bought these shares, nor does it receive an inflow of money to invest. Shares simply transfer in the open market, the secondary market for ETF shares, from one investor (the seller) to another (the buyer) and go through a settlement process based on the local exchange where the transaction took place. The process sounds simple, but if you can only buy ETF shares from another investor, where do the shares come from initially? How does money get invested into the fund?

The only investors who can create or redeem new shares of an ETF are a special group of institutional investors called *authorized participants*. APs are large broker/dealers, often market makers, who are authorized by the ETF issuer to participate in the creation/redemption process. The AP creates new ETF shares by transacting in kind with the ETF issuer. This in-kind swap happens off the exchange, in the primary market for the ETF, where APs transfer securities to (for creations) or receive securities from (for redemptions) the ETF issuer, in exchange for ETF shares. This is a prescribed, structured transaction with its own set of rules.

Each business day, the ETF manager publishes a list of required in-kind securities for each ETF. For instance, an S&P 500 Index ETF will typically list the index securities in quantities that reflect the index weighting. The list of securities specific to each ETF and disclosed publicly each day is called the **creation basket**. This basket also serves as the portfolio for determining the intrinsic net asset value of the ETF based on prices during the trading day.

To create new shares, an AP acquires the securities in the creation basket in the specified share amounts (generally by transacting in the public markets or using securities the AP happens to have in inventory). The AP then delivers this basket of securities to the ETF manager in exchange for an equal value in ETF shares. This exchange of shares happens after markets are closed through the settlement process. Importantly, the pricing of both the ETF and the basket is of minimal concern in this exchange: If the issuer receives 100 shares of a certain stock as part of the creation basket, the price the AP might have paid to acquire that stock or what its price happens to be at the end of the day is not relevant to the exchange taking place. Because it is an in-kind transaction, all that matters is that 100 shares of the required stock move from the AP's account to the ETF's account. Similarly, when the issuer delivers ETF shares to an AP, the ETF's closing NAV is not relevant.

These transactions between the AP and the ETF manager are done in large blocks called **creation units**, usually but not always equal to 50,000 shares of the ETF. This in-kind exchange involves the basket of underlying securities in exchange for a number of ETF shares of equal value.

The process also works in reverse: If the AP has a block of ETF shares it no longer wants (usually because it bought them from other market participants), the AP presents these shares for redemption to the ETF manager and receives in return the basket of underlying securities, which the AP can then sell in the market if it chooses. This basket often has the same security composition as the creation basket, but it may be different if the ETF portfolio manager is trying to sell particular securities for tax, compliance, or investment reasons. The basket of securities the AP receives when it redeems the ETF shares is called the **redemption basket**.

Although the actual process of exchanging baskets and blocks of ETF shares happens after the markets are closed, the AP is able to execute ETF trades throughout the trading day because the AP knows the security composition of the basket needed for ETF share creation or redemption, because of the fund's daily holdings disclosure to APs. If, during the course of the trading day, the AP wants to sell 50,000 shares of an ETF to investors in the secondary market, the AP can do so while simultaneously buying the securities in the creation basket. If the ETF and the securities in the creation basket are fairly priced, the AP faces no economic exposure in this transaction, because the value of the ETF shares sold and the value of the creation basket purchased are identical.

Why would APs engage in these transactions? Because there's a financial incentive to do so. The creation/redemption mechanism is key to keeping the price of an ETF in a tight range around the NAV of the portfolio of securities it holds, and it rewards the AP for this activity.

When the value of the security basket is different from the value of the corresponding ETF shares it represents, a potential arbitrage opportunity exists for APs to step in and transact in the ETF market. If the current per-share market value of the basket of underlying securities is greater than the quoted price of the ETF shares, the AP can simultaneously sell (or short) the basket of securities and buy ETF shares, to make a profit. In this situation, where the ETF share is undervalued, the ETF is said to be trading at a discount. If shares of the ETF are quoted at a higher price than the per-share market value of the basket of securities, the ETF is trading at a premium, and the AP can make a profit by simultaneously selling the ETF shares in the market and buying the basket of securities.

Because prices of the ETF and the basket securities are continuously changing on the basis of market conditions, APs monitor both for discrepancies, looking for opportunities to make arbitrage profits. The factors that drive the width of the ETF's bid–ask spread and trading range around intraday NAV include the cost of arbitrage (buying the securities and selling the ETF) and a risk premium to compensate for volatility and liquidity risk (ongoing volume in the securities and the ETF).

The *arbitrage gap*—the price(s) at which it makes sense for ETF market makers to step in and create or redeem shares—vary with the liquidity of the underlying securities and a variety of related costs; in some ETFs, the gap can be as small as the minimum tick size in the local market (e.g., −$0.01 in the US markets), whereas for other ETFs with underlying securities that are hard to trade (e.g., high-yield bonds), the arbitrage gap can be more than 1% wide. For any ETF, however, the gap creates a band or range around its fair value inside which the ETF will trade. In other words, arbitrage keeps the ETF trading at or near its fair value.

2.1.1. ETF Share Creation

Let's examine how this works in practice. In the scenario shown in Exhibit 1, the ETF is trading in the market at $25.10. The fair value of the ETF based on its underlying securities, however, is only $25.00. So, an AP will step in to transact and buy the basket of securities (at ETF fair value of $25.00) and simultaneously sell ETF shares on the open market for $25.10, realizing the $0.10 per share difference. (The AP may choose to create additional ETF shares by exchanging the basket securities for ETF shares with the fund's issuer).

EXHIBIT 1   An ETF Share Price at a Premium to NAV

This action puts downward pressure on the ETF price because the AP is selling shares out into the market and puts upward pressure on the prices of the underlying securities because the AP went out into the market and bought the underlying shares. APs will repeat this process until no further arbitrage opportunity exists.

2.1.2. ETF Share Redemption

As shown in Exhibit 2, the price of the ETF is $24.90. The fair value of the underlying stocks is $25.00. Here, the AP market maker steps in and purchases ETF shares on the open market while simultaneously selling the stocks on the exchange, realizing the $0.10 per share price difference. Once again, if the share price continues to be at a discount, the AP will continue this process until no further arbitrage opportunity exists. (The AP may choose to redeem ETF shares by exchanging them for the basket securities with the fund's issuer).

EXHIBIT 2   An ETF Share Price at a Discount to NAV

These profit-making scenarios do not include the costs that the APs incur related to ETF trading or any fees the issuer may charge for creating or redeeming shares. The AP generally pays all trading costs associated with buying or selling the securities in the baskets or the ETF shares and pays an additional fee to the ETF provider to cover processing fees associated with creation/redemption activities. APs may also have settlement costs, taxes, or other expenses based on their local markets and the markets for the underlying securities of the ETF.

The scenarios also do not account for risks in trading the basket of securities. If the underlying securities are difficult to access contemporaneously (for instance, if a US-listed ETF holds Japanese securities), then the AP will have to wait before completing one half of the transaction (e.g., selling the ETF shares but waiting until the Japanese market opens to buy the basket securities). These timing differences create uncertainty, which will generally cause the AP to wait for a wider arbitrage gap before stepping in. Similarly, if the basket securities are illiquid (such as high-yield bonds), the AP may need additional time to buy or sell the holdings. In both cases, the AP bears the market risk of the basket transaction.

A significant advantage of the ETF creation/redemption process is that the AP absorbs all costs of transacting the securities for the fund's portfolio. APs pass these costs to investors in the ETF's bid–ask spread, incurred by ETF buyers and sellers. Thus, non-transacting shareholders of an ETF are shielded from the negative impact of transaction costs caused by other investors entering and exiting the fund. In contrast, when investors enter or exit a traditional mutual fund, the mutual fund manager incurs costs to buy or sell investments arising from this activity, which affect all fund shareholders. This makes the ETF structure inherently more fair: Frequent ETF traders bear the cost of their activity, whereas buy-and-hold ETF shareholders are shielded from those costs.

Additionally, because creation and redemption happen in kind, they allow the ETF's portfolio managers to manage the cost basis of their holdings by selecting low-basis holdings for redemptions, leading to greater tax efficiency. Put simply, when an issuer is presented with a redemption request from an AP, the issuer can select which tax lots of the underlying securities to deliver. In addition, issuers may choose to publish customized redemption baskets, which allows them to target specific low-basis securities for removal from the portfolio. By delivering out shares that were originally acquired at low costs, the issuer can continuously raise the average acquired cost (or cost basis) of each position, thereby minimizing the position's unrealized gains.

The ETF issuer has the ability to determine how the process works for a fund. If the issuer requires that a creation basket be 200,000 shares instead of 50,000 shares, the AP will have less incentive to step in to arbitrage when net new demand is lower than 200,000 shares per day. Basket sizes range from 10,000 shares to 600,000 shares. If the ETF holds highly illiquid securities, the issuer can alter the basket that APs must deliver, thereby lowering the costs of creation. In the most extreme case, the fund may allow for the creation of ETF shares in exchange for cash. Issuers can also charge minimal or large fees for creation and redemption, which affect an AP's profit consideration and transactions, to keep prices in line with fair value. Consider the fee of $50 for the Vanguard Short-Term Inflation-Protected Securities ETF (VTIP) versus the fee of $28,000 for the Vanguard FTSE All-World Ex-US Small-Cap ETF (VSS).

Creation/Redemption Asset Class Differences

The creation/redemption mechanism described is broadly representative of how most ETFs work, regardless of their particular legal structure. However, depending on the asset class, some differences exist.

Fixed-income ETFs generally hold large amounts of bonds, which may be illiquid to trade (for example, a high-yield municipal bond ETF holds securities that might trade only every few days). Because of this, ETF issuers may choose not to do in-kind creations and redemptions but instead accept equivalent cash value. This makes the process easier for APs, encouraging greater ETF activity, but does result in trading costs and tax impact for the ETF. ETF issuers must balance those costs against the benefit of having the AP participate more actively in the market, keeping spreads tight and the price of the ETF close to fair value.

> Similarly, many leveraged and inverse ETFs and commodity ETFs may use cash creation/redemption because it makes managing their underlying swap positions easier. Since swaps are generally negotiated over-the-counter transactions, it would be difficult to have APs participate in increasing or decreasing those swap positions.

2.2. Trading and Settlement

There is much confusion in the investor community regarding the underlying mechanics of ETF trading and settlement. Whether this confusion relates to shorting, how shares are created/redeemed or settled, or how they trade, ETFs are potentially confusing to many investors. From the perspective of an investor buying on the open market, ETFs go through the same settlement and clearing process as other listed stocks. This section explains that process.

2.2.1. US Settlement: National Security Clearing Corporation and Depository Trust Company

In the United States, all trades that have been entered into on a given business day are submitted at the end of the day to the National Security Clearing Corporation (NSCC). As long as both parties of a transaction agree that Party 1 sold to Party 2 *N* shares of XYZ stock, the NSCC becomes the guarantor of that transaction—the entity that ensures all parties are immunized against the financial impact of any operational problems—on the evening of the trade, and the trade is considered "cleared." After this point, the buyer is guaranteed beneficial ownership in the stock (or ETF) as of the time the trade was marked "executed," even if something (e.g., bankruptcy) happens to the seller before the trade is settled.

The Depository Trust Company (DTC), of which the NSCC is a subsidiary, holds the book of accounts—the actual list of security holders and ownership. This information is aggregated at the member firm level, rather than at the individual investor level. For instance, the DTC keeps track of how many shares of Microsoft are currently held by J.P. Morgan or Charles Schwab, but Charles Schwab is responsible for keeping track of which of its customers own how many shares.

After each trade is cleared, the DTC then adds up the total of all trades in a process of continuous net settlement. For example, suppose at the end of a trading day the following is true:

- E*TRADE owes Schwab 1,000 shares of SPY.
- Schwab owes Bank of America Merrill Lynch 1,000 shares of SPY.

Then, from the DTC's perspective, Schwab is "whole": It both is owed and owes 1,000 shares of SPY. To settle the day's transactions, E*TRADE's account will be debited the 1,000 shares of SPY and Bank of America Merrill Lynch will be credited 1,000 shares.

The NSCC has two days to complete this process and have each firm review its records and correct any discrepancies. We refer to this two-day period as T+2 (trade date + 2 days). This T+2 settlement process works for the vast majority of ETF transactions.

Market makers receive special treatment on settlement requirements. Because the role of market makers is to make a continuous market in a given security by standing ready to buy or sell the security on the basis of demand/supply imbalances, they are more likely to end up truly short at the end of a given day. Because of the time required to create or borrow ETF shares, market makers are given up to six days to settle their accounts.

2.2.2. European Trading and Settlement

In Europe, the majority of ETF owners are institutional investors. Additionally, the market is fragmented across multiple exchanges, jurisdictions, and clearinghouses. This fragmentation results in the use of many different trading strategies by investors in both the primary and secondary markets for ETFs. Fundamentally, trading works the same as in the United States: An investor purchases shares in the secondary market from a market maker or other counterparty. APs use the creation/redemption mechanism, which helps keep the ETF share price in line with its fair value.

However, Europe's trading and settlement system is fragmented. The majority of trading happens in negotiated over-the-counter trades between large institutions, and although those trades are reported, they don't appear as "live" or published bids and asks on the public markets prior to their execution. Most ETFs in Europe are also cross-listed on multiple exchanges and may have different share classes available that vary in their treatment of distributions or currency hedging. In addition, the European settlement process is fragmented. In the United States, trades are cleared and settled centrally. In Europe, they are cleared to one of 29 central securities depositories (or CSDs). From a practical standpoint, this has no direct impact on investors other than the inherent complexity of such a system, which may result in wider spreads and higher local market trading costs.

3. UNDERSTANDING ETFs

Among the most important questions an investor can ask about an ETF is, Does the fund deliver on its promise? The best-managed ETFs charge low and predictable investment costs, closely track the indexes on which they are based, and provide investors with the lowest possible tax exposure for the investment objective. Additionally, these funds provide complete, accurate information in their prospectuses and marketing materials and explain the fund's structure, composition, performance, and risks. To best understand an ETF's ability to meet expectations, its expense ratio, index tracking, tax treatment, and potential costs and risks should be considered.

3.1. Expense Ratios

Fund expense ratios are often one of the first factors investors look at when evaluating ETFs. ETFs generally charge lower fees than mutual funds, in part because ETF providers do not have to keep track of individual investor accounts, since ETF shares are held by and transacted through brokerage firms. Nor do ETF issuers bear the costs of communicating directly with individual investors. In addition, index-based portfolio management, used by most ETFs, does not require the security and macroeconomic research carried out by active managers, which increases fund operating costs.

The actual costs to manage an ETF vary, depending on portfolio complexity (for example, how many securities the fund holds, how often rebalancing or strategy implementation occurs, difficulty in maintaining portfolio exposures), issuer size (economies of scale apply), and the competitive landscape.

ETF expense ratios have been one of the most visible areas of competitive differentiation for issuers, which has led to an overall decline in fees. Exhibit 3 shows average US-domiciled ETF expense ratios by asset class at the end of 2018.

EXHIBIT 3   Average US-Domiciled ETF Expense Ratios by Asset Class at the End of 2018

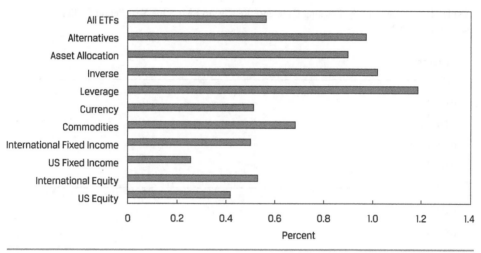

Sources: ETF.com and FactSet, as of 31 December 2018.

Because the average numbers include complex and expensive funds, they dramatically overstate the cost of accessing the most common ETF investment strategies and indexes.

As of the end of 2018, expense ratios for broad-based, capitalization-weighted indexes were as low as 0.03% for US equities, 0.11% for emerging market equities, and 0.04% for US bonds.

3.2. Index Tracking/Tracking Error

Even though an ETF's expense ratio is useful, it doesn't fully reflect the cost of holding an ETF. To understand how well an ETF delivers on its mandate, it is critical to assess the ETF's ability to track its underlying index.

For index-tracking ETFs, which represented 98% of the US ETF market as measured by assets under management (AUM) as of December 2018, ETF managers attempt to deliver performance that tracks the fund's benchmark as closely as possible (after subtracting fees). This can be measured by comparing ETF performance with index returns. The comparison can be done using daily or periodic returns but should always include both a central tendency, such as mean or median, and an expression of variability, such as standard deviation or range.

3.2.1. Daily Differences

Index tracking is often evaluated using the one-day difference in returns between the fund, as measured by its NAV, and its index. Exhibit 4 shows the daily tracking difference between the iShares MSCI Emerging Markets ETF (EEM) and its underlying index, the MSCI Emerging Markets Index (EMI), for a one-year period. EMI is a multicurrency international index containing hundreds of illiquid securities in more than 20 emerging markets. The index represents large- and mid-cap stocks in each of these markets. At the end of November 2018, EEM held approximately 900 of the 1,150 constituents in EMI.

EXHIBIT 4   EEM Daily Tracking Difference Relative to EMI, One-Year Period Ending 30 November 2018

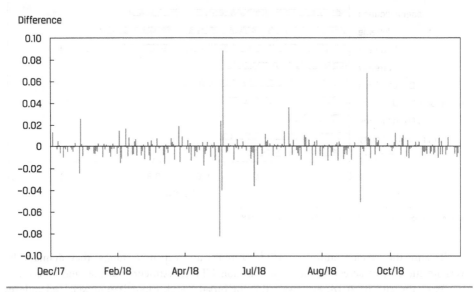

Source: FactSet.

3.2.2. Periodic Tracking

Tracking error is defined as the standard deviation of differences in daily performance between the index and the fund tracking the index, and a reported tracking error number is typically for a 12-month period. Over the period shown, EEM's standard deviation of daily performance differences to its index was 0.012%.

But importantly, tracking error does not reveal the extent to which the fund is under- or overperforming its index or anything about the distribution of errors. Daily tracking error could be concentrated over a few days or more consistently experienced. Therefore, tracking error should be assessed with the mean or median values.

An alternative approach is to look at tracking differences calculated over a longer holding period. A series of rolling holding periods can be used to represent both central tendencies and variability. This approach allows investors to see the cumulative effect of portfolio management and expenses over an extended period. Exhibit 5 shows the 12-month rolling return (or cumulative annual) tracking difference between EEM and its index.

EXHIBIT 5   EEM 12-Month Rolling Tracking Difference Relative to EMI, One-Year Periods
Ending 30 November 2018

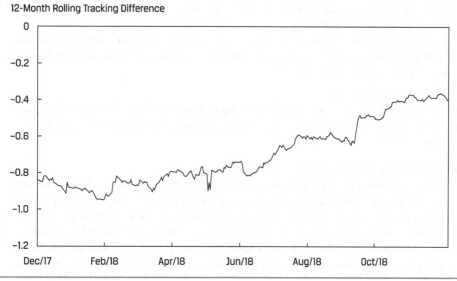

Source: FactSet.

One benefit of the rolling annual analysis is that it allows for comparison with other
annual metrics, such as the fund's expense ratio. All else equal, one would normally expect an
index fund to underperform its benchmark on an annual basis by the amount of its expense
ratio. In Exhibit 5, EEM's median tracking difference of 0.79% exceeded its 0.69% expense
ratio by 0.10%. Notably, the range of EEM's annual tracking difference showed some
variability, with underperformance as low as 0.38% and as high as 0.95%.

3.2.3. Sources of Tracking Error
Numerous factors can account for differences between an ETF's expected and actual
performance and the range of results with respect to its index. An ETF's fees, portfolio
construction and management approach, accounting practices, regulatory and tax requirements, and asset manager operations all contribute to tracking error. Because of this, funds
tracking the same underlying index can have very different index tracking results.

Sources of benchmark tracking error include the following:

- Fees and expenses—Index calculation generally assumes that trading is frictionless and
occurs at the closing price. A fund's operating fees and expenses reduce the fund's return
relative to the index.
- Representative sampling/optimization—Rather than fully replicate the index, funds may
hold only a subset of index securities to track the benchmark index.
- Depositary receipts and other ETFs—Funds may hold securities that are different from
those in the index, such as American depositary receipts (ADRs), global depositary receipts
(GDRs), and other ETFs.
- Index changes—Funds may trade index changes at times and prices that are different from
those of the benchmark tracked.

- Fund accounting practices—Fund accounting practices may differ from the index calculation methodology—for example, valuation practices for foreign exchange and fixed income.
- Regulatory and tax requirements—Funds may be subject to regulatory and tax requirements that are different from those assumed in index methodology, such as with foreign dividend withholding.
- Asset manager operations—ETF issuers may attempt to offset costs through security lending and foreign dividend recapture. These act as "negative" costs, which enhance fund performance relative to the index.

3.2.4. Fees and Expenses

As outlined in the prior sections, fund operating expenses vary by ETF, but all else equal, one would normally expect an index fund to underperform its benchmark on an annual basis by the amount of its expense ratio.

3.2.5. Representative Sampling/Optimization

For funds tracking index exposure to small or illiquid markets, owning every index constituent can be difficult and costly. Therefore, fund managers may choose to optimize their portfolios by holding only a portion, or representative sample, of index securities. A striking example is the SPDR S&P Emerging Asia Pacific ETF (GMF). As of 7 December 2018, GMF held only 763 of the 2,342 securities in the S&P Asia Pacific Emerging BMI Index. As shown in Exhibit 6, sampling has caused some sizable discrepancies between the fund's daily return and the index.

EXHIBIT 6   GMF Daily Tracking Difference Relative to the S&P Asia Pacific Emerging BMI Index, One-Year Period Ending 30 November 2018

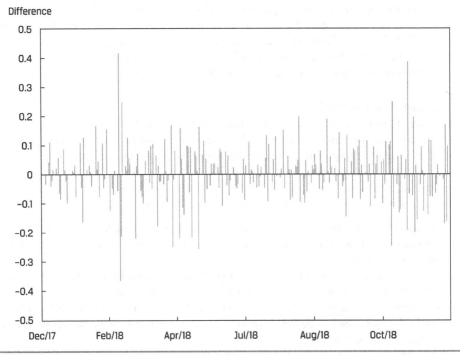

Source: FactSet.

Sampling, or optimization, can affect long-term tracking in two ways. First, it can make the median value unpredictive of future median values, especially if market regimes shift. Second, it dramatically expands the range of results. Exhibit 7 and the table below illustrate these effects, using trailing 12-month (TTM) rolling comparisons. Exhibit 7 contrasts EEM's median trailing 12-month tracking difference with GMF's more variable results.

EXHIBIT 7   Trailing 12-Month Tracking Difference: EEM and GMF

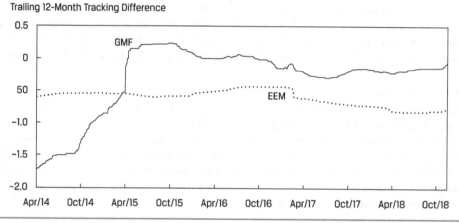

Source: FactSet.

A high level of optimization causes GMF's portfolio to underperform in certain market regimes and outperform in others. Looking at the differences between GMF and its underlying index explains why. As of 30 November 2018, GMF's median constituent market cap was $2.8 billion, whereas the S&P Asia Pacific Emerging BMI's was $0.695 billion, indicating that by holding approximately one-third of index constituents, GMF's portfolio omits many of the index's mid-caps and small-caps. Therefore, GMF will likely underperform the index during times when emerging market mid-caps and small-caps outperform emerging market large-caps, and vice versa.

As illustrated in the following table, GMF's tracking range—the spread between its maximum and minimum trailing 12-month tracking difference—is nearly 4 times that of EEM. A higher level of optimization within GMF causes it to have a wider range of tracking difference relative to its index.

EEM and GMF Tracking Range, One Year Ending 30 November 2018

	EEM	GMF
Maximum TTM	−0.38%	1.14%
Minimum TTM	−0.95%	−0.81%
Range	0.57%	1.95%

Source: FactSet.

Representative sampling/optimization, therefore, enhances or detracts from fund returns relative to the index depending on whether ETF portfolio holdings outperform or underperform those in the index. Compared with a full replication approach, representative sampling/optimization introduces greater potential for tracking error.

3.2.6. Depositary Receipts and ETFs

When local market shares are illiquid, ETF portfolio managers may choose to hold depositary receipts instead of local constituent shares. Although the economic exposure is equivalent, exchange trading hours for these securities differ. Differences in trading hours and security prices create discrepancies between portfolio and index values. Similarly, ETF issuers may choose to hold ETFs as underlying holdings. This also creates discrepancies between fund NAV and index value, because the ETFs' holdings are valued at their closing market price and not their NAV.

3.2.7. Index Changes

An index provider will periodically change index constituents or weights to comply with its index methodology. In the real world, portfolio managers may transact these changes before or after the effective date or time of the index change/closing prices, at different prices. The more volatile the market, the wider the bid–offer spreads and range of traded prices. ETF portfolio managers can use the creation/redemption process to manage rebalance trades, by cooperating with APs to ensure market-on-close pricing on the rebalance date, thus minimizing this source of tracking error.

3.2.8. Fund Accounting Practices

Differences in valuation practices between the fund and its index can create discrepancies that magnify daily tracking differences. Some ETF issuers follow the index industry's convention of establishing (striking) currency valuations using WM/Reuters rates, which are set at 4:00 p.m. GMT (11:00 a.m. EST), whereas others conform to established mutual fund industry practices of striking currency valuations at the close of ETF trading. In the United States, equity markets close at 4:00 p.m. ET. Many fixed-income ETF portfolios value bond positions at the time of the equity market close, in keeping with ETF industry custom. However, fixed-income indexes often follow the bond market's practice of valuing bonds at an earlier time. These practices may create valuation discrepancies between the ETF's NAV and the index value, particularly in volatile segments of the bond market, such as long-dated maturities. Valuation discrepancies can also occur for ETFs holding futures, foreign securities, physical metals, and currencies held in specie.

3.2.9. Regulatory and Tax Requirements

Regulatory and tax requirements may cause a fund to mis-track its index. For example, non-domestic holders of a nation's securities owe tax on distributions received from securities of companies domiciled in that nation. The tax withholding rate charged is determined by treaty and investor domicile. Index providers who offer a "net" return series adjust the dividends received to account for the tax charged, usually from the point of view of US-domiciled investors. However, index providers may use rates different from those experienced by the ETF, which can create return differences between the ETF and its index. For many years, Brazil imposed a tax on foreign investments coming into the country. Although this tax did not affect the closing prices of the local stocks and, therefore, was not reflected in index calculation methodology, non-local ETFs domiciled outside Brazil paid this tax whenever they acquired Brazilian stocks. This caused fund underperformance relative to the index.

3.2.10. Asset Manager Operations

ETF issuers may engage in security lending or foreign dividend recapture to generate additional income to offset fund expenses. These can be considered "negative" costs. Many ETFs (and mutual funds) lend a portion of their portfolio holdings to short sellers. In exchange, the ETF receives a fee and earns interest on the collateral posted by the borrower (generally, overnight fixed-income securities). This creates income for the portfolio. Since securities-lending income is not accounted for in the index calculation, it is a source of tracking error. Asset managers may work with foreign governments to minimize tax paid on distributions received.

3.3. Tax Issues

Two kinds of tax-based evaluations must be made for all ETFs: First, the investor must consider the likelihood of an ETF distributing capital gains to shareholders. Second, the investor must consider what happens when the investor sells the ETF. These two actions are distinct; the tax efficiency of a fund regarding its capital gains distributions has no relation to its tax efficiency at the time of investor sale.

3.3.1. Capital Gains Distributions

The issue of capital gains distributions affects all investors in taxable accounts. In general, funds must distribute any capital gains realized during the year. Funds typically make these distributions at year-end, although they may make them quarterly or on another periodic schedule.

ETFs are said to be "tax fair" and "tax efficient" because they have certain advantages over traditional mutual funds regarding capital gains distributions. On average, they distribute less in capital gains than competing mutual funds for two primary reasons.

3.3.1.1. Tax Fairness

In a traditional mutual fund, when an investor sells, the fund must (with a few exceptions) sell portfolio securities to raise cash to pay the investor. Any securities sold at a profit incur a capital gains charge, which is distributed to remaining shareholders. Put another way, in a traditional mutual fund, shareholders may have to pay tax liabilities triggered by other shareholders redeeming out of the fund.

In contrast, an investor sells ETF shares to another investor in the secondary market. The ETF manager typically does not know that the sale is occurring and does not need to alter the portfolio to accommodate this transaction. Thus, the selling activities of individual investors in the secondary market do not require the fund to trade out of its underlying positions. If an AP redeems ETF shares, this redemption occurs in kind and is not a taxable event. Thus, redemptions do not trigger capital gain realizations. This aspect is why ETFs are considered "tax fair": The actions of investors selling shares of the fund do not influence the tax liabilities for remaining fund shareholders.[1]

3.3.1.2. Tax Efficiency

The redemption process allows portfolio managers to manage the fund's tax liability. When an authorized participant submits shares of an ETF for redemption, the ETF manager can choose

---

[1]This is not always the case. US-domiciled "no K-1" funds—those that use an open-ended 1940 Act structure to hold a subsidiary that, in turn, holds futures contracts—cannot redeem in kind and, therefore, must distribute gains anytime an AP redeems shares. ETFs operating in certain Asian markets, such as China, South Korea, and Malaysia, are vulnerable to capital gains liabilities, because these markets prohibit in-kind redemptions.

which underlying share lots to deliver in the redemption basket. By choosing shares with the largest unrealized capital gains—that is, those acquired at the lowest cost basis—ETF managers can use the in-kind redemption process to reduce potential capital gains in the fund. Tax lot management allows portfolio managers to limit the unrealized gains in a portfolio.

Capital gains can still occur with ETFs. For example, in the case of an index delete in which an index constituent is being replaced, the outgoing constituent must be sold and the new constituent purchased. If the sale price is higher than the fund's original purchase price for the deleted company, a taxable gain occurs. Similarly, many indexes have rebalancing periods, and funds tracking these indexes must trade those changes. Rebalancing increases the potential for capital gains to occur. Tax efficiency can be improved if redemptions occur on index rebalance dates, because this allows the portfolio manager to remove appreciated securities via in-kind exchanges, rather than selling and realizing a capital gain.

Certain types of ETF portfolios are particularly vulnerable to capital gains. The most notable are bond funds, which can realize capital gains when bonds bought at a discount mature or when bonds must be sold to conform to investment objectives, such as when the day comes that a bond has only 12 months remaining to maturity and, therefore, can no longer be held in an intermediate-term bond fund. In addition, bond ETF portfolio managers sometimes offer cash redemptions to APs, to promote ETF liquidity. If the portfolio manager needs to raise cash by selling appreciated bonds in the open market, it may result in capital gains.

3.3.2. Other Distributions

Other events, such as security dividend distributions, can trigger tax liabilities for investors. In most markets, ETFs distribute their accumulated dividends; however, in some jurisdictions— notably in Europe—ETFs may have share classes that accumulate and automatically re-invest dividends into the fund. Because not all distributions are treated alike, investors must ensure they understand the tax treatment specific to each fund's domicile, legal structure, and portfolio type.

3.3.3. Taxes on Sale

In most jurisdictions, ETFs are taxed according to their underlying holdings. For example, in the United States, an ETF holding equities or bonds will itself be subject to the same capital gain, dividend, and return-of-capital tax rules that apply to its underlying stock or bond holdings. However, there can be nuances in individual tax jurisdictions that require investor analysis. For example, in the United States, exchange-traded notes tracking commodity indexes are treated differently from exchange-traded funds holding commodity futures contracts, creating a preferential tax treatment. A thorough analysis of ETF efficiency should take into account the ETF structure, the local market's taxation regime, and the individual tax situation of the end investor.

3.4. ETF Trading Costs

In comparing ETF and mutual fund costs, the usual starting point is management fees, which are often lower for an ETF because most are index based and traded in a highly competitive market. However, there are other important costs that should be considered.

An ETF has the advantage that it can be purchased whenever exchanges are open—as well as at closing NAV of the fund (similar to mutual fund purchases and sales) when a transaction is large enough to qualify for a creation or redemption. ETF investors usually pay a commission and incur a trading cost related to the liquidity factors associated with the ETF.[2] The trading, or market impact, costs are influenced by the bid–ask spread of the ETF, the size of the trade relative to the normal trading activity of the ETF, and the ease of hedging the ETF by the market-making community. The closing price of the ETF on the exchange may include a premium or discount to the NAV, driven by supply and demand factors on the exchange and the market impact costs of executing an exchange transaction.

3.4.1. ETF Bid–Ask Spreads

One of the most important drivers of ETF bid–ask spreads and liquidity is the market structure and liquidity of the underlying securities held. Fixed-income securities, which trade in a dealer market, tend to have much wider bid–ask spreads than large-capitalization stocks. The bid–ask spread of an ETF holding stocks traded in other markets and time zones is influenced by whether the markets for the underlying stocks are open during the hours in which the ETF trades. For specialized ETFs—such as those tracking commodities, volatility futures, or even small-cap stocks—bid–ask spreads can be wide simply because the risk of holding a position even for a short period of time can be high. For some ETFs, even though the underlying securities are liquid, bid–ask spreads may be wide simply because the ETF trades so infrequently the market maker or liquidity provider may need to carry ETF positions for some time before they accumulate sufficient size to create or redeem. Generally, as long as the liquidity in the underlying securities is adequate or hedging instruments can be easily sourced, an ETF trade can usually be executed in a cost-effective manner.

The primary factors that determine the width of the quoted bid–ask spread for a particular transaction size are the amount of ongoing order flow in the ETF, as measured by daily share volume (more flow means lower spreads); the amount of competition among market makers for that ETF (more competition means lower spreads); and the actual costs and risks for the liquidity provider. The bid–ask spread represents the market maker's price for taking the other side of the ETF transaction, which includes the costs and risks to carry the position on his or her books or to hedge the position using underlying securities or closely related ETFs or derivatives.

More specifically, ETF bid–ask spreads are generally less than or equal to the combination of the following:

- ± Creation/redemption fees and other direct trading costs, such as brokerage and exchange fees
- + Bid–ask spreads of the underlying securities held in the ETF
- + Compensation (to market maker or liquidity provider) for the risk of hedging or carrying positions for the remainder of the trading day
- + Market maker's desired profit spread, subject to competitive forces
- −Discount related to the likelihood of receiving an offsetting ETF order in a short time frame

---

[2]Some brokerage firms, especially those that also are ETF sponsors, have begun competing aggressively for business and offer trading with no commissions on ETFs to attract retail investor funds into their brokerage platforms.

Large, actively traded ETFs have narrow bid–offer spreads and the capacity (or liquidity) for large transaction sizes. For very liquid US-listed ETFs, such as SPY (the SPDR S&P 500 ETF), VOO (the Vanguard S&P 500 ETF), EEM (the iShares MSCI Emerging Markets ETF), or TLT (the iShares 20+ Year Treasury Bond ETF), buyers and sellers are active throughout the trading day and market makers have a high likelihood of finding the other side or hedging larger orders. Therefore, because most of these ETF trades are matched quickly and never involve the creation/redemption process, the first three factors do not contribute heavily in their spreads. For liquid ETFs, the bid–ask spread can be significantly tighter than the spreads on the underlying securities.

However, the quoted ETF bid–ask spread is generally for a specific, usually small, trade size and does not always reflect ETF liquidity for larger transactions (more than 10% of average daily volume). For larger trades, posted spreads may not reflect trading costs, and these trades may best be handled by negotiation. Investors looking to trade larger ETF sizes often work with capital market specialists at ETF managers and broker/dealer ETF desks to understand the various ETF execution options and associated trading costs.

Exhibit 8 shows the asset-weighted average and median bid–ask spreads for various ETF categories traded in the United States.

EXHIBIT 8   Average and Median Bid–Ask Spreads for US-Traded ETFs

US-Traded ETF Category	AUM ($ millions)	Average Spread ($ asset-weighted)	Median Spread
US Equity	1,871,942	0.03%	0.16%
International Equity	731,251	0.05%	0.24%
US Fixed Income	589,851	0.02%	0.14%
International Fixed Income	65,159	0.06%	0.24%
Commodities	62,620	0.05%	0.24%
Leveraged	29,633	0.29%	0.32%
Inverse	11,315	0.10%	0.21%
Asset Allocation	9,318	0.21%	0.29%
Alternatives	4,388	0.18%	0.38%
All US-Traded ETFs*	3,377,276	0.04%	0.20%

* Includes currency ETFs in addition to ETFs listed. Total currency ETF assets are $1,799 million.
Source: FactSet, as of the end of December 2018, based on 60-day averages.

The overall median bid–ask spread for ETFs traded in the United States as of the end of 2018 was 0.20%. US equity and fixed-income ETFs have the tightest asset-weighted spreads, as low as 0.02%, with the median level closer to 0.15%. International equity and international fixed-income spreads are wider, because the underlying securities trade in different market structures, making it difficult to price simultaneously, and because the underlying security exchanges may be closed during a portion of the US trading day. ETF categories representing longer-term strategies, such as asset allocation and alternatives, are less actively traded and have lower asset levels and wider spreads, in part because they have less ongoing two-way order flow and, therefore, depend more on market makers to source liquidity through the underlying securities. Bid–ask spreads are dynamic and vary by trade, depending on trade size and market conditions. Spreads tend to widen when market volatility increases or when significant information relating to the underlying index securities is expected.

Understanding spreads for non-equity ETFs is more complex. Although the fixed-income ETFs give investors access to a portfolio of debt securities trading with transparent bid–ask spreads in the stock market (via the ETF), the actual market for the underlying bonds is far less transparent. Most bonds trade over the counter, with traders at banks and large bond desks who offer quotes on demand but do not post bids or offers on an exchange, although they may participate in some electronic trading.

Some bonds, such as US Treasury securities, are actively traded and have tight bid–ask spreads and bid–ask prices regularly advertised on electronic platforms. Other corporate debt and high-yield bonds, and some municipals and international bonds, trade actively only around the time of issuance, after which they may be held until maturity. Therefore, bond ETFs that track indexes containing corporate and high-yield debt often invest only in a subset of the most liquid high-yield securities. Their bid–ask spreads tend to be wider than those of ETFs based on stocks or US Treasuries because of the risk to dealers in hedging inventory and the default risk of the securities, especially in periods of weak economic conditions.

3.4.2. Premiums and Discounts

In addition to commissions and bid–ask spreads, ETF premiums and discounts are also important components of ETF trading costs.

At the end of the trading day, each ETF has an end-of-day NAV at which shares can be created or redeemed and with which the ETF's closing price can be compared. Most investors rely on return calculations based on this closing NAV. NAV is intended to be an accurate assessment of the ETF's fair value. This is the case when the underlying securities trade on the same exchange as the one where the ETF is listed (or trades), because these securities trade in the same market structure and have the same closing price time as the ETF.

During the trading day, exchanges disseminate ETF **iNAVs**, or "indicated" NAVs; iNAVs are intraday "fair value" estimates of an ETF share based on its creation basket composition for that day. An ETF is said to be trading at a premium when its share price is higher than iNAV and at a discount if its price is lower than iNAV.

The calculation for end-of-day and intraday premiums/discounts is as follows:

End-of-day ETF premium or discount (%) = (ETF price − NAV per share)/NAV per share.

Intraday ETF premium or discount (%) = (ETF price − iNAV per share)/iNAV per share.

Like tracking error, premiums/discounts are driven by a number of factors, including timing differences and stale pricing.

3.4.2.1. Timing Differences

NAV is often a poor fair value indicator for ETFs that hold foreign securities because of differences in exchange closing times between the underlying (e.g., foreign stocks, bonds, or commodities) and the exchange where the ETF trades. For example, if a commodity held in the fund stops trading in the futures market at 3:00 p.m., the issuer may elect to retain that price for a 4:00 p.m. valuation. If a fund holds securities in a different currency, it may choose to "strike" or value the currency at 4:00 p.m. ET—or occasionally, at 4:00 p.m. London time. In the case where international stocks are held in US-traded ETFs, the NAV may be based on a market closing price in Asia or Europe that occurred hours ahead of when the ETF stops trading on the US exchange.

Because bonds do not trade on an exchange, no true "closing prices" are available for valuing the bonds in a portfolio. Instead, ETF issuers rely on bids from bond desks or pricing services for proxy prices. In the case of bonds that have not traded near the close of the dealer market, index providers and bondholders typically use pricing services for bond valuation. These pricing services often use more liquid bonds that have similar features to estimate where the non-traded bond would have closed.

Sometimes, bond pricing model inputs reflect the price at which a dealer is willing to buy the bonds and the risk and cost to a dealer in carrying the bonds in inventory. In such cases, the ETF's closing price is often higher than the bid prices of the underlying bond holdings used to calculate NAV, making it appear that the ETF is at a premium. During times of market stress, few bonds may trade, leaving pricing services without updated inputs for their models. Like ETFs holding foreign securities, this causes NAVs to be "stale" and, in this case, with possibly too high a valuation given market conditions. In this case, fixed-income ETFs with sufficient trading volume may appear to be trading at discounts to NAV. In these cases, by reflecting the market's most current assessment of value, liquid ETFs become "price discovery" vehicles.

ETFs also provide price discovery for after-hours markets. For example, US-listed ETFs holding European stocks trade until 4:00 p.m. ET, hours after European markets have closed. In these cases, premiums or discounts resulting from closed underlying markets are not mispricing; rather, they are the market's best estimate as to where the fund holdings would trade if the underlying markets were open.

3.4.2.2. Stale Pricing

ETFs that trade infrequently may also have large premiums or discounts to NAV. If the ETF has not traded in the hours leading up to the market close, NAV may have significantly risen or fallen during that time owing to market movement. In this case, comparing the last ETF trade price—for example, at 1:00 p.m.—with the end-of-day 4:00 p.m. NAV would result in a premium (or discount) if the market and corresponding NAV fell (or rose) sharply between 1:00 and 4:00 p.m.

This situation can be compounded if days or weeks elapse between the ETF's trades. Some premium/discount calculations use a strict last price input, whereas others use a closing midpoint. The strict pricing will quote the last trade price, no matter how distant the ETF trade date, which can lead to severe premiums or discounts as NAVs are updated on the basis of the latest market closing prices while the ETF price remains unchanged at last trade.

ETF prices may be a more accurate reflection than NAVs or iNAVs in the following situations: when the underlying securities are less actively traded (less liquid or volatile markets), when the underlying market is closed, and when the underlying market has time lags (such as the early-closing commodity markets) with respect to the market where the ETF trades.

Comparison of US ETF Trading Costs

A good way to assess the liquidity and potential trading costs of ETFs is to compare various measures of trading activity among similar funds. Exhibit 9 shows trading measures for some of the most liquid ETFs—the SPDR S&P 500 ETF (SPY), the iShares Core S&P 500 ETF (IVV), and the Vanguard S&P 500 ETF (VOO) benchmarked to the S&P 500 Index; another large-cap ETF, the iShares MSCI USA Equal Weighted ETF (EUSA), benchmarked to the MSCI USA Equal Weighted Index; and a liquid small-cap ETF, the iShares Russell 2000 ETF (IWM), benchmarked to the Russell 2000 Index.

EXHIBIT 9   Selected US Equity Index ETF Trading Measure Comparison

ETF Ticker	SPY	IVV	VOO	EUSA	IWM
Benchmark				MSCI USA	
Index	S&P 500	S&P 500	S&P 500	Equal Weighted	Russell 2000
Volume in US dollars					
Daily average volume	24.47 billion	1.22 billion	819.28 million	1.32 million	3.90 billion
Median volume	20.23 billion	1.08 billion	739.69 million	0.94 million	3.81 billion
Other trading characteristics					
Average spread (%)	0.00%	0.01%	0.01%	0.12%	0.01%
Average spread ($)	$0.01	$0.03	$0.03	$0.07	$0.01
Median premium/ discount (%)[a]	0.00%	0.00%	0.00%	0.04%	0.01%
Maximum premium (%)[a]	0.12%	0.13%	0.18%	0.96%	0.12%
Maximum discount (%)[a]	−0.19%	−0.11%	−0.08%	−0.38%	−0.13%

[a] Over previous 12 months.
Source: FactSet, as of 7 November 2018.

SPY, the largest ETF by AUM and the first ETF traded in the United States, is one of the most liquid securities in the world. IVV and VOO, with the same benchmark, are used more by intermediate- and longer-horizon investors but also have very tight spreads because of liquidity in the underlying securities and ease of hedging for market makers. SPY trades a median of $20 billion a day, compared with a median of $1 billion for IVV. The average bid–ask spread shows that both are highly liquid. In addition, both have tight premiums and discounts to NAV.

In contrast, EUSA has a larger spread, 0.12%. The lower liquidity and higher trading cost for EUSA can be attributed to the fact that the benchmark index does not have futures and other index products available for hedging use by market makers. The MSCI USA Equal Weighted Index also includes close to 600 stocks—100 more than the S&P 500 Index has.

IWM, benchmarked to the Russell 2000 Index of US small-cap stocks, holds far more securities than any of the previously mentioned ETFs, and many are small-cap stocks that have wide spreads. IWM, however, trades with spreads and premiums/discounts close to those of SPY.

How is that possible? First, trading activity in IWM is high (median daily dollar volume of $4 billion) and continuous throughout the trading day. Second, the Russell 2000 Index has an active futures market, making it easy for market makers and APs to quickly hedge the risk of large trades.

Exhibit 10 shows three US fixed-income ETFs—one US-Treasury based and two benchmarked to US high-yield indexes. All three are among the most liquid fixed-income ETFs and have tight average bid–ask spreads. The iShares iBoxx $ High Yield Corporate Bond ETF (HYG) is the most liquid, with median daily volume of $1.4 billion and a higher median premium (0.20%) than the iShares 20+ Year Treasury Bond ETF (TLT). These positive median premiums indicate that the SPDR Bloomberg Barclays High Yield Bond ETF (JNK) and HYG have been in a net demand position over most of the 12-month period covered in Exhibit 10 and investors have typically paid above fair value for ETF access to a high-yield portfolio.

The maximum premium and discount have generally been much larger for bond ETFs compared with the equity ETFs shown in Exhibit 9. This is because the underlying fixed-income securities trade in a dealer market and are not continuously priced. In this case, the fixed-income ETFs, which trade on an exchange with more continuous pricing, may be a better reflection of true supply and demand for the portfolio since the underlying bonds may not trade as frequently, particularly in extreme market conditions.

EXHIBIT 10   Selected US Fixed-Income ETF Trading Measure Comparison

ETF Ticker	TLT	JNK	HYG
Benchmark Index	ICE US Treasury 20+ Year Bond Index	Bloomberg Barclays High Yield Very Liquid Index	Markit iBoxx USD Liquid High Yield Index
Volume in US dollars			
Daily average volume	1.04 billion	0.46 billion	1.50 billion
Median volume	0.97 billion	0.41 billion	1.44 billion
Other trading characteristics			
Average spread (%)	0.01%	0.03%	0.01%
Average spread ($)	$0.01	$0.01	$0.01
Median premium/discount (%)[a]	0.03%	0.10%	0.20%
Maximum premium (%)[a]	0.68%	0.41%	0.59%
Maximum discount (%)[a]	−0.52%	−0.67%	−0.75%

[a] Over previous 12 months.

Source: FactSet, as of 7 November 2018.

3.5. Total Costs of ETF Ownership

Exhibit 11 provides a summary of cost factors when considering ETFs and mutual funds. Some of these costs are explicit, whereas others are implicit and reflected in net investment returns. Both ETFs and mutual funds typically pay lower institutional commission rates for trades because of their asset size. ETF transaction costs are incurred at purchase and sale regardless of holding period, whereas other costs, such as management fees, increase as the holding period lengthens. Ongoing costs, such as management fees, portfolio turnover, and security lending proceeds, have a consistent impact on investment returns based on holding period. ETF trading costs, such as commissions and bid–ask spreads, are incurred only at purchase and sale, and their return impact diminishes over longer holding periods, whereas management fees and other ongoing costs become a more significant proportion of total costs. Tracking error can be considered a positive or negative implicit cost.

For active short-term ETF investors who trade frequently, the cost of entering and exiting their ETF positions (commissions, bid–ask spreads, premiums/discounts) is a far more significant consideration than management fees, tracking error, and other costs that accumulate over longer holding periods.

ETFs may trade at market prices higher (premiums) or lower (discounts) than NAV, which is based on closing prices for the fund's underlying securities. Premiums and discounts may reflect a lag in the timing of the underlying security valuations relative to current market conditions and can be considered positive costs (in the case of premiums) or negative costs (in the case of discounts).

There are additional implicit trading costs of fund management, such as portfolio turnover costs that are reflected in fund returns. These are incurred within the fund as the portfolio manager buys and sells securities to execute the investment strategy and manage fund cash flows. Portfolio turnover costs reduce returns and affect performance for all investors in the fund. Many ETFs are based on indexes that have lower portfolio turnover than actively managed funds. Taxable gains incurred upon sale can be considered positive costs for the investor, whereas taxable losses represent negative costs. Security lending income for the fund represents negative costs.

EXHIBIT 11   Cost Factor Comparison—ETFs and Mutual Funds

Fund Cost Factor	Function of Holding Period?	Explicit/Implicit	ETFs	Mutual Funds
Management fee	Y	E	X (often less)	X
Tracking error	Y	I	X (often less than comparable index mutual funds)	(index funds only)
Commissions	N	E	X (some free)	
Bid–ask spread	N	I	X	
Premium/discount to NAV	N	I	X	
Portfolio turnover (from investor flows and fund management)	Y	I	X (often less)	X
Taxable gains/losses to investors	Y	E	X (often less)	X
Security lending	Y	I	X (often more)	X

3.5.1. Trading Costs vs. Management Fees

To illustrate the effect of management fees versus trading costs, consider an investor who pays a commission of $10 on a $20,000 trade (0.05% each way) combined with a 0.15% bid–ask spread on purchase and sale. The round-trip trading cost is, therefore, 0.25% and is calculated as follows:

Round-trip trading cost (%) = (One-way commission % × 2) + (½ Bid–ask spread % × 2)
= (0.05% × 2) + (½ × 0.15% × 2)
= 0.10% + 0.15%
= 0.25%.

For a round-trip trade that happens over a year, 0.25% can be larger than the annual expense ratios of many ETFs. If held for less than a year, the trading costs may be far larger than the expense ratio paid on the ETF.

To see the impact of holding period, consider the 3-month versus 12-month versus 3-year holding period costs for an ETF with a 0.15% annual fee, one-way commissions of 0.05%, and a bid–ask spread of 0.15%. Holding period costs can be calculated as follows:

Holding period cost (%) = Round-trip trade cost (%) + Management fee for period (%).

Specific holding period costs can be calculated as follows:

3-month holding period cost (%) = 0.25% + 3/12 × 0.15% = 0.29%.
12-month holding period cost (%) = 0.25% + 12/12 × 0.15% = 0.40%.
3-year holding period cost (%) = 0.25% + 36/12 × 0.15% = 0.70%.

Exhibit 12 illustrates that for holding periods of 3 and 12 months, trading costs represent the largest proportion of annual holding costs (0.86% and 0.625%, respectively). Excluding the compounding effect, for a three-year holding period, management fees represent a much larger proportion of holding costs (0.64%).

EXHIBIT 12   ETF Management Fee and Trading Cost Comparison

Holding Period	3 Months	12 Months	3 Years
Commission	0.10%	0.10%	0.10%
Bid–Ask Spread	0.15%	0.15%	0.15%
Management Fee	0.0375%	0.15%	0.45%
Total	**0.29%**	**0.40%**	**0.70%**
Trading Costs % of Total	0.86%	0.625%	0.36%
Management Fees % of Total	0.14%	0.375%	0.64%

For broad-based, capitalization-weighted equity index ETFs that have the lowest fees, trading costs represent the largest cost in using an ETF. The longer an ETF is held, the greater the proportion of total costs represented by the management fee component.

Tactical traders will generally choose an ETF on the basis of its liquidity and trading costs (e.g., commissions, bid–ask spreads). In many cases, shorter-term tactical traders may use an ETF with a higher management fee but a tighter bid–ask spread and more active or continuous two-way trading flow to avoid incurring the capital commitment cost of a market maker or the cost of arbitrage for the ETF versus the underlying securities. The size of the management fee is typically a more significant consideration for longer-term buy-and-hold investors.

3.6. Risks

ETFs introduce several unique risks because of their structure, fund holdings, and underlying exposure.

3.6.1. Counterparty Risk

Some ETF legal structures involve dependence on a counterparty. A counterparty failure can put the investor's principal at risk of default or affect a portion of the assets via settlement risk. Likewise, counterparty activity can affect a fund's economic exposure. Therefore, investors should carefully assess counterparty risk.

Although exchange-traded notes (ETNs) trade on exchanges and have a creation/redemption mechanism, they are not truly funds because they do not hold underlying securities. ETNs are unsecured debt obligations of the institution that issues them and are structured as a promise to pay a pattern of returns based on the return of the stated index minus fund expenses. The issuer of the note takes responsibility for setting up the counterbalancing hedges it believes necessary to meet the obligations.

In the United States, ETNs are registered under the Securities Act of 1933 because they are general obligation debt securities of a bank and are not managed by an investment firm for a fee. Similar ETN structures exist in most markets where ETFs are listed.

ETNs have the largest potential counterparty risk of all exchange-traded products because they are unsecured, unsubordinated debt notes and, therefore, are subject to default by the ETN issuer. Theoretically, an ETN's counterparty risk is 100% in the event of an instantaneous default by the underwriting bank, and should an issuing bank declare bankruptcy, any ETNs issued by the bank would effectively be worthless. Because baskets of notes may be redeemed back to the issuer at NAV, however, it is likely that only an extremely rapid and catastrophic failure would take investors by surprise. This happened once, in 2008, with three Lehman Brothers–backed ETNs, but it has not happened since.

In the United States, some funds offering exposure to non-US-dollar currencies achieve this via offshore bank deposits. These funds bear default risk at the deposit-holding bank.

Because ETNs and deposit-based ETFs are backed by banks, their default risk can be monitored via the issuing bank's credit default swap (CDS) pricing.

The credit spreads for one-year CDSs by issuer at the end of October 2018 are shown in Exhibit 13.

EXHIBIT 13   One-Year CDS Spreads for ETN Issuers, 24 October 2018

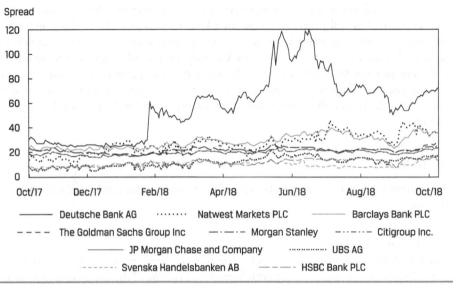

Spread

———— Deutsche Bank AG	········ Natwest Markets PLC	———— Barclays Bank PLC
– – – – The Goldman Sachs Group Inc	—·—·— Morgan Stanley	—··—··— Citigroup Inc.
———— JP Morgan Chase and Company	············ UBS AG	
·······- Svenska Handelsbanken AB	— — — - HSBC Bank PLC	

Source: Bloomberg.

The quoted CDS rates represent the cost to insure debt, in basis points per year; so, for example, investors could "insure" $1 million in Goldman Sachs bonds for just under $30,000 per year. Although the insurance rate should never be considered an estimate of actual default risk for a 12-month period, it does provide a reasonable gauge of the relative risk of the various issuers. In general, a one-year CDS rate above 5% should raise significant concerns among investors because it foretells a significant default risk in the year to come.

3.6.1.1. Settlement Risk

A fund that uses over-the-counter (OTC) derivatives, such as swaps, to gain market exposure has settlement risk; that is, mark-to-market (unrealized) gains are subject to counterparty default. Such ETFs include many European swap-based funds (or synthetic ETFs), funds using leverage (or geared funds), some currency funds, and some actively managed portfolios. To minimize settlement risk, OTC contracts are typically settled frequently—usually on a daily or weekly basis. This frequent settlement reduces the exposure the swap partners face if a company goes bankrupt, but there is a theoretical risk of counterparty default between settlement periods. In addition, the majority of the contract collateral is held in low-risk instruments, such as US T-bills, at a custodian bank.

Swap exposures are not unique to ETFs. Many mutual funds also use swaps and other derivatives to gain exposure. With ETFs, swap exposures are somewhat transparent because these holdings are disclosed daily by the ETF provider, although full information on counterparties and terms may not be disclosed.

3.6.1.2. Security Lending

ETF issuers (in addition to traditional mutual fund managers and institutions) lend their underlying securities to short sellers, earning additional income for the fund's investors.

Securities lent are generally overcollateralized, to 102% (domestic) or 105% (international), so that the risk from counterparty default is low. Cash collateral is usually reinvested into extremely short-term fixed-income securities with minimal associated risk. At the time of this chapter, there has been no instance of shareholder loss due to security lending in an ETF since ETF product inception in the early 1990s. A well-run security lending program can generate significant income for the ETF issuer, sometimes entirely offsetting the fund's operating expenses. Most ETF issuers credit all profits from this activity back to shareholders, although information about issuer lending programs is sometimes not well disclosed.

3.6.2. Fund Closures

Similar to mutual fund closures, ETF issuers may decide to close an ETF. In such a case, the fund generally sells its underlying positions and returns cash to investors. This activity can trigger capital gain events for investors and the need to find a replacement investment. Primary reasons for a fund to close include regulation, competition, and corporate activity. "Soft" closures—which do not involve an actual fund closing—include creation halts and changes in investment strategy.

3.6.2.1. Regulations

Security regulators can change the regulations governing certain types of funds, resulting in forced closure of those funds. For example, commodity futures are under constant regulatory scrutiny, and position limits can make it impossible for some funds to function. In 2018, the Israeli security regulator banned the ETN structure, forcing over 700 products to close and reopen as traditional ETFs.

3.6.2.2. Competition

Investors have benefited from a growing number of ETFs and increased competition. As ETFs proliferate, some funds fail to attract sufficient assets and are shut down by the ETF issuer. A fund's assets under management, in addition to those of any competitor, and the ETF's average daily liquidity are indications of market support. Low AUM and trading volumes over a significant period could indicate potential fund closure.

3.6.2.3. Corporate Actions

Mergers and acquisitions between ETF providers can prompt fund closures. When ETF families merge or are sold to other ETF providers, new ETF owners may close underperforming ETFs (from an asset-gathering perspective) and invest in new, higher-growth opportunities.

3.6.2.4. Creation Halts

ETN issuers may halt creations and redemptions when the issuer no longer wants to add debt to its balance sheet related to the index on which the ETN is based. A recent example of this occurred in September 2018, when ETN issuer UBS issued a "sales halt" for its ETRACS Monthly Pay 2xLeveraged Mortgage REIT ETN (MORL), effectively suspending further sales from its outstanding inventory of the ETN and preventing new shares from being created. When creations are halted, the ETN can trade at a substantial premium over fair value, as the arbitrage mechanism breaks down. In this case, MORL traded at a premium of more than 5%. Although all ETFs can theoretically close creations in extraordinary situations, in practice, it happens more commonly with ETNs.

3.6.2.5. *Change in Investment Strategy*

Some ETF issuers find it easier to repurpose a low-asset ETF from their existing lineup than to close one fund and open another. Issuers simply announce a change in the fund's underlying index—a common occurrence in the ETF industry. However, although most index changes result in small adjustments to an ETF's portfolio and economic exposure, these "soft closures" can result in a complete overhaul, changing exposures to countries, industries, or even asset classes.

3.6.3. Investor-Related Risk

ETFs provide access to sometimes complex asset classes and strategies. For all ETFs, it is important that investors understand the underlying exposure provided by the ETF; otherwise, ETFs may introduce risks to investors who do not fully understand them. For many investors, leveraged and inverse ETFs fall into this category by failing to meet investor expectations. Index methodology (e.g., constituent universe, weighting approach) and the fund's portfolio construction approach are central to understanding an ETF's underlying exposure and related performance.

Leveraged and inverse funds generally offer levered (or geared), inverse, or levered and inverse exposure to a given index and have a daily performance objective that is a multiple of index returns. These products must reset or adjust their exposure daily to deliver the target return multiple each day.

For example, consider a fund offering 300% exposure (3 times or 3×) to the FTSE 100 Index with a net asset value of £100. It uses swaps to get a notional exposure of £300. If the one-day FTSE 100 Index return is 5%, the £300 in exposure becomes £315 (a 5% increase), and the ETF's end-of-day NAV is £115: $100 \times (1 + 3 \times 5\%)$.

In order to deliver 300% of the index's daily performance for the following day, the ETF, now valued at £115, requires notional exposure of £345 for 3 times exposure. Because at the end of the day the ETF has only £315 in exposure, it must reset its exposure—in this case, increasing notional swap exposure by £30.

This example is outlined in Exhibit 14.

EXHIBIT 14   Example of Levered 3× ETF Exposure

	Index Level	One-Day Index Return (%)	3× ETF NAV (£)	Notional Swap Exposure (£)	3× Swap Exposure (£)	Swap Exposure Adjustment (£)
Day 1	100	—	100	300	300	0
Day 2	105	5%	115	315	345	30

If these ETFs are held for longer than a one-day period, the math of compounding and resetting exposure is such that an investor will not see the return multiple—for example, a 200% or −100% return in the case of a 2× ETF or inverse ETF, respectively—over his or her holding period.

Exhibit 15 presents a levered, inverse fund offering 2 times (−200%) exposure to the S&P 500 Index. The fund (−2× ETF) has a starting net asset value of $100 and uses swaps to obtain notional exposure.

EXHIBIT 15   Example of Levered and Inverse 2× ETF Daily Return vs. Holding Period Return

	Index Level	One-Day Index Return (%)	Index Period Return (%)	−2× ETF NAV	One-Day ETF Return (%)	2× ETF Holding Period Return (%)
Day 1	100	—		100	—	—
Day 2	110	10%	10%	80	−20%	−20%
Day 3	99	−10%	−1%	96	20%	−4%

Day 1: Both the index and the −2× fund are at a starting level of 100.
Day 2: The index increases to 110, a one-day return of 10%.

The −2× ETF daily return is calculated as follows:
= −2 × [(110 − 100)/100]
= −2 × (10%)
= −20%.

The −2× ETF NAV is calculated as follows:
= 100 × (1 + −0.2)
= 80.

Day 3: The index falls to 99, a one-day return of −10%.
The 2× ETF daily return is calculated as follows:
= −2 × [(99 − 110)/110]
= −2 × (−10%)
= 20%.

The −2× ETF NAV is calculated as follows:
= 80 × (1 + 0.2).
= 96.

This example shows the fund delivering its promised performance, −2× the daily index return, but it also shows how the return may not be what is naively expected over periods longer than a day.

Over the three days, the index return is −1%: (99 − 100)/100. A naive expectation might assume that over the same period the −2× ETF would return 2% (= −2 × −1%). Over the three days, the fund's actual return was −4%: (96 − 100)/100.

Because of these compounding effects in leveraged ETFs, the funds are generally not intended to be buy-and-hold products for more than a one-month horizon. If investors are planning to hold them long term, they must rebalance the funds periodically to maintain the desired net exposure.

4. ETFs IN PORTFOLIO MANAGEMENT

ETFs have become valuable tools for both institutional and retail investors. Available on a wide range of passive, systematic (rules-based) active, and traditional active strategies and segments of the stock, bond, and commodity markets, ETFs are used for both top-down (based on macro views) and bottom-up (focused on security selection) investment approaches. In addition to their use in implementing long-term strategic exposure to asset classes and risk factors, ETFs are used for tactical tilts, portfolio rebalancing, and risk management.

4.1. ETF Strategies

Most institutional asset managers and hedge fund managers, Registered Investment Advisers (RIAs), and financial advisers use ETFs for a wide range of strategies. These strategies serve many different investment objectives—some strategic, some tactical, and some dynamic, where the timing of changes is based on market conditions. Other ETF applications help in managing portfolios more efficiently and are used primarily for operational purposes. As we discuss the diverse set of strategies that can be found in an ETF structure, it is apparent that they are not easily classified as either active or passive. Except for core asset class and portfolio efficiency investment applications that use ETFs based on market-capitalization weighted benchmarks, almost all ETF-related strategies have some component of active investing, either within the ETF strategy or in the way the ETF is used.

Not all strategies are suitable in an ETF structure. The disclosure of holdings may be undesirable for an active manager who invests in less liquid securities or pursues a concentrated investment strategy or one that relies on an approach that cannot be easily described (such as a "black box" methodology) or disclosed without compromising the strategy. The liquidity of the underlying investments must also be high enough to accommodate daily creations and redemptions. Such factors as tax efficiency, low fees, and available product make ETFs competitive alternatives to traditional mutual funds and active managers. The primary applications in which ETFs are used include the following:

Portfolio efficiency: The use of ETFs to better manage a portfolio for efficiency or operational purposes. Applications include cash or liquidity management, rebalancing, portfolio completion, and active manager transition management.
Asset class exposure management: The use of ETFs to achieve or maintain core exposure to key asset classes, market segments, or investment themes on a strategic, tactical, or dynamic basis.
Active and factor investing: The use of ETFs to target specific active or factor exposures on the basis of an investment view or risk management need.

4.2. Efficient Portfolio Management

ETFs are useful tools for managing portfolio activity necessitated by cash flows and changes in external managers. In addition, ETFs can be used to easily accommodate portfolio rebalancing needs and unwanted gaps in portfolio exposure.

4.2.1. Portfolio Liquidity Management

One of the primary institutional applications of ETFs is cash flow management. ETFs can be used to invest excess cash balances quickly (known as cash equitization), enabling investors to remain fully invested in target benchmark exposure, thereby minimizing potential cash drag. Cash drag refers to a fund's mis-tracking relative to its index that results from holding uninvested cash. Managers may also use ETFs to transact small cash flows originating from dividends, income, or shareholder activity. Some portfolio managers hold small portions of their funds in ETFs in anticipation of future cash outflows. Transacting the ETF may incur lower trading costs and be easier operationally than liquidating underlying securities or requesting funds from an external manager.

4.2.2. Portfolio Rebalancing

Many investors rebalance portfolios on the basis of a specified time interval, usually at least quarterly, and some may adjust whenever the market value of a portfolio segment, or allocation, deviates from its target weight by a threshold, such as 2%. For tighter rebalancing thresholds and more frequent rebalancing time intervals, using liquid ETFs with tight bid–ask spreads allows the portfolio manager to execute the rebalance in a single ETF trade and ensures the portfolio remains fully invested according to its target weights. For investors who have the ability to sell short, reducing exposure associated with a rebalance can be done quickly using an ETF, and as the underlying securities are sold off, the short position can be covered.

4.2.3. Portfolio Completion Strategies

ETFs can also be used for completion strategies to fill a temporary gap in exposure to an asset class, sector, or investment theme or factor. Gaps may arise with changes in external managers or when an existing manager takes an active view that moves the portfolio out of a market segment to which the investor wishes to have continued exposure. The investor may want to retain the manager but use a tactical ETF strategy to maintain exposure to the desired market segment. If external managers are collectively underweighting or overweighting an industry or segment, such as technology, international small-cap stocks, or high-yield bonds, ETFs can be used to adjust exposure up or down to the desired level without making changes to underlying external manager allocations.

4.2.4. Transition Management

Transition management refers to the process of hiring and firing managers—or making changes to allocations with existing managers—while trying to keep target allocations in place. Since ETFs exist on most domestic, international, and global equity benchmarks, a newly appointed transition manager can invest in an ETF to maintain market exposure as she undergoes the process of selling the unwanted positions of the manager she is replacing (the terminated manager). The new transition manager can then take her time to invest in positions for her strategy and gradually reduce the ETF holding.

Asset owners can use ETFs to maintain desired market or asset class exposure in the absence of having an external manager in place. For example, if a fixed-income manager benchmarked to the Bloomberg Barclays US Aggregate Bond Index is terminated, the asset owner may wish to invest in the iShares Core US Aggregate Bond ETF (AGG) to maintain benchmark exposure until a replacement manager can be hired. In some cases, asset owners will "fund" new managers with ETF positions. The new manager will then sell off his ETF positions in the benchmark index as he invests in the underlying securities that meet his desired investment objectives and valuation criteria.

For very large asset owners, there are three potential drawbacks to using ETFs for portfolio management: (1) Given the asset owner size, they may be able to negotiate lower fees for a dedicated separately managed account (SMA) or find lower-cost commingled trust accounts that offer lower fees for large investors, (2) an SMA can be customized to the investment goals and needs of the investor, and (3) many regulators require large ETF holdings (as a percentage of ETF assets) to be disclosed to the public. This can detract from the flexibility in managing the ETF position and increase the cost of shifting investment holdings.

Exhibit 16 provides a summary of ETF portfolio efficiency applications, covering their roles in the portfolio, and examples by benchmark type. Applications include (1) transacting cash flows for benchmark exposure, (2) rebalancing to target asset class or risk factor weights, (3) filling exposure gaps in portfolio holdings of other strategies and funds, and (4) temporarily holding during transitions of strategies or managers.

EXHIBIT 16   ETF Portfolio Applications—Portfolio Efficiency

Portfolio Application	Role in Portfolio	Examples of ETFs by Benchmark Type
Cash Equitization/ Liquidity Management	Minimize cash drag by staying fully invested to benchmark exposure, transact small cash flows	Liquid ETFs benchmarked to asset category
Portfolio Rebalancing	Maintain exposure to target weights (asset classes, sub-asset classes)	Domestic equity, international equity, domestic fixed income
Portfolio Completion	Fill gaps in strategic exposure (countries, sectors, industries, themes, factors)	International small cap, Canada, bank loans, real assets, health care, technology, quality, ESG
Manager Transition Activity	Maintain interim benchmark exposure during manager transitions	ETFs benchmarked to new manager's target benchmark

4.3. Asset Class Exposure Management

Investors have used index exposure in core asset classes for decades, but one of the fastest-growing areas of ETF usage, especially by institutional investors, is fixed income. Since the financial crisis of 2008, the reduced capital available for banks (to participate in dealer bond markets) has contributed to greater use of fixed-income ETFs for core exposure. Except for the largest institutional investors, trading portfolios of bonds is much more difficult and expensive than similar portfolio trades in stocks. Fixed-income ETFs, especially those benchmarked to indexes containing corporates and high-yield securities, provide bond investors with a more efficient (lower cost, more continuous pricing, agency market) and liquid means of obtaining core fixed-income exposure.

4.3.1. Core Exposure to an Asset Class or Sub-asset Class
The primary strategic use of ETFs is to gain core index exposure to various asset classes and sub-asset classes. ETFs make doing so easy—across global equities, bonds, commodities, and currencies—and investors regularly use ETFs for broad portfolio diversification. Investors also use ETFs for more targeted strategic exposure to such segments as high-yield debt, bank

loans, and commodities (including crude oil, gold and other metals, and agricultural products).

A financial adviser can use ETFs to build a diversified portfolio on the basis of ETF recommendations from his or her firm's wealth management research team. Benchmarked to broad asset classes, portfolio choices for equity ETF exposure might include domestic large- and small-cap equities, sectors, such risk factors as dividend growth or momentum, industries, and international regions or countries with or without currency exposure. Choices for fixed-income ETF exposure might include government and corporate debt of various maturities, emerging market debt, bank loans, and possibly floating interest rate strategies. Commodity ETF exposure could include gold and other metals, broad commodity indexes, agriculture products, and oil. Similarly, brokerage firms and robo-advisers may offer more-automated solutions that select an ETF allocation based on the investor's risk and return profile. These firms offer a range of ETF investment choices from a preapproved product list to fit different asset class and risk factor categories.

4.3.2. Tactical Strategies

ETFs can also be used to implement market views and adjust portfolio risk on a more short-term, tactical basis. Some financial advisers and institutional investors allocate a portion of their portfolios for opportunistic trading based on their firm's (or strategist's) research or short-term outlook. Others make tactical adjustments in a range around target weights for asset classes or categories within an asset class. ETFs based on risk factors, country exposure, credit or duration exposure, currencies, or even volatility, crude oil, or metals can be used to express tactical views. To profit from an expected price decline, investors can sell ETFs short in a margin account.

Thematic ETFs are also used to implement investment views. Thematic ETFs hold stocks passively but allow investors to take an active view on a market segment they believe will deliver strong returns. These ETFs typically cover a narrow or niche area of the market not well represented by an industry. Examples include focused areas of technology, such as cybersecurity and robotics. Other themes accessed via ETFs are global infrastructure, regional banks, semiconductors, and gold mining. Generally, thematic ETFs are tactical tools that serve as substitutes for buying individual stocks or an industry ETF that is too broad to adequately represent the investor's investment view. Holdings may overlap with those of other ETFs or other portfolio positions but play a role when the investor wants to overweight this segment in the portfolio. Thematic ETFs should be evaluated similarly to stocks because they tend to have comparable levels of volatility and represent specialized active views.

ETFs that have the highest trading volumes in their asset class category are generally preferred for tactical trading applications, and the liquidity in many of the largest ETFs offered in each region makes them well suited for this purpose. Trading costs and liquidity, rather than management fees, are the important criteria in selecting an ETF for tactical adjustments. To identify the most commonly used ETFs for tactical strategies, one can look at the ratio of average dollar volume to average assets for the ETF.

Exhibit 17 provides a summary of ETF asset class exposure applications, covering their roles in the portfolio, categories of use, and examples by benchmark type. These applications relate to using ETFs for strategic, tactical, and dynamic asset class exposure.

EXHIBIT 17   ETF Portfolio Applications—Asset Class Exposure Management

Portfolio Application	Category	Role in Portfolio	Examples of ETFs by Benchmark Type
Core asset class or market	Strategic or tactical	Core long-term, strategic weighting Tactical tilt to enhance returns or modify risk Ease of access vs. buying underlying securities	Domestic equity, international equity, fixed income, commodities
Equity style, country, or sector; fixed income or commodity segment	Strategic or tactical	Tactical tilt to enhance returns or modify risk depending on short-term views Hedge index exposure of active stocks or bond strategy Ease of access vs. buying underlying securities	Value, growth, Japanese, Chinese, UK, Canadian, or Mexican equities; corporate or high-yield debt; gold; oil; agriculture
Equity sector, industry, investment theme	Dynamic or tactical	Tactical or dynamic active tilt to enhance returns or modify risk Efficient implementation of a thematic/industry vs. single-stock view Capture performance on an emerging theme or innovation not reflected in industry categories	Technology, financials, oil and gas, biotech, infrastructure, robotics, gold mining, buybacks, internet innovation, cybersecurity

4.4. Active and Factor Investing

In the mid-2000s, quantitative or rules-based strategies became available in ETFs. These strategies had "active" weights different from market capitalization and were able to disclose holdings because the stock selection and weighting was not chosen by a discretionary portfolio manager but, rather, by a set of quantitative rules, disclosed in the index methodology.

The first smart beta ETFs were indexes weighted by company fundamentals, such as dividends, or quantitatively screened on stock features. Although adoption was initially slow, institutional investors and RIAs now use smart beta ETF strategies to gain systematic active exposure to persistent common return drivers or factors. Global assets in smart beta equity funds, including both single-factor and multi-factor strategies, now represent approximately 20% of ETF assets.

Active ETFs, where the investment strategy is benchmarked but managed with discretion, have also gained assets, especially in fixed income, but they still represent a relatively small percentage of global ETF assets, at 2%–3%.

4.4.1. Factor (smart beta) ETFs

Factor ETFs are usually benchmarked to an index created with predefined rules for screening and/or weighting constituent holdings. The strategy index rules are structured around return drivers or factors, such as value, dividend yield, earnings or dividend growth, quality, stock volatility, or momentum. Some of these factors, such as size, value, and momentum, have academic support as equity risk premiums that may be rewarded over the long term. Within each single factor category, a range of offerings from competing ETF providers exists, differentiated by the criteria used to represent the factor and the weights applied to constituent holdings (equal, factor, or cap weighted). Their application is typically in providing longer-term, buy-and-hold exposure to a desired factor based on an investment view. Factor ETFs can be used to add risk factor allocations that might not be present in a benchmark or portfolio—for example, adding an equity index ETF with stocks screened for quality to add desired exposure to a quality factor.

Multi-factor ETFs that combine several factors also exist. They may adjust their weights dynamically as market opportunities and risk change. In a multi-factor ETF, strategy design involves factor selection, factor strategy construction, and a weighting scheme across factors that is managed over time. A multi-factor approach typically has lower return volatility than a single-factor approach over time but may also have less return potential for investors who want to capitalize on factor timing.

The success of active strategy ETFs is related to (1) whether the factor, as represented by a target benchmark factor index, performs well relative to expectations and (2) how effective the selected ETF is at delivering the benchmark factor return. Just as with traditional active investing, the success of active investing with ETFs depends on the skill of the ETF portfolio manager as well as the end investor's decision to undertake the investment strategy.

4.4.2. Risk Management

Some smart beta ETFs are constructed to deliver lower or higher risk than that of their asset class benchmark. For example, low-volatility factor ETFs select stocks on the basis of their relative return volatility and seek to represent a portfolio that offers a lower or target volatility return profile. These low-volatility rules-based factor ETFs have gained assets within each segment of the global equity market (domestic, developed international, and emerging markets) as investors have moved to lower volatility in portfolios. Other ETFs based on the beta characteristics of the constituent stocks can be used to adjust the portfolio's beta profile to desired levels.

ETFs are also used to manage other portfolio risks, such as currency and duration risk. ETFs that provide international exposure with a hedge on all or part of the associated currency risk are available. With respect to interest rate risk management, several smart beta fixed-income ETFs hold long positions in corporate or high-yield bonds and hedge out the duration risk of these bonds with futures or short positions in government bonds. These ETFs enable investors to add a position to their portfolio that seeks returns from taking credit risk with minimal sensitivity to movements in interest rates. Active investors with a negative macro view can use inverse asset class or factor ETF exposure to temporarily reduce benchmark holding risk. Doing so allows them to implement a macro view on a short-term basis and minimize turnover in underlying portfolio holdings.

4.4.3. Alternatively Weighted ETFs

ETFs that weight their constituents by means other than market capitalization, such as equal weighting or weightings based on fundamentals, can also be used to implement investment views—for example, ETFs that weight constituent stocks on the basis of their dividend yields. These ETFs select or overweight stocks with higher dividend yields, subject to other fundamental criteria or constraints, and are used by investors seeking income-generating strategies.

4.4.4. Discretionary Active ETFs

The largest active ETFs are in fixed income, where passive management is much less prominent than in equities. The PIMCO Active Bond ETF (BOND) launched in 2012 with an investment objective similar to that of the world's largest mutual fund at that time, the PIMCO Total Return Fund. Shorter-maturity, actively managed ETFs are also available in fixed income. Other active ETFs include exposure to senior bank loans, floating rate debt, and mortgage securities. Active equity ETFs have also been launched in areas of the technology industry.

"Liquid alternative" ETFs are based on strategy indexes that attempt to deliver absolute return performance and/or risk diversification of stock and bond holdings. Some of the first liquid alternative ETFs used rules-based strategies to replicate broad hedge fund indexes. Other strategy indexes offer transparent, rules-based, "hedge fund–like" strategies in specific types of alternatives. Such strategies include long–short, managed futures, private equity, and merger arbitrage.

4.4.5. Dynamic Asset Allocation and Multi-asset Strategies

ETF availability across a wide range of equity and bond risk exposures has fostered greater use of dynamic, top-down investment strategies based on return and risk forecasts. Asset managers, hedge funds, and asset owners have increasingly used ETFs for discretionary asset allocation or global macro strategies. Dynamic asset allocation ETF strategies are also available in commodities. Although some strategies allocate holdings on the basis of their relative risk contribution and others are return focused, all involve adjustments back to target weights, as defined by a dynamic investment process. Some pension and sovereign wealth funds implement these strategies in house, whereas other investors hire asset managers that offer multi-asset strategies. Implementation is done using ETFs, along with futures and swaps where available and when they are more efficient to trade.

Proper use of an active or factor strategy ETF requires investors to research and assess the index construction methodology and performance history and to ensure consistency with their investment view.

Exhibit 18 provides a summary of active and factor ETF portfolio applications, covering their roles in the portfolio, categories of use, and examples by benchmark type. These applications relate to ETFs as alternatives to other fund products, such as active mutual funds. In these cases, ETF evaluation is based on features of the investment approach, holdings, cost, risk, and return potential, as well as the impact to the portfolio's overall risk and return.

EXHIBIT 18   ETF Portfolio Applications—Active and Factor Investing

Portfolio Application	Category	Role in Portfolio	Examples of ETFs by Benchmark Type
Factor exposure	Strategic, dynamic, or tactical	Capture risk premium for one or more factors driving returns or risk Overweight or underweight depending on factor return or risk outlook Seek to capture alpha from rules-based screening and rebalancing (systematic active)	Quality, dividend growth, value, momentum, low volatility, liquidity screen, multi-factor
Risk management	Dynamic or tactical	Adjust equity beta, duration, credit, or currency risk	Currency-hedged, low-volatility, or downside-risk-managed ETFs
Leveraged and inverse exposure	Tactical	Access leveraged or short exposure for short-term tilts or risk management Limit losses on shorting to invested funds	ETFs representing asset classes, countries, or industries with leveraged or inverse daily return targets
Alternative weighting	Strategic, dynamic, or tactical	Seek outperformance from weighting based on one or more fundamental factors Balance or manage risk of security holdings	ETFs weighted by fundamentals, dividends, or risk; equal-weighted ETFs
Active strategies within an asset class	Strategic	Access discretionary active management in an ETF structure	ETFs from reputable fixed income or equity managers with active approach or theme
Dynamic asset allocation and multi-asset strategies	Dynamic or tactical	Seek returns from active allocation across asset classes or factors based on return or risk outlook Invest in a multi-asset-class strategy in single product	ETFs that allocate across asset categories or investment themes based on quantitative or fundamental factors

5. SUMMARY

In this chapter, we have examined important considerations for ETF investors, including how ETFs work and trade, tax efficient attributes, and key portfolio uses. The following is a summary of key points:

- ETFs rely on a creation/redemption mechanism that allows for the continuous creation and redemption of ETF shares.
- The only investors who can create or redeem new ETF shares are a special group of institutional investors called authorized participants.
- ETFs trade on both the primary market (directly between APs and issuers) and on the secondary markets (exchange-based or over-the-counter trades like listed equity).
- End investors trade ETFs on the secondary markets, like stocks.
- Holding period performance deviations (tracking differences) are more useful than the standard deviation of daily return differences (tracking error).
- ETF tracking differences from the index occur for the following reasons:
  - fees and expenses,
  - representative sampling/optimization,
  - use of depositary receipts and other ETFs,
  - index changes,
  - fund accounting practices,
  - regulatory and tax requirements, and
  - asset manager operations.
- ETFs are generally taxed like the securities they hold, with some nuances:
  - ETFs are more tax fair than traditional mutual funds, because portfolio trading is generally not required when money enters or exits an ETF.
  - Owing to the creation/redemption process, ETFs can be more tax efficient than mutual funds.
  - ETF issuers can redeem out low-cost-basis securities to minimize future taxable gains.
  - Local markets have unique ETF taxation issues that should be considered.
- ETF bid–ask spreads vary by trade size and are usually published for smaller trade sizes. They are tightest for ETFs that are very liquid and have continuous two-way order flow. For less liquid ETFs, the following factors can determine the quoted bid–ask spread of an ETF trade:
  - Creation/redemption costs, brokerage and exchange fees
  - Bid–ask spread of underlying securities held by the ETF
  - Risk of hedging or carry positions by liquidity provider
  - Market makers' target profit spread
- ETF bid–ask spreads on fixed income relative to equity tend to be wider because the underlying bonds trade in dealer markets and hedging is more difficult. Spreads on ETFs holding international stocks are tightest when the underlying security markets are open for trading.
- ETF premiums and discounts refer to the difference between the exchange price of the ETF and the fund's calculated NAV, based on the prices of the underlying securities and weighted by the portfolio positions at the start of each trading day. Premiums and discounts can occur because NAVs are based on the last traded prices, which may be observed at a time lag to the ETF price, or because the ETF is more liquid and more reflective of current information and supply and demand than the underlying securities in rapidly changing markets.
- Costs of ETF ownership may be positive or negative and include both explicit and implicit costs. The main components of ETF cost are
  - the fund management fee;

- tracking error;
- portfolio turnover;
- trading costs, such as commissions, bid–ask spreads, and premiums/discounts;
- taxable gains/losses; and
- security lending.

- Trading costs are incurred when the position is entered and exited. These one-time costs decrease as a portion of total holding costs over longer holding periods and are a more significant consideration for shorter-term tactical ETF traders.
- Other costs, such as management fees and portfolio turnover, increase as a proportion of overall cost as the investor holding period lengthens. These costs are a more significant consideration for longer-term buy-and-hold investors.
- ETFs are different from exchange-traded notes, although both use the creation/redemption process.
  - Exchange-traded notes carry unique counterparty risks of default.
  - Swap-based ETFs may carry counterparty risk.
  - ETFs, like mutual funds, may lend their securities, creating risk of counterparty default.
  - ETF closures can create unexpected tax liabilities.

- ETFs are used for core asset class exposure, multi-asset, dynamic, and tactical strategies based on investment views or changing market conditions; for factor or smart beta strategies with a goal to improve return or modify portfolio risk; and for portfolio efficiency applications, such as rebalancing, liquidity management, completion strategies, and transitions.
- ETFs are useful for investing cash inflows, as well as for raising proceeds to provide for client withdrawals. ETFs are used for rebalancing to target asset class weights and for "completion strategies" to fill a temporary gap in an asset class category, sector, or investment theme or when external managers are underweight. When positions are in transition from one external manager to another, ETFs are often used as the temporary holding and may be used to fund the new manager.
- All types of investors use ETFs to establish low-cost core exposure to asset classes, equity style benchmarks, fixed-income categories, and commodities.
- For more tactical investing, thematic ETFs are used in active portfolio management and represent narrow or niche areas of the equity market not well represented by industry or sector ETFs.
- Systematic, active strategies that use rules-based benchmarks for exposure to such factors as size, value, momentum, quality, or dividend tilts or combinations of these factors are frequently implemented with ETFs.
- Multi-asset and global asset allocation or macro strategies that manage positions dynamically as market conditions change are also areas where ETFs are frequently used.
- Proper utilization requires investors to carefully research and assess the ETF's index construction methodology, costs, risks, and performance history.

PRACTICE PROBLEMS

1. Which of the following statements regarding exchange-traded funds (ETFs) is *correct*?
   ETFs:
   A. disclose their holdings on a quarterly basis.
   B. trade in both primary and secondary markets.
   C. offer a creation/redemption mechanism that allows any investor to create or redeem shares.

2. The list of securities that a particular ETF wants to own, which is disclosed daily by all ETFs, is referred to as the:
   A. creation unit.
   B. creation basket.
   C. redemption basket.

3. When an authorized participant transacts to create or redeem ETF shares, the related costs are ultimately borne:
   A. solely by the ETF sponsor.
   B. solely by the AP.
   C. proportionally by all existing ETF shareholders.

4. Assuming arbitrage costs are minimal, which of the following is *most likely* to occur when the share price of an ETF is trading at a premium to its intraday NAV?
   A. New ETF shares will be created by the ETF sponsor.
   B. Redemption baskets will be received by APs from the ETF sponsor.
   C. Retail investors will exchange baskets of securities that the ETF tracks for creation units.

5. An ETF's reported tracking error is typically measured as the:
   A. standard deviation of the difference in daily returns between an ETF and its benchmark.
   B. difference in annual return between an ETF and its benchmark over the past 12 months.
   C. annualized standard deviation of the difference in daily returns between an ETF and its benchmark.

6. To best assess an ETF's performance, which reflects the impact of portfolio rebalancing expenses and other fees, an investor should:
   A. review daily return differences between the ETF and its benchmark.
   B. perform a rolling return assessment between the ETF and its benchmark.
   C. compare the ETF's annual expense ratio with that of other ETFs in its asset class category.

7. An ETF's tracking error, as traditionally reported, indicates to investors:
   A. whether the ETF is underperforming or outperforming its underlying index.
   B. the magnitude by which an ETF's returns deviate from its benchmark over time.
   C. the distribution of differences in daily returns between the ETF and its benchmark.

8. For a typical ETF, which of the following sources of tracking error is *most likely* to be the smallest contributor to tracking error?
   A. Representative sampling
   B. Fees and expenses incurred by the ETF
   C. Changes to the underlying index securities

9. Which of the following statements relating to capital gains in ETFs and mutual funds is *correct*?
   A. ETFs tend to distribute less in capital gains than mutual funds do.
   B. Mutual funds may elect not to distribute all realized capital gains in a given year.
   C. The selling of ETF shares by some investors may create capital gains that affect the remaining ETF investors in terms of taxes.

10. Which of the following statements regarding distributions made by ETFs is *correct*?
    A. Return-of-capital (ROC) distributions are generally not taxable.
    B. ETFs generally reinvest any dividends received back into the ETF's holdings.
    C. A dividend distribution is a distribution paid to investors in excess of an ETF's earnings.

11. Such factors as regulations, competition, and corporate actions relate to:
    A. fund-closure risk.
    B. counterparty risk.
    C. expectation-related risk.

12. John Smith has invested in an inverse ETF. Smith is a novice investor who is not familiar with inverse ETFs, and therefore, he is unsure how the ETF will perform because of a lack of understanding of the ETF's risk and return characteristics. This risk is *best* described as:
    A. counterparty risk.
    B. holdings-based risk.
    C. expectation-related risk.

13. Investors buying ETFs:
    A. incur management fees that decrease with the length of the holding period.
    B. are assured of paying a price equal to the NAV if they purchase shares at the market close.
    C. incur trading costs in the form of commissions and bid–ask spreads at the time of purchase.

14. Consider an ETF with the following trading costs and management fees:
    • Annual management fee of 0.40%
    • Round-trip trading commissions of 0.55%
    • Bid–offer spread of 0.20% on purchase and sale
    Excluding compound effects, the expected total holding-period cost for investing in the ETF over a nine-month holding period is *closest* to:
    A. 1.05%.
    B. 1.15%.
    C. 1.25%.

15. The bid–ask spread for very liquid, high-volume ETFs will be *least* influenced by the:
    A. market maker's desired profit spread.
    B. creation/redemption fees and other direct costs.
    C. likelihood of receiving an offsetting ETF order in a short time frame.

16. Factor (smart beta) strategy ETFs are *least likely* to be used by investors:
    A. to modify portfolio risk.
    B. for tactical trading purposes.
    C. to seek outperformance versus a benchmark.

17. Which of the following statements regarding applications of ETFs in portfolio management is correct?
    A. Equity ETFs tend to be more active than fixed-income ETFs.
    B. The range of risk exposures available in the futures market is more diverse than that available in the ETF space.
    C. ETFs that have the highest trading volumes in their asset class category are generally preferred for tactical trading applications.

The following information relates to questions 18–23

Howie Rutledge is a senior portfolio strategist for an endowment fund. Rutledge meets with recently hired junior analyst Larry Stosur to review the fund's holdings.

Rutledge asks Stosur about the mechanics of exchange-traded funds (ETFs). Stosur responds by making the following statements:

Statement 1. Unlike mutual fund shares that can be shorted, ETF shares cannot be shorted.
Statement 2. In the ETF creation/redemption process, the authorized participants (APs) absorb the costs of transacting securities for the ETF's portfolio.
Statement 3. If ETF shares are trading at a discount to NAV and arbitrage costs are sufficiently low, APs will buy the securities in the creation basket and exchange them for ETF shares from the ETF sponsor.

Rutledge notes that one holding, ETF 1, is trading at a premium to its intraday NAV. He reviews the ETF's pricing and notes that the premium to the intraday NAV is greater than the expected arbitrage costs.

Stosur is evaluating three ETFs for potential investment. He notes that the ETFs have different portfolio characteristics that are likely to affect each ETF's tracking error. A summary of the characteristics for the ETFs is presented in Exhibit 1.

EXHIBIT 1 ETF Characteristics Affecting Tracking Error

	ETF 2	ETF 3	ETF 4
Portfolio Construction Approach	Full Replication	Representative Sampling	Full Replication
Type of Foreign Holdings	Local shares	ADRs*	ADRs*
Engagement in Securities Lending	Yes	Yes	No

*ADRs are American Depositary Receipts.

Rutledge and Stosur discuss the factors that influence ETF bid–ask spreads. Stosur tells Rutledge that quoted bid–ask spreads for a particular transaction size are (1) negatively related to the amount of the ongoing order flow in the ETF, (2) positively related to the costs and risks for the ETF liquidity provider, and (3) positively related to the amount of competition among market makers for the ETF.

As ETF shares may trade at prices that are different from the NAV, Rutledge examines selected data in Exhibit 2 for three ETFs that might have this problem.

EXHIBIT 2   Selected Data on ETFs

	ETF 5	ETF 6	ETF 7
Percentage of Foreign Holdings	10%	50%	90%
Trading Frequency	High	Low	Low

Rutledge considers a new ETF investment for the fund. He plans to own the ETF for nine months. The ETF has the following trading costs and management fees:

- Annual management fee of 0.32%
- Round-trip trading commissions of 0.20%
- Bid–offer spread of 0.10% on purchase and sale

Rutledge asks Stosur to compute the expected total holding period cost for investing in the ETF.

18. Which of Stosur's statements regarding ETF mechanics is correct?
    A. Statement 1
    B. Statement 2
    C. Statement 3

19. Given the current pricing of ETF 1, the *most likely* transaction to occur is that:
    A. new ETF shares will be created by the APs.
    B. redemption baskets will be received by APs from the ETF sponsor.
    C. retail investors will exchange baskets of securities that the ETF tracks for creation units.

20. Which ETF in Exhibit 1 is *most likely* to have the lowest tracking error?
    A. ETF 2
    B. ETF 3
    C. ETF 4

21. Stosur's statement about quoted bid–ask spreads is *incorrect* with respect to the:
    A. amount of the ongoing order flow in the ETF.
    B. costs and risks for the ETF liquidity providers.
    C. amount of competition among market makers for the ETF.

22. Which ETF in Exhibit 2 is *most likely* to trade at the largest premium or discount relative to NAV?
    A. ETF 5
    B. ETF 6
    C. ETF 7

23. Excluding the compounding effect, the expected total holding period cost for investing in the ETF over a nine-month holding period is *closest* to:

    A. 0.54%.

    B. 0.62%.

    C. 0.64%.

CHAPTER 10

CASE STUDY IN PORTFOLIO MANAGEMENT: INSTITUTIONAL

Gabriel Petre, CFA

LEARNING OUTCOMES

The candidate should be able to:

- discuss tools for managing portfolio liquidity risk;
- discuss capture of the illiquidity premium as an investment objective;
- analyze asset allocation and portfolio construction in relation to liquidity needs and risk and return requirements and recommend actions to address identified needs;
- analyze actions in asset manager selection with respect to the Code of Ethics and Standards of Professional Conduct;
- analyze the costs and benefits of derivatives versus cash market techniques for establishing or modifying asset class or risk exposures;
- demonstrate the use of derivatives overlays in tactical asset allocation and rebalancing.

1. INTRODUCTION

The development of a strategic asset allocation (SAA) for long-horizon institutional investors like university endowments raises special challenges. These include supporting spending policies while ensuring the long-term sustainability of the endowment and establishing optimal exposure to illiquid investment strategies in the context of a diversified portfolio.

Large university endowments typically have significant exposure to illiquid asset classes. The exposure to illiquid asset classes impacts the portfolio's overall liquidity profile and

Portfolio Management, Second Edition, by Gabriel Petre, CFA. Copyright © 2019 by CFA Institute.

requires a comprehensive liquidity management approach to ensure liquidity needs can be met in a timely fashion.[1] In addition, capital market conditions and asset prices change, resulting in a need to change asset allocation exposures and/or rebalance the portfolio to maintain a profile close to the strategic asset allocation.

Derivatives are often used by institutions to manage liquidity needs and implement asset allocation changes. The cash-efficient nature of derivatives and their high levels of liquidity in many markets make them suitable tools for portfolio rebalancing, tactical exposure changes, and satisfying short-term liquidity needs—all while maintaining desired portfolio exposures.

This case study explores these issues from the perspective of a large university endowment undertaking a review of its asset allocation and then implementing proposed allocation changes and a tactical overlay program. Rebalancing needs for the endowment arise as market moves result in drift of the endowment's asset allocation.

The case is divided into two major sections. The first section addresses issues relating to asset allocation and liquidity management. The case introduces a framework to support management of liquidity and cash needs in an orderly and timely manner while avoiding disruption to underlying managers and potentially capturing an illiquidity premium. Such concepts as time-to-cash tables and liquidity budgets are explored in detail. Aspects relating to rebalancing and maintaining a risk profile similar to the portfolio's strategic asset allocation over time are also covered.

The second section explores the use of derivatives in portfolio construction from a tactical asset allocation (TAA) overlay and rebalancing perspective. The suitability of futures, total return swaps, and exchange-traded funds (ETFs) is discussed based on their characteristics, associated costs, and desired portfolio objectives. The case also presents a cost–benefit analysis of derivatives and cash markets for implementing rebalancing decisions.

2. BACKGROUND: LIQUIDITY MANAGEMENT

For an institutional investor, such as an endowment or a pension fund, liquidity management refers to the set of policies and practices that ensure the portfolio complies with investment policy yet can meet cash outflow needs in a timely and orderly manner without incurring excessive costs. Optimal liquidity management helps ensure that distressed sales of illiquid assets are avoided, especially in weak market conditions, and that the portfolio can benefit from the expected illiquidity premium associated with long-term private market allocations.

The importance of liquidity management was emphasized in the 2008 global financial crisis when many institutional investors with significant allocations to illiquid asset classes and regular cash outflow requirements struggled to meet these outflows.

During this time, public markets experienced significant losses, liquidity conditions deteriorated, and distributions from many private market investments stopped. For many university endowments, another source of liquidity—donations—also dropped significantly, further amplifying liquidity issues. In some cases, endowments were forced to liquidate securities at steep discounts, drastically cut funding for some programs dependent on endowment distributions, and/or borrow funds collateralized by the endowment, increasing leverage and the risk profile of the portfolio.

---

[1]In this context, "liquidity" refers to the ability to exchange assets into cash for an expected value within a known time frame.

Institutional investors have several important "tools" at their disposal to manage a portfolio's liquidity risk. These include:

- liquidity profiling and time-to-cash tables,
- rebalancing and commitment strategies,
- stress testing analyses, and
- derivatives.

2.1. Liquidity Profiling and Time-to-Cash

For any investor, the assessment of liquidity needs starts with identifying potential cash inflows and cash outflows for a defined investment horizon. In the case of endowments, cash outflows include distributions to the university and meeting capital call requirements for illiquid investments (e.g., real assets, private equity, hedge funds, and structured products). Once the sources and uses of cash have been identified, the institutional investor establishes the need for liquidity and the desired liquidity maturity profile for the overall portfolio. As part of this process, a **liquidity classification schedule (time-to-cash table)** is created and an overall **liquidity budget** is defined.[2] The liquidity classification schedule defines portfolio categories (or "buckets") based on the estimated time it would take in the normal course of business to convert assets in that particular category into cash. The liquidity budget assigns portfolio weights considered acceptable to each liquidity classification in the time-to-cash table and establishes a liquidity benchmark for the portfolio construction process.

An example of a time-to-cash table is provided in Exhibit 1. It defines liquidity classifications based on the time expected to liquidate an investment without liquidation having a significant impact on market conditions and the resulting sale price for the investment. The impact on market conditions is based on the expected market price immediately before and after trading if the sell order was executed. In the case of investments managed by third-party managers, the time-to-cash also depends on the contractual terms governing the type of investment vehicle used. Typically, private investments requiring more than one year to exit are viewed as illiquid. In the case of hedge funds, contractual terms (e.g., lockups, notification periods, withdrawal windows) vary based on the manager and underlying strategy. A manager's ability to deny withdrawal requests during stress periods ("to activate gates") to protect fund investors and prevent forced liquidations will impact time-to-cash.

EXHIBIT 1   Time-to-Cash Table and Liquidity Budget

Time to Cash	Liquidity Classification	Liquidity Budget (% of portfolio)
<1 Week	Highly Liquid	At Least 10%
<1 Quarter	Liquid	At Least 35%
<1 Year	Semi-Liquid	At Least 50%
>1 Year	Illiquid	Up to 50%

The granularity of a time-to-cash table may vary to include monthly or semi-annual categories depending on the investor's liquidity preferences, liquidity needs, and other

---

[2]See also Russell Investments (2013).

circumstances. The core principle is to identify liquidity categories relevant to the types of cash outflows the investor will face and to match overall portfolio characteristics with liquidity needs through the design of the resulting asset allocation. The next step is to define an overall liquidity budget specifying portfolio allocations for the different time-to-cash buckets (as shown in the last column of Exhibit 1).[3] In the case of highly liquid, liquid, and semi-liquid categories, minimum portfolio weights are identified. For the illiquid category, a maximum portfolio weight is identified.

The liquidity budget reflects the acceptable liquidity requirements that the portfolio must meet, even in a liquidity stress scenario. The results of stress test analyses are therefore important inputs in developing the liquidity budget.

To operationalize the concepts represented in the liquidity budget, the institutional investor does an analysis of the underlying liquidity characteristics of the portfolio investments and monitors these characteristics over time. The analysis should look through the broad definition of asset classes to the underlying investments used for exposure. Different investments within the same asset class (such as public equities) may have very different liquidity profiles. Commingled funds (funds that are pooled and managed together in a single account) may be less liquid than exchange-traded funds (ETFs) or mutual funds and may have different liquidity profiles than separate accounts. Furthermore, there could be differences in the liquidity profile of similar investment vehicles in the same asset class depending on the underlying strategy used by the investment manager. For example, a commingled fund following a concentrated, small-cap active strategy in emerging market equities may offer investors only quarterly liquidity as compared to a commingled fund investing in large-cap emerging market equities, which may offer monthly or weekly liquidity. For these reasons, it is appropriate to conduct liquidity analysis on a bottom-up basis for each investment, aggregate at the portfolio level, and monitor changes over time to keep the portfolio within liquidity budget parameters. An example of liquidity profiling for a portfolio's underlying investments is shown in Exhibit 2. The portfolio example uses investments in separate accounts, commingled funds, futures, ETFs, and active managers to achieve its asset class exposure to both public and private markets.

EXHIBIT 2   Liquidity Profiling for a Portfolio

| Asset Class | Asset Class Allocation (% of portfolio) | Investment Allocation (% of overall portfolio) | Investment Vehicle | Liquidity Classification | | | |
				Highly Liquid	Liquid	Semi-Liquid	Illiquid
Cash	1%	1%	Separate Account	100%	0%	0%	0%
Fixed Income	14%	5%	Separate Account	100%	0%	0%	0%
		8%	Commingled Fund	100%	0%	0%	0%
		1%	Futures	100%	0%	0%	0%

---

[3]Mercer (2015).

Asset Class	Asset Class Allocation (% of portfolio)	Investment Allocation (% of overall portfolio)	Investment Vehicle	Liquidity Classification			
				Highly Liquid	Liquid	Semi-Liquid	Illiquid
Domestic Equity	17%	8%	Commingled Fund	0%	50%	50%	0%
		8%	Separate Account	0%	100%	0%	0%
		1%	Futures	100%	0%	0%	0%
International Developed Equity	10%	6%	Commingled Fund	0%	50%	30%	20%
		4%	Separate Account	0%	80%	20%	0%
Emerging Market Equity	12%	9%	Commingled Fund	0%	75%	25%	0%
		3%	ETF	100%	0%	0%	0%
Private Equity	18%	18%	Funds 1–85	0%	0%	0%	100%
Real Assets	13%	4%	Funds 1–8	0%	0%	75%	25%
		6%	Funds 9–33	0%	0%	0%	100%
		3%	Funds 34–50	0%	0%	20%	80%
Diversifying Strategies	15%	4%	Funds 1–5	0%	0%	100%	0%
		6%	Funds 6–11	0%	25%	25%	50%
		5%	Funds 12–19	0%	0%	75%	25%
Overall Portfolio	**100%**	**100%**		**19%**	**26%**	**22%**	**33%**

2.2. Rebalancing, Commitments

The discussion so far has focused on liquidity management and the ability of an institutional portfolio to meet cash outflows in an orderly manner as they come due. Another consideration is the impact of changes in the liquidity profile on the overall risk of the investment portfolio and the ability to keep the portfolio close to desired risk targets. Illiquid assets carry extremely high rebalancing costs. Because asset liquidity tends to decrease in times of market stress, it is important to have sufficient liquid assets and rebalancing mechanisms in place. This will ensure the portfolio's risk profile remains within acceptable risk targets and does not "drift" as the relative valuations of different asset classes fluctuate during stress periods. Rebalancing mechanisms include the following:

Systematic rebalancing policies. Rebalancing disciplines, such as calendar rebalancing and percent-range rebalancing, are intended to control risk relative to the strategic asset allocation. In these cases, pre-specified tolerance bands for asset class weights are used. The size or width of the bands should consider the underlying volatility of each investment category to minimize transaction costs.

This means more-volatile investment categories should usually have wider rebalancing bands. Transaction costs, correlations between asset classes, and investor risk tolerance are other factors that may influence the size of the band selected.

Automatic adjustment mechanisms. These are mechanisms designed to maintain a stable risk profile when exposure drifts from targeted exposure. An example is using adjustments to a public market allocation that is correlated to a private market allocation to rebalance private market risk. This approach uses liquid public assets as a proxy for illiquid private assets. For example, assume private equity investments have an equity beta of 1. In a situation where the allocation to private equity increases by 1% versus the target, the allocation to public equities would automatically be adjusted down by 1% to maintain a stable systematic market risk profile. Note, however, that although systematic market risk is unchanged, illiquidity risk of the portfolio is now higher. Alternatively, the adjustment could be further refined to maintain a constant equity beta, assuming private equity has a beta to public equities of greater than 1 (caused by leverage, for example).[4] Similar public market proxies can be used to represent private real estate, infrastructure, or other illiquid instruments based on their underlying risk characteristics.

Multi-year funding strategies for private markets that incorporate a steady pace of commitments to reach a target allocation and/or to keep the allocation close to target over time are other means to ensure the portfolio remains consistent with desired risk objectives. Private market funds pose specific challenges for investors in maintaining a desired exposure over time as investors do not control the pace at which committed capital is drawn or the pace at which capital distributions are returned. Although unpredictable at an individual fund level, these patterns become more predictable within a portfolio of private market investments.

The objective of a multi-year funding strategy is to design a commitment-pacing strategy that will result in the desired portfolio exposure to the asset class over time. The commitment-pacing strategy translates into an annual level of commitments and is typically the result of a cash flow modeling exercise that takes into account expectations about the speed at which committed capital is drawn, the pace of distributions, the evolution in overall asset size, as well as other circumstances specific to the investor. The cash flow modeling exercise would project forward the expected asset class exposure (as a percentage of the overall portfolio) at various commitment levels, thus reducing the risk of overshooting the target allocation. Scenario analysis should also be used to consider the impact of different market stress conditions. The evolution of the asset allocation must be monitored over time with adjustments to the commitment pace made as necessary.

2.3. Stress Testing

A robust liquidity framework ensures that liquidity needs can be met in a timely fashion during periods of normal market and stress market conditions. Understanding how the portfolio's liquidity profile may change in addition to how the liquidity needs of the institution may change during stress periods is therefore critical. Comprehensive stress testing exercises would seek to "stress" (i.e., presume extremely adverse market conditions for) both assets and liabilities simultaneously to understand how these may be impacted during stress conditions. With respect to assets, the stress test can cover distributional assumptions

---

[4]See also Raymond (2009).

regarding prices (e.g., volatility, return), correlations across assets, as well as liquidity characteristics. Liability shocks can also be factored in, for example, by increasing expected endowment distributions to support the university during the stress periods. The design of the stress tests can be informed by historical events (e.g., the 2008 crisis), statistical models (e.g., extreme value theory), and/or by scenario analysis (e.g., analyzing the potential impact of a hypothetical scenario with respect to a set of variables on the overall portfolio).

2.4. Derivatives

Derivatives can be used to manage cash outflow needs and changing risk exposures. The cash-efficient nature of derivatives makes them desirable tools for rebalancing. A futures overlay program allows an institutional investor to rebalance exposures to public asset classes (for example, on a monthly or quarterly basis) while leaving allocations to external active managers unchanged. Derivatives can also be used to modify a portfolio's liquidity profile through the use of leverage—for example, using futures contracts (long futures position) to gain economic exposure to US equities and then deploying the cash that is not required for posting margin into other investments with different liquidity profiles or to satisfy short-term liquidity needs. Derivatives can also be used to generate additional cash by employing leverage at the overall portfolio level.

2.5. Earning an Illiquidity Premium

An attractive feature for investors in illiquid investments, such as private equity or private real estate, is the expectation of extracting an illiquidity premium in addition to premiums associated with underlying market risk factor exposures in an illiquid strategy. The illiquidity premium (also called the liquidity premium) is the expected compensation for the additional risk of tying up capital for a potentially uncertain time period. Quantitative estimates for the illiquidity premium suggest evidence of a positive illiquidity premium in private equity and private real estate and of illiquidity premium size being positively correlated to the length of the illiquidity horizon.[5]

An alternative approach for estimating the illiquidity risk premium is based on the idea that the size of the discount an investor should receive in return for committing capital for an uncertain period of time can be represented by the value of a put option with an exercise price equal to the marketable price of the illiquid asset at the time of purchase. (The "marketable price" is a hypothetical price at which the illiquid asset could be sold if it were freely traded; it can be estimated by various means.) In this case, the price of the illiquid asset can be derived by subtracting the put price from the marketable price of the asset. If both the marketable price and the illiquid asset price are estimated or known, then the expected return for each can be calculated, with the difference in expected returns representing the illiquidity premium (in %). This approach was initially developed by Chaffe (1993) and later improved upon by Staub and Diermeier (2003). They also find there should be a positive correlation between the length of the illiquidity horizon and the size of the illiquidity premium.

A significant body of literature documents a positive relationship between lack of liquidity and expected returns in the case of public equity. For example, Pastor and Stambaugh (2001) find that expected returns are impacted by systematic liquidity risk and estimate a 3% return over the 1996–2003 period in the US for a zero-net investment portfolio that holds low-liquidity stocks long and high-liquidity stocks short.

---

[5]See also Green (2015).

Overall, though, it is difficult to isolate the illiquidity premium with precision and separate its effects from such other risk factors as the market, value, and size in the case of equity investments. Furthermore, estimates of the illiquidity premium are based on broad market indexes, yet an investor in these asset classes would typically invest in only a small subset of the universe with the result that individual investment experience could be very different and more susceptible to idiosyncratic factors.[6] These challenges further emphasize the importance of liquidity budgeting in facilitating capture of the illiquidity premium while controlling for risk.

3. QUINCO CASE

Quadrivium University (QU) is an independent liberal arts college located in a vibrant mid-sized city with a growing and diverse population. The university was founded in 1916 by James Greaves and Colin Healey, two entrepreneurs with a passion for astronomy and mathematics who settled in the area in the early 1900s. Over time, the university has built an outstanding reputation as one of the top schools in the country. Consistent with the founders' interests, the programs in astronomy and mathematics are highly regarded, attracting applicants from all over the world.

The Quadrivium University endowment was established in 1936 through a $15 million donation from Mr. Healey, with the goal of providing financial aid to new undergraduate students. A quarter of new students receive Healey grants, and this percentage has increased steadily over time.

QU has an endowment of $8 billion as of the current fiscal year, of which $6 billion represents funds used for general unrestricted support and unrestricted funds functioning as endowment. The remaining funds have various donor-specified use restrictions. Although a significant portion of the endowment's growth has been from investment returns, the endowment also benefits from a strong and deep alumni network that provides regular donations and access to highly regarded industry contacts and money managers. Exhibit 3 shows the market value of the endowment over recent years, and Exhibit 4 shows the realized investment returns over the same period.

EXHIBIT 3   Market Value of QU Endowment

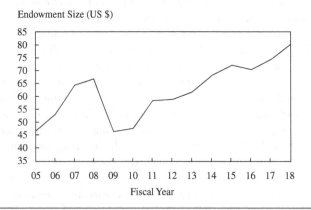

[6]Ang, Papanikolaou, and Westerfield, (2014).

EXHIBIT 4   Investment Returns for QU Endowment

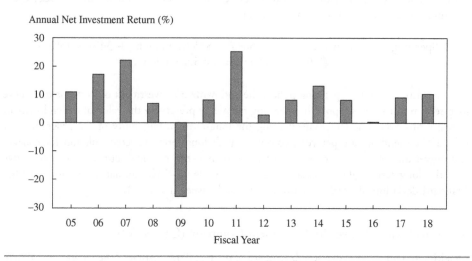

Annual Net Investment Return (%)

Fiscal Year

QU has an annual operating budget of $583 million, and 70% of the operating budget is used to fund salaries and benefits for faculty and administrative staff. In addition, the budget is used to pay down debt associated with a major upgrade of the main campus facilities, pay expenses associated with the maintenance of physical infrastructure, and fund various research and financial aid programs.

Annual distributions from the endowment provide funding for approximately 60% of the university's operating budget, including its financial aid programs. In absolute dollar terms, the size of annual distributions has increased steadily in the last five years as the size of the endowment fund has grown. Similarly, the percentage of the operating budget covered by distributions from the endowment has increased. The board of the university has recently expressed a preference for a predictable pattern of distributions to allow for better planning of resource deployment through its programs. Consistent with that preference, the spending policy of the endowment was changed following the 2008 global financial crisis. Pre-crisis, the university used a simple spending rule: Spending equaled the long-term desired spending rate of 5% multiplied by the market value of the endowment at the beginning of the fiscal year. Post-crisis, the university changed its spending rule to a geometric smoothing rule, sometimes called the Yale formula.

The current spending rule is designed to produce a 5% long-term spending rate in a way that shields annual distributions from fluctuations in the endowment's market value. The endowment uses a weighted-average formula of the previous year's spending amount and the endowment's market value at the end of the previous fiscal year multiplied by the long-term desired spending rate:

Spending for current fiscal year = (66% × Spending for previous fiscal year) + 34% × (5% × Endowment market value at the end of previous fiscal year)

For QU, the previous fiscal year's spending was $358.1 million, while the endowment's market value at the end of the previous fiscal year was $7,002.3 million. In this case, QU's spending for the current fiscal year would be:

$$\text{Spending for current fiscal year} = (66\% \times \$358.1 \text{ million}) + 34\% \times (5\% \times \$7,002.3 \text{ million}) = \$355.4 \text{ million}$$

Consistent with the spending policy, the endowment's investment objective is to achieve long-term returns that support the spending rate while preserving the value of the endowment in real terms over time (thus safeguarding the long-term sustainability of the program). For QU, a 5% spending rate per year, combined with long-term expected inflation for colleges and universities of 2–3% per year, translates into an 7–8% nominal return per year objective over the long term. QU's associated risk objective is 12–14% annualized return volatility (standard deviation of portfolio returns must be between 12–14%).

3.1. Quadrivium University Investment Company (QUINCO)

Quadrivium University is overseen by a board of trustees ("the Trustees"), generally consisting of prominent, wealthy alumni who are elected to the position. QUINCO is the university investment office, which manages QU's endowment. The office was established in 1993 at a time when endowment assets were $1 billion. From a governance perspective, the office is organizationally distinct from the university, although it is not a separate legal entity. The president of the investment office, Aaron Winter, reports to the university president and to the QUINCO board of directors ("the Board"). The Board is comprised of 11 members appointed by the Trustees. The president of QUINCO, the university president, and the treasurer of the university serve as ex-officio members. The QUINCO Board is responsible for approving investment policy and guidelines and providing guidance on key policy matters. Implementation of the investment policy has been fully delegated to QUINCO staff, who are empowered to make changes to the portfolio within the parameters of the investment guidelines.

QUINCO has 13 investment professionals who are university employees. The investment model is one where the investment strategy is implemented through external investment managers. The Board has consistently re-affirmed its view that such a model provides greater flexibility for changing investment portfolio exposures when circumstances warrant while reducing internal staffing needs compared to an in-house investment management model. Internal investment staff are focused on asset allocation, risk management, and selecting, monitoring, and terminating external investment managers.

The following five investment categories are part of the current asset allocation: fixed income, public equities, private equity, real assets (composed of primarily private real estate and natural resources), and diversifying strategies (primarily hedge fund strategies targeting high absolute returns with low correlations to traditional asset classes like public equity and fixed income). Alternative investments are considered to be private equity, real assets, and diversifying strategies. Private equity and real assets are recognized as illiquid (alternative) investments. The investment team is organized by investment category, with a senior portfolio manager leading each area and supported by an analyst. In addition, the team includes a portfolio strategist in charge of asset allocation and risk management, also supported by an analyst, and the president of the office who acts as the chief investment officer (CIO). Senior portfolio managers have primary responsibility for investment decisions within their investment category, while the portfolio strategist has responsibility for ongoing endowment rebalancing decisions, overlays, and tactical asset allocation tilts. All external investment manager decisions and tactical asset allocation deviations are discussed and approved by the internal investment committee. Winter chairs the committee, which includes all senior portfolio managers and the portfolio strategist. The QUINCO Board is responsible for granting final approval of external investment managers.

3.2. Investment Strategy: Background and Evolution

QUINCO has distinguished itself as a steady and progressive institutional investor with a focus on long-term objectives; it is unlikely to make abrupt wholesale changes to its investment strategy. This strategy is, in part, driven by leadership stability, with the office having had the same president (Winter's predecessor) for the first 25 years of existence. Another important factor has been an established culture focused on maintaining best-in-class investment practices and institutionalizing that knowledge through robust processes and systems.

For the first years of existence, the endowment invested only in public markets, mostly equities and bonds. In its early days, the belief was that the limited size and investment resources of the endowment would present challenges in accessing, monitoring and properly managing complex, nontraditional investment strategies. Since the mid-1990s, as the size of the endowment grew, the QUINCO Board has embraced the belief that exposure to nontraditional, or alternative, asset categories is beneficial for the long-term prospects of the endowment— enhancing investment risk diversification and providing potentially higher risk-adjusted returns in a greater variety of market environments. To express this belief, the Board has supported an increase in internal investment expertise, hiring seasoned investment professionals, and expanding QUINCO's investment staff. Over the next two decades, the endowment portfolio increased its exposure to such alternative investments as private equity, real assets, and hedge funds.

These investments have performed well for the endowment; in particular, private equity and real assets were very strong contributors to the portfolio return over that period, in line with expectations. In aggregate, however, exposure to alternatives in the portfolio is still below the average exposure of other large university endowments that are considered by the Board to be the endowment's relevant peer universe.

The evolution of the endowment's asset allocation is shown in Exhibit 5.

EXHIBIT 5   Evolution of the Strategic Asset Allocation

	Evolution of Investment Policy Targets							
	1996	1999	2002	2005	2008	2011	2014	2017
Cash	1%	1%	1%	1%	1%	1%	1%	1%
Fixed Income	29%	24%	24%	19%	16%	16%	14%	14%
Domestic Equity	40%	35%	26%	24%	23%	21%	20%	17%
International Developed Equity	24%	24%	20%	17%	15%	15%	12%	10%
Emerging Market Equity	0%	3%	10%	15%	15%	12%	12%	12%
Private Equity	3%	5%	8%	10%	12%	14%	16%	18%
Real Assets	3%	5%	6%	7%	9%	11%	12%	13%
Diversifying Strategies	0%	3%	5%	7%	9%	10%	13%	15%

The QUINCO Board oversees a comprehensive strategic asset allocation review every three years. The last review of the asset allocation occurred two years ago, and at that time, the Board approved a continued increase to alternative investments at the expense of developed market equities (both domestic and international).

3.2.1. Current Scenario

Winter, a QU alumnus who joined QUINCO five years ago, took over the role of president and CIO last year. This is the first time he will be overseeing an asset allocation review. The endowment's current asset allocation is shown in Exhibit 6.

EXHIBIT 6   Current Strategic Asset Allocation

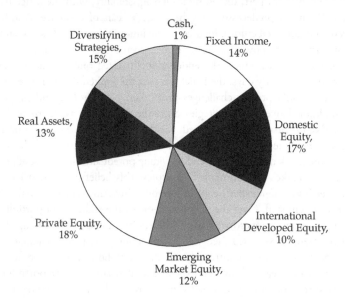

Based on discussions with the Board, Winter asks his portfolio strategy team—consisting of team lead Julia Thompson, her asset allocation analyst, and the senior portfolio managers for fixed income and public equities—to address the following considerations during the review process:

• The desired liquidity profile for the endowment and corresponding framework for liquidity management.
• The investment outlook and efficiency of the strategic asset allocation. A long period of falling interest rates and rising asset prices in the developed world drove most traditional listed asset classes to the upper bounds of historical valuation ranges, lowering future expected returns in these markets.
• The role of tactical asset allocation (TAA) in QU endowment's investment strategy. Given the long-term nature of the strategic asset allocation, some Board members are wondering whether a tactical asset allocation program might improve risk-adjusted returns for the portfolio.

- Endowment underperformance relative to a peer universe of large endowments. Although the QU endowment had better returns than most of those institutions during the 2008 global financial crisis, the portfolio has largely underperformed its peers since then.

3.3. Strategic Asset Allocation

Thompson and the strategy team have completed their analysis, including the considerations raised by Winter and the Board, and are now ready to present to the Board. As part of their work, Thompson updated the long-term, forward-looking capital market assumptions used for the mean–variance optimization process and asset allocation recommendations.

In developing their long-term capital market assumptions, Thompson and the strategy team considered and applied unsmoothing (or de-smoothing) techniques. These techniques were applied to illiquid investments to remove the impact of positive serial correlation on risk estimates caused by stale market pricing. From experience, Thompson knows that the uncertainty of risk and return estimates for illiquid assets is amplified by such aspects as infrequent trading, associated leverage, and long investment horizons. In attempting to estimate risk for illiquid assets, the team's challenges include the availability, quality/reliability, and frequency of pricing data. Thompson knows these issues would result in stale pricing or a smoother pattern of reported returns because of fewer data points with lower observed return volatility. If used as an input in their mean–variance optimization models without adjustment, the artificially low volatility would make illiquid asset classes appear more attractive, resulting in higher allocations to illiquids in the "optimal" portfolio. To prevent this, Thompson and her team applied unsmoothing techniques to better reflect the underlying risk of illiquid asset classes. After applying unsmoothing techniques to private equity, resulting volatility ends up being significantly higher than volatility that is observed or experienced for these assets. Exhibits 7 and 8 show these updated assumptions.

EXHIBIT 7   Long-Term Expected Return (Net of Fees) and Volatility Assumptions

Asset Class	Expected Real Return (annual geometric mean, next 10 years)	Expected Nominal Return (annual geometric mean, next 10 years)	Standard Deviation of Returns (annual)	Sharpe Ratio
Cash	0.9%	3.4%	1.7%	
Fixed Income	1.8%	4.3%	6.3%	0.14
Domestic Equity	5.0%	7.6%	18.1%	0.23
International Developed Equity	4.8%	7.4%	19.7%	0.20
Emerging Market Equity	6.0%	8.7%	26.6%	0.19
Private Equity	8.5%	11.2%	24.0%	0.32
Real Assets	4.5%	7.1%	13.3%	0.27
Diversifying Strategies	4.0%	6.6%	10.0%	0.31

Note: Inflation assumed to be 2.5% p.a.

EXHIBIT 8   Forward-Looking Correlation Matrix

	Cash	Fixed Income	Domestic Equity	International Developed Equity	Emerging Market Equity	Private Equity	Real Assets	Diversifying Strategies
Cash	1.00							
Fixed Income	0.11	1.00						
Domestic Equity	0.03	0.13	1.00					
International Developed Equity	0.02	0.14	0.91	1.00				
Emerging Market Equity	0.04	(0.18)	0.69	0.71	1.00			
Private Equity	0.02	(0.11)	0.68	0.65	0.59	1.00		
Real Assets	0.07	(0.16)	0.35	0.35	0.25	0.42	1.00	
Diversifying Strategies	0.18	0.18	0.40	0.40	0.45	0.35	(0.04)	1.00

Analysis by Thompson and her team uncovered the main reasons for peer underperformance since the 2008 crisis: a lower risk profile of the portfolio and a lower allocation to illiquid investments, in particular, private equity. As such, an important change being proposed by Thompson and the team is an increase in exposure to private markets. The change would increase the private equity allocation from 18% to 23% and the real assets allocation from 13% to 16%. To accommodate both increases, the allocations to public equities and fixed income would decrease. The proposed target allocations are presented in Exhibit 9.

In terms of implementation, Thompson and her team expect that the transition to the higher target allocations in private equity and real assets will occur gradually over the next two to three years.

EXHIBIT 9   Proposed Strategic Asset Allocation Targets

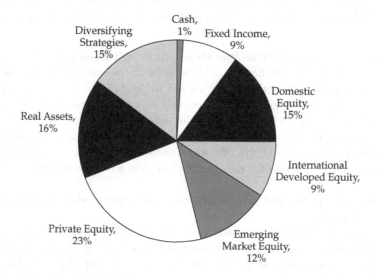

Optimization results in Exhibit 10 are based on the team's assumptions (Exhibits 7 and 8) and show that a higher allocation to private equity and real assets would improve the expected long-term risk–return profile of the endowment. The team also includes the results of Monte Carlo simulations that show the probability of an erosion in longer term purchasing power. Thompson notes that the resulting risk profile measured by the volatility is consistent with quantitative guidelines developed for the endowment's risk tolerance. Based on interaction with the Board, the risk tolerance has been specified as a volatility range of 12% to 14% based on long-term measures of risk.

EXHIBIT 10   Proposed vs. Current SAA: Expected Risk/Return Properties

Portfolio Characteristic	Proposed SAA	Current SAA
Expected nominal return (annual average, geometric, next 10 years)	7.8%	7.5%
Expected real return (annual average, geometric, next 10 years)	5.3%	5.0%
Standard deviation of returns (annual)	13.2%	12.5%
Sharpe ratio	0.34	0.33
Probability of 25% erosion in purchasing power over 20 years with 5% spending rate	30%	35%

Note: The probability of erosion in purchasing power was derived based on a Monte-Carlo simulation with a 20-year investment horizon, assuming expected return and volatility characteristics will be the same as for the next 10 years.

When asked to justify the proposed strategic asset allocation (SAA), including the higher allocation to private markets, Thompson highlights the optimization results from Exhibit 10 to the Board, noting that the primary driver of the proposed asset allocation changes is the expected improvement in the portfolio's long-term risk/return profile.

Thompson is aware the proposed asset allocation implies a small increase in the overall risk profile of the endowment as measured by the volatility of portfolio returns (13.2% for the proposed SAA versus 12.5% for the current portfolio). She believes that the increase in risk is justified by:

- lower return expectations for all asset classes relative to past expectations due to higher current valuations. This implies that a higher level of risk must be taken to achieve the same level of returns. At the time of the last review, the then-current SAA had an expected return of 5.3% in real terms, although now it is expected to generate a 5.0% real return going forward. Lower return expectations can only be compensated in part by efficiency improvements in the asset allocation. Although the proposed SAA is slightly more efficient (higher Sharpe Ratio of 0.01), this efficiency improvement alone is not enough to generate a 5.3% expected real return for the same level of short-term risk/volatility as the current SAA;
- a portfolio risk profile that is currently more conservative when compared to other endowment peers;
- a lower expected Sharpe ratio (expected risk–return profile) for fixed income (compared with recent history), suggesting a lower allocation to these strategies may be warranted; and
- Monte-Carlo simulations, suggesting that the proposed asset allocation has a higher probability of achieving the real return target over a 20-year horizon while better preserving the purchasing power of the endowment with the current spending policy of 5%.

In-text questions:

1. Discuss arguments in favor of increasing the endowment's allocation to illiquid investments.
2. Using additional information provided in Exhibit 10, and your knowledge of illiquid investments from prior curriculum content, justify Thompson's proposed asset allocation and explain the trade-offs involved in terms of portfolio volatility.

Guideline Answers:

1. In general, for a long-horizon institutional investor, the ability to tolerate illiquidity creates an opportunity to improve portfolio diversification and expected returns as well as access a broader set of investment strategies. In mean–variance optimization models, the inclusion of illiquid assets in the eligible investment universe may shift the efficient frontier upwards, theoretically resulting in more-efficient investment portfolios (i.e., portfolios with a higher expected return for a given level of risk).

   Thompson and her team believe the above to be true in the case of QU's endowment. In addition, there are further arguments in favor of increasing the allocation to illiquidity risk. Thompson believes the specific circumstances of the endowment continue to support an increase in exposure to illiquid investments. To date, the team's historical experience with illiquid investments has been positive with strong realized returns. The endowment has been building exposure to these strategies over the last two decades in a gradual manner. As a result, the illiquid portfolios are now well-established, mature, and well-diversified in terms of fund managers, strategies, and vintages. At the same time, the long presence in the market and the ability to access QU alumni networks have helped the endowment develop a strong network of connections in the industry and gain access to best-in-class managers in these spaces—building a reputation as a well-informed, patient, and reliable long-term investor. As revealed in the case text, the QU endowment has a lower exposure to illiquid investments than most institutional investor peers with similar risk profiles and objectives. Analysis by Thompson and her team has identified this as one of the reasons for the QU endowment's underperformance in recent years relative to peers.

Thompson and the strategy team should also examine whether the allocation to private equity and real assets is exposed to idiosyncratic risk factors. Avoiding large allocations to a small number of funds helps ensure that idiosyncratic risk factors are largely diversified away.

2. As Thompson highlights to the Board, the primary driver of the proposed asset allocation is the expected improvement in the portfolio's long-term risk/return profile. The proposed SAA has a higher expected real return compared to the current SAA (5.3% vs. 5.0% in real terms) and a slightly higher Sharpe Ratio (0.34 vs. 0.33).

The proposed asset allocation also has a higher probability of achieving the endowment's return target over the long-term. One way to get a better sense of this is through Monte Carlo simulations. For example, using such simulations, the team concludes that there is a 70% chance of maintaining at least 75% of purchasing power over a 20-year horizon for the proposed SAA versus a 65% chance for the current SAA, assuming a 5% spending rate.

There is an implicit trade-off in this case between the short-term risk measure (volatility) and the long-term risk represented by the probability of purchasing power erosion over a 20-year horizon.

Tradeoff 1: Portfolio volatility

Thompson has considered the increase in overall risk profile for the endowment (portfolio return volatility increases from 12.5% to 13.2%) and believes the increase to be justified.

Thompson believes future returns will be lower for all asset classes. Lower return expectations imply that a higher level of risk must be taken to achieve the same level of returns. Although the proposed SAA is slightly more efficient, as indicated by its higher Sharpe ratio, this improvement in portfolio efficiency is not sufficient to generate the 5.3% expected real return for the same level of short-term risk/volatility as the current SAA.

Optimization results also suggest that the proposed asset allocation has a higher probability of achieving the real return target while preserving the purchasing power of the endowment given the current 5% spending policy. Finally, Thompson also considers that QU's portfolio risk profile is still currently more conservative than its peers.

Tradeoff 2: Implementation costs

Thompson and her team analyzed the costs associated with implementing the proposed portfolio allocation changes. Private equity and private real estate strategies typically have higher investment management fees and performance fees than fixed-income and public equity strategies. By using "net of fees" return assumptions, Thompson and her team incorporated the impact of higher expected investment management fees arising from higher allocations to more-illiquid investments.

Before concluding that the QU endowment should adjust its asset allocation to illiquid investments, Thompson should confirm that the resulting risk profile (return volatility of 13.2% and the probability of erosion in purchasing power shown in Exhibit 10) is consistent with the endowment's risk tolerance (willingness and capacity to bear risk). Thompson also should confirm that with the increased allocation to illiquid investments, the resulting asset allocation remains consistent with the liquidity budget.

3.4. Liquidity Management

Given the increasing complexity in the investment portfolio and the university's reliance on regular distributions from the endowment, QUINCO needs a robust framework for managing liquidity. During her time at QUINCO, Thompson has worked to enhance QUINCO's overall liquidity management framework. This includes improving the tools used in that process and taking a comprehensive, enterprise-wide approach. Using her approach, the expected cash outflows and inflows for the endowment portfolio are modeled over various time horizons both under normal circumstances and in periods of severe market stress.

Thompson is concerned that the portfolio's liquidity characteristics will deteriorate in periods of severe market stress. She believes a deterioration in liquidity could potentially occur for the following reasons:

- **Capital calls in private markets exceeding capital distributions.** This would increase the allocation to private markets in the overall portfolio.
- **Activation of gates.** Some investment vehicles that provide quarterly or annual liquidity, like hedge funds or real estate funds, have provisions in their investment prospectuses allowing the investment manager to refuse investor withdrawal requests (activate gates) during stress periods to protect remaining investors in the fund. The inability to withdraw from funds leads to a more illiquid profile overall.
- **The smoothing effect.** Investments in private markets tend to incorporate market valuations with a lag that leads to a relative increase in their portfolio weighting during periods of market stress and a relative decrease in the portfolio weighting of more liquid assets. This does not reduce the effective liquidity of the portfolio in dollar terms, but it does impact the percentage of assets in the overall portfolio that could be used to satisfy liquidity needs in periods of market stress.

To address her concerns, Thompson asks her team for an analysis of the current and proposed QU portfolios under normal and stress market conditions. The team's analysis of each portfolio's liquidity profile is shown in Exhibits 11 and 12.

Exhibit 11 shows the current QU portfolio under normal and stress conditions.

EXHIBIT 11   QU Endowment Liquidity Profile: Current Portfolio (Normal and Stress Conditions)

A. Liquidity Profile - Normal Conditions

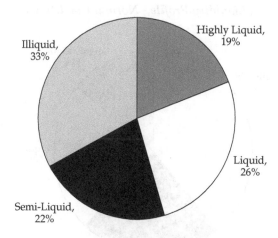

B. Liquidity Profile - Stress Conditions

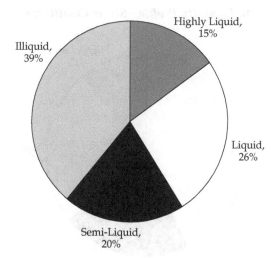

Exhibit 12 shows the proposed QU strategic asset allocation portfolio under normal and stress conditions.

EXHIBIT 12   QU Endowment Liquidity Profile: Proposed Strategic Asset Allocation (Normal and
Stress Conditions)

A. Liquidity Profile - Normal Conditions

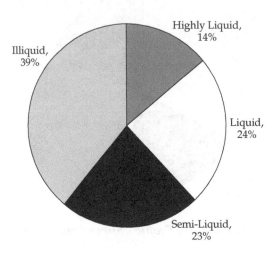

B. Liquidity Profile - Stress Conditions

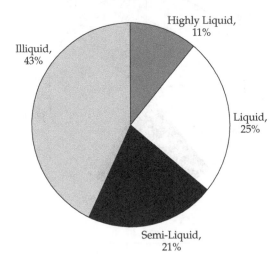

In-text questions:

1. Explain how current spending policy might affect liquidity needs in a market downturn.
2. Describe various tools that QUINCO might use to manage its portfolio liquidity risk.
3. What impact will the proposed asset allocation changes have on the endowment's liquidity profile?

Guideline Answers:

1. The design of the spending rate policy incorporates a smoothing, countercyclical element leading to spending rates below 5% in a period of sustained strong investment returns but higher than 5% in a protracted weak return environment. This design of the spending rate policy exacerbates the endowment's liquidity needs in severe market downturns.
2. Among the tools QUINCO could use are cash flow-forecasting and commitment-pacing models, liquidity budgets, and stress test analyses. To begin, Thompson estimates expected cash outflows and inflows. For cash outflows, Thompson projects distributions from the endowment to the university. These uses of cash can then be factored into the estimation of expected outflows and inflows through the spending rate policy in which the university seeks to spend, on average, 5% annually of the endowment while preserving the endowment's purchasing power over time.

   For the private equity and real estate portfolios, Thompson and her team can use cash flow-forecasting models and commitment-pacing models to project the expected increase in the allocation to private markets. These help the team project cash outflows needed for future investment commitments (committed but undrawn capital calls) in private markets. These flows could become particularly relevant in stress periods when distributions from prior investments in those markets might cease as general partners find it difficult to exit investments (because of depressed valuations and lack of transaction activity). Future investment commitments are legal obligations of the endowment, so the staff needs to ensure capital calls are met because the general partner may accelerate capital calls as opportunities arise in depressed markets. Thompson and her team should ensure diversification across fund vintage years to avoid overexposure to particular parts of the economic cycle and should also follow a strategy that commits capital on a steady and regular basis to minimize the need to make large allocation changes (or adjustments) with associated transaction costs. Avoiding large allocations to very few funds will help minimize idiosyncratic portfolio risk.

   At the same time, cash inflows into the endowment from donors will likely drop significantly during stress periods, further increasing liquidity needs. Liquidating risk assets or high-beta assets after periods of negative return is often not desirable from a valuation standpoint when future returns may be expected to be more attractive, particularly following periods of sharp drawdowns. Given her experience with these markets, Thompson should recognize the need for the team's approach to be flexible. Access to the top private market managers is often highly competitive, and opportunities to invest with these managers may not be available at times when the portfolio is making allocation increases.

Incorporating this information, Thompson can develop a liquidity budget for the endowment like that shown in Exhibit 1, which specifies minimum acceptable liquidity targets based on the expected time needed to convert portfolio holdings to cash. The liquidity budget should be monitored by Thompson and her team on a regular basis as part of the liquidity management framework in place at QUINCO. Thompson and her team can also do an analysis of the portfolio's current liquidity characteristics under normal market conditions, like that shown in Exhibit 2.

Thompson and her team should continue to undertake regular stress tests (such as the liquidity profile analysis done by her team) using historical and hypothetical scenarios to estimate how much the liquidity profile of the portfolio could drift under certain assumptions and to assess whether the minimum liquidity budget is still satisfied. The analysis can also be used to inform the team's asset allocation and implementation decisions for investment vehicles and strategies.

3. Compared to the liquidity profile of the current portfolio, the proposed asset allocation implies a shift toward more-illiquid investments, as shown in the following table:

Liquidity Category	Current Portfolio: Normal (%)	Current Portfolio: Stress (%)	Current Portfolio: Stress vs. Normal (%)	Proposed: Normal (%)	Proposed Portfolio: Stress (%)	Proposed Portfolio: Stress vs. Normal (%)	Proposed vs. Current: Normal (%)	Proposed vs. Current: Stress (%)
Highly Liquid	19	15	–4	14	11	–3	–5	–4
Liquid	26	26	0	24	25	1	–2	–1
Semi-Liquid	22	20	–2	23	21	–2	1	1
Illiquid	33	39	6	39	43	4	6	4

As a result, there will be a reduction in the highly liquid and liquid categories in the endowment's liquidity profile and a commensurate increase in the semi-liquid and illiquid categories under both normal and stress conditions. The proposed allocation results in an increase in the overall illiquidity profile because a higher percentage of the portfolio will be invested in private equity and private real estate, which are the most illiquid asset classes in the portfolio.

Thompson needs to ensure that even under stress conditions the proposed allocation continues to comply with the liquidity budgeting framework in place for the fund, which satisfies the various liquidity needs of the portfolio for both cash outflows and rebalancing. From an ongoing management perspective, and particularly at times when the liquidity profile of the proposed allocation is closer to the minimum thresholds set through the liquidity budget, Thompson and her team should plan to closely monitor the portfolio's liquidity profile and stress test it periodically to make sure portfolio liquidity remains adequate.

Based on this analysis, the QUINCO Board approves the proposed changes to the asset allocation and instructs the team to proceed with implementation. These changes are also presented to the Quadrivium Trustees as part of the university treasurer's financial report at the Trustees' next regular meeting.

3.5. Asset Manager Selection

It is now three months later, and Winter, Thompson, and the rest of the QUINCO team have begun implementing changes to the strategic asset allocation by seeking additional external managers. Winter is very pleased with their progress to date but has encountered a somewhat interesting situation.

Among the firms responding to QUINCO's request for proposal (RFP) seeking a new private equity manager is Genex Venture Capital (GVC). GVC is proposing that QUINCO invest in its new "GVC Fund II" offering. GVC is a US-based venture capital fund operating in the biotech space. GVC would be a new relationship for QUINCO. The firm has adopted the CFA Institute Asset Manager Code of Conduct for its employees. The founder and managing partner at GVC is Virginia Hall, CFA, a prominent alumna of Quadrivium University, elected to the university's board of trustees three years ago. Hall has made several generous donations to the university over the years, and the building that houses the school's student center and main dining facility is named in her honor. Both the university president and university treasurer have urged Winter to favorably consider GVC's proposal given Hall's importance to the university. Winter has suspicions that Hall has contacted the president and treasurer to advocate for her company.

The investment committee narrows the competition for the allocation of QUINCO's private market assets to GVC and Beacher Venture Investments (Beacher). Beacher is another venture capital investment firm operating in the same space and is a direct competitor to GVC.

Both GVC and Beacher are invited to make a presentation to QUINCO's investment committee. GVC's presentation is led by Jason Allen, one of Winter's former colleagues from the endowment they both worked for previously. Allen has joined GVC as a managing director as part of GVC's efforts to build the team in preparation for Fund II. Although Allen's presentation on behalf of GVC is thorough and well-documented, Winter is troubled by two aspects. The presentation is targeted to QUINCO but clearly incorporates information that is based on or could only have come from the university treasurer's non-public reports to the Quadrivium board of trustees or another university source. In addition, the performance presentation of GVC's historical returns shows substantially higher returns than performance reported by third-party performance databases.

Of the two finalists, Beacher has a longer track record and is a more established name in the industry; however, there are some concerns over the historical performance of its previous fund. At the same time, some investment committee members have expressed reservations over GVC's short track record. Given the overlap in sector and strategy between the two firms, the investment committee asks Bud Davis, a CFA charterholder and senior portfolio manager on QUINCO's private equity team, to return with a formal proposal to invest in one of the firms.

Davis presents an update on the fundraising efforts of each firm's fund and notes that GVC is facing challenges in raising the desired fund amount of $300 million for Fund II. Potential investors are apparently concerned with the significant increase in funding size of the fund (Fund I had raised $100 million) and question whether GVC has the infrastructure to scale operations.

Davis makes a strong case for investing with GVC, highlighting confidence in the manager and their differentiated approach to sourcing and growing portfolio companies in the biotech space. Davis tells the investment committee that because of the longer-than-expected fundraising period, GVC is eager to secure QU's commitment for Fund II; as a result, Davis has negotiated a discount on GVC's investment management fee. Following that discussion, the investment committee approves the recommendation from the team to invest with GVC.

After the decision is made to hire GVC, Winter calls Allen to tell him the good news and offer his congratulations. During the conversation, Allen expresses his satisfaction in having QUINCO as one of the fund's investors and praises Davis's strong commitment and drive. Allen goes on to mention that Davis's spouse, Andrea, is Hall's daughter. Winter expresses his surprise at this fact and later asks Davis about his wife's relationship to Hall. Davis responds that he believes this information is common knowledge and that he thought Winter and members of the QUINCO investment committee knew this information.

In-text question:

What ethical considerations arise regarding the actions and conduct of individuals involved in manager selection?

Guideline Answer:

Aaron Winter, QUINCO CIO
Winter faces several ethical dilemmas in this case. The main issue is the disclosure of a potential conflict of interest, Standard of Professional Conduct VI(A), regarding the hiring of an external investment manager with close ties to the university. Winter's independence and objectivity, Standard of Professional Conduct I(B), in making the hiring recommendation could be compromised by the implicit and explicit pressure he is receiving to hire GVC. He should disclose this conflict to the QUINCO Board as part of the hiring recommendation. He should also disclose that the managing director for GVC is a former colleague; that relationship could also be perceived as impairing his independence and objectivity, creating a conflict of interest. During the presentation, it appears that GVC has based their proposal on confidential information, Standard of Professional Conduct III(E), about the university, potentially obtained by Hall through her role as a Quadrivium Trustee or others at the university. As an employee of the University and QUINCO, Winter should make them aware of the possible breach of confidentiality. He also apparently has questions about the accuracy of the performance information, Standards of Professional Conduct I(C) and III(D), presented by GVC but fails to exercise appropriate diligence, Standard of Professional Conduct V(A), by following up with GVC or investigating further to determine the veracity of the information.

Virginia Hall, CFA, Quadrivium University Trustee and Managing Partner at GVC
Virginia Hall has a conflict of interest, Standard of Professional Conduct VI(A), if she is pressuring university staff and QUINCO employees to influence the external manager hiring process in her company's favor. Hall's personal/business interests with GVC pose a potential conflict of interest with her duties as a Trustee of the university board. She has a duty as a board member to act in the best interest of the university without regard

to how it may benefit her, but she has an incentive to pressure the university to hire her company. She would be violating her duty of loyalty, Standard of Professional Conduct IV(A), to the university as a Trustee by putting her firm, and therefore her personal interest, ahead of the interests of the university. She should disclose her potential conflict and recuse herself from any part in the external manager hiring process. In addition, she has potentially gone further by sharing confidential information, Standard of Professional Conduct III(E), she has received as a trustee with GVC in an effort to assist GVC's response and boost the prospects of her company in being hired—another violation of her duty of loyalty as a Trustee. GVC neglected to disclose the relationship of one employee's relative (Hall's daughter, who is Davis's spouse) with QUINCO.

Quadrivium University President/Quadrivium University Treasurer
The university president and treasurer, as members of the QUINCO Board, have a duty to act in the best interest, Standard of Professional Conduct IV(A), of the university by hiring the external investment managers most appropriate for managing the private equity portion of the university's endowment. In pressuring Winter to hire GVC, they are clearly letting the outside consideration of maintaining good relations with a Trustee influence their hiring decision. It is also possible they provided confidential information, Standard of Professional Conduct III(E), to Hall or GVC to assist their bid to become an investment manager for QUINCO. They should disclose their conflict, Standard of Professional Conduct VI(A), and recuse themselves from decisions where their independence and objectivity, Standard of Professional Conduct I(B), are compromised. The university president and treasurer should also have in place a due diligence questionnaire/RFP to raise questions to new managers about potential conflicts of interest.

Jason Allen, Managing Director at GVC
Winter has noticed a discrepancy between the performance history of GVC in the presentation made by Allen and the performance record of the company as reported elsewhere. It is possible that Allen is inadvertently using inaccurate information or, worse, knowingly misrepresenting the performance record, Standards of Professional Conduct I(C) and III(D), of GVC.

Bud Davis, CFA, Senior Portfolio Manager at QUINCO
Through his spouse, Davis has a personal relationship with GVC, a company he is tasked with investigating and providing an opinion on the potential hiring as an outside manager. This could affect his independence and objectivity, Standard of Professional Conduct I(B), and create, at minimum, the perception of a conflict of interest, Standard of Professional Conduct VI(A), that should be disclosed when making his recommendation. Davis should not rely on his belief that the relationship is "common knowledge" or widely known but should make an explicit disclosure of this potential conflict.

3.6. Tactical Asset Allocation

As part of the investment strategy review, the Board decided to significantly increase the active risk budget assigned to the QUINCO team for use in a new tactical asset allocation (TAA) program. QUINCO's active risk budget measures the deviation of the endowment's portfolio from its investment policy targets and is expressed as an annual tracking error limit. The Board increased QUINCO's active risk budget from 100 bps to 250 bps to allow the team to pursue greater excess returns versus the strategic asset allocation. By taking active risk relative to investment policy benchmarks through external managers in public asset classes as well as TAA positions, the QUINCO team hopes to add additional portfolio performance.

The implementation of the tactical asset allocation program and associated risk budget was fully delegated to Winter and his staff. At that time, the Board also informed that up to 150 bps (of the 250 bps) active risk budget could be used to implement the TAA program. One consideration the Board discussed was the use of leverage. The TAA program implementation could result in a levered position of the endowment portfolio (because derivatives are likely to be used in implementation and not every overweight exposure would be offset by a corresponding underweight in another asset), so the Board agreed to permit a modest leverage position for the overall portfolio of up to 5% of the portfolio's value.

Winter believes that the tactical asset allocation program will accommodate two types of active decisions:

- Overweight and underweight positions in one or more of the asset classes included in the investment policy portfolio.
- Provide exposure to asset classes and/or investment strategies outside the policy portfolio benchmark universe but compliant with the investment policy (e.g., high yield, emerging market, fixed income).

Winter began implementing the TAA program by building on a framework and research by Thompson and the asset allocation team that was informed by external parties (e.g., investment consultants, external tactical asset allocation managers, investment research houses). Using concepts of fair value and mean reversion in financial markets, fair value models were developed for various financial assets. To do this, the framework incorporated economic and financial data that had exhibited predictive power for future returns and risk over an investment horizon of one to three years. Current market pricing was then compared with output from the valuation models to determine whether the deviation from "fair value" was large enough to be exploited in a cost-efficient manner.

In extensive out-of-sample backtests, the methodology had produced encouraging results. One of the strongest signals suggested that large-cap US equities, characterized broadly by the S&P 500 Index, were significantly below fair value with mean reversion expected over the next year. Based on this information, Thompson decides to implement a 1% overweight to US equities through a passive exposure.

Thompson is now considering three options to implement her decision: a total return swap, equity futures, and ETFs. Her goal is to implement the overweight position as effectively as possible from a cost and cash usage perspective. Thompson asks her team to look at the associated costs for each option.

The team's cost comparison analysis is shown in Exhibit 13.

EXHIBIT 13   Cost Comparison Assuming a Fully-Funded Mandate

Cost Component	ETF	Futures	Total Return Swap
Commission (round trip)	4.00	2.00	5.00
Management fee (annual)	9.50	0.00	0.00
Bid/offer spread (round trip)	2.50	2.00	6.00

Cost Component	ETF	Futures	Total Return Swap
Price impact (round trip)	15.00	10.00	0.00
Mispricing (tracking error, annual)	4.00	8.00	0.00
Cost to roll the futures contract	0.00	20.00	0.00
Funding cost	0.00	0.00	40.00
Total cost	**35.00**	**42.00**	**51.00**

Notes: The exhibit shows the team's cost comparison for the three implementation options—ETFs, futures, and total return swaps—for an $80 million notional exposure to the S&P 500 Index (assuming a fully funded mandate) over a one-year investment horizon. All numbers are in basis points (bps) unless otherwise indicated.

The comparison assumes no leverage for the ETF and that the entire mandate amount ($80 million) is deposited to earn the 3-month Libor rate for futures and the total return swap as to offset the 3-month Libor component of the implied financing rate (or the funding cost in the case of the swap).

After closely examining the cost comparison analysis, Thompson debates the pros and cons of each option with her team.

From a cash "usage" perspective, ETFs would be least efficient as she would need to finance the full notional value of the ETF or use the margin features of the account. Even when using the margin, regulations would limit the margin to 50% of account value, implying a maximum of two times the leverage ratio. For example, for an $80 million ETF exposure, the minimum margin that would have to be held in cash would be $40 million. Thompson knows that using futures and total return swaps could generate a similar economic exposure to ETFs with a much lower capital commitment.

From a liquidity perspective, Thompson likes ETFs and futures, which appear efficient given their liquid trading and narrow bid–ask spreads. She also values the flexibility they offer to terminate exposure before intended maturity should the team's views on the market change. Thompson is concerned about the operational implications of holding futures because they require daily monitoring of margin requirements. In addition, she also worries about interest rate risk and exposure of QU to counterparty credit risk.

In-text question:

Assuming a fully-funded position (no use of leverage), which implementation option should Thompson choose for the 1% tactical overweight to US equities?

Guideline Answer:
Expected Costs. In the case of the ETF, the most significant cost component is price impact—the expected impact on market price from entering into (buying) and exiting out of (selling) the ETF position. This is estimated to be approximately 15 bps. The second-largest cost component is the management fee charged by the ETF manager, which is expected to be 9.5 bps.

In the case of futures, the largest cost component is expected to be the cost to roll the futures contract on a quarterly basis (5 bps quarterly or 20 bps annual cost). This is driven by the upward-sloping (contango) shape of the yield curve. In addition to the futures roll cost and the price impact, another significant futures cost is the mispricing or tracking error of expected futures performance relative to the underlying index performance. Expected tracking error on the futures contracts is 8 bps.

Finally, for the total return swap, the cost is dominated by the funding cost, which is expected to be 40 bps.

From a total cost perspective, at 35 bps the ETF offers the most cost-efficient vehicle to implement the tactical overlay, with relatively tight bid–ask spreads that are similar to futures.

Other Considerations. ETFs and futures are typically standardized products that trade on exchanges. Total return swaps are over-the-counter contracts that are negotiated and customizable in such features as maturity, leverage, and cost. ETFs are the least cash-efficient option requiring the largest cash outlay, and Thompson would be able to gain similar economic exposure with futures and swaps using significantly less cash.

A position in futures contracts would need to be rolled over each quarter to maintain exposure. Given Thompson's concerns about the operational requirements for futures and the need for daily monitoring for margin requirements, a position in futures is likely less desirable to Thompson. For ETFs, ongoing management of the exposure is done by the ETF manager.

Futures and ETFs have associated tracking error versus the index intended to be replicated. For ETFs, the tracking error may result from premiums and discounts to net asset value, cash drag, or regulatory diversification requirements. For futures, tracking error arises because of liquidity (supply/demand conditions), dividend forecast errors, and interest rate differentials. For total return swaps, the replication is exact; Thompson would receive the total return of the index without incurring any tracking error to the benchmark S&P 500 Index because the swap counterparty is obligated to provide the index return.

However, Thompson is concerned about interest rate risk in the case of futures and swaps. She is also concerned about the counterparty credit risk that QUINCO would be exposed to through a swap, which would additionally create complexities in managing net exposures over the duration of the contract.

To implement the tactical overlay given Thompson's considerations, the ETF provides the most cost-efficient vehicle, with adequate liquidity and relatively tight bid–ask spreads. ETFs also provide Thompson with the flexibility (noted as being important to her) to modify exposure before the end of the one-year horizon should her and her team's investment views change.

After considering with her team, Thompson believes implementing with ETFs appears to be the best option.

Later that day after further discussion, Thompson and the management team decide to implement the overlay using leverage. Thompson asks her team to complete a cost comparison analysis assuming a permissible leverage level of 4 times for all three options (meaning that cash needed to support the position would be 25% of the overlay notional amount).[7] The team's work is shown in Exhibit 14.

EXHIBIT 14   Additional Information with Respect to Impact of Leverage

Cost Component	ETF	Futures	Total Return Swap
Cost of obtaining leverage	187.50	0.00	0.00
Additional financing/funding cost	0.00	150.00	150.00
Total additional cost	187.50	150.00	150.00

Notes: The additional cost components assume 4 times leverage over a one-year investment horizon. All numbers are in basis points (bps) unless otherwise indicated.

The team's assumptions for the analysis are as follows:

- The borrowing cost of obtaining leverage in the case of the ETF is assumed to be 3-month Libor +50 bps.
- The 3-month Libor assumption used is 2% (opportunity costs).
- The same Libor rate was used to calculate the additional implied financing cost in the case of futures and the additional funding cost for the total return swap.
- The analysis focuses on the implementation cost of trade and does not consider the additional return earned by investing the cash that is not needed to support the transaction (75% of the overlay notional amount).

In-text question:

Assuming a permissible leverage level of 4 times for all three options, and using the information in Exhibit 14, would Thompson change her decision?

Guideline Answer:
As shown in Exhibit 14, the additional information changes the total cost estimates for the different implementation options. In the case of ETFs, to generate 4 times leverage, 75% of the desired nominal exposure would have to be borrowed to provide an overall exposure 4 times higher than the original capital. That is, for a desired nominal exposure of $80 million, borrowing $60 million (75% of $80 million) provides 4 times leverage to an original capital amount of $20 million.

The additional cost of obtaining leverage for each option would be as follows:

1. ETFs. ($80 million × 0.75 × 2.5%)/$80 million = 1.875%.
2. Futures. ($80 million × 0.75 × 2%)/$80 million = 1.50%. The additional financing cost for futures in this case (compared to the unlevered option) would occur because 75% of the amount would not be invested in 3-month Libor to offset the financing cost, thus increasing the overall cost for the futures.

---

[7]Although in the case of the ETF the leverage at the instrument level may be regulated to not exceed 2 times (50% margin requirement), for the purposes of this exercise assume that the endowment can generate leverage at the plan level for ETF usage.

3. Swaps. (\$80 million × 0.75 × 2%)/\$80 million = 1.50%. The additional financing cost for swaps in this case (compared to the unlevered option) would occur because 75% of the amount would not be invested in 3-month Libor to offset the financing cost, thus increasing the overall cost for the swaps.

Total costs for each option (in bps):

	ETF	Futures	Total Return Swap
Unlevered	35.00	42.00	51.00
Incremental cost	187.50	150.00	150.00
Total	222.50	192.00	201.00

Looking at the data, total costs for futures appear to be the lowest cost alternative (192 bps) followed by the total return swap (201 bps). Given a permissible leverage level of 4 times for all three options, and based on the data in Exhibit 14, ETFs now look to be the most expensive option (222.50 bps).

Given the difference in costs, Thompson would consider implementation through futures. The main consideration between the use of ETFs and futures not captured in the comparative pricing analysis is the additional complexity and operational monitoring associated with a quarterly futures roll. If Thompson and the team can get comfortable with that risk, implementation through futures would be the more efficient option.

Looking at the data, and based on their desire to use leverage, Thompson believes that futures offer the more efficient alternative. She decides to establish a 1% long position to the S&P 500 Index using S&P 500 futures.

3.7. Asset Allocation Rebalancing

Three months have passed since Thompson and the team implemented the tactical overweight position to US equities. To date, the position has been performing well and in line with *ex ante* expectations. Global equity markets have rallied, reflecting a favorable global growth environment, and fixed-income markets have sold off as interest rates rose significantly in anticipation of higher inflationary pressures. As a result, the asset allocation of the endowment has drifted from policy targets.

QUINCO follows a calendar quarter rebalancing policy with a rebalancing corridor for each asset class. The allocation drift of the actual portfolio relative to the SAA is monitored monthly; however, to minimize transaction costs, short of extraordinary market circumstances, rebalancing decisions are implemented at the end of each quarter. For public asset classes, systematic rebalancing occurs when the allocation to these assets is outside the rebalancing corridor at quarter end. When the allocation moves outside the corridor, Thompson and her team do have discretion to rebalance back to the target allocation or to the edge of the corridor.

For illiquid asset classes, given high transaction costs and practical challenges in rebalancing the allocation, rebalancing is normally undertaken through the reinvestment/

commitment strategy as allocations approach the upper or lower edges of the corridor. In these cases, the pace of commitments could be altered from the expected pace to gradually shift the overall allocation to illiquid assets over time. The SAA, width of the rebalancing corridor, and the current allocation for the various asset classes are shown in Exhibit 15:

EXHIBIT 15   SAA, Rebalancing Corridors, and Current (Actual) Allocations

	Target Allocation (SAA)	Corridor	Min/Max Target	Current Allocation
Cash	1%	±1%	0%–2%	0.8%
Fixed Income	9%	±3	6%–12%	6.5%
Domestic Equity	15%	±2.5	12.5%–17.5%	17.3%
International Developed Equity	9%	±2%	7%–11%	11.5%
Emerging Market Equity	12%	±2%	10%–14%	13.9%
Private Equity	23%	±5%	18%–28%	19.2%
Real Assets	16%	±3%	13%–19%	13.8%
Diversifying Strategies	15%	±3%	12%–18%	17.1%
Total	**100.0%**			**100.0%**

Thompson observes that the allocation to international developed equity (11.50%) now exceeds the upper end of its corridor (9.00% + 2.00% − 11.00%) by 0.50%, while the allocation to fixed income (6.50%) is below target (9.00%) but still within its rebalancing corridor (6.00%–12.00%).

Current allocations to private equity (19.20%) and real assets (13.80%) are close to the lower ends of their rebalancing corridors of 18.00% − 28.00% and 13.00% − 19.00%, respectively, as the team works to move toward the new targets approved by the Board in Exhibit 9 (in the very short term, these allocations cannot be increased).

Based on the information in Exhibit 15, Thompson sees a need to decrease the international developed equity allocation and increase the fixed-income allocation by the same amount. She meets with the team to discuss whether they should execute the rebalancing through the cash or derivatives market.

During the discussion, Thompson and her team consider the following factors: transaction costs, tracking error of the implementation vehicle versus the desired index exposure, tracking error implied by the current and post-rebalancing deviations from the target SAA weights, opportunity cost/impact to active strategies due to manager withdrawals and reallocations, implementation speed, and time horizon of the rebalancing trade.

Thompson knows that executing through the cash markets takes longer to implement than executing in the derivatives markets. Still, allocating to, or reallocating from, external managers may be warranted in certain cases, such as when the adjustments are viewed as more permanent and/or more significant in nature (as compared to smaller, more temporary adjustments that may be reversed within a shorter time frame if investment views change).

After meeting with her team, Thompson decides to rebalance back to the upper edge of the corridor (11.00%), by reallocating 0.50% (50 bps) from international developed equities to fixed income. The team's cost analysis is shown in Exhibit 16.

EXHIBIT 16   Cost Information: 50 bps Rebalancing Option

Cost Component	Cash Market	Futures (Equity/Fixed Income)
Bid/offer spread	5.00	3.00
Price impact (total trades)	5.00	4.00
Mispricing (tracking error, quarterly)	0.00	17.00
Cash drag (impact of timing delays and disruptions to active manager portfolios)	20.00	0.00
Cost of rolling the futures contract	0.00	0.00
Total cost	**30.00**	**24.00**

Notes: This exhibit shows the costs of reallocating 0.5% from international developed equities to fixed income in the cash and futures markets. The analysis assumes a 3-month (one quarter) investment horizon because the expectation is that the change in portfolio allocation is for a relatively short time period. Given the length of the investment horizon, no rolling of futures occurs. All numbers are in basis points (bps) unless otherwise indicated.

In-text questions:

1. Using Exhibit 16, analyze the relative costs of the cash market and derivatives approaches to rebalancing.
2. Explain how considerations of implementation speed and time horizon of the rebalancing trade could affect the implementation choice.

Guideline Answers:
1. Looking at the data in Exhibit 16, Thompson can see that the two options appear similar from a cost perspective. The main cost driver associated with rebalancing through the cash market is cash drag (approximately 20 bps) caused by timing delays and disruptions to active manager portfolios. Rebalancing through cash markets would involve withdrawing funds from international developed equity active managers and increasing funds to current fixed-income managers and/or adding a new fixed-income manager. These activities would generate transaction costs and cash drag because the liquidation process for the equity manager(s) and the investment process for the fixed-income manager(s) would likely not happen simultaneously.

   In the case of derivatives (short equity futures position and long fixed-income futures position), the biggest cost component is mispricing or tracking error. Creating a short exposure position for the MSCI EAFE Index (the benchmark for international ex USA and Canada developed-market equities) and a long fixed-income futures position would involve a higher tracking error (17 bps) compared to the tracking error of using one S&P 500 futures contract discussed previously (8 bps). In this case, using multiple futures instruments increases associated tracking error.

2. An additional factor is speed of implementation. In general, depending on the availability of derivatives for the asset classes involved, rebalancing using derivatives is likely to result in a shorter implementation time frame while leaving the active managers in place. Given high levels of liquidity in the equity futures that would be used for MSCI EAFE Index replication, implementing with derivatives could occur quickly.

Another important aspect is rebalancing size and expected time horizon of the trade. The larger the rebalancing, the more likely the rebalance would represent a more permanent re-alignment as opposed to a temporary adjustment that could be reversed the next quarter.

Based on the expected costs and considerations and the relatively small size of the adjustment, using derivatives to rebalance the portfolio appears to be the best option. Implementing with derivatives gives the team the flexibility to tactically adjust exposure to international developed equities if desired and the ability to quickly reverse decisions in full or in part while leaving the current external managers in place.

After further discussion with her team, Thompson decides to instead rebalance the international developed equity allocation back to the target allocation by reallocating 2.5% from the international developed equity allocation into fixed income. The team's current analysis is shown in Exhibit 17.

EXHIBIT 17   Cost Information on Rebalancing Options

Cost Component	Cash Market	Futures (Equity/Fixed Income)
Bid/offer spread	5.00	4.00
Price impact (total trades)	5.00	4.00
Mispricing (tracking error, annual)	0.00	68.00
Cash drag (impact of timing delays and disruptions to active manager portfolios)	50.00	0.00
Cost of rolling the futures contract	0.00	6.00
Total cost	**60.00**	**82.00**

Notes: This exhibit shows the costs of reallocating 2.5% from international developed equities to fixed income in the cash and futures markets. The analysis assumes a one-year investment horizon because the expectation is that the change in portfolio allocation is more permanent. Under normal market conditions, it would not be expected for these asset classes to move outside of the corridor again over that investment horizon. All numbers are in basis points (bps) unless otherwise indicated.

In-text question:

What implementation option should Thompson use in this case?

Guideline Answer:
Based on relative expected costs, Thompson would likely decide to rebalance the portfolio in the cash markets by reallocating between international developed equity and fixed-income investment managers.

Exhibit 17 shows that the cost of rebalancing back to target allocation using derivatives is higher than implementing through the cash markets. Specifically, the implementation cost with derivatives is 82 bps, while the implementation cost for the cash markets is 60 bps. The higher derivatives cost is primarily caused by expected tracking error of the replication using derivatives, which is 68 bps on an annual basis. In general, the cost of rebalancing through futures is expected to increase with investment time horizon as mispricing or tracking risk increases. In this case, the impact of the cost of rolling the futures is not viewed as material given that the roll of the short equity futures position would likely offset most of the cost of holding the long fixed-income futures position. With respect to the cash market implementation, given the size of the rebalancing trade (2.5% of the overall portfolio), potential cash drag is expected to increase to 50 bps as compared to the previous scenario.

Other considerations besides expected cost may be relevant. A faster desired speed of implementation would favor implementation using derivatives, while the size of the planned rebalancing implies a longer time horizon for the trade and favors implementation through the cash market. Based on the facts given, Thompson would likely decide to rebalance the portfolio in the cash markets.

4. SUMMARY

The QU endowment case study covers important aspects of institutional portfolio management involving the illiquidity premium capture, liquidity management, asset allocation, and the use of derivatives versus the cash market for tactical asset allocation and portfolio rebalancing. In addition, the case examines potential ethical violations in manager selection that can arise in the course of business.

From an asset allocation perspective, the case highlights potential risk and rewards associated with increasing exposure to illiquidity risk through investments like private equity and private real estate. Although this exposure is expected to generate higher returns and more-efficient portfolios in the long run, significant uncertainties are involved both from a modeling and implementation perspective.

REFERENCES

Ang, Andrew, Dimitris Papanikolaou, and Mark M. Westerfield. 2014. "Portfolio Choice with Illiquid Assets." *Management Science* 60 (11). https://pubsonline.informs.org/doi/abs/10.1287/mnsc.2014.1986.

Chaffe, David B.H., III. 1993. "Option Pricing as a Proxy for Discount for Lack of Marketability in Private Company Valuations." *Business Valuation Review* 12 (4): 182–88.

Green, Katie. 2015. "The Illiquidity Conundrum: Does the Illiquidity Premium Really Exist?" Schroders (August). http://www.schroders.com/hu/sysglobalassets/digital/insights/pdfs/the-illiquidity-conundrum.pdf.

Investments, Russell. 2013. "Liquidity Management: A Critical Aspect of a Successful Investment Program for Non-Profit Organizations" (October). https://russellinvestments.com/-/media/files/nz/insights/1310-liquidity-management.pdf.

Mercer. 2015. "Setting an Appropriate Liquidity Budget: Making the Most of a Long Investment Horizon" (February). https://www.mercer.com/content/dam/mercer/attachments/global/investments/setting-an-appropriate-liquidity-budget-mercer-february-2015-a4.pdf.

Pastor, Lubos, and Robert F. Stambaugh. 2001. "Liquidity Risk and Expected Stock Returns." NBER Working Paper w8462. https://ssrn.com/abstract=282688.

Raymond, Donald M. 2009. "Integrating Goals, Structure, and Decision-Making at Canada Pension Plan Investment Board." *Rotman International Journal of Pension Management* 2 (1).

Staub, Renato, and Jeffrey Diermeier. 2003. "Segmentation, Illiquidity and Returns." *Journal of Investment Management* 1 (1).

PRACTICE PROBLEMS

The following information relates to Questions 1–2

Joe Bookman is a portfolio manager at State Tech University Foundation and is discussing the $900 million university endowment with the investment committee.

Exhibit 1 presents selected data on the current university endowment.

EXHIBIT 1   Selected Data for State Tech University Endowment

Asset Class	Investment Allocation (% of portfolio)	Semi-Liquid	Liquid	Illiquid	Rebalancing Band Policy	Standard Deviation of Returns (annual)
Cash	1%	100%	0%	0%	0% – 15%	1.5%
Fixed Income	24%	100%	0%	0%	20% – 30%	5.9%
Public Equity	39%	50%	50%	0%	30% – 40%	15.4%
Private Equity	21%	0%	0%	100%	20% – 25%	27.2%
Real Assets	15%	0%	50%	50%	10% – 20%	11.7%

The university investment committee is performing its quarterly assessment and requests that Bookman review the rebalancing band policy.

1. **Identify** which asset class(es) Bookman is *most likely* to note as in need of rebalancing band policy adjustment. **Justify** your selection(s).

Identify which asset class(es) Bookman is *most likely* to note as in need of rebalancing band policy adjustment. [Circle choice(s)]	**Justify** your selection(s).
Cash	
Fixed Income	
Public Equity	
Private Equity	
Real Assets	

The investment committee also asks Bookman to investigate whether the endowment should increase its allocation to illiquid investments to take advantage of higher potential returns. The endowment's liquidity profile policy stipulates that at least 30% of investments must be classified as liquid to support operating expenses; no more than 40% should be classified as illiquid. Bookman decides to perform a bottom-up liquidity analysis to respond to the committee.

2. **Discuss** the elements of Bookman's analysis and the conclusions he will draw from it.

The following information relates to Question 3

Laura Powers is a senior investment analyst at Brotley University Foundation and works for the university endowment. Powers is preparing a recommendation to allocate more funds into illiquid investments for a higher potential return and is discussing the rationale with junior analyst Jasper Heard. Heard makes the following statements to Powers:

Statement 1. The endowment should shift funds into private equity and real estate. Specifically, within these asset classes the endowment should target shorter-term investments. These tend to be the most illiquid and offer the highest liquidity premium.

Statement 2. The endowment should consider low liquidity public equity investments because they are shown to be close substitutes for private equity and real estate investments in terms of liquidity premium.

3. **Determine if** Heard's statements are correct. **Justify** your response.

Determine if Heard's statements are correct.

Statement 1 (Circle one)	Statement 2 (Circle one)
Correct Incorrect	Correct Incorrect
Justify your response.	**Justify** your response.

The following information relates to Questions 4–5

Rob Smith, as portfolio manager at Pell Tech University Foundation, is responsible for the university's $3.5 billion endowment. The endowment supports the majority of funding for the university's operating budget and financial aid programs. It is invested in fixed income, public equities, private equities, and real assets.

The Pell Tech Board is conducting its quarterly strategic asset allocation review. The board members note that while performance has been satisfactory, they have two concerns:

1. Endowment returns have underperformed in comparison to university endowments of similar size.
2. Return expectations have shifted lower for fixed-income and public equity investments.

Smith attributes this underperformance to a lower risk profile relative to its peers due to a lower allocation to illiquid private equity investments. In response to the board's concerns, Smith proposes an increase in the allocation to the private equity asset class. His proposal uses option price theory for valuation purposes and is supported by Monte Carlo simulations.

Exhibit 1 presents selected data on the current university endowment.

EXHIBIT 1   Selected Data for Pell Tech University Endowment

Portfolio Characteristic	Current Allocation	Proposed Allocation
Expected return (next 10 years)	7.8%	8.3%
Standard deviation of returns (annual)	13.2%	13.9%
Sharpe ratio	0.44	0.45
Probability of 30% erosion in purchasing power over 10 years	25%	20%

4. **Discuss** Smith's method for estimating the increase in return expectations derived from increasing the endowment allocation to private equity.
5. **Discuss** *two* reasons why the increased risk profile is appropriate. **Justify** your response.

The following information relates to Questions 6–7

Frank Grides is a portfolio manager for Kemney University Foundation and manages the liquidity profile of the university endowment. This endowment supports some of the funding for the university's operations. It applies the following spending policy designed to produce a 5% long-term spending rate while shielding annual distributions from fluctuations in its market value:

Spending for current fiscal year = (60% × Spending for previous fiscal year) + [40% × (5% × Endowment market value at the end of previous fiscal year)].

Grides is considering allocating more funds to illiquid investments to capture higher potential returns and is discussing this strategy with senior analyst Don Brodka. Brodka has three related concerns given that the higher allocation to illiquid investments may

- reduce the liquidity profile of the endowment,
- induce "drift" in the portfolio's risk profile in times of market stress, or
- alter the endowment's overall risk profile.

Assessing his concerns, Brodka performs a stress test on the portfolio with both current and proposed investments.

Exhibit 1 presents selected data on the university endowment.

EXHIBIT 1   Selected Data for Kemney University Endowment

Liquidity Category	Current Portfolio: Normal	Current Portfolio: Stress	Proposed Portfolio: Normal	Proposed Portfolio: Stress
Liquid	42%	38%	37%	33%
Semi-liquid	31%	28%	31%	28%
Illiquid	27%	34%	32%	39%

6. **Discuss** the relevance of the endowment's spending policy to Brodka's expressed concerns.
7. **Discuss** actions that Grides should take to alleviate Brodka's concerns.

The following information relates to Question 8

Mason Dixon, CFA, a portfolio manager with Langhorne Advisors (Langhorne), has just completed the request for proposal (RFP) for the Academe Foundation's (the Foundation) $20 million fixed-income mandate. In the performance section of the RFP, Dixon indicated that Langhorne Advisors is a member firm of CFA Institute and has prepared and presented this performance report in compliance with the Global Investment Performance Standards (the GIPS® standards). The performance report presented Langhorne's fixed-income composite returns on the actual net-of fees basis and benchmark returns net of Langhorne's highest scheduled fee (1.00% on the first $5 million; 0.60% thereafter). The report also indicated that as of the most recent quarter, the composite comprised 10 portfolios totaling $600 million of assets under management (AUM).

Upon returning the completed RFP, Dixon thanked the Foundation's chief investment officer, who is also a charterholder, for considering Langhorne. Dixon also indicated that regardless of the outcome of the manager search, he would like to have the CIO and the Foundation's president join him on Langhorne's corporate jet to spend a day at an exclusive California golf club where the firm maintains a corporate membership.

8. **Identify** the ethical concerns posed by Dixon's actions and conduct.

The following information relates to Question 9

In its quarterly policy and performance review, the investment team for the Peralandra University endowment identified a tactical allocation opportunity in international developed equities. The team also decided to implement a passive 1% overweight ($5 million notional value) position in the asset class. Implementation will occur by either using an MISC EAFE Index ETF in the cash market or the equivalent futures contract in the derivatives market.

The team determined that the unlevered cost of implementation is 27 basis points in the cash market (ETF) and 32 bps in the derivatives market (futures). This modest cost differential prompted a comparison of costs on a levered basis to preserve liquidity for upcoming capital commitments in the fund's alternative investment asset classes. For the related analysis, the team's assumptions are as follows:

- Investment policy compliant at 3 times leverage
- Investment horizon of one year
- 3-month Libor of 1.8%
- ETF borrowing cost of 3-month Libor plus 35 bps

9. **Recommend** the most cost-effective strategy. **Justify** your response with calculations of the total levered cost of each implementation option.

The following information relates to Question 10

Clive Staples is a consultant with the Leedsford Organization (Leedsford), a boutique investment consulting firm serving large endowments and private foundations. Leedsford consults on tactical asset allocation (TAA) program development, implementation, and ongoing TAA idea generation.

Staples has just completed his quarterly client review of the Narnea Foundation. Based on the Foundation's current asset allocation and Leedsford's updated fair value models, Staples believes there is an exploitable TAA opportunity in US large-cap growth stocks. He recommends a 2% overweight position to the US equities policy allocation either through an unlevered ETF or total return swap exposures to the Russell 1000 Growth Index.

10. **Compare** the efficiency of the ETF and total return swap TAA implementation alternatives from the perspectives of capital commitment, liquidity, and tracking error.

Compare the efficiency of the ETF and total return swap TAA implementation alternatives from the perspectives of capital commitment, liquidity, and tracking error.

Capital Commitment:

Liquidity:

Tracking Error:

The following information relates to Question 11

The Lemont Family Foundation follows a systematic quarterly rebalancing policy based on rebalancing corridors for each asset class. In the latest quarter, a significant sell-off in US public equities resulted in an unusually large 1.2% underweight position relative to the applicable lower corridor boundary. This is the only policy exception requiring rebalancing attention.

The Foundation's investment team views the sell-off as temporary and remains pleased with the performance of all external managers, including that of its US public equities manager. However, the sell-off has increased the significance of liquidity and flexibility for the team. As a result, the team now considers whether to rebalance through the cash market or the derivatives market.

11. **Determine** the *most appropriate* rebalancing choice for the Foundation's investment team. **Justify** your response.

Determine the *most appropriate* rebalancing choice for the Foundation's investment team. (Circle one)

Cash Market	Derivatives Market

Justify your response.

GLOSSARY

Active risk budgeting Risk budgeting that concerns active risk (risk relative to a portfolio's benchmark).

Asset class A group of assets that have similar characteristics, attributes, and risk/return relationships.

Asset-only With respect to asset allocation, an approach that focuses directly on the characteristics of the assets without explicitly modeling the liabilities.

Authorized participants (APs) A special group of institutional investors who are authorized by the ETF issuer to participate in the creation/redemption process. APs are large broker/dealers, often market makers.

Back-fill bias The distortion in index or peer group data which results when returns are reported to a database only after they are known to be good returns.

Best-in-class An ESG implementation approach that seeks to identify the most favorable companies in an industry based on ESG considerations.

Business cycle Fluctuations in GDP in relation to long-term trend growth, usually lasting 9-11 years.

Calendar rebalancing Rebalancing a portfolio to target weights on a periodic basis; for example, monthly, quarterly, semiannually, or annually.

Capital market expectations (CME) Expectations concerning the risk and return prospects of asset classes.

Constituent securities With respect to an index, the individual securities within an index.

Creation basket The list of securities (and share amounts) the authorized participant (AP) must deliver to the ETF manager in exchange for ETF shares. The creation basket is published each business day.

Creation units Large blocks of ETF shares transacted between the authorized participant (AP) and the ETF manager that are usually but not always equal to 50,000 shares of the ETF.

Creation/redemption The process in which ETF shares are created or redeemed by authorized participants transacting with the ETF issuer.

Cross-sectional consistency A feature of expectations setting which means that estimates for all classes reflect the same underlying assumptions and are generated with methodologies that reflect or preserve important relationships among the asset classes, such as strong correlations. It is the internal consistency across asset classes.

Decision-reversal risk The risk of reversing a chosen course of action at the point of maximum loss.

Diffusion index An index that measures how many indicators are pointing up and how many are pointing down.

Divisor A number (denominator) used to determine the value of a price return index. It is initially chosen at the inception of an index and subsequently adjusted by the index provider, as necessary, to avoid changes in the index value that are unrelated to changes in the prices of its constituent securities.

Dynamic asset allocation A strategy incorporating deviations from the strategic asset allocation that are motivated by longer-term valuation signals or economic views than usually associated with tactical asset allocation.

Econometrics The application of quantitative modeling and analysis grounded in economic theory to the analysis of economic data.

Economic balance sheet A balance sheet that provides an individual's total wealth portfolio, supplementing traditional balance sheet assets with human capital and pension wealth, and expanding liabilities to include consumption and bequest goals. Also known as *holistic balance sheet*.

Economic indicators Economic statistics provided by government and established private organizations that contain information on an economy's recent past activity or its current or future position in the business cycle.

Equal weighting An index weighting method in which an equal weight is assigned to each constituent security at inception.

ESG integration The integration of qualitative and quantitative environmental, social, and governance factors into traditional security and industry analysis; also known as *ESG incorporation*.

Exclusionary screening An ESG implementation approach that excludes certain sectors or companies that deviate from an investor's accepted standards. Also called *negative screening* or *norms-based screening*.

Extended portfolio assets and liabilities Assets and liabilities beyond those shown on a conventional balance sheet that are relevant in making asset allocation decisions; an example of an extended asset is human capital.

Float-adjusted market-capitalization weighting An index weighting method in which the weight assigned to each constituent security is determined by adjusting its market capitalization for its market float.

Fundamental weighting An index weighting method in which the weight assigned to each constituent security is based on its underlying company's size. It attempts to address the disadvantages of market-capitalization weighting by using measures that are independent of the constituent security's price.

Goals-based investing With respect to asset allocation or investing, an approach that focuses on achieving an investor's goals (for example, related to supporting lifestyle needs or aspirations) based typically on constructing sub-portfolios aligned with those goals.

Grinold–Kroner model An expression for the expected return on a share as the sum of an expected income return, an expected nominal earnings growth return, and an expected repricing return.

Hedge funds Private investment vehicles that typically use leverage, derivatives, and long and short investment strategies.

Home-country bias The favoring of domestic over non-domestic investments relative to global market value weights.

Impact investing Selecting an investment opportunity primarily based on its expected social or environmental benefits with measurable investment returns.

iNAVs "Indicated" net asset values are intraday "fair value" estimates of an ETF share based on its creation basket.

Input uncertainty Uncertainty concerning whether the inputs are correct.

Intertemporal consistency A feature of expectations setting which means that estimates for an asset class over different horizons reflect the same assumptions with respect to the potential paths of returns over time. It is the internal consistency over various time horizons.

Leading economic indicators A set of economic variables whose values vary with the business cycle but at a fairly consistent time interval before a turn in the business cycle.

Liability glide path A specification of desired proportions of liability-hedging assets and return-seeking assets and the duration of the liability hedge as funded status changes and contributions are made.

Liability-driven investing An investment industry term that generally encompasses asset allocation that is focused on funding an investor's liabilities in institutional contexts.

Liability-relative With respect to asset allocation, an approach that focuses directly only on funding liabilities as an investment objective.

Liquidity budget The portfolio allocations (or weightings) considered acceptable for the liquidity categories in the liquidity classification schedule (or time-to-cash table).

Liquidity classification schedule   A liquidity management classification (or table) that defines portfolio liquidity "buckets" or categories based on the estimated time it would take to convert assets in that particular category into cash.

Market float   The number of shares that are available to the investing public.

Market-capitalization weighting   An index weighting method in which the weight assigned to each constituent security is determined by dividing its market capitalization by the total market capitalization (sum of the market capitalization) of all securities in the index. Also called *value weighting*.

Minimum-variance portfolio   The portfolio with the minimum variance for each given level of expected return.

Model uncertainty   Uncertainty as to whether a selected model is correct.

Multi-market indexes   Comprised of indexes from different countries, designed to represent multiple security markets.

Negative screening   An ESG investment style that focuses on the exclusion of certain sectors, companies, or practices in a fund or portfolio on the basis of specific ESG criteria.

Nonstationarity   A characteristic of series of data whose properties, such as mean and variance, are not constant through time. When analyzing historical data it means that different parts of a data series reflect different underlying statistical properties.

Nonsystematic risk   Unique risk that is local or limited to a particular asset or industry that need not affect assets outside of that asset class.

Parameter uncertainty   Uncertainty arising because a quantitative model's parameters are estimated with error.

Passive management   A buy-and-hold approach to investing in which an investor does not make portfolio changes based upon short-term expectations of changing market or security performance.

Percent-range rebalancing   An approach to rebalancing that involves setting rebalancing thresholds or trigger points, stated as a percentage of the portfolio's value, around target values.

Portfolio planning   The process of creating a plan for building a portfolio that is expected to satisfy a client's investment objectives.

Price index   Represents the average prices of a basket of goods and services.

Price return index   An index that reflects *only* the price appreciation or percentage change in price of the constituent securities. Also called *price index*.

Price weighting   An index weighting method in which the weight assigned to each constituent security is determined by dividing its price by the sum of all the prices of the constituent securities.

Rebalancing policy   The set of rules that guide the process of restoring a portfolio's asset class weights to those specified in the strategic asset allocation.

Rebalancing range   A range of values for asset class weights defined by trigger points above and below target weights, such that if the portfolio value passes through a trigger point, rebalancing occurs. Also known as a corridor.

Rebalancing   In the context of asset allocation, a discipline for adjusting the portfolio to align with the strategic asset allocation.

Re-base   With reference to index construction, to change the time period used as the base of the index.

Redemption basket   The list of securities (and share amounts) the authorized participant (AP) receives when it redeems ETF shares back to the ETF manager. The redemption basket is published each business day.

Reduced-form models   Models that use economic theory and other factors such as prior research output to describe hypothesized relationships. Can be described as more compact representations of underlying structural models. Evaluate endogenous variables in terms of observable exogenous variables.

Regime   The governing set of relationships (between variables) that stem from technological, political, legal, and regulatory environments. Changes in such environments or policy stances can be described as changes in regime.

Risk budgeting The establishment of objectives for individuals, groups, or divisions of an organization that takes into account the allocation of an acceptable level of risk.

Sector indexes Indexes that represent and track different economic sectors—such as consumer goods, energy, finance, health care, and technology—on either a national, regional, or global basis.

Security market index A portfolio of securities representing a given security market, market segment, or asset class.

Security selection The process of selecting individual securities; typically, security selection has the objective of generating superior risk-adjusted returns relative to a portfolio's benchmark.

Self-investment limits With respect to investment limitations applying to pension plans, restrictions on the percentage of assets that can be invested in securities issued by the pension plan sponsor.

Shareholder engagement The process whereby companies engage with their shareholders.

Shortfall probability The probability of failing to meet a specific liability or goal.

Shrinkage estimation Estimation that involves taking a weighted average of a historical estimate of a parameter and some other parameter estimate, where the weights reflect the analyst's relative belief in the estimates.

Strategic asset allocation The set of exposures to IPS-permissible asset classes that is expected to achieve the client's long-term objectives given the client's investment constraints.

Structural models Models that specify functional relationships among variables based on economic theory. The functional form and parameters of these models are derived from the underlying theory. They may include unobservable parameters.

Survivorship bias Bias that arises in a data series when managers with poor track records exit the business and are dropped from the database whereas managers with good records remain; when a data series of a given date reflects only entitites that have survived to that date.

Sustainable investing The practice of identifying companies that can efficiently manage their financial, environmental, and human capital resources to generate attractive long-term profitability; often synonymous with *responsible investing*.

Systematic risk Risk that affects the entire market or economy; it cannot be avoided and is inherent in the overall market. Systematic risk is also known as non-diversifiable or market risk.

Tactical asset allocation The decision to deliberately deviate from the strategic asset allocation in an attempt to add value based on forecasts of the near-term relative performance of asset classes.

Taylor rule A rule linking a central bank's target short-term interest rate to the rate of growth of the economy and inflation.

Thematic investing An ESG implementation approach that focuses on investing in companies within a specific sector or industry theme.

Time-series estimation Estimators that are based on lagged values of the variable being forecast; often consist of lagged values of other selected variables.

Time-to-cash table See *liquidity classification schedule*.

Total factor productivity A variable which accounts for that part of Y not directly accounted for by the levels of the production factors (K and L).

Total return index An index that reflects the price appreciation or percentage change in price of the constituent securities plus any income received since inception.

Tracking risk The standard deviation of the differences between a portfolio's returns and its benchmarks returns. Also called *tracking error*.

Trigger points In the context of portfolio rebalancing, the endpoints of a rebalancing range (corridor).

Unsmoothing An adjustment to the reported return series if serial correlation is detected. Various approaches are available to unsmooth a return series.

Value at risk (VaR) A money measure of the minimum value of losses expected during a specified time period at a given level of probability.

Volatility clustering The tendency for large (small) swings in prices to be followed by large (small) swings of random direction.

ABOUT THE AUTHORS

Bidhan L. Parmar, PhD, is at the University of Virginia (USA).

Dorothy C. Kelly, CFA, is at McIntire School of Commerce, University of Virginia (USA).

Colin McLean, MBA, FIA, FSIP, is at SVM Asset Management (United Kingdom).

Nitin M. Mehta, CFA (United Kingdom).

David B. Stevens, CIMC, CFA, is at Wells Fargo Private Bank (USA).

Robert Kissell, PhD, is at Molloy College and Kissell Research Group (USA).

Barbara J. Mack is at Pingry Hill Enterprises, Inc. (USA).

Christopher D. Piros, PhD, CFA (USA).

William W. Jennings, PhD, CFA, is at the US Air Force Academy (USA).

Eugene L. Podkaminer, CFA, is at Franklin Templeton Investments (USA).

Jean L.P. Brunel, CFA, is at Brunel Associates LLC (USA).

Thomas M. Idzorek, CFA, is at Morningstar (USA).

John M. Mulvey, PhD, is at the Bendheim Center for Finance at Princeton University (USA).

Peter Mladina is at Northern Trust and UCLA (USA).

Brian J. Murphy, CFA, is at Willis Towers Watson (USA).

Mark Ruloff, FSA, EA, CERA, is at Aon (USA).

William A. Barker, PhD, CFA (Canada).

Bernd Hanke, PhD, CFA, is at Global Systematic Investors LLP (United Kingdom).

Brian J. Henderson, PhD, CFA, is at The George Washington University (USA).

James Adams, Ph.D, CFA is at New York University (USA).

Donald J. Smith, PhD, is at Boston University Questrom School of Business (USA).

James Clunie, PhD, CFA, is at Jupiter Asset Management (United Kingdom).

James Alan Finnegan, CAIA, RMA, CFA (USA).

David M. Smith, PhD, CFA, is at the University at Albany, New York (USA).

Kevin K. Yousif, CFA, is at LSIA Wealth & Institutional (USA).

Bing Li, PhD, CFA, is at Yuanyin Asset Management (Hong Kong SAR).

Yin Luo, CPA, PStat, CFAx, is at Wolfe Research LLC (USA).

Pranay Gupta, CFA, is at Allocationmetrics Limited (USA).

Barclay T. Leib, CFE, CAIA, is at Sand Spring Advisors LLC (USA).

Kathryn M. Kaminski, PhD, CAIA, is at Alpha Simplex Group, LLC (USA).

Mila Getmansky Sherman, PhD, is at Isenberg School of Management, UMASS Amherst (USA).

Christopher J. Sidoni, CFP, CFA, is at Gibson Capital, LLC (USA).

Vineet Vohra, CFA, is at Cognasia Talent (Singapore and Hong Kong SAR).

Paul Bouchey, CFA, is at Parametric Portfolio Associates, Seattle, WA, (USA).

Helena Eaton, PhD, CFA, is at J.P. Morgan, London, (UK).

Philip Marcovici is at Offices of Philip Marcovici, Hong Kong SAR, (China).

Arjan Berkelaar, PhD, CFA, is at KAUST Investment Management Company (USA).

Kate Misic, CFA, is at Telstra Super Pty Ltd (Australia).

Peter C. Stimes, CFA, is a private investor in Fallbrook, California (USA).

Connie Li (USA).

Roberto Malamut (USA).

Marc A. Wright, CFA, is at Russell Investments (USA).

Jeffrey C. Heisler,, PhD, CFA is at TwinFocus Capital Partners (USA).

Donald W. Lindsey, CFA (USA).

ABOUT THE CFA PROGRAM

If the subject matter of this book interests you, and you are not already a CFA Charterholder, we hope you will consider registering for the CFA Program and starting progress toward earning the Chartered Financial Analyst designation. The CFA designation is a globally recognized standard of excellence for measuring the competence and integrity of investment professionals. To earn the CFA charter, candidates must successfully complete the CFA Program, a global graduate-level self-study program that combines a broad curriculum with professional conduct requirements as preparation for a career as an investment professional.

Anchored in a practice-based curriculum, the CFA Program body of knowledge reflects the knowledge, skills, and abilities identified by professionals as essential to the investment decision-making process. This body of knowledge maintains its relevance through a regular, extensive survey of practicing CFA charterholders across the globe. The curriculum covers 10 general topic areas, ranging from equity and fixed-income analysis to portfolio management to corporate finance—all with a heavy emphasis on the application of ethics in professional practice. Known for its rigor and breadth, the CFA Program curriculum highlights principles common to every market so that professionals who earn the CFA designation have a thoroughly global investment perspective and a profound understanding of the global marketplace.

www.cfainstitute.org

INDEX